Psychology of Aging

The International Library of Psychology
Series Editor: David Canter

Titles in the Series:

Human Perception
Marco Bertamini and Michael Kubovy

Hypnosis
Michael Heap and Irving Kirsch

Interpersonal Development
Brett Laursen and Rita Žukauskienė

Counseling Psychology
Frederick T.L. Leong and Mark M. Leach

Psychology of Aging
Martin Orrell and Aimee Spector

**Psychology and Law:
Criminal and Civil Perspectives**
Ronald Roesch and Nathalie Gagnon

Clinical Forensic Psychology and Law
Ronald Roesch and Kaitlyn McLachlan

Parapsychology
Richard Wiseman and Caroline Watt

Psychology of Aging

Edited by

Martin Orrell and Aimee Spector

University College London, UK

ASHGATE

© Martin Orrell and Aimee Spector 2009. For copyright of individual articles please refer to the Acknowledgements.

All rights reserved. No part of this publication may be reproduced, stored in a retrieval system or transmitted in any form or by any means, electronic, mechanical, photocopying, recording or otherwise without the prior permission of the publisher.

Wherever possible, these reprints are made from a copy of the original printing, but these can themselves be of very variable quality. Whilst the publisher has made every effort to ensure the quality of the reprint, some variability may inevitably remain.

Published by
Ashgate Publishing Limited
Wey Court East
Union Road
Farnham
Surrey GU9 7PT
England

Ashgate Publishing Company
Suite 420
101 Cherry Street
Burlington, VT 05401-4405
USA

Ashgate website: http://www.ashgate.com

British Library Cataloguing in Publication Data
Psychology of aging. – (International library of
  psychology)
  1. Aging – Psychological aspects
  I. Orrell, Martin II. Spector, Aimee
  155.6'7

Library of Congress Control Number: 2008939260

ISBN: 978-0-7546-2789-0

Mixed Sources
Product group from well-managed
forests and other controlled sources
www.fsc.org Cert no. SGS-COC-2482
© 1996 Forest Stewardship Council
FSC

Printed and bound in Great Britain by
TJ International Ltd, Padstow, Cornwall

Contents

Acknowledgements ix
Series Preface xiii
Introduction xv

PART I   COGNITION AND AGING

1 Ian J. Deary, Lawrence J. Whalley, Helen Lemmon, J.R. Crawford and John M. Starr (2000), 'The Stability of Individual Differences in Mental Ability from Childhood to Old Age: Follow-up of the 1932 Scottish Mental Survey', *Intelligence*, **28**, pp. 49–55. 3

2 Patrick Rabbitt, Peter Diggle, Fiona Holland and Lynn McInnes (2004), 'Practice and Drop-Out Effects During a 17-Year Longitudinal Study of Cognitive Aging', *Journals of Gerontology*, **59**, pp. P84–P97. 11

3 Paul B. Baltes and Ulman Lindenberger (1997), 'Emergence of a Powerful Connection Between Sensory and Cognitive Functions Across the Adult Life Span: A New Window to the Study of Cognitive Aging?', *Psychology and Aging*, **12**, pp. 12–21. 25

4 Yaakov Stern (2002), 'What is Cognitive Reserve? Theory and Research Application of the Reserve Concept', *Journal of the International Neuropsychological Society*, **8**, pp. 448–60. 35

5 Paul B. Baltes and Margret M. Baltes (1990), 'Psychological Perspectives on Successful Aging: The Model of Selective Optimization with Compensation', in Paul B. Baltes and Margret M. Baltes (eds), *Successful Aging: Perspectives from the Behavioural Sciences*, New York, NY: Cambridge University Press, pp. 1–34. 49

PART II   SOCIAL AND EMOTIONAL FUNCTIONING IN OLD AGE

6 B. Nygren, L. Aléx, E. Jonsén, Y. Gustafson, A. Norberg and B. Lundman (2005), 'Resilience, Sense of Coherence, Purpose in Life and Self-Transcendence in Relation to Perceived Physical and Mental Health among the Oldest Old', *Aging and Mental Health*, **9**, pp. 354–62. 85

7 Jennifer B. Unger, Gail McAvay, Martha L. Bruce, Lisa Berkman and Teresa Seeman (1999), 'Variation in the Impact of Social Network Characteristics on Physical Functioning in Elderly Persons: MacArthur Studies of Successful Aging', *Journals of Gerontology*, **54**, S245–S251. 95

8 C. Donald Sherbourne, L.S. Meredith, W. Rogers and J.E. Ware Jr (1992), 'Social Support and Stressful Life Events: Age Differences in their Effects on Health-Related Quality of Life among the Chronically Ill', *Quality of Life Research*, **1**, pp. 235–46.   103

9 Laura L. Carstensen, Derek M. Isaacowitz and Susan T. Charles (1999), 'Taking Time Seriously: A Theory of Socioemotional Selectivity', *American Psychologist*, **54**, pp. 165–81.   115

PART III LIFESTYLE AND WELL-BEING IN OLD AGE

10 Hui-Xin Wang, Anita Karp, Bengt Winblad and Laura Fratiglioni (2002), 'Late-Life Engagement in Social and Leisure Activities is Associated with a Decreased Risk of Dementia: A Longitudinal Study from the Kungsholmen Project', *American Journal of Epidemiology*, **155**, pp. 1081–87.   135

11 Joe Verghese, Richard B. Lipton, Mindy J. Katz, Charles B. Hall, Carol A. Derby, Gail Kuslansky, Anne F. Ambrose, Martin Sliwinski and Herman Buschke (2003), 'Leisure Activities and the Risk of Dementia in the Elderly', *New England Journal of Medicine*, **348**, pp. 2508–16.   143

12 Nalin A. Singh, Karen M. Clements and Maria A. Fiatarone Singh (2001), 'The Efficacy of Exercise as a Long-term Antidepressant in Elderly Subjects: A Randomized, Controlled Trial', *Journals of Gerontology*, **56**, pp. M497–M504.   153

PART IV PSYCHOLOGICAL ASPECTS OF DEMENTIA

13 Tom Kitwood and Kathleen Bredin (1992), 'Towards a Theory of Dementia Care: Personhood and Well-being', *Ageing and Society*, **12**, pp. 269–87.   163

14 R.T. Woods, (2001) 'Discovering the Person with Alzheimer's Disease: Cognitive, Emotional and Behavioural Aspects', *Aging and Mental Health*, **5**, pp. S7–S16.   183

15 Lucille R. Taulbee and James C. Folsom (1966), 'Reality Orientation for Geriatric Patients', *Hospital and Community Psychiatry*, **17**, pp. 133–35.   193

16 Aimee Spector, Lene Thorgrimsen, Bob Woods, Lindsay Royan, Steve Davies, Margaret Butterworth and Martin Orrell (2003), 'Efficacy of an Evidence-Based Cognitive Stimulation Therapy Programme for People with Dementia: Randomised Controlled Trial, *British Journal of Psychiatry*, **183**, pp. 248–54.   197

17 Jiska Cohen-Mansfield (2001), 'Nonpharmacologic Interventions for Inappropriate Behaviors in Dementia: A Review, Summary, and Critique', *American Journal of Geriatric Psychiatry*, **9**, pp. 361–81.   205

18 Florence Pasquier (1999), 'Early Diagnosis of Dementia: Neuropsychology', *Journal of Neurology*, **246**, pp. 6–15.   227

19 E. Moniz-Cook, R. Woods and E. Gardiner (2000), 'Staff Factors Associated with Perception of Behaviour as "Challenging" in Residential and Nursing Homes', *Aging and Mental Health*, **4**, pp. 48–55.   237

PART V FAMILIES AND CARERS IN OLD AGE

20 Robin G. Morris, Lorna W. Morris and Peter G. Britton (1988), 'Factors Affecting the Emotional Wellbeing of the Caregivers of Dementia Sufferers', *British Journal of Psychiatry*, **153**, pp. 147–56.   247

21 Leonard I. Pearlin, Joseph T. Mullan, Shirley J. Semple and Marilyn M. Skaff (1990), 'Caregiving and the Stress Process: An Overview of Concepts and Their Measures', *The Gerontologist*, **30**, pp. 583–94.   257

22 Steven H. Zarit, Karen E. Reever and Julie Bach-Peterson (1980), 'Relatives of the Impaired Elderly: Correlates of Feelings of Burden', *The Gerontologist*, **20**, pp. 649–55.   269

23 Henry Brodaty, Alisa Green and Annette Koschera (2003), 'Meta-Analysis of Psychosocial Interventions for Caregivers of People with Dementia', *JAGS*, **51**, pp. 657–64.   277

24 Mary S. Mittelman, David L. Roth, David W. Coon and William E. Haley (2004), 'Sustained Benefit of Supportive Intervention for Depressive Symptoms in Caregivers of Patients with Alzheimer's Disease', *American Journal of Psychiatry*, **161**, pp. 850–56.   285

25 Judith Rodin and Ellen J. Langer (1977), 'Long-Term Effects of a Control-Relevant Intervention with the Institutionalized Aged', *Journal of Personality and Social Psychology*, **35**, pp. 897–902.   293

26 Sheryl Zimmerman, Philip D. Sloane, Christianna S. Williams, Peter S. Reed, John S. Preisser, J. Kevin Eckert, Malaz Boustani and Debra Dobbs (2005), 'Dementia Care and Quality of Life in Assisted Living and Nursing Homes', *The Gerontologist*, **45**, pp. 133–46.   299

PART VI PSYCHOLOGICAL ASPECTS OF MENTAL HEALTH PROBLEMS IN OLD AGE

27 Dan G. Blazer (2003), 'Depression in Late Life: Review and Commentary', *Journal of Gerontology*, **58**, pp. M249–M265.   315

28 V. Kraaij and E.J. de Wilde (2001), 'Negative Life Events and Depressive Symptoms in the Elderly: A Life Span Perspective', *Aging and Mental Health*, **5**, pp. 84–91.   333

29 Ken Laidlaw, Larry W. Thompson and Dolores Gallagher-Thompson (2004), 'Comprehensive Conceptualization of Cognitive Behaviour Therapy for Late Life Depression', *Behavioural and Cognitive Psychotherapy*, **32**, pp. 389–99.   341

30 Sharon Tennstedt, Jonathan Howland, Margie Lachman, Elizabeth Peterson, Linda Kasten and Alan Jette (1998), 'A Randomized, Controlled Trial of a Group Intervention to Reduce Fear of Falling and Associated Activity Restriction in Older Adults', *Journals of Gerontology*, **53**, pp. P384–P392.   353

31 Larry W. Thompson, Dolores Gallagher-Thompson, Andrew Futterman, Michael J. Gilewski and James Peterson (1991), 'The Effects of Late Life Spousal Bereavement over a 30-Month Interval', *Psychology and Aging*, **6**, pp. 434–41.   363

32 A. Hautamäki and P.G. Coleman (2001), 'Explanation for Low Prevalence of PTSD among Older Finnish War Veterans: Social Solidarity and Continued Significance given to Wartime Sufferings', *Aging and Mental Health*, **5**, pp. 165–74. 371

33 J.Q. Morse and T.R. Lynch (2004), 'A Preliminary Investigation of Self-Reported Personality Disorders in Late Life: Prevalence, Predictors of Depressive Severity, and Clinical Correlates', *Aging and Mental Health*, **8**, pp. 307–15. 381

Name Index 391

Acknowledgements

The editors and publishers wish to thank the following for permission to use copyright material.

American Psychological Association for the essays: Paul B. Baltes and Ulman Lindenberger (1997), 'Emergence of a Powerful Connection Between Sensory and Cognitive Functions Across the Adult Life Span: A New Window to the Study of Cognitive Aging?', *Psychology and Aging*, **12**, pp. 12–21. Copyright © 1997 American Psychological Association; Laura L. Carstensen, Derek M. Isaacowitz and Susan T. Charles (1999), 'Taking Time Seriously: A Theory of Socioemotional Selectivity', *American Psychologist*, **54**, pp. 165–81. Copyright © 1999 American Psychological Association; Judith Rodin and Ellen J. Langer (1977), 'Long-Term Effects of a Control-Relevant Intervention with the Institutionalized Aged', *Journal of Personality and Social Psychology*, **35**, pp. 897–902. Copyright © 1977 American Psychological Association; Larry W. Thompson, Dolores Gallagher-Thompson, Andrew Futterman, Michael J. Gilewski and James Peterson (1991), 'The Effects of Late-Life Spousal Bereavement over a 30-Month Interval', *Psychology and Aging*, **6**, pp. 434–41. Copyright © 1991 American Psychological Association.

Cambridge University Press for the essays: Paul B. Baltes and Margret M. Baltes (1990), 'Psychological Perspectives on Successful Aging: The Model of Selective Optimization with Compensation', in Paul B. Baltes and Margret M. Baltes (eds), *Successful Aging: Perspectives from the Behavioural Sciences*, New York, NY: Cambridge University Press, pp. 1–34. Copyright © 1990 European Science Foundation; Yaakov Stern (2002), 'What is Cognitive Reserve? Theory and Research Application of the Reserve Concept', *Journal of the International Neuropsychological Society*, **8**, pp. 448–60. Copyright © 2002 International Neuropsychological Society; Tom Kitwood and Kathleen Bredin (1992), 'Towards a Theory of Dementia Care: Personhood and Well-being', *Ageing and Society*, **12**, pp. 269–87. Copyright © 1992 Cambridge University Press; Ken Laidlaw, Larry W. Thompson and Dolores Gallagher-Thompson (2004), 'Comprehensive Conceptualization of Cognitive Behaviour Therapy for Late Life Depression', *Behavioural and Cognitive Psychotherapy*, **32**, pp. 389–99. Copyright © 2004 British Association for Behavioural and Cognitive Psychotherapies.

Copyright Clearance Center for the essays: Mary S. Mittelman, David L. Roth, David W. Coon and William E. Haley (2004), 'Sustained Benefit of Supportive Intervention for Depressive Symptoms in Caregivers of Patients with Alzheimer's Disease', *American Journal of Psychiatry*, **161**, pp. 850–56. Copyright © 2004 American Psychiatric Society; Lucille R. Taulbee and James C. Folsom (1966), 'Reality Orientation for Geriatric Patients', *Hospital and Community Psychiatry*, **17**, pp. 133–35. Copyright © 1966 American Psychiatric Association.

Elsevier for the essay: Ian J. Deary, Lawrence J. Whalley, Helen Lemmon, J.R. Crawford and John M. Starr (2000), 'The Stability of Individual Differences in Mental Ability from Childhood to Old Age: Follow-up of the 1932 Scottish Mental Survey', *Intelligence*, **28**, pp. 49–55. Copyright © 2000 Elsevier.

Lippincott Williams and Wilkins for the essay: Jiska Cohen-Mansfield (2001), 'Nonpharmacologic Interventions for Inappropriate Behaviors in Dementia: A Review, Summary, and Critique', *American Journal of Geriatric Psychiatry*, **9**, pp. 361–81.

Massachusetts Medical Society for the essay: Joe Verghese, Richard B. Lipton, Mindy J. Katz, Charles B. Hall, Carol A. Derby, Gail Kuslansky, Anne F. Ambrose, Martin Sliwinski and Herman Buschke (2003), 'Leisure Activities and the Risk of Dementia in the Elderly', *New England Journal of Medicine*, **348**, pp. 2508–16. Copyright © 2003 Massachusetts Medical Society.

Oxford University Press for the essays: Patrick Rabbitt, Peter Diggle, Fiona Holland and Lynn McInnes (2004), 'Practice and Drop-Out Effects During a 17-Year Longitudinal Study of Cognitive Aging', *Journals of Gerontology*, **59**, pp. P84–P97. Copyright © 2004 Gerontological Society of America; Jennifer B. Unger, Gail McAvay, Martha L. Bruce, Lisa Berkman and Teresa Seeman (1999), 'Variation in the Impact of Social Network Characteristics on Physical Functioning in Elderly Persons: MacArthur Studies of Successful Aging', *Journals of Gerontology*, **54**, S245–S251. Copyright © 1999 Gerontological Society of America; Nalin A. Singh, Karen M. Clements and Maria A. Fiatarone Singh (2001), 'The Efficacy of Exercise as a Long-term Antidepressant in Elderly Subjects: A Randomized, Controlled Trial', *Journals of Gerontology*, **56**, pp. M497–M504. Copyright © 2001 Gerontological Society of America; Leonard I. Pearlin, Joseph T. Mullan, Shirley J. Semple and Marilyn M. Skaff (1990), 'Caregiving and the Stress Process: An Overview of Concepts and Their Measures', *The Gerontologist*, **30**, pp. 583–94. Copyright © 1990 Gerontological Society of America; Sheryl Zimmerman, Philip D. Sloane, Christianna S. Williams, Peter S. Reed, John S. Preisser, J. Kevin Eckert, Malaz Boustani and Debra Dobbs (2005), 'Dementia Care and Quality of Life in Assisted Living and Nursing Homes', *The Gerontologist*, **45**, pp. 133–46. Copyright © 2005 Gerontological Society of America; Dan G. Blazer (2003), 'Depression in Late Life: Review and Commentary', *Journals of Gerontology*, **58**, pp. M249–M265. Copyright © 2003 Gerontological Society of America; Sharon Tennstedt, Jonathan Howland, Margie Lachman, Elizabeth Peterson, Linda Kasten and Alan Jette (1998), 'A Randomized, Controlled Trial of a Group Intervention to Reduce Fear of Falling and Associated Activity Restriction in Older Adults', *Journals of Gerontology*, **53**, pp. P384–P392. Copyright © 1998 Gerontological Society of America; Hui-Xin Wang, Anita Karp, Bengt Winblad and Laura Fratiglioni (2002), 'Late-Life Engagement in Social and Leisure Activities is Associated with a Decreased Risk of Dementia: A Longitudinal Study from the Kungsholmen Project', *American Journal of Epidemiology*, **155**, pp. 1081–87; Steven H. Zarit, Karen E. Reever and Julie Bach-Peterson (1980), 'Relatives of the Impaired Elderly: Correlates of Feelings of Burden', *The Gerontologist*, **20**, pp. 649–55.

Royal College of Psychiatrists for the essays: Robin G. Morris, Lorna W. Morris and Peter G. Britton (1988), 'Factors Affecting the Emotional Wellbeing of the Caregivers of Dementia

Sufferers', *British Journal of Psychiatry*, **153**, pp. 147–56; Aimee Spector, Lene Thorgrimsen, Bob Woods, Lindsay Royan, Steve Davies, Margaret Butterworth and Martin Orrell (2003), 'Efficacy of an Evidence-Based Cognitive Stimulation Therapy Programme for People with Dementia: Randomised Controlled Trial, *British Journal of Psychiatry*, **183**, pp. 248–54.

Springer for the essays: C. Donald Sherbourne, L.S. Meredith, W. Rogers and J.E. Ware Jr (1992), 'Social Support and Stressful Life Events: Age Differences in their Effects on Health-Related Quality of Life among the Chronically Ill', *Quality of Life Research*, **1**, pp. 235–46. Copyright © 1992 Rapid Communications of Oxford Ltd; Florence Pasquier (1999), 'Early Diagnosis of Dementia: Neuropsychology', *Journal of Neurology*, **246**, pp. 6–15. Copyright © 1999 Steinkopff Verlag.

Taylor and Francis Limited for the essays: B. Nygren, L. Aléx, E. Jonsén, Y. Gustafson, A. Norberg and B. Lundman (2005), 'Resilience, Sense of Coherence, Purpose in Life and Self-Transcendence in Relation to Perceived Physical and Mental Health among the Oldest Old', *Aging and Mental Health*, **9**, pp. 354–62. Copyright © 2005 Taylor & Francis Group Ltd; R.T. Woods (2001), 'Discovering the Person with Alzheimer's Disease: Cognitive, Emotional and Behavioural Aspects', *Aging and Mental Health*, **5**, pp. S7–S16. Copyright © 2001 Taylor & Francis Group Ltd; E. Moniz-Cook, R. Woods and E. Gardiner (2000), 'Staff Factors Associated with Perception of Behaviour as "Challenging" in Residential and Nursing Homes', *Aging and Mental Health*, **4**, pp. 48–55. Copyright © 2000 Taylor & Francis Group Ltd; V. Kraaij and E.J. de Wilde (2001), 'Negative Life Events and Depressive Symptoms in the Elderly: A Life Span Perspective', *Aging and Mental* Health, **5**, pp. 84–91. Copyright © 2001 Taylor & Francis Group Ltd; A. Hautamäki and P.G. Coleman (2001), 'Explanation for Low Prevalence of PTSD among Older Finnish War Veterans: Social Solidarity and Continued Significance given to Wartime Sufferings', *Aging and Mental Health*, **5**, pp. 165–74. Copyright © 2001 Taylor & Francis Group Ltd; J.Q. Morse and T.R. Lynch (2004), 'A Preliminary Investigation of Self-Reported Personality Disorders in Late Life: Prevalence, Predictors of Depressive Severity, and Clinical Correlates', *Aging and Mental Health*, **8**, pp. 307–15. Copyright © 2004 Taylor & Francis Group Ltd.

Wiley-Blackwell for the essay: Henry Brodaty, Alisa Green and Annette Koschera (2003), 'Meta-Analysis of Psychosocial Interventions for Caregivers of People with Dementia', *JAGS*, **51**, pp. 657–64. Copyright © 2003 American Geriatrics Society.

Every effort has been made to trace all the copyright holders, but if any have been inadvertently overlooked, the publishers will be pleased to make the necessary arrangement at the first opportunity.

Series Preface

Psychology now touches every corner of our lives. No serious consideration of any newsworthy topic, from eating disorders to crime, from terrorism to new age beliefs, from trauma to happiness, is complete without some examination of what systematic, scientific psychology has to say on these matters. This means that psychology now runs the gamut from neuroscience to sociology, by way of medicine and anthropology, geography and molecular biology, connecting to virtually every area of scientific and professional life. This diversity produces a vibrant and rich discipline in which every area of activity finds outlets across a broad spectrum of publications.

Those who wish to gain an understanding of any area of psychology therefore either have to rely on secondary sources or, if they want to connect with the original contributions that define any domain of the discipline, must hunt through many areas of the library, often under diverse headings.

The volumes in this series obviate those difficulties by bringing together under one set of covers, carefully selected existing publications that are the definitive papers that characterize a specific topic in psychology.

The editors for each volume have been chosen because they are internationally recognized authorities. Therefore the selection of each editor, and the way in which it is organized into discrete sections, is an important statement about the field.

Each volume of the International Library of Psychology thus collects in one place the seminal and definitive journal articles that are creating current understanding of a specific aspect of present-day psychology. As a resource for study and research the volumes ensure that scholars and other professionals can gain ready access to original source material. As a statement of the essence of the topic covered they provide a benchmark for understanding and evaluating that aspect of psychology.

As this International Library emerges over the coming years it will help to specify what the nature of 21st century psychology is and what its contribution is to the future of humanity.

DAVID CANTER
Series Editor
Professor of Psychology
University of Liverpool, UK

Introduction

Producing a list of the best essays on the psychology of aging was not only a daunting task, but also variously described as bewildering, frightening and, according to a senior colleague, an impossible task. Perhaps we are not the first editors compiling such a volume to juggle the twin torments of procrastination and deadlines. It is, of course, tempting to ask ourselves what we can possibly write that will add anything to what these great essays have already said. Hopefully we can make a small contribution and it is at once an inspiration, a pleasure and an honour to have the task of drawing these essays together into a single volume and providing an Introduction by way of an appetizer.

Cognition and Aging

In the last few decades there have been some remarkable advances in cognition and aging. In practice, cognitive difficulties are often attributed to old age, but how far is deteriorating cognition a product of the aging process? What contributes to it, and what, if anything, can be done to reduce or forestall it? In old age in particular there are important questions as to whether differences in mental ability earlier in life contribute to the risk of dementia. In Part I, Ian Deary and his colleagues look at how mental ability changes from childhood to old age, Paul Baltes and Ulman Lindenberger examine the relationship between sensory and cognitive functions in aging and Patrick Rabbitt and his colleagues clarify the thorny issues of practice and drop-out effects in longitudinal studies of cognitive aging. Following on from these, Paul and Margret Baltes describe their eloquent model of selective optimization and compensation in successful aging and, finally, Yaakov Stern, in his seminal essay, examines the concept of cognitive reserve.

In a now classic essay on the stability of individual differences in mental ability from childhood to old age, Deary *et al.* (Chapter 1) raise the bar in terms of long-term studies in the cognition of aging. They point out that the stability of individual differences in mental abilities is of wide interest as it impinges upon questions about whether education initiatives boost ability levels and how far environmental factors (such as nutrition) lower cognitive performance. In this essay the authors present their spectacular longitudinal study starting at age 11 with a follow-up age of 77. Rightly, they point out that this addresses the stability of mental functions across most of the human lifespan and, with its unique data set, it is a major advance on similar studies. All Scottish children born in 1921 and attending school on 1 June 1932 (n = 7498) undertook a validated test of psychometric intelligence known as the Moray House Test. In June 1998, 101 people aged 77 were followed up and re-administered the same mental ability test, with most attending a group testing session in Aberdeen. The authors provided the same kind of exam conditions at both points of testing, with people in a large hall, seated at desks and chairs, and given the requisite 45 minutes and same test instructions. As a blueprint for a high-quality longitudinal study we found this uncannily hard to fault. The Moray House test closely relates to what used to be the English 11-plus school entrance examination, testing a range of verbal, mathematical and intellectual abilities. Interestingly, the effect of time was highly significant, with people scoring the equivalent of nine IQ points better at the age of 77 than at age 11. The authors draw attention to the importance of a person's premorbid mental ability in the investigation of cognitive decline or possible dementia. The results suggest that broad stability of individual differences in mental abilities might be expected across the human lifespan, many of which appear to remain stable. This may be accounted for by either genetic differences coming into play in later life that may impact on cognitive decline or environmental effects.

Understandably, after the 66-year interval Ian Deary *et al.* do not dwell on the potential practice effects of repeating the same test. However, the next essay by Patrick Rabbitt *et al.* (Chapter 2) addresses the issues of practice and drop-out effects during a 17-year longitudinal study of cognitive aging. They draw attention to a number of problems with previous studies of cognitive change. These include methodological difficulties and how repeated assessments result in practice, which can lead to underestimates of true rates of change and even disguise cognitive decline. Moreover, if some people improve more on some tasks than others, the analyses may incorrectly suggest that certain mental abilities decline at different rates. For example, less able and also older individuals show greater initial improvement on easy tasks, whereas on difficult tasks the more able and younger show greater and more sustained gain. Thus there is a need to understand the relative contributions of practice to the different characteristics of the individuals and different mental-ability tasks.

The authors analysed data from four successive presentations of several intelligence tests administered over a 17-year period to 5,899 community residents from Manchester and Newcastle aged 49–92 years. They found that, practice effects on intelligence tests accounted for around 4.5 per cent of gains and were retained even over a seven-year gap between successive assessments. In addition, there were cohort effects related to differing levels of ability, which affected the interpretation of verbal learning and intelligence tests. In contrast there were negligible effects in relation to vocabulary tests. Tactfully, Rabbitt *et al.* refrain from speculating about why Manchester residents performed significantly better than Newcastle residents for some of the tests, even when the effects of socioeconomic status and gender were taken into account.

Adjusting for practice and drop-out effects revealed accelerating declines in fluid intelligence and cumulative learning, but linear declines in verbal free recall showed no substantial change in vocabulary. Socioeconomic status and basal levels of general fluidity did not seem to affect rates of decline. After adjusting for demographic factors, variability between individuals increased as the sample aged, as might be expected with a group in which a proportion would be in the process of cognitive decline.

The advances documented in both the Deary and Rabbitt essays signal a clear sense of progress towards a better understanding of cognitive aging. However, the essay by Paul Baltes and Ulman Lindenberger (Chapter 3) provides such a dramatic new insight into the impact of sensory impairment and cognitive function across the adult lifespan that we need to adapt our view of cognitive aging still further. Baltes and Lindenberger point out that the role of sensory functions in intellectual functioning has generally not been a high priority for research on aging and intelligence, perhaps due to a focus on testing adults and children and the lack of samples covering advanced old age. However, one of their earlier studies (Lindenberger and

Baltes, 1994), using a sample from the Berlin aging study, found that simple measures of visual and auditory acuity together accounted for 49 per cent of the total and 93 per cent of the age-related variance in intellectual functioning. The authors suggested three possible hypotheses accounting for these findings: (a) sensory deprivation; (b) an aging-induced increase in the cognitive load of sensory performance; and (c) a brain-related common cause.

The focus of the Baltes and Lindenberger study reproduced in this volume is the common cause hypothesis which argues that correlation between measures of sensory and intellectual functioning may increase in old age because both sets of measures are an expression of the physiological architecture of the aging brain. Moreover, other indices of sensory motor function such as balance and gait also strongly correlate with intellectual functioning. The study included three samples: a younger adult group aged 25–69 years, the Berlin aging study sample aged 70–103 years, and a composite of both groups. Visual and auditory acuity was measured with standard tests, and a total of 14 tests were administered as part of the cognitive test battery. The initial results showed that controlling for vision was associated with a 3.9-fold reduction of age-related individual differences in cognitive functioning and that controlling for hearing led to an 8.8-fold reduction, whereas controlling for both vision and hearing led to an 18.5-fold reduction of age differences in cognitive functioning. Baltes and Lindenberger point out that a high degree of predictive overlap between age and sensory functioning for fluid abilities in both groups is consistent with the notion that mechanisms associated with chronological age explain the sensory/cognitive link across the entire age range and that the increase in the strength of the connection between sensory and intellectual functioning with advancing age is a reflection of the acceleration of negative age-based changes during the last decades of the lifespan. They also note that the link between cognition and sensory impairment was stronger for fluid intellectual abilities than for crystalline intellectual performance. However, they acknowledge that the results do not allow for conclusive distinction between the three hypotheses or specify the underlying mechanisms. Nevertheless, this essay makes a significant contribution to our understanding of the relationship between cognitive and sensory impairments, particularly taking into account the impact of dementia on cognitive deterioration.

Models for the potential role of education in cognitive aging have been discussed by Orrell and Sahakian (1995). However, the essay by Yaakov Stern (Chapter 4) presents a critical review of the concept of cognitive reserve. Stern highlights the research evidence on the poor correlation between the degree of pathological damage and the level of clinical impairment in people with dementia. For example, Katzman *et al.* (1989) described ten cases of cognitively normal older people who at post mortem were found to have advanced Alzheimer's disease pathology in their brains. Stern eloquently categorizes reserve into brain reserve and cognitive reserve. He describes brain reserve as a type of passive protection against clinical symptoms from brain damage, which is associated with structural features such as the overall size of the brain, the number of neurons and synapses. He suggests that this is a passive type of protection against dementia, as the person already has a degree of reserve and can thus lose more neurons and neuronal connections before starting to show clinical symptoms. In parallel he develops the idea of 'cognitive reserve' as an active process of compensation allowing the brain to use networks more efficiently or recruit alternative networks to offset the potential impairment caused by pathological brain damage. He talks about this as the ability of the cognitive paradigm underlying a task to sustain disruption and still operate effectively. He also highlights the role of IQ and educational levels, acknowledges the limitations of the model and notes that the actual level of reserve may be a combination both of the brain reserve capacity and the cognitive reserve capacity to resist the effects of damage.

Although Stern was not the first author to look at the neuropsychological mechanisms potentially underlying the idea of cognitive reserve (see, for example, Katzman, 1993), he did so in a way that provided a particularly lucid explanation of the two concepts. Surprisingly, he did not reference Baltes' work and the optimization/compensation paradigm. However, the next essay in this volume, which addresses the psychological perspectives on successful aging and the model of selective optimization with compensation, provides us with a landmark in the quest to better understand the adaptive potential of cognitive functioning in the context of the areas of decline associated with the aging process.

This seminal essay by Paul and Margret Baltes, published as a book chapter in 1990 and reproduced here as Chapter 5, provided new insight and clarity into the nature of aging. Rather than just framing it as a period of decline and disability, the authors presented a more developmental model involving selection, optimization and compensation. This immensely thoughtful and scholarly review has influenced our own approach to the potential for improving the functioning and well-being of older people, including those with dementia. Baltes and Baltes introduce the chapter by looking at the concept of intra-individual variability and plasticity and highlighting these as cornerstones for a developmental theory of human adaptation. Quoting Cicero, they note that old age offers many opportunities for positive change and productive functioning, hence constructing a positive image of old age and aging. They note that Cicero himself was in his early 60s when he wrote *De Senecucte*. Highlighting the paradox of 'successful aging', they observe that old age conjures up a picture of loss, decline and approaching death whereas 'success' indicates gains, winning and a positive balance in life, and that even defining the nature of success is elusive. Should it be judged on length of life? Physical health? Mental health? Cognitive performance? Social competence? Productivity? Personal control? Or life satisfaction? Concluding that a single dimension is not sufficiently adequate to describe successful aging but that an integration of subjective and objective criteria is needed, they set out seven propositions about the nature of human aging from the psychological perspective: 1) there are major differences between normal, optimal and pathological aging; 2) there is much variability in aging; 3) there is much latent reserve (plasticity); 4) there is an aging loss near the limits of reserve; 5) knowledge-related pragmatics and technology can offset age-related decline in cognitive mechanics; 6) with aging, the balance between gains and losses becomes less positive; and 7) the self remains resilient in old age.

This provides a sound conceptual basis for understanding the psychological dimensions for aging, and many of the studies cited by Baltes and Baltes are of major importance to our understanding of psychological changes in old age. For instance, Salthouse (1984) examined the performance of younger and older typists and found that although older typists were slower in tapping speed, some of them exhibited superior typing performance and this may be because they compensated for the reduction in speed by reading ahead in the text. Finally, Baltes and Baltes provide a model for improving performance in aging known as selective optimization with compensation. This model is then used to characterize certain aspects of old age, such as care in nursing homes, and is well illustrated by a description of how the famous pianist Anton Rubenstein managed to maintain his virtuoso performances in old age.

In this way, the model suggests that individuals can optimize their performance in old age by carefully considering their skills, limitations and priorities. This particularly resonant essay provides not only hope, but also a very constructive theoretical approach for improving people's performance and well-being in old age.

Social and Emotional Functioning in Old Age

Positive psychology has recently been highlighted in a number of aging-related studies. In Chapter 6 B. Nygren and his colleagues look at various aspects of positive psychological approaches to aging, including resilience, sense of coherence, purpose in life and self-transcendence. Their work advances the field because it looks at this important combination of factors in a sample of people 85 years and older, commonly referred to as the 'oldest old'. The positive psychology approach in aging is developing, despite the acknowledged difficulties of the limitations found in old age such as losses associated with physical capacity and cognitive resources, social status, friends and family members. Resilience is most distinctly described as a personal characteristic that influences one's ability to recover from adverse experience. According to Antonovsky (1987), 'sense of coherence' involves three dimensions with regard to the world and one's life, including: comprehensibility, manageability and meaningfulness. The concepts of purpose in life and self-transcendence help to enhance meaningfulness and sense of worth.

Nygren *et al.*'s study looks at these four key variables (resilience, sense of coherence, purpose in life and self-transcendence), as well as mental and physical health, in 125 participants in relation to the SF36 health survey questionnaire. The authors find significant correlations between the scores for resilience, sense of coherence, purpose in life and self-transcendence. But there were also correlations between these scales and the mental health element of the SF36 amongst women, but not in men. There were no significant correlations between perceived physical and mental health and the results suggest that the oldest old have the same or higher scores than younger age groups. Nygren *et al.* conclude that the scales measure some dimension of inner strength, and the oldest old have this strength to the same extent as younger adults. For men, the positive psychology variables accounted for only 6 per cent of the variance in mental health and the model was not significant. However, for women, these variables accounted for 30 per cent of the variance in mental health and the model reached statistical significance. Nygren *et al.* describe the characteristics of resilience, sense of coherence, purpose in life and self-transcendence as aspects of inner strength that are crucial for retaining health and handling adversity. These inner strengths might be open to enhancement and they may be particularly important in helping to counterbalance the negative views of the aging process within healthcare systems.

The relationship between social networks, social support and physical aspects of well-being in old age is not clearly understood. In a major piece of research from the MacArthur Studies of Successful Aging, Jennifer Unger *et al.* (Chapter 7) examine in-depth the possible moderating effect of high health status and socioeconomic factors on physical health. Unger *et al.* highlight many previous studies on social support in relation to mortality and physical disorders and put this in the context of the idea of successful aging, whereby people maintain a good quality of life and functional independence. The MacArthur Studies of Successful Aging comprise a longitudinal study of relatively high-functioning men and women aged 70–79, based in three centres in the USA. Over 4,000 men and women fulfilled the age criteria, but only 1,330 of these were identified as high-functioning on the basis of four criteria of physical abilities and two criteria of cognitive functioning; of this potential sample 90 per cent agreed to participate. The baseline data were collected in 1998 and 1999. The mean follow-up was 86 months. Unger *et al.* find that increased social support is associated with less functional decline after controlling for various potential confounding variables. The beneficial effects of social support are higher for males and those with lower baseline physical performance, suggesting that having a good social network may be protective against physical decline. The authors acknowledge that using a high-functioning cohort may limit generalizability, but highlight the importance of their research in gaining a better understanding of what can be done to promote more successful aging.

In a classic study looking at social support and health, Donald Sherbourne *et al.* (Chapter 8) examine quality-of-life differences in relation to social support, stressful life events and age in people with chronic illness. They note that as chronic diseases are long-term by their nature, treatment and care outcomes often need to be geared towards maintaining adequate functioning and improving quality of life. Often, variations in physical well-being and functional status cannot be accounted for solely by looking at either age or type of disorder, so a better understanding is required of what other factors determine good health outcomes. Stressful life events, for example, may have differential effects for older and younger adults, depending on the particular type of event, yet most studies have generally focused on healthy older people and it is not known how far these and other factors, such as social support, might influence the outcome of chronic diseases.

Sherbourne *et al.*'s study examines the extent to which social support and stressful life events affected long-term physical functioning and mental health in 1,402 adults between the ages of 19 and 98 (average age 59 years) with one of four chronic illnesses (diabetes, coronary heart disease, hypertension and depression). Low levels of social support appeared to be particularly damaging for the physical functioning of older people. However, stressful life events seemed to have varying effects. Relationship events had an immediate effect on well-being, which diminished over time whereas financial events had an immediate negative effect on functioning and well-being, which persisted over time for middle-aged patients. Bereavement seemed to have a delayed impact on quality of life, with younger adults being more vulnerable to the negative effects. Work-related events had a variety of negative and positive effects, depending on the age group. Retirement as a work event had no negative health impact on older people, perhaps because it is usually considered a normal experience. It should also be acknowledged that the authors used a checklist approach to measuring events and so, in many instances, the events may have been precipitated by the person themselves and the level of threat for the event would vary according to the context of the person experiencing the event. The authors conclude that professionals dealing with patients with chronic diseases need to be aware of the importance of identifying and dealing with psychosocial factors such as social support and life events.

According to Laura Carstensen, Derek Isaacowitz and Susan Charles who discuss socioemotional selectivity theory in Chapter 9, across the life cycle social motives fall into two categories: knowledge acquisition and emotional regulation. They go on to describe, with engaging clarity, the principles of socioemotional selectivity theory which argues that time left in life and chronological age tend to determine social goals. When time is perceived as open-ended, knowledge-based goals are prioritized whereas when time is perceived as more limited emotional goals are prioritized. However, the authors argue that perception of time is malleable and that social goals change in both older and younger people when time constraints are imposed. They support the theoretical model with evidence from a novel programme of studies comparing older and younger people but also looking at the effects that constraints (for example, terminal illness) have on the prioritization of goals. This remarkable, provocative, and intriguing essay is likely to be influential for many years ahead.

Lifestyle and Well-being in Old Age

One of the running themes throughout this Introduction is the potential for people to be able to influence their own functioning, well-being and performance through changes in their lifestyle, behaviour and activities. In Part III, two essays look at social and leisure activities in relation to reducing the risk of dementia. The first by Hui-Xin Wang *et al.* (Chapter 10) examines older people's engagement in social and leisure activities in a longitudinal study from the Kungsholmen project. The authors suggest that a rich social network might decrease the risk of developing dementia, due some kind of protective effect of social interaction and intellectual stimulation. To test this hypothesis, they investigated whether engagement in different activities was related to a decreased incidence of dementia at follow-up, on average 6.4 years later. The long follow-up period is worthy of remark as it could be argued that this would pre-date any early symptoms of dementia. Wang *et al.* cite previous studies suggesting that an inactive life is related to a higher risk of dementia, but note that case control studies have been criticized because of possible biases in selection and recall. There is also the problem that in the early stages of dementia people may reduce their activities for a variety of reasons, including cognitive impairment.

Wang *et al.*'s study involved all inhabitants of the Kungsholmen district of Stockholm aged 75 years (or older) in October 1987 and without a diagnosis of dementia. The participants were interviewed at baseline and at two further follow-ups. Social and leisure activities were assessed by means of a personal interview covering types of activity (mental, physical, social and productive) and frequency of participation. Social network was classified in four ways: extensive, moderate, limited or poor. At follow-up, 123 incident cases of dementia were identified and, after adjustment for baseline variables, frequency of engagement in mental, social or productive activities was related to a reduced risk of dementia. The authors suggest that mental stimulation itself may play a role in preserving cognition, but also that participation in productive or social activities may help sustain a person's self-concept of usefulness and competence. With hindsight, perhaps the categorization of the activities could be challenged in that it may have been better to try to emphasize activities that were mental, social or physical. For example, playing cards or board games was categorized as a social activity, but might also be considered as highly mentally stimulating. The authors conclude that stimulating activity involving either mental or psychosocial components may help to preserve cognition or hinder cognitive decline, although their study did not find a causal relationship.

Soon after Wang *et al.*'s essay was published in 2002, Joe Verghese *et al.* (Chapter 11) reported on a similar study looking at leisure activities and the risk of dementia in a prospective cohort of 469 people aged over 75 living in the community and without dementia at baseline. They carried out an extensive battery of neuropsychological tests at study visits, and the potential study period consisted of 21 years between 1980 and 2001. The average length of follow-up overall was just over five years. Verghese *et al.* classified activities into either cognitive or physical, and recorded the frequency of participation. They used responses to generate a scale corresponding to one point for each activity per day per week, so that subjects would receive seven points for participating in one activity every day. Diagnosis of dementia was rigorous, and all cases were discussed at case conferences. The authors found that dementia developed in 124 people. Among leisure activities, reading, playing board games, playing musical instruments and dancing were associated with reduced risk of dementia, but they also found that a one-point increment in the cognitive activity score was associated with a reduced risk of dementia. These findings persisted when other factors were controlled for and after excluding subjects with possible pre-clinical dementia at baseline. In the third of the overall group with the highest rate of activities there was a 63 per cent lower rate of developing dementia. Even when they only included cases that had more than seven years' follow-up, this association was still present. For future research they suggest that clinical trials are needed to define the possible role of leisure activities in reducing the rate of dementia.

Physical exercise may have a range of physical and mental benefits in older people, and in Chapter 12 Nalin Singh *et al.* examine the efficacy of exercise as a long-term antidepressant in older people in a randomized controlled trial. Exercise is now more widely recognized as having worthwhile antidepressant effects particularly in younger adults, but the authors state that they found little evidence for its effectiveness for depression in older people. This study is particularly interesting as it examines long-term, rather than acute, effects in a group of older people in the community with diagnosed depression. The authors note that existing research raises the following questions: were the antidepressant effects of weight-lifting sustainable over the long term? Was the efficacy of exercise in depression dependent on a supervised method of delivery? Would a short period of training lead to long-term exercise use?

This study followed on from an earlier study examining the effects on a group of ten weeks of intensive exercise running three times a week, and followed up participants during weeks 10–20 and months 6–26, when the exercise intervention group continued unsupervised and was only monitored through a brief weekly phone call. During the first follow-up period the exercise group were offered three alternatives, continued supervised training at the sports centre, continued training at a community health facility or home-based training with free weights and written materials. Depression in those who exercised was significantly reduced at the 20-week and 26-month follow-ups compared with controls. The benefits of treatment were most pronounced in those with more severe depression and persisted even when the supervision in group training had been withdrawn.

In terms of mechanisms, Singh *et al.* suggest that the exercisers developed a more positive attitude towards their aging whereas ratings of loneliness and agitation did not differ between the groups. They also suggest that a more optimistic view of the aging process may help minimize depressive reactions to the stresses and events that might be experienced. In this way, increased self-efficacy may help disrupt the maladaptive cognitive processes of people with depression. The authors recommend that randomized controlled trials are needed to evaluate the potency of exercise in comparison with standard pharmacological and psychological treatments. They conclude that progressive resistance training exercise is safe, feasible and effective for depression. This study adds to the growing body of work indicating that changes to mental and physical activity may be beneficial to mental health.

Psychological Aspects of Dementia

The importance of psychology in the understanding, diagnosis and treatment of dementia has grown considerably in recent years. In a move away from the traditional medical model of dementia, it is becoming increasingly accepted that dementia is influenced by numerous factors in addition to neurological damage – in other words, that it is a biopsychosocial illness (Downs, Clare and Anderson, 2008). This thinking has had a huge impact on the ability of psychologists to intervene and has been paralleled by an increase in the development, as well as more rigorous evaluations, of psychological interventions for dementia.

Part IV of this volume opens with a seminal essay by Tom Kitwood – whose ideas have had a great influence on the way dementia is perceived, particularly within care settings – and Kathleen Bredin (Chapter 13). Kitwood and Bredin propose that the process of dementia should be viewed as a dialectical interplay between two tendencies – neurological impairment and psychological factors (involving both personal and social psychology) – on the basis that the degree of neuropathology often correlates poorly with the level of functional, psychological and social impairment. In their essay, Kitwood and Bredin introduce the idea of 'personhood', which emphasizes treating individuals as people rather than sufferers of an illness. Although simple, these concepts still remain hugely neglected in many care settings.

In later writings Kitwood described a 'malignant social psychology', whereby the negative psychology surrounding people with dementia can have a significant impact on their impairment and well-being. He described 17 factors which occur in the interactions between many care staff and people with dementia, including treachery, disempowerment and infantilization (Kitwood, 1997). Kitwood referred to such negative care environments as the 'old culture of dementia care', presenting the challenge of moving towards a new, more positive 'culture'. More than a decade on, this still remains a challenge, but Kitwood's ideas have become very influential in care practice and national policy.

Research demonstrating the inconsistent and often weak relationship between the presenting dementia in the living person and neurological changes post mortem continues to provide support for the notion that dementia is influenced by an array of factors. Although Kitwood's 'dialectical model of dementia' is still used, more recent research points to the influence of additional factors on the presenting dementia. These include pre-morbid intelligence (Stern, Chapter 4), cognitive stimulation (Spector *et al.*, Chapter16), and life events (Orrell and Bebbington, 1998).

In Chapter 14 R.T. Woods eloquently summarizes his biopsychosocial approach towards dementia and describes the cognitive, emotional and behavioural aspects. He highlights the fact that people may suffer considerable disability over and above what would be expected from the level of their neurological impairment. Woods reviews a number of theories and intervention studies – for example, describing phases of adaptation to dementia and paying attention to different coping mechanisms and their effect on a person's experience of the disease – and goes on to emphasize the importance of holding on cognitively and outline key cognitive rehabilitation techniques. In a discussion of the emotional response to dementia, he reviews emotionally-oriented approaches such as validation therapy, which focuses on the emotional meaning of people's behaviour and speech rather than the factual content. Finally, he provides a beautiful description of the way in which challenging behaviour is a result of unmet or poorly communicated needs – for example, shouting might be reflecting a physical pain which cannot be adequately communicated. Woods concludes by talking about the need to respond flexibly in supporting 'personhood' as an individual's capacities diminish.

This increased understanding of the psychological and social factors affecting dementia has coincided with the development of interventions and therapies which tap in to these areas. The key aims of the multitude of approaches appear to be: (1) improving emotional well-being and quality of life; (2) improving cognitive function; and/or (3) improving behavioural function (Woods and Clare, 2008). To illustrate this, we have included in Part IV two essays on cognitive stimulation, and another that reviews behavioural interventions for dementia.

It has long been known that mental activities and stimulation are important in slowing down mental deterioration in dementia – for example Lorand (1913) stated that '[w]ork of any kind, even mental work alone, is a means of preventing precocious senility'. The development of reality orientation (RO) and reminiscence therapy (RT) in the 1960s made a significant impact at the time, in that these approaches began to introduce the concept of rehabilitation in dementia. It started to become apparent that people with dementia could take a more active role in their treatment and that, as a consequence, aspects of their well-being could actually improve. In an essay dating from that period Lucille Taulbee and James Folsom (Chapter 15) describe reality orientation – the re-teaching of orientation information to 'confused geriatric' or brain-damaged patients. Their intervention involved activities such as relearning to write your name in a classroom-type environment, led by an 'instructor'. The authors describe how their approach 'makes the patient feel that he is worth something after all, that he can still accomplish something, that life has not passed him by and that there are still people in the world who care about him' (p. 194). Although such ideas are now the accepted norm of person-centred care, this essay provides an interesting insight into the way in which people with dementia were treated at the time as passive recipients of care. Although now largely superseded by new approaches and philosophy, this work was ground-breaking because it introduced the idea that people with dementia can take an active role in their rehabilitation.

Orrell and Woods (1996) highlighted the enormous discrepancy between the quality of research on pharmacological therapies and on psychological therapies for dementia. Whereas most of the former had been evaluated through large, double-blind randomized controlled trials, trials in the latter tended to be small and contain methodological weaknesses such as a lack of control group. Consequently, although there was much anecdotal evidence that psychological therapies were beneficial and the effectiveness of most of the drugs was limited, the major emphasis in terms of treatment for dementia was pharmacological. Subsequently, their group developed an evidence-based psychological therapy programme for dementia known as cognitive stimulation therapy (CST). As explained by Aimee Spector *et al.*, (Chapter 16), CST was developed by systematically reviewing all the research on the major psychological therapies for dementia. Using these reviews, Spector and her colleagues extracted features from trials with significant outcomes and combined these to create a 14-session programme of themed, stimulating activities over seven weeks. This was evaluated as a multi-centre randomized controlled trial (RCT) for 201 people with dementia. Results showed that CST led to significant benefits in cognition and quality of life, was cost-effective, and that the magnitude of changes in cognition were similar in scale to that achieved by the major drugs used to treat dementia. As a consequence, the recent UK guidelines produced by the National Institute of Clinical Excellence (NICE) recommend the use of structured group CST for cognitive symptoms and maintenance of function in dementia, regardless of medication used. CST is now widely used in the UK and in a number of other countries. This is a clear example of the need to use evidence-based research with strong methodology in order to have a wider political impact. Despite the encouraging results, however, the study conducted by Spector *et al.* was only short-term and there is a need to know more about the possible longer-term effects of CST. In addition, little is known about the effects of CST (and related therapies) in combination with drugs for dementia: are the effects synergistic or is there little or no benefit from a combined approach?

Jiska Cohen-Mansfield (Chapter 17) provides a review of non-pharmacological interventions for 'inappropriate behaviour' in dementia. Inappropriate behaviour is defined as 'inappropriate verbal, vocal or motor activity that is not judged by an outside observer to be an obvious outcome of the needs or confusion of the individual' (p. 205). Behaviours are then divided into four categories: (1) physically aggressive behaviour (for example, biting); (2) physically non-aggressive behaviour (for example, pacing); (3) verbally non-aggressive agitation (for example, repetition); and verbal aggression (for example, screaming). Cohen-Mansfield describes how such behaviours have historically been treated with psychotropic drugs or physical restraints, or have been ignored. She subsequently reviews some psychological theories which provide an understanding of the cause of these behaviours: as an expression of unmet needs, as a learnt behaviour, or as a result of environmental vulnerability. She argues that these models are not mutually exclusive and may be complementary, but most importantly that they indicate the need for more psychological interventions to target these behaviours because these would be more appropriate to addressing the biopsychosocial cause of the behaviours. She also points out that medication may mask a person's actual need by eliminating the behaviour that signals the need, hence reducing a person's already limited communication. The systematic review includes trials of all methodology. This yields 83 articles, which she divides into: sensory enhancement/relaxation methods (for example, music and sensory stimulation), behavioural interventions, staff training, structured activities, environmental design, medical/nursing interventions and combination interventions. She finds that 91 per cent of studies reported some benefit and 53 per cent reported a significant improvement from baseline. Cohen-Mansfield's thoughtful discussion offers some principles which should be considered as primary targets for future non-pharmacologic interventions, including provision of social contact and meaningful stimuli or activity, and tailoring the intervention to the individual. This review is really helpful in providing the reader with a theoretical rationale for using some of these interventions, an overview of what might be used, and some practical guidance to follow when working clinically with people presenting with such problems.

In dementia, the results of neuropsychological testing may be crucial – for example, in localizing specific deficits, distinguishing between depression and dementia or identifying subtypes of dementia. The skills of psychologists are also often drawn upon for the more sensitive issue of feedback, diagnosis and emotional support. The next essay by Florence Pasquier (Chapter 18) neatly summarizes the importance of neuropsychology in the diagnosis of dementia. It reviews the commonly used neuropsychological tools and the main cognitive functions assessed, including memory, language and visuospatial ability. It then offers a description of the neuropsychological profiles of the main dementia syndromes at early stages. This essay merited inclusion as it provides a much needed and accessible overview of the area.

In the UK many people with dementia live in formal care settings. The negative psychological consequences of such institutionalization been widely researched (see, for example, Woods and Clare, 2008). In Chapter 19 E. Moniz-Cook, R. Woods and E. Gardiner address the critical issue of the relationship between formal care staff and people with dementia, looking at staff factors associated with their perception of behaviour as challenging. The study involved 326 staff working in 14 residential and nursing homes across England, who were given a number of vignettes describing 'challenging resident behaviour' and asked to appraise the vignettes. Staff factors were also evaluated. Staff anxiety, supervisor support and the potential to relate to residents as individuals predicted 'perceived management difficulty'. These findings have important implications for clinical psychologists, who are often referred clients with dementia displaying 'challenging behaviour' in care homes. The authors suggest that the problem might lie as much within the care staff as within the person with dementia, and that providing support and advocating a person-centred approach is essential.

Families, Carers and the Care Environment

With the rapid increase in life expectancy, more people are living to an age at which they become dependent on others. Care may be 'informal', involving family members, friends and volunteers, or 'formal', involving paid carers and staff. Over the years, the tendency for many families to live further apart, the increased emphasis on women in the workforce and people having fewer children have all combined to reduce the availability of family carers. Most of the carer literature focuses on home carers and tends also to concentrate on primary, as opposed to secondary, caregivers, implying that the carer takes on most caregiving activities (often living with the person they care for). Caring for a disabled older person has been identified as one of the most stressful and disruptive events in the family life cycle (Zarit and Edwards, 2008). There is great variation in the way in which people adapt to caring, just as any potentially stressful situation will be perceived differently by different people. Their approach will be affected by their own histories, personalities, coping mechanisms and support systems. Caring for older people with any physical or mental health issue can be a huge strain on the caregiver and although the majority of studies have focused on dementia, many of the issues are very relevant to other populations of carers.

Robin Morris, Lorna Morris and Peter Britton (Chapter 20) provide an excellent summary of research from psychiatry, clinical and social psychology, looking at factors which mediate the emotional well-being of carers of dementia sufferers. Differentiating between objective burden (the behavioural challenges of caring and their effect on the person's life) and subjective burden (the carer's emotional reaction to this), they argue that there is a weak correlation between degree of symptoms and emotional disturbance or strain. Subsequently, the essay focuses on factors affecting the subjective burden, including the meaning a person attributes to their situation, the quality of the relationship between the carer and the cared-for, the carer's coping strategies and the availability of formal and informal support. The essay raises interesting areas for debate, including the association between a low past level of marital intimacy and depression and the differing perceptions of caring between genders.

The stress process model of Leonard Pearlin *et al.* (Chapter 21) is arguably the most influential conceptual model for understanding caregiver stress. The essay looks beyond factors that influence stress to the 'process' by which they interact. For example, stress will be processed differently according to a person's social support or coping mechanisms. Within this model, the authors present four domains: the background and context of stress; the stressors themselves (with a distinction between primary and secondary stressors); the mediators of stress; and the outcomes or manifestations of stress. Primary and secondary stressors correspond to objective and subjective burden – for example, they include cognitive impairment and problematic behaviour as primary stressors and family conflict and loss of self-esteem as secondary. This model can be very easily applied when formulating a carer's individual difficulties and in considering how to intervene clinically. As well as presenting a thorough and coherent model, the authors developed a number of measures to assess components of the model and used the largest (555) sample of carers to that date.

One of the challenges in understanding the relative effects on carers is how to measure carer stress. In 1980 Steven Zarit, Karen Reever and Julie Bach-Peterson developed the leading scale for evaluating carer burden, widely known as the Zarit Burden Interview (although the original title was simply the Burden Interview). Their essay (Chapter 22) describes the need for, and the development of, the scale, noting that earlier studies 'have not clarified how specific behaviors contribute to the burden of home care' (p. 270). The study looked at level of burden in relation to cognitive function, duration of illness, memory and behaviour problems, and living skills. The authors find that only family visits were associated with reduced feelings of burden by the primary carer. This leads them to argue that interventions involving the family could be worthwhile to help support the carer and so reduce institutionalization.

There is a huge variety of ways in which caregivers can be supported, such as through providing education (about the illness and what to expect) or practically through help with legal issues or respite care. With such a range of psychosocial interventions available for carers, the next study by Henry Brodaty, Alisa Green and Annette Koschera (Chapter 23) includes a meta-analysis of 30 controlled trials of different interventions, including individual and family counselling, stress management, training and education. This review finds that caregiver interventions have modest but significant benefits on caregiver knowledge, psychological morbidity, coping skills and social support. When looking at depression as an outcome, Brodaty, Green and Koschera find a mean effect size across studies of 0.3, implying that the average patient in the treatment group was less depressed than about 62 per cent of patients in the control group. This effect size is even greater for increase in caregiver knowledge. The authors suggest that the results should be interpreted with caution, due to the heterogeneity of the studies. One factor which emerges as significant across studies is the involvement of the person with dementia in a structured programme, such as teaching the carer problem-solving skills in the care of the patient. Qualitatively important features include involvement of the extended family, structured individual counselling and the flexible provision of a consistent professional to provide long-term support.

Brodaty, Green and Koschera state that the quality of research into carer interventions is advancing, but that there is considerable room for methodological improvement. Thus the next essay describes the ground-breaking study by Mary Mittelman *et al.* (Chapter 24), a large, randomized controlled trial looking at the effects of enhanced counselling and support for caregivers over three years – a longer time period than that of most other intervention studies. This study included 406 spouse caregivers who were randomized into two groups, one receiving a structured counselling intervention followed by a weekly support group and continuous availability of ad hoc counselling and the other receiving usual care, involving receiving information and advice on request, and the option to take part in support groups and ad hoc counselling if they so chose. In the first year, the authors found a significant decrease in depressive symptoms in those receiving enhanced treatment, but an increase in those receiving usual care. Sustained improvements were found more than three years after the programme began, despite comparison with a control group who had received more support than care normally offered. This was a strong study due to its size, methodology and long follow-up. However, how much such an intense support system would cost, and hence how practical it would be to implement on a large scale, remains to be seen.

In recent years there has been a growing emphasis, in both research and practice, on the quality of care, choice and empowerment in the care of older people in institutions such as residential homes or nursing homes. Thirty years ago there was almost no research on the care of people in nursing home settings and no consistent recommendations for good practice to improve people's quality of life. This is one of the reasons why the essay by Judith Rodin and Ellen Langer (Chapter 25) on the long-term effects of an intervention with the 'institutionalized aged' is so important and remains influential today. This study was based on an earlier field study to assess the effect of an intervention designed to encourage elderly residents of nursing homes to make more choices in their everyday life and to experience more control over, and responsibility for, events. The hope was that the intervention could potentially help reduce the decline in health, alertness and activity which often seemed to occur in older people in care home settings. The population was divided into a treatment group in which the hospital administrator emphasized to residents their responsibility for themselves, and a control group in which the administrator emphasized to residents the staff responsibility for them as patients. The treatment group were given plants to look after, whereas the control group were given plants that were watered by the staff. The authors state that the treatment induction 'was intended to bolster individual predispositions for increased choice and control' (p. 293). The study found that people in the treatment (responsibility) group appeared to be more active and sociable and showed more initiative than the comparison group. Moreover, there the death rate at 18 months follow-up was 30 per cent in the control group compared to 15 per cent in the treatment group. The groups were not randomized, and the authors acknowledge that they 'simply cannot know everything about the equivalency of these subjects prior to the intervention' (p. 296). However, this was a novel study which made efforts to reduce bias and have some degree of blindness for the researchers completing the ratings. Rodin and Langer suggest that further studies should look at patient–nurse interaction to assess if and how this factor relates to patients' health. Their work has helped to lay the foundations for social models of intervention in care home settings and emphasizes the importance of staff and resident interactions.

Our final essay in Part V by Sheryl Zimmerman *et al.* (Chapter 26) addresses the crucial issue of formal care, this time looking at factors related to quality of life (QoL) in assisted living and nursing homes. In order to gather information needed to guide policy and the development of best practice, the authors recruited 421 randomly selected residents with dementia, living in 35 care facilities over four states in the USA. They used a variety of report and observational measures to examine the structure and process of care, such as looking at staff turnover, job satisfaction and attitudes towards dementia. They then directly observed resident-staff relationship, looking at factors such as communication and 'positive person work' (Kitwood). Further, they measured QoL using standardized measures, three of which were direct resident measures, six of which were measured by care providers and three observational measures. This study is therefore unusual in terms of its large sample size and multi-method and multi-informant outcome approach. The authors collected data cross-sectionally at baseline and at six-month follow-up. They found that change in QoL was better in facilities which used a specialized worker approach, trained more staff in domains central to dementia care and encouraged activity participation. Of interest, residents perceived their QoL as better when staff were more involved in care planning and when their attitudes were more favourable. This latter finding was mirrored in our own study which showed a link between staff hope and resident QoL in care homes (Spector and Orrell, 2006). Zimmerman also found that QoL was lower in facilities that used more drug treatment such as antipsychotics, and when residents were ungroomed. The results lead to some extremely helpful guidance as to how care should be offered to maximize well-being and quality of life. These include training all staff in domains central to dementia, encouraging participation in activities and involving staff in care planning, and finding ways of encouraging more hope.

Psychological Aspects of Mental Health Problems in Old Age

In Part VI our first three selected essays provide an overall review of depression in later life, some ideas of how events across the lifetime contribute to late-life depression and a model of how CBT, the therapeutic intervention for depression recommended in the NICE guidelines may be adapted for late-life depression. Anxiety disorders are common in older people (Manela, Katona and Livingston, 1996), and the next essay describes an RCT to reduce fear of falling, a common and disabling anxiety disorder in older people. Two further essays look at major life stress and its consequences for mental health, and our final essay in this section considers the issue of personality disorders in later life, which introduces some provocative thoughts as to how clinical psychologists might understand the presentation of some of our older patients.

Dan Blazer (Chapter 27) provides a timely and comprehensive review and commentary of depression in late life. His essay covers diagnostic criteria, epidemiology, outcomes, aetiology, diagnostic evaluation and treatment. In the psychological sphere Blazer offers examples of behavioural, psychodynamic and cognitive causes of late-life depression. For example, the behavioural theory of 'learned helplessness' can be applied to older people who suffer from continued losses and thus may feel that they have no control over their life. He also highlights the key psychological interventions for depression, including CBT and psychodynamic therapy. We included this essay as it provides an excellent overview of most of the key issues with regard to depression in old age.

To introduce the debate as to what causes depression in late life, we follow up with an interesting essay by V. Kraaij and E.J. de Wilde (Chapter 28), which looks at events across the lifespan as contributors to depression. Kraaij and de Wilde point out that recent negative life events, such as experiences of loss and severe illness, are widely studied and linked to depression, but with little focus on events occurring in earlier life. They interviewed 194 older people and found that death of significant others, sexual abuse and relational stress, occurring throughout life, were all significantly related to depression after controlling for age and gender. In contrast, physical abuse and crime, disaster and war events were not associated with depressive symptoms. However, studies have found that extreme war events are related to depression, suggesting that more exploration is needed into which specific war events have long-lasting effects on well-being. An important consideration is the fact that correlation does not imply causation – there may have been a number of other causes of depression in each individual, which were not measured within this study.

Cognitive behavioural therapy (CBT) has established efficacy for depression in older people, yet research generally seems to focus on outcome, as opposed to process issues. Ken Laidlaw, Larry Thompson and Dolores Gallagher-Thompson (Chapter 29) provide an excellent model that addresses age-related issues within a CBT framework. They begin by stating that one might debate the point of this exercise in the light of evidence suggesting that CBT may not benefit older people. Nonetheless, in their view, anecdotal evidence that, for example, 'cognitive restructuring' may seem too abstract for many older people, suggests that some modifications may improve the standard model. Laidlaw, Thompson and Gallagher-Thompson present a conceptual framework, featuring the standard CBT model for depression at its centre, but with five added elements. The first is cohort beliefs – for example, a person from an older cohort may have different beliefs about lifestyle choices or gender roles which could affect the therapeutic relationship. Further, the stigma of mental illness is far greater in the current cohort of older people than in younger generations; older people might be more likely to attribute their problems to physical, as opposed to emotional, symptoms, making depression harder to detect. The second new element is 'intergenerational linkages' which can cause tensions due to misunderstandings and expectations about notions of family and 'milestones' in life progression. For example, older generations may be disappointed by their offspring if they have not 'settled down' and had children by the age of 30. It is common for relationship strains between older adults and their children to precipitate a depressive episode. The other three remaining elements are transitions in role investments, sociocultural context and physical health. The authors provide case examples throughout, making this model extremely tangible, and state that mapping out these domains has helped many therapists to conduct treatments and interventions.

To highlight one of the key influences on anxiety in older age, our next essay by Sharon Tennstedt *et al.* (Chapter 30) involves a randomized controlled trial of a group intervention (named 'a matter of balance') to reduce fear of falling (FOF) and associated activity restriction in older people. It had previously been shown that FOF was the most common fear in a sample of older people living in the community, and that it commonly leads to restricted physical and social activity. Further, FOF may become a risk factor for further falls, due to deconditioning and associated muscle weakness. Tennstedt *et al.* recruited 434 people over the age of 60. Participants either received a brief group intervention, involving cognitive restructuring, goal-setting, environmental change and increasing physical exercise or a brief social control group (only lasting two hours). The study showed that this eight-session intervention led to an immediate effect of increasing the level of intended activities and mobility control, although the effects were lost at six-month follow-up. The authors argue that one or more booster sessions would therefore be needed to reinforce the changes made, although they acknowledge that an intervention which is in itself an 'activity' might not be greatly appealing to people who are by definition 'inactive'. Hence in-home, individualized interventions may have greater effects than the group intervention they present. Interestingly, the actual number of falls did not significantly differ between the two groups for up to 12 months. The relationship between increased activity and expected number of falls is unclear in the authors' discussion. On the one hand, increased activity may lead to physical deconditioning and a subsequent reduction of falls; on the other hand, the more active people are, the more likely they are to fall. Measures of well-being, mood and anxiety would have enhanced this study, as they are likely to be knock-on effects of FOF and the impact of the group on these factors would be interesting to know.

Bereavement, one of the most serious of all stressful life events, can occur at all ages, and a common complication of bereavement is depression. The essay by Larry Thompson *et. al.* (Chapter 31) was an important step forward because it looked at the long-term effects of late-life spousal bereavement over 30 months. The authors compared 212 bereaved older people with a control group who were either currently married or, if single, had not lost a spouse through death or divorce in the past five years, although, interestingly, the controls had to have experienced the death of another family member or a close friend during that period. The groups were roughly comparable in terms of age (55–63 years) and years of marriage. Structured interviews were carried out three times following the loss of spouse at two months, 12 months and 30 months. The authors found that differences in levels of depression at two months post loss had diminished to non-significant levels at 12 and 30 months. However, on measures of grief, the bereaved spouses were still significantly different from the controls at 30 months. Women reported more distress than men, regardless of bereavement status, yet did not report more symptoms of grief following the loss. Thompson *et al.* suggest that expressions of grief are consistent across both male and female genders, but expressions of depression are not. In the context of previous literature, their findings suggest that men and women express longing for their lost spouse in similar ways. This study provides important new information about the nature of bereavement and the differences between bereavement experiences and depression.

By the time they reach old age, many people have experienced a wide variety of stressful life experiences. In the current cohort of older people, their experiences during the Second World War may be some of the most traumatic stresses they have had to encounter. Many war veterans go on to have persistent mental health problems, particularly post-traumatic stress disorder (PTSD). In their seminal essay, A. Hautamaki and P.G. Coleman (Chapter 32) look at the experiences of older Finnish war veterans from the Second World War (which involved two wars with the Soviet Union and one to remove German forces from Northern Finland). Out of 700,000 men and women serving, almost half were either killed or injured. Despite these heavy losses, Finland retained its independence. Remarkably, earlier studies had found a very low rate of PTSD (under 10 per cent) in Finnish war veterans despite the multiplicity of medical problems and physical disabilities. In order to examine possible explanations for this, Hautamäki and Coleman carried out a qualitative study using in-depth interviews with 30 veterans with an average age of 77 years from a disabled veteran's hospital and a rehabilitation centre. They found low levels of PTSD and relatively high levels of subjective well-being. The veterans looked back on the war as an honourable task and emphasized Finnish fighting spirit and the strong bonds of loyalty with their comrades. War featured prominently as part of their current identity. The study suggested that a strong community spirit, together with continuing esteem from Finnish society, were the key factors contributing to the high levels of well-being expressed by the survivors. They described how individual and group resilience helped to make sense of a crisis situation and endow it with a deep meaning. Hautamäki and Coleman do, however, indicate one limitation to the study, namely that some of the less resilient may not have survived up to old age. This essay not only tells us much about adaptability and resilience in old age, but also neatly illustrates how qualitative research can provide deep and meaningful insight into the processes of human experience.

There is an interesting debate as to what happens to personality disorders (PDs) in later life, touched on by J.Q. Morse and T.R. Lynch in Chapter 33. Their study examined self-reported personality disorder traits in 65 depressed older people. They found that, in line with past research, clusters A (odd and eccentric, such as paranoid or schizoid PD) and C (anxious and inhibited, such as avoidant or dependent PD) were most prevalent. They also found that the presence of PD predicted the maintenance or re-emergence of depressive symptoms, as did hopelessness and ambivalence regarding emotional expression. They offer some theories as to why certain disorders do not change with age. For example, people may favour information which confirms, rather than challenges, their self-beliefs. A person with avoidant PD may repeatedly avoid social situations and hence never learn that they may be able to cope with them. It may also be that lifestyle habits which had helped the person cope with the disorder are no longer available in older age, leaving them vulnerable. For instance, a person with obsessive-compulsive PD may have used work as a coping strategy. In contrast, cluster B disorders (dramatic and erratic, such as antisocial or borderline PD) appeared to decline with old age. This may be because people have less energy for impulsive or reckless behaviour or have died or been imprisoned or become institutionalized (for example, some people with antisocial PD may have become criminals). Further, disconfirming environmental feedback, such as revulsion following self-harming, may slowly extinguish behaviours. This is a provocative debate which may raise questions for clinicians about appropriate diagnoses of some of our clients.

Conclusion

Many of the essays in this volume represent landmarks in the field of the psychology of aging, and we think that many others will be recognized as seminal contributions in the years to come. We hope you find this volume as exciting, challenging and stimulating as we have. It has been a source of inspiration and reflection for us.

Acknowledgement

We are grateful to Professor Bob Woods and Professor Ian Stuart Hamilton for suggesting some of the essays for inclusion.

References

Antonovsky, A. (1987), *Unraveling the Mystery of Health: How People Manage Stress and Stay Well*, San Francisco: Jossey-Bass Inc.

Downs, M., Clare, L. and Anderson, E. (2008), 'Dementia as a Biopsychosocial Condition: Implications for Practice and Research', in R.T. Woods and L. Clare (eds), *Handbook of the Clinical Psychology of Ageing*, Chichester: Wiley.

Katzman, R. (1993), 'Education and the Prevalence of Dementia and Alzheimer's Disease', *Neurology*, **43**, pp. 13–20.

Katzman, R., Aronson, M., Fuld, P., Kawas, C., Brown, T., Morgenstern, H., Frishman, W., Gidez, L., Eder, H. and Ooi, W.L. (1989), 'Development of Dementing Illnesses in an 80-year-old Volunteer Cohort', *Annals of Neurology*, **25**, pp. 317–24.

Kitwood, Tom (1997), *Dementia Reconsidered: The Person Comes First*, Buckingham: Open University Press.

Lindenberger, U. And Baltes, P.B. (1994), 'Sensory Functioning and Intelligence in Old Age: A Strong Connection', *Psychology and Aging*, **9**, pp. 339–55.

Lorand, A. (1913), *Old Age Deferred: The Causes of Old Age and its Postponement by Hygienic and Therapeutic Measures*, Philadelphia, PA: F.A. Davis Co.

Manela, M., Katona, C. and Livingston, G (1996), 'How Common are the Anxiety Disorders in Old Age?', *International Journal of Geriatric Psychiatry*, **11**(11), pp. 65–70.

Orrell, M.W. and Bebbington, P.E. (1998), 'Life Events and Cognition in Dementia', *Ageing and Mental Health*, **2**(1), pp. 53–59.

Orrell, M.W. and Sahakian, B. (1995), 'Education and Dementia: Research Evidence Supports the Concept of "Use it or Lose it"', *British Medical Journal*, **310**, pp. 951–52.

Orrell, M.W. and Woods, B. (1996), 'Tacrine and Psychological Therapies in Dementia – No Contest?', Editorial, *International Journal of Geriatric Psychiatry*, **11**, pp. 189–92.

Salthouse, T.A. (1984), 'The Skill of Typing', *Scientific American*, **250**, pp. 128–29.

Spector, A. and Orrell, M.W. (2006), 'Quality of Life in Dementia: A Comparison of the Perceptions of People with Dementia and Care Staff in Residential Homes', *Alzheimer's Disease and Associated Disorders*, **20**(3), pp. 160–65.

Woods, R.T. and Clare, L. (2008), 'Psychological Interventions for People with Dementia', in R.T. Woods and L. Clare (eds), *Handbook of the Clinical Psychology of Ageing*, Chichester: Wiley.

Zarit, S. and Edwards, A. (2008), 'Family Caregiving: Research and Clinical Intervention', in R.T. Woods and L. Clare (eds), *Handbook of the Clinical Psychology of Ageing*, Chichester: Wiley.

Part I
Cognition and Aging

[1]
The Stability of Individual Differences in Mental Ability from Childhood to Old Age: Follow-up of the 1932 Scottish Mental Survey

IAN J. DEARY
University of Edinburgh, Edinburgh, Scotland, UK

LAWRENCE J. WHALLEY
HELEN LEMMON
J.R. CRAWFORD
University of Aberdeen, Aberdeen, Scotland, UK

JOHN M. STARR
Royal Victoria Hospital, Edinburgh, Scotland, UK

All Scottish children born in 1921 and attending school on June 1, 1932 ($N = 87,498$) undertook a validated test of psychometric intelligence, The Moray House Test. We followed up 101 of these people at age 77 and re-administered the same mental ability test. Concurrent validity data are provided for the Moray House Test at age 11 ($n = 1,000$) and age 77 years ($n = 97$). The correlation between Moray House Test scores at age 11 and age 77 was 0.63, which adjusted to 0.73 when corrected for attenuation of ability range within the re-tested sample. This, the longest follow-up study of psychometric intelligence reported to date, shows that mental ability differences show substantial stability from childhood to late life.

INTRODUCTION

The stability of individual differences in human mental abilities is of scientific and popular interest (Jensen, 1980). In childhood, it is of interest to discover whether educational initiatives can boost ability levels and whether environmental insults—such as poor nutrition or lead pollution—can lower cognitive functions. In old age, there is intense

Table 1. Summary of Some Key Studies of the Stability of Individual Differences in Psychometric Intelligence

Study	Mean initial age (years)	Mean follow-up age	Correlation	Test used
Humphreys (1989)	2	9	0.56	Wechsler Preschool and Primary Scale of Intelligence and Wechsler Intelligence Scale for Children
	9	15	0.47	
	2	15	0.78	
Kangas and Bradway (1971)	4	42	0.41	Stanford–Binet
	14	42	0.68	
	30	42	0.77	
Eichorn et al. (1981)	17–18	36–48	0.83 (men), 0.77 (women)	Stanford–Binet or Wechsler Bellevue (initial) and Wechsler Adult Intelligence Scale (follow-up)
Plassman et al. (1995)	Approx. 18	Mid-60s	0.46	Army General Classification Test (initial) and Telephone Interview for Cognitive Status (follow-up)
Owens (1966)	19	50	0.79	Army Alpha
	50	61	0.92	
	19	61	0.78	
Nisbet (1957)	22	47	0.48	Simplex Group Test
Schwartzman et al. (1987)	25	65	0.78	Revised Examination "M"
Tuddenham et al. (1968)	30[a]	43	0.64–0.79	Army General Classification Test
Mortensen and Kleven (1993)	50	60	0.94	Wechsler Adult Intelligence Scale
	60	70	0.91	
	50	70	0.90	
Deary et al. (present study)	11	77	0.63	Moray House Test

[a]Subjects were probably 7 years younger than this making the follow-up interval 20 rather than 13 years.

interest in whether mental ability differences earlier in life contribute to the risk of dementia and other syndromes of cognitive decline (Snowdon et al., 1996).

There are reports of the stability of measures of mental ability: (a) within childhood (Humphreys, 1989); (b) from childhood to mid-adulthood (Kangas & Bradway, 1971); (c) across young- to mid-adulthood (Eichorn, Hunt, & Honzik, 1981; Nisbet, 1957; Owens, 1966; Plassman et al., 1995; Schwartzman, Gold, Andres, Arbuckle, & Chaikelson, 1987; Tuddenham, Blumenkrantz, & Wilkin, 1968); and (d) in old age (Mortensen & Kleven, 1993). Table 1 summarizes these studies, showing the duration across which stability of individual differences was assessed and the stability coefficients obtained. The studies collected in Table 1 show that intellectual ability differences become increasingly stable throughout childhood, and have high stability across many years of adulthood. Both the Concordia study (Schwartzman et al., 1987) and the Intergenerational Studies (Eichorn et al., 1981) found higher stability across adulthood for verbal abilities than for non-verbal/performance IQ-type abilities.

The value of knowing the stability of mental ability differences from early adulthood to old age was emphasized in two long-term follow-up studies. In the "Nun Study," the linguistic complexity of hand-written autobiographies in early adulthood correlated with the incidence of dementia and mental ability level in late life (Snowdon et al., 1996). In a separate study, recruits from the American armed forces in the early 1940s were administered the Army General Classification Test and followed up 50 years later using a brief telephone-administered cognitive interview (Plassman et al., 1995). This latter study made particular mention of the necessity yet rarity of having early life cognitive estimates in the interpretation of cognitive scores in old age. Therefore, though it is a research priority, we do not know the stability of psychometric intelligence differences from early to late life. The principal reason for this gap in our knowledge is the rarity of samples of the population who were tested in youth and then followed up in old age.

We now report the first follow-up study of human cognitive ability that extends from childhood (mean age 11 years) to old age (mean age 77 years), and is thus informative about the stability of mental functions across most of the human lifespan. Further improvements upon the best currently available studies (Plassman et al., 1995; Schwartzman et al., 1987; Snowdon et al., 1996) include: (i) the use of the same validated mental test at baseline and follow-up using identical instructions; (ii) characterization of the follow-up sample in terms of age, sex, and initial IQ with respect to the entire relevant Scottish population; and (iii) concurrent validation of the mental test at first testing (age 11 years) and follow-up (age 77).

BACKGROUND TO THE PRESENT STUDY

We used data from the 1932 Scottish Mental Survey to investigate the stability of psychometric intelligence differences across a gap of 66 years. The Scottish Mental Survey 1932, under the auspices of the Scottish Council for Research in Education (SCRE), sought to quantify the number of people in Scotland who were "mentally deficient." It was broadened to "obtain data about the whole distribution of the intelligence of Scottish pupils from one end of the scale to the other" (Scottish Council for Research in Education, 1933). On June 1, 1932, all children at school in Scotland and born in the calendar year 1921 undertook a group-administered mental ability test, including some practice items. Children were tested in classrooms by teachers who followed detailed printed instructions. The number of children tested was 87,498 (44,210 boys and 43,288 girls). A very small number of private schools and those children absent owing to sickness were the only 1921-born children not tested.

The group mental ability test used in the Survey is referred to in the original publication as the "Verbal Test" (Scottish for Council for Research in Education, 1933). The test comprises a variety of types of item as follows: following directions (14 items), same-opposites (11), word classification (10), analogies (8), practical items (6), reasoning (5), proverbs (4), arithmetic (4), spatial items (4), mixed sentences (3), cypher decoding (2), and other items (4). The test has 71 numbered items, 75 items in total, and the maximum possible score is 76. The test was closely related to the Moray House Test No. 12, which was used in "eleven-plus" examinations in England. We shall hereafter refer to the test as the Moray House Test. The scores on the Moray House Test in 1932 were validated by individually re-testing a representative sample of 1,000 of the children (500 boys, 500 girls) on the Stanford Revision of the Binet-Simon scale. Those who administered the individual Stanford-Binet tests had special training in mental testing.

METHOD

Subjects

The Scottish Council for Research in Education made the complete data set for the 1932 Scottish Mental Survey available to the authors. From January to May 1998, we traced local (North-East Scotland) survivors of the 1932 Scottish Mental Survey. With the approval of the Grampian Ethics of Research Committee and family doctors, we contacted 199 survivors randomly selected from the Community Health Index (the local register of people's allocations to family physicians in the UK's National Health Service) and 35 other locals who volunteered on hearing media reports of the study. Of the 234 potential subjects, 208 people agreed to a full physical and mental health assessment and 73 agreed, in addition to the aforementioned health checks, to re-take the Moray House Test precisely 66 years to the day after the first sitting. The 73 attended a group testing session at a large public hall in Aberdeen town center on June 1, 1998, the 66th anniversary of the original testing session. The hall was specially furnished with desks and chairs for a group examination. Some 28 other subjects attended on dates up to 5 months later at times convenient to them. All but one—who attended in a wheelchair—of the 101 re-tested subjects were ambulant. None of the 101 was suffering from any major physical or mental illness or medication known to affect cognitive functioning.

Mental Test and Procedure

The Moray House Test was administered in a group fashion using the same instructions as those used in 1932 (Scottish Council for Research in Education, 1933). Forty-five minutes were allowed for the completion of the test. Only two of the tests' items required minor altering from the 1932 version. A question involving shillings and pence was altered to feet and inches because, whereas money altered to a decimal format in the UK in 1971, the measurement of distance is still principally duodecimal, especially among old people. Another question archaically referring to "vitamine" was changed to read "vitamins." In addition to the newly gathered 1998 test scores, all subjects' Moray House Test scores were identified from the records of the 1932 sitting.

On a separate occasion, 97 of the 101 subjects completed a further mental ability test to provide concurrent validity for the 1998 scores on the Moray House Test. The test was Raven's Progressive Matrices (Raven, Court, & Raven, 1977), a non-verbal pattern-completion test. Raven's Matrices test is a good indicator of general intelligence (Spearman's g; Carroll, 1993). The Raven test was administered to subjects individually by trained researchers using a time limit of 20 min.

RESULTS

The mean score on the Moray House Test for the 101 subjects in 1932 was 43.3 (SD = 11.9), and for the same subjects in 1998 was 54.2 (11.8) (Table 2). Mean scores for men and women were very similar at age 11 but, at age 77, men scored higher than women by almost three points. A mixed model analysis of variance of Moray House Test scores was carried out with time as a repeated measure (1932 score vs. 1998 score) and sex as a between subjects factor. The effect of time was highly significant, with people scoring better at age 77 years than at age 11 (F = 118.0, df = 1.99, $p < 0.001$). There was no

Table 2. Descriptive Statistics of, and Correlations among, Mental Tests for All Subjects and Separately for Men and Women

	Mean (SD)	N	MHT 1932	MHT 1998
All subjects				
MHT 1932	43.3 (11.9)	101		
MHT 1998	54.2 (11.8)	101	0.63	
Raven	28.8 (8.5)	97	0.48	0.57
Men				
MHT 1932	43.1 (13.3)	49		
MHT 1998	55.6 (11.8)	49	0.62	
Raven	30.2 (8.6)	47	0.43	0.58
Women				
MHT 1932	43.5 (10.5)	52		
MHT 1998	52.8 (11.8)	52	0.67	
Raven	27.5 (8.3)	50	0.55	0.55

Note: All correlations are $p<0.01$. MHT = Moray House Test; Raven = Raven's Standard Progressive Matrices.

significant overall effect of sex on test scores ($F = 0.3$, $df = 1.99$, $p = 0.6$). There was a statistical trend in the interaction between time and sex, with men tending to gain higher scores over the 66-year gap between tests ($F = 2.6$, $df = 1.99$, $p = 0.1$).

The population mean score for the Moray House Test in 1932 was 34.5 (34.5 for 44,210 boys, and 34.4 for 43,288 girls), and the standard deviation was 15.5 (15.9 for boys, and 15.0 for girls). Thus, the sample re-tested in 1998 had a 1932 Moray House Test score mean that was 0.57 standard deviation units higher than the population mean—equivalent to 8.9 IQ points on a standard IQ-type scale with $\mu = 100$, $\sigma = 15$. The standard deviation in the re-tested sample was only 77% of that found in the population.

Concurrent Validity of the Moray House Test

From the re-test in 1998, the mean score on Raven's Standard Progressive Matrices was 28.8 ($SD - 8.5$) (Table 2). There was a trend toward higher mean scores among men ($t = 1.6$, $df = 95$, $p = 0.1$). Table 2 shows concurrent validity coefficients for the Moray House Test at both the 1932 and 1998 test waves. As described above, after taking the Moray House (group-administered) Test in 1932, 1,000 children (500 boys, 500 girls) were tested individually on the Stanford revision of the Binet intelligence test battery. The correlation between the Moray House Test and the Stanford–Binet test was 0.81 for the boys and 0.78 for the girls. In the 1998 re-tested sample, the correlation between Moray House Test raw score and raw score on Raven's Standard Progressive Matrices was 0.57 (Table 2). All coefficients have p values of < 0.001. The coefficients of men and women did not differ significantly.

Lifetime Stability of Mental Ability Differences

The Pearson r-correlation between the Moray House Test scores in 1932 and 1998 was 0.63 ($p < 0.001$). The 95% confidence limits on this correlation are from 0.50 to 0.74. This raw correlation is an underestimate of the true correlation in the population because of the attenuation of the re-tested sample with respect to variance on the 1932 Moray House Test scores. The disattenuated correlation across the 66-year gap, allowing for the restricted range of the sample, is 0.73. This corrected coefficient, too, is an underestimate of the true value because the correlation is further attenuated by measurement error on both testing occasions. The stability coefficients are similar for men and women (Table 2). The correlation between the Moray House Test scores in 1932 and the Raven test taken in 1998 was 0.48 ($p < 0.001$), not significantly different from the correlation between Raven and the Moray House Test taken in 1998.

Discussion

To our knowledge, this is the longest follow-up study of human psychometric intelligence differences reported to date. The interval between the two testing sessions comprises most of the normal human lifespan. The present study has design features which rarely occur together in other studies: the same test was used at first test and follow-up; the test had concurrent validation at both test sessions; the original and follow-up samples can be compared quantitatively with the entire age-relevant population; men and women were tested; and the initial and follow-up tests were conducted with identical delays for all subjects. The corrected correlation between the Moray House Test scores at age 11 and 77 years informs us that, for community-resident old people in relative good health, psychometric intelligence differences show high stability across most of the human lifespan. The majority—just—of the variance in test scores at age 77 is to be found as early as age 11 years. The possibility that men and women might show different patterns of change for the Moray House Test scores needs establishing in a larger study. The larger gain in the scores of men is in accord with the results of Kangas and Bradway (1971) who reported data on 48 people studied using the Stanford–Binet and/or Wechsler Adult Intelligence Scale at ages 4, 14, 30, and 42 years.

The new data provided here have implications for both applied and basic science. In the field of cognitive gerontology, the results underscore the importance of taking into account the pre-morbid mental ability of a person in the investigation of cognitive decline or dementia in old age (Deary, 1995). Moreover, the results validate the assumption implicit in pre-morbid ability estimates: that in the absence of disease processes, we might expect broad stability of individual differences in mental abilities across the human lifespan.

In the field of differential psychology, the genetic and environmental sources of this remarkable stability of individual differences in human intelligence must be sought. The stability exists in the face of a change in the genetic contribution to intelligence differences over the lifespan: counter-intuitively, perhaps, genes might account for more of the variance in intelligence differences in old age than in childhood and young adulthood (Plomin, Pedersen, Lichtenstein, & McLearn, 1994). And we must seek an account of the half of the variance that is not stable over the lifespan. Some of this will be error variance that properly belongs to stability. Some of it will be found in the genetic differences, coming in to play later in life, that protect us from cognitive decline or accelerate it (MacLullich, Seckl, Starr, & Deary, 1998). And some of it will be found in individual differences in the slings and arrows of fortune. The present results help us to apportion these sources of variance more clearly.

Acknowledgements: The study was supported by a grant to LJW from Henry Smith's Charities. Patricia Whalley and Mariesha Struth assisted in collection and collation of data. We are indebted to the Scottish Council for Research in Education—especially Graham Thorpe, Rosemary Wake and Professor Wynne Harlen—for providing data from the 1932 Scottish Mental Survey.

REFERENCES

Carroll, J. B. (1933). *Human mental abilities: A survey of factor-analytic studies.* Cambridge, UK: Cambridge University Press.

Deary, I. J. (1995). Age-associated memory impairment: A suitable case for treatment? *Ageing and Society, 15,* 393–406.

Eichorn, D. H., Hunt, J. V., & Honzik, M. P. (1981). Experience, personality, and IQ: Adolescence to middle age. In D. H. Eichorn, J. A. Clausen, N. Haan, M. P. Honzik, & P. H. Mussen (Eds.), *Present and past in middle life.* New York: Academic Press.

Humphreys, L. G. (1989). Intelligence: Three kinds of instability and their consequences for policy. In R. L. Linn (Ed.), *Intelligence.* Urbana: University of Illinois Press.

Jensen, A. R. (1980). *Bias in mental testing.* London: Methuen.

Kangas, J., & Bradway, K. (1971). Intelligence at middle age: A thirty-eight-year follow-up. *Developmental Psychology, 5,* 333–337.

MacLullich, A. M. J., Seckl, J. R., Starr, J. M., & Deary, I. J. (1998). The biology of intelligence: From association to mechanism. *Intelligence, 26,* 63–73.

Mortensen, E. L., & Kleven, M. (1993). A WAIS longitudinal study of cognitive development during the life span from ages 50 to 70. *Developmental Neuropsychology, 9,* 115–130.

Nisbet, J. D. (1957). Intelligence and age: Retesting with twenty-four years' interval. *British Journal of Educational Psychology, 27,* 190–198.

Owens, W. A. (1966). Age and mental abilities: A second adult follow-up. *Journal of Educational Psychology, 57,* 311–325.

Plassman, B. L., Welsh, K. A., Helms, M., Brandt, J., Page, W. F., & Breitner, J. C. S. (1995). Intelligence and education as predictors of cognitive state in late life: A 50-year follow-up. *Neurology, 45,* 1446–1450.

Plomin, R., Pedersen, N. L., Lichtenstein, P., & McClearn, G. E. (1994). Variability and stability in cognitive abilities are largely genetic in later life. *Behavior Genetics, 24,* 207–215.

Raven, J. C., Court, J. H., & Raven, J. (1977). *Manual for Raven's progressive matrices and vocabulary scales.* London: Lewis.

Schwartzman, A. E., Gold, D., Andres, D., Arbuckle, T. Y., & Chaikelson, J. (1987). Stability of intelligence—A 40 year follow up. *Canadian Journal of Psychology, 41,* 244–256.

Scottish Council for Research in Education (1933). *The intelligence of Scottish children: A national survey of an age-group.* London: University of London Press.

Snowdon, D. A., Kemper, S. J., Mortimer, J. A., Greiner, L. H., Wekstein, D. R., & Markesbery, W. R. (1996). Linguistic ability in early life and cognitive function and Alzheimer's disease in late life: Findings from the Nun Study. *Journal of the American Medical Association, 275,* 528–532.

Tuddenham, R. D., Blumenkrantz, J., & Wilkin, W. R. (1968). Age changes on AGCT: A longitudinal study of average adults. *Journal of Consulting and Clinical Psychology, 32,* 659–663.

[2]
Practice and Drop-Out Effects During a 17-Year Longitudinal Study of Cognitive Aging

Patrick Rabbitt,[1] Peter Diggle,[2] Fiona Holland,[2] and Lynn McInnes[3]

[1] Age and Cognitive Performance Research Centre, University of Manchester, England.
[2] Department of Biomathematics and Statistics, University of Lancaster, England.
[3] Department of Psychology, University of Northumbria, England.

> Interpretations of longitudinal studies of cognitive aging are misleading unless effects of practice and selective drop-out are considered. A random effects model taking practice and drop-out into account analyzed data from four successive presentations of each of two intelligence tests, two vocabulary tests, and two verbal memory tests during a 17-year longitudinal study of 5,899 community residents whose ages ranged from 49 to 92 years. On intelligence tests, substantial practice effects counteracted true declines observed over 3 to 5 years of aging and remained significant even with intervals of 7 years between successive assessments. Adjustment for practice and drop-out revealed accelerating declines in fluid intelligence and cumulative learning, linear declines in verbal free recall, and no substantial change in vocabulary. Socioeconomic status and basal levels of general fluid ability did not affect rates of decline. After further adjustment for demographics, variability between individuals was seen to increase as the sample aged.

MANY excellent longitudinal studies of cognitive change have had the same basic aims. The most general has been to determine the average form of the trajectory of age-related change and, in particular, whether or not the average rates of change accelerate in old age (e.g., Hertzog & Schaie, 1988; Rabbitt, 1993a; Schaie & Strother, 1968). A corollary aim has been to determine whether rates of change differ between different mental abilities or are similar for all (e.g., Arenberg 1974; Colsher & Wallace, 1991; Heron & Chown, 1967; Hertzog & Schaie, 1988; Hultsch, Hertzog, Small, McDonald-Miszczak, & Dixon 1992; Johansson, Zarit, & Berg, 1992; Lansen, 1997; Owens, 1953, 1966; Powell, 1994; Rabbitt, 1993a; Schaie, 1996; Schaie & Labouvie-Vief, 1974; Schaie & Strother, 1968; Schaie & Willis, 1993; Terman & Oden, 1947, 1959). A third aim has been to test how rates of cognitive change are affected by demographic factors such as educational and social advantage (e.g., Bosworth, Schaie, & Willis, 1999; Evans et al., 1993; Forner, 1972), by gender (e.g., Bosworth et al., 1999; Voitenko, & Tokar, 1983), by epidemiological factors such as general health (e.g., Bell, Rose, & Damon, 1972; Birren, Butler, Greenhouse, Sokoloff, & Yarrow, 1963; Costa & McCrae, 1980; McInnes & Rabbitt, 1997; Rabbitt, Bent, & McInnes, 1997), by specific pathologies (e.g., Hertzog, Schaie, & Gribbin, 1978), by maintenance of physical mobility and engagement in everyday physical activities (e.g., Clark, 1960; Clement, 1974; Dirken, 1972; McInnes & Rabbitt, 1997), or by genetic factors (e.g., Bank & Jarvik, 1978; Payton et al., 2003; Pendleton et al., 2002; Terman & Oden, 1947, 1959). This raises the general issue of the extent and etiology of individual differences in trajectories of aging. Prima facie, because individuals are affected in different ways and to different extents by their lifestyles, health histories, and genetic factors, we might expect that their trajectories of aging correspondingly diverge so that variance in performance between members of a sample will increase as the members age (Morse, 1993; Rabbitt, 1982, 1993a). It follows that individual differences in rates of change provide more information about the functional determinants of cognitive aging than do average trajectories of decline.

Achievement of these general aims has been frustrated by persistent methodological problems. One issue is that analyses have simply regressed performance data across successive time–assay points. Neglect of longitudinal correlations in the data can lead to incorrect inference. A second issue is that when participants are repeatedly assessed on the same or similar tasks, improvements with practice may lead to underestimates of true rates of change and, in particular, may disguise an age-related acceleration of rate of decline. Further, if participants improve more on some tasks than others, analyses may incorrectly conclude that the particular mental abilities that support these tasks decline at different rates. Useful discussions and some empirical investigations (e.g., Zelinski & Burnight, 1997; Zelinski, Gilewski, & Stewart, 1993; Zelinski & Stewart 1998) suggest that, because patterns of correlations between scores on different tests remain stable across successive assessments, improvements are similar across tasks and thus do not mimic or mask differences in the rates of decline of different mental abilities. This hope has been vitiated by cross-sectional studies showing that practice effects vary with complex interactions between individuals' overall levels of general fluid mental ability and the particular kinds of tasks on which they are compared. Less able and older individuals show greater initial and overall improvements on easy tasks (Rabbitt, 1993b), but on difficult tasks the more able and younger show much greater immediate and sustained gains (Rabbitt, Banerji, & Szemanski, 1989). Similar interactions among the effects of practice, of individual differences in ability, and of task difficulty in longitudinal data would conceal age-related declines on simple tasks on which less able older individuals show relatively greater improvements and exaggerate apparent declines on difficult tasks on which they show relatively smaller improvements. Unless analyses determine the relative sizes of practice effects both for different tasks and for older and younger and more and less able individuals, they will incorrectly estimate true rates of overall age-related decline and may also misleadingly suggest that performance declines more rapidly on some tasks than on others.

A third, well-documented, but incompletely resolved methodological problem has been that older, frailer, and less able participants drop out of longitudinal studies earlier than the younger, healthier, and more able. Thus, successive data points reflect the performance of a progressively more elite subset of the original sample, and the true extent of cognitive changes is disguised (e.g., Baltes, 1968; Forner, 1972; Lachman, Lachman, & Taylor, 1982; Lindenberger, Singer, & Baltes, 2002; Mason & Mason, 1973; Nesselrode & Baltes, 1979; Palmore, 1978; Schaie, Labouvie, & Barrett, 1973; Schlesselman, 1973a, 1973b; Schulsinger, Knop, & Mednick, 1981).

Parenthetically, a typical practice in longitudinal investigations is not to recruit a single sample of participants who are thereafter followed until the study ends but rather to continue to recruit new waves of participants, at least throughout the early years. The possibility that the cohorts recruited in successive waves may differ from each other both in demographics and in overall levels of ability gives rise to a corollary, and largely unexplored, methodological problem that may be termed the "drop-in effect." Unless analyses take recruitment cohort differences into account, estimates of rates of cognitive decline will be misleading, especially if cohorts differ more on performance of some tasks than of others.

Apart from obvious age differences, participants who withdraw early from longitudinal studies tend to have poor levels of general health, education, and socioeconomic advantage. Men also tend to drop out earlier than women (Rabbitt, Watson, Donlan, Bent, & McInnes, 1994). Such trends can lead to complex misinterpretations. For example, because women tend to perform better than men on some verbal learning tasks (Rabbitt, Donlan, Watson, McInnes, & Bent, 1996; Rabbit et al., 2002), the rates at which verbal learning declines with age may be underestimated unless gender differences in dropout are taken into consideration.

Some investigators have estimated the effects of selective drop-out by comparing patterns of differences between age groups observed in initial cross-sectional screenings of a volunteer population against the patterns of age-related changes that become apparent as longitudinal data are accumulated. Because patterns of age-related differences revealed by cross-sectional and longitudinal comparisons seem very similar, investigators have concluded that selective drop-out may not always lead to serious misinterpretations (e.g., Sliwinski & Bushke, 1999; Zelinski & Burnight, 1997; Zelinski et al., 1993; Zelinski & Stewart, 1998). The comparison of cross-sectional against longitudinal trends is a useful exploratory step that can tell us whether drop-out affects the relative amount of change in different cognitive abilities, but it does not reveal the extent to which drop-out has masked the actual amount of changes. In particular, such comparisons do not show whether substantial progressive increases in variability between members of an aging population have been masked by selective withdrawal of the oldest and less able. We believe that only longitudinal studies can properly address all of the effects of drop-out on population changes in performance over time.

Thus, a main aim of the analyses described here was to model changes over time to take account of drop-out effects.

To consider how this may be done, we find it important to distinguish among three different drop-out scenarios (Lindenberger, 2002; Rubin, 1976). The first is the completely random drop-out: The drop-out process is independent of the measurement process. The second is the random drop-out: The drop-out process is dependent on the observed measurements prior to drop-out but is independent of the measurements that would have been observed had the participant not withdrawn. The third is the informative drop-out: The drop-out process is dependent on the measurements that would have been observed had the participant not dropped out. Not surprisingly, analyses made under the informative drop-out assumption are fraught with difficulty. The results of such analyses typically depend on modeling assumptions that are difficult or impossible to check from observed data. For example, in most observational studies it is extremely difficult even to identify the precise time at which a participant made a decision to drop out. In contrast, analyses under the assumption of completely random drop-out are generally straightforward because no distinction need be made between measurements that are unavailable because of drop-out and those that are unavailable because they were never intended. Put another way, completely random drop-out implies that the incomplete data can simply be treated as if from an unbalanced experimental design, with no commonality to the times at which measurements are made on different subjects.

The simplicity of analysis under the completely random drop-out assumption is bought at a price. If this assumption is invalid, then so may be the resulting inferences about the measurement process. However, if likelihood-based methods of inference are used, validity is retained under the weaker assumption of random drop-out. This is important because longitudinal data are typically correlated over time. This means that even when the true drop-out process is informative, the most recent measurements on a given subject before drop-out are partially predictive of the missing measurements after drop-out. By allowing for the effects of these measurements on dropout (which is what the random drop-out assumption implies), we can partly compensate for the missing information (see, e.g., Scharfstein, Rotnitzky, & Robins 1999, and the associated discussion). To appreciate how the likelihood-based methods automatically make this kind of compensation, Diggle, Liang, and Zeger (1994, chap. 11) showed a simulated data set from a model in which the mean response is constant over time, but the probability of drop-out for any given subject at any given time is a decreasing function of that subject's most recent measurement. The effect of this random drop-out mechanism is that low-responding subjects progressively drop out, leading to an apparent rising trend in the mean response over time as the observed mean is calculated from the progressively more selective subpopulation of survivors. This rising trend is what would be estimated by a naive regression analysis of the data that ignores both the drop-out process and the longitudinal correlation in the data.

An important implication is that, for longitudinal data with drop-out, there is no reason why a fitted mean response curve should track the observed mean response trajectory of the survivors. In contrast, a model fitted by likelihood-based

Table 1. Schedule of Recruitment and Testing of Volunteers (Newcastle)

Wave	TB 1 Administered (1982–1985)	TB 1 (1985–1986)	Robbins & Sahakian Battery (1985–1986)	TB 2 (1985–1991)	TB 1 (1991–1992)	Currently Registered
Wave 1–2 (1982–1985)	2,052 (first test)	1,578 (retest 1)	828 (first test)	1,167 (first test)	977 (second test)	977
Wave 3 (1988)		629 (first test)		492 (first test)	425 (second test)	425
Wave 4 (1989–1990)				607 (first test)	601 (first test)	601
Wave 5 (1991–1992)					67 (first test)	67

Notes: TB = test battery. Total tested on at least one battery = Waves 1 and 2 (2,048) = Wave 3 (629) + Wave 4 (601) + Wave 5 (67) = 3,345. Total retested once on Battery 1 = Wave 1 (1,578) + Wave 2 (425) = 2,003. Total tested at least once on both Battery 1 and Battery 2 = Wave 1 (1,167) + Wave 2 (492) = 1,659. Total still registered on panel = 2,070.

methods under the assumption of random drop-outs estimates what the mean response would have been if it had been possible to follow up the entire study population. That is, the observed means are estimating the mean response conditional on not dropping out before the end of a determined census period. The unconditional and conditional means coincide only if the data are uncorrelated in time, or if the drop-out process is completely random. We would argue that neither of these assumptions is plausible for most data from longitudinal studies of cognitive aging. We therefore conclude that a likelihood-based analysis under a random drop-out assumption is a sensible analytic strategy because it focuses on the complete study population, rather than on the progressively self-selected subpopulation of subjects who do not drop out of the study. We used this analysis to examine the data set described in the paragraphs that follow.

The present study was made to investigate the extent to which improvements associated with repeated testing and by selective drop-out and drop-in effects have obscured answers to the basic questions about the nature of age-related cognitive changes. The analyses also addressed substantive hypotheses on the true relationships that would be revealed when practice effects have been identified and drop-out has been taken into consideration.

First, practice effects would be found to be substantial and large enough to disguise the true rates and forms of trajectories of longitudinal changes. Second, the sizes of practice effects would be found to differ both between different kinds of tasks and also between more and less intellectually able, and so implicitly younger and older, participants (as has been found in brief, cross-sectional laboratory studies by Rabbitt, 1993b, and Rabbitt et al., 1989). Third, when the true forms of trajectories of age-related changes can be established, rates of cognitive change will be found to accelerate with age and to differ with task demands. It will also be possible to more accurately determine the extents to which individual differences in rates of change vary with demographic variables such as gender and socioeconomic status and with individual differences in level of general fluid mental ability (gf). Fourth, after the effects of demographics, gender, and individual differences in ability have been taken into consideration, variance in cognitive performance between participants will be found to increase significantly as the sample ages.

To examine the effects of practice, we used a drop-out and drop-in random effects model to analyze data from successive presentations of the same battery of six different tasks during a 17-year longitudinal study of 5,899 healthy, community resident, older people. The model allowed us to determine the true sizes of practice effects, the extent to which practice effects differ between tasks, and the extent to which practice effects and Task × Practice interactions differed between individuals of different ages and levels of gf.

METHODS

Participants

Details of recruitment of the sample are given elsewhere (Rabbitt, Donlan, Bent, McInnes, & Abson, 1993). The data analyzed here were obtained from 5,899 active community residents from Newcastle-upon-Tyne ($n = 3,261$) and Greater Manchester ($n = 2,638$) who ranged in age from 49 to 92 years on entry. Years of education varied from 5 to 21 ($M = 11.7$, $SD = 4.2$). Numbers of health complaints recorded on the Cornell Medical Index (Brodman, Erdman, & Wolff, 1949) varied from 2 to 18 ($M = 6.4$, $SD = 3.2$). Table 1 shows the time pattern of successive waves of recruitment and the subsequent retesting schedule by city of residence. Participants experienced the battery between one and four times, depending on when they were recruited and whether, and when, they dropped out. Tables 1 and 2 detail the patterns of successive waves of recruitment and the extent of drop-out in Newcastle and Manchester.

The index of socioeconomic advantage was the categories for Classification of Occupation published by the (U.K.) Office of Population Censuses & Surveys (1980).

Procedure

Volunteers traveled independently to laboratories in Manchester or Newcastle-upon-Tyne, where they were tested in groups of 10 to 15. Sessions were conducted in large quiet rooms by two experimenters who checked that participants with visual or auditory problems had brought their prescribed prostheses and were not inconvenienced. Sessions lasted, on average, for 90 min with 15-min tea and coffee breaks. Volunteers each received £5 (U.K.) for each session to cover their travel expenses. The tests were administered over two successive sessions within a period of 8 weeks.

Cognitive Tests

During the first testing session, volunteers completed the Heim (1970) AH4-1 and AH4-2 intelligence tests, and the Raven (1965) Mill Hill "A" and "B" (MHA and MHB) vocabulary tests. During the second session, they completed a cumulative verbal learning (CVL) task and a verbal free recall (VFR) task.

Both AH4 tests are well-standardized measures of gf and correlate strongly ($R = .7–.8$) with instruments such as the

Table 2. Schedule of Recruitment and Testing of Volunteers (Manchester)

Wave	TB 1 (1985–1988)	TB 2 (Oct. 1988–Sept. 1990)	TB 1 (Oct. 1990–Aug. 1992)	Currently Registered
Waves 1, 2, and 3 (recruited 1985–1988)	2,361	1,452	1,147	1,147
Wave 4 (recruited 1989–1990)		522 (first test)	256 (first test)	256
Wave 5 (recruited 1991–1992)			104 (first test)	104

Notes: TB = test battery; Oct. = October; Sept. = September; Aug. = August. Total tested on at least one battery = Waves 1–3 (2,361) + 522 (Wave 2) + 104 (Wave 3) = 2,992. Total retested once on Battery 1 (Waves 1–3) = 1,147. Total tested at least once on both Battery 1 and Battery 2 = Waves 1–3 (1,452) + Wave 4 (256) = 1,708. Total still registered on panel = Waves 1–3 (1,147) + Wave 4 (256) + Wave 5 (104) = 1,507.

Wechsler Adult Intelligence Scale battery (see Heim, 1970). In each test, volunteers are given untimed and unscored practice on 5 demonstration problems with provided solutions and then have 10 min to solve as many as possible out of a total of 65 problems. AH4-1 problems include equal numbers of logical reasoning tests, verbal comparisons, and arithmetic and number series problems. AH4-2 problems are nonverbal, involving addition and subtraction of complex shapes, completion of logical series of shapes, and matching by mental rotation of irregular shapes. For each AH4 test the scores analyzed are the numbers of problems correctly solved in 10 min.

The MHA recognition vocabulary test comprises a list of 33 different rare words, each accompanied by a set of 6 different words from which participants must select the most appropriate synonym. The MHB production vocabulary test comprises a list of 33 different rare words for each of which participants provide an accurate and concise definition as possible (Raven, 1965). Both MH tests are untimed. Scores analyzed consist of the number of correct synonyms identified or definitions given.

In the CVL test, a list of 15 different three-syllable words matched for concreteness and for frequency (1/10,000, Kucera & Francis, 1967, norms) are projected, one item at a time, by a Kodak "Carousel" projector at a rate of 1.5/s. Words appear in Times Roman print, boldface, as a string that is 150 cm long and 15 cm high on a projection screen that is no further than 5 m from any member of the group tested. The room is blacked out to maximize visibility, and participants' results are not recorded unless the participants remembered to bring prescribed spectacles and have no difficulty reading the displays. After the first presentation of the 15 words, participants write down as many as they can recall, in any order they wish, on the first page of an answer booklet. They then turn to a new page and the 15 words are then presented in a new random order, and recall is again attempted. Scores analyzed are the total numbers of words correctly recalled over four such presentations.

In the VFR test, 30 words, selected and matched as for the CVL task, are presented once, in random order, at a rate of 1 item/1.5 s. Volunteers then immediately write down as many as they can recall in any order they wish. Scores analyzed are the total numbers of words correctly recalled.

Description of Test Data and Exploratory Analysis

Because the tests have total scores ranging from 30 to 65, each participant's raw scores were converted to a percentage correct to provide a common measurement scale. Mean scores at entry, broken down by the selected demographic groups, are shown in Table 3.

Choice of scores.—We made the decision to use percentage correct scores rather than standardized scores for the following reasons: Let Y_{ijk} denote the raw score on test i recorded by subject j on the kth testing occasion. Our models for these data take the generic form

$$Y_{ijk} = x'_{ijk}\beta + A_{ij} + B_{ij}t_{jk} + E_{ijk}, \quad (1)$$

in which x_{ijk} is a vector of explanatory variables, with associated regression parameters β; A_{ij} and B_{ij} are subject-specific random effects, assumed to be normally distributed and realized independently for different subjects, but possibly correlated within subjects; t_{jk} is the age of the jth subject on the kth testing occasion; and E_{ijk} are measurement errors, assumed to be mutually independent, and normally distributed.

Our substantive hypotheses concern claims that, first, particular elements of β are nonzero, reflecting real, group-level effects on test outcomes; second, particular terms in the variance matrix of the random effects are nonzero, reflecting dependencies between the different outcomes achieved by a given subject on different tests or between a given subject's general level of achievement and his or her rate of change with age (in both cases, measured relative to the subject's peer group as defined by the explanatory variables).

The normalized score corresponding to each Y_{ijk} is Y^*_{ijk}, where

$$Y^*_{ijk} = (Y_{ijk} - m_i)/s_i \quad (2)$$

and m_i is the observed mean of Y_{ijk} for a given cognitive test, i; s_{ik} is the observed standard deviation of Y_{ijk} for a given cognitive test, i.

Combining Equations 1 and 2 leads to

$$Y^*_{ijk} = x'_{ijk}\beta^*_i + A^*_{ij} + B^*_{ij}t_{jk} + E^*_{ijk}. \quad (3)$$

Comparing Equations 1 and 3 with respect to the random effect terms A and B, we see that they are essentially identical. Specifically, if the A_{ij} and B_{ij} are multivariate normally distributed, then so are A^*_{ij} and B^*_{ij} and vice versa. Further, because the transformations from the variants with and without asterisks are made componentwise, then any two random effects that are uncorrelated before transformation remain so after transformation and vice versa. In particular, a test for whether any two "without asterisk" random effects are or are not

Table 3. Mean Percentage of Correct Scores at Initial Test by Selected Demographics

Demographic	Participants n (%)	AH4-1 M (SD)	AH4-2 M (SD)	MHA M (SD)	MHB M (SD)	CVL M (SD)	VFR M (SD)
Gender							
Female	4,176 (71)	47.5 (17.3)	42.9 (16.2)	66.2 (14.2)	48.5 (18.5)	70.4 (14.3)	28.0 (11.1)
Male	1,735 (29)	50.8 (17.8)	49.0 (17.0)	70.5 (14.1)	52.1 (18.5)	66.4 (15.0)	25.7 (11.1)
City							
Manchester	2,646 (45)	49.7 (17.8)	45.7 (16.9)	69.8 (13.8)	54.8 (17.9)	71.2 (14.0)	28.3 (11.6)
Newcastle	3,265 (55)	47.6 (17.3)	43.8 (16.4)	65.6 (14.5)	45.4 (18.0)	67.5 (14.9)	26.4 (10.8)
Social class							
Category 1, professional	266 (4.5)	61.5 (13.9)	59.5 (14.6)	79.0 (11.1)	63.5 (15.7)	71.8 (13.9)	29.5 (12.2)
Category 2, intermediate	1,876 (31.7)	56.4 (16.6)	51.0 (16.0)	74.1 (12.2)	58.3 (16.6)	73.0 (13.3)	30.3 (11.8)
Category 3 (N), nonmanual skilled	2,080 (35.2)	48.4 (14.9)	43.6 (14.3)	66.5 (12.4)	48.1 (16.3)	70.2 (13.6)	27.4 (10.4)
Category 3 (M), manual skilled	765 (12.9)	38.6 (15.4)	37.5 (15.3)	60.7 (13.3)	40.3 (16.7)	63.0 (14.6)	22.7 (9.5)
Category 4, partly skilled or Category 5, unskilled	488 (8.3)	34.7 (14.7)	33.5 (15.1)	55.9 (13.8)	34.9 (16.4)	61.3 (15.1)	22.0 (9.2)
Missing/uncoded	436 (7.4)	39.7 (17.9)	38.0 (17.4)	61.4 (16.5)	42.7 (19.9)	61.4 (17.9)	24.3 (10.8)
Entry age (years)							
49–59	1,418 (24)	55.2 (17.2)	53.0 (16.2)	68.3 (13.9)	51.4 (18.0)	75.0 (13.2)	31.6 (12.2)
60–69	2,910 (49)	49.4 (16.7)	45.3 (15.6)	67.3 (14.1)	49.4 (18.3)	69.8 (13.8)	27.6 (10.6)
70–79	1,431 (24)	41.6 (16.5)	36.6 (14.7)	67.2 (15.0)	48.3 (19.4)	64.1 (14.5)	23.5 (9.9)
80+	152 (3)	33.7 (15.6)	29.6 (12.8)	68.0 (15.3)	40.4 (19.7)	56.7 (17.2)	21.2 (10.9)

Notes: For participants, $N = 5,911$; MHA and MHB = Mill Hill A and Mill Hill B (tests). AH4-1 and AH4-2 are intelligence tests. CVL = cumulative verbal learning; VFR = verbal free recall.

correlated is equivalent to a test that the corresponding "with asterisk" random effects are or are not correlated.

With respect to the regression parameters, the important difference between Equations 1 and 3 is that the β* parameter has acquired a subscript i. This implies that the substantive meaning of a hypothesis involving interactions between explanatory variables and cognitive tests is indeed different on the raw and standardized scales (e.g., a hypothesis that the average effect of a 1-year increase in age is numerically the same across all cognitive tests). However, the substantive meaning of a hypothesis concerning main effects is unchanged (e.g., a hypothesis that an increase in age does or does not affect the average response to a particular cognitive test).

The overall conclusion is that although the numerical values of estimated parameters would be affected by a change from raw to standardized scores, the substantive conclusions sought from the analysis and claimed in this article are not.

Model specification.—The first methodological issue to which we have drawn attention is the need to take account of the fact that measurements taken over time on the same individual tend to be correlated. There are several approaches to model this correlation structure, and the choice depends on the main scientific questions of interest. Our present aims are (a) to identify factors predictive of cognitive decline at the population level and (b) to gain insight into individual differences relative to the population levels. This leads us naturally to the random effects model, which has two parts: a model for the average response over time for respondents with given values of all explanatory variables, and a model for the random variation about the mean response. For the second component, we postulate a set of latent variables, or "random effects," which represent deviations of individual respondents from the population average for some relevant features. This random variation occurs in addition to the residual variation.

To address the substantive hypotheses set out in the introduction, we need to describe for each cognitive test how the population-average scores depend on the following set of explanatory variables: age, gender, socioeconomic status (SES), city of origin (Manchester or Newcastle), wave of recruitment to the study (cohort), level of general intellectual ability (gf) as indexed by AH4 test scores, and whether tests are being taken for the first, second, third, or fourth time (practice effects). Accordingly, the analysis was made to address the combined effects of age, gender, SES, and practice effects, which are of substantive interest, whereas effects distinguishing cities and year-of-entry cohorts are included as a means of adjusting for unidentified confounding factors. The effects of differences in level of intellectual ability (I gf) are then also explored.

We now introduce the following notation. For a given response, let Y_{ij} denote the percent correct score for the ith subject on the jth occasion. Hence $i = 1-n$ (the number of subjects with at least one response measure) and $j = 1-4$. We use x_{ijk}, where $k = 1-p$, to denote the values of the set of p explanatory variables associated with each Y_{ij}. In particular, let x_{ij1} denote age (in years over 49, the minimum entry age) and x_{ij2} denote age squared. Improvement at the three repeat test occasions ($j \geq 2$) is modeled as a series of step functions. Then the mean value of Y_{ij} is μ_{ij} defined by

$$\mu_{ij} = \beta_0 + \beta_1 x_{ij1} + \beta_2 x_{ij2} + \cdots + \beta_p x_{ijp},$$

and the measured value Y_{ij} is

$$Y_{ij} = \mu_{ij} + A_i + B_i x_{ij1} + E_{ij},$$

where A_i and B_i are subject-specific parameters giving the deviation of the ith subject's intercept and slope from the average population response. We assume these to be random variables drawn from a bivariate normal distribution with mean zero and covariance matrix

$$\Sigma = \begin{bmatrix} \sigma_A^2 & \rho_{AB}\sigma_A\sigma_B \\ \rho_{AB}\sigma_A\sigma_B & \sigma_B^2 \end{bmatrix}$$

independent of E_{ij}, which follows a univariate normal distribution with mean zero and variance σ^2_E. Further random effects (such as quadratic age terms or practice effects) are not considered. As described in the paragraphs that follow, age appears to have little or no effect on the MH tests. For this pair of tasks, we therefore omitted the subject-specific random slope effects B_i from the model.

We used maximum likelihood, using the $mle(\ )$ function within the Splus software environment, for model estimation under the assumption that drop-out was random (i.e., the probability that a respondent drops out may depend on his or her observed measurement history, but not on the unobserved responses).

We fitted separate models to each response, adopting the same method for selecting the mean structure.

RESULTS

Not all participants provided scores on all measures. Thus a total of 5,894–5,899 individuals with at least one response measure were included in the AH4 and MH analyses. As already mentioned, the CVL and VFR tests were performed on a second session. Because substantial numbers withdrew after the first testing session of the first data collection, only 5,254 participants also had a CVL or a VFR result.

Selection of the Mean Structure

Based on the empirical evidence of a declining age effect for the AH4-1, AH4-2, CVL, and the VFR tests, the following steps are used to derive a mean model for these responses.

Assuming that the relationship between cognitive decline and age is captured adequately by a linear and a quadratic term, we adopt the following step-down approach to test whether there is any evidence that the overall age trajectory differs with SES, gender, or practice. Based on participants from Newcastle who, overall, were followed up for longer than those from Manchester, a sequence of models is fitted. Under the assumption that the improvement at the second data-collection point adequately captures the Practice × Age interaction, we fit models allowing the quadratic curve to depend on any combination of SES, gender, and improvement. We then fit simpler interaction models, retaining the simpler model at each step if the generalized likelihood ratio test (LRT) for the additional terms is nonsignificant at the conventional 5% level. We do not separately test for an interaction with the linear or quadratic component of age. Hence, a test comprises $2(m-1)$ degrees of freedom, where m is the number of levels of the factor in question.

There are no significant interactions with age for AH4-1 or VFR, whereas there is a significant single interaction for Improvements at Visit 2 × Age for AH4-2, and Gender × Age for CVL. Repeating these steps but considering only main effect practice terms results in the same "final" models for AH4-1, CVL, and VFR, whereas for AH4-2 the age quadratic now depends on the Gender × SES combination. Although they are statistically significant, all these interactions have very small effects that we considered unimportant in substantive terms. We also noted that the covariance matrix estimates for the random effects were robust to the choice of mean model (i.e., main effects only or with age interactions). For these reasons we proceed to fit models without interactions to the combined data set, including a term for city of residence, and test the quadratic age trend against the linear term for these four responses. In all cases this was highly significant ($p < .0001$, 2 df).

For the vocabulary tests the linear age term based on the complete Manchester and Newcastle data set was statistically significant for MHB but not MHA scores, with estimated mean declines of -0.06 and -0.03 per annum, respectively. Although these trends are clearly too slight to be of substantive importance, predicting a decline of only 0.6% and 0.3% respectively over 10 years, the linear age term was retained in order to better estimate the covariance structure.

Before describing the mean estimates for each response pair and comparing the parameter estimates of substantial interest, namely the age trends and practice components across tests, we now give a brief explanation of the parameter estimates. In all models the first level of each factor is the reference group. Thus, the intercept parameter represents the percentage score for a respondent who is in socioeconomic category (C) 1; female; of age 49; and a resident in Manchester and taking the test for the first time in 1983. The improvement parameters measure the average step increase between successive testing occasions ($j \geq 2$). The effects for socioeconomic categories (Cs) from 2 to 4–5 represent the estimated difference in mean percent correct scores between socioeconomic groups 2 to 4–5 and socioeconomic group 1. The entry year values represent the difference in scores between 1984–1992 and 1983, and the city term gives the mean difference between Newcastle and Manchester participants. This allows us to test the substantive working hypotheses that, when practice and drop-out have been taken into consideration, tests will show accelerated age-related declines, and that rates of decline will be seen to differ between tests, and also between individuals of higher and lower gf.

AH4-1 and AH4-2 Scores

Tables 4 and 5 summarize the estimated mean effects for AH4-1 and AH4-2, respectively. The AH4-1 intercept of 66.0 is 4.9 points higher than the AH4-2 intercept. The fact that both quadratic coefficients are negative indicates that scores on both these tests show accelerated decline with age. The rates of decline are very similar. For example, consider the entry scores: On AH4-1, the average score for a 60-year-old would be 64.6, and for a 70-year-old, 58.6 (a 6-point drop), falling to 46.5 (a further 12-point fall) for an 80-year-old. On the AH4-2 task, the corresponding scores would be 58.2, 52.1 (6-point drop), and 38.6 (a further 13-point drop). This supports the first working hypothesis that, after practice and drop-out are taken into consideration, at least on tests of gf, the rates of decline are seen to accelerate with increasing age.

The next substantive hypothesis to be tested is that practice effects would differ between tests and age groups, and possibly also between sexes, between demographic groups and as a function of overall level of gf. Tables 4 and 5 show that the average practice step increase for AH4-2 on the second occasion of

Table 4. AH4-1 Model Estimates

Mean Response Model Parameter	Estimate	SE	t Value	p Value	95% CI
Intercept	66.03	1.53	43.08	<.001	63.03, 69.03
age − 49	0.04	0.05	0.74	.459	−0.07, 0.15
(age − 49)^2	−0.02	0.001	−17.57	<.001	−0.03, −0.02
Improvement					
$j \geq 2$	4.51	0.16	27.58	<.001	4.19, 4.83
$j \geq 3$	2.21	0.21	10.28	<.001	1.79, 2.63
$j \geq 4$	1.90	0.36	5.25	<.001	1.19, 2.61
Male vs. female	2.20	0.44	5.02	<.001	1.34, 3.07
Socioeconomic status					
C2 vs. C1	−3.77	0.96	−3.94	<.001	−5.64, −1.89
C3 (N)	−10.53	0.98	−10.72	<.001	−12.45, −8.60
C3 (M)	−19.94	1.04	−19.19	<.001	−21.98, −17.91
C4/5	−23.20	1.13	−20.56	<.001	−25.41, −20.99
Missing	−19.12	1.16	−16.44	<.001	−21.40, −16.84
Newcastle vs. Manchester	−3.20	1.07	−3.00	.003	−5.29, −1.11
Entry year					
1984 vs. 1983	0.71	0.64	1.12	.261	−0.53, 1.96
1985	−0.82	1.25	−0.65	.515	−3.27, 1.64
1986	−0.50	1.28	−0.39	.699	−3.05, 2.04
1987	−1.54	1.33	−1.16	.245	−4.14, 1.06
1988	1.97	0.74	2.65	.008	0.51, 3.43
1989	4.64	0.89	5.24	<.001	2.90, 6.37
1990	5.37	1.47	3.65	<.001	2.49, 8.25
1991	1.19	1.84	0.65	.516	−2.41, 4.79
1992	1.64	1.55	1.06	.289	−1.39, 4.68

Notes: CI = confidence interval; C = category; N = nonmanual skilled; M = manual skilled. Covariance and residual parameters: For σ_A, estimate = 15.43 and 95% CI = 14.71, 16.18; for σ_B, estimate = 0.41 and 95% CI = 0.36, 0.47; for ρ_{AB}, estimate = −0.51 and 95% CI = −0.58, −0.44; for σ_E, estimate = 5.71 and 95% CI = 5.58, 5.84.

Table 5. AH4-2 Model Estimates

Mean Response Model Parameter	Estimate	SE	t Value	p Value	95% CI
Intercept	61.12	1.44	42.57	<.001	58.31, 63.94
age − 49	−0.17	0.06	−3.01	.003	−0.28, −0.06
(age − 49)^2	−0.02	0.00	−15.57	<.001	−0.02, −0.02
Improvement					
$j \geq 2$	5.58	0.17	32.94	<.001	5.24, 5.91
$j \geq 3$	4.72	0.22	21.07	<.001	4.28, 5.15
$j \geq 4$	5.88	0.38	15.34	<.001	5.13, 6.64
Male vs. female	5.14	0.41	12.62	<.001	4.34, 5.93
Socioeconomic status					
C2 vs. C1	−5.96	0.89	−6.73	<.001	−7.70, −4.23
C3 (N)	−11.36	0.91	−12.50	<.001	−13.14, −9.58
C3 (M)	−17.58	0.96	−18.25	<.001	−19.47, −15.69
C4/5	−20.37	1.04	−19.50	<.001	−22.42, −18.33
Missing	−17.56	1.08	−16.22	<.001	−19.68, −15.44
Newcastle vs. Manchester	−0.57	0.99	−0.58	.564	−2.51, 1.37
Entry year					
1984 vs. 1983	−0.27	0.59	−0.46	.646	−1.42, 0.88
1985	2.22	1.16	1.91	.056	−0.05, 4.50
1986	2.58	1.21	2.14	.032	0.22, 4.94
1987	2.22	1.23	1.80	.071	−0.19, 4.63
1988	3.19	0.69	4.64	<.001	1.84, 4.54
1989	9.03	0.82	11.00	<.001	7.42, 10.64
1990	8.50	1.37	6.22	<.001	5.82, 11.17
1991	7.41	1.71	4.34	<.001	4.07, 10.75
1992	4.25	1.45	2.93	<.001	1.41, 7.08

Notes: CI = confidence interval; C = category; N = nonmanual skilled; M = manual skilled. Covariance and residual parameters: For σ_A, estimate = 14.63 and 95% CI = 13.94, 15.35; for σ_B, estimate = 0.43 and 95% CI = 0.38, 0.49; for ρ_{AB}, estimate = −0.58 and 95% CI = −0.63, −0.51; for σ_E, estimate = 6.22 and 95% CI = 6.09, 6.36.

testing are comparable (gains of 4.5 and 5.6 points, respectively). On the third and fourth occasions the level falls to under 2.5 on AH4-1, but it remains above 4.5 for AH4-2, corresponding to a cumulative gain of 5.6, 10.3, and 16.2. Thus practice effects differ, even between tests that putatively measure the same performance index, gf. Although initial improvements are similar on the two AH4 tests, in the longer term, AH4-2 scores show greater and more sustained gains.

On average, men performed significantly better than women on both of the AH4 tests. Tables 4 and 5 show that, after the other covariates in the model are adjusted for, scores on both AH4 tests markedly vary with SES category. Participants in C1 score at least 20 points more, on average, than participants in C4–5. Another demographic factor, city of residence, also affects AH4 test scores. On the AH4-1, Manchester residents score higher than Newcastle residents, but on the AH4-2, this city effect is not significant. Implications of this male advantage are discussed in the paragraphs that follow. The overall effects of SES are as expected.

There are also significant differences between waves of recruitment; that is, there are significant drop-in effects. Individuals who entered the study in 1989 and 1990 have markedly higher scores on both AH 4 tests than those who entered in the first year of the study, 1983. Note that a principal aim of the analysis is to examine the hypothesis that rates of change over time are affected both by demographic factors and by overall levels of gf, and this cannot be properly addressed if this drop-in effect is neglected.

Cumulative Verbal Learning and Verbal Free Recall Scores

Tables 6 and 7 summarize these results for CVL and VFR, respectively. Note that the intercept estimate of 75.6 for CVL is more than double the 35.5 point score on VFR, which is the lowest score overall.

As for the AH4 responses, the quadratic term is negative for both tests, indicating some acceleration of decline with age. However, the deviation from linearity is small. As an example, the average CVL entry score is 73.6 for a 60-year-old, 68.6 for a 70-year-old, and falls to 60.2 for an 80-year-old; that is, there are declines of 5.0 and 8.4 points. The corresponding VFR scores of 32.4, 28.6, and 23.8 points equate to declines of 3.8 and 4.8 points over the successive 10-year intervals. The average improvement on the second experience of CVL was 1.0. This, although statistically significant, is slight. The equivalent improvement for VFR was negative and nonsignificant. On the third and fourth testing occasions, an improvement followed by a decline occurred for both these tests. These fluctuations remain unexplained.

On both the CVL and VFR tests, women performed significantly better than men. On the CVL and VFR tests, the differ-

Table 6. CVL Model Estimates

Mean Response Model Parameter	Estimate	SE	t Value	p Value	95% CI
Intercept	75.57	1.37	55.14	<.001	72.89, 78.26
age − 49	0.07	0.06	1.06	.290	−0.06, 0.19
(age − 49)^2	−0.02	0.00	−13.36	<.001	−0.03, −0.02
Improvement					
$j \geq 2$	0.97	0.20	4.75	<.001	0.57, 1.37
$j \geq 3$	5.51	0.28	19.50	<.001	4.95, 6.06
$j \geq 4$	−3.16	0.48	−6.53	<.001	−4.11, −2.21
Male vs. female	−4.28	0.39	−11.01	<.001	−5.04, −3.52
Socioeconomic status					
C2 vs. C1	−0.58	0.82	−0.71	.478	−2.18, 1.02
C3 (N)	−3.76	0.84	−4.47	<.001	−5.40, −2.11
C3 (M)	−8.63	0.90	−9.61	<.001	−10.38, −6.87
C4/5	−10.88	0.98	−11.09	<.001	−12.80, −8.96
Missing	−9.12	1.16	−7.83	<.001	−11.40, −6.84
Newcastle vs. Manchester	−1.09	0.97	−1.12	.262	−2.98, 0.81
Entry year					
1984 vs. 1983	4.57	0.54	8.53	<.001	3.52, 5.62
1985	6.96	1.12	6.23	<.001	4.77, 9.14
1986	4.98	1.15	4.33	<.001	2.73, 7.23
1987	6.05	1.19	5.10	<.001	3.72, 8.37
1988	8.31	0.74	11.25	<.001	6.86, 9.75
1989	7.59	0.77	9.88	<.001	6.09, 9.10
1990	7.97	1.27	6.27	<.001	5.48, 10.46
1991	4.99	1.64	3.05	<.001	1.78, 8.19
1992	3.87	1.37	2.83	<.001	1.19, 6.55

Notes: CVL = cumulative verbal learning; CI = confidence interval; C = category; N = nonmanual skilled; M = manual skilled. Covariance and residual parameters: For σ_A, estimate = 10.24 and 95% CI = 9.28, 11.29; for σ_B, estimate = 0.49 and 95% CI = 0.44, 0.56; for ρ_{AB}, estimate = −0.45 and 95% CI = −0.57, −0.32; for σ_E, estimate = 7.59 and 95% CI = 7.43, 7.76.

Table 7. VFR Model Estimates

Mean Response Model Parameter	Estimate	SE	t Value	p Value	95% CI
Intercept	35.46	1.07	33.10	<.001	33.36, 37.55
age − 49	−0.23	0.05	−4.41	<.001	−0.34, −0.13
(age − 49)^2	−0.01	0.00	−4.01	<.001	−0.01, 0.00
Improvement					
$j \geq 2$	−0.16	0.18	−0.91	.365	−0.51, 0.19
$j \geq 3$	1.96	0.24	8.14	<.001	1.49, 2.44
$j \geq 4$	−0.93	0.40	−2.33	.020	−1.72, −0.15
Male vs. female	−2.07	0.29	−7.01	<.001	−2.65, −1.49
Socioeconomic status					
C2 vs. C1	0.05	0.62	0.07	.942	−1.18, 1.27
C3 (N)	−2.99	0.64	−4.65	<.001	−4.24, −1.73
C3 (M)	−5.83	0.68	−8.56	<.001	−7.17, −4.50
C4/5	−6.71	0.75	−8.99	<.001	−8.17, −5.25
Missing	−4.99	0.91	−5.48	<.001	−6.77, −3.21
Newcastle vs. Manchester	−1.21	0.72	−1.68	.092	−2.61, 0.20
Entry year					
1984 vs. 1983	1.21	0.41	2.94	<.001	0.41, 2.02
1985	1.35	0.84	1.61	.107	−0.29, 3.00
1986	0.52	0.86	0.61	.545	−1.17, 2.22
1987	1.06	0.89	1.18	.237	−0.69, 2.80
1988	2.30	0.56	4.09	<.001	1.20, 3.41
1989	1.77	0.58	3.03	.002	0.63, 2.92
1990	2.07	0.98	2.12	.034	0.15, 3.98
1991	2.11	1.26	1.67	.094	−0.36, 4.58
1992	0.11	1.05	0.10	.917	−1.95, 2.17

Notes: VFR = verbal free recall; CI = confidence interval; C = category; N = nonmanual skilled; M = manual skilled. Covariance and residual parameters: For σ_A, estimate = 9.67 and 95% CI = 8.95, 10.46; for σ_B, estimate = 0.23 and 95% CI = 0.16, 0.31; for ρ_{AB}, estimate = −0.72 and 95% CI = −0.78, −0.65; for σ_E, estimate = 7.00 and 95% CI = 6.87, 7.15.

ences in trends for SES Cs are much less marked than on the AH4 tests. Again, the largest difference is between C1 and C4–5 (10.9% and 6.7% points for CVL and VFR, respectively). On these tests, as on all others, average scores are higher for Manchester than for Newcastle residents, but in this case these differences are not significant. Interestingly, the mean CVL scores are from 3.9 to 8.3 points higher for participants who entered the study from 1984 onward, compared with those entering in 1983. VFR scores show a similar but less marked recruitment wave, or drop-in effect.

Mill Hill A and Mill Hill B Scores

Tables 8 and 9 show the results for MHA and MHB, respectively. The intercept estimate for the MHA test is 80.6, which is higher than for any other test and is 15.4 points higher than the intercept estimate of 65.1 for the MHB test.

Assuming that the age trajectories for MHA and MHB are described by a linear term, there is a nonsignificant decline of −0.03 points per year for MHA, and a significant decline of −0.06 points per year for MHB. Assuming a mean rate corresponding to the lower confidence interval for MHB, we find that this equates to a decline of only 1.2% over 10 years.

Tables 7 and 8 show negligible positive or negative changes of 1.5 or less on MHA at all repeat testings, and on MHB for the first and second repeat testings. The estimated improvement of 9% points on MHB on the last testing occasion is an unexplained anomaly. Scores on both the MHA and MHB tests are significantly higher for men than for women, and for Manchester residents than for Newcastle residents. The differences between SES Cs were substantial, and they were comparable in magnitude with the effect sizes for AH4. Note that, in contrast to all other tests, on MHA the average entry year scores for cohorts recruited from 1984 onward were lower, though not significantly so for those starting in 1983. There was no clear pattern for MHB. This illustration that successive recruitment cohorts may differ on some tests though not on others emphasizes that drop-in effects may be complex and must be taken into consideration when one analyzes longitudinal data.

Comparisons of Practice Effects Between Tasks

For AH4-1, AH4-2, and CVL, rates of decline are similar and accelerate with age. For VFR, the rate of decline is linear, and MH scores remain stable over time. The size of the average practice effect on the second occasion varies between tasks: Gains of over 4.5% points on the AH4 tests contrast with gains of 1% or less on the other tasks. On the third and fourth occasion, a gain of over 4.5 for AH4-2 and CVL contrasts with negative estimates for several other tasks. However, note that these differences may reflect a lack of fit between the quadratic and improvement parameters at older ages for which relatively few data points are available.

A further question about practice effects is whether their sizes vary with the interval between successive repetitions of the tasks. The fact that some individuals missed particular retesting sessions but later returned to the study allowed us to make a secondary analysis to determine whether the substantial practice effect of over 4.5 points on the second occasion of taking the AH4-1 and AH4-2 tests varies with the duration of the interval between initial and second experiences. Restricting the analysis to individuals with scores at entry and at the second scheduled visit for each test, we found that the interval between these two time points ranged from 1 to 8 years. Because of small numbers in the lowest and highest categories, the categories we used were ≤ 2, 3, 4, 5, 6, or 7+ years. We fitted a model to each response, replacing the single-step function at the second occasion by a six-level term corresponding to the gap times. For the AH4-1 response, the mean practice effects are similar across the intervals, ranging from 3.5 to 5.2 points, with no clear trend over time. The estimates are slightly more variable for AH4-2, ranging from 3.8 to 7.9. For both responses, this model provides an improvement in fit compared with the simpler model with practice at the second visit coded as a two-level factor ($p = .006$ and $p < .0001$, 5 df). That is to say, the average sizes of improvement caused by a previous experience of either AH4 test remained the same over intervals of 2 to 7 years.

Deviation Around the Mean Response: Random Effects

The final hypotheses examined are that participants' rates of cognitive decline vary with their overall levels of gf, and that variance in performance between participants increases as the study continues, and the mean age of the sample increases.

In these models, the A_is reflect the extent to which individuals deviate from the average response value, and the B_is measure their deviations in slope, that is, in rates of decline. The maximum likelihood estimates (and 95% confidence intervals, or CIs) of the standard deviations (σ_A and σ_B) and correlation (ρ_{AB}) of these random effects, assumed to be normally distributed with mean zero, are presented in the table notes of Tables 4 through 9. After adjustment for covariates, the individual estimates of the A_i and B_i are of interest as they can be used to predict intercepts and slopes of individual trajectories of change. They are usually estimated as the conditional expectation of the effects given the observed data, and they are sometimes termed empirical Bayes (EB) estimates. In addition, histograms and scatterplots can be used to detect unusual individuals.

From values of $\hat{A}_i$ and $\hat{B}_i$ estimates for individuals based on the AH4-1 model, we calculate sample standard deviation estimates of 12.84 and 0.15. These are considerably smaller than the *mle* estimates of 15.43 and 0.41. The estimated sample correlation is weakly negative ($\hat{\rho} = -0.29$), whereas the *mle* is strongly negative ($\hat{\rho}_{AB} = -0.51$, 95% CI of -0.58 to -0.44). Discrepancies of similar magnitudes are observed for the other responses. This suggests that the empirically observed estimates do indeed substantially underestimate the true variability in the random effects. Actually, for any linear combination of the random effects, the EB estimates are less than or equal to the true variability in the random effects (Verbeck & Molenberghs,

Table 8. MHA Model Estimates

Mean Response Model Parameter	Estimate	SE	t Value	p Value	95% CI
Intercept	80.56	1.33	60.61	<.001	77.96, 83.16
age − 49	−0.03	0.02	−1.41	.155	−0.07, 0.01
Improvement					
$j \geq 2$	1.07	0.16	6.57	<.001	0.75, 1.39
$j \geq 3$	−1.48	0.21	−7.02	<.001	−1.90, −1.07
$j \geq 4$	1.47	0.34	4.32	<.001	0.80, 2.13
Male vs. female	1.89	0.39	4.82	<.001	1.12, 2.66
Socioeconomic status					
C2 vs. C1	−3.18	0.85	−3.73	<.001	−4.85, −1.51
C3 (M)	−17.09	0.93	−18.41	<.001	−18.91, −15.27
C3 (N)	−10.35	0.88	−11.82	<.001	−12.06, −8.63
C4/5	−21.11	1.01	−20.95	<.001	−23.08, −19.14
Missing	−16.20	1.04	−15.61	<.001	−18.23, −14.16
Newcastle vs. Manchester	−4.21	0.96	−4.39	<.001	−6.08, −2.33
Entry year					
1984 vs. 1983	−0.44	0.57	−0.78	.433	−1.55, 0.66
1985	−1.44	1.12	−1.28	.200	−3.64, 0.76
1986	−1.72	1.16	−1.48	.139	−4.00, 0.56
1987	−2.15	1.19	−1.81	.071	−4.47, 0.18
1988	−0.18	0.66	−0.27	.790	−1.47, 1.12
1989	−1.24	0.79	−1.56	.120	−2.79, 0.32
1990	−1.14	1.32	−0.86	.388	−3.74, 1.45
1991	−2.56	1.65	−1.55	.121	−5.79, 0.68
1992	−2.57	1.40	−1.84	.066	−5.30, 0.17

Notes: MHA = Mill Hill A; CI = confidence interval; C = category; N = nonmanual skilled; M = manual skilled. Covariance and residual parameters: For σ_A, estimate = 11.84 and 95% CI = 11.59, 12.09; for σ_E, estimate = 6.07 and 95% CI = 5.97, 6.18.

1997, chap. 3). This latter result provides theoretical support for our findings.

Within this model, the issue of whether individuals' trajectories of cognitive decline vary with their basal levels of mental ability (AH4 test scores) can be approached only if we make a strong assumption that there is a particular age before which decline proceeds at a constant rate. Given this assumption, we see that estimates $\hat{\rho}_{AB}$ from the models have substantive value. Assuming that this critical age is the lowest entry age in the sample, 49 years, we find that the outcome is that, among individuals who were aged 49 at entry, those with higher initial AH4-1 scores tended to show relatively more rapid cognitive decline on AH4-1 than did those with lower initial scores. As shown in Tables 4 through 7, the correlation estimates for AH4-1, AH4-2, CVL, and VFR are all significantly negative.

Nevertheless, it is important to note that these correlations are arbitrary and depend on the age used for "centering." For example, if age 65 is used instead of age 49, the correlation is approximately zero for the AH4-1 scores, indicating parity in rates of change for individuals at all levels of AH4-1 scores. They become increasingly positive as centering ages older than 65 are selected, indicating faster rates of decline for individuals with lower AH4-1 scores.

The question of whether variability between participants increases with sample age can be addressed in a similar way. For each response, the σ_A standard deviation estimate can be used to calculate the 95% expected range (the range over which 95% of

Table 9. MHB Model Estimates

Mean Response Model Parameter	Estimate	SE	t Value	p Value	95% CI
Intercept	65.13	1.59	40.91	<.001	62.01, 68.25
age − 49	−0.06	0.03	−2.35	.019	−0.12, −0.01
Improvement					
$j \geq 2$	0.97	0.23	4.28	<.001	0.53, 1.42
$j \geq 3$	−1.31	0.30	−4.39	<.001	−1.89, −0.76
$j \geq 4$	9.31	0.49	18.93	<.001	8.34, 10.27
Male vs. female	0.94	0.47	2.01	.045	0.02, 1.86
Socioeconomic status					
C2 vs. C1	−4.28	1.02	−4.21	<.001	−6.27, −2.29
C3 (N)	−13.60	1.04	−13.03	<.001	−15.64, −11.55
C3 (M)	−21.64	1.11	−19.55	<.001	−23.81, −19.48
C4/5	−26.26	1.20	−21.82	<.001	−28.62, −23.90
Missing	−19.78	1.25	−15.88	<.001	−22.22, −17.34
Newcastle vs. Manchester	−3.71	1.15	−3.23	<.001	−5.96, −1.46
Entry year					
1984 vs. 1983	−2.49	0.67	−3.71	<.001	−3.81, −1.18
1985	2.32	1.35	1.72	.085	−0.32, 4.96
1986	−0.04	1.39	−0.03	.976	−2.77, 2.69
1987	0.69	1.42	0.49	.627	−2.10, 3.48
1988	0.79	0.79	1.00	.318	−0.76, 2.33
1989	−1.01	0.95	−1.06	.287	−2.87, 0.85
1990	−2.42	1.59	−1.52	.128	−5.54, 0.70
1991	−3.70	1.98	−1.86	.062	−7.58, 0.19
1992	−2.01	1.68	−1.20	.230	−5.29, 1.27

Notes: MHB = Mill Hill B; CI = confidence interval; C = category; N = nonmanual skilled; M = manual skilled. Covariance and residual parameters: For σ_A, estimate = 13.53 and 95% CI = 13.22, 13.85; for σ_E, estimate = 9.00 and 95% CI = 8.84, 9.16.

the population values would fall) for the intercept. For example, the 95% expected ranges for the AH4-1 and AH4-2 mean entry levels are 66.0 + 1.96 × 15.4 = [35.8–96.3] and [32.5–89.8], respectively. The expected ranges for the other tests are smaller because the $\hat{\sigma}_A$ are less. We can also examine the relative variability of the A_i with respect to the corresponding fixed effect estimate. Based on the parameter estimates presented in Table 4, the relative variability is 15.4/66.0 = 23% for AH4-1. Estimates of similar size were obtained for AH4-2 (24%), VFR (27%), and MHB (21%), whereas CVL and MHA showed markedly less relative variability (14% and 15%).

The σ_B estimates ranged from 0.41 to 0.49 on the AH4 and CVL responses, whereas there was less variability in the individual slopes for the VFR response ($\hat{\sigma}_B = 0.23$). Approximately 95% of the individual B_i values lie within $\pm 1.96\,\hat{\sigma}_B$ of the zero mean. Although the σ_B estimates for these four responses appear small, they are amplified by the multiplication with age (in years over 49) in the model. For example, a difference of 0.45 (roughly 1 SD on the AH4 and CVL tests) in the slopes for any two participants with equal cognitive function on entry to the study would result in a difference of 4.5 and 9.0 percentage points after 10 and 20 years, respectively. Because participants have different rates of decline, this implies that between-individual variability in performance increases with sample age and also that this increase in variability is most marked for those tasks with large between-participant variability. It is important to note that, because the effects of covariates such as gender, SES, and city of residence were taken into consideration in computing this variance, they cannot provide functional explanations for it. Because age is modeled as a quadratic function in the mean part of the models, neither the expected ranges nor the relative variability of the B_i can be calculated. Finally, under the specified random effect models, the residual standard deviation estimates were similar between tests and ranged from 5.7 to 9.0 percentage points.

DISCUSSION

It has long been recognized that longitudinal data may be seriously misinterpreted if participants in longitudinal studies improve because they repeatedly take the same tests. The current analyses tested the working hypothesis that practice effects do occur in a longitudinal study, that they are substantial enough to mask age-related declines, and that they vary between tasks and between individuals of different ages and levels of ability.

Practice Effects

Practice effects are significant and substantial on both AH4 tests and on the CVL test. For example, on the second occasion, gains of over 4.5 percentage points on the AH4 tests contrast with improvements of 1% or less on the other tests. On the third and fourth occasions, an improvement of over 4.5 is predicted for AH4-2 and CVL, contrasting with negative estimates for several other tasks. Note that these gains from practice are comparable with the declines in average scores, after practice and drop-out have been taken into consideration, of 6 points between age 60 and 70 (64.6 and 58.6, respectively) on the AH4-1 and 6 points (58.2 to 52.1, respectively) on the AH4-2.

The sizes of practice effects do differ between tasks, and between older and younger individuals. On AH4-1 and AH4-2 tasks, practice effects were indeed markedly greater for older than for younger participants, with estimated improvements between first and second testing of 1.5–2.5% for a 49-year-old as against over 4.5% for a 70-year-old. On all other tasks they ranged from only 0.1 to 1.6 points, and they were independent of age. Neglect of practice effects leads to underestimation of the true extent of age-related changes and may disguise the fact that they are accelerated rather than linear. Further, marked differences in practice effects between tasks and age groups may be misinterpreted as evidence that brain aging affects performance on some tasks, and so some mental abilities, earlier and more severely than others.

Practice improvements were greatest between the first and second encounters with a task, and were thereafter modest. At first sight this seems paradoxical because considerable bodies of evidence, such as those reviewed by Kausler (1990), show that age slows the learning of novel tasks. This would lead us to expect that, the older individuals are, the less they should improve during a longitudinal study. One explanation for this counterintuitive finding is that older individuals perform poorly when they first encounter novel cognitive tests because they need longer to understand what the tests demand of them and to accommodate to an unfamiliar environment (Rabbit, 1993b). On this premise the large and long-lasting practice gains observed between the first and subsequent test sessions during this longitudinal study not only reflect specific task learning but also general familiarity with the testing environment and procedures. Note that this possibility carries the awkward methodological implication that, even if particular tasks are not repeated, for example, by using "parallel forms," increasing familiarity with the general testing procedures may benefit older participants more than younger participants and so counteract age differences in rates of decline. We suggest that these findings also have theoretical implications. Difficulties in coping with task novelty, and marked gains once initial problems have been overcome, are characteristics of patients with focal prefrontal cortical damage (Burgess, 1997). In this context the present findings may be interpreted as further evidence for age-related declines in "executive" functions supported by the prefrontal cortex that enable us to cope with novel tasks (Burgess & Shallice, 1996; Lowe & Rabbitt, 1998; Shallice & Burgess, 1991) This behavioral evidence has been assumed to reflect neurophysiological findings that the prefrontal cortex suffers earlier and more rapid neurophysiological and cerebrovascular changes than other areas (Gur, Gur, Orbist, Skolnik, & Reivitch, 1987; Haugh & Eggers, 1991; Scheibel & Scheibel, 1975; Shaw et al., 1984). In this framework of interpretation, it is a surprising new finding that, once experienced, tasks and testing situations do not regain "novelty" through disuse, even over periods as long as 7 years.

Drop-Out

We have argued that these likelihood-based analyses under random drop-out assumptions allow good estimates of what actual trajectories of change would have been had drop-out not occurred and so permit more realistic estimates of how rates of age-related cognitive change differ between age groups, socioeconomic groups, and gender groups. Note, however, that these analyses adjust for, but do not give information about, drop-out effects. The relationship between volunteers' propensity to drop out and their cognitive measurement profiles, their gender, socioeconomic category, or general health status are different questions of substantive interest in their own right. We propose to investigate these relationships by using informative drop-out models. The results will be reported separately in due course.

The analysis also detected, and took into consideration, significant differences between the average levels of ability of cohorts recruited at different points during the study. These drop-in effects differed between tasks. On the AH4 and CVL tests, cohort recruitment differences were large enough so that interpretation of the data would have been affected if they had been neglected. In contrast, they were negligible on the MH vocabulary tests. This implies that analyses must not assume that cohort differences on any single "benchmark" test can be taken as representative of differences on all other tests.

The remaining working hypotheses were that, after practice and drop-out effects had been considered, it would be possible to more accurately determine actual rates of changes, and so to discover whether these are constant or are accelerated by increasing age, and whether they differ between different kinds of tasks, between more and less able individuals, and with demographic factors such as gender and socioeconomic advantage. Finally, it was predicted that after all of the aforementioned factors had been taken into consideration, variance in cognitive performance between members of a sample would be seen to significantly increase as the members age.

Does Rate of Cognitive Decline Accelerate With Sample Age?

After practice and drop-out effects were adjusted for, there was clear evidence that rates of decline accelerated with age on the two AH4 tests and the CVL task.

Do Scores on Different Cognitive Tests Decline at Different Rates?

On the AH4-1 and AH4-2 tests and on the CVL task, declines accelerated with age. Declines in VFR scores were less marked and were linear rather than accelerated. On the MHA and MHB vocabulary tests, there was little or no decline. This last finding agrees with the consensus of previous studies that declines in tasks that are assumed to be supported by gf contrasts with stability on tests such as the MHA and MHB vocabulary tests, in which performance is supported by "crystallized" knowledge acquired over a lifetime and maintained by practice in old age (Horn, 1982). The different trajectories of change for the CVL and VFR tests also provide a longitudinal confirmation of Horn's (1982) many cross-sectional demonstrations that age affects performance on some tests of fluid mental abilities more than on others.

How Are Rates of Decline Affected by Gender, by Level of Socioeconomic Advantage, and by Individual Differences in General Intellectual Ability?

On average, men performed better than women on the AH4-1 and AH4-2 and MHA and MHB, but women performed better than men on the CVL and VFR tasks. Superiority of men on the AH4 and MH tests may partly be explained by the fact that, for these generations of participants, women had much poorer educational and career opportunities, most especially in the industrial North of England. The finding of superiority of women on CVL and VFR tests confirms and extends cross-sectional comparisons within this sample by Rabbitt and colleagues (1996). The gender effect on CVL scores appears to be complex, because it also depends on age. The advantage in CVL scores for women is relatively small at young to middle ages and thereafter widens. One possible explanation for this might be that because women live longer they also retain mental competence later in life. However, this seems unlikely because there is no similar Gender × Age interaction on any other task. In our view, and in the absence of other evidence, the particular advantage for verbal learning (CVL) is as likely to reflect lifestyle factors as intrinsic differences in the level and the maintenance of particular mental abilities. These and other hints of interactions between differences in lifestyle and preservation of particular abilities in old age require further investigation.

There were marked differences in cognitive performance between socioeconomic categories on all tests. The mean difference between occupational groups C1 and C4–5 was over 20 percentage points on the AH4 and MH tasks and 7–11 percentage points on the CVL and VFR tasks. In spite of this clear evidence that SES affects overall levels of performance, there is no evidence that it differentially affects rates of decline. This is unexpected because SES is a good proxy for many factors that are known to slow biological decline, such as level of general health and of lifetime health care, level of education, and exposure to toxicity (Kitagawa & Hauser, 1973). Socioeconomic disadvantage is also associated with higher and earlier mortality in later life, and there is robust evidence that approach to death reduces level of cognitive performance during longitudinal studies (Berkowitz, 1964; Bosworth et al., 1999; Botwinick, West, & Storandt, 1978; Jarvik & Blum, 1971; Johannsen & Berg, 1989; Lieberman, 1965; Rabbitt et al., 2002; Reimanis & Green, 1971; Riegel & Riegel, 1972; Riegel, Riegel, & Myer, 1967; Small & Backman, 1997). There is also evidence that socioeconomic disadvantage, and in particular lower educational attainment, is linked to the prevalence of Alzheimer's disease in old age (Bonaiuto, Rocca, & Lippi, 1990; Evans et al., 1993; Korczyn, Kahana, & Galper, 1991). Obviously, more detailed analyses exploring relationships among socioeconomic factors, age, and cognition in this particular population sample are required.

Even when effects of SES and gender are taken into account, Manchester residents perform significantly better than Newcastle residents on the AH4-1, MHA, and MHB tests. There is no evidence of any difference in performance between cities on CVL or VFR. These differences remain cryptic because the city term is likely to be a proxy for a variety of unidentified factors for which the modeling process could not control.

These analyses also suggest that the level of general intellectual ability of participants on entry to a longitudinal study may affect their rates of subsequent cognitive change, though not in the direction that previous research has led us to expect. If we make the reasonable assumption that, in members of this sample, cognitive decline can be dated from age 49 (the age of the youngest volunteers on entry to the study) and that individuals' rates of decline previous to age 49 had been constant, the analysis shows that after practice and drop-out effects had been considered, individuals who entered the study with higher overall levels of ability declined more rapidly than those who entered with lower levels of ability. This finding is inconsistent with previous suggestions that higher levels of performance in young adult life may be associated with longer retention of ability and with lower incidence of dementias and predementing conditions in old age (see, e.g., Snowden et al., 1996). It does, however, agree with an analysis of data from a subgroup of this sample by Rabbitt, Chetwynd, and McInnes (2003) based on the entirely different premise that, because individuals' scores on the MHA vocabulary test do not change with age, they can be used as proxies for their AH4 test scores in middle age and so can be compared against their current, observed AH4 test scores to estimate age-related losses.

Note, however, that the outcome of the present analysis depends on the age used for "centering" in the population. If age 65 is used for "centering," then rates of decline do not vary with levels of gf, and if ages older than 65 are used for "centering," then it appears that the less able decline more rapidly than the more able. The implications of these findings with regard to methods of analysis of individual differences in the forms of trajectories of cognitive change are currently being further explored.

As a Population Ages Does Variability Between Its Members Increase?

The standard deviation estimates provide useful insight into the amount of variability between individuals on each task. The estimated standard deviation for the linear rate of decline was similar for the AH4 and CVL tasks, ranging from 0.41 to 0.49, but for VFR it was only 0.23. The differences between the slopes for individuals give rise to increased variability in performance with age. For example, a pair of participants with equal cognitive function on entry to the study whose slopes differed by 0.4 would differ by 4 points after 10 years and by 8 points after 20 years. Differences of this size are of practical importance because they are large enough to provide useful insights into the functional causes of marked individual differences in rates of cognitive decline in old age.

There are two quite different reasons why, as the members of a sample age, they should increasingly diverge in terms of their levels of cognitive performance. One is that differing genetic legacies and lifetime health histories bring about differences in trajectories of biological aging, which will diverge over time (Rabbitt, 1982, 1993a). A second is that as people age and so become less able, their performance on any task on which they are tested varies more from moment to moment and, as a direct consequence, their average levels of performance also vary more from session to session and from day to day (Rabbitt, 1999; Rabbitt, Osman, Stollery, & Moore, 2001). As day-to-day variability increases for all members of a sample, so they will differ more with respect to each other when they are all tested on any single occasion. Thus, increasing variability between members of aging samples has at least two, functionally different, causes. The possibility of confounds between these effects means that any single, cross-sectional observation of members of a population at a particular time point will give us an inaccurate, and probably exaggerated, estimate of actual individual differences in trajectories of cognitive aging. For better estimates to be obtained, longitudinal data are essential; ideally, we also need to estimate, as far as possible, the effects of session-to-session or day-to-day variability by taking several samples of performance on each task at each successive longitudinal data point. Estimates of intrinsic within-participant variability obtained from these samples will allow long-term trends resulting from differences in trajectories of change to be more precisely determined. Such data will also be useful in showing the extent to which increases in the intrinsic variability of individuals' performance, as distinct from changes in their mean levels of performance, alter as they age.

ACKNOWLEDGMENT

Address correspondence to Patrick Rabbitt, Age and Cognitive Performance Research Centre, Zochonis Building, University of Manchester, Manchester, M13 9PL, United Kingdom. E-mail: rabbitt@psy.man.ac.uk

REFERENCES

Arenberg, D. (1974). A longitudinal study of problem solving in adults. *Gerontology, 29,* 650–658.

Baltes, P. B. (1968). Longitudinal and cross-sectional sequences in the study of age and generation effects. *Human Development, 11,* 145–171.

Bank, L., & Jarvik, L. F. (1978). A longitudinal study of aging human twins. In Schneider, E. L. (Ed.), *The genetics of aging* (pp. 303–333). New York: Plenum Press.

Bell, B., Rose, C. L., & Damon, A. (1972). The normative aging study: Interdisciplinary and longitudinal study of health and aging. *Aging and Human Development, 3,* 5–17.

Berkowitz, B. (1964). Changes in intellect with age: IV. Changes in achievement and survival. *Newsletter for Research in Psychology, 6*, 18–20.

Birren, J. E., Butler, R. N., Greenhouse, S. W., Sokoloff, L., & Yarrow, M. R. (1963). *Human aging* (Publication No. 986). Washington, DC: U.S. Government Printing Office.

Bonaiuto, S., Rocca, W. A., & Lippi, A. (1990). Impact of education and dementia: Clinical issues. In H. A. Whitaker (Ed.), *Neuropsychological studies of non-focal brain damage* (pp. 1–15). New York: Springer.

Bosworth, H. B., Schaie, K. W., & Willis, S. L. (1999). Cognitive and sociodemographic risk factors for mortality in the Seattle Longitudinal Study. *Journal of Gerontology: Psychological Sciences, 54B*, P273–P282.

Botwinick, J., West, R. L., & Storandt, M. (1978). Predicting death from behavioral test performance. *Journal of Gerontology, 33*, 755–762.

Brodman, E., Erdman, A. J., Jr., & Wolff, H. G. (1949). *Manual for the Cornell Medical Index Health Questionnaire*. New York: Cornell University Medical School.

Burgess, P. W. (1997). Theory and methodology in executive function research. In P. M. A. Rabbitt (Ed.), *Methodology of frontal and executive function* (pp. 81–116). Hove, England: Psychology Press.

Burgess, P. W., & Shallice, T. (1996). Bizarre responses, rule detection and frontal lobe lesions. *Cortex, 32*, 241–259.

Busse, E. W., Maddox, G. L., Buckley, C. E., III., Burger, P. C., George, L. K., March, G. R., et al. (1985). *The Duke Longitudinal Studies of Normal Aging: 1955–1980*. New York: Springer.

Clark, J. W. (1960). The ageing dimension. A factorial analysis of individual differences with age on psychological and physiological measurement. *Gerontology, 15*, 183–187.

Clement, F. J. (1974). Longitudinal and cross-sectional assessments of age-changes in physical strength as related to sex, social class and mental ability. *Gerontology, 15*, 94–116.

Colsher, P. L., & Wallace, R. B. (1991). Longitudinal application of cognitive measures in a defined population of community dwelling elders. *Annals of Epidemiology, 3*, 71–77.

Costa, P. T., & McCrae, R. R. (1980). Somatic complaints in males as a function of age and neuroticism: A longitudinal analysis. *Journal of Behavioral Medicine, 3*, 245–253.

Diggle, P. J., Liang, K. Y., & Zeger, S. L. (1994). *Analysis of longitudinal data*. Oxford, England: Oxford University Press.

Dirken, J. M. (1972). *Functional age of industrial workers*. Groningen, The Netherlands: Wolters-Noordhof.

Evans, D. A., Beckett, L. A., Albert, M. S., Hebert, L. E., Scherr, P. A., Funkenstein, H. H., et al. (1993). Level of education and change in cognitive function in a community population of older persons. *Annals of Epidemiology, 3*, 77–81.

Forner, A. (1972). *Aging and society* (Vol. III). New York: Sage.

Gur, R. C., Gur, R. E., Orbist, W. D., Skolnik, B. E., & Reivitch, M. (1987). Age and regional cerebral blood flow at rest and during cognitive activity. *Archives of General Psychiatry, 44*, 617–621.

Haugh, H., & Eggers, R. (1991). Morphometry of the human cortex cerebri and cortex striatum during aging. *Neurobiology of Aging, 12*, 336–338.

Heim, A. W. (1970). *The AH4 group tests of intelligence*. Windsor, England: NFER/Nelson.

Heron, A., & Chown, S. (1967). *Age and function*. London: Churchill.

Hertzog, C., & Schaie, K. W. (1988). Stability and change in adult intelligence: 2. Simultaneous analysis of longitudinal means and covariance structures. *Psychology and Aging, 3*, 122–130.

Hertzog, C., Schaie, K. W., & Gribbin, K. (1978). Cardiovascular disease and changes in intellectual function from middle to old age. *Journal of Gerontology, 33*, 872–883.

Horn, J. L. (1982). The theory of fluid and crystallized intelligence in relation to concepts of cognitive psychology and aging in adulthood. In F. I. M. Craik & S. Trehub (Eds.), *Aging and cognitive processes* (pp. 237–278). Boston: Plenum Press.

Hultsch, D. F., Hertzog, C., Small, B. J., McDonald-Miszczak, L., & Dixon, R. A. (1992). Short-term longitudinal change in cognitive performance in later life. *Psychology and Aging, 7*, 571–584.

Jarvik, L., & Blum, K. (1971). Cognitive declines as predictors of mortality in twin pairs. In E. Palmore & F. Jeffers (Eds.), *Prediction of life span* (pp. 46–73). Lexington, MA: Heath.

Johansson, B., & Berg, S. (1989). The robustness of the terminal decline phenomenon: Longitudinal data from the Digit-Span Memory Test. *Journal of Gerontology: Psychological Sciences, 44*, P184–P186.

Johansson, B., Zarit, S. H., & Berg, S. (1992). Changes in cognitive function of the oldest old. *Journal of Gerontology: Psychological Sciences, 47*, P75–P80.

Kausler, D. H. (1990). *Experimental psychology, cognition and human aging*. New York: Springer-Verlag.

Kitagawa, E. M., & Hauser, P. M. (1973). *Differential mortality in the United States: A study in socioeconomic epidemiology*. Cambridge, MA: Harvard University Press.

Korczyn, A. D., Kahana, E., & Galper, Y. (1991). Epidemiology of dementia in Ashkelon, Israel. *Neuroepidemiology, 10*, 100.

Kucera, H., & Francis, N. (1967). *Frequency and word association norms*. Providence, RI: Brown University Press.

Lachman, R., Lachman, J. L., & Taylor, D. W. (1982). Reallocation of mental resources over the productive lifespan: Assumptions and task analyses. In F. I. M. Craik & S. Trehub (Eds.), *Aging and the cognitive process* (pp. 227–252). New York: Plenum Press.

Lansen, P. (1997). The impact of aging on cognitive functions: An 11-year follow up study of four age cohorts. *Acta Neurologica Scandinavica Supplimentum, 96* (No. 172), 172–193.

Lieberman, M. A. (1965). Psychological correlates of impending death: Some preliminary observations. *Journal of Gerontology, 20*, 181–190.

Lindenberger, U., Singer, T., & Baltes, P. B. (2002). Longitudinal selectivity in aging populations: Separating mortality-associated versus experimental components in the Berlin Aging Study (BASE). *Journal of Gerontology: Psychological Sciences, 57B*, P474–P482.

Lowe, C., & Rabbitt, P. M. A. (1998). Test/re-test reliability of the CANTAB and ISPOCD neuropsychological batteries: Theoretical and practical issues. *Neuropsychologia, 36*, 915–923.

Mason, K., & Mason, W. (1973). Some methodological issues in cohort analysis of archival data. *American Sociological Review, 38*, 242–258.

McInnes, L., & Rabbitt, P. M. (1997). The relationship between functional ability and cognitive ability among elderly people. In *Facts and research in gerontology* (pp. 34–45). Paris: Serdi.

Moller, J. T., Cluitmans, P., Rasmussen, L. S., Houx, P., Canet, J., Rabbitt, P., et al. (1998). Long-term post-operative cognitive dysfunction in the elderly: ISPOCD1 study. *The Lancet, 351*, 857–861.

Morse, C. K. (1993). Does variability increase with age? An archival study of cognitive measures. *Psychology and Aging, 8*, 156–164.

Nesselrode, J. R., & Baltes, P. B. (1979). *Longitudinal research in the study of behaviour and development*. New York: Academic Press.

Office of Population Censuses & Surveys. (1980). *Classification of occupations*. London: Her Majesty's Stationary Office.

Owens, W. A. (1953). Age and mental abilities; a longitudinal study. *Genetic Psychological Monographs, 48*, 3–54.

Owens, W. A. (1966). Age and mental abilities: A second adult follow-up. *Journal of Educational Psychology, 57*, 311–325.

Palmore, E. (1978). When can age, period and cohort be separated? *Social Forces, 57*, 282–295.

Payton, A., Holland, F., Diggle, P., Rabbitt, P., Horan, M., Davidson, Y., et al. (2003). Cathepsin D exon 2 polymorphism associated with general intelligence in a healthy older population. *Molecular Psychiatry, 8*, 14–18.

Pendleton, N., Payton, A., van den Boogerd, E. H., Holland, F., Diggle, P., Rabbitt, P. M. A., et al. (2002). Apolipoprotein E genotype does not predict decline in intelligence in older adults. *Neurosciences Letters, 324*, 74–76.

Powell, D. H. (1994). *Profiles in cognitive aging*. Cambridge, MA: Harvard University Press.

Rabbitt, P. M. A. (1982). Cognitive psychology needs models for old age. In A. D. Baddeley & J. Long (Eds.), *Attention and performance IX* (pp. 142–165). Hove, England: Erlbaum.

Rabbitt, P. M. (1993a). Does it all go together when it goes? *Quarterly Journal of Experimental Psychology, 46(A)*, 385–433.

Rabbitt, P. M. (1993b). Crystal quest: An examination of the concepts of "fluid" and "crystallised" intelligence as explanations for cognitive changes in old age. In A. D. Baddeley & L. Weiskrantz (Eds.), *Attention, selection, awareness and control* (pp. 197–231). Oxford, England: Oxford University Press.

Rabbitt, P. M. A. (1999). Measurement indices, functional characteristics and psychometric constructs in cognitive ageing. In T. J. Perfect & E. A. Maylor (Eds.), *Models of cognitive aging* (pp. 160–187). Oxford, England: Oxford University Press.

Rabbitt, P. M. A., Banerji, N., & Szemanski, A. (1989). Space Fortress as an IQ test? Predictions of learning and of practised performance in a complex video game. *Acta Psychologica, 71*, 243–257.

Rabbitt, P., Bent, N., & McInnes, L. (1997). Health, age and mental ability. *The Irish Journal of Psychology, 18*, 104–131.

Rabbitt, P. M., Chetwynd, A., & McInnes, L. (2003). Do clever brains age more slowly? Further exploration of a Nun result. *British Journal of Psychology, 94*, 63–71.

Rabbitt, P. M., Donlan, C., Bent, N., McInnes, L., & Abson, V. (1993). The University of Manchester Age and Cognitive Performance Research Centre and North East Age Research longitudinal programmes 1982 to 1997. *Zeitschrift Gerontology, 26*, 176–183.

Rabbitt, P. M. A., Donlan, C., Watson, P., McInnes, L., & Bent, N. (1996). Unique and interactive effects of depression, age socio-economic advantage and gender on cognitive performance of normal healthy older people. *Psychology & Aging, 10*, 221–235.

Rabbitt, P. M. A., Osman, P., Stollery, B., & Moore, B. (2001). There are stable individual differences in performance variability, both from moment to moment and from day to day. *Quarterly Journal of Experimental Psychology, 54A*, 981–1003.

Rabbitt, P. M., Watson, P., Donlan, C., Bent, L., & McInnes, L. (1994). Subject attrition in a longitudinal study of cognitive performance in community-based elderly people. In B. J. Vellas, J. L. Albarede, & P. J. Garry (Eds.), *Facts and research in gerontology* (pp. 203–207). Paris: Serdi.

Rabbitt, P., Watson, P., Donlan, C., McInnes, L., Horan, M., Pendleton, N., et al. (2002). Effects of death within 11 years on cognitive performance in old age. *Psychology and Aging, 17*, 1–14.

Raven, J. C. (1965). *The Mill Hill Vocabulary Scale*. London: Lewis.

Reimanis, G., & Green, R. (1971). Immanence of death and intellectual decrement in the aging. *Developmental Psychology, 5*, 270–272.

Riegel, K. F., & Riegel, R. M. (1972). Development, drop and death. *Developmental Psychology, 6*, 306–348.

Riegel, K. F., Riegel, R. M., & Myer, G. (1967). A study of the drop-out rates in longitudinal research on aging and the prediction of death. *Journal of Personality and Social Psychology, 5*, 342–348.

Rubin, D. B. (1976). Inference and missing data. *Biometrika, 63*, 581–592.

Schaie, K. W. (1996). *Intellectual development in adulthood: The Seattle Longitudinal Study*. New York: Cambridge University Press.

Schaie, K. W., & Labouvie-Vief, G. (1974). Generational versus ontogenetic components of change in adult cognitive functioning: A fourteen-year cross-sequential study. *Developmental Psychology, 10*, 305–320.

Schaie, K. W., Labouvie, G. V., & Barrett, T. J. (1973). Selective attrition effects in a fourteen-year study of adult intelligence. *Gerontology, 28*, 328–334.

Schaie, K. W., & Strother, C. R. (1968). A cross-sequential study of age changes in cognitive behaviour. *Psychological Bulletin, 70*, 671–680.

Schaie, K. W., & Willis, S. L. (1993). Age difference patterns of psychometric intelligence in adulthood: Generalizability within and across ability domains. *Psychology and Aging, 8*, 44–55.

Scharfstein, D. O., Rotnitzky, A., & Robins, J. M. (1999). Adjusting for non-ignorable drop-out using semiparametric non-response models (with discussion). *Journal of the American Statistical Association, 94*, 1096–1120.

Scheibel, M. E., & Scheibel, A. B. (1975). Structural changes in the aging brain. In H. Brody, D. Harmon, & J. M. Ordy (Eds.), *Aging* (Vol. 1, pp. 11–37). New York: Raven Press.

Schlesselman, J. J. (1973a). Planning a longitudinal study: I. Sample size determination. *Journal of Chronic Diseases, 26*, 532–560.

Schlesselman, J. J. (1973b). Planning a longitudinal study: II. Frequency of measurement and study duration. *Journal of Chronic Diseases, 26*, 561–570.

Schulsinger, F., Knop, J., & Mednick, S. A. (1981). *Longitudinal research*. Lexington, MA: Hinghams.

Shallice, T., & Burgess, P. W. (1991). Higher-order cognitive impairments and frontal lobe lesions in man. In H. S. Levin, H. M. Eisenberg, & A. L. Benton (Eds.), *Frontal lobe function and dysfunction* (pp. 211–259). New York: Oxford University Press.

Shaw, T. G., Mortel, K. F., Meyer, J. S., Rogers, R. L., Hardenberg, J., & Cutaia, M. M. (1984). Cerebral blood flow changes in benign aging and cerebrovascular disease. *Neurology, 34*, 855–862.

Shock, N. W., Greulich, R. C., Andres, R., Arenberg, D., Costa, P. T., Jr., Lakatta, E. G., et al. (1984). *Normal human aging: The Baltimore Longitudinal Study of Aging* (NIH Publication No. 84-2450). Washington DC: U.S. Government Printing Office.

Sliwinski, M., & Buschke, H. (1999). Cross-sectional and longitudinal relationships among age, cognition and information processing speed. *Psychology and Aging, 14*, 18–33.

Small, B. J., & Backman, L. (1997). Cognitive correlates of mortality: Evidence from a population-based sample of very old adults. *Psychology and Aging, 12*, 309–313.

Snowden, D. A., Kemper, S. J., Mortimer, J. A., Greinier, L. H., Wekstein, D. R., & Markesbery, W. R. (1996). Linguistic ability in early life and cognitive function and Alzheimer's disease in later life. Findings from the Nun study. *Journal of the American Medical Association, 21*, 528–532.

Terman, L. M., & Oden, M. H. (1947). *Genetic studies of genius. Vol. 4: The gifted child grows up*. Stanford, CA: Stanford University Press.

Terman, L. M., & Oden, M. H. (1959). *Genetic studies of genius. Vol. 5: The gifted group at mid life*. Stanford, CA: Stanford University Press.

Verbeck, G., & Molenberghs, S. (1997). *Linear mixed models in practice. A SAS-oriented approach*. New York: Springer-Verlag.

Voitenko, V. P., & Tokar, A. V. (1983). The assessment of biological age and sex differences of human aging. *Experimental Aging Research, 9*, 239–244.

Zelinski, E. M., & Burnight, K. P. (1997). Sixteen-year longitudinal and time lag changes in memory and cognition in older adults. *Psychology and Aging, 12*, 503–513.

Zelinski, E. M., Gilewski, M. J., & Stewart, K. W. (1993). Individual differences in cross-sectional and 3 year longitudinal memory performance across the adult life span. *Psychology and Aging, 8*, 176–186.

Zelinski, E. M., & Stewart, S. T. (1998). Individual differences in 16-year memory changes. *Psychology and Aging, 13*, 622–630.

Received February 8, 2001
Accepted August 18, 2003
Decision Editor: Margie E. Lachman, PhD

[3]

Emergence of a Powerful Connection Between Sensory and Cognitive Functions Across the Adult Life Span: A New Window to the Study of Cognitive Aging?

Paul B. Baltes and Ulman Lindenberger
Max Planck Institute for Human Development and Education

Six hundred eighty seven individuals ages 25–103 years were studied cross-sectionally to examine the relationship between measures of sensory functioning (visual and auditory acuity) and intelligence (14 cognitive tasks representing a 5-factor space of psychometric intelligence). As predicted, the average proportion of individual differences in intellectual functioning connected to sensory functioning increased from 11% in adulthood (25–69 years) to 31% in old age (70–103 years). However, the link between fluid intellectual abilities and sensory functioning, albeit of different size, displayed a similarly high connection to age in both age groups. Several explanations are discussed, including a "common cause" hypothesis. In this vein, we argue that the increase in the age-associated link between sensory and intellectual functioning may reflect brain aging and that the search for explanations of cognitive aging phenomena would benefit from attending to factors that are shared between the 2 domains.

The role of sensory functions (such as vision and hearing) as antecedents, correlates, and consequents of intellectual functioning has not been at the center of research on the aging of intelligence, some exceptions notwithstanding (Granick, Kleban, & Weiss, 1976; MacFarland, 1968; Nettelbeck & Rabbitt, 1992; Stelmach & Hömberg, 1993). To be sure, sensory functioning has been mentioned in general conceptual frameworks developed to index the realm of intellectual functioning (e.g., Carroll, 1993; Horn & Hofer, 1992). Moreover, certain movements in the history of psychological theory, such as British empiricism or German elementarism (Herrnstein & Boring, 1965; Hilgard, 1987), have attended to the role of sensory input in the development and regulation of cognitive behavior. However, despite these lines of argument, in hundreds of studies on cognitive aging (for reviews, see Craik & Salthouse, 1992; Salthouse, 1991b), sensory functioning and its relationship to complex intellectual functioning has rarely been part of the research agenda.

This relative disinterest in the role of sensory functioning in efforts to understand the aging of intelligence is probably due to at least three perspectives. First, there is the tradition of intelligence testing (Dixon & Baltes, 1986; Sternberg & Detterman, 1986), with its primary focus on complex and knowledge-based problem-solving tasks (however, see Vernon, 1987). Simple measures of visual and auditory acuity seemed ill-suited to capture the complexity of intelligence and related phenomena. Second, there is an age bias in research on intellectual development, with the vast majority of intelligence-related research being conducted with children and younger adults such as college students. Similarly, in cognitive aging research, samples rarely reach into advanced old age. If sensory systems operate at relatively high levels in most individuals during these earlier age periods, the likelihood of finding strong relations to other domains of functioning would seem to be reduced. Third, there possibly was a lack of knowledge among gerontological researchers interested in the study of intellectual functioning about the brain-based sources of age differences in visual and auditory acuity. Only more recently, cognitive aging researchers have begun to recognize more fully that age-related individual differences in visual and auditory functioning are not only peripheral phenomena but also reflect age-based changes in the central nervous system (cf. Fozard, 1990).

It would be dishonest to imply that the present line of work was primarily the outcome of hypothesis-guided research or of anticipatory insights into the potential role of sensory factors in cognitive aging. It is more accurate to state that, aside from an early interest in the topic by one of us (Schaie, Baltes, & Strother 1964), the initial impetus was more due to the serendipities arising from interdisciplinary collaboration. In part, the data for the present study are taken from the Berlin Aging Study (BASE; Baltes, Mayer, Helmchen, & Steinhagen-Thiessen,

---

Data on the old-age sample (70–103 years) were collected as part of the Berlin Aging Study, which was sponsored by the Berlin–Brandenburg Academy of Sciences.

We express our gratitude to our many colleagues in this project, especially Markus Borchelt (Max Burger Hospital, Berlin) and Hans Scherer (professor and chairman of the Department of Otolaryngology, Free University of Berlin, Benjamin Franklin Medical College), who were significant partners in the decision to include sensory and sensorimotor measures in the assessment protocol of the Berlin Aging Study. In addition, we acknowledge helpful discussions with Chris Hertzog. Finally, we thank Annette Rentz, Anita Günther, Daniela Jopp, Karola Kersting, Gisela Schubert, Angelika Stöber, and Manfred Weilandt for assistance in data collection and project management regarding the younger sample (25–69 years).

Correspondence concerning this article should be addressed to either Paul B. Baltes or Ulman Lindenberger, Center of Psychology and Human Development, Max Planck Institute for Human Development and Education, Lentzeallee 94, 14195 Berlin, Germany.

1993). Because of its interdisciplinary emphasis, researchers in BASE range widely across disciplines and include biological, medical, behavioral, and social scientists. Not surprisingly, therefore, the measurement scheme developed for BASE (which covered for each participant a total of 14 sessions of assessment) included measures of sensory functioning.

In our first report from BASE on the interface between sensory functioning and intelligence in old age (Lindenberger & Baltes, 1994), the promise of interdisciplinary research materialized in a new finding. When considering the age range from 70 to 103 years, simple identification and threshold measures of visual and auditory acuity together accounted for 49% of the total and 93% of the age-related reliable variance in intellectual functioning. A large and fairly comprehensive battery of 14 tests of cognitive functioning (Lindenberger, Mayr, & Kliegl, 1993) had been used to mark the intellectual ability domain. Thus, it was difficult to argue that this finding was specific to one type of cognitive task. Moreover, the findings presented in Lindenberger and Baltes (1994) were not of the significant-but-low-effect-size kind. On the contrary, the pattern of outcomes suggested that, in old age, measures of visual and auditory acuity were as good in predicting age-related individual differences in intellectual abilities as measures from the realm of intellectual functioning itself that are known to excel in this regard (e.g., measures of perceptual speed; cf. Salthouse, 1991a). In fact, the connection between sensory functioning and intelligence was so strong that the data were consistent with a structural model (Bentler, 1989) in which age differences in intelligence (as indexed by the common variance of perceptual speed, reasoning, memory, knowledge, and fluency) were completely mediated by differences in visual and auditory acuity.

In our first efforts at accounting for these findings (Baltes & Lindenberger, 1995; Lindenberger & Baltes, 1994) we identified three different but possibly interrelated interpretations: (a) the sensory deprivation hypothesis, (b) the hypothesis of an aging-induced increase in the cognitive load of sensory performance, and (c) the brain-related "common cause" hypothesis. The common cause explanation, which is at the focus of the present study, was based on the argument that correlations between measures of sensory and intellectual functioning may increase in old age because "both sets of measures are an expression of the physiological architecture . . . of the [aging] brain" (Lindenberger & Baltes, 1994, p. 339).

The common cause hypothesis was further supported by data analyses showing that the magnitude of the relation between sensory and cognitive functioning was largely invariant across types of cognitive tests, levels of sensory or cognitive performance, and absence versus presence of brain-related pathology (i.e., dementia). Moreover, an index of sensorimotor functioning—balance/gait—was found to display as high a connection to intellectual functioning as visual and auditory acuity. It should be noted, however, that the common cause interpretation of the age-based link between sensory and cognitive functioning is a third-variable hypothesis. Thus, in principle, the ensemble of common cause factors promoting the strong connection between the two domains of functioning may not only involve age-related changes in brain integrity, but also age-based changes in other bodily functions. Finally, we cannot exclude the possibility that age- or cohort-associated changes in experiential conditions, such as differences in life contexts and life events, also contribute to the connection.

The present study has two major goals: to replicate the original finding of a strong link between sensory functioning and intelligence in old age, and to explore differences in the magnitude of this link across the entire adult age span. The findings reported in Lindenberger and Baltes (1994) were based on the opening participant wave of BASE, which provided a random sample of 156 persons stratified by age and gender ranging from 70 to 103 years. The first objective of the present study—replication—was achieved by extending that sample to the now available entire BASE sample, which consists of 516 persons, again stratified by age and gender and ranging from 70 to 103 years. The second objective—comparisons across a broader age span—was achieved by considering younger individuals. Specifically, we collected the same sensory and intellectual measures in a sample of younger adults ($N = 171$) ranging from 25 to 69 years.

Method

Samples and Procedure

Younger adult sample (25–69 years). Younger individuals ($N = 171$, M age = 48.2 years, $SD = 14.7$, 58% women) were recruited by a survey research institute to obtain a heterogeneous sample base and were tested individually at our laboratory in two sessions. In the first session, a general information questionnaire (modeled after the Intake Assessment of BASE; cf. Baltes et al., 1993) as well as measures related to vision and hearing were given. The battery of cognitive tests was administered in the second session. Procedures for sensory and cognitive assessments (see below) were identical to those used in BASE and have been reported in more detail elsewhere (Baltes & Lindenberger, 1995; Lindenberger et al., 1993; Steinhagen-Thiessen & Borchelt, 1993).

BASE sample (70–103 years). Older individuals ($N = 516$, M age = 84.9 years, $SD = 8.66$) represent the total sample of BASE (cf. Baltes et al., 1993). The sample is stratified by gender and six age brackets (70–74, 75–79, 80–84, 85–89, 90–94, and 95+ years), with 43 individuals in each of the resulting 12 design cells. Measures of distance visual acuity were given at the beginning, the battery of cognitive tests in the middle, and measures of hearing and close visual acuity toward the end of the 14-session multidisciplinary assessment protocol (for details, see Lindenberger & Baltes, 1994).

Composite sample (25–101 years). Some of the results reported below are based on regression analyses that cover an age range from 25 to over 100 years. For these analyses, the new younger sample was combined with a subsample from BASE rather than with all 516 participants to ensure that all levels of the independent variable (i.e., chronological age) were given about equal weight in the regression equations. Specifically, 12 individuals were drawn at random from each of the 12 Gender (2) × Age Group (6) design cells of BASE, with the constraints that they had not received a clinical diagnosis of dementia according to criteria from the revised third edition of the *Diagnostic and Statistical Manual of Mental Disorders (DSM–III–R;* American Psychiatric Association, 1987) and that they were not part of the sample reported in Lindenberger and Baltes (1994). The resulting sample of 144 individuals was combined with the new younger sample to yield a composite sample ($N = 315$) that spanned an age range from 25 to 101 years (M age = 64.9 years, $SD = 22.0$).

Measures

Visual acuity. Visual acuity was measured in Snellen decimal units at two different distances using two different standard reading tables containing digits and letters (Geigy, 1977). Distance visual acuity was assessed binocularly using a reading table presented at a standard distance of 2.5 m to the participant. Close visual acuity was measured separately for the left and the right eye using a reading table presented at reading distance. All three measurements were taken without and with the best optical correction (i.e., glasses) available to the participant. Ninety two percent of the participants in the BASE sample and 74% of the participants in the younger sample had at least one pair of glasses. The analyses reported in this article are based on the better values, which in most cases referred to corrected vision. The decision to use corrected rather than uncorrected vision is in line with our earlier work (Baltes & Lindenberger, 1995; Lindenberger & Baltes, 1994). It also provides for a better test of the common cause hypothesis because corrective devices should filter out, to a certain degree, peripheral variance (e.g., variance due to individual differences in the refractory properties of the lens), thereby allowing for a more direct assessment of the portion of sensory loss that is central-neuronal in nature.

Auditory acuity. Measures related to auditory acuity were assessed with a Bosch ST-20-1 pure tone audiometer using headphones. Thresholds were measured separately for the right and left ears at eight different frequencies. Sixteen percent of the individuals in the BASE sample and none of the individuals in the younger sample had hearing aids. For technical reasons, thresholds were assessed without hearing aids only. Testing started with the better ear; for participants who did not know which ear was their better one, testing started with the right ear. Within ears, frequencies were tested in the following order: 1.00, 2.00, 3.00, 4.00, 6.00, 8.00, 0.50, and 0.25 kHz.

Cognitive test battery. A total of 14 tests was administered measuring five different intellectual abilities: perceptual speed (Digit Letter Test, Digit Symbol Substitution, Identical Pictures), reasoning (Figural Analogies, Letter Series, Practical Problems), memory (Activity Recall, Memory for Text, Paired Associates), knowledge (Practical Knowledge, Spot-a-Word, Vocabulary), and fluency (Animals, Letter "S"). Perceptual speed, reasoning, and memory represent the broad fluid domain (Horn, 1982) or the relatively knowledge-free "mechanics" of cognition (Baltes, 1987, 1993). In contrast, knowledge and fluency represent the broad crystallized domain of cognitive functioning, or the knowledge-saturated "pragmatics." Stimulus presentation and data collection were supported by a Macintosh SE30 personal computer equipped with a MicroTouch Systems touch-sensitive screen. A detailed description of the tests and their psychometric and structural properties can be found elsewhere (Lindenberger et al., 1993). The 14 measures have satisfactory internal consistencies, high interrater reliabilities, and substantial loadings on their latent factors (Lindenberger et al., 1993). Using exploratory and confirmatory factor-analytic techniques (cf. Hertzog, 1990; McArdle & Nesselroade, 1994), structural differentiation into the five expected latent ability factors could be demonstrated for all three samples reported in this study.

Results

Overview

Results are reported in three sections. First, we report cross-sectional age gradients (Baltes, 1968; Schaie, 1965) of the five intellectual abilities in the composite life span sample (age range = 25–101 years) and examine the extent to which age gradients in intellectual abilities are attenuated after regressing intellectual abilities on vision, hearing, or both. Second, we investigate whether vision and hearing are more strongly related to individual differences in intellectual abilities in the old sample than in the younger sample. Third, we examine whether intercorrelations within the sensory and cognitive domains were higher in the older sample. To minimize the complexity of statistical procedures, the relevant variables of sensory and cognitive functioning are based on composites of their standardized indicators and were scaled in a T-score metric (i.e., $M = 50$, $SD = 10$). Thus, measures are not corrected for unreliability through the use of structural modeling techniques, as we had done in previous work (Lindenberger & Baltes, 1994). In analyses not reported here, equivalent results were obtained using structural modeling techniques.

Cross-Sectional Age Gradients in Intellectual Abilities From Age 25 to 101 Years: The Connection to Vision and Hearing

Figure 1 and the top rows of Table 1 display the relation of vision, hearing, and intellectual abilities to the linear and quadratic trends of age.[1] The table also contains an "intellectual ability composite" computed as the unit-weighted average over the five intellectual abilities to represent the centroid of the intellectual ability factor space as assessed with our battery. On average, the age gradients of vision and hearing were more negative than the age gradients of the three fluid-mechanical intellectual abilities of perceptual speed, reasoning, and memory ($z = 3.76$, $p < .01$), which in turn—as predicted by life span theories of psychometric intelligence (Baltes, 1993; Horn & Hofer, 1992; Schaie, 1965)—had more negative gradients than knowledge and fluency, the two crystallized pragmatic abilities ($z = 8.77$, $p < .01$).[2] Post hoc comparisons revealed the following order in the magnitude of negative age relations ($p < .01$): hearing > perceptual speed > (reasoning = vision = memory) > (knowledge = fluency).

Next, we examined whether age-related individual differences in the two domains were relatively independent of each other, or whether a large portion of the age-related variance in the two domains was shared. The middle rows of Table 1 provide a clear answer to this question. Averaged across the five intellectual abilities, controlling for vision was associated with a 3.9-fold reduction of age-related individual differences in cognitive functioning. Controlling for hearing led to a 8.8-fold reduction, and controlling for both vision and hearing to a 18.5-fold reduction of age differences in cognitive functioning. In fact, most linear and quadratic age trends in intellectual abilities were no longer significantly different from zero ($p < .01$) after controlling for either hearing alone or vision and hearing.[3]

---

[1] The quadratic age trend was computed by regressing age squared on age and saving the residuals (i.e., the quadratic component that is orthogonal to the linear component of age).

[2] Within-sample differences in age gradients were tested for significance using the formulae described in Meng, Rosenthal, and Rubin (1992). Correlations of intellectual abilities with both linear and quadratic age trends were taken into consideration when testing for differences in age gradients [i.e., $R(\text{age}) = (r^2_{\text{age linear}} + r^2_{\text{age quadratic}})^{1/2}$].

[3] When regressing the five intellectual abilities on vision and hearing in the composite sample (i.e., $N = 315$, age range = 25–101 years), the Vision × Hearing interaction accounted for about an additional 1% of predicted variance ($p < .01$) in all five intellectual abilities. For this reason, the interaction term was included in regression equations with the composite sample when both vision and hearing served as predictor variables.

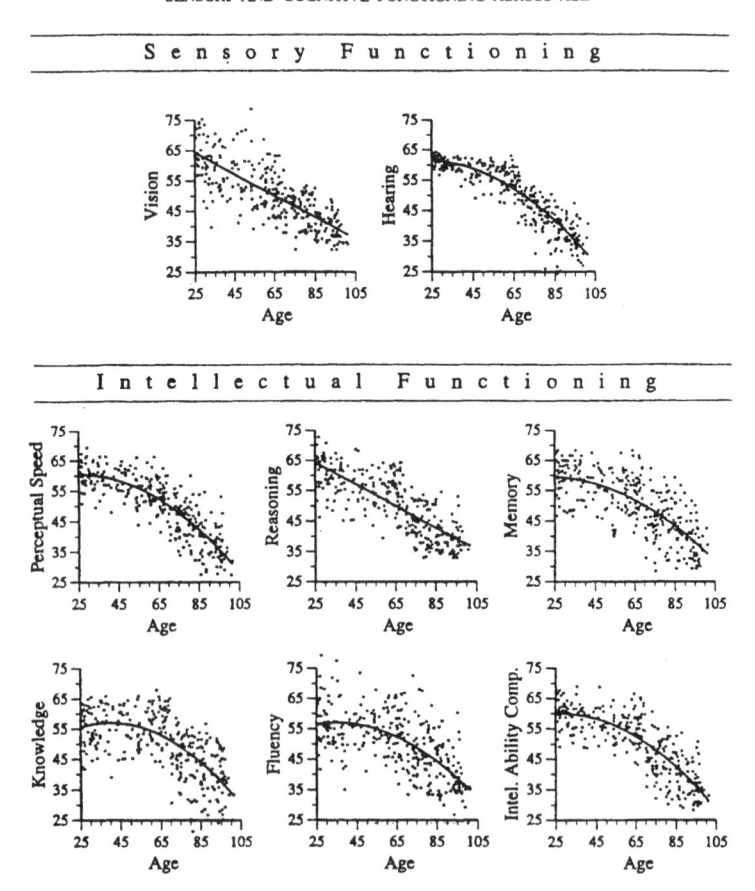

Figure 1. Cross-sectional age gradients for vision, hearing, five intellectual abilities, and the intellectual ability composite ($N = 315$, age range = 25–101 years). Linear and quadratic age trends are reported in the top rows of Table 1. With respect to vision and reasoning, quadratic age trends did not differ significantly from zero ($p > .01$). Intel. Ability Comp. = intellectual ability composite.

The bottom rows of Table 1 also show that controlling for individual differences in vision and hearing was about as effective in reducing the age-related variance in the remaining four intellectual abilities as controlling for perceptual speed, the intellectual ability with the strongest negative relationship to age (cf. Lindenberger & Baltes, 1994; Lindenberger et al., 1993). This is important because perceptual speed has been widely discussed as a primary mediator of negative age differences in adult cognition (Salthouse, 1991b).

Table 2 displays the link between sensory and cognitive functioning before and after regressing the intellectual abilities on linear and quadratic trends of age. On average, controlling for age was associated with a 14.1-fold reduction in the amount of variance in intellectual functioning associated with vision and hearing.

Finally, Table 3 reports the unique and shared variance components of the main effects of vision, hearing, and age as predictors of the intellectual ability composite (commonality analysis; cf. Hertzog, 1989). Vision, hearing, or both accounted for 67.7% of the total, 94.7% of the age-related, but only 12.6% of the total age-independent variance in the intellectual ability composite. The latter figure (i.e., 12.6%) was computed as the age-independent variance predicted by vision and hearing over the total amount of age-independent variance—that is, $100 * \{(2.5 + 1.1 + 0.5)/[100 - (3.8 + 3.2 + 12.9 + 47.5)]\}$. Moreover, 66.4% of the predicted variance was shared among all

Table 1
Correlations of Intellectual Abilities With Simple (i.e., Linear) and Quadratic Age Trends Before and After Controlling for Individual Differences in Vision, Hearing, Vision and Hearing, or Perceptual Speed

	Sensory functioning		Cognitive functioning (intelligence)					
Correlation	Vision	Hearing	Perceptual speed	Reasoning	Memory	Knowledge	Fluency	Composite
Zero-order age correlations								
Linear age	−.78	−.87	−.82	−.79	−.71	−.61	−.60	−.79
Quadratic age	−.05	−.21	−.22	−.12	−.17	−.28	−.22	−.23
Variance predicted (%)	60.6	79.2	71.5	64.1	52.8	45.0	40.4	67.4
Age correlations of residuals controlled for individual differences in vision								
Linear age	—	−.44	−.36	−.34	−.29	−.18	−.16	−.32
Quadratic age	—	−.25	−.27	−.12	−.18	−.32	−.24	−.28
Variance predicted (%)	—	27.7	19.0	15.5	15.8	12.1	8.5	16.7
Age correlations of residuals controlled for individual differences in hearing								
Linear age	−.22	—	−.21	−.20	−.13	−.06	−.10	−.17
Quadratic age	.15	—	−.09	−.06	−.04	−.19	−.12	−.10
Variance predicted (%)	9.5	—	9.1	7.2	4.6	4.4	5.8	7.0
Age correlations of residuals controlled for individual differences in vision and hearing								
Linear age	—	—	−.16	−.13	−.10	−.02	−.05	−.12
Quadratic age	—	—	−.05	.01	.01	−.13	−.10	−.07
Variance predicted (%)	—	—	4.6	3.4	2.7	1.8	2.3	3.0
Age correlations of residuals controlled for individual differences in perceptual speed								
Linear age	−.26	−.36	—	−.21	−.10	.01	.01	—
Quadratic age	.17	−.05	—	.11	.00	−.18	−.09	—
Variance predicted (%)	9.0	16.5	—	4.3	1.2	1.5	0.4	—

Note. N = 315, age range = 25–101 years. The quadratic component of age was computed by regressing age squared on age (i.e., linear age). Residual age correlations were computed by correlating residuals controlled for individual differences in the corresponding variable(s) with linear and quadratic trends of age. Portions of variance associated with linear and quadratic age trends were obtained by means of hierarchical regressions and may differ somewhat from the sum of squared linear and quadratic age trends due to collinearities among predictors. Coefficients not significantly different from zero at the .01 level are in boldface. Dashes refer to values that were not computed because of complete or partial identity between the dependent and independent variables.

three predictors, and a substantial portion of the total variance, 12.9%, was shared between age and hearing only.

The results reported in this section show a powerful intersystemic connection. Age gradients in five different intellectual abilities were extremely well predicted by individual differences in vision and hearing. An average of 92.9% of the predictive variance in vision and hearing was shared with age. In the next section, we investigate whether this link between sensory and intellectual functioning increases from adulthood to old age.

Age Differences in the Link Between Sensory and Intellectual Functioning: 25–69 Years Versus 70–103 Years

Figure 2 shows the amount of total variance accounted for by vision and hearing in the five different intellectual abilities and the intellectual ability composite.[4] Averaged over the five different intellectual abilities, vision and hearing predicted about 11% of the total variance in the younger sample (N = 171, age range = 25–69 years), but about 31% of the total variance in the old sample (N = 516, age range = 70–103 years). Except for reasoning (z = 1.94, p = .026), the amount of variance predicted by vision and hearing was significantly larger in the old-age sample (perceptual speed: z = 2.98; memory: z = 3.67; knowledge: z = 4.93; fluency: z = 3.28; intellectual ability composite: z = 3.46; for all z values, ps < .01). Within the old-age sample, vision and hearing predicted more variance in perceptual speed than in the other four intellectual abilities (z = 5.57). An examination of the joint and unique contributions of vision and hearing suggested that this surplus covariance was due, for the most part, to individual differences in vision, and possibly reflects the visual nature of the perceptual speed measures (see also Lindenberger & Baltes, 1994).

The data summarized in Figure 2 lend strong support to our

---

[4] In both samples, quadratic age trends did not differ from zero (all ps > .01), and Vision × Hearing interactions did not explain a significant additional amount of variance in any of the variables from the intellectual domain. Therefore, results reported in this section are based on linear age trends and on main effects of vision and hearing only.

Table 2
Correlations of Intellectual Abilities With Vision and Hearing Before and After Controlling for Individual Differences in Linear and Quadratic Age

Correlations	Perceptual speed	Reasoning	Memory	Knowledge	Fluency	Composite
Zero-order correlations						
Vision	.74	.71	.62	.60	.60	.73
Hearing	.80	.76	.71	.66	.59	.79
Variance predicted (%)	70.5	63.9	53.3	48.7	42.3	68.9
Correlations of residuals controlled for linear and quadratic age trends						
Vision	.18	.15	**.09**	.15	.16	.19
Hearing	**.08**	**.09**	**.09**	**.10**	**.04**	**.10**
Variance predicted (%)	3.6	3.2	3.2	5.4	4.3	4.5

Note. N = 315, age range = 25–101 years. Residual correlations were computed by correlating residuals controlled for individual differences in linear and quadratic age trends with vision or hearing. Portions of variance associated with vision and hearing were obtained by means of hierarchical regressions and differ from the sum of squared vision and hearing correlations because of collinearities among the two predictors. Coefficients not significantly different from zero at the .01 level are in boldface.

expectation (Lindenberger & Baltes, 1994) that vision and hearing are more closely related to intelligence in old age than during earlier periods of the adult life span. From the perspective of the common cause hypothesis, this age-associated increase in the link between sensory functioning and intelligence is induced by an age-based acceleration of changes in the central nervous system that affect both sensory and cognitive systems of functioning.

To further explore this idea, we examined whether the proportion of the predictive variance in vision and hearing that is shared with age would differ between the two age groups. As can be seen in Figure 3, shared variance proportions were high in both age groups for the three fluid abilities representing the mechanics of cognition, with no evidence for an increase between age groups. In contrast, values were considerably lower in the younger age group than in the old-age sample for knowledge and fluency, the two crystallized abilities representing the pragmatics of cognition.[5] This is not surprising because these two abilities showed no significant negative relation to age in the age range between 25 and 69 years (knowledge: r = .06, ns; fluency: r = −.13, ns). The finding is also theoretically meaningful as life span theories of intelligence (Baltes, 1993; Horn & Hofer, 1992) postulate that, during adulthood, crystallized pragmatic abilities primarily reflect cultural–experiential rather than biological factors.

The high degree of predictive overlap between age and sensory functioning for fluid abilities in both age groups is consistent with the notion that mechanisms associated with chronological age are the driving force behind the sensory–cognitive link across the entire age range considered in this study. From this perspective, the increase in the strength of the connection between sensory and intellectual functioning with advancing age is due to an acceleration of negative age-based changes in both domains during the last decades of the life span.

Age Differences in Magnitude of Correlations Within Cognitive and Sensory Domains

According to our common cause hypothesis, mechanisms related to brain aging function as a general and increasingly severe "common" constraint for many different functional systems of the brain. A corollary prediction emanating from this common causes–based view is that relations within sensory and cognitive domains should also increase with advancing age, reflecting the increasing importance of this general set of constraints (cf. the dedifferentiation hypothesis of old-age intelligence; Reinert, 1970). Thus, because of the increasing role of a common cause, not only the across-domain connections, but also the within-domain correlations should be higher in the old sample (70–103 years) than in the younger sample (25–69 years).

The relevant correlations for the younger and the old-age

Table 3
Predicting Interindividual Differences in the Intellectual Ability Composite: Unique and Shared Variance Components of Age, Vision, and Hearing

Component	Variance explained (%)
Unique age	3.8
Unique vision	2.5
Unique hearing	1.1
Shared age, vision	3.2
Shared age, hearing	12.9
Shared vision, hearing	0.5
Shared age, vision, hearing	47.5
Total variance explained	71.5

Note. N = 317, age range = 25–101 years. Variance components are based on unweighted composites and were computed by regressing the intellectual ability composite on all possible combinations of the main effects of age (linear and quadratic), vision, and hearing.

---

[5] A statistical test for across-sample differences in variance proportions is difficult to obtain because they represent different amounts of total variance.

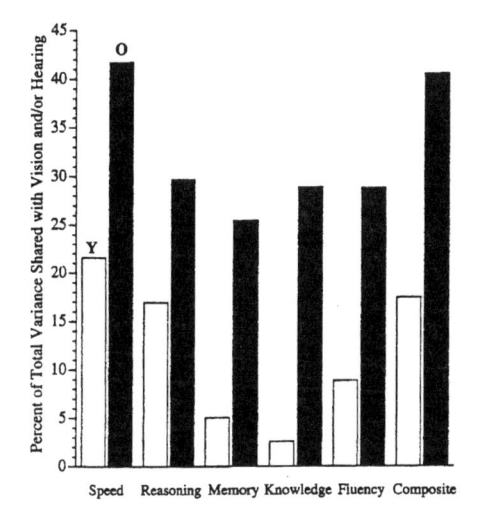

Figure 2. Amount of total variance in intellectual functioning accounted for by vision and hearing in two age groups. Bars represent the amount of total variance predicted by the main effects of vision and hearing. Light bars refer to the younger (Y) sample ($N = 171$, age range = 25–69 years), and dark bars to the old-age (O) sample ($N = 516$, age range = 70–103 years). Except for reasoning, differences in predicted variance were significant at the .01 level.

sample are reported in Table 4. The median correlation among the five intellectual abilities was $r = .38$ in the younger and $r = .71$ in the old sample; the difference was statistically significant ($z = 5.48, p < .01$). For the correlation between vision and hearing, the difference was in the expected direction but statistically not reliable (younger sample: $r = .36$; old sample: $r = .45; z = 1.17, p > .05$).

Summary

Results can be summarized in five points. First, simple measures of vision and hearing showed negative cross-sectional age gradients of substantial magnitude over an age range of 25 to 101 years (Figure 1). Second, negative age gradients in intellectual abilities were extremely well predicted by individual differences in vision and hearing (Table 1). Third, as revealed by age group comparisons (i.e., 25–69 vs. 70–103 years), the link between sensory and intellectual functioning increased substantially from adulthood to old age (Figure 2). Fourth, with respect to fluid intellectual abilities or the mechanics of cognition, a high degree of age-relatedness of the link between sensory and intellectual functioning was observed in both age groups (Figure 3). Finally, intercorrelations within the cognitive domain were higher in the old-age than in the younger group (Table 3).

Before discussing these results, a methodological issue related to the interpretation of group differences in prediction needs to be addressed. If the variances of the relevant measures were systematically smaller in one of the two groups, such differences would tend to favor smaller covariances and, as a consequence, smaller regression coefficients in the less variable group (the so-called restriction-of-range problem). Compared with the old-age sample, the younger sample was actually more heterogeneous in three variables: age (Cochran's $C = .74$), vision ($C = .71$), and fluency ($C = .57$; for all differences, $N_1 = 171, N_2 = 516, p < .01$). It was less heterogeneous in four variables: hearing (probably because hearing was measured in decibel units; $C = .67$), perceptual speed ($C = .70$), memory ($C = .60$), and knowledge ($C = .66$; for all differences, $N_1 = 171, N_2 = 516, p < .01$). No significant group differences in heterogeneity were found for reasoning (Cochran's $C = .56, p > .01$). Note also that the median correlation between vision and the five intellectual abilities was higher in the old-age sample, despite the fact that vision was more variable in the younger group ($r = .29$ vs. $r = .49; z = 2.57, p < .01$). On the basis of these analyses, it is unlikely that the observed age-group differences in the strength of the connection between sensory and intellectual functioning were largely due to statistical differences in sample variability.

Discussion

The main objective of this report is to present a new finding concerning the magnitude of the relationship between sensory

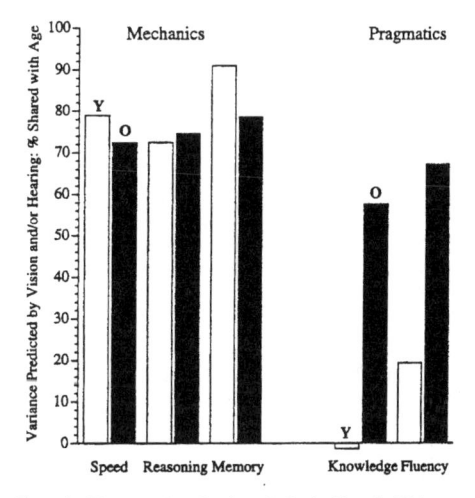

Figure 3. The proportion of variance in five intellectual abilities predicted by vision and hearing that is shared with age. Bars indicate how much of the variance predicted by vision and hearing is also predicted by age. The 100% reference points refer to the total amount of variance predicted by vision and hearing. For the mechanics of intelligence, the results show that the age-relatedness of the link between sensory and cognitive functioning is of equal magnitude in the two samples. Light bars refer to the younger (Y) sample ($N = 171$, age range = 25–69 years), and dark bars to the old-age (O) sample ($N = 516$, age range = 70–103 years).

Table 4
Intercorrelations Among Vision, Hearing, and the Five Intellectual Abilities in the Younger (25–69 Years) and the Old (70–103 Years) Samples

Item	1	2	3	4	5	6	7	8
1. Vision	—	.45	.59	.50	.43	.49	.47	−.59
2. Hearing	.36	—	.50	.42	.42	.42	.44	−.57
3. Perceptual speed	.43	.32	—	.72	.71	.71	.73	−.59
4. Reasoning	.39	.26	.42	—	.64	.70	.63	−.51
5. Memory	.20	**.17**	.42	.40	—	.66	.70	−.49
6. Knowledge	**.14**	**−.02**	.22	.42	.42	—	.70	−.41
7. Fluency	.29	**.05**	.36	.30	.25	.33	—	−.46
8. Age	−.51	−.63	−.49	−.41	−.30	**.05**	**−.13**	—

Note. Correlations for the old sample ($N = 516$, $M = 84.9$ years, range = 70–103 years) are shown above the main diagonal, and correlations for the younger sample ($N = 171$, $M = 48.2$ years, range = 25–69 years) are shown below the main diagonal. Coefficients not significantly different from zero at the .01 level are in boldface.

systems and intelligence in old age. We submit that this new finding deserves serious consideration in adult-developmental and gerontological research on the aging mind. At the same time, we are aware that the work presented here needs to be complemented by other strategies of data collection such as cohort longitudinal methods to examine individual trends and possible cohort effects (Hultsch et al., 1992; Magnusson, Bergman, Rudinger, & Törestad, 1991; Nesselroade & Baltes, 1979; Schaie, 1995), more fine-grained and comprehensive methods of sensory assessment (Corso, 1987; Fozard, 1990), and componential analyses of the relevant cognitive and sensory tasks.

As is often true for novel findings obtained serendipitously in interdisciplinary research, the finding of a strong age-based and aging-induced link between sensory and cognitive functioning poses more questions than answers. Besides brain integrity, additional bodily and experiential factors may be involved (e.g., Welford, 1984; cf. Anstey, Lord, & Williams, 1997). However, the magnitude of the intersystemic connection observed and the putative clarity of the data are promising and lend further support to the findings reported in Lindenberger and Baltes (1994). First, the replication part of the study showed that the results from the opening wave of BASE can be generalized to a larger sample. Second, the extension to younger age levels resulted in the predicted outcome: The relationship between sensory and cognitive functioning was much lower between 25 and 69 than between 70 and 103 years of age. At the same time, vision and hearing were excellent predictors of age differences in intellectual functioning across the entire age range represented in this study. This pattern of findings suggests that the mechanisms underlying the connection between sensory and cognitive functioning are similar across the entire adult life span, but that their expression is amplified in old and very old age.

In our previous work (Baltes & Lindenberger, 1995; Lindenberger & Baltes, 1994), we offered three hypotheses to explain the strong age-based connection between sensory and intellectual functioning: the sensory deprivation hypothesis, the aging-induced cognitive load hypothesis of sensory performance, and the common cause hypothesis. Currently, we favor the common cause hypothesis, according to which negative age differences in sensory and cognitive domains are the outcome of a third common factor or ensemble of factors, namely, the integrity of brain structure and function and its aging-induced changes. In contrast, the sensory deprivation hypothesis states that sensory functioning is closely related to intellectual functioning because protracted sensory underload and degradation of sensory input interfere with cognitive efficacy and, in the long run, reduce the likelihood of productive cognitive engagements. Further, the aging-induced cognitive load hypothesis would submit that seemingly "simple" sensory tasks increase in cognitive complexity and demands as participants reach old age.

The present results do not allow for a conclusive distinction among the three hypotheses and do not allow for the specification of underlying mechanisms. However, we believe that there is some further empirical support for the notion of a common cause. First, as reported elsewhere (Lindenberger & Baltes, 1994, p. 347), another measure of sensorimotor functioning, balance/gait, was found to show as high a connection to intellectual functioning in old age as measures of visual and auditory acuity. Second, the strong connection between sensory and intellectual functioning was also present when older adults with large losses in hearing and vision were excluded from the analysis (Baltes & Lindenberger, 1995; Lindenberger & Baltes, 1994). A third reason is based on the present finding that the high degree of predictive overlap between sensory functioning and age is also observed at younger ages when sensory deprivation is unlikely to be present, but only in that category of intellectual functioning—the fluid mechanics—in which individual differences, according to life span theory (Baltes, 1993; Horn & Hofer, 1992), are dominated by factors associated with the current functional status of the brain.

As is often true for third-variable explanations, the common cause hypothesis in its current form is both theoretically and empirically underidentified. Some of the work needed to test its implications are under way in our laboratory. For instance, we are exploring whether temporary reductions in sensory performance levels through vision-impairing lenses and hearing-impairing earshields are able to simulate cognitive aging losses in middle-aged adults. According to the common cause hypothesis, simulated reductions of peripheral input should not result in major and generalized performance decrements in middle-aged adults because such treatments do not alter the neurophysiological status of the brain. In addition, we are in the process of examining whether sensory and sensorimotor tasks require an increasing amount of cognitive resources (e.g., attention) with advancing age. Finally, we are exploring the sensory demand characteristics of the cognitive tests of our battery. Except for some surplus covariance between visual acuity and perceptual speed, the evidence with older participants thus far does not suggest that cognitive tests with relatively high sensory demands or sensory specificity exhibit a stronger or more modality-specific relation to sensory functioning than tests with low or less specific sensory demands (see also Lindenberger & Baltes, 1994, Table 7).

In conclusion, the present data suggest that a large portion of the mechanisms that drive negative age differences in sensory performance also bring about the aging of complex cognition. This finding has implications regarding the search for "psychological primitives" of negative age differences in cognition (Hertzog, 1996; Lindenberger & Baltes, 1994; Salthouse, 1991a, 1991b) and gives new impetus to the dedifferentiation or neo-integration hypothesis of adult intellectual development (Baltes, Cornelius, Spiro, Nesselroade, & Willis, 1980; Reinert, 1970; Schaie, Willis, Jay, & Chipuer, 1989). The very high degree of commonality between the age-related variance of the two domains is consistent with the notion that at least a major portion of these primitives is operating at a relatively global, rather than modular or domain-specific, level. At the same time, it is important to note that there also was some evidence for specificity in our data. For instance, in their role as predictors of individual differences in intelligence, hearing and age had more variance in common than vision and age, which is reminiscent of earlier findings regarding the diagnosticity of hearing loss for cognitive aging phenomena (Granick et al., 1976).

We argue, then, that the present findings open a new window to the investigation of negative age differences in adult cognition by redirecting the explanatory search. The strong connection between sensory and intellectual functioning in old age points to inquiries into sources, factors, and mechanisms that are common to both domains. Specifically, and in line with some earlier work (MacFarland, 1968; Walsh, 1976), our data suggest that the investigation of negative age differences in sensory and perceptual tasks may contribute in important ways to our understanding of aging losses in cognitive functioning. Most likely, sensory tasks are more easily amenable to task decomposition, cognitive psychophysics (e.g., Kliegl, Mayr, & Krampe, 1994), and neuroscience procedures than complex cognitive tasks. Age-comparative research on sensory tasks using these and other approaches may enhance our understanding of negative age differences in adult cognitive development.

References

American Psychiatric Association. (1987). *Diagnostic and statistical manual of mental disorders* (3rd ed., rev.). Washington, DC: Author.

Anstey, K. J., Lord, S. R., & Williams, P. (1997). Strength in the lower limbs, visual contrast sensitivity, and simple reaction time predict cognition in older women. *Psychology and Aging, 12,* 137–144.

Baltes, P. B. (1968). Longitudinal and cross-sectional sequences in the study of age and generation effects. *Human Development, 11,* 145–171.

Baltes, P. B. (1987). Theoretical propositions of life-span developmental psychology: On the dynamics between growth and decline. *Developmental Psychology, 23,* 611–626.

Baltes, P. B. (1993). The aging mind: Potential and limits. *The Gerontologist, 33,* 580–594.

Baltes, P. B., Cornelius, S. W., Spiro, A., Nesselroade, J. R., & Willis, S. L. (1980). Integration versus differentiation of fluid/crystallized intelligence in old age. *Developmental Psychology, 16,* 625–635.

Baltes, P. B., & Lindenberger, U. (1995). Sensorik und Intelligenz: Intersystemische Wechselwirkungen und Veränderungen im hohen Alter [Sensory functioning and intelligence: Intersystemic dependencies and changes in old age]. *Akademie-Journal, 1,* 20–28.

Baltes, P. B., Mayer, K. U., Helmchen, H., & Steinhagen-Thiessen, E. (1993). The Berlin Aging Study (BASE): Overview and design. *Ageing and Society, 13,* 483–515.

Bentler, P. M. (1989). *EQS: Structural equations manual.* Los Angeles: BMDP Statistical Software.

Carroll, J. B. (1993). *Human cognitive abilities.* Cambridge, England: Cambridge University Press.

Corso, J. F. (1987). Sensory-perceptual processes and aging. In K. W. Schaie & C. Eisdorfer (Eds.), *Annual review of gerontology and geriatrics* (pp. 29–55). New York: Springer.

Craik, F. I. M., & Salthouse, T. A. (Eds.). (1992). *The handbook of aging and cognition.* Hillsdale, NJ: Erlbaum.

Dixon, R. A., & Baltes, P. B. (1986). Toward life-span research on the functions and pragmatics of intelligence. In R. J. Sternberg & R. K. Wagner (Eds.), *Practical intelligence: Nature and origins of competence in the everyday world* (pp. 203–234). New York: Cambridge University Press.

Fozard, J. L. (1990). Vision and hearing in aging. In J. E. Birren & K. W. Schaie (Eds.), *Handbook of the psychology of aging* (3rd ed., pp. 150–170). San Diego, CA: Academic Press.

Geigy, J. R. (1977). *Wissenschaftliche Tabellen* [Scientific tables]. Basel, Switzerland: J. R. Geigy AG.

Granick, S., Kleban, M. H., & Weiss, A. D. (1976). Relationships between hearing loss and cognition in normally hearing aged persons. *Journal of Gerontology, 31,* 434–440.

Herrnstein, R. J., & Boring, E. G. (1965). *A source book in the history of psychology.* Cambridge, MA: Harvard University Press.

Hertzog, C. (1989). Influences of cognitive slowing on age differences in intelligence. *Developmental Psychology, 25,* 636–651.

Hertzog, C. (1990). On the utility of structural equation models for developmental research. In P. B. Baltes, D. L. Featherman, & R. M. Lerner (Eds.), *Life-span development and behavior* (Vol. 10, pp. 257–290). Hillsdale, NJ: Erlbaum.

Hertzog, C. (1996). Research design in studies of aging and cognition. In J. E. Birren & K. W. Schaie (Eds.), *Handbook of the psychology of aging* (4th ed.). New York: Academic Press.

Hilgard, E. R. (1987). *Psychology in America: A historical survey.* San Diego, CA: Harcourt Brace Jovanovich.

Horn, J. L. (1982). The theory of fluid and crystallized intelligence in relation to concepts of cognitive psychology and aging in adulthood. In F. I. M. Craik & S. Trehub (Eds.), *Aging and cognitive processes* (pp. 237–278). New York: Plenum Press.

Horn, J. L., & Hofer, S. M. (1992). Major abilities and development in the adult period. In R. J. Sternberg & C. A. Berg (Eds.), *Intellectual development* (pp. 44–99). Cambridge, England: Cambridge University Press.

Hultsch, D. F., Hertzog, C., Small, B. J., McDonald-Miszczak, L., et al. (1992). Short-term longitudinal change in cognitive performance in later life. *Psychology and Aging, 7,* 571–584.

Kliegl, R., Mayr, U., & Krampe, R. T. (1994). Time-accuracy functions for determining process and person differences: An application to cognitive aging. *Cognitive Psychology, 26,* 134–164.

Lindenberger, U., & Baltes, P. B. (1994). Sensory functioning and intelligence in old age: A strong connection. *Psychology and Aging, 9,* 339-355.

Lindenberger, U., Mayr, U., & Kliegl, R. (1993). Speed and intelligence in old age. *Psychology and Aging, 8,* 207-220.

MacFarland, R. A. (1968). The sensory and perceptual processes in aging. In K. W. Schaie (Ed.), *Theory and methods of research on aging* (pp. 9-52). Morgantown: West Virginia University.

Magnusson, D., Bergman, L. R., Rudinger, G., & Törestad, B. (Eds.). (1991). *Problems and methods in longitudinal research: Stability and change.* Cambridge, England: Cambridge University Press.

McArdle, J. J., & Nesselroade, J. R. (1994). Using multivariate data to structure developmental change. In S. H. Cohen & H. W. Reese (Eds.), *Life-span developmental psychology: Methodological contributions* (pp. 223-267). Hillsdale, NJ: Erlbaum.

Meng, X.-L., Rosenthal, R., & Rubin, D. B. (1992). Comparing correlated correlation coefficients. *Psychological Bulletin, 111,* 172-175.

Nesselroade, J. R., & Baltes, P. B. (Eds.). (1979). *Longitudinal research in the study of behavior and development.* New York: Academic Press.

Nettelbeck, T., & Rabbitt, P. (1992). Aging, cognitive performance, and mental speed. *Intelligence, 16,* 189-205.

Reinert, G. (1970). Comparative factor analytic studies of intelligence throughout the life span. In L. R. Goulet & P. B. Baltes (Eds.), *Life-span developmental psychology: Research and theory* (pp. 476-484). New York: Academic Press.

Salthouse, T. A. (1991a). Mediation of adult age differences in cognition by reductions in working memory and speed of processing. *Psychological Science, 2,* 179-183.

Salthouse, T. A. (1991b). *Theoretical perspectives on cognitive aging.* Hillsdale, NJ: Erlbaum.

Schaie, K. W. (1965). A general model for the study of developmental problems. *Psychological Bulletin, 64,* 92-107.

Schaie, K. W. (1995). *Adult intellectual development: The Seattle Longitudinal Study.* New York: Cambridge University Press.

Schaie, K. W., Baltes, P. B., & Strother, C. R. (1964). A study of auditory sensitivity in advanced age. *Journal of Gerontology, 19,* 453-457.

Schaie, K. W., Willis, S. L., Jay, G., & Chipuer, H. (1989). Structural invariance of cognitive abilities across the adult life span: A cross-sectional study. *Developmental Psychology, 25,* 652-662.

Steinhagen-Thiessen, E., & Borchelt, M. (1993). Health differences in advanced old age. *Ageing and Society, 13,* 619-656.

Stelmach, G. E., & Hömberg, V. (1993). (Eds.). *Sensorimotor impairment in the elderly.* Dordrecht, The Netherlands: Kluwer.

Sternberg, R. J., & Detterman, D. K. (Eds.). (1986). *What is intelligence?* Norwood, NJ: Ablex.

Vernon, P. A. (1987). *Speed of information-processing and intelligence.* Norwood, NJ: Ablex.

Walsh, D. A. (1976). Age differences in central perceptual processing: A dichoptic backward masking investigation. *Journal of Gerontology, 31,* 178-185.

Welford, A. T. (1984). Between bodily changes and performance: Some possible reasons for slowing with age. *Experimental Aging Research, 10,* 73-88.

Received March 12, 1996
Revision received May 15, 1996
Accepted June 15, 1996 ■

[4]

What is cognitive reserve? Theory and research application of the reserve concept

YAAKOV STERN

Cognitive Neuroscience Division, G.H. Sergievsky Center, The Taub Institute, and Departments of Neurology, Psychiatry, and Psychology, Columbia University College of Physicians and Surgeons

(RECEIVED August 22, 2000; REVISED February 26, 2001; ACCEPTED February 28, 2001)

Abstract

The idea of reserve against brain damage stems from the repeated observation that there does not appear to be a direct relationship between the degree of brain pathology or brain damage and the clinical manifestation of that damage. This paper attempts to develop a coherent theoretical account of reserve. One convenient subdivision of reserve models revolves around whether they envision reserve as a passive process, such as in brain reserve or threshold, or see the brain as actively attempting to cope with or compensate for pathology, as in cognitive reserve. Cognitive reserve may be based on more efficient utilization of brain networks or of enhanced ability to recruit alternate brain networks as needed. A distinction is suggested between reserve, the ability to optimize or maximize normal performance, and compensation, an attempt to maximize performance in the face of brain damage by using brain structures or networks not engaged when the brain is not damaged. Epidemiologic and imaging data that help to develop and support the concept of reserve are presented. (*JINS*, 2002, *8*, 448–460.)

Keywords: Functional imaging, Alzheimer's disease, Compensation, Brain damage, Epidemiology

INTRODUCTION

The idea of reserve against brain damage stems from the repeated observation that there does not appear to be a direct relationship between the degree of brain pathology or brain damage and the clinical manifestation of that damage. For example, Katzman et al. (1989) described 10 cases of cognitively normal elders who were discovered to have advanced Alzheimer's disease (AD) pathology in their brains at death. They speculated these women did not express the clinical features of AD because their brains were larger than average. Similarly, most clinicians are aware of the fact that a stroke of a given magnitude can produce profound impairment in one patient and while having minimal effect on another. Something must account for the disjunction between the degree of brain damage and its outcome, and the concept of reserve has been proposed to serve this purpose.

There have been many attempts to produce a coherent theoretical account of reserve. This paper will attempt to review and synthesize concepts that have been suggested, such as threshold, compensation, neuronal or brain reserve, and cognitive reserve. Many of these terms have been used interchangeably by previous authors, and they have not had well-accepted definitions. Specific definitions will be offered for these concepts that attempt to capture potential theoretical distinctions between them.

The concept of reserve should be relevant to any situation where the brain sustains injury. In addition, it will be argued that the concept of reserve should be extended to encompass variation in healthy individuals' performance, particularly when they must perform at their maximum capacity. Nevertheless, many of the concrete examples will be framed around AD, with the implicit assumption that the discussion has implications for brain damage in general. AD has some unique advantages for examining disease-induced changes in brain function. AD pathology affects cortical circuitry that subserves a wide range of cognitive functions, and its pathology is more likely than conditions

Reprint requests to: Yaakov Stern, Sergievsky Center, 630 W. 168th Street, New York, NY 10032. E-mail: ys11@columbia.edu such as stroke to affect similar anatomic sites across subjects, allowing better generalization. AD is also slowly but inexorably progressive, providing a more sensitive indicator of the severity of brain insult required before cognitive networks change. On the other hand, the potential for adaptation of recovery might vary between slowly progressive and acute pathologies, so studies of AD may not always have direct implications for studies of other conditions.

Finally, it should be noted that this paper is not intended to be a comprehensive review of all of the literature relevant to the concept of reserve. For example, there is a large body of work investigating the concept of reserve in the context of HIV-related cognitive functioning that will not be addressed here (Basso & Bornstein, 2000; Pereda et al., 2000; Satz et al., 1993; Starace et al., 1998; Stern et al., 1996). Rather, work has been selected that helps to develop and support the ideas that will be presented.

DEFINING RESERVE

One convenient, although not entirely accurate, subdivision of reserve models revolves around whether they envision reserve as a passive process, or see the brain as actively attempting to cope with or compensate for pathology. In passive models, reserve is defined in terms of the amount of damage that can be sustained before reaching a threshold for clinical expression. In the active models, reserve revolves around differences in how the task is processed. These two approaches are not mutually exclusive. Ultimately, some combination of these two approaches might best describe the empirical observations that have prompted us to develop the concept of reserve.

Passive Models: Brain Reserve or Threshold

Many investigators have proposed passive models including Katzman (1993; *brain reserve*) and Mortimer et al. (1981; *neuronal reserve*). This type of model has also long been implicitly adopted by most clinicians. The threshold model, critically reviewed by Satz (1993), is one of the best articulated passive models. The threshold model revolves around the construct of *brain reserve capacity* (BRC). While BRC is a hypothetical construct, concrete examples of BRC might include brain size or synapse count. The model recognizes that there are individual differences in BRC. It also presupposes that there is a critical threshold of BRC. Once BRC is depleted past this threshold, specific clinical or functional deficits emerge.

This formulation, illustrated in Figure 1 (derived from Satz, 1993b), is sufficient to account for many clinical observations. Assume that two patients have two different amounts of BRC. A lesion of a particular size might result in a clinical deficit in a person with less BRC (Patient 2), because it exceeds the threshold of brain damage sufficient to produce that deficit. However, an individual with greater BRC (Patient 1) could remain unaffected, because this

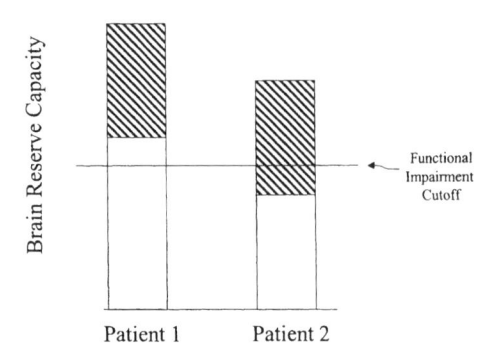

Fig. 1. The threshold or brain reserve model. In 2 patients with different amounts of brain reserve capacity (BRC), a lesion of a particular size results in a clinical deficit in a person with less BRC (Patient 2), because it exceeds the threshold of brain damage sufficient to produce that deficit. However, an individual with greater BRC could remain unaffected.

threshold is not exceeded. Thus, more BRC can be considered protective factor, while less BRC would impart vulnerability. An apparently intact individual with pre-existing brain damage can tolerate less new brain damage than another individual without this underlying pathology: the pre-existing damage reduces the amount of remaining BRC, so the new lesion is sufficient to exceed the functional impairment cutoff.

Many observations about the prevalence and incidence of AD are consistent with the threshold model. Figure 2 (based on Katzman, 1993) illustrates that the progression of AD pathology and the clinical expression of AD can be discontinuous. AD pathology probably begins to develop many years before the disease is expressed clinically and

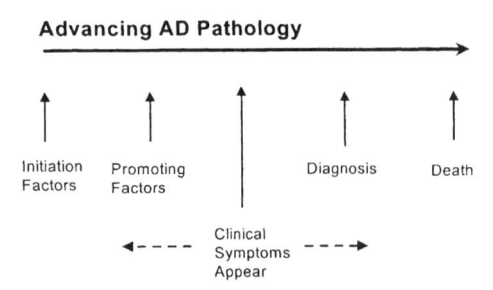

Fig. 2. AD pathology probably begins to develop many years before the disease is expressed clinically and slowly becomes more severe. At some point symptoms of sufficient severity allow the diagnosis of AD. The arrows surrounding the point in the figure where clinical symptoms appear denote the fact that there are individual differences in reserve capacity, and these differences result in later or earlier expression of clinical symptoms.

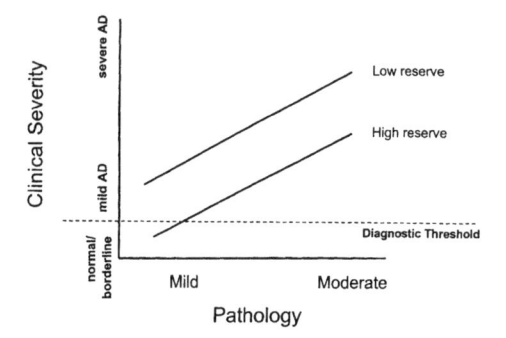

Fig. 3. Because reserve mediates between the pathology and its clinical outcome, the level of reserve should also influence the severity of clinical symptoms after the threshold for their appearance has occurred. Here, at any level of disease pathology, patients with more reserve evidence more mild levels of clinical severity

slowly becomes more severe. The threshold model would assume that when synapses are depleted beyond some critical point[1] the initial symptoms of dementia will appear. At some point after this, depletion will result in symptoms of sufficient severity to allow the diagnosis of AD. The arrows surrounding the point in the figure where clinical symptoms appear denote the fact that there are individual differences in reserve capacity, and these differences result in later or earlier expression of clinical symptoms. In patients with more reserve, synapse loss must be more severe before clinical symptoms appear and the symptoms appear later. Conversely, symptoms would appear earlier in a patient with less reserve.

The threshold approach can be extended to account for more than just differences in the onset of a clinical outcome. Because reserve mediates between the pathology and its clinical outcome, the level of reserve should also influence the severity of clinical symptoms after the threshold for their appearance has occurred. This is demonstrated schematically in Figure 3 with regard to AD. Almost all patients in this scheme are demented, except those with mild pathology and high levels of reserve. Two levels of pathologic severity are illustrated. Within any level, patients with more reserve show less severe clinical signs of AD as assessed by global measures such as mental status tests or by more focused measures such as memory tests. Still, at any level of reserve, more severe pathology results in more severe clinical deficits.

Some research that supports the threshold or brain reserve model in AD will be reviewed below. To give one concrete example, several studies have found that individuals with larger brain size or head circumference have less severe AD or are less likely to develop AD (Graves et al., 1996; Schofield et al., 1997), or are more likely to have less severe AD. Ostensibly, individuals with larger brain size would have more synapses to lose before the critical threshold for AD is reached.

There are several reasons why threshold or brain reserve models can be termed *passive* models of reserve. First, this type of model assumes that there is some fixed cut-off or threshold at which functional impairment will occur for everyone. In the case of AD, this threshold might be depletion of synapses to the point where only a specific number remain. Second, threshold models are essentially quantitative models. They assume that a specific type of brain damage will have the same effect in each person, and that repeated instances of brain damage sum together. Individuals differ only in their overall brain capacity, and brain damage is either sufficient or insufficient to deplete BRC to some critical level. The model does not account for individual differences in how the brain processes cognitive or functional tasks in the face of the disruption caused by brain damage. It also does not address potential qualitative differences between different types of brain damage.

These observations do not negate the importance of the threshold model. They just suggest that this model alone is probably not sufficient to explain all features of reserve and that extensions of the threshold model need to be considered.

Active Models

The active models of reserve suggest that the brain actively attempts to compensate for brain damage. I suggest that in its active form, there can be at least two types of reserve. The first is *cognitive reserve*. This could take the form of using brain networks or cognitive paradigms that are less susceptible to disruption. I propose that this type of reserve is a normal process used by healthy individuals when coping with task demands. The second is *compensation*: using brain structures or networks not normally used by individuals with intact brains in order to compensate for brain damage.

Cognitive reserve

Cognitive reserve parallels the concept of brain reserve in that it is a potential mechanism for coping with brain damage. In the threshold model, the reserve capacity typically consists of additional synapses or an increased number of redundant neuronal networks. Cognitive reserve focuses more on the "software." This could consist of the ability of the cognitive paradigm underlying a task to sustain disruption and still operate effectively. Alternately, this could consist of the ability to use alternate paradigms to approach a problem when the more standard approach is no longer operational.

The concept of cognitive reserve provides a ready explanation for why many studies have demonstrated that higher

---

[1] For the purposes of discussion, we can treat the advancing AD pathology as loss of synapses. Loss of synapses is the facet of AD pathology that has been most reliably linked to cognitive change and disease severity (DeKosky & Scheff, 1990; Terry et al., 1991).

levels of intelligence, and of educational and occupational attainment are good predictors of which individuals can sustain greater brain damage before demonstrating functional deficit. Rather than positing that these individuals' brains are grossly anatomically different than those with less reserve (e.g., they have more synapses), the cognitive reserve hypothesis posits that they process tasks in a more efficient manner.

The concept of cognitive reserve also differs from the passive threshold approach in other important ways. Recall that in the passive model, individuals may have different levels of BRC and a lesion of the same size is sufficient to deplete BRC below the critical threshold in some individuals but not others (see Figure 1). The cognitive reserve model is illustrated in Figure 4. Here the 2 patients have the *same* amount of BRC (again, let's say, the same number of synapses). However, Patient 1 has more cognitive reserve than Patient 2, in that Patient 1 uses more efficient processing mechanisms. As a result, Patient 1 can tolerate a *larger* lesion than Patient 2 before functional impairment is apparent. Thus, the cognitive reserve model does not assume that there is some fixed cut-off or threshold at which functional impairment will occur. The critical threshold differs from one person to the next, depending on how efficient or resilient the "software" is in using the remaining neural substrate. Putting it another way, the threshold approach supposes that the person with more BRC has more to lose before they reach some clinical cut-point. The cognitive reserve hypothesis focuses less on what is lost and more on what is left. In the case of AD, one individual may begin to express clinical features when synapses are depleted to a particular number, while an individual with more cognitive reserve may be able to operate effectively with the same number of synapses.

From a strict point of view, the differences in cognitive processing envisioned by the cognitive reserve model must also have a physiologic basis, in that the brain must ultimately mediate all cognitive function. The difference is in terms of the level of analysis. Presumably, the physiologic variability subsumed by cognitive reserve is at the level of variability in synaptic organization, or in relative utilization of specific brain regions. Thus cognitive reserve implies anatomic variability at the level of brain networks, while brain reserve implies differences in the quantity of available neural substrate.

The cognitive reserve model also does not assume that a specific type of brain damage will have the same effect in each person. Because of individual variability in how they cope with brain damage, the same amount of damage will have different effects on different people, even if BRC is held constant.

A proposed definition of cognitive reserve is: the ability to optimize or maximize performance through differential recruitment of brain networks, which perhaps reflect the use of alternate cognitive strategies. Since the changes in brain recruitment associated with reserve are a normal response to increased task demands, this definition suggests that cognitive reserve is present in both healthy individuals and those with brain damage, and is reflected in the modulation of the same brain networks. In essence, an individual who uses a brain network more efficiently, or is more capable of calling up alternate brain networks or cognitive strategies in response to increased demand may have more cognitive reserve. The definition encompasses two possibilities, differences in recruitment of the same network, and differential ability to recruit alternate networks. These possibilities will be discussed in turn. This discussion is extremely speculative, although some evidence to support these speculative lines will be reviewed.

More efficient use of brain networks

This idea is based on studies of how normal individuals respond as tasks are made increasingly difficult and of individual differences in task performance. The rough parallel here is that, in effect, brain damage acts to increase task difficulty. Several functional imaging studies suggest that a common response to increasing task difficulty in normal individuals is increased activation of areas involved in an easier version of the task and/or the recruitment of additional brain areas (Grady et al., 1996; Grasby et al., 1994; Gur et al., 1988; Rypma et al., 1999). There are also individual differences in how this additional recruitment occurs. For any level of task difficulty, more skilled individuals typically show less task-related recruitment than less skilled individuals. When the more skilled individual exerts herself maximally, she can perform better than the less skilled one. This increased efficiency and larger dynamic range can be considered reserve. If brain damage is considered a form of demand (similar to increased task difficulty), then a person with more cognitive reserve would be able to cope with more brain damage and still maintain effective functioning. Often, increased task difficulty results in the recruitment of additional brain areas or networks. We might

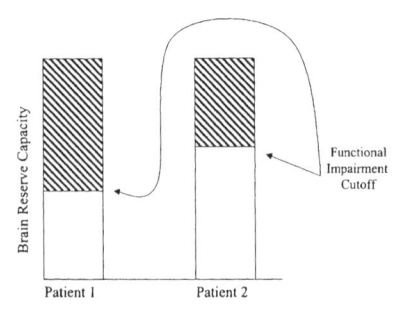

Fig. 4. The cognitive reserve model. Two patients have the *same* amount of brain reserve. However, Patient 1 has more cognitive reserve than Patient 2, in that Patient 1 uses more efficient processing mechanisms. As a result, Patient 1 can tolerate a *larger* lesion than Patient 2 before functional impairment is apparent.

speculate that, in a person with more reserve, this additional recruitment would occur at a higher difficulty level.

Differential ability to recruit alternate networks

This possibility is more speculative, but is consistent with the concept of cognitive reserve. The point is simply that a person with more reserve might be able to call on a larger array of alternate networks for solving the problem at hand. As a concrete example, a trained mathematician might be able to solve a mathematics problem many different ways, while a less experienced individual might have only one possible solution strategy available. The mathematician would have more flexibility in solving the problem if any particular solution strategy was precluded. This built in redundancy would permit greater resilience in the face of brain damage.

These two ideas about reserve might form a heuristic framework for designing studies about cognitive reserve. Studies can be aimed at behavior in unimpaired individuals, taking advantage of inherent inter-individual differences in skills or intelligence. Predictions can then be made about how these individual differences might affect response to brain damage.

Compensation

The term cognitive reserve can be limited to the variability seen in non-brain damaged individuals, which distinguishes it from compensation, which might be reserved for a specific response to brain damage. This distinction emerges from the consideration of findings in functional imaging studies that compared task-related activation in impaired and unimpaired groups with a more critical eye. For example, several functional neuroimaging studies comparing task-related activation in AD patients and controls found more marked and extensive activation in the patients (Becker et al., 1996; Deutsch et al., 1993; Grady et al., 1993). These findings have been interpreted as evidence that the patients compensated for AD pathology. That is, since pathology impaired the patients' ability to mediate the task through the same brain network used by the controls, the patients compensated by engaging alternate brain areas during task performance. One may ask whether this observed "compensation," as the investigators called it, is the same thing as cognitive reserve. If compensation truly represents a change that is induced by brain damage, then it might be important to distinguish between compensation and cognitive reserve. This distinction has not been commonly used in the reserve literature. However, recent functional imaging studies are often carefully designed to ensure that observed group differences are not simply a function of task difficulty.

Compensation is thus first defined in the negative, in that it cannot be simply a normal response to difficulty. In addition, the term compensation implies an attempt to maximize performance in the face of brain damage by using brain structures or networks not engaged when the brain is not damaged.

One of the theoretical reasons why discriminating between reserve and compensation might be important is that it helps critically evaluate the results of studies comparing impaired and unimpaired populations. For example, one study (Becker et al., 1996) reported a comparison of PET rCBF in AD patients and elderly controls performing a verbal list-learning task. Three list-lengths, of one, three, and eight were used. In the eight-word task (compared to the three-word task), patients showed decreased activation of the lateral frontal cortex relative to controls. However, dorsolateral prefrontal cortex and areas surrounding the angular gyrus were more active than in the controls. The authors suggested that this may represent a response to neuropathologic changes that is specific to AD patients. In the proposed classification scheme, this would be considered compensation. Later, using another analytic technique, the same authors concluded that both patients and controls used the same underlying network to mediate the memory task (Herbster et al., 1996). They reported that observed group differences they originally reported were a result of differential activation of this network, probably because the task was more difficult for the AD patients. In the proposed classification scheme, this would be considered cognitive reserve. In assessing the brain's response to damage, it clearly will be important to know which responses are within the range of normal behavior and which only occur in the presence of pathology.

Disentangling compensation and reserve presents a specific experimental design problem. Studies must use tasks that allow for systematic manipulation of task difficulty. Ideally, task difficulty should be equated across individuals, not just subject groups. Once task difficulty is equated, group differences in patterns and levels of functional activation are more likely to represent compensation, and not reserve.

Stern et al. (2000) tried to determine whether the pathology of Alzheimer's disease (AD) alters the brain networks subserving performance on a memory task, while carefully controlling for task difficulty. $H_2[^{15}O]$ PET was used to measure regional cerebral blood flow in patients and healthy elders during the performance of a verbal recognition task. Task difficulty was matched across participants by adjusting the size of the list that each subject had to remember such that each subject's recognition accuracy was 75%. In the healthy elders, a network of brain areas involving left anterior cingulate, anterior insula, and left basal ganglia was activated during task performance. Higher study list size (SLS) was associated with increased recruitment of this network, indicating that this network was associated with task performance and that subjects who could recruit the network to a greater degree could perform the task better. Only 3 AD patients also expressed this network in a similar manner. This network used by the controls and a minority of AD patients may mediate reserve, in that it appears to be recruited to cope with the demands presented by the activation task, and differential recruitment of the network is directly related to the ability to perform the task. Individuals who are able to activate this network to a greater degree may have more reserve against brain damage.

The remaining 11 AD patients recruited a different network during task performance, consisting of left posterior temporal cortex, calcarine cortex, posterior cingulate, and the vermis. Again, in these patients, higher SLS was associated with increased activation of this network. Thus the majority of AD patients did not use the same network as controls to mediate task performance, but rather used an alternate network. The healthy elders also expressed this network during task performance, but it did not mediate their performance of the task, as indicated by the lack of correlation between their expression of this network and their SLS.

Whether the patients' use of the alternate network represents compensation is a matter of definition. The alternate network was used by patients in the place of the normal network in an attempt to mediate task demands, suggesting that its use was compensatory. However, this network was also activated by the healthy elders, indicating that it was not unique to the patients. If the term compensation is reserved for the use of a novel network that emerges in response to pathology, then the alternate network does not meet this criterion. On the other hand, the role played by the alternate network differed in patients and controls, in that it appeared to be mediating the ability to achieve larger study list sizes in the patients but not the healthy elders. This novel use of the network may arise out of the inability to use the standard network, and thus may be considered compensation. Studies such as this one may lead to better understanding of the brain mechanisms underlying compensation and reserve.

Similar considerations of compensation and reserve apply when examining other issues, such as recovery from stroke. Some aspects of recovery simply rely on resolution of factors such as edema. More interesting from our perspective is recovery of function that results from alterations in the brain networks that underlie specific behavior. Thus it is important to demonstrate that the patient is really using a novel brain network, as opposed to a degraded version of the "normal" network.

RESEARCH APPROACHES TO RESERVE

Research investigating reserve must focus on three components: brain damage, clinical expression of the brain damage, and the theoretical mediation of reserve. Of course, the key question to be answered is what actually mediates the relationship between brain damage and its clinical outcome. Most typically, study designs attempt to establish some operational definition for at least two of the three components. By measuring these two components they attempt to make inferences about the third. This theme will be developed further in the discussion below, which reviews some operational definitions that have been used for each component of the model, and describes some representative studies that have used these definitions.

Indices of Pathology

The problem of assessing the nature and degree of brain damage is a familiar one in neuropsychological studies. The optimal measure of brain damage would be some anatomic index of that damage. In some cases, these indices can be relatively direct, even without resorting to post mortem studies. In stroke, for example, direct measures of the volume of stroke, in combination with some consideration of their location, might be useful. Most often, we must resort to proxy measures of pathology. In studies of head trauma, for example, we have no direct measure of neuronal damage, but clinical indices have been established that appear to capture that severity to some degree. These include measures of the severity of the head trauma itself or measures of its sequela, including the duration of loss of consciousness. In AD, there is no existing direct measure of pathologic severity. In addition, we run a danger of confusing measures of outcome with measures of pathologic severity; because they are outcomes, clinical measures of disease severity, such as mental status or activities of daily living scales cannot be used to estimate the pathologic burden. An optimal approach to this problem is clinicopathologic studies, where postmortem indices of pathology, such as synapse loss, or amyloid burden, are related to aspects of the clinical presentation observed during life. Several studies of reserve have used this challenging approach. In particular, Snowdon et al. have demonstrated a relation between measures of linguistic ability acquired at an early age, and the presence of AD pathology noted post mortem (Snowdon et al., 1996).

An alternate approach is to develop a proxy measure for pathology that can be used during life. Some studies of AD have used the characteristic reduction in parietotemporal and frontal perfusion and metabolism seen at rest in AD (Prohovnik et al., 1988) as an index of the severity of AD pathology. The perfusion deficit correlates with disease severity and increases with disease progression (Foster et al., 1984) and its distribution overlaps with the cortical areas with the greatest density of histopathological abnormalities (Brun & Englund, 1981; Pearson et al., 1985; Rogers & Morrison, 1985). Because this perfusion pattern is not unique to AD (Schapiro et al., 1993), the degree of CBF deficit might be used as a marker of the severity of AD pathology, but not necessarily as a diagnostic indicator.

One functional imaging study found that, in patients matched for overall severity of dementia, the parietotemporal flow deficit was greater in those with more years of education (Stern et al., 1992). This observation was confirmed in a later PET study (Alexander et al., 1997). After controlling for clinical dementia severity, higher education was correlated with reduced cerebral metabolism in prefrontal, premotor, and left superior parietal association areas.

These studies support the idea that although pathology was more advanced in patients with higher education, the clinical manifestations of the disease were comparable to those in patients with lower education and less pathology. Presumably the patients with more education had more cognitive reserve.

Because of the general difficulty in ascertaining or quantifying pathology, many research designs do not attempt to do so. In general, if a research design specifies two of the three components, the third can be inferred. Thus often studies measure clinical outcomes while specifying some index of reserve, and then attempt to make inferences about underlying pathology. One such study (Stern et al., 1995a) matched AD patients for clinical severity and followed them prospectively. AD patients with greater education or occupational attainment died sooner than those with less attainment. Here, the proxy for reserve is the level of educational and occupational attainment. The outcome is death, which is more likely when AD pathology is more advanced. The observed relation between the level of reserve and mortality implies that at any level of assessed clinical severity, the underlying pathology of AD is more advanced in patients with more educational or occupational attainment. This would result in shorter duration of diagnosed disease before death. A recent study did not replicate this finding (Geerlings et al., 1997), but a follow-up study by the same group, using patients with more advanced dementia, did (Geerlings et al., 1999).

Outcome Measures

One of the key outcomes in the study of reserve is the presence or absence of some clinical entity. For example in AD, many studies have attempted to determine whether there is a relation between some measure of reserve, such as education, and the prevalence or incidence of AD. Many studies have observed higher prevalence of AD in individuals with lower education (Bonaiuto et al., 1990; Callahan et al., 1996; The Canadian Study of Health and Aging, 1994; Glatt et al., 1996; Gurland et al., 1995; Hill et al., 1993; Korczyn et al., 1991; Mortel et al., 1995; Ott et al., 1995; Prencipe et al., 1996; Sulkava et al., 1985; Zhang et al., 1990). Note that the assumption here is that since education is associated with reserve against the expression of AD pathology, AD should be less prevalent in individuals with higher education. These studies do not directly measure AD pathology, and assume that its prevalence is relatively equal across education groups.

A major weakness of prevalence studies for the study of reserve is the potential confounding of the determination of the outcome with the measure of reserve. For example, the diagnosis of dementia relies on the presence of cognitive deficit. Individuals with lower educational attainment may simply perform worse on the psychometric tests used to identify these deficits, while those with higher education perform better. It is possible to eliminate some of this diagnostic bias with incidence studies, where the outcome is the new diagnosis of dementia in a previously non-demented individual. If all subjects originally have the same diagnostic evaluation and are judged to be nondemented, the diagnosis of incident dementia at followup necessarily implies major decline from initial performance. This minimizes the chance of misdiagnosing a nondemented individual who could never have passed the diagnostic tests. Several groups have reported that the relative risk of incident dementia was increased in subjects with low education (Evans et al., 1993; Letenneur et al., 1994; Stern et al., 1994; White et al., 1994). Other prevalence (Beard et al., 1992; Fratiglioni et al., 1991) and incidence (Cobb et al., 1995) studies have not found an education effect for AD. Between-study differences are probably a function of differences in study samples. For example, in contrast to studies with positive findings, the Cobb et al. (1995) study had only a small percentage of subjects who did not complete grade school (8.1%), perhaps limiting power to observe an educational effect. Also, lower educational attainment was strongly confounded with increased age in that study.

The incidence studies suggest that higher prevalence of dementia in the low education/occupation group is not simply a result of detection bias, because all subjects pass the screens and are rated as nondemented at least once. Still the possibility of bias exists even in incidence studies. It may have been more difficult to detect new dementia in the high education and occupation groups because of lowered sensitivity of neuropsychological tests in these groups. The Stern et al. (1994) study tried two approaches to address this issue. First, subjects with "questionable dementia" were eliminated from analyses. This ensured a substantial change in performance for the diagnosis of dementia. They also evaluated the validity of the dementia diagnoses by investigating functional decline. Functional scores in the newly demented patients from both high and low education groups declined significantly from baseline values, while those in the nondemented groups remained stable. To the extent that the diagnosis of dementia corresponds to changes in performance that disrupt daily activities, the possibility of detection bias is minimized.

The epidemiologic studies above used a dichotomous outcome, the presence or absence of AD. Neuropsychologists excel in developing and applying measures that ascertain the effects of brain damage. Standard measures of cognition, both global and specific can be used as outcome measures in the study of reserve. A great advantage of continuous outcome measures is that they provide more statistical power than dichotomous variables.

The value of a continuous outcome measure is demonstrated by a study in which AD patients were matched for clinical severity and performance on a memory test (Stern et al., 1999). Patients with higher educational and occupational attainment showed more rapid decline in their memory functioning. A similar relationship between educational attainment and rate of decline in memory scores was also noted in another study (Teri et al., 1995). A cognitive-reserve-based explanation for these findings would be that, because patients with higher educational and occupational attainment have more cognitive reserve, more pathology is required before memory begins to be affected. However, AD pathology progresses independently of educational and occupational attainment, and when pathology becomes very severe there is no longer a substrate for cognitive reserve to come into play. Thus, the severity of AD pathology at the initiation of memory deficit varies as a function of reserve, but the level of pathology associated with severe clinical dysfunction does not vary as a function of reserve. The result is a shorter time between the initiation of memory loss and severe memory disability in patients with higher educational and occupational attainment. Note that this interpretation relies on the assumption that AD pathology progresses independently of reserve. Thus, differential rates of clinical progression can provide insight into how reserve may mediate the relation between pathology and outcome. This approach does not rely a direct measure of pathology but rather on the progressive nature of the pathology.

In contrast to the findings in AD, several studies of normal aging have found more rapid cognitive decline in individuals with lower educational attainment (Albert et al., 1995; Butler et al., 1996; Farmer et al., 1995). Similarly, lower education has been associated with greater risk of functional decline in nondemented individuals (Snowdon et al., 1989). These findings, in healthy individuals, suggest that reserve is allowing them to cope more successfully with age-related changes.

It is also important to consider noncognitive outcomes that may be mediated by reserve. Among these are changes in day-to-day function, which are assessed by measures of basic and instrumental activities of daily living as well by other indices of function such as vocational measures. In addition, it is important to consider whether reserve may mediate the affective consequences of brain damage, such as depression. One epidemiologic study of AD is instructive in this regard (Geerlings et al., 2000). The authors found a reduced incidence of AD in individuals with higher *versus* lower educational attainment. However, the presence of depression was predictive of incident dementia only in the higher education group. They reasoned that cognitive reserve allowed individuals with more education to cope with AD pathology longer, thus delaying the cognitive symptoms of AD. However, the reserve was not successful in coping with another outcome of AD pathology, depression. Thus individuals with higher education were more likely to manifest an early depression as an early sign of the disease.

Measures of Reserve

The selection of research measures to represent reserve is dependent on the investigator's theoretical concept of what reserve is. When selecting a proxy for reserve, one must keep in mind that its true mode of action may not be in accord with the theoretical reason for its selection.

For advocates of the idea of brain reserve, anatomic measures such as brain size, head circumference, synaptic count, or dendritic branching are effective measures of reserve.

A direct test of the brain reserve hypothesis is to determine whether larger head or brain size is associated with reduced prevalence, risk, or severity of dementia. Several studies have showed such a relationship (Aksari & Stoppe, 1996; Graves et al., 1996; Mori et al., 1997; Schofield et al., 1997). Schofield et al. (1997) conducted a dementia prevalence study in 649 community-dwelling elders. Head circumference was measured in a standardized fashion. Analyses controlled for age, education, ethnicity, and height. Women in the lowest head circumference quintile were 2.9 times more likely to have AD than those in the upper four quintiles. Similarly, men in the lowest quintile were 2.3 times more likely to have AD. These findings suggest that individuals with larger brains may have more reserve against AD pathology.

Even in passive models such as threshold models, it is clear that there are demographic features that serve as proxies for reserve. These include measures of socioeconomic status, such as income or occupational attainment. Educational attainment has also been a widely used proxy for reserve, probably because it is relatively easy to ascertain. Finally, specific measured attributes have been used as indices of reserve, including literacy, IQ, and measures of specific cognitive functions.

Great care must be taken not to confound measures of reserve with measures of outcome. For example, many studies have evaluated the relation between IQ or education and the prevalence or incidence of AD. In these studies, as explained above, the possibility that education or IQ simply confounds the diagnosis of AD must be addressed. Kittner (1986) suggested adjusting for education when screening for dementia, in order to avoid ascertainment bias. In a dissenting view, Berkman (1986) suggested that we must remain open to the view that "educational level and/or socioeconomic behavior correlated with it may be genuine risk factors for senile dementia and are worthy of scientific exploration in their own right." Simply controlling for education during assessment will not supply the solution to this question.

In 1981, Gurland wrote:

> It is still an open matter whether there is an important sociocultural contribution to the prevalence of Alzheimer's and other forms of dementia occurring in the senium, but the evidence now available is sufficiently intriguing to warrant further study of the issue.

Similar considerations were raised by other investigators (Mortimer, 1988). The reason that education or SES might serve as proxies for reserve is an important issue for research. Lower SES is associated with increased risk for toxic or environmental exposures, nutritional deficiencies, or perinatal insult (Katzman, 1993; Mortimer & Graves, 1993). Thus, some studies have noted an association between education and vascular or alcohol-related dementia but not AD (Cobb et al., 1995; Del Ser et al., 1997; Fratiglioni et al., 1991), suggesting that education may simply be a proxy for other factors or exposures that mediate risk. Some studies have controlled for conditions observable in adults, such as stroke (Stern et al., 1994) and still found relationships between education and dementia. Still, the potential interactions between proxies for reserve and clinical outcomes requires careful investigation. In particular, the important issue of the effect of perinatal or early childhood exposures will require prospective studies that follow children from before birth.

Education might also be a marker for innate intelligence, which may in turn be genetically based or a function of exposures. Some studies suggest that an estimate of IQ, or premorbid IQ might actually be a more powerful measure of reserve in some cases (Albert & Teresi, 1999; Alexander et al., 1997). One study had the unique opportunity to evaluate the relation between mental ability, as assessed in 1932 at age 11, and the incidence of dementia (Whalley et al., 2000). It found that mental ability scores were significantly lower in children who developed late-onset dementia when compared to those who remained nondemented.

Still, education, or other life experiences, may impart reserve over and above that obtained from innate intelligence. Studies have demonstrated separate or synergistic effects for higher educational and occupational attainment, suggesting that each of these life experiences contributed independently to increased reserve (Evans et al., 1993; Mortel et al., 1995; Rocca et al., 1990; Stern et al., 1994, 1995b). Occupational attainment also served as a measure of reserve in CBF studies of AD patients (Stern et al., 1995b). Thus several variables that are descriptive of life experiences might influence the cognitive reserve in the same way that education does. In addition to occupational attainment, these may include leisure activity (Bickel & Cooper, 2000; Fabrigoule et al., 1995; Hultsch et al., 1999; Kondo et al., 1994), and literacy (Manly et al., 1999). Also, recent analyses in our group suggest that, after controlling for educational level and measures of intelligence, Spanish-speaking individuals who learned to speak English have reduced risk of incident dementia when compared to those who never learned to speak English. This might suggest that the experience of acquiring another language imparts reserve.

ASSUMPTIONS OF BOTH ACTIVE AND PASSIVE MODELS: CAUTIONS FOR DESIGNING AND INTERPRETING RESEARCH

Research investigating reserve tends to treat the three components of the reserve model as if they are independent. This assumption is probably not true. As discussed above, many of our proxies for reserve are not independent of the outcome measures. This section reviews other areas of potential interaction between components of the reserve model.

A straightforward explication of either the threshold or cognitive reserve model assumes independence between the source of brain damage and reserve. For example, when exploring reserve in AD, it is convenient to begin by assuming that the progression of AD pathology is independent of the number of neurons a person has or their level of education. This simplifying assumption may not be valid, however. Some investigators (Friedland, 1993; Swaab et al., 1998) have suggested several mechanisms by which chronic neuronal activation stemming from educational exposure or other sources might actually be protective against the development of AD pathology. Also, the genetic determinants that influence reserve factors such as brain size, intelligence, or memory capacity might also influence the advent of the brain pathology. For example, APOE influences the timing of the onset of AD, but also has been related to the rate of change in memory capacity in nondemented elders (O'Hara et al., 1998). Alternately, one study found that linguistic ability evidenced in a writing sample produced at age 22 was predictive of later AD, controlling for education (Snowdon et al., 1996). This might suggest that lowered linguistic capacity, even at that early age, was due to existing pathology.

A related assumption is that the BRC remains relatively constant. For brain reserve, this simply means that there are a fixed number of neurons or synapses to lose. For cognitive reserve this means that the brain substrate remains stable, while the cognitive functions which that substrate mediates can vary. Again, this simplifying assumption may not be valid. It has been suggested that education may stimulate increased synaptic growth in the developing infant or child (Katzman, 1993), similar to that seen in animals reared in an enriched environment (Diamond, 1988). Increased dendritic branching has been noted in individuals with more education (Jacobs et al., 1993), although the causal direction of this relationship cannot be determined. Recently, it has been recognized that the adult brain is continuously generating new, functioning, neurons (Gould et al., 1999). Further, animal studies suggest that aspects of life experience, including enriched environment (Kemperman et al., 1997) and exercise (van Praag et al., 1999) can increase the amount of new neurons that are generated in mature animals. Thus some variable ostensibly associated with cognitive reserve, such as education, may dynamically influence the underlying neural substrate.

DIFFERENTIAL IMPLICATIONS OF ACTIVE AND PASSIVE MODELS

The active and passive models of reserve can often lead to the same predictions, so it is useful to consider the differential implications of the two types of models. As stated, the brain reserve, passive, models rely on actual anatomic differences to determine who has more or less reserve. Thus, there is no ready explanation in these models for why educational and occupational attainment, or IQ, should impart reserve other than to rely on the assumption that these experiences must modify brain anatomy in some way. The cognitive reserve hypothesis does not rely on gross differences in brain anatomy.

Some of the research findings described above are more easily explained using an active reserve model. For example, two functional imaging studies described above found that, in patients matched for overall severity of dementia, the parietotemporal flow deficit was greater in those with more years of education. These studies suggest that although pathology was more advanced in patients with higher education, the clinical manifestations of the disease were comparable to those in patients with lower education and less pathology. Given no gross difference in brain size, passive models do not have a ready explanation for why the patients with more education can tolerate more pathology. Some studies described above have also shown that AD patients with higher educational attainment have more rapid memory decline and die sooner. There is no ready explanation for this observation using a passive model. In fact, the explanation put forward above using an active reserve model relies on the assumption that "brain reserve" does *not* differ as a function of education, and essentially posits that there comes a point when pathology becomes so severe that there is no longer a substrate for cognitive reserve to come into play. Thus the active and passive models can produce different predictions and can differ in their ability to explain observed phenomena.

CONCLUSION

Cognitive reserve is a rich concept that has great heuristic value for research. While reserve is basically a simple concept, upon consideration there can be many layers of theoretical complexity. Consideration of the concept of reserve suggests that it cannot be considered as a unidimensional entity. While they overlap to some degree, the concepts of brain reserve and cognitive reserve may produce different predictions about the impact of brain pathology on function. Further, the differentiation of reserve and compensation may have practical utility particularly when attempting to study reserve using functional imaging.

Careful thought must go into translating theories about reserve into a research design. Also, we must resist the urge to invoke reserve reflexively to explain any anomalous result. Still, the concept of reserve does have great salience for the investigation of variability in individual performance and for understanding how the brain responds to challenge and pathology.

ACKNOWLEDGMENTS

This work was supported by a grant from the National Institutes on Aging (RO1 AG14671).

REFERENCES

Aksari, P. & Stoppe, G. (1996). Risk factors in Alzheimer's dementia. *Fortschritte der Neurologie-Psychiatrie, 64*, 425–432.

Albert, M.S., Jones, K., Savage, C.R., Berkman, L., Seeman, T., Blazer, D., & Rowe, J.W. (1995). Predictors of cognitive change in older persons: MacArthur studies of successful aging. *Psychology and Aging, 10*, 578–589.

Albert, S.M. & Teresi, J.A. (1999). Reading ability, education, and cognitive status assessment among older adults in Harlem, New York City. *American Journal of Public Health, 89*, 95–97.

Alexander, G.E., Furey, M.L., Grady, C.L., Pietrini, P., Mentis, M.J., & Schapiro, M.B. (1997). Association of premorbid function with cerebral metabolism in Alzheimer's disease: Implications for the reserve hypothesis. *American Journal of Psychiatry, 154*, 165–172.

Basso, M.R. & Bornstein, R.A. (2000). Estimated premorbid intelligence mediates neurobehavioral change in individuals infected with HIV across 12 months. *Journal of Clinical and Experimental Neuropsychology, 22*, 208–218.

Beard, C.M., Kokmen, E., Offord, K., & Kurland, L.T. (1992). Lack of association between Alzheimer's disease and education, occupation, marital status, or living arrangement. *Neurology, 42*, 2063–2068.

Becker, J.T., Mintun, M.A., Aleva, K., Wiseman, M.B., Nichols, T., & DeKosky, S.T. (1996). Compensatory reallocation of brain resources supporting verbal episodic memory in Alzheimer's disease. *Neurology, 46*, 692–700.

Berkman, L.F. (1986). The association between educational attainment and mental status examinations: Of etiologic significance for senile dementias or not? *Journal of Chronic Diseases, 39*, 171–174.

Bickel, H. & Cooper, B. (2000). Incidence and relative risk of dementia in an urban elderly population: Findings of a prospective field study. *Psychological Medicine, 24*, 179–192.

Bonaiuto, S., Rocca, W. A., Lippi, A., Luciani, P., Turtu, F., Cavarzeran, F., & Amaducci, L. (1990). Impact of education and occupation on prevalence of Alzheimer's disease (AD) and multi-infarct dementia (MID) in Appignano, Macerata Province, Italy. *Neurology, 40* (Suppl. 1), 346–346.

Brun, A. & Englund, E. (1981). Regional pattern of degeneration in Alzheimer's disease: Neuronal loss and histopathological grading. *Histopathology, 5*, 549–564.

Butler, S.M., Ashford, J.W., & Snowdon, D.A. (1996). Age, education, and changes in the Mini-Mental State Exam scores of older women: Findings from the Nun Study. *Journal of the American Geriatrics Society, 44*, 675–681.

Callahan, C.M., Hall, K.S., Hui, S.L., Musick, B.S., Unverzagt, F.W., & Hendrie, H.C. (1996). Relationship of age, education, and occupation with dementia among a community-based sample of African Americans. *Archives of Neurology, 53*, 134–140.

Cobb, J.L., Wolf, P.A., Au, R., White, R., & D'Agostino, R.B. (1995). The effect of education on the incidence of dementia and Alzheimer's disease in the Framingham Study. *Neurology, 45*, 1707–1712.

DeKosky, S.T. & Scheff, S.W. (1990). Synapse loss in frontal cortex biopsies in Alzheimer's disease: Correlation with cognitive severity. *Annals of Neurology, 27*, 457–464.

Del Ser, T., Gonzalez-Montalvo, J.-I., Martinez-Espinosa, S., Delgado-Villapalos, C., & Bermejo, F. (1997). Estimation of premorbid intelligence in Spanish people with the Word Accentuation Test and its application to the diagnosis of dementia. *Brain and Cognition, 33*, 343–356.

Deutsch, G., Halsey, J.H., & Harrell, L.E. (1993). Exaggerated cortical blood flow reactivity in early Alzheimer's disease during successful task performance. *Journal of Clinical and Experimental Neuropsychology, 15*, 71.

Diamond, M.C. (1988). *Enriching heredity: The impact of the environment on the anatomy of the brain.* New York: The Free Press.

Evans, D.A., Beckett, L.A., Albert, M.S., Hebert, L.E., Scherr, P.A., Funkenstein, H.H., & Taylor, J.O. (1993). Level of education and change in cognitive function in a community population of older persons. *Annals of Epidemiology, 3,* 71–77.

Fabrigoule, C., Letenneur, L., Dartigues, J.F., Zarrouk, M., Commenges, D., & Barberger-Gateau, P. (1995). Social and leisure activities and risk of dementia: A prospective longitudinal study. *Journal of American Geriatrics Society, 43,* 485–490.

Farmer, M.E., Kittner, S.J., Rae, D.S., Bartko, J.J., & Regier, D.A. (1995). Education and change in cognitive function: The epidemiologic catchment area study. *Annals of Epidemiology, 5,* 1–7.

Foster, N.L., Chase, T.N., Mansi, L., Brooks, R., Fedio, P., Patronas, N.J., & Dichiro, G. (1984). Cortical abnormalities in Alzheimer's disease. *Annals of Neurology, 16,* 649–654.

Fratiglioni, L., Grut, M., Forsell, Y., Viitanen, M., Grafstrom, M., Holmen, K., Ericsson, K., Backman, L., Ahlbom, A., & Winblad, B. (1991). Prevalence of Alzheimer's disease and other dementias in an elderly urban population: Relationship with age, sex and education. *Neurology, 41,* 1886–1892.

Friedland, R. (1993). Epidemiology, education, and the ecology of Alzheimer's disease. *Neurology, 43,* 13–20.

Geerlings, M.I., Deeg, D.J.H., Penninx, B.W., Schmand, B., Jonker, C., Bouter, L.M., & van Tilberg, W. (1999). Cognitive reserve and mortality in dementia: The role of cognition, functional ability and depression. *Psychological Medicine, 29,* 1219–1226.

Geerlings, M.I., Deeg, D.J.H., Schmand, B., Lindeboom, J., & Jonker, C. (1997). Increased risk of mortality in Alzheimer's disease patients with higher education? A replication study. *Neurology, 49,* 798–802.

Geerlings, M.I., Schmand, B., Braam, A.W., Jonker, C., Bouter, L.M., & Van Tilburg, W. (2000). Depressive symptoms and risk of Alzheimer's disease in more highly educated older people. *Journal of the American Geriatric Society, 48,* 1092–1097.

Glatt, S.L., Hubble, J.P., Lyons, K., Paolo, A., Tröster, A.I., Hassanein, R.E., & Koller, W.C. (1996). Risk factors for dementia in Parkinson's disease: Effect of education. *Neuroepidemiology, 15,* 20–25.

Gould, E., Reeves, A.J., Graziano, M.S.A., & Gross, C.G. (1999). Neurogenesis in the neocortex of adult primates. *Science, 286,* 548–552.

Grady, C.L., Haxby, J.V., Horwitz, B., Gillette, J., Salerno, J.A., Gonzalez-Aviles, A., Carson, R.E., Herscovitch, P., Schapiro, M.B., & Rapoport, S.I. (1993). Activation of cerebral blood flow during a visuoperceptual task in patients with Alzheimer-type dementia. *Neurobiology of Aging, 14,* 35–44.

Grady, C.L., Horwitz, B., Pietrini, P., Mentis, M.J., Ungerleiter, L., Rapoport, S.I., & Haxby, J. (1996). The effect of task difficulty on cerebral blood flow during perceptual matching of faces. *Human Brain Mapping, 4,* 227–239.

Grasby, P.M., Frith, C.D., Friston, K.J., Simpson, J.F.P.C., Frackowiak, R.S.J., & Dolan, R.J. (1994). A graded task approach to functional mapping of areas implicated in auditory–verbal memory. *Brain, 117,* 1271–1282.

Graves, A.B., Mortimer, J.A., Larson, E.B., Wenzlow, A., Bowen, J.D., & McCormick, W.C. (1996). Head circumference as a measure of cognitive reserve. Association with severity of impairment in Alzheimer's disease. *British Journal of Psychiatry, 169,* 86–92.

Gur, R.C., Gur, R.E., Skolnick, B.E., Resnick, S.M., Silver, F.L., Chawluk, J.M.L., Obrist, W.D., & Reivich, M. (1988). Effects of task difficulty on regional cerebral blood flow: Relationships with anxiety and performance. *Psychophysiology, 25,* 392–399.

Gurland, B.J. (1981). The borderlands of dementia: The influence of sociocultural characteristics on rates of dementia occurring in the senium. In Miller, N.E. & Cohen, G.D. (Eds.), *Clinical aspects of Alzheimer's disease and senile dementia* (pp. 61–84). New York: Raven Press.

Gurland, B.J., Wilder, D., Cross, P., Lantigua, R., Teresi, J.A., Barret, V., Stern, Y., & Mayeux, R. (1995). Relative rates of dementia by multiple case definitions, over two prevalence periods, in three cultural groups. *American Journal of Geriatric Psychiatry, 3,* 6–20.

Herbster, A.N., Nichols, T., Wiseman, M.B., Mintun, M.A., DeKosky, S.T., & Becker, J.T. (1996). Functional connectivity in auditory-verbal short-term memory in Alzheimer's disease. *Neuroimage, 4,* 67–77.

Hill, L.R., Klauber, M.R., Salmon, D.P., Yu, E.S.H., Liu, W.T., Zhang, M., & Katzman, R. (1993). Functional status, education, and the diagnosis of dementia in the Shanghai survey. *Neurology, 43,* 138–145.

Hultsch, D.F., Hertzog, C., Small, G.W., & Dixon, R.A. (1999). Use it or lose it: Engaged lifestyle as a buffer of cognitive decline in aging? *Psychology and Aging, 14,* 245–263.

Jacobs, B., Schall, M., & Scheibel, A.B. (1993). A quantitative dendritic analysis of Wernicke's area in humans. II. Gender, hemispheric, and environmental factors. *Journal of Comparative Neurology, 327,* 97–111.

Katzman, R. (1993). Education and the prevalence of dementia and Alzheimer's disease. *Neurology, 43,* 13–20.

Katzman, R., Aronson, M., Fuld, P., Kawas, C., Brown, T., Morgenstern, H., Frishman, W., Gidez, L., Eder, H., & Ooi, W.L. (1989). Development of dementing illnesses in an 80-year-old volunteer cohort. *Annals of Neurology, 25,* 317–324.

Kemperman, G., Kuhn, H.G., & Gage, F.H. (1997). More hippocampal neurons in adult mice living in an enriched environment. *Nature, 386,* 493–495.

Kittner, S.J., White, L.R., Farmer, M.E., Wolz, M., Kaplan, E., Moes, E., Brody, J.A., & Feinleib, M. (1986). Methodological issues in screening for dementia: The problem of education adjustment. *Journal of Chronic Diseases, 39,* 163–170.

Kondo, K., Niino, M., & Shido, K. (1994). A case-control study of Alzheimer's disease in Japan—significance of life-styles. *Dementia, 5,* 314–326.

Korczyn, A.D., Kahana, E., & Galper, Y. (1991). Epidemiology of dementia in Ashkelon, Israel. *Neuroepidemiology, 10,* 100.

Letenneur, L., Commenges, D., Dartigues, J.F., & Barberger-Gateau, P. (1994). Incidence of dementia and Alzheimer's disease in elderly community residents of south-western France. *International Journal of Epidemiology, 23,* 1256–1261.

Manly, J.J., Jacobs, D.M., Sano, M., Bell, K., Merchant, C.A., Small, S.A., & Stern, Y. (1999). Effect of literacy on neuropsychological test performance in nondemented, education-matched elders. *Journal of the International Neuropsychological Society, 5,* 191–202.

Mori, E., Hirono, N., Yamashita, H., Imamura, T., Ikejiri, Y., Ikeda, M., Kitagaki, H., Shimomura, T., & Yoneda, Y. (1997). Premorbid brain size as a determinant of reserve capacity against intellectual decline in Alzheimer's disease. *American Journal of Psychiatry, 154,* 18–24.

Mortel, K.F., Meyer, J.S., Herod, B., & Thornby, J. (1995). Education and occupation as risk factors for dementia of the Alzheimer and ischemic vascular types. *Dementia, 6,* 55-62.

Mortimer, J.A. (1988). Do psychosocial risk factors contribute to Alzheimer's disease. In Henderson, A.S. & Henderson, J.H. (Eds.), *Etiology of dementia of Alzheimer's type* (pp. 39-52). Chichester, UK: John Wiley and Sons.

Mortimer, J.A. & Graves, A. (1993). Education and other socioeconomic determinants of dementia and Alzheimer's disease. *Neurology, 43* (Suppl. 4), 39-44.

Mortimer, J.A., Schuman, L., & French, L. (1981). Epidemiology of dementing illness. In Mortimer, J.A. & Schuman, L.M. (Eds.), *The epidemiology of dementia: Monographs in epidemiology and biostatistics* (pp. 323-333). New York: Oxford University Press.

O'Hara, R., Yesavage, J.A., Kraemer, H.C., Mauricio, M., Friedman, L.F., & Murphy, G.M., Jr. (1998). The APOE epsilon4 allele is associated with decline on delayed recall performance in community-dwelling older adults. *Journal of the American Geriatrics Society, 46,* 1493-1498.

Ott, A., Breteler, M.M., van Harskamp, F., Claus, J.J., van der Cammen, T.J., Grobbee, D.E., & Hofman, A. (1995). Prevalence of Alzheimer's disease and vascular dementia: association with education. The Rotterdam study [see comments]. *British Medical Journal, 310,* 970-973.

Pearson, R.C.A., Esiri, M.M., Hiorns, R.W., Wilcock, G.K., & Powell, T.P.S. (1985). Anatomical correlates of the distribution of pathological changes in the neocortex in Alzheimer's disease. *Proceedings of the National Academy of Sciences, 82,* 4531-4534.

Pereda, M., Ayuso-Mateos, J.L., Gomez Del Barrio A., Echevarria, S.F.M.C., Garcia Palomo, D., Gonzalez Macias J., & Vazquez-Barquero, J.L. (2000). Factors associated with neuropsychological performance in HIV-seropositive subjects without AIDS. *Psychological Medicine, 30,* 205-217.

Prencipe, M., Casini, A.R., Ferretti, C., Lattanzio, M.T., Fiorelli, M., & Culasso, F. (1996). Prevalence of dementia in an elderly rural population: Effects of age, sex, and education. *Journal of Neurology Neurosurgery and Psychiatry, 60,* 628-633.

Prohovnik, I., Mayeux, R., Sackeim, H.A., Smith, G., Stern, Y., & Alderson, P.O. (1988). Cerebral perfusion as a diagnostic marker of early Alzheimer's disease. *Neurology, 38,* 931-937.

Rocca, W.A., Bonaiuto, S., Lippi, A., Luciani, P., Turtu, F., Cavarzeran, F., & Amaducci, L. (1990). Prevalence of clinically diagnosed Alzheimer's disease and other dementing disorders: A door-to-door survey in Appignano, Macerata Province, Italy. *Neurology, 40,* 626-631.

Rogers, J. & Morrison, J.H. (1985). Quantitative morphology and regional and laminar distributions of senile plaques in Alzheimer's disease. *Journal of Neuroscience, 5,* 2801-2808.

Rypma, B., Prabhakaran, V., Desmond, J.E., Glover, G.H., & Gabrieli, J.D. (1999). Load-dependent roles of frontal brain regions in the maintenance of working memory. *Neuroimage, 9,* 216-226.

Satz, P. (1993). Brain reserve capacity on symptom onset after brain injury: A formulation and review of evidence for threshold theory. *Neuropsychology, 7,* 273-295.

Satz, P., Morgenstern, H., Miller, E.N., Selnes, O.A., McArthur, J.C., Cohen, B.A., Wesch, J., Becker, J.T., Jacobson, L., D'Elia, L.F., van Gorp, W., & Visscher, B. (1993). Low education as a possible risk factor for cognitive abnormalities in HIV-1: Findings from the Multicenter AIDS Cohort Study (MACS).

Journal of Acquired Immune Deficiency Syndromes, 6, 503-511.

Schapiro, M.B., Pietrini, P., Ball, M.J., DeCarli, C., Kumar, A., Kaye, J.A., & Haxby, J.V. (1993). Reductions in parietal and temporal cerebral metabolic rates for glucose are not specific for Alzheimer's disease. *Journal of Neurology, Neurosurgery, and Psychiatry, 56,* 859-864.

Schofield, P.W., Logroscino, G., Andrews, H., Albert, S., & Stern, Y. (1997). An association between head circumference and Alzheimer's disease in a population-based study of aging. *Neurology, 49,* 30-37.

Snowdon, D.A., Kemper, S.J., Mortimer, J.A., Greiner, L.H., Wekstein, D.R., & Markesbery, W.R. (1996). Linguistic ability in early life and cognitive function and Alzheimer's disease in late life. Findings from the Nun Study. *Journal of the American Medical Association, 275,* 528-532.

Snowdon, D.A., Ostwald, S.K., & Kane, R.L. (1989). Education, survival and independence in elderly Catholic sisters, 1936-1988. *American Journal of Epidemiology, 130,* 999-1012.

Starace, F., Baldassarre, C., Biancolilli, V., Fea, M., Serpelloni, G., Bartoli, L., & Maj, M. (1998). Early neuropsychological impairment in HIV-seropositive intravenous drug users: Evidence from the Italian Multicentre Neuropsychological HIV Study. *Acta Psychiatrica Scandinavica, 97,* 132-138.

Stern, R., Silva, S., Chaisson, N., & Evans, D.L. (1996). Influence of cognitive reserve on neuropsychological functioning in asymptomatic human immunodeficiency virus-1 infection. *Archives of Neurology, 53,* 148-153.

Stern, Y., Albert, S., Tang, M.-X., & Tsai, W.-Y. (1999). Rate of memory decline in AD is related to education and occupation: Cognitive reserve? *Neurology, 53,* 1942-1947.

Stern, Y., Alexander, G.E., Prohovnik, I., & Mayeux, R. (1992). Inverse relationship between education and parietotemporal perfusion deficit in Alzheimer's disease. *Annals of Neurology, 32,* 371-375.

Stern, Y., Alexander, G.E., Prohovnik, I., Stricks, L., Link, B., Lennon, M.C., & Mayeux, R. (1995b). Relationship between lifetime occupation and parietal flow: Implications for a reserve against Alzheimer's disease pathology. *Neurology, 45,* 55-60.

Stern, Y., Gurland, B., Tatemichi, T.K., Tang, M.X., Wilder, D., & Mayeux, R. (1994). Influence of education and occupation on the incidence of Alzheimer's disease. *Journal of the American Medical Association, 271,* 1004-1010.

Stern, Y., Moeller, J.R., Anderson, K.E., Luber, B., Zubin, N., Dimauro, A., Park, A., Campbell, C.E., Marder, K., Van Heertum, R.L., & Sackeim, H.A. (2000). Different brain networks mediate task performance in normal aging and AD: Defining compensation. *Neurology, 55,* 1291-1297.

Stern, Y., Tang, M.X., Denaro, J., & Mayeux, R. (1995a). Increased risk of mortality in Alzheimer's disease patients with more advanced educational and occupational attainment. *Annals of Neurology, 37,* 590-595.

Sulkava, R., Wikstrom, J., Aromaa, A., Raitasalo, R., Lahtinen, V., Lahtela, K., & Palo, J. (1985). Prevalence of severe dementia in Finland. *Neurology, 35,* 1025-1029.

Swaab, D.F., Lucassen, P.J., Salehi, A., Scherder, E.J., van Someren, E.J., & Verwer, R.W. (1998). Reduced neuronal activity and reactivation in Alzheimer's disease. *Progress in Brain Research, 117,* 343-347.

Teri, L., McCurry, S.M., Edland, S.D., Kukull, W.A., & Larson, E.B. (1995). Cognitive decline in Alzheimer's disease: A longitudinal investigation of risk factors for accelerated decline. *Journals of Gerontology: Biological Sciences & Medical Sciences, 50A,* M49–M55.

Terry, R.D., Masliah, E., Salmon, D.P., Butters, N., DeTeresa, R., Hill, R., Hansen, L.A., & Katzman, R. (1991). Physical basis of cognitive alterations in Alzheimer's disease: Synapse loss is the major correlate of cognitive impairment. *Annals of Neurology, 30,* 572–580.

The Canadian Study of Health and Aging. (1994). Risk factors for Alzheimer's disease in Canada. *Neurology, 44,* 2073–2080.

van Praag, H., Kemperman, G., & Gage, F.H. (1999). Running increases cell proliferation and neurogenesis in the adult mouse dentate gyrus. *Nature Neuroscience, 2,* 266–270.

Whalley, L.J., Starr, J.M., Athawes, R., Hunter, D., Pattie, A., & Deary, I.J. (2000). Childhood mental ability and dementia. *Neurology, 55,* 1455–1459.

White, L., Katzman, R., Losonczy, K., Salive, M., Wallace, R., Berkman, L., Taylor, J., Fillenbaum, G., & Havlik, R. (1994). Association of education with incidence of cognitive impairment in three established populations for epidemiological studies of the elderly. *Journal of Clinical Epidemiology, 47,* 363–374.

Zhang, M., Katzman, R., Salmon, D., Jin, H., Cai, G., Wang, Z., Qu, G., Grant, I., Yu, E., Levy, P., Klauber, M.R., & Liu, W.T. (1990). The prevalence of dementia and Alzheimer's disease in Shanghai, China: Impact of age, gender and education. *Annals of Neurology, 27,* 428–437.

[5]

Psychological perspectives on successful aging: The model of selective optimization with compensation

PAUL B. BALTES AND MARGRET M. BALTES

The purpose of this chapter is twofold. First, we review research on the nature of psychological aging in terms of seven propositions. Second, we present a psychological model for the study of successful aging that, we contend, is consistent with the propositional framework. The approach advanced is based on the premise that successful, individual development (including aging) is a process involving three components: selection, optimization, and compensation. How these components of adaption are realized depends on the specific personal and societal circumstances individuals face and produce as they age.

Introduction

Two scientific concepts have had a major impact on our thinking about successful aging: interindividual *variability* and intraindividual *plasticity* (M. Baltes & P. Baltes, 1982; P. Baltes & M. Baltes, 1980; P. Baltes & Schaie, 1976). Reflection on the theoretical and policy-related implications of both concepts has suggested to us that there is much opportunity for the continual optimization of human development (see also Brim & Kagan, 1980; Labouvie-Vief, 1981; Lerner, 1984). Over the years, we have begun to believe that systematic age-related shifts in the extent of variability and plasticity are cornerstones for a developmental theory of human adaptation. Initial evidence for this perspective is available in our first attempt to formulate an agenda for successful aging (P. Baltes & M. Baltes, 1980). After reviewing research on variability and plasticity, we laid the groundwork for a prototheory of successful aging as an adaptive process involving the components of selection, optimization, and compensation. The present chapter builds on this earlier effort and the contributions of others (Brim, 1988; Featherman, Smith, & Peterson, this volume) who have followed similar lines of reasoning and worked toward similar goals.

Because this is the opening chapter of this volume, we begin with some general introductory observations. In these observations, we comment first on the role of beliefs about old age. We suggest that optimism about old age influences research and personal action by directing it toward the search for positive aspects of aging. For this purpose, we invoke the Roman philosopher Cicero. Second, we comment on the general nature of criteria of successful aging and the question of subjective versus objective modes of assessment. Thereafter, we shift to the main focus of this chapter: the presentation of several propositions about the nature of aging and an exposition of one possible model of successful aging.

A precursor: Cicero's *De Senectute*

It was the Roman philosopher and statesman Cicero (106–43 B.C.) who produced perhaps the first powerful statement on the nature of good aging with his essay *De Senectute* (44 B.C./1979). Cicero wrote this essay in his early sixties to show that old age is not a phase of decline and loss. Instead, Cicero argued that old age, if approached properly, harbors many opportunities for positive change and productive functioning.

In our view, in *De Senectute* Cicero implicitly proceeds from the assumption that aging is a variable and plastic phenomenon and offers a persuasive demonstration of the power of the individual mind in constructing a positive image of old age and aging. Applying principles of stoicism (a school of philosophy that emphasized the virtues of the mind and argued that the body is often a negative force in achieving willful behavior), Cicero extols the potential strengths of old age for exactly the same reasons that others have viewed old age as a phase of loss and decline. Cicero contends, from a stoicist perspective, that in old age it is *finally* possible for the individual to focus on further development and enjoyment of the mind and not to be distracted by bodily needs and pleasures: "Nothing [is] more directly destructive to the dignity of man than the pursuit of bodily pleasure" (p. 82).

Cicero's essay is full of supporting arguments and creative observations about old age, many of which pass the test of modern psychological gerontology. Unfortunately, a few examples must suffice. In his philosophical journey toward the stoicist conclusion that old age offers the capstone experience of the human mind, Cicero refutes a number of expectations that cloud everyday views of old age. For example, Cicero introduces the distinction between "normal" and "sick" old age and argues that we should not confuse old age with illness. Illness is a condition that, for some people, is added on to old age. Furthermore, Cicero discusses various negative expectations about old age such as failing memory. If older persons had a failing memory, he queries, how could they reach the highest level of mindful performance? Cicero's rejoinder has two parts. First, he rejects memory loss as a general phenomenon and concludes that only those older persons who also suffer from a brain disease have memory deficits. Second, he emphasizes that memory loss is selective. Older persons forget only those facts and cognitive skills in which they are no longer interested and, therefore, do not care to practice in their everyday lives. Cicero's witty example speaks for itself: "Have you heard of an old man who forgot where he hid his treasure?"

As an effective human being and as a good practical philosopher, Cicero is highly confident about the value of his propositions on old age and about the advice he offers his young students. Using himself as an example for the effectiveness of his discourse on aging, Cicero reports having attained a new view on his own impending old age. Fears and anxieties about old age made way for new feelings of harmony and satisfaction. Surely Cicero's account of old age is optimistic, a psychological utopia based on the power of the human mind to design and control thoughts, feelings, and aspirations beyond the constraints of one's biology. However, utopias are powerful vehicles to help us think in ways that reality would not suggest to us: "Utopias have their value – nothing so wonderfully expands imaginative horizons of human potentialities" (Berlin, 1988, p. 16).

Cicero's essay provides an encouragement for efforts to explore the nature of successful aging. Even so, current efforts are unlikely to be fully consistent with Cicero's approach. In our own case, for instance, we will propose a model of successful aging that departs from Cicero's view in one very significant aspect: It does not ignore the biology of the aging body. Thus, although we adapt Cicero's optimism and stoicist belief in the power of the human mind and will (see also Langer, 1989, for a current version of this position), we propose a model in which the aging body, with its reduced reserves and increased vulnerability to illness, is part of the story.

The concept of successful aging

The concept of successful aging dates back several decades (e.g., Havighurst, 1963; Palmore, 1979; Williams & Wirths, 1965), although it has only recently been forcefully promoted as a guiding theme in gerontological research and as a challenge for the design of social policy (M. Baltes, 1987; Butt & Beiser, 1987; Rowe & Kahn, 1987; Ryff, 1982). The fact that the theme of successful aging has attracted much attention recently is due not only to the catchword-like qualities of the term itself and the importance of issues of aging in a modern world. It most likely also reflects a newfound optimism in the field of gerontology itself (e.g., P. Baltes, 1987; Birren & Bengtson, 1988; Labouvie-Vief, 1981; Langer, 1989; Lehr, 1987; Riley, 1983). For example, there is an increasing body of knowledge about untapped reserves of the elderly and their potential for change. Thus, a discussion about successful aging converges with the search for factors and conditions that help us to understand the potential of aging and, if desirable, to identify ways to modify the nature of human aging as it exists today. Whether in the long run the concept of successful aging will remain a scientifically viable topic is perhaps less significant than its power in identifying and organizing questions and research directions that reflect the current dynamics of the field.

At first glance, aging and success seem to represent a contradiction: Aging conjures a picture of loss, decline, and approaching death, whereas success connotes gains, winning the game, and a positive balance. Thus, the association of aging with success seems intellectually and emotionally a paradox. There is also the possible critique that the notion of successful aging may be a latent vestige of social Darwinism, a rampant competitive spirit, and one of the less desirable excesses of Western capitalist traditions. Even the last phase of life, critics can argue, is about to be captured by the view that success, defined by standards external to the individual, is a necessary part of the good life.

At second glance, however, the association of aging with success might indicate that the apparent contradiction is intended to provoke a probing analysis of the nature of old age as it exists today. We are asked not only to reflect upon but also to participate in the creation of aging, instead of passively experiencing it as a given reality that is "natural" only for the reason that it exists. In this sense, the concept of successful aging suggests a vigorous examination of what might in principle be possible. Moreover, a critical but constructive analysis of the concept may indeed serve to articulate the idea that forms and vehicles of "success" in old age may be different from those in earlier phases of life.

The problem of indicators

Defining the nature of success is elusive. Even in such areas as sports, for instance, consensus about the definition of success is difficult to achieve.

In gerontology, length of life is most often proposed as the prototypical indicator of successful aging.

Which criteria?

To live as long as possible, to be the oldest living human, is a dream or desire that, to some, is a persuasive criterion of success. Yet, there is no need to call upon Darwin's often-used notion of "survival of the fittest" bestowing success upon a world-record holder for the number of years lived, because there is another side to this coin. The world-record holder in length of life will also have experienced many undesirable events. He or she also might be the one who has most often lost friends, most often stood at open graves, and perhaps most often endured illness. The first motto of the Gerontological Society of America illustrates this two-sided view. This motto in 1955 called for "adding life to years, not just more years to life."

As this example emphasizes, the search for indicators of successful aging is a complex endeavor. It is not possible to solve this problem without invoking values and without a systemic view. Quantitative and qualitative aspects of life need to be balanced. A first step toward identifying an all-encompassing definition of successful aging is to think in terms of multiple criteria. From such a *multicriteria approach*, the following characteristics frequently appear either as concurrent or as outcome criteria in the literature (Bengtson & Kuypers, 1985; Palmore, 1979; Rowe & Kahn, 1987; Ryff, 1982):

- length of life
- biological health
- mental health
- cognitive efficacy
- social competence and productivity
- personal control
- life satisfaction

Existing research on successful aging reflects this multicriteria approach, although a consensus on their interrelationship or relative importance has not been achieved. In general, it seems fair to conclude that the criteria mentioned exhibit a positive manifold. However, the positive interrelations are not of sufficient magnitude so that a single latent dimension is indicated. Moreover, at least in psychological gerontology, research has not yet reached a point where there is good "causal" evidence about predictor variables or about the role of risk and protective factors.

Integrating subjective and objective criteria

In addition to the question of dimensionality and relative weight of the criteria, a further issue concerns the categorization of criteria along yet another dimension, namely, *subjective versus objective* indicators. In psychological and social science research, there is a preponderance of the use of subjective criteria such as measures of life satisfaction, self-concept, and self-esteem and, more recently, measures of perceived or personal control. This emphasis on subjective indicators reflects the assumption that a certain parallelism exists between the subjective and objective world and also the view that, for the social scientist, reality is in part socially and personally constructed. It also reflects the value judgment that the perceiving self ought to be the litmus test for the quality of life (Bengtson, Reedy, & Gordon, 1985; Schwartz, 1974).

The usefulness of subjective criteria is somewhat undermined, in our view, by the fact that the human psyche is extraordinarily plastic, adaptive, and able to compensate (see also Brim, 1988; Epstein, 1981; Filipp & Klauer, 1986; Greenwald, 1980; Markus & Wurf, 1987). By the use of various psychological mechanisms, humans are able to "successfully" adapt their subjective assessments to objectively quite diverse conditions. It is astonishing, for instance, how little difference has been found in life satisfaction between people who live in objectively adverse life conditions (such as during wartime or in prisons or slums) and those who live under normal or even superior life conditions.

Consequently, we submit that subjective indicators are possibly overweighted in typical definitions of successful aging. They are necessary but not sufficient conditions for an adequate definition of successful aging. Moreover, we contend that subjective assessments of well-being might even be misleading if used as the only indicators. For example, because of the mind's power to transform reality and in the extreme even to ignore it, the sole use of subjective indicators is likely to underestimate both the existence of behavioral and ecological deficiencies and the potential for further progress. Thus, for the planning of environments aimed at the optimization of individual development, it seems essential to supplement subjective criteria with objective ones.

The search for objective criteria for life quality seems to proceed generally along two avenues. The first is based on a *normative* definition of an ideal state. Such a normative definition describes developmental outcomes (such as mental health) and goals (life goals and patterns) that are used as a standard for success. Erikson's theory of lifelong personality development, with generativity and wisdom as the central themes of later life, is an example of such an approach (Erikson, Erikson, & Kivnick,

1986; Ryff, 1984). Achieving generativity and wisdom, then, becomes the yardstick for successful aging. The fundamental objection to such models is that they start, as the label *normative* suggests, with the assumption of a highly standardized society. In addition, the standards chosen often reflect the priorities and values of the middle and upper classes. Successful aging should not be a phenomenon restricted to a given social class.

The second avenue leading toward a specification of objective measures of successful aging is based on the concept of *adaptivity* (or *behavioral plasticity*). This approach seems more general because it does not imply a single outcome, specific contents, or life goals. Rather, its focus is on the measurement of the efficacy of a system. Adaptivity or behavioral plasticity is a measure of potential and preparedness for dealing with a variety of demands (M. Baltes, 1987; P. Baltes, 1987; Coper, Jänicke, & Schulze, 1986; Shock, 1977). Illustrations of adaptivity in the psychological realm are the quality of one's memory and cognition and the quality of one's ability to cope with stressful events. Taken together, such measures are expected to yield indicators of the adaptive plasticity and potential of a person.

In summary, an encompassing definition of successful aging requires a value-based, systemic, and ecological perspective. Both subjective and objective indicators need to be considered within a given cultural context with its particular contents and ecological demands. However, both the objective aspects of medical, psychological, and social functioning and the subjective aspects of life quality and life meaning seem to form a Gordian knot that no one is prepared to untie at the present time. Our suggested solution is to use multiple subjective and objective criteria and to explicitly recognize individual and cultural variations.

A framework of propositions

In the following, seven propositions about the nature of human aging are presented from a psychological point of view. It is argued that a conception of successful aging needs to be placed into the context of this framework. Subsequently, we will derive one prototheoretical model of successful aging that in our view is consistent with this framework.

Proposition 1: There are major differences between normal, optimal, and sick (pathological) aging

The first proposition concerns the differentiation among normal, optimal, and sick aging (Cicero, 44 B.C./1979; Rowe & Kahn, 1987; Whitbourne, 1985). Normal aging refers to aging without biological or mental pathology. It thus concerns the aging process that is dominant within a society for persons who are not suffering from a manifest illness. Optimal aging refers to a kind of utopia, namely, aging under development-enhancing and age-friendly environmental conditions. Finally, sick or pathological aging characterizes an aging process determined by medical etiology and syndromes of illness. A classical example is dementia of the Alzheimer type.

This distinction among normal, optimal, and pathological aging is not unequivocal, but it is useful as a heuristic. Whether there is aging without pathology is an open question. Fries (this volume), for example, argues that it is possible, in principle, to either reduce or postpone the occurrence of chronic diseases such that the "natural and fixed" biological life span can run its course into old age before illness becomes overtly manifest. Death would end life before disease hampers daily living, similar to a clock that suddenly stops ticking without warning or any appearance of damage. Whether this futuristic propositon of Fries will become reality is not essential to the basic argument. The important point is that it is pathological incidents that primarily produce a qualitatively different organism in old age and not aging itself.

Proposition 2: There is much heterogeneity (variability) in aging

The second proposition is that aging is characterized by large interindividual variability in level, rate, and direction of change. Aging is a very individual and differential process with regard to mental, behavioral, and social outcome variables. There are 70-year-olds who look and think like 50-year-olds and vice versa.

Why is there so much variability in aging? Three sources seem to produce this effect. First, there are differences in genetic factors and environmental conditions that act cumulatively over ontogenetic time. For example, some genetic effects may be augmented over the life span, and there are also late-life genes (Plomin & Thompson, 1986). Second, there are individualizing effects resulting from the way each person influences his or her own life course (Brandtstädter, 1984; Brandtstädter, Krampen, & Heil, 1986; Lerner, 1984). Finally, and especially in the late decades of life, variability may increase because the course of normal aging can be modulated by a variety of different patterns of pathologies (Proposition 1).

The notion of interindividual variability or heterogeneity of aging receives much support from longitudinal studies on adulthood and old age (Maddox, 1987; Thomae, 1979, 1987). In our assessment, five longitudinal projects are of particular significance. Historically, the Kansas City

Studies of Adult Life conducted by Havighurst, Henry, Neugarten, and associates opened the way for a differential perspective (Neugarten, 1968, 1987). Subsequently, the Duke Longitudinal Studies (Busse & Maddox, 1985; Maddox, 1987), the Baltimore Longitudinal Study on Aging (Costa & Andres, 1986; Shock et al., 1984), the Bonn Longitudinal Study of Aging (Lehr & Thomae, 1987; Thomae, 1979), and Schaie's Seattle Longitudinal Study of Intellectual Aging (Schaie, 1979, 1983) produced converging evidence. Each of these longitudinal studies documented that aging was not a general and uniform process. Instead, individuals were shown to age very differently.

Research on the sociology (Dannefer, 1984; Featherman, 1983; Maddox, 1987; Riley, 1985) and the biology of aging (Finch, 1988; Fries & Crapo, 1981; Rowe & Kahn, 1987) further strengthened the view that aging in Western societies is a highly heterogeneous process. A general perspective on aging evolved and took hold. This perspective stated that human biology and human culture set the "genotypic" stage for a remarkable degree of "phenotypic" individuality and variability.

Although large heterogeneity in old age is a widely accepted fact, nevertheless, there is disagreement about whether interindividual variability increases with age (Bornstein & Smircina, 1982). Aside from the empirical evidence in current data, there is a new theoretical issue associated with future changes in length of life. If more and more people approach their "maximum" biological life span, as Fries (1983) suggests, the unifying force of a common biological program of aging and dying may actually contribute to a reduction of interindividual variability in future cohorts of very old persons.

Proposition 3: There is much latent reserve

The concept of plasticity provides a conceptual foundation for this proposition and emerges in conjunction with another kind of longitudinal research, that is, gerontological intervention studies. When individuals were subjected to targeted interventions, whether in the area of self-care, social behavior, or perceived control or in the domain of cognitive functioning, evidence for a sizable amount of intraindividual plasticity was obtained. Studies repeatedly demonstrated that most old people, like young people, possess sizable reserves that can be activated via learning, exercise, or training. As a result, the focus has been on the concept of *reserve capacity*, a concept whose utility in clinical diagnosis was advanced, for example, as early as 1934 by Vygotsky (see Guthke, 1972, 1982; Roether, 1983; Schmidt, 1971).

In operant-experimental research on dependent versus independent behavior, for instance, many different types of dependent behavior have been examined (for reviews see M. Baltes & Barton, 1979; Mosher-Ashley, 1986–87; Wisocki, 1984). Using diverse reinforcement and stimulus control procedures, researchers have demonstrated substantial behavioral plasticity in the elderly. These laboratory-type findings support the possibility of behavioral optimization and corrective compensation in old age. The important role of environmental conditions in determining the emittance of either dependent or independent behavior has been validated by observational studies in the field (see M. Baltes, 1988; M. Baltes & Wahl, 1987). The findings appear to represent a dependence–support script: The social environment (the social partners) of the elderly reinforces dependent behavior and ignores independent behavior. Consequently, it is likely that the reserve capacities of older persons are not fully activated in their everyday lives.

Similar evidence for substantial reserve capacity also exists in the domain of cognitive functioning. Here, the data show that healthy elderly people in the age range between 60 and 80 benefit from practice (like younger adults do) and show an increase in performance on the specific abilities trained that is comparable in its magnitude to the aging decline found in untrained persons in longitudinal studies (P. Baltes & Lindenberger, 1988; Schaie & Willis, 1986). Moreover, it has been shown that a variety of cognitive interventions can be effective, even ones that involve a minimum amount of instruction and practice (Denney, 1984; Labouvie-Vief, 1985; Roether, 1986; Willis, 1987).

For example, when comparing the effects of tutor-guided and self-guided practice for fluid intelligence (this cluster of intellectual abilities shows consistent aging loss), P. Baltes, Sowarka, and Kliegl (1989) found that healthy older adults were able to generate, by themselves, levels of performance that hitherto were attributed to guided instruction by others (Figure 1.1). In addition, it has been shown that healthy old people are able to learn new cognitive skills, for instance, by becoming memory experts (Kliegl, J. Smith, & P. Baltes, 1989). Such findings suggest that for many older adults the mechanics of the cognitive system continue to function during old age in the same general way as they do during earlier phases of the life course. Thus, older adults are able to use their cognitive mechanics to acquire new forms of declarative and procedural knowledge.

The fact that older adults have the cognitive reserves to acquire new forms of factual and procedural knowledge is important because it suggests that cognitive aging does not only consist of the maintenance of past functioning. Based on the fact that *new learning* is possible, one can argue that older adults may continue to produce new forms of adaptive capacity

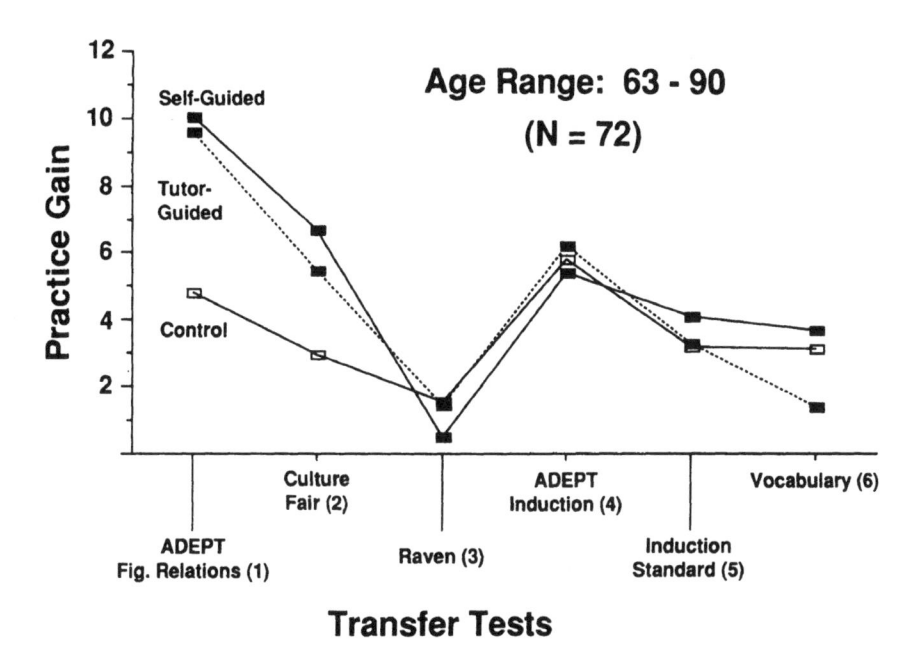

Figure 1.1. Pattern of transfer gains following training in one fluid ability (figural relations) for two training groups (tutor-guided, self-guided) and a control group (data from P. Baltes, Sowarka, & Kliegl, 1989). The results show that older adults have the capacity for self-directed learning involving certain domains of fluid intelligence.

(P. Baltes, 1987; Charness, 1985; Dixon & P. Baltes, 1986; Featherman, 1986; Hoyer, 1985; Labouvie-Vief, 1981; Perlmutter, in press; Roether, 1983; Rybash, Hoyer, & Roodin, 1986). This is relevant, for instance, regarding the acquisition, maintenance, and transformation of expertise in the professional world.

The capacity for new learning has implications for domains of life that have been identified for late-life growth, as perhaps most forcefully argued on the conceptual level by Labouvie-Vief (1981). Wisdom, in particular, has been singled out as a candidate (P. Baltes & J. Smith, 1990; Holliday & Chandler, 1986; Meacham, 1982; Perlmutter, in press; J. Smith, Dixon, & P. Baltes, 1989; Sternberg, in press). Indeed, in cross-sectional studies on wisdom and life knowledge, it has been shown that some older adults are in the group showing top levels of performance (P. Baltes & J. Smith, 1990; J. Smith & P. Baltes, 1990; Sowarka, 1989; Staudinger, 1989). In addition, scholars have argued for positive (desirable) late-life changes in certain aspects of personality such as a movement toward interiority, less dominance, social generativity, and emotional integrity (Gutmann, 1987; Henry, 1988; Labouvie-Vief, 1981,

1986; Ryff, 1984). It has been proposed (e.g., by Gutmann, Labouvie-Vief, and Henry) that such advances in psychological functioning may even be facilitated by losses or transformations in biological status. For instance, a reduction of male hormones in men could result in an increase in the reserve capacity for positive change toward a less aggressive style of human functioning.

One note of caution, however: Current evidence does not indicate that the majority of older adults, in areas such as professional expertise, wisdom, or personality, demonstrate superior performances when compared with the young. All that has been shown is that under favorable environmental and medical conditions, many older adults continue to have the potential to function at high levels and to acquire new domains of factual and procedural knowledge associated with the "pragmatics" of intelligence or "advanced" levels of personality and social functioning.

Proposition 4: There is an aging loss near limits of reserve

During recent years, an additional perspective has emerged that is essential to the understanding of aging. This perspective involves the search for *limits* to behavioral plasticity or adaptivity. Consequently, a *Janus-like*, dual view on plasticity and its limits has resulted (P. Baltes, 1987; Kliegl & P. Baltes, 1987).

Despite sizable reserve capacities in the old, evidence is mounting that shows, at the same time, aging-correlated limits to the magnitude and scope of cognitive reserve capacity. Similar to biological and physical functioning (M. Baltes & Kindermann, 1985; Coper et al., 1986; Stones & Kozma, 1985; Whitbourne, 1985), psychological researchers have now begun to examine this issue more closely. The key test is whether under conditions most favorable to optimal performance, older adults can reach the same levels of top performance as the young. Testing-the-limits is a methodological strategy to estimate levels of current and future reserve capacity. The three levels to be explored are baseline performance, baseline reserve capacity, and developmental reserve capacity (Table 1.1).

Evidence for the contention that there is definite aging loss in cognitive reserve capacity is available from long-term training studies involving reaction time and other speed-related indicators of information-processing capacity (Craik, 1983; Salthouse, 1985). For example, it does not appear possible for older adults to reach the same level of top performance as younger adults in reaction time on either simple- or complex-choice reaction tasks. This aging loss at limits is most evident for abilities characterized as part of the "mechanics" of the mind (P. Baltes, 1987; Hunt, 1978; Kliegl & P. Baltes, 1987).

Table 1.1. *Three tiers of reserve capacity*

Baseline performance	Assessment of performance under standardized conditions without intervention
Baseline reserve capacity	Assessment of current maximum performance potential by strategies aimed at optimization through variation of performance factors (context, instruction, motivation, etc.)
Developmental reserve capacity	Assessment of future performance potential by means of development-enhancing interventions

Note: Modified from P. Baltes, Dittmann-Kohli, & Dixon, 1984; Kliegl & Baltes, 1987.

In the cognitive laboratory of the Berlin Max Planck Institute, this approach has been extended using a testing-the-limits paradigm in the area of memory functioning. Applying principles of cognitive psychology as well as theoretical suggestions from research on memory experts (Ericsson, 1985), we engineer high levels of a cognitive expertise, such as a mnemonic skill, in the laboratory and have subjects of different adult ages practice these skills for extended periods of time. To date, the evidence indicates that older adults, despite their sizable reserve capacity, are not able to reach the same level of performance in such memory skills as young adult subjects of comparable IQ levels. Results from a study by Kliegl, J. Smith, and P. Baltes (1989) are shown in Figure 1.2 to illustrate this finding.

Further research (P. Baltes & Kliegl, 1989; Kliegl, 1989) has demonstrated that the aging loss apparent at limits of performance cannot be fully eliminated even when older adults participate in extended programs of practice. In addition, this result has been obtained even when older adults are selected based on their history of professional accomplishments. For instance, healthy, older graphic designers who, because of their professional specializations, excel in some of the skills that are part of the memory system to be trained are unable to reach the same level of performance as younger, adult graphic designers (Lindenberger, 1990).

Evidence from testing-the-limits research on maximum levels of performance adds a new dimension to past research on reserve capacity (see also Ericsson, this volume, who explores a similar question for middle adulthood). On the one hand, it provides further support for the existence of a substantial reserve capacity (Proposition 3). Most older adults can reach high levels of cognitive performance and exhibit new forms of cognitive skills. On the other hand, age differences are magnified when performances are studied at levels that approximate limits of performance

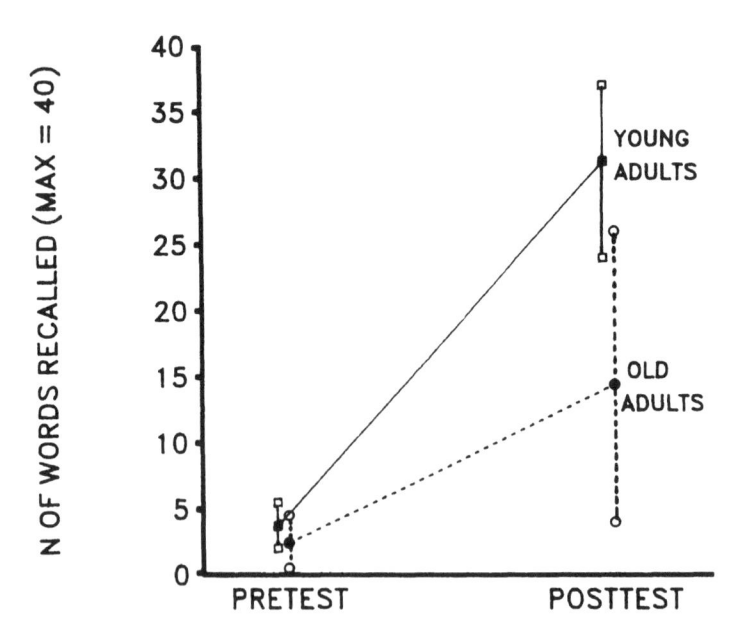

Figure 1.2. Plasticity and limits to plasticity in testing-the-limits research on memory functioning. Bar lines indicate range of scores (data from Kliegl, J. Smith, & P. Baltes, 1989).

potential. In fact, in the study of expert memory (see Figure 1.2), age-group differences were so large at posttest that almost none of the elderly persons could operate at the same level as many young adults.

This series of initial studies seems to suggest almost unchangeable or fixed limits to the efficiency of the mechanics of intelligence and memory. Obviously, much more work is needed to substantiate this claim. Nevertheless, if considered in conjunction with other theoretical positions associated with the concept of limited capacity (Craik, 1977, 1983; Salthouse, 1985), available evidence is highly suggestive of the conclusion that the magnitude of cognitive reserve capacity is reduced in old age and that this reduction is conspicuous when limits of performance and developmental reserve are tested. It is our prediction that a similar reduction would be found if energy-related, motivational resources were studied. Older adults report having less energy, and animal studies with old rats (Coper et al., 1986), for example, seem to demonstrate less physical vigor on energy-intensive tasks, such as running in a drum-wheel.

Is a reduced range of cognitive and motivational reserve capacity relevant for everyday behavior? It depends. In two cases the answer is affirmative. First, reduced reserve capacity affects behavior on any task that requires levels of functioning beyond the limits available. In everyday life such instances may be rare and only experienced when the range (limits) of reserve capacity has dropped extensively (e.g., onset of Alzheimer's disease). Second, the consequences of a reduced reserve capacity may accumulate over a series of tasks. Thus, it is likely that elderly adults are able to perform fewer strenuous behaviors within a given time unit, such as an hour, a day, or a week, without exhausting their reserve capacity.

Proposition 5: Knowledge-based pragmatics and technology can offset age-related decline in cognitive mechanics

Propositions 3 and 4 offer somewhat contradictory evidence: evidence for latent potential (reserve capacity) but also aging-related losses in the range of such latent potential. Proposition 5 addresses the dynamics between the processes associated with these two propositions. We illustrate the important role of knowledge (and technology) in offsetting certain losses in reserve capacity using the area of intellectual functioning as a sample case.

The domain of intellectual functioning encompasses two major, distinct categories: the fluid, cognitive mechanics and the crystallized, cognitive pragmatics (P. Baltes, 1987; Cattell, 1971; Horn, 1970). Consideration of the interplay between cognitive mechanics and pragmatics offers an important avenue for understanding how successful aging is possible. The suggestion is that cognitive pragmatics can compensate for losses (differences) in cognitive mechanics. This conclusion is based on the view that any given intellectual product such as performance on a given test of intelligence or remembering a long poem or story is the outcome of a *multitude* of component skills involving both the mechanics and the knowledge-based pragmatics as building blocks.

Knowledge is a powerful enricher and modulator of the mind. The amount and quality of factual and procedural knowledge available determine to a very large extent what can be achieved with a particular set of cognitive mechanics. Thus, even if some individuals have "worse" cognitive mechanics, if their task-related knowledge is "better," these persons will excel in performance on that task (Staudinger, Cornelius, & P. Baltes, 1989). The effects of knowledge and of associated strategies of cognitive engineering can be quite large indeed, as illustrated in the work on expert memory summarized earlier. Individuals from most walks of life (including the elderly) can become memory experts by using and practicing mnemonic techniques, which essentially comprise the acquisition of factual and procedural knowledge.

From the perspective of the aging individual, therefore, a loss in cognitive mechanics can be overcome to a large degree by the development of pragmatic knowledge. The powerful compensatory and enriching effect of knowledge is perhaps best demonstrated by research that has focused on adults in real life who excel in their performance (i.e., experts). This research takes advantage of the practice, training, and knowledge acquisition that occur in natural settings and over extended periods of time. For example, in a creatively designed study, Salthouse (1984) examined the performance of younger and older good typists. He found that tapping speed, a component skill involved in typing, was significantly slower in the older typists. However, some older typists exhibited superior typing performance. How was this possible? The findings of Salthouse's study made it possible to argue that older typists likely compensated for the decline in tapping speed by reading farther ahead in the text to be typed. In our interpretation, tapping speed is an indicator of cognitive mechanics, whereas reading of text is a measure of the knowledge-based pragmatics. Older typists can overcome their deficit in tapping speed by developing a strategy that is based on what psychologists call declarative and procedural knowledge (Brown, 1982; Mandl & Spada, 1988; Weinert, 1986).

Knowledge, of course, is available not only as an "internal component" of an individual's mind but also as a cultural product. Therefore, technology and other support systems can facilitate the enrichment and compensation of individual differences in cognitive and motivational reserve capacities. Society is challenged to invest some of its resources with the particular goal of generating pragmatic knowledge and technical support systems to compensate for losses due to aging (e.g., cognitive mechanics, physical vigor).

Proposition 6: With aging the balance between gains and losses becomes less positive

The essence of Proposition 6 is a summary statement about the relative balance of positive and negative changes with development. The proposition proceeds from the view that development at any life period reflects a dynamic interplay between gains and losses. We contend that this dynamic becomes one involving an increasingly less positive balance in old age. This trend toward a less positive balance is evident on the level of both subjective expectations as well as objective behavioral assessment.

There are two major causes for this phenomenon. The first is inherent in any developmental process because development is never only a gain. This is so because every developmental change is an adaptive specialization (P. Baltes, 1987; Featherman et al., this volume; Greenough, 1986;

Labouvie-Vief, 1981; Singer, 1987). Because of this specialization, any given developmental process that entails a positive change in some kind of adaptive capacity also contains the loss of other developmental capacities and future options.

This point is illustrated well by examples in social, cognitive, and biological domains. Professional career development, for instance, involves a decreasing probability of alternative career lines. Another example is the fact that becoming a multilingual speaker always involves the possibility of positive and negative transfer regarding the acquisition of additional languages. Likewise in the cognitive domain, as children become experts in highly regulated forms of logical thinking, they are likely to lose some of their capacity for fantasy and playfulness. Finally, similar perspectives are part of developmental biology (e.g., canalization): The differentiation of certain neuronal developmental paths occurs at the cost of other possible developmental pathways. Thus, every realized developmental process is not merely progress in adaptive capacity but also implies at the same time some degree of loss.

The second cause is unique to aging and is associated with an aging-related loss in adaptivity or plasticity. Why should the balance between gains and losses become less and less positive in old age? We propose that a change in the balance between gains and losses toward a less positive balance is a necessary product of the aging-related reduction in the scope of cognitive and motivational reserve capacity (Proposition 4). Therefore, life tasks exceed more easily the limits of reserve capacity. Such a shift in the balance between gains and losses could be avoided or minimized only if societies were structured in a way that their age-related allocation of resources would fully compensate for the aging loss in "biological" reserve capacity.

The phenomenon of an increasingly negative balance between gains and losses is also part of subjective expectations about old age. Proceeding from the existence of a negative aging stereotype, Heckhausen, Dixon, and P. Baltes (1989), for example, predicted that adults would attribute an increasingly larger number of losses to the later periods of the life span. A gain was defined as an expectation of a change with age that was desirable (such as becoming more intelligent); a loss was defined as an expected change that was undesirable (such as becoming less healthy).

In this study, adults were asked about the desirability of changes expected to occur throughout adulthood from ages 20 to 90 on a large number of attributes. On the average, subjects reported less desirable change expectations for attributes having an expected onset of change at older ages (see Figure 1.3). If one aggregates all expectations, the balance between expected gains and losses shifts toward a less and less positive

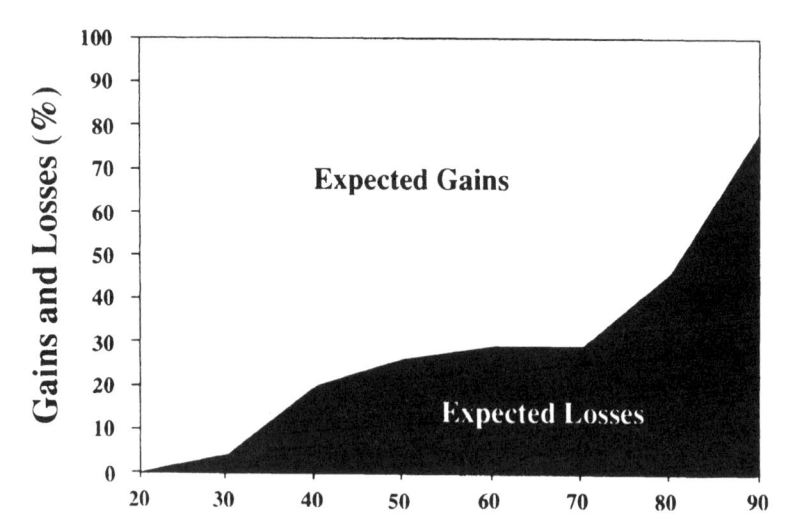

Figure 1.3. Age-related pattern involving 163 psychological attributes: expected gains (increase in desirable attributes) and losses (increase in undesirable attributes) across the adult life span (data from Heckhausen, Dixon, & P. Baltes, 1989).

pattern with age. At the same time, even in very old age, some positive changes were expected. For instance, there was the expectation that wisdom and dignity emerge during late life.

Proposition 7: The self remains resilient in old age

Proposition 7 addresses the aging self. Research has yielded counterintuitive evidence on this topic that is critical for an adequate conception of mastery in old age. Because of a negative aging stereotype (Harris, 1975), one might easily expect that older persons would hold less positive views of themselves and their efficacy to control their own lives. Contradictory to this expectation, however, old people on the average do not differ from young people in reports of their subjective life satisfaction or on self-related measures such as personal control or self-efficacy (M. Baltes & P. Baltes, 1986; Butt & Beiser, 1987; Felton, 1987; Filipp & Klauer, 1986; Lachman, 1986; Veroff, Douvan, & Kulka, 1981).

Three factors are probably responsible for the fact that older adults do not differ from younger adults when asked about their own views of self and life satisfaction. First, there is the phenomenon of multiple selves. Research suggests that people hold more than one view of the self (Filipp & Klauer, 1986; Markus & Nurius, 1986; Neisser, 1988). We all have a number of quite different images of who we are, who we were, who we want to be, or who we could be. The existence of multiple selves and the images connected to them are an effective mechanism for adjustment to diverse life situations. Second, it is possible that there is a change in goals and levels of aspiration (Abeles, 1987; Brandtstädter & Baltes-Götz, this volume; Brim, 1988). Based on experiences of failure and success as well as expectations about the nature of life stages with their own changing scenarios, individuals are quite capable of adjusting their expectations to new levels. Third, there is the process of social comparison. Adjustment to new goals and expectations, which is part of many major life transitions, is facilitated by life events and often leads to a change in one's reference groups (Schwarzer, Lange, & Jerusalem, 1982; Suls & Mullen, 1982; Wills, 1981; Wood, 1989). Old people, for instance, even if they are worse off than the rest of the population, tend to orient their comparison standards toward other old people in similar situations. The result is an adjusted assessment that allows one's own life situation and one's self to appear in a new frame of reference.

These observations on the relative resilience of views of self in old age do not imply that all older adults have intact selves and a high level of self-esteem or personal control. Of course, as is true for younger age-groups as well, there are sizable individual differences among the elderly in indicators of selfhood and the ability to adjust and cope. For example, Brandtstädter and Baltes-Götz (this volume) found in a longitudinal study on partnership relationships during adulthood that people differed markedly in their ability to adjust their individual and mutual developmental goals. Proposition 7 only suggests that, on the average, older adults do not appear to differ markedly from younger age-groups in indicators of what Brewster Smith (1978) has called "selfhood."

Strategies for successful aging

General principles

Based on this framework of propositions about the nature of aging, a series of general principles can be derived with regard to potential strategies for successful aging. Aside from the general optimism associated with these perspectives, these guidelines are not earthshaking if taken individually. However, as a pattern they suggest a coordinated and focused approach.

First, it seems desirable to engage in a healthy life-style in order to reduce the probability of pathological aging conditions (Proposition 1). Second, because of considerable heterogeneity in the onset, direction, and diversity of aging, it is important to avoid simple solutions and to encourage individual and societal flexibility (Proposition 2). Third, it is desirable to strengthen one's reserve capacities (Proposition 3) via educational, motivational, and health-related activities as well as the formation and nurturance of social convoys (Antonucci & Jackson, 1987; Kahn & Antonucci, 1980). The greater one's reserve capacities, be they physical, mental, or social reserves, the more likely successful aging will take place. This is also true because a larger reserve capacity facilitates the search for and creation of optimizing environments, as implied, for instance, in Lawton's conception of "environmental proactivity" (Lawton, 1988; Parmelee & Lawton, 1990). In order to enact these general strategies, the provision of societal resources and opportunities is a prerequisite. Development-enhancing societal opportunities and supports need to be offered.

Limits to reserve capacity (Proposition 4) and the enriching and compensatory role of knowledge and technology (Proposition 5) suggest another general strategic principle. Because of loss in adaptive capacity, particularly at limits of capacity, older adults will need special compensatory supports. A creative search is required for substitute and prosthetic devices, age-appropriate life-styles, and age-friendly environments (M. Baltes, 1987; Lawton, 1982, 1988; Lehr & Thomae, 1987; Thomae, 1987). This is perhaps the most underdeveloped part of our culture. Age-friendly environments refer to ecologies that, in addition to providing development-enhancing conditions, are less taxing on person's reserve capacities and, furthermore, contain prosthetic devices. Examples from diverse areas of life are environmental supports for the handicapped in traffic and public buildings, home health care systems, and day clinics for the elderly.

The changing balance in gain/loss ratios (Proposition 6) and the continued resilience of the self (Proposition 7) suggest the consideration of strategies that facilitate adjustments to "objective" reality without loss of selfhood. By definition, life-span development and aging cannot only be a "winning game" (P. Baltes & Kliegl, 1986; Brim, 1988). In terms of absolute criteria of functional capacity, losses will occur. The central task will be to assist individuals in acquiring effective strategies involving changes in aspirations and the scope of goals.

The facilitation of changes in aspirations and goals is complicated by the question of when to accept the fact of loss and reorient one's life. Brim (1988) has proposed a criterion of "performance standard/capacity ratio" associated with the notion of "just manageable difficulty." Using a performance standard/capacity ratio approach, it may be possible to specify when objective reality would mandate the acceptance of a loss. Acceptance of certain losses would be necessary, for example, when the same behaviors can be displayed only if a dysfunctionally high level of reserve capacity (performance standard/capacity ratio) is required for their execution; that is, if the target behavior overtaxes the system of mental, social, and motivational resources. Such a view is consistent with the position that dependency in old age can be an effective strategy for avoiding overtaxing or depletion of one's reserve (M. Baltes & Wahl, 1987).

Taken together, these perspectives underscore the theme of heterogeneity and variability (Proposition 2). Because aging is a highly individual process, societal input should be primarily geared toward the individualization of resources and opportunities. Because of large variability in aging, a parallel diversity of societal resources must be offered that would allow each person to find his or her personal form and expression of aging. It is likely that no single set of conditions and no single trajectory of aging would qualify as *the* form of successful or optimal aging.

The principle of selective optimization with compensation

Is it possible to specify a model that reflects this dynamic interplay between gains and losses, between development-oriented plasticity and age-related boundaries of such plasticity? Can we devise a model that could serve as a guideline for an individual's thoughts and actions and for social policy? Can we envision a prototypical strategy of effective aging that allows for self-efficacy and growth in the context of increasing biological vulnerability and reduced reserve capacity?

During the last decade we have begun to articulate such a prototypical strategy of successful aging and named it "selective optimization with compensation" (P. Baltes & M. Baltes, 1980; M. Baltes, 1987; P. Baltes, 1987; P. Baltes, Dittmann Kohli, & Dixon, 1984; see also Featherman et al., this volume). Figure 1.4 summarizes the dynamics of this process of adaptation. In our view, the key concept, selective optimization with compensation, describes a *general* process of adaptation. Individuals are likely to engage in this process throughout life. We believe, however, that the process of selective optimization with compensation takes on a new significance and dynamic in old age because of the loss of biological, mental, and social reserves.

In the model of selective and compensatory optimization, there are three interacting elements and processes. First, there is the element of *selection*, which refers to an increasing restriction of one's life world to fewer domains of functioning because of an aging loss in the range of adaptive potential. It is the adaptive task of the person and society to concentrate on those domains that are of high priority and involve a convergence of environmental demands and individual motivations, skills, and biological

Antecedent Conditions → **Processes** → **Outcome**

Life Development as Specialized and Age-Graded Adaptation

Reduction in General Reserve Capacity

Losses in Specific Functions

→ Selection
Optimization
Compensation →

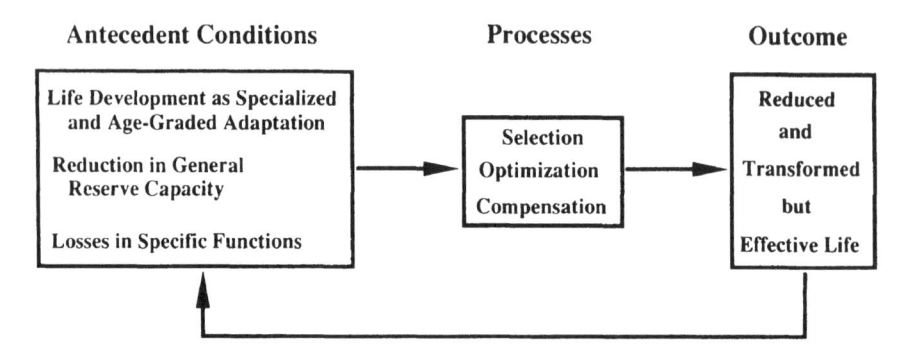

Reduced and Transformed but Effective Life

Figure 1.4. The ongoing dynamics of selective optimization with compensation. The process is a lifelong phenomenon, but it is amplified in old age. The essentials of the process are universal. Its phenotypic manifestation, however, varies widely between individuals.

capacity. Although selection connotes a reduction in the number of high-efficacy domains, it can also involve new or transformed domains and goals of life. Thus, the process of selection implies that an individual's expectations are adjusted to permit the subjective experience of satisfaction as well as personal control.

The second element, *optimization*, reflects the view that people engage in behaviors to enrich and augment their general reserves and to maximize their chosen life courses (and associated forms of behavior) with regard to quantity and quality. Intervention studies on plasticity have demonstrated that old people continue to be able to implement this optimizing process.

The third element, *compensation*, results also (like selection) from restrictions in the range of plasticity or adaptive potential. It becomes operative when specific behavioral capacities are lost or are reduced below a standard required for adequate functioning. This restriction is experienced particularly at a time when situations and goal characteristics require a wide range of activity and a high level of performance (e.g., mountain climbing, competitive sports, risky traffic situations, daily hassles, and situations that require quick thinking and memorization). The element of compensation involves aspects of the mind and technology. Psychological compensatory efforts include, for instance, the use of new mnemonic strategies (including external memory aids) when internal memory mechanics or strategies are insufficient. The use of a hearing aid would be an instance of compensation by means of technology.

Example: Cognitive functioning. Table 1.2 describes the process of selective optimization with compensation for the domain of intellectual aging. The

Table 1.2. *Selective optimization with compensation: A process prototypical of adaptive life-span development of cognitive functioning*

- A general feature of life-span development is an age-related increase in specialization (selection) of motivational and cognitive resources and skills.
- There are two main features of the aging of cognitive functions:
  (1) The reserve capacity for peak or maximum performances in fluid functioning (mechanics of intelligence) is reduced.
  (2) Some procedural and declarative knowledge systems (pragmatics of intelligence) can continue to evolve and function at peak levels.
- When and if limits of reserve capacity (especially in the mechanics) are exceeded during the course of aging for a given individual, the following developmental consequences result:
  (1) Increased selection (channeling) and further reduction of the number of high-efficacy domains.
  (2) Development of compensatory and/or substitute mechanisms.

Note: Modified from P. Baltes & M. Baltes, 1980.

example is drawn from a research program on the aging of intelligence (P. Baltes, 1987; Kliegl & P. Baltes, 1987; J. Smith et al., 1989; Staudinger et al., 1989; Thompson & Kliegl, 1989). In this research program, two large systems of intelligence are differentiated: the knowledge-free, fluid mechanics and the knowledge-rich, crystallized pragmatics. Using a computer analogy, this distinction is similar to the hardware–software distinction. With respect to the fluid cognitive mechanics, a loss with age in efficiency and speed is posited. At the same time, it is argued that select aspects of the crystallized pragmatics of intelligence can be maintained into old age, perhaps even evincing some further growth.

The interesting question involving the process of selective optimization with compensation refers to the interaction between these two cognitive systems and the use of pragmatics to prevent or balance the aging decline in the mechanics of intelligence. As discussed in Proposition 5, this can be accomplished, for instance, via optimization of knowledge systems and the acquisition of compensatory thinking and memory strategies. In that context, research on mnemonic training in old age and on expert older typists was presented.

Example: Nursing homes. The process of selective optimization with compensation can be further illustrated by reference to the design and use of age-friendly environments such as nursing homes. In this instance, the process is evident at both the macrolevel and the microlevel.

At the macrolevel, the intent of nursing homes is to create a special world that, by definition, includes aspects of increased selection, optimization, and compensation. Selection is expressed by the provision of a less demanding physical and social ecology, optimization by opportunities given for practice in domains targeted for further growth, and compensation by the availability of technological and medical systems to support functions with diminished reserve capacities. It is uncertain, of course, whether all these goals are sufficiently met.

On the microlevel, research by Margret Baltes and her colleagues (M. Baltes & Reisenzein, 1986; M. Baltes & Wahl, 1987, in press; M. Baltes, Kindermann, Reisenzein, & Schmid, 1987) demonstrates how the process of selective optimization with compensation operates within the nursing home in the social interactions between elderly residents and staff. Using detailed observations of the flow of interactional patterns between elderly residents and staff, this research demonstrates two phenomena that are consistent with a model of selective optimization with compensation on a microsocial level.

First, selection and compensation are evident in the fact that elderly residents and staff display a definite pattern (social script) of resident dependency that is followed by staff support for dependency. We argue that this script implies that dependent behaviors are judged to be appropriate, and that the weaknesses of the elderly are to be compensated for by the staff. This focus on the dependence–support script is so strong that when independent behavior on the part of the elderly occurs, such behavior is ignored by the staff (see Figure 1.5). Second, this concentration on the dependence–support script enables elderly residents, at the same time, to achieve optimization in another aspect, that is, social contact. After elderly residents engage in dependent behaviors (e.g., request for bodily care), these result in prompt and reliable consequences on the part of the staff involving not only care but also social attention. Therefore, although dependent behavior may result in a lack of and possibly a loss in self-care behavior, it gives elderly nursing home residents a strategy for exerting control over their social environment, gaining social contact, and, thereby, perhaps avoiding isolation (M. Baltes, 1988; M. Baltes & Wahl, 1987).

Other examples. Selective optimization with compensation allows the elderly to engage in life tasks that are important to them despite a reduction in energy or in biological and mental reserves. As such, the strategy of selective and compensatory adaptation is hypothesized to have general or universal application. The individualization of this prototypical strategy of mastery lies in the individual patterning, which may vary according to interests, health, preferences, and resources. In each case of successful aging, there is likely to be a creative, individualized, and societally appropriate combination of selection, optimization, and compensation.

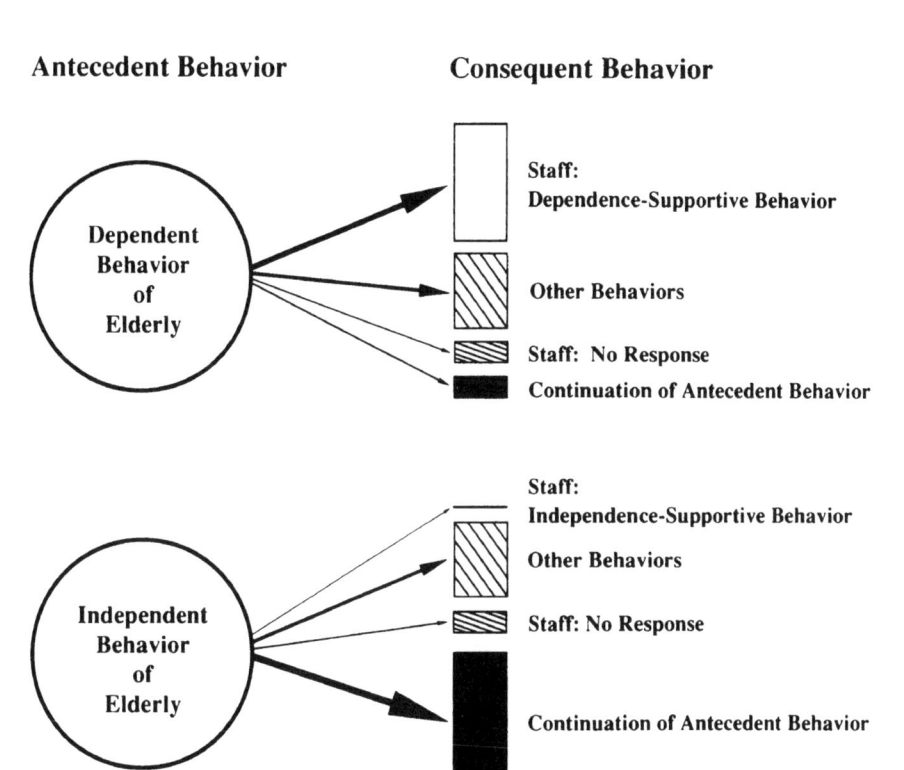

Figure 1.5. The dependence-support script in nursing homes. Dependent behavior of the elderly is firmly associated with the staff's offering of physical care. Independent behavior, however, is ignored (data from M. Baltes & Wahl, in press). A by-product is that physical care also offers the primary occasion for social contact.

Consider, for example, a person who has excelled as a marathon runner all of his or her adult life and wants to continue this activity into old age. If this runner wants to stay at the same performance level, more time and energy will need to be invested in running. As a consequence, the person will have to reduce or give up other activities (selection). At the same time, the runner will have to increase his or her training and knowledge about optimizing conditions such as the influence of daily rhythms and dieting (optimization), and finally he or she will have to become an expert in techniques aimed at reducing the impact of loss in functioning (compensation). Which shoes to use and how to treat injuries are examples of such compensatory strategies. By combining these elements of selection, optimization, and compensation, a high level of performance in marathon running might be retained into old age.

Similar selection and compensatory strategies can be imagined for almost any domain of life. For instance, the pianist Rubinstein remarked in a television interview that he conquers weaknesses of aging in his piano playing in the following manner: First, he reduces his repertoire and plays a smaller number of pieces (selection); second, he practices these more often (optimization); and third, he slows down his speed of playing prior to fast movements, thereby producing a contrast that enhances the impression of speed in the fast movements (compensation).

Summary and outlook

The search for conditions and variations of successful (good) aging is a meaningful scientific and societal agenda, even if no simple answer can be expected. Because of the seeming contradiction in terms, research attempting to understand the criteria, conditions, and variations of successful aging is likely to contribute to a critical analysis of the idea of success itself as well as its varying cultural and personal manifestations. In addition, such research will provide knowledge on the range and limits of human potential. The magic of human cultural evolution can be found in attempts to understand not only the factors of the current realities of aging but also the conditions and range of alternative scenarios. In general, we maintain that old age is the last "incomplete" part of cultural evolution.

We have presented a summary of findings about the nature of psychological aging. In our view, this summary can serve as a framework within which constructive discussions about current and future patterns of human aging can take place. Aside from the unresolved questions about appropriate criteria for successful aging, we have emphasized seven propositions or themes: (1) the distinction between normal, pathological, and optimal aging; (2) interindividual variability (heterogeneity); (3) plasticity and latent reserve capacity; (4) aging loss in the range of reserve capacity or adaptivity; (5) the enriching and compensatory role of individual and social knowledge, including technology; (6) aging-related changes toward an increasingly negative balance in gain-loss ratios; and finally (7) the phenomenon of a resilient self.

It is likely that there are several ways to derive models of successful aging from this framework of propositions (see the chapters by Featherman et al. and Fries in this volume for alternative but related conceptions). We have argued that a joint consideration of all propositions is essential for the identification of a prototypical strategy of successful aging.

One such prototypical strategy is the model of selective optimization with compensation. This model, which in its constituent features is implemented at any age, gains increasing importance in old age because of two empirical facts specific to old age: (1) The primary biological feature of normal aging is increased vulnerability and a concomitant reduction in general adaptability (reserve capacity) to environmental variation, and (2) the normal trajectory of psychological and biological development and aging is a continual evolution of specialized forms of adaptation, that is, increasing individualization of life trajectories. There are two other corollaries. First, individuals' subjective views of the self are constructed to deal well with such changes, and psychological mechanisms are available to adjust life goals and aspirations in the face of changing internal and external circumstances. Second, the process of selective optimization with compensation, although general in its "genotypic" characteristics, is quite diverse in its phenotypic manifestations. Depending on individual and societal conditions, it can take many forms in content and timing.

We contend that by using strategies of selection, optimization, and compensation, individuals can contribute to their own successful aging. On the one hand, then, it is correct that the biological nature of human aging limits more and more the overall range of possibilities in old age. On the other hand, however, the adaptive task of the aging individual is to select and concentrate on those domains that are of high priority and that involve a convergence of environmental demands and individual motivations, skills, and biological capacity. Under these conditions, Cicero's basic view may be useful after all. Although his stoicist optimism about the power of the human mind is certainly an oversimplification of the mind–body interface, forming a coalition between the human mind and society to outwit the limits of biological constraints in old age seems an obtainable and challenging goal for cultural evolution.

NOTE

In addition to the reviewers, we especially thank Steven W. Cornelius for extensive comments and helpful suggestions on an earlier draft of this chapter.

REFERENCES

Abeles, R. P. (Ed.). (1987). *Life-span perspectives and social psychology*. Hillsdale, NJ: Lawrence Erlbaum.

Antonucci, T. C., & Jackson, J. S. (1987). Social support, interpersonal efficacy, and health: A life course perspective. In L. L. Carstensen & B. A. Edelstein (Eds.), *Handbook of clinical gerontology* (pp. 291–311). New York: Pergamon Press.

Baltes, M. M. (1987). Erfolgreiches Altern als Ausdruck von Verhaltenskompetenz und Umweltqualität. In C. Niemitz (Ed.), *Der Mensch im Zusammenspiel von Anlage and Umwelt* (pp. 353–377). Frankfurt: Suhrkamp.

Baltes, M. M. (1988). The etiology and maintenance of dependency in the elderly: Three phases of operant research. *Behavior Therapy, 19*, 301–319.

Baltes, M. M., & Baltes, P. B. (1982). Microanalytic research on environmental factors and plasticity in psychological aging. In T. M. Field, A. Huston, H. C. Quay, C. Troll, & G. E. Finley (Eds.), *Review of human development* (pp. 524–539). New York: Wiley.

Baltes, M. M., & Baltes, P. B. (Eds.). (1986). *The psychology of control and aging.* Hillsdale, NJ: Lawrence Erlbaum.

Baltes, M. M., & Barton, E. M. (1979). Behavioral analysis of aging: A review of the operant model and research. *International Journal of Behavioral Development, 2*, 297–320.

Baltes, M. M., & Kindermann, T. (1985). Die Bedeutung der Plastizität für die klinische Beurteilung des Leistungsverhaltens im Alter. In D. Bente, H. Coper, & S. Kanowski (Eds.), *Hirnorganische Psychosyndrome im Alter: Vol. 2. Methoden zur Objektivierung pharmakotherapeutischer Wirkung* (pp. 171–184). Berlin: Springer Verlag.

Baltes, M. M., Kindermann, T., Reisenzein, R., & Schmid, U. (1987). Further observational data on the behavioral and social world of institutions for the aged. *Psychology and Aging, 2*, 390–403.

Baltes, M. M., & Reisenzein, R. (1986). The social world in long-term care institutions: Psychological control toward dependency. In M. M. Baltes & P. B. Baltes (Eds.), *The psychology of control and aging* (pp. 315–343). Hillsdale, NJ: Lawrence Erlbaum.

Baltes, M. M., & Wahl, H.-W. (1987). Dependency in aging. In L. L. Carstensen & B. A. Edelstein (Eds.), *Handbook of clinical gerontology* (pp. 204–221). New York: Pergamon Press.

Baltes, M. M., & Wahl, H.-W. (in press). The behavioral system of dependency in the elderly: Interaction with the social environment. In M. Ory & R. P. Abeles (Eds.), *Aging, health, and behavior.* Baltimore, MD: Johns Hopkins University Press.

Baltes, P. B. (1987). Theoretical propositions of life-span developmental psychology: On the dynamics between growth and decline. *Developmental Psychology, 23*, 611–626.

Baltes, P. B., & Baltes, M. M. (1980). Plasticity and variability in psychological aging: Methodological and theoretical issues. In G. E. Gurski (Ed.), *Determining the effects of aging on the central nervous system* (pp. 41–66). Berlin: Schering.

Baltes, P. B., Dittmann-Kohli, F., & Dixon, R. A. (1984). New perspectives on the development of intelligence in adulthood: Toward a dual-process conception and a model of selective optimization with compensation. In P. B. Baltes & O. G. Brim, Jr. (Eds.), *Life-span development and behavior* (Vol. 6, pp. 33–76). New York: Academic Press.

Baltes, P. B., & Kliegl, R. (1986). On the dynamics between growth and decline in the aging of intelligence and memory. In K. Poeck, H.-J. Freund, & H. Gänshirt (Eds.), *Neurology* (pp. 1–17). Heidelberg: Springer.

Baltes, P. B., & Kliegl, R. (1989). *Testing-the-limits research suggests irreversible aging loss in mental imagery.* Unpublished manuscript, Max Planck Institute for Human Development and Education, Berlin, Federal Republic of Germany.

Baltes, P. B., & Lindenberger, U. (1988). On the range of cognitive plasticity in old age as a function of experience: 15 years of intervention research. *Behavior Therapy, 19*, 283–300.

Baltes, P. B., & Schaie, K. W. (1976). On the plasticity of intelligence in adulthood and old age: Where Horn and Donaldson fail. *American Psychologist, 31*, 720–725.

Baltes, P. B., & Smith, J. (1990). Toward a psychology of wisdom and its ontogenesis. In R. J. Sternberg (Ed.), *Wisdom: Its nature, origins, and development* (pp. 87–120). New York: Cambridge University Press.

Baltes, P. B., Sowarka, D., & Kliegl, R. (1989). Cognitive training research on fluid intelligence in old age: What can older adults achieve by themselves? *Psychology and Aging, 4*, 217–221.

Bengtson, V. L., & Kuypers, J. A. (1985). The family support cycle: Psychosocial issues in the aging family. In J. M. A. Munnichs, P. Mussen, & E. Olbrich (Eds.), *Life-span and change in a gerontological perspective* (pp. 61–77). New York: Academic Press.

Bengtson, V. L., Reedy, M., & Gordon, C. (1985). Aging and self-concept: Personality processes and social contexts. In J. E. Birren & K. W. Schaie (Eds.), *Handbook of the psychology of aging* (2nd ed., pp. 544–593). New York: Van Nostrand Reinhold.

Berlin, I. (1988). On the pursuit of the ideal. *New York Review of Books, 35*, 16.

Birren, J. E., & Bengtson, V. L. (Eds.). (1988). *Emergent theories of aging*. New York: Springer.

Bornstein, R., & Smircina, M. T. (1982). The status of empirical support for the hypothesis of increased interindividual variability in aging. *Gerontologist, 22*, 258–260.

Brandtstädter, J. (1984). Personal and social control over development: Some implications of an action perspective in life-span developmental psychology. In P. B. Baltes & O. G. Brim, Jr. (Eds.), *Life-span development and behavior* (Vol. 6, pp. 1–32). New York: Academic Press.

Brandtstädter, J., Krampen, G., & Heil, F. E. (1986). Personal control and emotional evaluation of development in partnership relations during adulthood. In M. M. Baltes & P. B. Baltes (Eds.), *The psychology of control and aging* (pp. 265–296). Hillsdale, NJ: Lawrence Erlbaum.

Brim, O. G., Jr. (1988). Losing and winning: The nature of ambition in everyday life. *Psychology Today, 9*, 48–52.

Brim, O. G., Jr., & Kagan, J. (1980). Constancy and change: A view of the issues. In O. G. Brim, Jr., & J. Kagan (Eds.), *Constancy and change in human development* (pp. 1–25). Cambridge: Harvard University Press.

Brown, A. L. (1982). Learning and development: The problem of compatibility, access, and induction. *Human Development, 25*, 89–115.

Busse, E. W., & Maddox, G. L. (1985), *The Duke Longitudinal Studies of normal aging: 1955–1980*. New York: Springer.

Butt, D. S., & Beiser, M. (1987). Successful aging: A theme for international psychology. *Psychology and Aging, 2*, 87–94.

Cattell, R. B. (1971). *Abilities: Their structure, growth, and action*. Boston: Houghton Mifflin.

Charness, N. (Ed.). (1985). *Aging and human performance*. Chichester, England: John Wiley & Sons.

Cicero, M. T. (44 B.C.) *Cato major – De senectute*. (Original work translated by J.

Logan and published by B. Franklin 1744 as *Cato major; or, His discourse of old age*. Philadelphia, PA: Benjamin Franklin.) Reprinted by Arno Press, 1979.

Coper, H., Jänicke, B., & Schulze, G. (1986). Biopsychological research on adaptivity across the life span of animals. In P. B. Baltes, D. L. Featherman, & R. M. Lerner (Eds.), *Life-span development and behavior* (Vol. 7, pp. 207–232). Hillsdale, NJ: Lawrence Erlbaum.

Costa, P. T., Jr., & Andres, R. (1986). Patterns of age changes. In I. Rossman (Ed.), *Clinical geriatrics* (pp. 23–30). New York: Lippincott.

Craik, F. I. M. (1977). Age differences in human memory. In J. E. Birren & K. W. Schaie (Eds.), *Handbook of the psychology of aging* (pp. 384–420). New York: Van Nostrand Reinhold.

Craik, F. I. M. (1983). On the transfer of information from temporary to permanent memory. *Philosophical Transactions of the Royal Society of London, B-302*, 341–359.

Dannefer, D. (1984). Adult development and social theory: A paradigmatic reappraisal. *American Sociological Review, 49*, 100–116.

Denney, N. W. (1984). A model of cognitive development across the life span. *Developmental Review, 4*, 171–191.

Dixon, R. A., & Baltes, P. B. (1986). Toward life-span research on the functions and pragmatics of intelligence. In R. J. Sternberg & R. K. Wagner (Eds.), *Practical intelligence: Nature and origins of competence in the everyday world* (pp. 203–235). New York: Cambridge University Press.

Epstein, S. (1981). The unity principle versus the reality and pleasure principles, or the tale of the scorpion and the frog. In M. D. Lynch, A. A. Norem-Hebeisen, & K. J. Gergen (Eds.), *Self-concept: Advances in theory and research* (pp. 27–38). Cambridge, MA: Ballinger.

Ericsson, K. A. (1985). Memory skill. *Canadian Journal of Psychology, 39*, 188–231.

Erikson, E. H., Erikson, J. M., & Kivnick, H. (1986). *Vital involvement in old age: The experience of old age in our time*. London: Norton.

Featherman, D. L. (1983). The life-span perspective in social science research. In P. B. Baltes & O. G. Brim, Jr. (Eds.), *Life-span development and behavior* (Vol. 5, pp. 1–59). New York: Academic Press.

Featherman, D. L. (1986). Biography, society, and history: Individual development as a population process. In A. B. Sørensen, F. E. Weinert, & L. R. Sherrod (Eds.), *Human development and the life course: Multidisciplinary perspectives* (pp. 99–149). Hillsdale, NJ: Lawrence Erlbaum.

Felton, B. J. (1987). International cohort variation on happiness: Some hypotheses and exploratory analyses. *International Journal of Aging and Human Development, 25*, 27–42.

Filipp, S.-H., & Klauer, T. (1986). Conceptions of self over the life span: reflections on the dialectics of change. In M. M. Baltes & P. B. Baltes (Eds.), *The psychology of control and aging* (pp. 167–205). Hillsdale, NJ: Lawrence Erlbaum.

Finch, C. E. (1988). Neural endocrine approaches to the resolution of time as a dependent variable in the aging processes of mammals. *Gerontologist, 28*, 29–42.

Fries, J. F. (1983). The compression of morbidity. *Milbank Memorial Fund Quarterly, 61*, 397–419.

Fries, J. F., & Crapo, L. M. (1981). *Vitality and aging*. San Francisco: Freeman & Co.

Greenough, W. T. (1986). What's special about development? Thoughts on the bases of experience-sensitive synaptic plasticity. In W. T. Greenough & J. M. Juraska (Eds.), *Developmental Neuropsychology* (pp. 387–407). Orlando, FL: Academic Press.

Greenwald, A. G. (1980). The totalitarian ego: Fabrication and revision of personal history. *American Psychologist, 35,* 603–618.

Guthke, J. (1972). *Zur Diagnostik der intellektuellen Lernfähigkeit.* Berlin: Deutscher Verlag der Wissenschaften.

Guthke, J. (1982). The learning test concept: An alternative to the traditional static intelligence test. *German Journal of Psychology, 6,* 306–324.

Gutmann, D. (1987). *Reclaimed powers: Toward a new psychology of men and women in later life.* New York: Basic Books.

Harris, L. (1975). *The myth and reality of aging in America.* Washington, DC: National Council on the Aging.

Havighurst, R. J. (1963). Successful aging. In R. H. Williams, C. Tibbits, & W. Donahue (Eds.), *Processes of aging* (Vol. 1, pp. 299–320). New York: Atherton Press.

Heckhausen, J., Dixon, R. A., & Baltes, P. B. (1989). Gains and losses in development throughout adulthood as perceived by different adult age groups. *Developmental Psychology, 25,* 109–121.

Henry, J. P. (1988). The archetypes of power and intimacy. In J. E. Birren & V. L. Bengtson (Eds.), *Emergent theories of aging* (pp. 269–298). New York: Springer.

Holliday, S. G., & Chandler, M. J. (1986). Wisdom: Explorations in adult competence. In J. A. Meacham (Ed.), *Contributions to human development* (Vol. 17, pp. 1–96). Basel: Karger.

Horn, J. L. (1970). Organization of data on life-span development of human abilities. In L. R. Goulet & P. B. Baltes (Eds.), *Life-span developmental psychology: Research and theory* (pp. 423–466). New York: Academic Press.

Hoyer, W. J. (1985). Aging and the development of expert cognition. In T. M. Schlechter & M. P. Toglia (Eds.), *New directions in cognitive science* (pp. 69–87). Norwood, NJ: Ablex.

Hunt, E. (1978). Mechanics of verbal ability. *Psychological Review, 85,* 109–130.

Kahn, R.L., & Antonucci, T. C. (1980). Convoys over the life course: Attachment, roles, and social support. In P. B. Baltes & O. G. Brim, Jr. (Eds.), *Life-span development and behavior* (Vol. 3, pp. 253–286). New York: Academic Press.

Kliegl, R. (1989). *Formation of expert knowledge in a mnemonic skill: Twelve case studies of young and old adults.* Unpublished manuscript, Max Planck Institute for Human Development and Education, Berlin, Federal Republic of Germany.

Kliegl, R., & Baltes, P. B. (1987). Theory-guided analysis of development and aging mechanisms through testing-the-limits and research on expertise. In C. Schooler & K. W. Schaie (Eds.), *Cognitive functioning and social structure over the life course* (pp. 95–119). Norwood, NJ: Ablex.

Kliegl, R., Smith, J., & Baltes, P. B. (1989). Testing-the-limits and the study of adult age differences in cognitive plasticity of a mnemonic skill. *Developmental Psychology, 25,* 247–256.

Labouvie-Vief, G. (1981). Proactive and reactive aspects of constructivism: Growth and aging in life-span perspective. In R. M. Lerner & N. A. Busch-Rossnagel (Eds.), *Individuals as producers of their development* (pp. 197–230). New York: Academic Press.

Labouvie-Vief, G. (1985). Intelligence and cognition. In J. E. Birren & K. W. Schaie (Eds.), *Handbook of the psychology of aging* (2nd ed., pp. 500–530). New York: Van Nostrand Reinhold.

Labouvie-Vief, G. (Ed.). (1986). *Developmental dimensions of adult adaptation: Perspectives on mind, self, and emotion.* Unpublished manuscript, Wayne State University, Department of Psychology, Detroit.

Lachman, M. E. (1986). Personal control in later life: Stability, change, and cognitive correlates. In M. M. Baltes & P. B. Baltes (Eds.), *The psychology of control and aging* (pp. 207–236). Hillsdale, NJ: Lawrence Erlbaum.

Langer, E. (1989). *Mindfulness.* Reading, MA: Addison-Wesley.

Lawton, M. P. (1982). Environments and living arrangements. In R. H. Binstock, W.-S. Chow, & J. H. Schulz (Eds.), *International perspectives on aging* (pp. 159–192). New York: United Nations Fund for Population Activities.

Lawton, M. P. (1988). Behavior-relevant ecological factors. In K. W. Schaie & C. Schooler (Eds.), *Social structures and aging: Psychological processes* (pp. 57–78). Hillsdale, NJ: Lawrence Erlbaum.

Lehr, U. (1987). *Zur Situation der älterwerdenden Frau.* Munich: C. H. Beck.

Lehr, U., & Thomae, H. (Eds.). (1987). *Formen seelischen Alterns.* Stuttgart: Enke.

Lerner, R. M. (1984). *On the nature of human plasticity.* New York: Cambridge University Press.

Lindenberger, U. (1990). *The effects of professional expertise and cognitive aging on skilled memory performance.* Unpublished doctoral dissertation, Free University of Berlin.

Maddox, G. L. (1987). Aging differently. *Gerontologist, 27,* 557–564.

Mandl, H., & Spada, H. (Eds.). (1988). *Wissenspsychologie.* Munich and Weinheim: Psychologie Verlags Union.

Markus, H., & Nurius, P. (1986). Possible selves. *American Psychologist, 41,* 954–969.

Markus, H., & Wurf, E. (1987). The dynamic self-concept: A social psychological perspective. *Annual Review of Psychology, 38,* 299–337.

Meacham, J. A. (1982). Wisdom and the context of knowledge: Knowing that one doesn't know. In D. Kuhn & J. A. Meacham (Eds.), *On the development of developmental psychology* (pp. 111–134). Basel: Karger.

Mosher-Ashley, P. M. (1986–1987). Procedural and methodological parameters in behavioral-gerontological research: A review. *International Journal of Aging and Human Development, 24,* 189–229.

Neisser, U. (1988). Five kinds of self-knowledge. *Philosophical Psychology, 1,* 35–59.

Neugarten, B. L. (Ed.). (1968). *Middle age and aging: A reader in social psychology.* Chicago: University of Chicago Press.

Neugarten, B. L. (1987). Kansas City studies of adult life. In G. L. Maddox (Ed.), *The encyclopedia of aging* (pp. 372–373). New York: Springer.

Palmore, E. (1979). Predictors of successful aging. *Gerontologist, 19,* 427–431.

Parmelee, P. A., & Lawton, M. P. (1990). The design of special environments for the aged. In J. E. Birren & K. W. Schaie (Eds.), *Handbook of the psychology of aging* (3rd ed., pp. 464–488). New York: Van Nostrand Reinhold.

Perlmutter, M. (Ed.). (in press). *Late-life potential.* Washington, DC: Gerontological Society of Ameria.

Plomin, R., & Thompson, L. (1986). Life-span developmental behavioral genetics. In P. B. Baltes, D. L. Featherman, & R. M. Lerner (Eds.), *Life-span development and behavior* (Vol. 8, pp. 1–31). Hillsdale, NJ: Lawrence Erlbaum.

Riley, M. W. (1983, December). *Aging and society: Notes on the development of new understandings*. The Leon and Josephine Winkelman Lecture, School of Social Work, University of Michigan.

Riley, M. W. (1985). Age strata in social systems. In R. H. Binstock & E. Shanas (Eds.), *Handbook of aging and the social sciences* (Vol. 3, pp. 369–411). New York: Van Nostrand Reinhold.

Roether, D. (1983). Entwicklungspsychologische Beiträge zum lebenslangen Lernkonzept. *Zeitschrift für Gerontologie, 16*, 234–240.

Roether, D. (1986). *Lernfähigkeit im Erwachsenenalter: Ein Beitrag zur klinischen Entwicklungspsychologie.* Leipzig: Hirzel.

Rowe J. W., & Kahn, R. L. (1987). Human aging: Usual and successful. *Science, 237*, 143–149.

Rybash, J. M., Hoyer, W. J., & Roodin, P. A. (1986). *Adult cognition and aging: Developmental changes in processing, knowing, and thinking.* Elmsford, NY: Pergamon Press.

Ryff, C. D. (1982). Successful aging: A developmental approach, *Gerontologist, 22*, 209–214.

Ryff, C. D. (1984). Personality development from the inside: The subjective experience of change in adulthood and aging. In P. B. Baltes & O. G. Brim, Jr. (Eds.), *Life-span development and behavior* (Vol. 6, pp. 243–279). New York: Academic Press.

Salthouse, T. A. (1984). Effects of age and skill in typing. *Journal of Experimental Psychology: General, 113*, 345–371.

Salthouse, T. A. (1985). *A theory of cognitive aging.* Amsterdam: North-Holland.

Schaie, K. W. (1979). The primary mental abilities in adulthood: An exploration in the development of psychometric intelligence. In P. B. Baltes & O. G. Brim, Jr. (Eds.), *Life-span development and behavior* (Vol. 3, pp. 67–115). New York: Academic Press.

Schaie, K. W. (Ed.). (1983). *Longitudinal studies of adult psychological development.* New York: Guilford Press.

Schaie, K. W., & Willis, S. L. (1986). Can adult intellectual decline be reversed? *Developmental Psychology, 22*, 223–232.

Schmidt, L. R. (1971). Testing the limits im Leistungsverhalten: Möglichkeiten und Grenzen. In E. Duhm (Ed.), *Praxis der klinischen Psychologie* (Vol. 2, pp. 9–29). Göttingen: Hogrefe.

Schwartz, A. N. (1974). Staff development and morale building in nursing homes. *Gerontologist, 14*, 50–53.

Schwarzer, R., Lange, B., & Jerusalem, M. (1982). Selbstkonzeptentwicklung nach einem Bezugsgruppenwechsel. *Zeitschrift für Entwicklungspsychologie und Pädagogische Psychologie, 14*, 125–140.

Shock, N. W. (1977). System integration. In C. E. Finch & L. Hayflick (Eds.), *Handbook of the biology of aging* (pp. 639–665). New York: Van Nostrand Reinhold.

Shock, N. W., Greulich, R. C., Costa, P. T., Andres, R., Lakatta, E. G., Arenberg, D., & Tobin, J. D. (1984). *Normal human aging: The Baltimore Longitudinal Study on Aging* (Report No. 84-2450). Washington, DC: NIH Publications.

Singer, W. (1987). Activity-dependent self-organization of synaptic connections as a substrate of learning. In J.-P. Changeux & M. Konishi (Eds.), *The neural and molecular bases of learning* (pp. 301–336). New York: John Wiley & Sons.

Smith, J., & Baltes, P. B. (1990). Wisdom-related knowledge: Age/cohort differences in response to life-planning problems. *Development Psychology, 26*, 494–505.

Smith, J., Dixon, R. A., & Baltes, P. B. (1989). Expertise in life planning: A new research approach to investigating aspects of wisdom. In M. L. Commons, J. D. Sinnott, F. A. Richards, & C. Armon (Eds.), *Adult development: Vol. 1. Comparisons and applications of developmental models* (pp. 307–331). New York: Praeger.

Smith, M. B. (1978). Perspectives on selfhood. *American Psychologist, 33*, 1053–1063.

Sowarka, D. (1989). Weisheit und weise Personen: Common-Sense-Konzepte älterer Menschen. *Zeitschrift für Entwicklungspsychologie und Pädagogische Psychologie, 21*, 87–109.

Staudinger, U. M. (1989). *The study of life review: An approach to the investigation of intellectual development across the life span* (Studien und Berichte des Max-Planck-Instituts für Bildungsforschung, No. 47). Stuttgart: Klett Verlag.

Staudinger, U. M., Cornelius, S. W., & Baltes, P. B. (1989). The aging of intelligence: Potential and limits. *Annals of the Academy of Political and Social Sciences, 503*, 43–59.

Sternberg, R. J. (Ed.). (in press). *Wisdom: Its nature, origins, and development.* New York: Cambridge University Press.

Stones, M. J., & Kozma, A. (1985). Physical performance. In N. Charness (Ed.), *Aging and human performance* (pp. 261–291). New York: John Wiley & Sons.

Suls, J. N., & Mullen, B. (1982). From the cradle to the grave: Comparison and self-evaluation across the life span. In J. N. Suls (Ed.), *Psychological perspectives on the self* (Vol. 1, pp. 97–128). Hillsdale, NJ: Lawrence Erlbaum.

Thomae, H. (1979). The concept of development and life-span developmental psychology. In P. B. Baltes & O. G. Brim, Jr. (Eds.), *Life-span development and behavior* (Vol. 2, pp. 282–312). New York: Academic Press.

Thomae, H. (1987). Altersformen: Wege zu ihrer methodischen und begrifflichen Erfassung. In U. Lehr & H. Thomae (Eds.), *Formen seelischen Alterns* (pp. 173–195). Stuttgart: Enke.

Thompson, L. A., & Kliegl, R. (1989). *Adult age differences in connecting thoughts during elaborative encoding.* Manuscript submitted for publication.

Veroff, J., Douvan, E., & Kulka, R. A. (1981). *The inner American: A self-portrait from 1957 to 1976.* New York: Basic Books.

Weinert, F. E. (1986). Developmental variations of memory performance and memory-related knowledge across the life-span. In A. B. Sørensen, F. E. Weinert, & L. R. Sherrod (Eds.), *Human development and the life course: Multidisciplinary perspectives* (pp. 535–554). Hillsdale, NJ: Lawrence Erlbaum.

Whitbourne, S. K. (1985). *The aging body.* New York: Springer.

Williams, R. H., & Wirths, C. G. (1965). *Lives through the years: Styles of life and successful aging.* New York: Atherton Press.

Willis, S. L. (1987). Cognitive training and everyday competence. In K. W. Schaie (Ed.), *Annual Review of Gerontology and Geriatrics* (Vol. 7, pp. 159–188). New York: Springer.

Wills, T. A. (1981). Downward comparison principles in social psychology. *Psychological Bulletin, 90*, 245–271.

Wisocki, P. (1984). Behavior modification in the elderly. In M. Hersen, R. M. Eisler, & P. Miller (Eds.), *Progress in behavioral modification* (Vol. 16, pp. 121–157). New York: Academic Press.

Wood, J. V. (1989). Theory and research concerning social comparisons of personal attributes. *Psychological Bulletin, 106*, 231–248.

Part II
Social and Emotional Functioning in Old Age

[6]

Resilience, sense of coherence, purpose in life and self-transcendence in relation to perceived physical and mental health among the oldest old

B. NYGREN[1], L. ALÉX[1], E. JONSÉN[1], Y. GUSTAFSON[2], A. NORBERG[1], & B. LUNDMAN[1]

[1]*Department of Nursing &* [2]*Department of Community Medicine and Rehabilitation, Geriatric Medicine, Umeå University, Umeå, Sweden*

(*Received 5 December 2003; accepted 4 August 2004*)

Abstract

Different concepts have been presented which denote driving forces and strengths that contribute to a person's ability to meet and handle adversities, and keep or regain health. The aim of this study, which is a part of The Umeå 85+ study, was to describe resilience, sense of coherence, purpose in life and self-transcendence in relation to perceived physical and mental health in a sample of the oldest old. The study sample consisted of 125 participants 85 years of age or older, who ranked themselves on the Resilience Scale, Sense of Coherence Scale, Purpose in Life Scale and Self-Transcendence Scale and answered the SF-36 Health Survey questionnaire. The findings showed significant correlations between scores on the Resilience Scale, the Sense of Coherence Scale, the Purpose in Life Test, and the Self-Transcendence Scale. Significant correlations were also found between these scales and the SF-36 Mental Health Summary among women but not among men. There was no significant correlation between perceived physical and mental health. The mean values of the different scales showed that the oldest old have the same or higher scores than younger age groups. Regression analyses also revealed sex differences regarding mental health. The conclusions are that, the correlation between scores on the different scales suggests that the scales measure some dimension of inner strength and that the oldest old have this strength at least in the same extent as younger adults. Another conclusion is that the dimensions that constitute mental health differ between women and men.

Introduction

Recent research has highlighted positive aspects of, and gains associated with becoming old. Several studies including a study by Baltes, Kuehl and Sowarka (1992) note that people continue to mature in old age, both intellectually and with regard to skills. Other reports focus on a high degree of well-being (Kunzmann, Little & Smith, 2000), a high quality of life (Sarvimaki & Stenbock Hult, 2000) and absence of limitations in old age (Bould, Smith & Longino, 1997). Nonetheless becoming old in Westernized societies has traditionally been seen as a downward curve with losses as well as declines of body and mind. Losses associated with becoming old involve not only physical capacity and cognitive resources, but also social status, friends and family members (Femia, Zarit & Johansson, 2001; Pascucci & Loving, 1997). With advanced age the prevalence of physical diseases and impairments increases (Clarke & Cook, 1989; Dening et al., 1998; Jagger, Jagger, Spiers & Clarke, 1993; Zarit, Johansson & Malmberg, 1995) as do limitations in the ability to manage activities of daily living (ADL) (Bould et al., 1997), and high rates of depression have been reported (Stouffer Calderon, 2001).

There are several models describing adaptive strategies in every day life as resources against negative ageing. Selective optimisation with compensation is a model described in Lang, Rieckmann & Baltes (2002) for the understanding of how people master the challenge of ageing and experience well-being. According to Lang, Rieckmann and Baltes (2002) selection in every day life can for instance be to reduce the number of daily activities, actively or passively. Compensation in every day life is, for example, to use new and alternative means to reach a goal. Optimisation can be to use more time and efforts in specific tasks or activities. Baltes (1997) even states that the theory of selective optimisation with compensation is highly general and a meta-theory of development in general. Carstensen, Isaacowitz and Charles (1999) claims from a socio-emotional selectivity theory, that time plays a fundamental role in the selection and pursuit of personal goals. They found that in old age, the emotional goals predominate in contrast to younger people, when cognitive goals are dominant. The oldest old in their study had fewer social partners and were more focused on relationships with relatives than younger persons who were interested in new relationships and cognitive goals. Tornstam (1997) argues that well-being in old age is based on experiences of meaning and purpose in life and the possibility to transcend.

In order to better understand how some of the elderly appear to have more strengths, and better ability than others to compensate for various losses, bodily decline and other functional health limitations, research has focused on the personal power and driving forces of individuals in this age group. Research on people's ways of handling adversities and retaining health and strength has resulted in theoretical constructions described by concepts such as 'resilience' (Wagnild & Young, 1990), 'sense of coherence' (Antonovsky & Sagy, 1986), 'purpose in life' (Frankl, 1963) and 'self-transcendence' (Reed, 1991a). In this paper we describe various concepts aimed at elucidating this type of strength in relation to perceived physical and mental health among the oldest old.

Resilience has been described as a personal characteristic that influences the ability to recover from adverse experiences (Dyer & McGuinness, 1996; Wagnild & Young, 1990) as well as a protective strength (Dyer & McGuinness, 1996). For older people resilience has been described as flexibility and as a type of adaptive capacity (Staudinger, Marsiske & Baltes, 1993) that may be activated and contribute to maintenance of independent functioning and well-being (Rowe & Kahn, 2000). Richardson (2002) described research of resilience as 'three waves of resilience inquiry', in which resilience as a trait is the first wave and resilience as a process is the second. The third wave is research on resilience as identification of motivational forces within individuals or groups. Based on interviews with elderly women, Wagnild and Young (1990) identified five interrelated components that constitute resilience: Equanimity (a balanced perspective of one's life and experience); perseverance (a willingness to continue to reconstruct one's life and to remain involved); self-reliance (a belief in oneself and one's capabilities); meaningfulness (an understanding that life has a purpose); and existential aloneness (a realization that each person's life path is unique).

Sense of coherence is seen as a way of viewing the world and one's life, and as a kind of motivational force. Antonovsky (1987) described three dimensions which constitute sense of coherence: Comprehensibility (the extent to which an individual perceives the situation that confronts her or him as cognitively meaningful and predictable); manageability (the degree to which an individual perceives her or his resources to be sufficient to meet internal and external demands); and meaningfulness (the degree to which an individual feels that life is emotionally meaningful and that some of her or his problems are perceived as challenges rather than hindrances). Sense of coherence develops from experiences during life (Antonowsky, 1987), and Rennemark and Hagberg (1997) found indications that the more positive the evaluation of one's life history among elderly men and women, the stronger the sense of coherence. Sense of coherence has been shown to correlate positively with health related factors such as global health (Callahan & Pincus, 1995), hope (Coward, 1996), concern about symptoms such as shortness of breath, pain and fatigue (Nesbitt & Heidrich, 2000), purpose in life (Sarvimäki & Stenbock-Hult, 2000), and hardiness (Williams, 1990). Rennemark and Hagberg (1999) found strong connection between sense of coherence and physical symptoms from muscles, bones and joints as well as between sense of coherence and mental symptoms such as depression.

Purpose in life as a concept originates from the orientation of humanistic psychology and is based in Frankl's (1963) concept 'will to meaning'. Frankl described the will to meaning as the primary motivational force and argues that frustration of this force will give a desperate feeling of existential vacuum. Rappaport, Fossler, Bross and Gilden (1993) found a positive correlation between purpose in life and a positive view of the future.

Self-transcendence has been seen as a major psychosocial resource of developing maturity, which enables a person to extend personal boundaries. Self-transcendence is defined as expansion of one's boundaries inwardly in various introspective activities, outwardly through concerns about others and temporally, whereby the perceptions of one's past and future enhance the present (Reed, 1991a). Self-transcendence enhances one's feeling of self-worth (Coward, 1990) and has been linked to feelings of spiritual connectedness (Bauer & Barron, 1995) as well as ADL abilities (Upchurch, 1999).

The above concepts have been described in an attempt to provide a theoretical basis for illuminating driving forces and strengths in relation to various forms of adversity or strain. It seems reasonable to assume that the described qualities denoted by the concepts, will affect perceived physical and mental health. Research on the relationship between physical and mental health among the oldest old is scarce. Heidrich and D'Amico (1993) found a positive correlation between perceived physical and perceived mental health among individuals over the age of 80 in the USA. Bryant, Beck and Fairclough (2000) found experiences of health, despite severe physical limitations, in the elderly. The aim of the present study was to describe resilience, sense of coherence, purpose in life, and self-transcendence in relation to perceived physical and mental health in a sample of the oldest old.

Method

Participants

The participants were people living in a mid-sized town in northern Sweden. This study forms part of a larger study, The Umeå 85+ study. The inclusion criteria were being 95 years of age and older, being 90 years old, or being 85, the year the study was carried out. We invited all those being 95 years of age or older, and all 90 year olds, and a random sample of individuals who were 85 years old. The specific inclusion criteria for this study were being able to answer questionnaires of the Likert type and having the strength to participate in narrative interviews. The study sample consisted of a total of 125 participants including 86 women (69%). Twenty-six participants (21%) were 95 years or older, 46 (37%) were 90, and 53 (42%) were 85 years of age. Eleven participants (9%) had more than nine years of education and eight participants (6%) had less than six years of education. Ninety-three (75%) participants were living in ordinary housing and 106 (85%) were living alone. The participants had a mean score of 18.7 (SD ± 5.7) on Barthel's index assessing personal ADL (Mahoney & Barthel, 1965) and 38 participants (30%) were totally independent in both instrumental and personal ADL assessed with 'The Staircase of ADL' (Sonn, 1996). The cognitive status of the participants was assessed with the Mini Mental State Examination (out of 30). The participants in this study had a mean score of 25.6 (SD ± 3.9). Scores below 24 (out of 30) indicate impaired cognition (Folstein, Folstein & McHugh, 1975). The only variable that showed differences between women and men were that significantly more women lived alone (91% versus 72%, $p = 0.006$).

Measurements

The Resilience Scale (RS) (Wagnild & Young, 1993), which was developed from a qualitative study among elderly women (Wagnild & Young, 1990), consists of 25 items. Respondents rate statements about their personal view of themselves on a Likert scale ranging from 1–7. The possible scores range from 25–175, and the higher the score, the higher the degree of resilience. The scale was translated into Swedish and the translated version was translated back into English and the back-translated version was sent to one of the original authors for comments, resulting in a minor modification of one of the items. Alpha coefficients between 0.76–0.91 have been reported for the English version (Wagnild & Young, 1993) and between 0.88–0.90 for the Swedish version (unpublished data). In the present study Cronbach's alpha was 0.83.

The Sense of Coherence Scale (SOC) was developed from interviews with people who had recovered after adverse experiences. The focus was on salutogenesis (Antonovsky, 1987). The original scale comprises 29 statements. In the present study the 13-item version of the SOC (Antonovsky, 1993) was used. The scale is of Likert type with item ranges from 1–7. The range of possible scores is 13–91, and the higher the score, the stronger the sense of coherence. The scale was translated into Swedish by Langius and Bjoervell (1993) and has been proved to be psychometrically sound. For the Swedish 13-item version, alpha coefficients between 0.74–0.91 have been reported (Langius & Bjoervell, 1993). In the present study Cronbach's alpha was 0.77.

The Purpose in Life Test (PIL) (Crumbaugh, 1968; Crumbaugh & Maholick, 1964;) was developed to detect existential vacuum, which Frankl (1963) viewed as the opposite of purpose in life. The scale consists of 20 items of the Likert type with item ranges from 1–7. The range of possible scores is 20–140, with 140 representing the highest degree of purpose in life. The PIL has been translated into several languages and has been used for more than 30 years (Crumbaugh & Henrion, 1988). Concept and concurrent validity have been reasonably well established (Crumbaugh & Henrion, 1988). Meier and Edwards (1974) have reported test-retest reliability to 0.83. Åkerberg (1987) tested the Swedish version of PIL and found it to be valid. In the present study Cronbach's alpha was 0.85.

The Self-Transcendence Scale (STS) was developed to identify intrapersonal, interpersonal and temporal experiences characteristic of later life and reflect expanded boundaries of self (Reed, 1989). The STS is a 15-item scale with item ranges from 1–4. The possible range of scores is 15–60, with 60 representing the highest degree of self-transcendence (Reed, 1989). Construct validity has been tested by multiple testing, both in a phenomenological study and in analysis of data from correlation and longitudinal studies (Coward, 1990, 1996; Reed, 1991b). Studies using the STS report a Cronbach's alpha ranging from 0.52–0.86 (Coward, 1996; Ellermann & Reed, 2001). The scale was translated into Swedish and the translated version was translated back into English and then the back-translated version was sent to the original author, who approved the back-translation. The reliability and construct validity of the Swedish version of the STS have been evaluated and reported in a paper for a Master's degree, and the internal consistency of the Swedish version was 0.70–0.85 (unpublished data). In the present study Cronbach's alpha was 0.70.

The SF-36 Health Survey (SF-36) was used as an outcome measure. The SF-36 is a health-related quality of life instrument that was developed in the USA and has been used in a number of countries (Ware & Sherbourne, 1992). The SF-36 is organized into two main dimensions of health: the Physical Health Dimension (SF-36 physical component summary [PCS]) and the Mental Health Dimension (SF-36 mental component summary [MCS]). These two main dimensions comprise eight sub-scales representing eight aspects of health: Physical Functioning, Role-Physical, Bodily Pain, General Health, Vitality, Social Functioning, Role-Emotional and Mental Health. The first four makes the Physical Heath sum index and the last four makes the Mental Health sum index. The SF-36 is a 36-item, Likert type scale. It gives scores on each sub-scale and on the two main dimensions. A higher score indicates better health. The norm mean values for the general Swedish population aged 75 and older are for women: PCS = 37.0 and MCS = 46.5. The corresponding values for men are: PCS = 40.5 and MCS = 52.3. The SF-36 has been translated and tested in a general Swedish population. Reliability values for internal consistency, as measured by Cronbach's alpha, have ranged from 0.79–0.93 (Sullivan, Karlsson & Ware, 1995). In the present study Cronbach's alpha for both PCS and MCS was 0.83.

Procedure

We informed the respondents of the study and its purpose by letter and by telephone. After informed consent was received an appointment was made. The data collection took place in the respondents' home. For the majority of the participants, the questionnaires were answered on two occasions. The researcher read the statements out aloud and the participants had an enlarged copy of the answering alternatives in front of them. Sometimes they chose to answer orally and at other times they responded by just pointing at a figure on the copy of the answering alternatives. When the participants had chosen their alternative the researcher filled in the answer on the questionnaire. The procedure for filling in the questionnaires was agreed upon among the researchers who carried out the data collection. The response rate varied among the scales. The study was approved by the Ethics Committee of the Medical Faculty, Umeå University (No. 99–326).

Analysis

A simultaneous multiple regression analysis was preformed with PCS and MCS as depending variables. Missing internal values were replaced with the mode value for the actual item. Altogether 31 mode values (RS, $n=11$; SOC, $n=6$; PIL, $n=5$; STS, $n=9$) in 22 subjects were imputed. No more than three mode values were replaced for an individual participant.

Results

The mean scores and SD of the RS, the SOC, the PIL and the STS are given in Table I. The only statistically significant difference in mean scores between women and men was found in PIL, where men had higher scores (110 versus 103, $p=0.017$).

Table I. Mean scores (±SD) for the RS, SOC, PIL, STS and SF-36 PCS and SF-36 MCS among total sample, women and men.

	n	Total ($n=125$)	Women ($n=86$)	Men ($n=39$)	p-value
RS	117	148 ± 16.0	148 ± 16.9	150 ± 13.7	0.45
SOC	116	73 ± 10.3	72 ± 10.7	74 ± 9.2	0.22
PIL	115	106 ± 15.7	103 ± 16.3	110 ± 13.3	0.02
STS	122	47 ± 5.1	47 ± 5.3	47 ± 4.8	0.97
SF-36 PCS	110	37 ± 10.9	36 ± 11.1	40 ± 10.2	0.07
SF-36 MCS	110	54 ± 8.4	54 ± 8.7	53 ± 7.8	0.37

Table II. Correlation coefficients for RS, SOC, PIL and STS scores and the SF-36 PCS and SF-36 MCS scores for the total sample, women and men.

	RS	SOC	PIL	STS	PCS	MCS
RS Total	–					
RS Women	–					
RS Men	–					
SOC Total	0.35**	–				
SOC Women	0.34**	–				
SOC Men	0.37**	–				
PIL Total	0.53**	0.57**	–			
PIL Women	0.53**	0.57**	–			
PIL Men	0.53**	0.55**	–			
STS Total	0.49**	0.33**	0.58**	–		
STS Women	0.49**	0.37**	0.60**	–		
STS Men	0.48**	0.23	0.56**	–		
PCS Total	0.08	0.07	0.21*	0.12	–	
PCS Women	0.03	−0.00	0.18	0.22	–	
PCS Men	0.19	0.23	0.19	−0.15	–	
MCS Total	0.37**	0.30**	0.38**	0.30**	0.18	–
MCS Women	0.45**	0.34**	0.50**	0.36**	−0.11	–
MCS Men	0.15	0.21	0.09	0.12	−0.15	–

**$p<0.01$; *$p<0.05$.

There were no significant differences between the age groups in terms of mean scores (data not shown). Correlation coefficients between the scores on RS, SOC, PIL and STS, as well as between the two main SF-36 dimensions of physical (PCS) and mental (MCS) health in relation to the other scales, are shown in Table II. Looking at the total sample there were significant correlations between the scores on RS, SOC, PIL, STS and SF-36 MCS scores. Only one scale, the PIL, correlated significantly to SF-36 PCS. When comparing women and men, the significant correlations between scores on RS, SOC, PIL, STS and SF-36 MCS only applied for the women. There were no significant correlations between scores on RS, SOC, PIL, STS and SF-36 PCS for women or for men. Likewise, there was no significant correlation between scores on SF-36 PSC and SF-36 MCS.

To further examine the relationship and unique effects of RS, SOC, PIL and STS on physical and mental health, multiple regression analyses were preformed for the total sample and for women and men separately. The regression analyses are showed in Tables III and IV. As the variable 'living alone'

Table III. Summary of simultaneous regression analysis for variables predicting mental health for total sample, women and men.

Variable	B	SE B	Beta	Sig.
(constant)				
Total	16.69	8.59		0.055
Women	12.49	9.49		0.193
Men	31.85	18,79		0.102
RS				
Total	0.11	0.06	0.22	0.055
Women	0.13	0.06	0.25	0.054
Men	0.05	0.13	0.09	0.69
SOC				
Total	0.09	0.09	0.11	0.341
Women	0.05	0.1	0.07	0.589
Men	0.1	0.19	0.23	0.324
STS				
Total	0.11	0.19	0.07	0.573
Women	0.05	0.21	0.03	0.826
Men	0.18	0.39	0.11	0.654
PIL				
Total	0.09	0.07	0.16	0.22
Women	0.17	0.08	0.32	0.04
Men	−0.09	0.16	−0.15	0.597

$R^2 = 0.192$ and Adjusted $R^2 = 0.160$ for Total sample; $R^2 = 0.302$ and Adjusted $R^2 = 0.260$ for Women; $R^2 = 0.061$ and Adjusted $R^2 = -0.078$ for Men.

Table IV. Summary of simultaneous regression analysis for variables predicting physical health for total sample, women and men.

Variable	B	SE B	Beta	Sig.
(constant)				
Total	26.08	12.14		0.034
Women	24.12	13.96		0.089
Men	28.06	23.02		0.233
RS				
Total	−0.03	0.08	−0.05	0.707
Women	−0.09	0.09	−0.13	0.353
Men	0.17	0.16	0.22	0.306
SOC				
Total	−0.07	0.13	−0.07	0.558
Women	−0.16	0.15	−0.15	0.286
Men	0.11	0.24	0.10	0.650
STS				
Total	0.43	0.27	0.02	0.870
Women	0.46	0.32	0.22	0.147
Men	−0.91	0.47	−0.42	0.065
PIL				
Total	0.18	0.10	0.26	0.076
Women	−0.14	0.12	0.20	0.245
Men	0.20	0.20	0.26	0.321

$R^2 = 0.047$ and Adjusted $R^2 = 0.009$ for Total sample; $R^2 = 0.081$ and Adjusted $R^2 = 0.026$ for Women; $R^2 = 0.179$ and Adjusted $R^2 = 0.057$ for Men.

showed significant differences between women and men it was included in the regression but it did not change the regression models. As seen in Table III, the included variables explained 19% of the variance in mental health. The model itself reaches statistical significance ($p < 0.0005$), in spite of that none of the single predictors showed significant values. When looking at the models for women and men separately it was found that the model for women accounted for 30% of variance in mental health and that this model also reached statistical significance ($p < 0.005$). One of the variables (PIL) made a significant contribution. The model for the men accounted for only 6% of the variance in mental health and did not reach statistical significance. The models presented in Table IV shows that the variables had little influence on physical health for the women or the men.

Discussion

The aim of this study was to describe resilience, sense of coherence, purpose in life and self-transcendence in relation to perceived physical and mental health in a sample of the oldest old with high levels of cognition. The findings showed mean scores on RS and SOC that were higher among this aged population than reported for younger age groups. Mean scores for PIL and STS were comparable to those reported from younger age groups. We found significant correlations between scores on all the scales aimed to measure resilience, sense of coherence, purpose in life and self-transcendence. We also found that there were significant correlations between scores on these scales and perceived mental health among the women but not among the men. There were no correlations between scores on these scales and physical health, and no correlations between physical and mental health.

The mean RS score of 148 is the same as reported by Wagnild and Young (1993). Their sample consisted of the readership of a major senior citizen periodical in the USA, whose age span was 53–95 years. Participants in their study were more well-educated (with 66% having received education beyond high school level) than the participants in our study (9%). Three studies presented by Wagnild and Young (1993) with female samples, mean age of 31–33 years, showed mean RS scores of 139–142.

Wagnild and Young (1993) in their study among elderly people found that high RS scores were positively correlated to physical health and negatively correlated to depression. Our study shows that perceived physical health in our study population did not significantly correlate to resilience, although Staudinger and Fleeson (1996) remark that extreme physical constraint appears to limit the possibilities of resilience. The results of the present study correspond to those of other studies about resilience related to psychological health. In a study of Irish immigrants in the USA, Christopher (2000) found that a higher degree of resilience and greater life satisfaction were the strongest predictors of psychological well-being. Aroian and Norris (2000) reported that high resilience among Russian immigrants to Israel decreased the risk of being depressed by about two-fold.

The mean SOC score in the present study was 73. Sarvimäki and Stenbock Hult (2000) reported a mean score of 65 among people aged 75–97 living in Finland. Other studies using the 13-item scale have reported mean scores of between 58 and 69 (Carmel, Anson, Levenson, Bonneh & Maoz, 1991; Post-White et al., 1996). These studies were performed on people aged 21–74 years. Only the study by Ekman, Fagerberg and Lundman (2002) which included older people with heart failure (mean age 81 years) and healthy controls, had results comparable to the results of this study. In the literature only minor differences in mean SOC scores between women and men have been found (Schumacher, Gunzelmann & Braehler, 2000). The relationship between the SOC score and various aspects of perceived health has been demonstrated in many studies among people at different ages and in different life circumstances (Carmel et al., 1991; Chamberlain, Petrie & Azariah, 1992; Coward, 1996). Sagy and Antonovsky (1990) found positive correlations between the SOC and the Multidimensional Health Scale, and between activities and life satisfaction among Israeli retirees. Based on a path analysis, they proposed a model which shows that a person with a strong SOC, leading to maintenance of a high level of health, will score high on life satisfaction. Several studies report a correlation between SOC and perceived health (Langius & Lind, 1995; Sanden Eriksson, 2000) but no study has been found that relates SOC to both physical and mental health.

The mean PIL score of 106 in the present study is comparable to that reported in other studies among elderly people. Klaas (1998) reports mean scores of 109 in a convenience sample of 75–91-year-old people in the USA. Meier and Edwards (1974) in their study of >65-year-old Canadians found mean scores of 109 for men and 116 for women. In a Finnish study with a random sample of people aged 75–97 years living in ordinary housing, the mean score of PIL for the total sample was 103, but for the oldest old aged 85 years or older the mean score was 99 (Sarvimaki & Stenbock Hult, 2000). It seems therefore that our mean PIL scores are comparable to those reported elsewhere although our results show higher scores among the oldest old compared with the Finnish sample. In this study a relationship was found between perceived mental health and PIL scores. A positive correlation between well-being and PIL in older individuals has been found in several studies (Coward, 1996; Klaas, 1998; Sarvimaki & Stenbock Hult, 2000). In addition, Coward (1996) stresses that PIL is a strong predictor of well-being, based on her study using the PIL and a factor score of well-being.

The mean score of 47 on the STS is comparable to results from Upchurch's (1999) study of older persons aged 65–93 years, participants in a senior citizen organization with a mean score of 48, and to results in a study by Klaas (1998), who found a mean score of 46 among people aged 75–91 years.

Both these studies were carried out in the USA. We found only one other study that had a sample of only oldest old persons (aged 80+ years), and that was a convenience sample of independently living persons. In that study the mean STS score was 50 (Reed, 1991a). Other studies have included purposive samples. Mellors, Riley and Erlen (1997), for instance, measured self-transcendence in women with human immunodeficiency virus (HIV) and report a mean score of 46, while Chin-A-Loy and Fernsler (1998) report a mean score of 50 among older men aged 61–84 years with prostate cancer. A positive correlation between STS score and well-being/health has been established in several studies. Klaas (1998) showed correlations between STS scores and perceived health and Coward (1996) found a correlation between STS scores and self-assessed physical health among people aged 19–85. Upchurch (1999) also found a correlation between the STS results and self-rated physical health among people aged 65–93. Reed (1991b) reports a correlation between STS scores and mental health among the oldest old.

Many studies have shown a correlation between separate scales intended to measure resilience, sense of coherence, purpose in life, self-transcendence and, either health in general or physical or mental health. We have not found any study that has used all the scales we have used and correlated these to both physical and mental health. An interesting finding was the positive correlation to perceived mental health and the lack of significant correlations to physical health. To grow old means both gains and losses. Among the losses are physical diseases and disabilities (Dening et al., 1998). It is possible that development of mental resilience constitutes a form of compensation for losses of functional capacity and physical health, in accordance with selective optimisation as described by Lang et al. (2002). This fact can be understood in the light of the gains and losses described in relation to growing old.

The fact that in our study the correlation between the scales and mental health only applied to the women is difficult to explain, since the mean scores for RS, SOC, PIL and STS as well as for the SF-36 PSC and SF-36 MCS was quite comparable between the sexes. The higher proportion of women can be one explanation to the sex differences found, even if the sample size for the men ought to be sufficient for the analyses. Another question that arises is whether the questions in the questionnaires are gender biased. The RS was developed from a qualitative study among women (Wagnild & Young, 1990) and so far mostly been used in studies with a predominance of women (e.g., Christopher, 2000; Wagnild & Young, 1993). Gibson and Cook (1997) found sex differences when looking at scores of subscales of the SOC and psychological well-being measured with the 12-item General Health Questionnaire. They argue that women and men cope differently with different types of stressful situations due to their variations in both personality and their approach to health. Men born in the early 20th century in western societies have lived in the dominating male discourse stressing men as the breadwinner, and women have lived in the dominating discourse of stressing women as taking care of children and home (Hirdman, 1994). It is questionable if these perspectives have been taken into account while constructing these scales. One conclusion from our study is that there are a lack of studies looking at items and scales from a gender perspective. Sex differences among the oldest old in the area of well-being have been reported (e.g., the Berlin Aging Study). Smith, Fleeson, Geiselmann, Settersten and Kunzman (1999) concluded that women aged 85 and over reported less frequent experiences of positive emotions which are an important part of well-being and also that women represent a risk factor for lower subjective well-being. Our findings regarding sex differences shown in the regression analysis suggests a difference in the constitution of mental health among the oldest old, which should be a field for further research.

The absence of correlation between mental and physical health can be interpreted as that the bodily decline have less impact on well-being among the oldest old compared with younger people. This can be understood from the model of selective optimisation with compensation (Baltes & Carstensen, 1996) as well as from theories of transcendence such as Reed's (1991a) theory of self-transcendence, and Tornstam's (1997) theory of gerotranscendence where a shift in perspective from preoccupation with the physical self to an increased awareness of the mental self is described.

The findings could also be looked upon in the light of the driving force and strengths that can be seen as constituent elements in the concepts of resilience, sense of coherence, purpose in life and self-transcendence. The fact that the RS, SOC, PIL and STS scores correlated to each other could suggest that, what the concepts denote are similar or that the concepts share a common 'area'. As all the concepts imply some sort of process of inner growth, on the one hand, and some driving force and/or strength within oneself, on the other, this common 'area' could be looked upon as a person's inner strength. We have not found any uniform definition of the concept 'inner strength', but several studies (e.g., Coward, 1994; Rose, 1990) have been presented to give additional insight into the meaning of the concepts. In some of these studies, a phenomenological or hermeneutic approach was used and the focus was on adversities. In the descriptions of the meaning of inner strength many connections with resilience, sense of coherence, purpose in life and self-transcendence can be found. Among the components Wagnild and Young (1990) identified as constituting resilience there are self-reliance, meaningfulness and existential aloneness. Relating themes can be seen in studies on inner strength. In Coward's (1991) description of inner strength among women with breast cancer, finding purpose in life and increasing self-worth are two components that were found. Moch (1990) as well as Coward (1994) described meaning and purpose in life as components of inner strength and Coward (1994) also described aloneness as a theme. Rose (1990) found having capacity as one theme in her description of inner strength, which can be compared to self-reliance. As mentioned previously, self-transcendence is linked to spiritual connectedness. Burkhardt (1993) described the connection between spirituality and inner strength while Kinney (1996) listed trusting one's inner voice, self-reliance and transcendence as important constituents when mobilizing inner strength. In addition, in a concept analysis of inner strength, Dingley, Roux and Bush (2000) reported that sense of coherence is a concept related to inner strength. They also found that one of the consequences of inner strength is psychological well-being/health, which corresponds with the results of the present study.

Summary and implications

The myth that the older a person gets, the frailer in all aspects of life she or he becomes has not been supported in our study. The findings show that the oldest old in this study in northern Swedish had higher (or at least the same level of) sense of coherence, resilience, purpose in life and self-transcendence as younger persons. This study shows correlations between scores on scales aimed to measure what these concepts denote and mental health and it can be assumed that good mental health helps persons overcome negative experiences such as physical limitations and losses. The study also shows connections between resilience, sense of coherence, purpose in life and self-transcendence, and these concepts liaison to inner strength. As they represent aspects of a driving force and strengths which are crucial for retaining health and handling adversities it is of utmost importance that these inner strengths are taken into consideration in health care and social care services, especially among older people who are more prone to diseases, impairments and losses. Inner strength can be enhanced (Dancy, 1994) suggesting that it might be a worthwhile area for interventions to improve health and coping. The different impact of various aspects of inner strength among women and men might be important in the perspective of promoting mental health in old age.

To focus on a person's inner strength is to apply a positive health perspective that is important as a counterbalance to the dominant dysfunctional perspective often taken in the health care system.

Acknowledgements

This work was supported by grants from The Vårdal Research Foundation (No. V2000379), The Swedish Research Council (No. 521-2002-6510), King Gustaf V and Queen Viktoria's Foundation, the Research Foundation of the Faculty of Medicine and Odontology at Umeå University and the Detlof Research Foundation.

References

Åkerberg, H. (1987). *Livet som utmaning: Existentiell ångest hos svenska gymnasieelever* (Life as a challenge: Existential anxiety among pupils of the Swedish upper secondary school) [In Swedish]. Stockholm: Norstedts.
Antonovsky, A. (1987). *Unraveling the mystery of health: How people manage stress and stay well.* San Francisco: Jossey-Bass Inc. Publisher.
Antonovsky, A. (1993). Complexity, conflict, chaos, coherence, coercion and civility. *Social Science and Medicine, 37*(8), 969–974.
Antonovsky, H., & Sagy, S. (1986). The development of a sense of coherence and its impact on responses to stress situations. *Journal of Social Psychology, 126*(2), 213–225.
Aroian, K. J., & Norris, A. E. (2000). Resilience, stress, and depression among Russian immigrants to Israel. *Western Journal of Nursing Research, 22*(1), 54–67.
Baltes, M. M., Kuehl, K. P., & Sowarka, D. (1992). Testing for limits of cognitive reserve capacity: A promising strategy for early diagnosis of dementia? *Journal of Gerontology, 47*(3), 165–167.
Baltes, M. M., & Carstensen, L. L. (1996). The process of successful aging. *Ageing and Society, 16*, 397–422.
Baltes, P. B. (1997). On the incomplete architecture of human ontogeny. selection, optimization, and compensation as foundation of developmental theory. *American Psychologist, 52* (4), 366-380.
Bauer, T., & Barron, C. R. (1995). Nursing interventions for spiritual care: Preferences of the community-based elderly. *Journal of Holistic Nursing, 13* (3), 268–279.
Bould, S., Smith, M. H., & Longino Jr, C. F. (1997). Ability, disability, and the oldest old. *Journal of Aging and Social Policy, 9*(1), 13–31.
Bryant, L. L., Beck, A., & Fairclough, D. L. (2000). Factors that contribute to positive perceived health in an older population. *Journal of Aging and Health, 12*(2), 169–192.
Burkhardt, M. A. (1993). Characteristics of spirituality in the lives of women in a rural Appalachian community. *Journal of Transcultural Nursing, 4*(2), 12–18.
Callahan, L. F., & Pineus, T. (1995). The sense of coherence scale in patients with rheumatoid arthritis. *Arthritis Care and Research, 8*(9), 28–35.
Carmel, S., Anson, O., Levenson, A., Bonneh, D. Y., & Maoz, B. (1991). Life events, sense of coherence and health: Gender differences on the kibbutz. *Social Science and Medicine, 32*(10), 1089–1096.
Carstensen, L., Isaacowitz, D., & Charles, S. (1999). Taking time seriously. *American Psychologist, 54*(3), 165-181.
Chamberlain, K., Petrie, K., & Azariah, R. (1992). The role of optimism and sense of coherence in predicting recovery following surgery. *Psychology and Health, 7*(4), 301–310.
Chin-A-Loy, S. S., & Fernsler, J. I. (1998). Self-transcendence in older men attending a prostate cancer support group. *Cancer Nursing, 21*(5), 358–363.
Christopher, K. A. (2000). Determinants of psychological well-being in Irish immigrants. *Western Journal of Nursing Research, 22*(2), 123–140.

Coward, D. D. (1990). The lived experience of self-transcendence in women with advanced breast cancer. *Nursing Science Quarterly, 3*(4), 162–169.
Coward, D. D. (1991). Self-transcendence and emotional well-being in women with advanced breast cancer. *Oncology Nursing Forum, 18*(5), 857–863.
Coward, D. D. (1994). Meaning and purpose in the lives of persons with AIDS. *Public Health Nursing, 11*(5), 331–336.
Coward, D. D. (1996). Self-transcendence and correlates in a healthy population. *Nursing Research, 45*(2), 116–121.
Crumbaugh, J. C., & Henrion, R. (1988). The PIL Test: Administration, interpretation, uses theory and critique. *International Forum for Logotherapy, 11*(2), 76–88.
Crumbaugh, J. C., & Maholick, L. T. (1964). An experimental study in existentialism: The psychometric approach to Frankl's concept of noogenic neurosis. *Journal of Clinical Psychology, 20*(2), 200–207.
Crumbaugh, J. C. (1968). Cross-validation of purpose-in-life test based on Frankl's concepts. *Journal of Individual Psychology, 24*(1), 74–81.
Dancy, B. L. (1994). African-American men: The ideal AIDS program. *Journal of National Black Nurses' Association, 7*(1), 60–67.
Dening, T. R., Chi, L. Y., Brayne, C., Huppert, F. A., Paykel, E. S., & O'Connor, D. W. (1998). Changes in self-rated health, disability and contact with services in a very elderly cohort: A 6-year follow-up study. *Age and Ageing, 27*(1), 23–33.
Dingley, C. E., Roux, G., & Bush, H. A. (2000). Inner strength: A concept analysis. *Journal of Theory Construction and Testing, 4*(2), 30–35.
Dyer, J. G., & McGuinness, T. M. (1996). Resilience: Analysis of the concept. *Archives of Psychiatric Nursing, 10*(5), 276–282.
Ekman, I., Fagerberg, B., & Lundman, B. (2002). Health-related quality of life and sense of coherence among elderly patients with severe chronic heart failure in comparison with healthy controls. *Heart and Lung: The Journal of Acute and Critical Care, 31*(2), 94–101.
Ellermann, C. R., & Reed, P. G. (2001). Self-transcendence and depression in middle-age adults. *Western Journal of Nursing Research, 23*(7), 698–713.
Femia, E. E., Zarit, S. H., & Johansson, B. (2001). The disablement process in very late life: A study of the oldest-old in Sweden. *Journal of Gerontology: Series B: Psychological Sciences and Social Sciences, 56b*(1), 12–23.
Folstein, M. F., Folstein, S. E., & McHugh, P. R. (1975). 'Mini-mental state'. A practical method for grading the cognitive state of patients for the clinician. *Journal of Psychiatric Research, 12*(3), 189–198.
Frankl, V. E. (1963). *Man's search for meaning: An introduction to logotherapy.* New York: Washington Square Press.
Gibson, L. M., & Cook, M. J. (1997). Do health questionnaires which do not consider sex differences miss important information? *Psychological Reports, 81*(1), 163–171.
Heidrich, S. M., & D'Amico, D. (1993). Physical and mental health relationships in the very old. *Journal of Community Health Nursing, 10*(1), 11–21.
Hirdman, Y. (1994). *Women—from possibility to problem.* Stockholm: Arbetslivscentrum.
Jagger, C., Clarke, M., & Cook, A. J. (1989). Mental and physical health of elderly people: Five-year follow-up of a total population. *Age and Ageing, 18*(2), 77–82.
Jagger, C., Spiers, N. A., & Clarke, M. (1993). Factors associated with decline in function, institutionalization and mortality of elderly people. *Age and Ageing, 22*(3), 190–197.
Kinney, C. K. (1996). Transcending breast cancer: Reconstructing one's self. *Issues in Mental Health Nursing, 17*(3), 201–216.
Klaas, D. (1998). Testing two elements of spirituality in depressed and non-depressed elders. *International Journal of Psychiatric Nursing Research, 4*(2), 452–462.

Kunzmann, U., Little, T. D., & Smith, J. (2000). Is age-related stability of subjective well-being a paradox? Cross-sectional and longitudinal evidence from the Berlin Aging Study. *Psychology and Aging*, *15*(3), 511–526.

Lang, F. R., Rieckmann, N., & Baltes, M. (2002). Adapting to aging losses: Do resources facilitate strategies of selection, compensation, and optimization in everyday functioning? *Journal of Gerontology*, *57*(6), 501–509.

Langius, A., & Bjoervell, H. (1993). Coping ability and functional status in a Swedish population sample. *Scandinavian Journal of Caring Sciences*, *7*(1), 3–10.

Langius, A., & Lind, M. G. (1995). Well-being and coping in oral and pharyngeal cancer patients. *European Journal of Cancer. Part B, Oral Oncology*, *31b*(4), 242–249.

Mahoney, R. I., & Barthel, D. W. (1965). Functional evaluation: The Barthel index. *Maryland State Medical Journal*, *14*, 56–62.

Meier, A., & Edwards, H. (1974). Purpose-in-life test: Age and sex differences. *Journal of Clinical Psychology*, *30*(3), 384–386.

Mellors, M. P., Riley, T. A., & Erlen, J. A. (1997). HIV, self-transcendence, and quality of life. *Journal of the Association of Nurses in AIDS Care*, *8*(2), 59–69.

Moch, S. D. (1990). Health within the experience of breast cancer. *Journal of Advanced Nursing*, *15*(12), 1426–1435.

Nesbitt, B. J., & Heidrich, S. M. (2000). Sense of coherence and illness appraisal in older women's quality of life. *Research in Nursing & Health*, *23*(1), 25–34.

Pascucci, M. A., & Loving, G. L. (1997). Ingredients of an old and healthy life: A centenarian perspective. *Journal of Holistic Nursing*, *15*(2), 199–213.

Post-White, J., Ceronsky, C., Kreitzer, M. J., Nickelson, K., Drew, D., Mackey, K. W., et al. (1996). Hope, spirituality, sense of coherence, and quality of life in patients with cancer. *Oncology Nursing Forum*, *23*(10), 1571–1579.

Rappaport, H., Fossler, R. J., Bross, L. S., & Gilden, D. (1993). Future time, death anxiety, and life purpose among older adults. *Death Studies*, *17*(4), 369–379.

Reed, P. G. (1989). Mental health of older adults. *Western Journal of Nursing Research*, *11*(2), 161–163.

Reed, P. G. (1991a). Toward a nursing theory of self-transcendence: Deductive reformulation using developmental theories. *Advances in Nursing Science*, *13*(4), 64–77.

Reed, P. G. (1991b). Self-transcendence and mental health in oldest-old adults. *Nursing Research*, *40*(1), 5–11.

Rennemark, M., & Hagberg, B. (1997). Social network patterns among the elderly in relation to their perceived life-history in an Eriksonian perspective. *Aging & Mental Health*, *1*, 321–331.

Rennemark, M., & Hagberg, B. (1999). What makes old people perceive symptoms of illness? The impact of psychological and social factors. *Aging & Mental Health*, *3*(1), 79–87.

Richardson, G. E. (2002). The metatheory of resilience and resiliency. *Journal of Clinical Psychology*, *58*(3), 307–321.

Rose, J. F. (1990). Psychologic health of women: A phenomenologic study of women's inner strength. *Advances in Nursing Science*, *12*(2), 56–70.

Rowe, J. W., & Kahn, R. L. (2000). Successful aging and disease prevention. *Advances in Renal Replacement Therapy*, *7*(1), 70–77.

Sagy, S., & Antonovsky, A. (1990). Coping with retirement: Does the sense of coherence matter less in the kibbutz? *International Journal of Health Sciences*, *1*(4), 233–242.

Sanden Eriksson, B. (2000). Coping with type-2 diabetes: The role of sense of coherence compared with active management. *Journal of Advanced Nursing*, *31*(6), 1393–1397.

Sarvimäki, A., & Stenbock-Hult, B. (2000). Quality of life in old age described as a sense of well-being, meaning and value. *Journal of Advanced Nursing*, *32*(4), 1025–1033.

Schumacher, J., Gunzelmann, T., & Braehler, E. (2000). Deutsche normierung der sense of coherence scale von Antonovsky. (Standardization of Antonovsky's sense of coherence scale in the German population) [In German]. *Diagnostica*, *46*(4), 208–213.

Smith, J., Fleeson, W., Geiselmann, B., Settersten Jr, R. A., & Kunzmann, U. (1999). Sources of well-being in very old age. In P. B. Baltes & K. U. Mayer (Eds), *The Berlin aging study: Aging from 70 to 100*. Cambridge: Cambridge University Press.

Sonn, U. (1996). Longitudinal studies of dependence in daily activities among elderly persons. *Scandinavian Journal of Rehabilitative Medicine*, *34*, 1–35.

Staudinger, U. M., & Fleeson, W. (1996). Self and personality in old and very old age: A sample case of resilience? *Development and Psychopathology*, *8*(4), 867–885.

Staudinger, U. M., Marsiske, M., & Baltes, P. B. (1993). Resilience and levels of reserve capacity in later adulthood: Perspectives from life-span theory. *Development and Psychopathology*, *5*(4), 541–566.

Stouffer Calderon, K. (2001). Making the connection between depression and activity levels among the oldest-old: A measure of life satisfaction. *Activities, Adaptation and Aging*, *25*(2), 59–73.

Sullivan, M., Karlsson, J., & Ware Jr, J. E., (1995). The Swedish SF-36 health survey-I. Evaluation of data quality, scaling assumptions, reliability and construct validity across general populations in Sweden. *Social Science & Medicine*, *41*(10), 1349–1358.

Tornstam, L. (1997). Gerotrancendence: The contemplative dimension of aging. *Journal of Aging Studies*, *11*(2), 143–154.

Upchurch, S. (1999). Self-transcendence and activities of daily living: The woman with the pink slippers. *Journal of Holistic Nursing*, *17*(3), 251–266.

Wagnild, G., & Young, H. M. (1990). Resilience among older women. *IMAGE: Journal of Nursing Scholarship*, *22*(4), 252–255.

Wagnild, G. M., & Young, H. M. (1993). Development and psychometric evaluation of the Resilience Scale. *Journal of Nursing Measurement*, *1*(2), 165–178.

Ware Jr, J. E., & Sherbourne, C. D. (1992). The MOS 36-item short-form health survey (SF-36): I. Conceptual framework and item selection. *Medical Care*, *30*(6), 473–483.

Williams, S. J. (1990). The relationship among stress, hardiness, sense of coherence, and illness in critical care nurses. *Medical Psychotherapy*, *3*, 171–186.

Zarit, S. H., Johansson, B., & Malmberg, B. (1995). Changes in functional competency in the oldest old: A longitudinal study. *Journal of Aging and Health*, *7*(1), 3–23.

[7]

Variation in the Impact of Social Network Characteristics on Physical Functioning in Elderly Persons: MacArthur Studies of Successful Aging

Jennifer B. Unger,[1] Gail McAvay,[2] Martha L. Bruce,[3] Lisa Berkman,[4] and Teresa Seeman[5]

[1]University of Southern California.
[2]Columbia University, New York City.
[3]Cornell University Medical College, Ithaca, New York.
[4]Harvard University School of Public Health.
[5]University of California, Los Angeles.

Objectives. Social support and social networks have been shown to exert significant effects on health and functioning among elderly persons. Although theorists have speculated that the strength of these effects may differ as a function of sociodemographic characteristics and prior health status, few studies have directly tested the moderating effects of these variables.

Methods. Longitudinal data from the MacArthur Study of Successful Aging were used to examine the effects of structural and functional social support on changes in physical functioning over a 7-year period, measured by the Nagi scale, in a sample of initially high-functioning men and women aged 70 to 79 years. Multiple regression analyses were used to test the main effects of social support and social network variables, as well as their interactions with gender, income, and baseline physical performance.

Results. After controlling for potential confounding effects, respondents with more social ties showed less functional decline. The beneficial effects of social ties were stronger for respondents who were male or had lower levels of baseline physical performance.

Discussion. The effects of social support and social networks may vary according to the individual's gender and baseline physical capabilities. Studies of functional decline among elderly persons should not ignore this population variation in the effects of social networks.

THE aging of the United States population, recent developments in medical treatment, and improvements in health behaviors have resulted in a dramatic increase in the elderly population. Unfortunately, many elderly people experience functional disabilities that compromise their quality of life, so the added years of life can be marred by physical impairment. As a consequence, preservation of functional independence in elderly persons has become an important goal of medical research. Although it was once commonly believed that functional decline was inevitable in old age, recent studies have revealed that some elderly people seem to be protected from functional decline, and a significant proportion of impaired elderly people regain physical functioning (Beckett et al., 1996; Crimmins & Saito, 1993).

Subsequent studies have identified the demographic, medical, behavioral, and psychological characteristics associated with maintenance of functional independence. Compared with elderly people who experience functional decline, "successful agers"—those who experience little or no decline—are more likely to be male, White, free of chronic disease, and have high levels of education and income (Mor, Wilcox, Rakowski, & Hiris, 1994; Seeman, Berkman, Blazer, & Rowe, 1994; Strawbridge, Cohen, Shema, & Kaplan, 1996). Those who practice healthy behaviors such as physical activity (Seeman et al., 1995; Simonsick et al., 1993; Strawbridge et al., 1996) and refrain from unhealthy behaviors such as smoking (Parker, Thorslund, Lundberg, & Kareholt, 1996) and heavy alcohol consumption (Scherr, LaCroix, Wallace, & Berkman, 1992) also are likely to age more successfully. In addition, psychosocial factors such as self-efficacy (Mendes de Leon, Seeman, Baker, Richardson, & Tinetti, 1996; Seeman & Unger, 1997), lack of depression (Strawbridge et al., 1996), and good self-rated health (Mor et al., 1994) are associated with more successful aging.

Social support and social networks also are associated with health outcomes in elderly persons, including a lower risk of mortality, cardiovascular disease, cancer mortality, and functional decline (for reviews, see Berkman, 1995; Seeman, 1996; Thoits, 1995). These protective effects of social networks may result from several processes. These include provision of access to information about health and health care services (Bloom, 1990), encouragement of healthy behaviors (Bovbjerg et al., 1995; Mermelstein, Cohen, Lichtenstein, Kanmark, & Baer, 1986), encouragement of health care utilization (Bleeker, Lamers, Leenders, & Kruyssen, 1995), provision of tangible aid (Thoits, 1995), provision of emotional support to facilitate coping with life stress (Thoits, 1995), enhancement of feelings of self-esteem and control (Krause & Borawski-Clark, 1994), and influences on neuroendocrine or immune functioning (Seeman, Charpentier, Berkman, et al., 1994; Uchino, Cacioppo, & Kiecolt-Glaser, 1996).

Although the main effects of social variables on health have been documented, the extent to which these effects may vary across population subgroups is not known. Three variables that may moderate the effects of social support/social networks on health are income, gender, and level of physical functioning, as described below.

Income

Social support may have stronger benefits for elderly people with low income. People with low income may have greater exposure to health threats including inadequate or unsafe housing conditions, crime-ridden neighborhoods, and inadequate nutrition (Robert & House, 1996). These people may have a greater need for social support and they may suffer more when they lack adequate social support. Conversely, elderly people with adequate income are able to afford health care, assistive devices, nutritious food, travel, and entertainment, and they are able to pay others to help them with household tasks. Therefore, elderly people with adequate income may be able to compensate for a lack of social support by paying for appropriate housing, household help, or travel to visit distant relatives or friends. This may result in an interaction between social support and income; lack of social support may lead to more negative health effects among people with low income.

Gender

The effects of social support also may differ by gender. Many elderly women may have devoted significant portions of their lives to caretaking and developing supportive friendships, so they may be more accustomed to marshaling social support networks and asking for help. Many elderly men, in contrast, may have devoted significant portions of their lives to career achievement, so they may not have developed supportive social networks or the skills to marshal social support. This gender difference in social networks can lead to two different predictions about the nature of gender differences in the effects of social support on health. First, because women may be more skilled at marshaling social support, the effects of social support may be stronger for women, because women are better prepared to recruit social network members to provide instrumental or emotional support in the appropriate ways at the appropriate times. Men, in contrast, may be reluctant to ask for support, or they may seek it less skillfully than women do. This would lead to the prediction that social support would have stronger effects for women, because women are able to obtain and use it more effectively.

Conversely, social support may have stronger effects for men. Because many men are unaccustomed to marshaling social support when they need it, those men with low levels of social support may be especially isolated, which may put them at especially high risk for negative health outcomes. Women with low social support, however, may be able to compensate for social isolation by forming new social contacts or strengthening weak ones. This scenario would predict that social support would show stronger effects for men, because there would be a greater disparity in health between people with low and high social support among men than among women.

It is not clear whether there are gender differences in the effects of social support on health outcomes. Some studies have found more beneficial effects for men (Barer, 1994; House, Robbins, & Metzner, 1982; Umberson, Wortman, & Kessler, 1992); some have found more beneficial effects for women (Tower & Kasl, 1996); and some have found no gender differences (Berkman & Syme, 1979; Umberson, 1996). In addition, most research on gender differences in the effects of social support has focused on mortality or psychological distress; few studies have used functional status as an outcome variable.

Health Status

Social support/social networks also may have stronger effects for elderly people who are in poorer health. The support and assistance provided by social network members might be more valuable for elderly people with lower levels of physical functioning, because these individuals require more assistance. Elderly people with high levels of physical functioning are more able to perform activities of daily living (ADLs), and they do not have to cope with the severe emotional consequences of chronic illness and functional limitations. Therefore, the buffering effects of social support and social networks may be especially powerful for those elderly people who have impaired physical functioning and who need to cope with the physical and psychological consequences of their limitations. The combination of poor physical functioning and low social support may have especially harmful consequences for health.

To date, most studies of social influences on health have concentrated on main effects; few have investigated whether these effects vary by gender, income, or health status. The present study examines two functional aspects of social ties (instrumental support and emotional support) and two structural aspects of social ties (marital status and number of other social ties) in relation to changes in self-reported physical functioning over a 7-year period. More specifically, this study investigates whether the strength of these relationships varies by gender, income, or health status. Analyses were performed to answer two research questions:

1. Are social support and social network characteristics associated with decline in self-reported physical functioning over a 7-year period?
2. Do the associations between social network characteristics and physical functioning differ according to gender, income, or baseline health status?

METHODS

Sample

The data used in this study are from the MacArthur Studies of Successful Aging, a longitudinal study of relatively high-functioning men and women ages 70–79 years. As described by Berkman et al. (1993), participants were subsampled on the basis of age and physical and cognitive functioning from three community-based cohorts of the National Institute on Aging's Established Populations for Epidemiologic Studies of the Elderly (EPESE) in Durham, North Carolina, East Boston, Massachusetts, and New Haven, Connecticut (Cornoni-Huntley et al., 1986). Only those respondents aged 70–79 were included in the study to minimize the effects of age on subsequent analyses of factors associated with the maintenance of health and functioning.

Of the 4,030 men and women who met the age criterion, 1,313 were identified as high functioning on the basis of four criteria of physical functioning (no ADL disability, no more than one reported mild disability on eight items tapping gross mobility and range of motion; ability to hold a semitandem balance for at least 10 seconds; and ability to stand from a seated position five times within 20 seconds) and two criteria of cognitive functioning (scores of 6 or more correct on the 9-item Short Portable Mental Status Questionnaire [Pfeiffer, 1975] and ability to remember at least three elements on a delayed recall of a short story).

Of the 1,313 men and women classified as high functioning, 1,189 (90.6%) agreed to participate and provided informed consent. Baseline data were collected between May 1988 and December 1989. The cohort was reinterviewed between October 1995 and February 1997. The mean time between interviews was 86 months. Of the 1,189 men and women interviewed at baseline, 273 (23%) died before the follow-up interview (32% of the men and 16% of the women). Of those who survived, complete data on physical functioning at both baseline and follow-up were available for 850 respondents. These 850 respondents, who represent 93% of those who were alive at follow-up and 71% of the original sample, constitute the sample used in this analysis.

Measures

Dependent variable.—The outcome measure used in this analysis is change in physical functioning from 1988 to 1995, as measured by the Nagi physical functioning scale (Nagi, 1976). This scale measures the respondent's perceived difficulty in performing five tasks: pushing/pulling large objects, stooping/kneeling, lifting/carrying 10 pounds, reaching/extending arms, and writing/handling small objects. The Nagi score represents the number of tasks that the respondent rated as "some difficulty," "a lot of difficulty," or "unable to do." Nagi scores can range from 0 to 5, with higher scores indicating more impairment. Because the baseline sample was restricted to individuals with Nagi scores of 0 or 1, the change in Nagi score could range from −1 (a 1-point improvement in functioning) to 5 (a 5-point decline in functioning).

Measures of social support and social networks.—Measures of both structural and functional aspects of social networks were included as predictors of impairment. Structural measures included marital status (married vs not married) and number of social ties, other than the spouse. Functional measures included emotional support and instrumental support. These constructs were measured separately for the respondent's spouse, children, and friends/relatives, and the three scores were averaged to create a single score for each type of functional support. Emotional support was measured based on the reported frequency with which the respondent's social network members "will listen when you have a problem" and make the respondent "feel loved and cared for." Instrumental support was measured based on the reported frequency with which network members "help with daily tasks" and "provide information." As previously reported (Seeman, Charpentier et al., 1994), these measures exhibit adequate test–retest reliability.

Covariates.—To control for confounding, variables found to be associated with social support and/or health status in previous studies were evaluated as potential covariates. Correlation analyses were conducted to determine which of these variables were associated significantly with the dependent variable, and these variables were retained for inclusion in subsequent multiple regression analyses.

Demographic variables included age, gender, ethnicity (White vs Black), education (high school graduate vs less than high school), and income (less than $10,000/year, over $10,000/year, or unknown). The education variable was dichotomized because its distribution was skewed. For income, the "unknown" category was included because a substantial proportion of the respondents (9%) either refused to provide income information or said they did not know their income. Rather than excluding these respondents from the analysis, we created dummy variables for income less than $10,000/year and income missing.

Baseline physical and psychological health status variables were included as covariates because older adults in poor health typically require and receive higher levels of social support (Wilcox, Kasl, & Berkman, 1994) and are at higher risk of functional decline (Seeman et al., 1995). These included a physical performance measure derived from tests of balance, gait, chair stands, foot taps, and manual ability (described in detail by Seeman, Charpentier, et al., 1994) and number of prevalent chronic conditions at baseline. Depressive symptoms were measured with the depression subscale of the Hopkins Symptom Checklist (Derogatis, Lipman, Rickels, Uhlenhuth, & Covi, 1974).

Health behaviors such as alcohol use, smoking, and physical activity also were included as covariates. Smoking was expressed in pack-years. Levels of physical activity were assessed based on self-reported frequency of current leisure- and work-related activity. Each activity mentioned was classified as light, moderate, or strenuous based on intensity codes (described by Seeman et al., 1995). Summary scales were derived by multiplying the frequency of activity (5 categories, ranging from never to 3+ times/week) by the intensity and summing over all activities. To assess alcohol use, respondents were asked how many days in the past month they had consumed beer, wine, or liquor, and how many drinks they had at a time. These responses were used to create an estimate of the amount of ethyl alcohol consumed in the past month (Armor, Polich, & Stambul, 1975).

Analysis

The model-building process involved several steps. First, correlations were computed between the dependent variable (change in Nagi impairment) and each hypothesized covariate (demographic and health status variables). The covariates that were significantly correlated with change in Nagi impairment were included along with the four social support/social network variables in a multiple regression model predicting change in Nagi impairment, to determine the effects of social support/social networks after controlling for the covariates. Finally, to determine whether the effects of the social support/social network variables were moderated by gender, income, or physical health status, interaction terms were added to the model. There were 12 interaction terms, representing the 4 social support/social network variables crossed with the 3 potential moderators.

RESULTS

Table 1 shows the baseline demographic characteristics of the 340 men and 510 women who were alive and had complete data in 1995. The mean age of the respondents was 74.2 years (standard deviation = 2.7 years). The mean change in Nagi impairment was 0.82 impairments (standard deviation = 1.36 impairments).

Several variables differed significantly by gender. The women in the sample were older than the men (t = 2.37, p < .05), were more likely to have income less than $10,000 per year (chi square = 95.09, p < .001), were less likely to be married (chi square = 142.46, p < .001), smoked less (t = 8.00, p < .0005), drank less alcohol (t = 7.56, p < .0005), had less physical activity (t = 4.38, p < .0005), had lower physical performance scores (t = 10.42, p < .0005), had higher emotional support (t = 3.11, p < .005), had fewer social ties (t = 3.61, p < .0005), and showed larger changes in Nagi impairment (t = 4.42, p < .0005). The other variables in the model did not differ significantly by gender.

The correlations between each hypothesized predictor variable and functional decline are shown in Table 2. Several of the hypothesized covariates were correlated significantly with functional decline. These included age, gender, income, baseline chronic conditions, alcohol use, physical activity, physical performance, and depressive symptoms. These variables were retained for inclusion in the multiple regression described below. In addition, the correlations between the social support/social network variables and functional decline were assessed. Marital status was correlated significantly with functional decline, and the correlation between emotional support and functional decline approached statistical significance (p = .0798).

Table 3 shows the results of the multiple regression analyses predicting change in Nagi impairment. In this model, the effects of each covariate and social support/social network variable are controlled for the effects of the other variables. Only those covariates found to be significantly correlated with change in Nagi impairment were retained for inclusion in the multiple regression model. Interaction terms were added to the model, as described in the Methods section, to evaluate the potential moderating influences of gender, income, and baseline physical functioning.

Social support/social networks.—The only social support/social network variable significantly associated with functional decline was number of social ties at baseline, which was associated with less functional decline. The main effects of the other social support/social network variables were not associated significantly with functional decline, after controlling for the other variables.

Some of the social support/social network variables were intercorrelated. However, these associations were only modest, so multicollinearity is not a problem. Instrumental support was correlated positively with emotional support (r = .34, p < .0005), marital status (r = .10, p < .005), and number of social ties (r = .22, p < .0005). Emotional support also was correlated positively with number of social ties (r = .19, p < .0005).

Although marital status was associated significantly with functional decline in the correlation analyses, additional stepwise analyses (not shown) indicated that it became nonsignificant after depressive symptoms, income, and age were added to the model. Number of social ties was not associated significantly with functional decline in the correlation analyses, but it became significant after controlling for income, depressive symptoms, age, physical activity, and emotional support.

Table 1. Demographic Characteristics of Respondents at Baseline (1988)

	n	Percent
Gender		
Male	340	40
Female	510	60
Age		
70–72	281	33
73–75	282	33
76–80	287	34
Ethnicity		
White	700	82
Other	146	17
Missing	4	0
Education		
<High school	433	51
High school +	417	49
Income		
≤$10,000	341	40
$10,000+	433	51
Missing	76	9
Marital status		
Married	399	47
Not married	450	53
Missing	1	0
Change in Nagi score 1998–1995		
−1	59	7
0	432	51
1	145	17
2	94	11
3	66	8
4	42	5
5	12	1
Instrumental support		
0–1	70	8
1.1–2	399	47
2.1–3	238	28
Missing	6	1
Emotional support		
0–1	14	2
1.1–2	169	20
2.1–3	662	78
Missing	5	1
Number of social ties		
0–5	177	21
6–10	326	38
11–15	218	26
16+	127	15
Missing	2	0

Covariates.—Several of the covariates were associated significantly with functional decline. These included older age, lower physical activity, lower physical performance, and higher levels of depressive symptoms.

Table 2. Correlations Between Hypothisized Covariates and Change in Nagi Impairment Scores

Variable	Correlation	p value
Hypothesized Covariates		
Age	.122	.0003
Female gender	.140	.0001
Black ethnicity	-.024	.4828
High school education	-.039	.2517
Income over $10,000	-.148	.0001
Income missing	-.012	.7208
Baseline chronic conditions	.071	.0396
Smoking	-.019	.5882
Alcohol use	-.103	.0027
Physical activity	-.116	.0007
Physical performance	-.131	.0001
Depressive symptoms	.127	.0001
Social Support / Social Network Variables		
Instrumental support	-.020	.5669
Emotional support	-.060	.0798
Married	-.126	.0002
Number of social ties	-.031	.3738

Table 3. Predictors of Change in Nagi Impairment

Variable	b	SE	t value	p value
Covariates				
Age	.041	.018	2.34	.0196
Female gender	-.443	.539	-0.82	.4109
Income over $10,000	-.560	.523	-1.07	.2839
Baseline chronic conditions	.077	.052	1.48	.1391
Alcohol use	-.008	.006	-1.40	.1614
Physical activity	-.003	.002	-2.19	.0291
Physical performance	-1.103	.530	-2.08	.0378
Depressive symptoms	.046	.015	3.15	.0017
Social Support / Social Networks				
Instrumental support	-.233	.555	-0.42	.6741
Emotional support	-.547	.765	-0.72	.4748
Married	-.175	.797	-0.22	.8263
Number of social ties	-.235	.070	-3.34	.0009
Interactions				
Female × Instrumental	.154	.154	1.00	.3184
Female × Emotional	-.099	.216	-0.46	.6464
Female × Married	.279	.226	1.23	.2189
Female × Social Ties	.044	.021	2.09	.0372
Income × Instrumental	.145	.142	1.02	.3095
Income × Emotional	.034	.206	0.17	.8683
Income × Married	-.125	.211	-0.59	.5543
Income × Social Ties	.011	.020	.054	.5872
Physical perf × Instrumental	-.023	.149	-0.15	.8774
Physical perf × Emotional	.184	.213	0.86	.3874
Physical perf × Married	-.100	.214	-0.47	.6416
Physical perf × Social Ties	.058	.109	3.11	.0019

Note: Unstandardized regression coefficients.

Interactions.—Two of the 12 interaction terms, both involving the number of social ties, were significant. The interaction between gender and number of social ties ($p < .05$) is shown in Figure 1. Overall, respondents with larger numbers of social ties at baseline reported less functional decline. As shown in Figure 1, the association between number of social ties and functional decline was stronger for men than for women. In other words, although social ties were beneficial for respondents of both genders, they had a stronger protective effect for men than for women. The largest gender differences in functional decline were observed at the highest levels of social ties.

The interaction between baseline physical performance and number of social ties ($p < .005$) is shown in Figure 2. Although baseline physical performance was analyzed as a continuous variable in the regression analyses, it is shown as a dichotomous variable to simplify the illustration. This interaction indicates that the association between number of social ties at baseline and subsequent functional decline was stronger for individuals who were below the mean on baseline physical performance. Social ties were protective regardless of baseline physical performance, but they were especially protective for respondents with low levels of baseline physical performance.

Because the analyses focused on changes in Nagi impairment, they did not include the 273 respondents who died before the 1995 follow-up interview. To confirm the effects with a less restricted sample, we ran a similar analysis on the entire baseline sample, using mortality as the dependent variable. The results of this analysis were consistent with the analyses of Nagi impairment (data not shown).

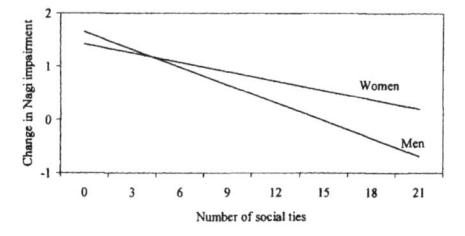

Figure 1. Change in Nagi impairment, according to gender and number of social ties.

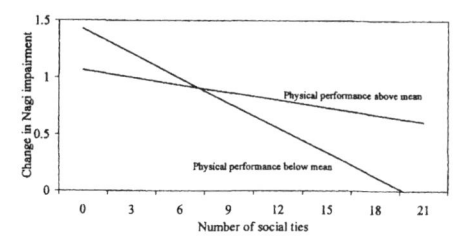

Figure 2. Change in Nagi impairment, according to baseline physical performance and number of social ties.

Discussion

These results indicate that the effects of social ties on the risk of functional decline in elderly persons are moderated by gender and baseline physical performance. Specifically, social ties had a stronger protective effect for men and for respondents with low levels of baseline physical performance.

Our finding that social support/social networks had a stronger effect on functional status for men than for women is consistent with other research findings for other health outcomes. A number of prospective studies have reported stronger effects for social support and/or social networks with respect to cardiovascular and all-cause mortality for men (Berkman et al., 1993; House et al., 1982; see also Seeman, 1996 for review). In particular, the harmful effect of widowhood on cardiovascular morbidity and mortality has been shown to be stronger among men than among women (Berkman et al., 1993). Because older men who are widowed or socially isolated are at high risk for functional decline and mortality, this high-risk group should be a target for health promotion interventions. Studies also are needed to determine what causes elderly men to become socially isolated, and how this social isolation and its associated harmful health effects can be prevented.

The stronger protective effect of social ties among respondents with low levels of baseline physical performance also has important implications for interventions to promote successful aging. Social ties appear to be most important for elderly people with more limited physical ability. This suggests that interventions to increase social support, such as arranging group activities for elderly people or pairing them with "buddies" in the community, may be especially powerful for those elderly people who already have some physical impairment or activity limitations. However, because of their restricted mobility, these older adults may pose the greatest challenge for health promotion programs and services. Greater efforts are needed to implement social activities that are accessible and can be enjoyed by people with physical impairments.

We had hypothesized that income also would moderate the effects of social support/social networks on functional decline. However, the moderating effects of income were not significant. Although higher income was associated with less functional decline in the correlational analysis, the main effect of income became nonsignificant in the multiple regression model, and none of the interaction terms involving income were significant. This suggests that the associations between income and functional status found in other studies (Berkman & Gurland, 1998) may be explained in part by differences in social support and social networks, and that social support may be a mediator, rather than a moderator, of the association between income and health status among elderly persons. Elderly people with higher incomes, for example, may be more able to remain integrated within a social network, because they are able to afford transportation and activities.

The significant interactions found in this study indicate that the beneficial effects of social variables are not equally strong for all elderly people. Although many previous studies have examined only the main effects of social variables, the present results indicate that the benefits of social variables may differ for men and women, and they may differ according to an individual's level of physical functioning. If studies evaluate only the main effects of social variables on health, they may fail to detect important subgroup differences in the effects of social support and social networks. Health promotion interventions for elderly people should focus on those elderly people who are most at risk of suffering harmful health effects as a result of social isolation. The results of this study suggest that men and people with physical impairments may be especially in need of interventions to enhance social support and social networks.

Limitations

Because this is a study of an initially high-functioning cohort, the generalizability of these findings may be limited. While this study suggests that social ties are more protective for people with lower levels of physical performance, all respondents in this study did in fact have relatively high levels of physical functioning, as evidenced by their lack of impairment in ADLs. This study does not clarify what the effects of social ties would be for elderly people with more severe functional limitations, because the initial selection criteria guaranteed that these individuals were not represented in the baseline cohort. Nevertheless, the significant moderating effect of physical performance found in this study indicates that even modest differences in physical performance within a high-functioning sample were associated with differential effects of social ties. One might hypothesize that the variation in effects would be even stronger in a cohort that included more severely impaired respondents.

Another possible limitation is that the data used in this study are based on respondents' self-reports of their physical functioning and social networks. Although attempts were made to control for variables that may confound the relationship between social variables and physical functioning (e.g., depressive symptoms, health behaviors, baseline health status), other variables not included in these analyses may have biased the accuracy of respondents' self-reports. Potential confounding variables that have been associated with both social networks and health outcomes include personality factors such as cynical hostility (Everson et al., 1997) and health behaviors other than those measured here (Lauver, Nabholz, Scott, & Tak, 1997).

Despite these limitations, these data provide important information about the effects of social support and social networks on physical functioning in elderly persons. More specifically, they highlight the fact that previously observed main effects might obscure important population variation in the effects of social ties and social support on health outcomes. As shown in these analyses, factors such as gender and baseline physical performance appear to moderate social network effects. Greater attention needs to be given to describing and understanding the complex interaction between social networks and individual characteristics if we are to gain the requisite understanding to design effective interventions to promote more successful aging.

Acknowledgments

Dr. Jennifer Unger was supported by a postdoctoral fellowship from the National Institute on Aging during the preparation of this article. Data collection for the MacArthur studies was supported by the MacArthur Foundation Research Network on Successful Aging through a grant from the John D. and Catherine T. MacArthur Foundation.

Address correspondence to Dr. Teresa Seeman, Division of Geriatrics, UCLA School of Medicine, 10945 Le Conte Avenue, Suite 2339, Los Angeles, CA 90095-1687. E-mail: TSeeman@mednet.UCLA.edu

REFERENCES

Armor, D. J., Polich, M., & Stambul, H. B. (1975). *Alcoholism and treatment*. (Appendix A). New York: John Wiley and Sons.

Barer, B. M. (1994). Men and women aging differently. *International Journal of Aging and Human Development, 38*, 29–40.

Beckett, L. A., Brock, D. B., Lemke, J. H., Mendes de Leon, C. F., Guralnik, J. M., Fillenbaum, G. G., Branch, L. G., Wetle, T. T., & Evans, D. A. (1996). Analysis of change in self-reported physical function among older persons in four population studies. *American Journal of Epidemiology, 143*, 766–778.

Berkman, L. F. (1995). The role of social relations in health promotion. *Psychosomatic Medicine, 57*, 245–254.

Berkman, C. S., & Gurland, B. J. (1998). The relationship among income, other socioeconomic indicators, and functional level in older persons. *Journal of Aging and Health, 10*, 81–98.

Berkman, L. F., Seeman, T. E., Albert, M., Blazer, D., Kahn, R., Mohs, R., Finch, C., Schneider, E., Cotman, C., & McClearn, G., (1993). High, usual and impaired functioning in community-dwelling older men and women: Findings from the MacArthur Foundation Research Network on Successful Aging. *Journal of Clinical Epidemiology, 46*, 1129–1140.

Berkman, L. F., & Syme, S. L. (1979). Social networks, host resistance, and mortality: A nine-year follow-up study of Alameda County residents. *American Journal of Epidemiology, 109*, 186–204.

Bleeker, J. K., Lamers, L. M., Leenders, I. M., & Kruyssen, D. C. (1995). Psychological and knowledge factors related to delay of help-seeking by patients with acute myocardial infarction. *Psychotherapy and Psychosomatics, 63*, 151–158.

Bloom, J. R. (1990). The relationship of social support and health. *Social Science and Medicine, 30*, 635–637.

Bovbjerg, V. E., McCann, B. S., Brief, D. J., Follette, W. C., Retzlaff, B. M., Dowdy, A. A., Walden, C. E., & Knopp, R. H. (1995). Spouse support and long-term adherence to lipid-lowering diets. *American Journal of Epidemiology, 141*, 451–460.

Cornoni-Huntley J., Ostfeld, A. M., Taylor, J. O., Wallace, R. B., Blazer, D., Berkman, L. F., Evans, D. A., Kohout, F. J., Lemke, J. H., & Scherr, P. A. (1986). Established Populations for Epidemiologic Studies of the Elderly: Study design and methodology. *Aging (Milano), 5*, 27–37.

Crimmins, E. M., & Saito, Y. (1993). Getting better and getting worse: Transitions in functional status among older Americans. *Journal of Aging and Health, 5*, 3–36.

Derogatis, L. R., Lipman, R. S., Rickels, K., Uhlenhuth, E. H., & Covi, L. (1974). The Hopkins Symptom Checklist (HSCL): A self-report symptom inventory. *Behavioral Science, 19*, 1–15.

Everson, S. A., Kauhanen, J., Kaplan, G., Goldberg, D. E., Julkunen, J., Tuomilehto, J., & Salonen, J. T. (1997). Hostility and increased risk of mortality and acute myocardial infarction: The mediating role of behavioral risk factors. *American Journal of Epidemiology, 146*, 142–152.

House, J., Robbins, C., & Metzner, H. (1982). The association of social relationships and activities with mortality: Prospective evidence from the Tecumseh Community Health Study. *American Journal of Epidemiology, 116*, 123–140.

Krause, N., & Borawski-Clark, E. (1994). Clarifying the functions of social support in later life. *Research on Aging, 16*, 251–279.

Lauver, D., Nabholz, S., Scott, K., & Tak, Y. (1997). Testing theoretical explanations of mammography use. *Nursing Research, 46*, 32–39.

Mendes de Leon C. F., Seeman, T. E., Baker, D. I., Richardson, E. D., & Tinetti, M. E. (1996). Self-efficacy, physical decline, and change in functioning in community-living elders: A prospective study. *Journal of Gerontology: Social Sciences, 51B*, S183–S190.

Mermelstein, R., Cohen, S., Lichtenstein, E., Kanmark, T., & Baer, J. S. (1986). Social support and smoking cessation and maintenance. *Journal of Consulting and Clinical Psychology, 54*, 447–453.

Mor, V., Wilcox, V., Rakowski, W., & Hiris, J. (1994). Functional transitions among the elderly: Patterns, predictors, and related hospital use. *American Journal of Public Health, 84*, 1274–1280.

Nagi, S. Z. (1976). An epidemiology of disability among adults in the United States. *Milbank Memorial Fund Quarterly, 54*, 439–468.

Parker, M. G., Thorslund, M., Lundberg, O., & Kareholt, I. (1996). Predictors of physical function among the oldest old: A comparison of three outcome variables in a 24-year follow-up. *Journal of Aging and Health, 8*, 444–460.

Pfeiffer, E. (1975). A Short Portable Mental Status Questionnaire for the assessment of organic brain deficit in elderly patients. *Journal of the American Geriatrics Society, 23*, 433–441.

Robert, S., & House, J. S. (1996). SES differentials in health by age and alternative indicators of SES. *Journal of Aging and Health, 8*, 359–388.

Scherr, P. A., LaCroix, A. Z., Wallace, R. B., & Berkman, L. (1992). Light to moderate alcohol consumption and mortality in the elderly. *Journal of the American Geriatrics Society, 40*, 651–657.

Seeman, T. E. (1996). Social ties and health. *Annals of Epidemiology, 6*, 442–451.

Seeman, T. E., & Unger, J. B. (1997, April). *Functional disability: The consequences of low self-efficacy beliefs*. Poster presented at the Society of Behavioral Medicine conference, San Francisco, CA.

Seeman, T. E., Berkman, L. F., Blazer, D., & Rowe, J. W. (1994). Social ties and support and neuroendocrine function: The MacArthur Studies of Successful Aging. *Annals of Behavioral Medicine, 16*, 95–106.

Seeman, T. E., Berkman, L. F., Charpentier, P., Blazer, D., Albert, M., & Tinetti, M. (1995). Behavioral and psychosocial predictors of physical performance: MacArthur Studies of Successful Aging. *Journal of Gerontology: Medical Sciences, 50A*, M177–M183.

Seeman, T. E., Charpentier, P. A., Berkman, L. F., Tinetti, M. E., Guralnik, J. M., Albert, M., Blazer, D., & Rowe, J. W. (1994). Predicting changes in physical performance in a high-functioning elderly cohort: MacArthur Studies of Successful Aging. *Journal of Gerontology: Medical Sciences, 49*, M97–M108.

Simonsick, E. M., Lafferty, M. E., Phillips, C. L., Mendes de Leon, C. F., Kasl, S. V., Seeman, T. E., Fillenbaum, G., Hebert, P., & Lemke, J. H. (1993). Risk due to inactivity in physically capable older adults. *American Journal of Public Health, 83*, 1443–1450.

Strawbridge, W. J., Cohen, R. D., Shema, S. J., & Kaplan, G. A. (1996). Successful aging: Predictors and associated activities. *American Journal of Epidemiology, 144*, 135–141.

Thoits, P. A. (1995). Stress, coping, and social support processes: Where are we? What next? *Journal of Health and Social Behavior, 36* (Extra issue), 53–79.

Tower, R. B., & Kasl, S. V. (1996). Gender, marital closeness, and depressive symptoms in elderly couples. *Journal of Gerontology: Psychological Sciences 51B*, P115–P129.

Uchino, B. N., Cacioppo, J. T., & Kiecolt-Glaser, J. K. (1996). The relationship between social support and physiological processes: A review with emphasis on underlying mechanisms and implications for health. *Psychological Bulletin, 119*, 488–531.

Umberson, D. (1996). The effect of social relationships on psychological well-being: Are men and women really so different? *American Sociological Review, 61*, 837–851.

Umberson, D., Wortman, C. B., & Kessler, R. C. (1992). Widowhood and depression: Explaining long-term gender differences in vulnerability. *Journal of Health and Social Behavior, 33*, 10–24.

Wilcox, V. L., Kasl, S. V., & Berkman, L. F. (1994). Social support and physical disability in older people after hospitalization: A prospective study. *Health Psychology, 13*, 170–179.

Received June 22, 1998
Accepted March 23, 1999

[8]

Social support and stressful life events: age differences in their effects on health-related quality of life among the chronically ill

C. Donald Sherbourne,* L. S. Meredith, W. Rogers and J. E. Ware Jr
RAND, 1700 Main Street, Santa Monica, CA 90407-2138 (C. Donald Sherbourne, L. S. Meredith and W. Rogers);
New England Medical Center, Box 345, 750 Washington St, Boston, MA 02111, USA (J. E. Ware).

There is substantial evidence of individual variation in health-related quality of life measures that is not accounted for by age or disease condition. An understanding of factors that determine good health is necessary for maintained function and improved quality of life. This study examines the extent to which social support and stressful life events were more or less beneficial for the long-term physical functioning and emotional well-being of 1402 chronically ill patients. Analyses, conducted separately in three age groups, showed that social support was beneficial for health over time regardless of age. In addition, low levels of support were particularly damaging for the physical functioning of older patients. Stressful life events impacted differentially on health-related quality of life: relationship events had an immediate effect on well-being which diminished with time; financial events had an immediate negative effect on functioning and well-being which persisted over time for middle-aged patients; bereavement had a delayed impact on quality of life, with the youngest patients especially vulnerable to its negative effects; work-related events had both negative and positive effects, depending on age group. Results reinforce the importance of identifying and dealing with psychosocial problems among patients with chronic disease.

Key words: Functional status, social support, stressful life events, well-being.

Introduction

The growth and increasing longevity of older Americans has led to the important goal of improving the quality of life for those persons faced with chronic diseases. Because chronic diseases are long-term in nature, treatment expectations have shifted from elimination of disease to maintenance of acceptable levels of functioning and improvements in the overall quality of life. Most elderly suffer from one or more chronic conditions and the number who are functionally impaired due to chronic disease increases from 41% for those aged 54–74 years to over 60% for those 85 years and older.[1] There is substantial evidence of great individual variation in functional status and well-being that is not accounted for by age or disease condition. An understanding of what determines good health outcomes is necessary in order to maintain function and therefore improve quality of life.

Social support is one factor that may play an important role in maintaining health and decreasing the impact of illness. Literally hundreds of articles have been published in recent years addressing the question of whether or not social support is related to health.[2,3] This interest in social support grew out of earlier research on stressful life events. The modest relationship found between stressful life events and health outcomes[4,5] led researchers to explore factors, such as social support, that might moderate this relationship. Research in this area has generally addressed the issue of whether social support benefits health directly, or instead acts as a buffer to lessen the negative impact of stressful life events on health. There is support for both points of view.[6-11] It appears that support can benefit health directly and also mediate the consequences of stressful life events,[12] depending upon the type of support and stressful event measured.[2,3]

Very little is known about age differences in the relationships among social support, stressful life

Supported by grants from the National Institute on Ageing, Bethesda, MD, the Henry J. Kaiser Family Foundation, Menlo Park, CA; The Robert Wood Johnson Foundation, Princeton, NJ; The Pew Charitable Trusts, Philadelphia, PA; the Agency for Health Care Policy and Research, Rockville, MD; the National Institute of Mental Health, Bethesda, MD; and RAND, Santa Monica, CA and the New England Medical Center, Boston, MA out of their own research funds.

* To whom correspondence should be addressed.

events and health outcomes.[13] The general belief has been that social support may play a particularly important role in maintaining health among the elderly, because the elderly are at high risk both for illness and for disruptions in their sources of support.[14] Although it has been suggested that the nature of social supports varies over the life course, little empirical evidence is available about the possible consequences of this variation for health.[15]

A few studies have revealed that symptoms of depression are more likely in older people who experience decreased social interaction[16] or receive less informational support when under financial strain.[17] Older individuals with satisfying relationships also had lower serum cholesterol and uric acid levels and higher indices of immune function than did older people with poorer social support systems.[18] On the other hand, emotional support was not related to self-ratings of functional health or distress from chronic health problems,[19] while strong-tie support explained significantly less of the variation in depression in subjects 50 years old and older than in younger subjects.[15] A study by George, Landerman, and Blazer[20] found no age differences in the effects of four dimensions of social support (network size, interaction frequency, instrumental assistance, and perception of support adequacy) on depression.

There is some evidence that older adults experience fewer stressful life events[21,22] and different types of events than younger adults.[22,23] For example, the stresses of young adulthood may be more likely to dissipate with time or involve challenges, whereas those of old age may be more chronic and involve threats and losses.[24,25] However, we do not know whether these differences in the experience of stress translate into a more or less favourable impact on health outcomes. There is some evidence that marital dissolution has a more negative effect for older than younger adults,[26] although one study[20] found no differences in the effects of life events on depression across young, middle and older age groups.

Most of these previous studies have focused on populations of generally healthy adults. However, once a person becomes ill, do these relationships among support, stress, and health remain the same across age groups? Or is one age group more vulnerable to the effects of lack of support or to the experience of stressful events?

In a longitudinal study of patients with one of four chronic illnesses (diabetes, coronary heart disease, hypertension, or depression), we examined the extent to which social support and stressful life events were more or less beneficial for physical functioning and emotional well-being in different age groups. We previously reported that social support affected mental health, but not physical functioning over a 1 year interval.[27] Results were not evaluated for different age groups or over a 2 year interval.

Methods

Study population and data collection

The data are from patients participating in the Medical Outcomes Study (MOS), an observational study of variations in physician practice styles and patient outcomes in one of three different systems of care: health maintenance organizations (HMOs), large multispecialty groups (LMSGs), and solo fee-for-service (SOLO) practice. Details regarding the study can be found elsewhere.[28,29] To summarize briefly, data for these analyses were obtained from patients visiting general medical physicians, psychologists, and other mental health providers practising in each of the three systems of care in Boston, Chicago, or Los Angeles. Providers were sampled from lists obtained from the HMOs and national professional associations; only those between the ages of 31 and 55 years, who were board eligible/certified or licensed for independent practice, and who had direct patient care as their primary professional activity were eligible. The final sample included 298 SOLO and 225 HMO and LMSG providers, representing a participation rate of 58% and 85%, respectively.

A representative cross-section of patients visiting participating providers was sampled ($n = 20\,223$) during an average 9 day screening period in 1986. Doctor and patient information was used to identify patients with hypertension, diabetes, or coronary heart disease. Depressed patients were sampled in a two-stage screening procedure.[30] A telephone interview (TCI) was then used to collect additional information on eligible patients ($n = 8\,040$). Of 5342 patients who took the TCI, a panel of 2546 patients were selected for further study. Selection criteria favoured patients with current or lifetime depression as opposed to depressive symptoms only, doctor-certified diabetes, hypertensives taking medications, and the elderly.

The information included in this paper is based on a subset of patients sampled from the offices of medical providers who enrolled in the 2 year longitudinal study during late 1986, completed the enrolment self-administered Form B Patient Assessment Questionnaire (PAQ) plus the 2 year follow-up assessment, and had complete data on all variables included in the analysis (n = 1402). Analyses excluded patients sampled from the offices of mental health providers, because medical and mental health provider groups deliver very different styles of mental health care and treat patients with different levels of functioning and disease severity.[31] For the analytic sample, ages ranged from 19–98 years (average age was 59 years), 42% were male, 18% were nonwhite, 61% were married, the average family size was 2.1, while average years of education was 13.3.

We evaluated the representativeness of the analytic sample (n = 1402) to the full MOS panel of patients sampled from the offices of general medical providers (n = 2181) in terms of demographic characteristics and enrolment health functioning. Results shown in Table 1 suggest that patients in the analytic sample were significantly more likely than those in the full panel to be male, white, older, married, with higher income, better baseline physical functioning and emotional well-being, and higher levels of social support. To correct for these differences, we weighted our analyses for sample non-response.

Measures

Health-related quality of life. We defined health-related quality of life in terms of patients' everyday physical functioning and their emotional well-being. Physical functioning assessed current capacity to perform a variety of physical activities such as bathing, dressing, running and participating in strenuous sports.[32,33] The internal-consistency reliability of this ten-item scale was high ($\alpha = 0.95$). Emotional well-being tapped feelings of anxiety, depression, loss of emotional/behavioural control and positive affect in the past month. This 16-item measure was derived from the 38-item Mental Health Inventory (MHI) developed for the Health Insurance Experiment,[34-36] represented both positive and negative emotional states, and has been shown to be highly reliable ($\alpha = 0.95$) and valid.[34,37,38] Both measures were developed for the MOS, represent the most important concepts in accepted definitions of health, and are universally valued regardless of an individual's age or medical condition.

Social support. Our support measure[39] focused on the perception of the current availability of functional support, one of the most essential components of social support.[2,40,41] The 19-item measure asked respondents to rate the perceived availability, if needed, of: (1) tangible support, involving the provision of material aid or behavioural assistance, (2) affectional support, involving expressions of love and affection, (3) positive social interaction, involving the availability of other persons to do fun things with you, and (4) emotional/informational support, involving the expression of positive affect, empathetic understanding and the offering of advice, guidance, or feedback.[39] For each item, respondents were asked to indicate how often each kind of support was available to them if needed. The five-choice response scale for each item ranged from 'none of the time' to 'all of the time'. The reliability of the overall support measure was very high ($\alpha = 0.97$).

Stressful life events were represented by four subscales from a longer 19-item life event battery.

Table 1. Average characteristics of patients in panel and analysis sample

Characteristics	Panel n = 2 181	Analysis sample n = 1 402
Male (%)	39	43
Nonwhite (%)	29	18
Income (adjusted 1 985 household dollars)	19 428	22 987
Age (years)	57	59
Married (%)	52	61
Physical functioning (mean level)	63	71
Emotional well-being (mean level)	69	76
Social support (mean level)	67	73

Note: Those in the analytic sample differed significantly from those missing due to form non-response or missing data on each of the characteristics.

C. Donald Sherbourne et al.

For each event which had occurred during the 12 months prior to baseline, respondents were asked to rate the perceived impact of the event on their life (e.g., happened, bad effect; happened, but no effect; happened, good effect; did not happen). Events were scored for their negative impact in which a '1' indicated that the event had a bad effect, a '0' indicated otherwise. The four clusters of events were derived by summing over relevant events.

Work-related events were represented by a six-item measure which included: arguments at work; laid off; resigned or retired; started a new job; changed duties at work; changed work or living surroundings. A two-item measure of financial events included minor financial problems and major financial crisis. Relationship events was a three-item measure including: serious arguments with others; serious problems with others; and separation, divorce or end of a relationship. The fourth event was a single-item measure of bereavement (death of someone close). These clusters of events were formed based on results from a factor analysis of the longer 19-item battery and were similar to events commonly grouped together for analysis.[3]

Analysis Plan

All analyses were conducted for patients in three age groups: ages 18–44 years ($n = 303$), 45–64 years ($n = 515$) and 65 years and older ($n = 584$). Because the MOS oversampled older patients, the split between patients ages 18–44 years and 45–64 years was determined primarily for reasons of sample size (e.g., to form groups with adequate numbers for analysis), while the split at age 65 years and older is common in studies of older people.

We first examined means and standard deviations for social support and stressul life events by age group. We then estimated the effects of social support and stressful life events on physical functioning and emotional well-being using multiple regression methods. Three types of models were examined: (1) baseline cross-sectional; (2) endpoint; and (3) change over time. The baseline cross-sectional model provided a point-in-time picture of outcome differences at the beginning of the study. The endpoint model provided a similar snapshot 2 years later. The change model provided a picture of the longitudinal course of outcomes over time. We did not control for baseline status in the endpoint and change models because ANOVA adjustment for baseline level of the outcome measure often leads to biased estimates of regression parameters.[42–44] Difference scores provide appropriately conservative tests of null hypotheses.[45–47] In cases where one of the life event subscales impacted significantly on health, a stress-buffering model was evaluated by adding a multiplicative term of social support and that subscale to the multivariate regression model. The stress-buffering model tested the hypothesis that social support had greater positive impact on health and well-being under high stress than under low stress conditions.

Covariates in each model included gender, race, education, study site, type of chronic disease condition (hypertension, diabetes, heart disease, depressive symptoms), and a count of 33 comorbid conditions. All covariates were measured prior to or at baseline.

To illustrate our results, we generated predicted means (using the parameters of the regression models) of the level of functioning and well-being for groups which differed in level of support and in the presence or absence of stressful life events. The predictions were generated for each individual, adjusting for covariates in the model and then averaged within groups. These predictions were weighted for sample non-response and to correct for the effects of sampling probabilities for patients and clinicians. The estimates represent the original population from which the sample was selected.

Results

Zero-order correlations among all variables studied are provided in the Appendix. The magnitude of the correlations among covariates included in the models are only weak to moderate. Thus, multicolinearity is not a problem in our analyses.

Table 2 presents unadjusted mean levels of social support and the percent of patients experiencing negative life events by age. The youngest age group (18–44 years) reported significantly less availability of social support. They were significantly more likely to experience work, financial and relationship events. The oldest patients were least likely to experience stressful events. There were no differences among age groups in the percentage of patients reporting the death of someone close.

Table 2. Unadjusted mean level of social support and percent of patients experiencing negative life events by age group

	18–44 years	Age group 45–64 years	65+ years
Social support			
Mean	68.1	73.9[a]	74.8[a]
SD	22.6	22.9	23.7
Work events (%)	31	16	03
Financial events (%)	30	12	04
Relationship events (%)	34	20	11
Bereavement (%)	15[a]	16[a]	16[a]

[a] Groups in each row that share a common letter do not differ significantly from one another.
Social support scores range from 0–100 with a high score indicating greater availability of social support.

Table 3 presents adjusted mean levels of physical functioning and emotional well-being at baseline and 2 years later for patients with low (25th percentile) and high (75th percentile) levels of social support by age group.

Patients with low social support reported significantly worse physical functioning and emotional well-being at baseline of the study than did patients with high social support. This was true for all but the oldest patients, whose baseline functioning did not differ by level of social support.

The pattern of significantly lower physical functioning and emotional well-being for patients with low rather than high levels of social support persisted over the 2 year study. Mean health levels remained constant over time with little change as a function of social support level. For patients aged 65 years and older, however, there were significant decrements in physical functioning for those with low social support; their physical functioning declined by 6.3% (6.3 points on a 0–100 distribution) over the 2 year interval. In contrast to the physical functioning results, the emotional well-being of the oldest patients with high social support declined significantly over time, although it remained higher than that of patients with low support.

Similar analyses were conducted for patients who did and did not experience financial, work-related, relationship events or bereavement in the 12 months prior to baseline (results not shown). We summarize those results here and provide selected figures to illustrate the major findings.

The occurrence of financial events was not related to physical functioning or emotional well-being except in patients 45–64 years old. Those

Table 3. Adjusted mean level of physical functioning and emotional well-being at baseline and 2 years later for patients with low (25th percentile) and high (75th percentile) social support by age group

Age group/ support level	Physical functioning Baseline	Year 2	Emotional well-being Baseline	Year 2
18–44 years				
Low support	80.8*	81.2*	64.8*	65.7*
	(1.6)	(1.6)	(2.0)	(1.3)
High support	85.2	86.1	70.8	72.6
	(1.8)	(1.6)	(1.5)	(1.5)
45–64 years				
Low support	75.2*	74.3*	73.8*	75.6*
	(1.3)	(1.4)	(0.7)	(0.8)
High support	79.4	78.8	81.0	80.9
	(1.4)	(1.4)	(0.9)	(0.9)
65+ years				
Low support	64.8	58.5*,[a]	79.0*	77.8*
	(1.6)	(1.5)	(0.7)	(0.8)
High support	66.9	65.4	86.2	82.6[a]
	(1.9)	(1.8)	(0.8)	(0.9)

Standard error in parentheses.
[a] Significant decline from baseline; *indicates significantly different from patients with high social support at $p < 0.05$.

C. Donald Sherbourne et al.

who reported financial problems had worse functioning and well-being at baseline and the 2 year follow-up than did similarly aged patients without financial problems. Health levels remained constant and did not worsen or improve significantly over time as a function of financial problems (see Figure 1 for an example of this pattern). At baseline, support buffered this relationship (see Figure 2) such that among patients with financial problems, those with high social support were 11.8 points higher in physical functioning than those with low support. In contrast, among patients without financial problems, there was only a 2.7 difference between those with high and low support.

The occurrence of bereavement was not related to physical functioning except at the 2 year follow-up for the youngest patients. Bereaved patients had significantly worse physical functioning after 2 years than did the non-bereaved (a 12 point difference). Support did not buffer this effect. There was no significant change in physical functioning over time as a function of bereavement in any of the age groups.

Bereavement was also related to follow-up emotional well-being for the youngest and oldest patients. As illustrated in Figure 3, the level of emotional well-being was similar at baseline between patients who had and had not experienced the death of someone close. Over time however, bereaved patients showed a significant decline in their emotional well-being. In contrast, for middle-aged patients, there was an immediate negative effect of bereavement on emotional well-being (a 4.7 difference between the bereaved and non-bereaved) that dissipated over time (only 1.8 points lower at year 2). Support did not buffer the effect of bereavement on emotional well-being.

Relationship events were not related to physical functioning in any of the age groups. However, emotional well-being was significantly lower at baseline for patients of all ages who had experienced one or more relationship events than for patients who did not report these events. The negative impact of relationship events did not persist over time, and among patients 45–64 years old, emotional well-being improved significantly for patients who had experienced these events (see Figure 4). Support did not buffer the effect of relationship events on emotional well-being.

Work events appeared to have a more varied impact that differed across age groups. Patients under 65 years old who had experienced work events did not appear to differ at baseline in their physical functioning from those who had not experienced work events. They did, however have worse emotional well-being. For the youngest patients, physical functioning declined significantly over time for those who had these types of events (see Figure 5), while emotional well-being

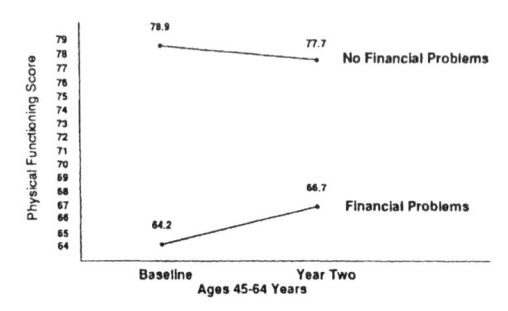

Figure 1. Mean level of physical functioning for groups differing in financial problems.

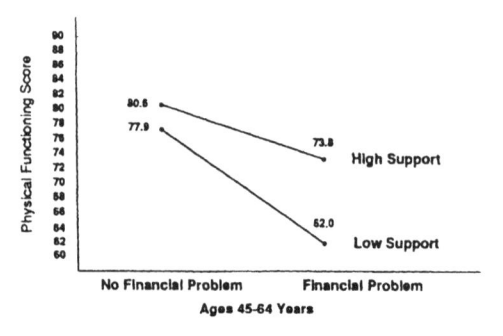

Figure 2. Mean level of baseline physical functioning for groups differing in financial events and level of social support.

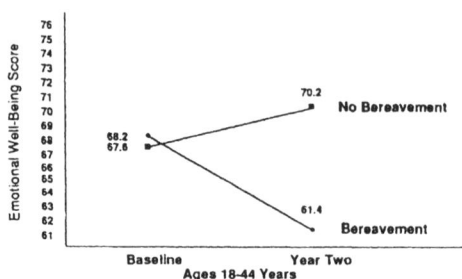

Figure 3. Mean level of emotional well-being for groups differing in bereavement.

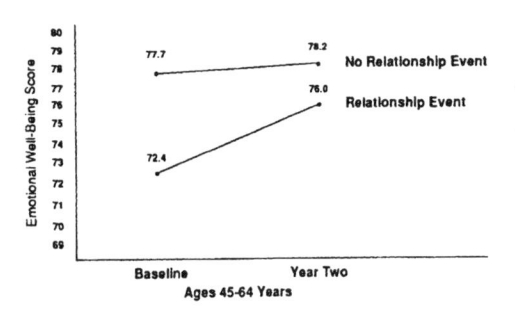

Figure 4. Mean level of emotional well-being for groups differing in relationship events.

Figure 5. Mean level of physical functioning for groups differing in work events.

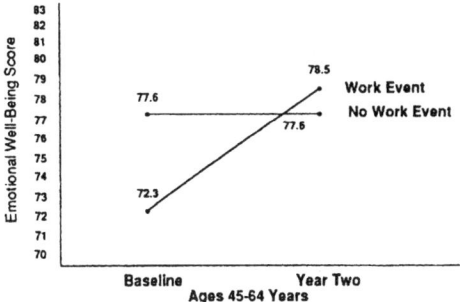

Figure 6. Mean level of emotional well-being for groups differing in work events.

remained impaired. The oldest patients who experienced work events actually had better physical functioning at both time periods and better emotional well-being at baseline than did their counterparts who had not experienced such events. For the oldest patients with these events, emotional well-being decreased (8 points) over time, while among middle-aged patients, their emotional well-being improved (see Figure 6). Support did not buffer the effect of work events on physical functioning or emotional well-being.

Discussion

This study focused on two important measures of health-related quality of life, physical functioning and emotional well-being. We determined the extent to which social support maintained health and decreased the impact of illness on these outcomes over time. The impact of stressful life events on quality of life was also evaluated. Analyses focused on a sample of chronically ill patients and differences in results among patients in three age groups were examined.

Although one might expect that older patients with chronic illnesses, like older people in general, are at increased risk for poor quality of life because they are more likely to have disruptions in their sources of support (e.g., through retirement, moves, deaths), our findings did not support the view that social support was less available for this group. It was the youngest patients who reported less availability of social support and the more frequent occurrence of work-related, financial and relationship events. Other recent studies have also found that older persons do not feel that they are suffering from insufficient social networks.[48] Instead, most elderly have fairly extensive contacts, are not isolated from family and friends, and are satisfied with the support available to them.[13] Similarly, older subjects have consistently been found to experience fewer life events than do younger subjects.[15,26]

Our findings support the idea that social support benefits health-related quality of life. Patients with high levels of social support had significantly better levels of physical functioning and emotional well-being than did patients with low levels of social support. These differences were evident at the beginning of the study and persisted over time. There was little change in levels of functioning or well-being over time for low and high support groups, suggesting that the effect of support on health is fairly stable. In fact, perceived social support itself was also very stable over time. Separate analyses of change in levels of social support (i.e., low, moderate, and high support) between baseline and one year later showed that

68% of the sample stayed in the same level. Less than 1% of the sample moved from low to high levels of perceived support or vice versa over the 1 year period. From this study, we cannot tell at which point in a patient's life support generated its beneficial effects—most likely before the study began. However, once patients achieved a level of support, our results suggest that the pattern of better health for patients with high levels of support persisted over time. Social support in chronically ill patients did not appear to improve their functioning and well-being but instead helped maintain the high level of health attained previously.

Social support appears to be beneficial regardless of age. In addition, there is some evidence from our results that low levels of support may be particularly damaging for older patients. We found that patients 65 years old and older with low levels of support had significant decrements in physical functioning over a 2 year interval. It may be particularly important for intervention purposes to target older patients who report low levels of social support, since this group is at particular risk for poor physical health outcomes.

We do not know why the very oldest patients with high levels of social support showed a significant decline in emotional well-being over time. Although well-being declined significantly, it remained significantly better than that of patients with low levels of support. In fact, the mean level of emotional well-being for patients 65 years old and older with high social support was higher than the level of any other age group, supported or unsupported. The decline in well-being for this group may be statistical regression to the mean.

Our results show how negatively perceived stressful life events affect health-related quality of life differentially by age. The sample considered here was chronically ill and thus already under stress to some extent. The occurrence of stressful events were expected to place additional demands on the chronically sick person which might impede their adjustment or accelerate the deterioration of their functioning and well-being.

As has been found in many other studies of stressful life events, when negatively perceived life events occurred, their impact on functioning and well-being was harmful. Emotional well-being was more likely to be affected than physical functioning. Traditionally, stress has been viewed in terms of its relevance for short-term (i.e., over 1 and 2 year periods) deterioration in function. Our results showed that there was some variation in the temporal impact of stressful life events on outcomes. In some cases, life events had an immediate effect which then diminished over time, presumably as the patient learned to cope with the event. This pattern was especially true for relationship events, where the occurrence of events such as divorce or arguments with significant others were particularly stressful initially. Over time, observed increases in emotional well-being may well represent a recovery from the stress reaction as people formed new relationships or distanced themselves from stressful encounters with others. To some extent, this pattern was also true for work events among middle-aged patients. Although patients in this age group who had experienced work-related events had poorer emotional well-being at baseline than those who had not experienced these events, over time there was significant improvement in well-being for those with these types of events.

A second pattern that emerged was one in which the stressful event had an immediate negative effect on quality of life which persisted over time. This pattern was true for the effect of financial events on both physical functioning and emotional well-being among middle-aged patients. Previous research has confirmed the relationship between financial strain and psychological well-being.[49] However, it is unclear why financial problems would not affect the health of all age groups equally. It may be that patients 45–64 years old are more likely than those younger and older to be dependent on their own incomes (younger patients may receive financial aid from their parents, while the oldest patients may have retirement income to draw upon or may receive financial aid from their adult children). In addition, older persons have been found to be more satisfied with their incomes, even when the income is of questionable adequacy.[50]

A third pattern that emerged was one in which there was a delayed impact of a stressful event, primarily bereavement, on quality of life. The youngest patients in our sample appeared to be especially vulnerable to the negative impact of bereavement on both physical functioning and emotional well-being. Those who had experienced the death of someone close had significantly worse outcomes more than 2 years after the event had occurred than did patients who had not experienced the death of someone close. The decline in emotional well-being was significant for the youngest patients and a similar pattern for emotional well-being emerged for the oldest bereaved patients. Past research has confirmed the finding of a strong adverse relationship between bereavement and health status.[14] In addition, there is similar evidence that younger bereaved individuals may be more at risk for adverse health outcomes than older bereaved individuals.[51] It has been suggested that older individuals are more prepared for this 'on-time' type of event.[52]

Interestingly, work-related events had a unique pattern of effects on quality of life among patients 65 years and older. These older patients who experienced work events had significantly better physical functioning both at baseline and 2 years later. Their emotional well-being was also better at baseline but declined over time to levels comparable to patients who had not experienced work events. There may be several explanations for this positive impact of work-related events on health. First, because the oldest patients were much less likely to be working, they reported significantly fewer work-related events. When they did report work-related events, they were more likely to endorse the item about a 'change in the surroundings where you live or work' as the event which had occurred. This item confounds work events with changes in living conditions. Thus, the extent to which this item reflects work-related events rather than other life changes is unclear. Second, by the age of 65 years, most people have retired. The fact that persons of this age were still working may have been due to their better health to begin with. Finally, a larger percentage of older patients endorsed 'retirement' as one of their work-related events. Retirement has not been found to have a negative health outcome for older people because it has increasingly become an expected and normative transition for most people.[53] However, this pattern would not be expected of people retiring early because of poor health (as would be true of the younger patients in our study).

We should recall that the stressful life events measured in this study were reported as occurring during the year prior to baseline and thus, in this example, almost 3 years prior to the 2 year outcome variables. We do not know what types of events ensued during the intervening years. In fact, for all the findings reported here, the test of the relationship between stressful life events and health-related quality of life is conservative due to the time lag between the measurement of events and health outcomes.

These findings confirm the beneficial role of perceived social support for the future health of chronically ill patients of all ages and suggest that lack of support may be particularly damaging for older patients. The fact that the effects of social support appear to be fairly stable over time argues for the importance of early intervention to foster high levels of support in patients with chronic conditions. From our findings we cannot tell the point in time that social support had its initial benefits on health. It may have occurred prior to or subsequent to the development of the chronic disease condition. Longitudinal research which tracks levels of functioning and well-being as well as changes in social support in an initially well population, some of whom develop a chronic illness, will be necessary before causal interpretations can be made with certainty. To the extent that perceived social support is a more stable personality attribute, such as coping style, interventions which actually increase quantitative levels of support may not be as effective for health-related quality of life as interventions designed to alter cognitive orientations.

Life events have a more varied impact on quality of life health outcomes. Identification of groups at risk for poor functioning and well-being should focus on those events, such as bereavement and financial problems, which either persist over time or show an increasingly negative impact over time. The young and middle-aged patients are particularly at risk for poor outcomes due to bereavement and financial problems, respectively. Our results suggest that social support may not lessen the negative impact of these events on health. In only one case (i.e., the effect of financial problems on the physical functioning of middle-aged patients at baseline) did social support buffer the effects of stressful life events on health.

The variation in results across health-related quality of life measures as well as across age groups emphasizes the importance of measuring dimensions of quality of life separately, rather than aggregating health concepts into a global measure of outcome. Measurement of separate dimensions allows a better understanding of the health consequences associated with the lack of social support and the occurrence of stressful life events. In recent years, there has been a trend toward incorporating health-related quality of life measures in a variety of applications, including clinical trials, clinical practice, as well as population-based studies. Professionals dealing with chronic disease patients should be aware of the importance of also identifying and dealing with psychosocial problems, such as social support and unique types of life events, in order to arrest

C. Donald Sherbourne et al.

further deterioration of the patient's functioning and well-being.

References

1. Kane RL, Ouslander JG, Abrass IB. *Essentials of Clinical Geriatrics.* New York: McGraw-Hill Book Co., 1984.
2. Cohen S, Wills TA. Stress, social support, and the buffering hypothesis. *Psychol Bull* 1985; 98(2): 310–357.
3. Kessler RC, McLeod JD. Social support and mental health in community samples. In: Cohen S, Syme SL, eds. *Social Support and Health.* Orlando: Academic Press, Inc., 1985.
4. Cohen S, Hoberman H. Positive events and social supports as buffers of life change stress. *J Appl Soc Psychol* 1983; 13: 99–125.
5. Murrell S, Norris F, Grote C. Life events in older adults. In: Cohen, L, ed. *Life Events and Psychological Functioning: Theoretical and Methodological Issues.* Beverly Hills, CA: Sage, 1988.
6. Andrews GC, Tennant D, Hewson D, Vaillant G. Life event stress, social support, coping style, and risk of psychological impairment. *J Nerv Ment Dis* 1978; 166(5): 307–316.
7. Aneshensel CS, Frericks RR. Stress, support, and depression: a longitudinal causal model. *J Comm Psychol* 1982; 10: 363–376.
8. Barrera M. Social support in the adjustment of pregnant adolescents: Assessment issues. In: Gottleib B, ed. *Social Networks and Social Support.* Beverly Hills, CA: Sage, 1981.
9. Kessler RC, Essex M. Marital status and depression: the importance of coping resources. *Social Forces* 1982; 61(1): 484–507.
10. Pearlin LI, Lieberman MA, Menagham E, Mullan J. The stress process. *J Health Soc Behav* 1981; 22: 337–356.
11. Williams AW, Ware JE Jr, Donald CA. A model of mental health, life events, and social supports applicable to general populations. *J Health Soc Behav* 1981; 22: 324–336.
12. Thoits PA. Social support and psychological well-being: theoretical possibilities. In: Sarason IG, Sarason BR, eds. *Social Support: Theory, Research, and Applications.* The Netherlands: Martinus Nijhoff Publishers, 1985.
13. George LK. Stress, social support, and depression over the life-course. In: Markides KS, Cooper CL, eds. *Aging, Stress, and Health.* New York: Wiley & Sons, 1989.
14. Minkler M. Social support and health of the elderly. In: Cohen S, Syme SL, eds. *Social Support and Health.* Orlando: Academic Press, Inc., 1985.
15. Lin N, Ensel WM, Dean A. The age structure and the stress process. In: Lin N, Dean A, Ensel WM, eds. *Social Support, Life Events, and Depression.* New York: Academic Press, Inc., 1986.
16. Lowenthal MF, Haven C. Interaction and adaptation: intimacy as a critical variable. *Am Social Rev* 1968; 33(1): 20–30.
17. Krause N. Chronic financial strain, social support, and depressive symptoms among older adults. *Psychol Aging* 1987; 2(2): 185–192.
18. Thomas PD, Goodwin JM, Goodwin JS. Effect of social support on stress-related changes in cholesterol level, uric acid level, and immune function in an elderly sample. *Am J Psychiatry* 1985; 142(6): 735–737.
19. Fuller SS, Larson SB. Life events, emotional support, and health of older people. *Res Nurs Health* 1980; 3: 81–89.
20. George LK, Landerman R, Blazer DG. Age differences in the antecedents of depression and anxiety: Evidence from the Duke Epidemiologic Catchment Area Program. Paper presented at the Annual Meetings of the America Association for the Advancement of Science, Chicago, 1987.
21. Chiriboga DA, Dean H. Dimensions of stress: Perspectives from a longitudinal study. *J Psychosom Res* 1978; 22: 47–55.
22. Hughes DC, Blazer DG, George LK. Age differences in life events: a multivariate controlled analysis. *Int J Aging Hum Dev* 1988; 27: 207–220.
23. Goldberg EG, Comstock GW. Epidemiology of life events: frequency in general populations. *Am J Epidemiol* 1980; 111: 736–752.
24. McCrae R. Age differences in the use of coping mechanisms. *J Gerontol* 1982; 37: 454–460.
25. Pearlin LI. Life strains and psychological distress among adults. In: Smelser N, Erikson E, eds. *Themes of Work and Love in Adulthood.* Cambridge, MA: Harvard University Press, 1980.
26. Chiriboga DA. The measurement of stress exposure in later life. In: Markides KS, Cooper CL, eds. *Aging, Stress, and Health.* New York: Wiley & Sons, 1989.
27. Sherbourne CD, Hays RD. Marital status, social support, and health transitions in chronic disease patients. *J Health Soc Behav* 1990; 31(4): 328–343.
28. Rogers W, McGlynn E, Berry S, et al. Methods of sampling. In: Stewart AL, Ware JE, eds. *Measuring Functioning and Well-Being: The Medical Outcomes Study Approach.* Duke University Press, 1992: 27–47.
29. Tarlov A, Ware JE Jr, Greenfield S, et al. The Medical Outcomes Study: an application of methods for evaluating the results of medical care. *J Am Med Assoc* 1989; 262(7): 925–930.
30. Burnam MA, Wells KB, Leake B, Landsverk J. Development of a brief screening instrument for detecting depressive disorders. *Med Care* 1988; 26: 775–789.
31. Wells KB, Hays RD, Burnam MA, et al. Detection of depressive disorder for patients receiving prepaid or fee-for-service care. *J Am Med Assoc* 1989; 263: 3298–3302.
32. Stewart AL, Ware JE Jr, Brook RH. Advances in the measurement of functional status: construction of aggregate indexes. *Med Care* 1981; 19: 473–488.
33. Stewart AL, Kamberg C. Physical functioning measures. In: Stewart AL, Ware JE Jr, eds. *Measuring Functioning and Well-Being: The Medical Outcomes Study Approach.* Duke University Press, 1992: 86–101.
34. Stewart AL, Ware JE Jr, Sherbourne CD, Wells KB. Psychological distress/well-being and cognitive

functioning measures. In: Stewart AL, Ware JE Jr, eds. *Measuring Functioning and Well-Being: The Medical Outcomes Study Approach.* Duke University Press, 1992: 102–142.
35. Veit CT, Ware JE Jr. The structure of psychological distress and well-being in general populations. *J Consult Clin Psychol* 1983; 51: 730–742.
36. Ware JE Jr, Johnston SA, Davies-Avery A, Brook RH. *Conceptualization and Measurement of Health for Adults in the Health Insurance Study, Vol. II, Mental Health.* R-1987/3-HEW, The RAND Corporation, Santa Monica, CA, 1979.
37. Cassileth BR, Lusk EJ, Strouse TB, et al. Psychosocial status in chronic illness: a comparative analysis of six diagnostic groups. *N Engl J Med* 1984; 311: 506–511.
38. Ware JE Jr, Davies-Avery A, Brook RH. *Conceptualization and Measurement of Health for Adults in the Health Insurance Study: Vol. VI, Analysis of Relationships Among Health Status Measures.* R-1987/6-HEW, The RAND Corporation, Santa Monica, CA, 1980.
39. Sherbourne CD, Stewart AL. The MOS social support survey. *Soc Sci Med* 1991; 32: 705–714.
40. Cohen S, Syme SL. Issues in the study and application of social support. In: Cohen S, Syme SL, eds. *Social Support and Health.* Orlando: Academic Press Inc., 1985.
41. House JS, Kahn RL. Measures and concepts of social support. In: Cohen S, Syme SL, eds. *Social Support and Health.* San Francisco: Academic Press, Inc., 1985.
42. Kaplan RM, Berry CC. Adjusting for confounding variables. In: L. Sechrest, E. Perrin, J. Bunker, eds. *Research Methodology: Strengthening Causal Interpretations of Nonexperimental Data.* USA Department of Health and Human Services, 1990.
43. Lord FM. A paradox in the interpretation of group comparisons. *Psychol Bull* 1967; 68: 304–305.
44. Porter AC, Raudenbush SW. Analysis of covariance: its model and use in psychological research. *J Counsel Psychol* 1987; 34: 383–392.
45. Allison PD. Change scores as dependent variables in regression analysis. *Sociol Methodol* 1990; 20: 93–114.
46. Overall JE. Contradictions can never a paradox resolve. *Appl Psychol Measurement* 1989; 13: 426–428.
47. Willett JB. Questions and answers in the measurement of change. In: Rothkipf EZ, ed. *Review of Research in Education, Volume 15.* Washington, D.C.: American Educational Research Association, 1988.
48. Antonucci TC. Personal characteristics, social support, and social behavior. In: Binstock RH, Shanas E, eds. *Aging and the Social Sciences.* New York: Van Nostrand Reinhold, 1985.
49. Krause N, Jay G, Liang J. Financial strain and psychological well-being among the American and Japanese elderly. *Psychol Aging* 1991; 6(2): 170–181.
50. Streib GF. Social stratification and aging. In: Binstock RH, Shanas E, eds. *Handbook of Aging and the Social Sciences.* New York: Van Nostrand Reinhold, 1985; 339–360.
51. Heyman D, Gianturco D. Long-term adaptation by the elderly to bereavement. *J Gerontol* 1973; 28: 359–362.
52. Neugarten B. Time, age and the life cycle. *Am J Psychiatry* 1979; 136: 887–894.
53. Markides KS, Cooper CL. Aging, Stress, Social Support and Health: An Overview. In: Markides, KS, and Cooper, CL, eds. *Aging, Stress, and Health.* New York: Wiley & Sons, 1989.

(*Received 21 April 1992;*
accepted 27 May 1992)

C. Donald Sherbourne et al.

Appendix 1. Zero Order Correlations Among Study Variables.

	1	2	3	4	5	6	7	8	9	10	11	12	13	14	15	16	17
1. Age	—																
2. Male	05	—															
3. Non-white	-14*	-09*	—														
4. Education	-26*	12*	-09*	—													
5. Current depression	-28*	-10*	01	04	—												
6. Depressive symptoms	-18*	-17*	06*	-04	-14*	—											
7. Heart disease	16*	12*	-06*	-03	-09*	-06*	—										
8. Hypertension	26*	04	01	-03	-24*	-23*	-19*	—									
9. Diabetes	04	03	14*	-07*	-14*	-03	02	-06*	—								
10. Comorbidity	06*	-09*	-02	-05	12*	02	08*	00	03	—							
11. Social support	10*	20*	-11*	02	-26*	-14*	06*	09*	06*	-14*	—						
12. Work events	-32*	-07*	08*	12*	26*	12*	-04	-18*	-07*	06	-18*	—					
13. Financial events	-30*	-14*	12*	05	29*	15*	-02	-15*	-07*	05	-21*	34*	—				
14. Relationship events	-21*	-13*	04	04	29*	16*	-06*	-16*	-08*	08*	-24*	24*	28*	—			
15. Bereavement	01	-09*	06*	-02	05	08*	-04	-01	01	07*	-08*	08*	13*	16*	—		
16. Physical functioning	-30*	18*	-01	22*	00	-14*	-19*	-01	-08*	-27*	15*	07*	-07*	-06*	-10*	—	
17. Emotional well-being	32*	14*	-04	01	-45*	-32*	07*	23*	08*	-15*	43*	-34*	-35*	-35*	-10*	22*	—

*Indicates correlation significant at $p < 0.05$ or less.

[9]

Taking Time Seriously
A Theory of Socioemotional Selectivity

Laura L. Carstensen — *Stanford University*
Derek M. Isaacowitz — *University of Pennsylvania*
Susan T. Charles — *Stanford University*

Socioemotional selectivity theory claims that the perception of time plays a fundamental role in the selection and pursuit of social goals. According to the theory, social motives fall into 1 of 2 general categories—those related to the acquisition of knowledge and those related to the regulation of emotion. When time is perceived as open-ended, knowledge-related goals are prioritized. In contrast, when time is perceived as limited, emotional goals assume primacy. The inextricable association between time left in life and chronological age ensures age-related differences in social goals. Nonetheless, the authors show that the perception of time is malleable, and social goals change in both younger and older people when time constraints are imposed. The authors argue that time perception is integral to human motivation and suggest potential implications for multiple subdisciplines and research interests in social, developmental, cultural, cognitive, and clinical psychology.

I often feel that death is not the enemy of life, but its friend, for it is the knowledge that our years are limited which makes them so precious.—Rabbi Joshua L. Liebman (1961, p. 106)

The monitoring of time is so basic to human functioning that it was likely instrumental in the evolution of human thought and cognition (Suddendorf & Corballis, 1997). Markings engraved in ancestral bones dating back to the Ice Age reflect systematic recordings of a lunar calendar (Marshack, 1972), and the sophistication of Aztec sundials reveals that time has been interwoven into the social and political fabrics of societies for centuries (Aveni, 1995). Although cultures clearly differ in their treatment of time, such as the tempo with which life is lived (Levine, 1997), a basic awareness of time is ubiquitous in all known cultures and peoples.

Scholars of theoretical physics, anthropology, astronomy, and philosophy have written extensively about people's perception of time; in contrast, psychologists have remained conspicuously silent on the topic. This is not to say that tacit conceptions of time have been absent in social science. On the contrary, psychologists have studied the influence of historical periods on human development (Elder & Clipp, 1994; Elder, Pavalko, & Hastings, 1991), life-stage effects on values and attitudes (Sears, 1981), cultural differences in the social norms pertaining to time (Jones, 1988), and individual differences in time orientation (Gonzalez & Zimbardo, 1985). To the extent that chronological age is an index of the passage of time, the entire subdiscipline of developmental psychology is inherently organized around this concept. Yet, if one really takes time seriously and acknowledges that time provides the structure from which people plan and implement all short- and long-term goals, the implications for psychology are far-reaching and have been largely ignored (Birren & Cunningham, 1985).

People are always aware of time—not only of clock and calendar time, but of lifetime. Biologist John Medina (1996) wrote,

When contemplating life we inevitably assume the presence of an internal clock. Wound to zero at birth, it incessantly and inherently ticks away during our entire terrestrial tenure. So solid are these concepts in our mind that we have coined the term, "life span" to denote its boundaries. (p. 9)

As people move through life they become increasingly aware that time is in some sense "running out." More social contacts feel superficial—trivial—in contrast to the ever-deepening ties of existing close relationships. It becomes increasingly important to make the "right" choice, not to waste time on gradually diminishing future payoffs. Increasingly, emotionally meaningful goals are pursued.

In the following pages we argue that the perception of time as constrained or limited as opposed to expansive or open-ended has important implications for emotion, cognition, and motivation. In particular, we argue that the ap-

---

Editor's note. Denise C. Park served as action editor for this article.

Author's note. Laura L. Carstensen and Susan T. Charles, Department of Psychology, Stanford University; Derek M. Isaacowitz, Department of Psychology, University of Pennsylvania.

Work on this article was supported by National Institute on Aging Grant RO1-8816. We are greatly indebted to Helene Fung and Eleanor Maccoby for their comments on drafts of this article.

Correspondence concerning this article should be addressed to Laura L. Carstensen, Department of Psychology, Stanford University, Stanford, CA 94305-2130.

Laura L. Carstensen
Photo by L. A. Cicero

proach of endings is associated with heightened emphasis on feelings and emotion states. Activities that are unpleasant or simply devoid of meaning are not compelling under conditions in which time is perceived as limited. Interest in novel information, because it is so closely intertwined with future needs, is reduced. Instead, when endings are primed people focus on the present rather than on the future or the past, and this temporal shift leads to an emphasis on the intuitive and subjective rather than the planful and analytical. The argument we make herein is that a temporal emphasis on the present increases the value people place on life and emotion, importantly influencing the decisions they make.

Subsequently, we argue that the perception of time is inevitably linked to the selection and pursuit of social goals. Our arguments are grounded in socioemotional selectivity theory (Carstensen, 1991, 1993, 1995, 1998; Carstensen, Gross, & Fung, 1997), which is a life-span theory of social motivation in which the perception of time plays a central role in the prioritization of social goals and subsequent preferences for social partners. Because chronological age is inextricably and negatively associated with the amount of time left in life, age-related patterns do emerge, but even these age patterns can be altered when individuals adopt a time perspective different from what is predicted by their place in the life cycle.

In the following pages, we overview socioemotional selectivity theory and describe a program of empirical research that tests its postulates. Because we believe that time is fundamental to human motivation, we then consider the broader implications that boundaries on time may have for theory building and research in psychology.

Socioemotional Selectivity Theory

General Tenets of the Theory

Socioemotional selectivity theory addresses the role of time in predicting the goals that people pursue and the social partners they seek to fulfill them. Three presumptions underlie the theory. First, the theory adopts as axiomatic the belief that social interaction is core to survival, with predispositions toward social interest and social attachment having evolved over the millennia. Second, it considers humans to be inherently agentic and to engage in behaviors guided by the anticipated realization of goals (Bandura, 1982, 1991, 1997). Third, it presumes that because people simultaneously hold multiple—sometimes opposing—goals, the selection of goals is a precursor to action. Socioemotional selectivity theory maintains that the view of time as expansive or limited influences the appraisal process that precedes goal selection.

Over the years, different motivation theorists have posited different sets of "basic" human needs or goals that instigate action (Deci & Ryan, 1991; James, 1890; Maslow, 1968; Ryan, 1991, 1993; White, 1959). Socioemotional selectivity theory is less concerned with which goals are essential than with how social goals function to direct behavior. According to the theory, diverse social goals, ranging from seeking the answer to a question about the weather to seeking emotional comfort, can be classified into one of two broad functional categories: those related to the acquisition of knowledge and those related to the regulation of emotion.

A tremendous amount of social behavior is motivated by the pursuit of information. Contact with other people provides a primary source of knowledge. Observations of others and direct instruction from them play a central role in human survival. Indeed, the intergenerational transmission of language, values, and culturally shared mental representations are accomplished largely through social means (D'Andrade, 1981; Shweder & Sullivan, 1990). Knowledge acquisition through social contact is typically necessary to master even nonsocial skills. And familiarizing oneself with a broad spectrum of people allows individuals to understand the social climate, come to know their own likes and dislikes, and begin to make evaluative comparisons of themselves in relation to others. Thus, the category of knowledge-related goals refers to acquisitive behavior geared toward learning about the social and physical world.

The category of emotion motives refers in its broadest sense to the regulation of emotional states via contact with others. As Rothbart (1994) states "from the earliest days, emotion is regulated by others, and many of our emotions and cognitions about emotion [are] developmentally shaped in a social context" (p. 371). Along with attempts to avoid negative states and experience positive ones (Higgins, 1997; Tomkins, 1970), the category of emotion motives also encompasses the desire to find meaning in life, gain emotional intimacy, and establish feelings of social embeddedness.

**Derek M.
Isaacowitz**

According to the theory, knowledge- and emotion-related goals together comprise an essential constellation of goals that motivates social behavior throughout life. On a day-to-day basis, social goals compete with one another, and often emotional goals vie with knowledge-related ones. Seeking information, for example, may entail emotional risks. A scientist interested in critical feedback from a colleague may expect to feel disheartened by it but will pursue the feedback nonetheless. In our culture, maintaining a satisfying relationship with an intimate partner typically requires that one refrain from seeking novel intimate experiences. In addition, although people are motivated in certain circumstances to seek confirmatory evidence of their self-views, the same people in other circumstances are motivated to disconfirm self-relevant views in order to stimulate growth. Even though the desire to experience positive emotions clearly motivates much behavior (Higgins, 1987, 1997), in some cases, social contact is pursued precisely because it elicits aversive emotions that motivate achievement in some other domain (Norem & Cantor, 1986). When knowledge-related goals compete with goals involving the regulation of emotions, the relative importance of the two goals is weighed, and action is taken or not taken accordingly.

The cardinal tenet of socioemotional selectivity theory is that the assessment of time plays a critical role in the ranking and execution of behaviors geared toward specific goals. Cognitive appraisal of time assists people in balancing long- and short-term goals in order to adapt effectively to their particular circumstances. An expansive future is associated with the pursuit of knowledge-related goals. The young boy talks to his older cousin about college, not because the information is relevant to him at the moment, but because it may become so at some point in the future.

The student arriving for her first year at college finds a wide range of social partners appealing and invests much time and energy in making new friends. The young newlywed couple spends considerable time trying to discover ways to solve problems in their relationship because solutions will allow them to avoid future conflicts. The theory predicts that future-oriented goals such as these will be adaptively prioritized when the future is perceived as expansive, and that this will be the case even when knowledge-related goals entail the delay of emotional rewards or emotional costs.

When the conclusion of the appraisal process is that time is limited, the acquisitive mode associated with unlimited time is transformed into a more present-oriented state. Present orientation is likely to involve goals related to feeling states, deriving emotional meaning, and experiencing emotional satisfaction. Relieved of concerns about the future, attention shifts to experiences occurring in the moment. When emotion regulation is the primary goal, people are highly selective in their choice of social partners, nearly always preferring social partners who are familiar to them, because with these partners emotions are predictable and often quite positive. Moreover, when time is limited social interactions are navigated carefully in order to ensure that their emotional quality is high. In contrast to the young couple described above, the elderly couple often decides to accept their relationship as it is, to appreciate what is good, and ignore what is troubling, rather than seek new solutions to problems. The college senior approaching graduation is uninterested in meeting new students and instead shows strong preferences for spending time with her best friends. And sadly, the young boy living in a crime-ridden neighborhood who believes that he will not live past the age of 20 is decidedly uninterested in conversations about college. According to the theory, he will pursue present-oriented goals, perhaps by establishing strong social bonds through gang membership. Like the older person, he perceives his future as largely irrelevant and focuses his attention on the present.

Clearly, the two classes of social goals described in socioemotional selectivity theory do not reflect absolute, nonoverlapping categories. First, there is an emotional component to all goal-directed behavior (Zajonc, 1997); even the accounting process by which informational goals are selected involves valenced evaluations of prospective targets. Therefore, any distinction among goals in which some are classified as emotional and others are classified as nonemotional is, in some ways, problematic. We do not dispute that there is an emotional component to information seeking or that, conversely, there are elements of information seeking in the pursuit of emotional goals. Clearly, there are. Second, there is ample evidence that when information holds relevance to the immediate situation, it will be sought regardless of temporal orientation (e.g., Turk-Charles, Meyerowitz, & Gatz, 1997). For example, a hungry person who perceives the future as limited will nonetheless speak to a waiter in a restaurant.

Rather, the delineation of social goals suggested by socioemotional selectivity theory concerns those that are

Susan T. Charles

primarily oriented to gaining knowledge or preparing for the future and those that are primarily aimed at satisfying emotional needs. Another way to think about the distinction is that one class of goals is related to preparedness and one to satisfaction in the moment. Interest in an attractive stranger, although likely to involve both positive and negative emotions (e.g., happiness and anxiety), is acted on primarily because of future possibilities. The potential emotional satisfaction that may result from contact remains largely unknown. We expect that much heterosocial contact in adolescence is governed more by excitement or the thrill of novelty than by emotional satisfaction. Young people may embark on an exploration of potential mates, for example, in order to find out what other people are like in this type of relationship. Such behaviors are far from unemotional, but the core motive underlying action is not a search for emotionally meaningful experience. Thus, although "knowledge-related" and "emotional" may be imperfect labels for motivations, we argue that the underlying heuristics point to coherent streams of behavior aimed at realizing goals and, more important, allow for complex human behavior to be distinguished on functional grounds such that useful predictions can be made.

Theoretical Relevance to Life Span Development

Human aging, inherently chronicled by the passage of time, provides an ideal ground for exploring differences in time perspective. Empirical studies suggest that people do carry with them diffuse expectations about the relatively expansive or limited future that awaits them. In our laboratory we have collected questionnaire data from highly diverse samples spanning adolescence through very old age that document clear associations between age and perceived time left in life (Carstensen & Lang, 1997a). Older people relative to their younger counterparts describe their futures as limited and recognize that they do not have "all the time in the world" left to pursue their goals. We expect that the monitoring of time occurs regularly at an unconscious level and is also primed acutely on a periodic basis by discrete events that mark time, such as a child's wedding or a friend's death.

Although research shows that older people consider the past as the time of greatest activity and potency in contrast to younger people's anticipation of future development (Shmotkin, 1991; see also Cross & Markus, 1991; Heckhausen, Dixon, & Baltes, 1989), the primary age difference in time orientation concerns not the past but the present. Older people are mostly present-oriented, less concerned than the young with the far distant future (Fingerman & Perlmutter, 1995). They do not dwell on the past, however, as popular stereotypes suggest.[1] Rather, more than other age groups, they focus on the here and now.

Socioemotional selectivity theory suggests that age-related differences in the anticipated future lead to developmental trends in the ranking of knowledge-related and emotional goals. The knowledge trajectory starts high during the early years of life and declines gradually over the life course as knowledge accrues and the future for which it is banked grows shorter. The emotion trajectory is high during infancy[2] and early childhood, declines from middle childhood throughout early adulthood, and rises from later adulthood into old age as future-oriented strivings become less relevant.

Because knowledge strivings are so important from late adolescence to middle adulthood, they are pursued relentlessly even at the cost of emotional satisfaction. By late adolescence and early adulthood, the regulation of feeling states is relegated lower status than acquiring knowledge. During this period of life, the exploration of the world demands emotional resilience in the face of failures and social rejections. Later in life, however, goals that are satisfied by the resulting "feeling" state are more likely to be pursued because they are experienced in the here and now, a valuable commodity in the face of limited time. Figure 1 provides the idealized trajectories of knowledge-related and emotional goal salience across the life span.

Finally, socioemotional selectivity theory predicts that endings are associated with qualitative changes in emotional experience. In part, this is the consequence of increasingly selective social partner choices and engagement in smaller, but more emotionally meaningful, social networks (Carstensen et al., 1997). By shaping the social world, negative emotional responses can be avoided and positive ones optimized. This form of emotion control, referred to in the literature as "antecedent regulation of

---

[1] Past orientation is associated with depressive symptoms (e.g., Holman & Silver, 1998), but age is not reliably associated with past focus.

[2] In very early childhood, limited cognitive capacity precludes the appreciation of abstract concepts of time. Subsequently, the type of goal competition predicted by the theory is minimal. Infants are highly motivated by both knowledge-related and emotional goals.

Figure 1
Idealized Model of Socioemotional Selectivity Theory's Conception of the Salience of Two Classes of Social Motives Across the Life Span

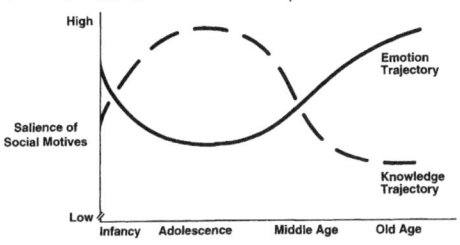

Note. From "The Social Context of Emotion," by L. L. Carstensen, J. Gross, & H. Fung, 1997, *Annual Review of Geriatrics and Gerontology, 17,* p. 331. Copyright 1997 by Springer Publishing Company, Inc. Reprinted with permission.

emotion" (see Gross, in press), is arguably the most effective way to manage emotional experience at any age, but theoretically improves over time. Older people not only interact with fewer people, they interact primarily with people who are well-known to them (Field & Minkler, 1988). In old age, people's inner social circles are composed primarily of old friends and family members. Kahn and Antonucci (1980) refer to the handful of significant others who accompany individuals through life as "social convoys." In old age, social convoys knit individuals into kin and friendship networks with unmatched capabilities to affirm the sense of self and provide support in times of need (Antonucci, 1990, 1991; Antonucci & Akiyama, 1997; Antonucci & Jackson, 1987). Moreover, the life-long history of support exchange in long-term relationships can allow even the very frail older person to feel needed by others (Carstensen & Lang, 1997b). In short, the predictability of interactions with familiar social partners permits people to better navigate difficult social transactions, to more reliably elicit positive emotions, and to obtain a sense of social embeddedness and meaning in life.

In addition, the theory suggests that the knowledge that time is limited has direct effects on emotional experience. Appreciation of the fragility of life, recognition that the passage of time cannot be stopped, and heightened awareness of one's immediate surroundings directly alters the experience of emotion.[3] We also expect that, relieved of concerns for the future, endings bring out the best qualities in people; kindness becomes a more prominent feature of social exchanges during graduations, funerals, or retirements. As people approach the ultimate ending—death—lives are evaluated, and a search for existential meaning in life places emotion at center stage.

We have conducted several lines of research and used a variety of research methods to test postulates from the theory. In keeping with theoretical and empirical links between time perspective and chronological age, much of this research has considered age a proxy for time left in life. Over the years, however, we have made repeated attempts to decouple age from time, by drawing on studies of naturally occurring subgroups (e.g., young people living with a terminal illness) and by using experimental methods to tease apart the effects of age and time. In the following section, we describe our program of empirical research. It is organized around four general research themes that reflect central postulates of socioemotional selectivity theory: (a) life-cycle differences in the salience of emotion, (b) age differences in the regulation of emotion, (c) age differences in social network composition, and (d) social preferences under conditions characterized by limited or expansive time.

Empirical Findings From Socioemotional Selectivity Theory

The Salience of Emotion as People Approach the End of Life

A central postulate of socioemotional theory is that the salience of particular social goals is influenced by the perception of time. According to the theory, open-ended time is associated with the pursuit of knowledge, and constraints on time are associated with the prioritization of emotional goals. Such changes are presumed to be evident in the ways that people think about social partners and the relative attention paid to emotion in cognitive operations. Below we summarize findings from three studies that examined the cognitive dimensions along which people mentally represent social partners and the relative weights placed on these dimensions at different points in the life cycle. At the close of this section, we also report findings from a study of age differences in incidental memory for social narrative.

Mental representations of social partners. We recognized early on in our research that we needed to obtain evidence that the goal dimensions posited in socioemotional selectivity theory are actually evident in people's thinking about social partners (Fredrickson & Carstensen, 1990). Because direct questions about social goals (e.g., Would you learn something new by interacting with your mother?) pose serious concerns about demand characteristics, we developed an experimental procedure based on similarity judgments. By asking people to classify various social partners on the basis of perceived similarities, we were able to explore the cognitive dimensions that people use to make such judgments.

This experimental approach also allowed us to examine the relative weights placed on specific cognitive dimen-

---
[3] Some previous research on time perspective associates present orientation, and the concomitant failure to delay gratification, with hedonism (Gonzalez & Zimbardo, 1985). However, these studies measure time orientation within a relatively narrow time period; for example, will a person study today or tomorrow? In contrast, "time" as construed in socioemotional selectivity theory spans the life course. Although an emphasis on the present is common to both, present orientation activated by awareness of mortality leads to mixed emotional reactions, such as poignancy, as opposed to hedonism.

sions by different groups of people. In two studies we examined age differences in samples that included participants as young as adolescents and as old as octogenarians. Samples in both studies spanned a similar age range, but the second was far more representative than the first in that it was constructed such that men and women, blue- and white-collar workers, and African and European Americans were evenly distributed across the targeted age range (Carstensen & Fredrickson, 1998). Together, these first two studies allowed us to examine both the reliability and generalizability of cognitive dimensions and their salience in different age groups.

The third sample differed importantly in that age was held constant across subsamples. In each subsample, the average age was 37 years, and all participants were male. However, each subsample differed by HIV status (Carstensen & Fredrickson, 1998). One subsample was HIV-negative, another HIV-positive but asymptomatic, and a third subsample was HIV-positive and actively experiencing symptoms of AIDS. Therefore, each subsample was comparably aged, but differed in life expectancy, allowing us to examine closeness to the end of life independent of the experience factor that typically confounds chronological age with place in the life cycle. Put differently, the first two samples allowed us to examine mental representations as a function of time since birth. The third sample allowed us to examine the same questions as a function of time until death. In all three studies, we predicted that identified cognitive dimensions would reflect emotional and knowledge-related qualities of others and that closeness to the end of life would be associated with greater emphasis on the emotional as opposed to the knowledge-related dimension.

The experimental procedures were identical in each study. Research participants were presented with a set of 18 cards, each of which described a particular type of social partner. The set of social partners was designed to span a broad spectrum of people, some of whom are likely to provide novel information in the course of social interaction (e.g., the author of a book you've read) and others who are more likely to yield emotional payoffs (e.g., a close friend). Participants were asked to sort the cards into as many or as few piles as they wished according to how similarly they would feel interacting with the person described on the card. After participants classified prospective social partners on the basis of similarity judgments, data were submitted to multidimensional scaling analysis, which revealed the dimensions along which people sorted the cards.

The same three dimensions accounted reliably for most of the variance in the mathematical solution in each study. The first dimension clearly represented a valenced (i.e., good–bad) dimension, which we labeled the "affective potential" of the social partners described on the cards. Both additional dimensions were consistent with knowledge-related qualities of the social partners: One was interpreted as "future contact" and the other as "information-seeking." Thus, people do indeed appear to think about others in terms of the trajectories posited in the theory.

More pertinent to the study hypotheses were group differences in the degree to which these dimensions governed their classifications. We found that successive age groups placed increasingly greater emphasis on the affective potential of social partners, whereas younger adults weighted the three dimensions fairly evenly. Not only was this true for the overall study samples, but within the samples the patterns held for men and women, blue- and white-collar workers, and African and European Americans. Moreover, in our study based on HIV status, the profile of findings paralleled those from our age-based samples. HIV-positive, symptomatic, male participants represented prospective social partners nearly exclusively along affective dimensions, just as our oldest participants did in our previous studies. We drew two conclusions from this series of studies. First, the goal categories posited in socioemotional selectivity theory are reliably reflected in people's thinking about others, and second, the importance of emotion in these assessments is more central in people nearing the end of life.

Memory for social narratives. If emotion is more salient to older as compared with younger adults, older adults may process emotional information more deeply and subsequently remember it better than nonemotional information. Using an incidental memory paradigm, we explored the type of information older and younger people recall about an emotionally charged social interaction (Carstensen & Turk-Charles, 1994). In light of well-documented age differences in memory performance (Smith, 1996), we did not predict that older adults would remember more emotional information than younger adults. Rather we predicted that of the material remembered, proportionately more would concern emotional aspects of the situation.

We recruited a sample of research participants aged 20 to 83 years and asked them to read a two-page selection drawn from a popular novel. At the end of an experimental hour in which participants completed other unrelated questionnaires, they were asked to recall all that they could about the story. Responses were transcribed and classified as emotional or nonemotional. We calculated the proportion of emotional to nonemotional information and examined its relationship to age. As depicted in Figure 2, the proportion of emotional material recalled increased with age. Each successive age group recalled proportionately more emotional material than nonemotional information from the narratives.

All told, the above findings suggest that emotion is an important dimension along which people consider others across adulthood. Findings also suggest that emotional qualities of others assume greater importance in mental representations about social partners and in memory about social interactions among increasingly older age-cohorts. A similar profile occurs among subsamples of younger people constructed according to their probable life expectancies; closeness to the end of life is related to the prominence of emotion in mental representations. The striking similarity between the profile of older adults and the profile of younger adults approaching death challenges a purely de-

Figure 2
Mean Proportion of Emotional Material Recalled in Four Adult Age Groups

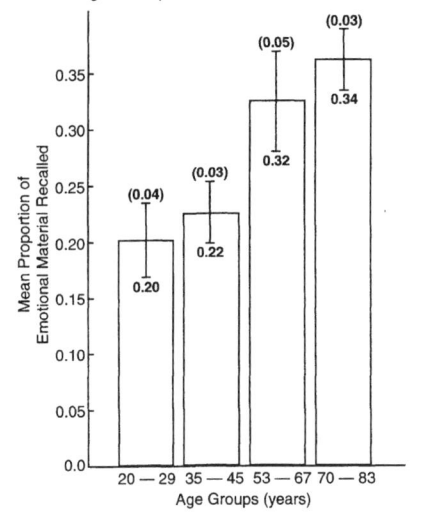

[Bar chart showing mean proportion of emotional material recalled by age group:
- 20–29: 0.20 (0.04)
- 35–45: 0.22 (0.03)
- 53–67: 0.32 (0.05)
- 70–83: 0.34 (0.03)
X-axis: Age Groups (years); Y-axis: Mean Proportion of Emotional Material Recalled]

Note. Error bars depict standard errors of the mean. From "The Salience of Emotion Across the Adult Life Course," by L. L. Carstensen and S. Turk-Charles, 1994, *Psychology and Aging, 9*, p. 262. Copyright 1994 by the American Psychological Association.

velopmental account of change and implicates the approach of an important ending in the instigation of cognitive shifts.

Age Differences in the Regulation of Emotion

Evidence that emotion is more prominent in social cognitive processing in groups of people nearing the end of life is consistent with socioemotional selectivity theory's contention that emotion and emotional goals are increasingly important as people approach endings. To the extent that greater value is placed on emotionally meaningful goals, there also should be a concomitant enhancement of emotional experience and, very likely, better regulation of emotional experience (see Carstensen & Charles, in press). That is, more investment in emotional goals should be related to more resource allocation to these goals. We argue that as people approach endings, they pay more attention to the emotional quality of social exchanges and engage in strategic attempts to optimize emotional aspects of important social relationships. In everyday terms, awareness of limited time provides the sense of perspective that softens the experience of negative emotions (why get angry now?) and enhances the appreciation of positive aspects of life. The sense that "this may be the last time" changes emotional reactions to positive and negative social exchanges.

We do not believe that this occurs only as people approach the end of life. On the contrary, the theory suggests that this experience is common. We expect that saying your last goodbyes to a friend (even if the friendship has been rocky), or approaching graduation or retirement, should also be characterized by efforts to make the experience emotionally positive. Yet, old age is the life stage where potential "last times" are ubiquitous, and thus the theory makes clear predictions about emotional functioning during the last stage of life.

Although emotion in old age has been decidedly understudied, diverse evidence from a number of laboratories is beginning to converge to suggest that people function very well in emotional domains of life in the later years. Studies examining social reasoning and decision making are suggestive of improved understanding of basic emotion states well into adulthood as well as better integration of emotion into cognitive processing (Blanchard-Fields, 1986; Labouvie-Vief, DeVoe, & Bulka, 1989; Labouvie-Vief, Hakim-Larson, DeVoe, & Schoeberlein, 1989). Mood inductions under controlled laboratory conditions result in subjective experiences that are comparably intense for younger and older adults (Levenson, Carstensen, Friesen, & Ekman, 1991), but older people nevertheless report superior self-regulation of emotion, including decreased lability and surgency and better control over negative emotions (Lawton, Kleban, Rajagopal, & Dean, 1992).

Although there have been no longitudinal studies of emotion regulation, leaving open the possibility that cohort differences are responsible for age differences, Gross et al. (1997) recently reported findings from a project based on multiple samples including Norwegians, Catholic nuns, African Americans, Chinese Americans, and European Americans. Across these diverse samples, older people reported better control of emotion, and consistent with Lawton et al.'s (1992) earlier report, older adults in all samples reported fewer negative emotions. Thus, if cohort accounts for generational differences in the perceived regulation of emotion, they are surprisingly widespread. Finally, the self-reported reduction in surgency (Gross et al., 1997; Lawton et al., 1992) finds convergent support from studies in which autonomic reactivity is measured directly during emotional episodes; older people display relatively lower levels of physiological activity during mood inductions and while engaging in discussions of emotionally charged topics (Levenson et al., 1991; Levenson, Carstensen, & Gottman, 1994). All told, empirical research on emotion and aging suggests that emotional functioning is at the least well-preserved in old age, and may even improve.

In an effort to understand the dynamics of emotional exchanges among intimates at different ages, Carstensen and two colleagues, John Gottman and Robert Levenson (1995; see also, Levenson, Carstensen, & Gottman, 1993, 1994), conducted a study of middle-aged and older couples who had been married for many years. After an initial screening to ensure that both happy and unhappy couples were included in both age groups, couples completed a number of questionnaires about married life. They indicated the degree to which various issues presented problems in their relationships (e.g., finances, children, in-laws) and the degree of pleasure they derived from other activities along with a variety of instruments that assessed emotional and physical health. Couples were then observed while they discussed a conflict in their relationship. After an experimenter helped couples agree on a conflict appropriate for discussion (e.g., both parties had to agree it was a conflict), they were left alone in a room equipped with remote cameras and asked to discuss the conflict for 15 minutes. Throughout the interaction, cameras recorded the interaction, and physiological activity was monitored as couples discussed conflictual aspects of their relationships.

Subjective evaluations and direct observations of discussions both pointed to superior emotion regulation in older couples. By self-report, the conflicts in a number of domains (e.g., finances, children, and so on) were less severe in older as compared with middle-aged couples; it is important to note that this was true even for unhappily married couples. Moreover, older couples reported that they derived greater pleasure than middle-aged couples in four arenas: talking about children and grandchildren, doing things together, taking vacations, and "dreaming." Thus, compared with middle-aged couples, older couples reported experiencing less conflict and taking greater pleasure in their marriages (Levenson et al., 1993).

However, this project went beyond self-reported evaluations of the relationships we studied. The videotaped discussions of conflict provided a rich source of observational data. Coding of specific affects revealed direct evidence for emotion regulation. Even after controlling for marital satisfaction, older couples, compared with their middle-aged counterparts, expressed lower levels of anger, disgust, belligerence, and whining. Moreover, they were more likely than middle-aged couples to express affection to one another, even as they discussed a problematic aspect of their relationship. Older couples were not less involved in the task; they displayed levels of tension and domineeringness similar to those of middle-aged couples. Rather, they interwove expressions of affection along with expressions of discontent (Carstensen et al., 1995; Carstensen, Graff, Levenson, & Gottman, 1996).

Previous research, our own included, suggests that where there are differences, older people experience fewer negative emotions and have greater control over their emotions in everyday life. Our observational research on married couples is certainly consistent with these reports. Still, the bulk of the evidence in the literature relies on self-reports, which are susceptible to distortion as a function of demand characteristics and implicit theories about what behavior "should be like" at different life stages. Very recently, we completed a project designed to sample emotions in everyday life (Carstensen, Pasupathi, & Mayr, 1998). The experience sampling method we adopted allowed us to examine emotional experience and regulation without asking participants for global judgments about regulatory control.

We recruited a sample spanning the ages of 18 to 95 years to participate in a study of emotions in everyday life.

We used an experience sampling technique that required participants to carry electronic pagers for a one-week period and to record their emotions each of 35 times they were paged. At random times, throughout the days and evenings, participants were paged. Each time they were signaled, they indicated which emotions they were experiencing and how intensely they were felt on a response sheet that listed 19 emotional states. Both positive and negative states were represented on the response sheet; some were basic emotions, like anger and sadness, and others were mood states, like anxiety or jealousy. At the end of each day, participants mailed their response sheets back to the laboratory for coding.

We tested several hypotheses about aging and emotion, based on socioemotional selectivity theory's general contention that emotional experience is optimized and better regulated in old age. We postulated that the frequency of positive emotions would be comparable across age groups, but the frequency of negative emotional experience would decline. Our findings showed that positive emotions are maintained in both frequency and intensity across adulthood. Negative emotions decline in frequency, but not intensity. This age trend persists across adulthood until very old age, at which point negative emotions do occur somewhat more frequently. At no point in old age, however, are negative emotions experienced more often than in young adulthood.

We examined the regulation of emotion by computing conditional probabilities that an emotion would occur given that it occurred on the previous page. Here we found that the natural duration of positive emotional experience is similar for old and young, but the duration of negative emotions, as indexed by conditional probabilities, is lesser for older as compared with younger adults.

Finally, we explored the postulate that emotional experience is more mixed in older as opposed to younger people. In day-to-day life, people frequently experience multiple emotions concurrently in response to an elicitor. Within a matter of seconds, they may feel anger, sadness, and perhaps even some degree of happiness (e.g., satisfaction that the villain has shown his true colors). Socioemotional selectivity theory predicts that emotional experience becomes more multifaceted with age because limited time changes the character of positive emotions and negative emotions. We tested this hypothesis in two ways. First, we computed the simple correlation between positive emotional experience and negative emotional experience and then assessed the degree to which positive and negative emotions are experienced simultaneously as a function of age. We found that the association increases with age. Second, we computed a factor analysis for each participant based on the 35 data points obtained during their participation. We then computed the correlation between age and the average number of factors that typified participants' responses. We reasoned that more differentiated experience would result in more factors, whereas less differentiated experience would result in fewer factors. Once again, the number of factors characterizing participants' emotional experiences was positively associated with age.

In summary, empirical evidence accrued during the past decade paints a distinctly positive picture of aging in the emotion domain. The theoretical postulate that emotion is better regulated at the end of life is supported in studies based on self-report, observational, and experience sampling methods. Improved emotion regulation with age, though interestingly inconsistent with the adulthood trajectory of cognitive functioning, is not terribly surprising. Experience, no doubt, plays a role in the regulation of emotion. However, if based purely on experience one might predict improvement through direct suppression of emotion or, alternatively, through emotional withdrawal. When experienced, however, negative and positive emotions are felt just as intensely among young and old. The principle age differences involve the frequency of negative emotional experience and the complexity of emotional experience. Anger is intertwined with affection; happiness and sadness are more likely experienced in the same moment. Far more research is needed to establish the reliability of these preliminary findings and the viability of our interpretations. Age differences in emotional experience are consistent, however, with theoretical predictions about the way that emotion may change under conditions that limit time. These findings, in conjunction with those described in the previous section, suggest that emotion is not only more salient when time in life is limited, but that the quality of these experiences may change as well.

Life Cycle Differences in the Composition of Social Networks

To the extent that mental representations of others and the prioritizing of emotion goals reflect social preferences, such preferences have implications for social networks. Socioemotional selectivity theory predicts that, ideally, older people have relatively small social networks concentrated with social partners who are most likely to provide a social climate in which they feel validated and loved. In contrast, younger people have relatively larger, more diverse social networks that include a high proportion of relatively novel social partners.

Age differences in social network size have been well-documented in social gerontology. Longitudinal and cross-sectional studies reveal far smaller social networks among older as compared with younger people (Lee & Markides, 1990; Palmore, 1981). Most theorizing about this highly reliable difference has focused on age-related losses, such as poor health, deaths of social partners, and ageist societal practices that limit access to other people (Havighurst & Albrecht, 1953). One highly influential model—disengagement theory—suggested that reduced social contact stems from the mutual, emotional withdrawal of individuals from societies (and societies from them) in symbolic preparation for death (Cumming & Henry, 1961). The motivational approach we have adopted, however, construes people as active agents who construct social worlds to match their social goals. In contrast to both disengagement theory, which suggests that people withdraw most from those closest to them, and explanations that hold social and physical barriers responsible for reduced social network size, we hypothesized that people systematically hone their social networks such that available social partners satisfy emotional needs. At the time we began our research on social networks, virtually all of the published research focused on comparisons of overall network size, typically between middle and old age. Given that losses do accumulate across this period of life, attributing age differences to loss was certainly reasonable; loss must play a role to some degree. Nevertheless, proactive processes may also contribute. Socioemotional selectivity theory suggests that goal trajectories change gradually across adulthood. If age differences in network size reflect the culmination of lifelong selection processes, evidence should be apparent relatively early in adulthood.

A study was designed to assess potential changes in social contact from early to middle adulthood (Carstensen, 1992) that involved the reanalysis of longitudinal data from the Child Guidance Study (MacFarlane, 1938). In 1930, MacFarlane selected a sample of infants whom she (and subsequently others) followed into adulthood, assessing and reassessing their status at regular time intervals. In adulthood, the participants in the Child Guidance Study were interviewed four times, at ages 18, 30, 40, and 50 years. Interviews addressed participants' satisfactions and sorrows associated with various types of social partners, ranging from acquaintances to close friends and relatives. Interviews also included questions about the frequency of contact with specific types of social partners. Thus, these data allowed the life course charting of a spectrum of relationships, some of which had considerable potential to provide novel information (e.g., acquaintances) and others which offered the potential for emotional satisfaction (e.g., intimates). We hypothesized that contact with acquaintances would decline over time, whereas contact with intimates (e.g., spouses, parents, children) would remain stable or increase.

As predicted, rates of interaction with acquaintances declined from early to middle adulthood, as did participants' satisfaction with remaining contact with acquaintances. Across the same years, however, interaction rates with spouses, parents, and siblings were maintained or increased. In other words, reductions in contact appeared to begin long before age-related loss could be the cause, and reductions were restricted to acquaintances. The picture that emerged was consistent with a selection process that begins by early adulthood, excludes novel social partners, and maintains emotionally close ones.

Returning to a consideration of old age, we conducted a cross-sectional comparison of the social networks of old and very old adults (Lang & Carstensen, 1994). Theoretically, selectivity should be greatest in old age because this is the time in life when endings are most salient. Our target sample was a representative group of old and very old people recruited to participate in the Berlin Aging Study (P. B. Baltes, Mayer, Helmchen, & Steinhagen-Thiessen, 1993). Research participants ranged in age from 69 to 104 years. Our results indicated that the oldest participants had fewer social partners compared with relatively younger participants. However, independent consideration of close and less close social partners revealed an interesting pattern. The number of peripheral social partners was greatly reduced among the very old compared with the young-old, yet there was little difference in the number of emotionally close social partners they reported. Even among the very old, the number of social partners identified as part of the participants' "inner circle" was virtually the same as it was among adults as much as 30 years their junior. In a subsequent study based on the same sample, we examined potential differences in selectivity as a function of personality and family status and found that the selectivity effect held across these individual difference variables (Lang, Staudinger, & Carstensen, 1998). Although the design of this cross-sectional comparison prohibits conclusions about developmental change, findings are consistent with a longitudinal analysis of a smaller sample of participants across a comparable time frame (Field & Minkler, 1988) and, moreover, fit well into the larger profile of findings generated by socioemotional selectivity theory.

In summary, research on social networks suggests that there are systematic age differences, not only in social network size, as have been reported repeatedly over the years, but also in composition. Across adulthood, an increasingly larger percentage of the total network is occupied by emotionally close social partners. This change begins far too early in life to consider loss the exclusive explanation, and because emotionally close social partners are systematically retained in the process, emotional disengagement is not likely the cause. We interpret these findings as evidence for a proactive pruning process that selectively emphasizes emotionally close social partners and disregards more peripheral ones as time in life grows increasingly limited.

Social Preferences as a Function of Time

With the exception of our research on HIV-positive and HIV-negative men, the work described so far treats age as a proxy for time. In this section we describe our experimental attempts to decouple age from time. In these studies, we have found reliably that time, as opposed to age per se, appears to be the critical factor in the age differences in social patterns we have observed.

Psychological theory and research published over the past two to three decades documents well the proactive, agentic nature of human functioning (Bandura, 1987; Ryan, 1993). People do not simply react to environments in which they find themselves; rather the choices that they make contribute actively to the creation of their social worlds. Socioemotional selectivity theory predicts that these choices are influenced by the perception of time. When time is perceived as expansive, social preferences reflect knowledge-related goals. When time is limited, they reflect emotional goals.

Several years ago, Fredrickson and Carstensen (1990) developed an experimental procedure in which social partner preferences were assessed under conditions of limited and open-ended time. Our original objective was to document age differences in social partner preferences predicted by the theory and, further, to assess whether social preferences could be modified by manipulating perceived time. Modified versions of this experimental approach have now been used in four other studies also described below (Fung, Carstensen, & Lutz, 1998).

In our first study we asked research participants aged 11 to 92 years to indicate which of three social partners they preferred under two experimental conditions. We hypothesized that older people, by virtue of age, face limited time and subsequently are likely to pursue emotionally relevant social contact. Younger people, in contrast, are more likely to prefer novel social partners because interactions with these types of social partners are more likely to yield new information. As a result, older people were expected to show a bias for familiar social partners, whereas younger people were not. In keeping with our thinking about the role of time in social goals, however, we also hypothesized that younger people would show a preference for familiar social partners if they perceived time to be limited.

Research participants were asked to choose from among three prospective social partners: (a) a member of their immediate family (the emotionally salient choice), (b) a recent acquaintance with whom they seemed to have much in common (novel partner related to future possibilities and knowledge gain), and (c) the author of a book they had read (novel partner who is a potential knowledge source). Selections were made under two experimental conditions. The first simply required participants to imagine that they had 30 minutes of free time and decided to spend it with another person. The second required participants to imagine a situation in which time was limited due to an approaching geographical move, and to choose again from among the same three social partners.

Our hypotheses were confirmed. Older people showed strong preferences for familiar social partners. This was true under both conditions. In contrast, younger adults' preferences differed by condition. Under open-ended conditions, younger people failed to show a preference for familiar social partners, but in the second condition, in which constraints were placed on time, responses of younger and older participants were indistinguishable.

Subsequently, we completed another study very similar to the first, but instead of an ending condition, participants were asked to imagine a hypothetical situation in which the future was expanded (Fung et al., 1998). The second experimental condition required participants to imagine that they had just received a telephone call from their physician, who had informed them of a new medical breakthrough that would likely add 20 years to their life. In this study, the social preferences of younger people were stable across experimental conditions but responses of older people changed. Once again, under the open-ended condition, which was a straight replication of the first condition in our initial study, social preferences of older people revealed a strong bias for familiar social partners. Under the expanded time condition, however, this bias disappeared. Older people were no more likely than younger people to prefer familiar social partners.

We recently completed two additional studies in Hong Kong (Fung et al., 1998). In one, we conducted a modified replication of our initial study in an Asian culture. We recruited Hong Kong participants aged 8 to 90 years and asked them to choose from among the three social partners listed previously. The first condition involved the selection of social partners under open-ended conditions. The second condition required that participants imagine an approaching emigration before they made their selection. Findings from our U.S. sample were replicated in Hong Kong. Under open-ended conditions, older Hong Kong citizens were more likely than their younger counterparts to select familiar social partners. When a hypothetical ending was imagined, however, younger people also favored familiar social partners.

Later the same year, Hong Kong's political return to the People's Republic of China became increasingly salient around the world, but especially among the people of Hong Kong. Newspaper headlines such as "Can Hong Kong Survive?" implied the certain end of a political era and possibly of a way of life. Calendars sold in Hong Kong in 1997 marked the number of days until the handover. Many Hong Kong citizens reported that they would likely emigrate (Skeldon, 1995). We postulated that this macrolevel political change was producing a sense of anticipated endings in an entire population. Because we had collected evidence about social preferences earlier the same year, we decided to repeat the procedure just four months before the handover. As we predicted, both younger and older adults at this time preferred familiar over novel social partners.

Very recently, we repeated the study again, one year after the handover, expecting that the sense of the Hong Kong "ending" would have passed. As expected, age associations with social preferences at this point in time were indistinguishable from those identified in our surveys one year before the handover. Thus, this set of findings suggests that endings other than death, such as geographical moves or political transitions, may instigate the same kinds of changes in social preferences observed in old age.

Taken as a whole, this body of research supports the contention that the anticipation of time plays an important role in social cognition and social behavior. We argue that socioemotional selectivity represents an adaptive process (see Lang & Carstensen, 1994). When the future is expansive, novel experiences with others are at a premium. Contact with a wide range of people helps individuals to prepare for an unknown future and the myriad experiences and challenges that await them. When time is limited, familiar social partners are valued because they are best able to influence emotional states and are realized immediately during the social exchange. Although, obviously, close social relationships are not uniformly positive, they nevertheless remain the relationships in which emotional support and emotional meaning are most likely to be found.

Broader Applicability of Time in Psychological Research

Throughout this article, we have outlined theoretical and empirical support for the contention that the perception of time, especially recognition of approaching endings, exerts a reliable influence on human behavior. Much of the research we have reviewed has focused on age differences predicted by the theory on the basis of time's relationship to age. However, in studies where we have eliminated age confounds—as in our study of HIV-infected men or in our experimental studies of time and social preferences—our predictions are also supported, strengthening our contention that time is an important factor in the ranking and execution of social goals. Because people approach endings in many different contexts and at many times during their lives, the remainder of our comments address broader theoretical implications as they apply to different subdisciplines within psychology.

Implications for life span developmental psychology. Socioemotional selectivity theory has obvious implications for the study of life span development, many of which we have alluded to above. It bears mentioning, however, that this program of research offers an important alternative to deficit models of aging. Our findings suggest that behavioral changes in old age do not simply reflect efforts to cope with loss, but rather reflect active adaptation to particular circumstances, social niches, and environments, which are inevitably framed by time. In this program of research, age is not construed as a fixed, intractable state; rather aging is conceptualized as providing a set of conditions that frequently alters behavioral, cognitive, and emotional goals and brings to the fore different, but nevertheless basic, human processes that operate throughout life.

Although there is no doubt that people experience an increasingly disproportionate number of losses as compared with gains as they age, and fully expect such changes to occur (Heckhausen et al., 1989), we argue that the program of research we have outlined contributes an important complement to theoretical models that presume age differences reflect the accommodation to actual or even anticipated loss (e.g., Brandtstädter & Greve, 1994; see Carstensen & Freund, 1994). In our theoretical formulation, loss is not a precondition for change; rather many changes reflect proactive shifts due to the salience of different goals at different points in the life cycle. Something in the finite nature of time appears to make life precious, especially as the end nears. Within this framework, age changes may reflect increased appreciation of life rather than despair about loss.

Socioemotional selectivity theory also complements well the model of selective optimization with compensation (SOC) introduced by P. B. Baltes and Baltes in 1990 (see also M. M. Baltes & Carstensen, 1996; P. B. Baltes, 1997). According to SOC, development (or adaptation) throughout life requires three essential processes: selection, optimization, and compensation. Because organisms inevitably pursue some specializations and not others (e.g., language, occupations, social relationships), *selection* is the cardinal feature of development. *Optimization* refers to the basic human drive to master environmental and self-related life tasks in a way that maximizes adaptation. *Compensation* involves the utilization of internal and external resources in order to obtain selected goals. Hence, SOC describes processes that are necessary for the realization of developmental goals.

However, the SOC model does not prescribe or predefine specific criteria or goals of development (M. M. Baltes & Carstensen, 1996). Thus, predictions about the types of goals that are selected, the compensatory strategies that people use, and the nature of optimization are left to domain-specific theories. Socioemotional selectivity theory makes specific predictions in the domains of emotion and social relations. When social endings are approached, the penultimate of which is represented by old age, emotional goals are selected (i.e., assume highest priority) over other goals (e.g., information seeking, making new friends, and so on). When the regulation of emotion assumes greatest priority among social motives, social partners are systematically selected to optimize emotional experience, and social interactions are navigated carefully to maintain an emotionally balanced and meaningful life. By narrowing the range of social partners, older people compensate for reductions in physical and cognitive resources, freeing time and energy to direct toward selected social relationships.

Implications for social and personality psychology. Of all the subdisciplines in psychology, time perspective has received most attention in social psychology (McGrath, 1988). Unfortunately, research on time in this subdiscipline has been highly instrumental in nature (cf. Freedman & Edwards, 1988) and even at its most philosophical has ignored the fact that time ends (McGrath, 1988). Rather, social psychological consideration of time has focused primarily on individual differences in time perspective among young college students. Moreover, in most of this research, even future and present orientation are operationalized within a relatively limited time frame (e.g., Do you put off until tomorrow what you can do today?). If, as we argue, the perception of time left in life is fundamental to motivation, it has far-reaching implications for the study of social behavior. Certainly, it underscores the inadequacy of the "college sophomore" as the prototype for human behavior. Not only is age correlated with time perspective, the college years are arguably unmatched in their emphasis on future preparedness.

Even in college student samples in which time orientation is inevitably restricted, those who are future-oriented place greater emphasis on goal-directed behavior and engage in a greater number of activities geared toward achieving long-term goals (Murrell & Mingrone, 1994). We expect, however, that the temporal framing of life has more subtle implications for motivation. Perceiving an ending may play an important role in identity processes, such that endings promote greater self-acceptance and less striving toward an abstract ideal. The concepts of past, present, and future selves (Markus & Nurius, 1986; Markus & Wurf, 1987) represent a notable exception in social psychology in that they are embedded within a life-course time frame. Indeed, research on age differences in self-concept suggests that advanced age is related to greater self-acceptance (Cross & Markus, 1991), and discrepancies between "actual" and "ideal" selves are reduced (Ryff, 1991).

Self-completion theory suggests that perceived inconsistencies between personal characteristics and important identity strivings lead to self-symbolizing behavior (Gollwitzer, 1986). For example, an athlete who is told that a personality inventory reveals that she is unlike most other athletes is likely to emphasize her athletic prowess on subsequent experimental tasks. Gollwitzer and his colleagues have demonstrated this effect in an elegant program of research. They interpreted the symbolic behavior as reparative; that is, individuals symbolically overcompensate for the threat by reasserting themselves. It is interesting that Wicklund and Gollwitzer (1981) found that expertise is inversely related to self-symbolizing. They suggest that people who are secure in their self-views are less likely than others to engage in symbolic representations. A slightly different take on the same effect relates to time: Implicit in self-completion theory is the notion that the threat to self has implications for future performance. If the negative predictive value is removed, the same information may not undermine the self at all. Indeed, it may serve to affirm a sense of individuality.

The approach of endings may affect the behavior of people moving to new areas, undergoing job relocations, or completing major life tasks, such as graduating from college or launching one's own children from the home "nest." Fredrickson (1995) compared college seniors with new college students and found that seniors preferred familiar partners over people they did not know, whereas entering college students were more interested in meeting others. And recall that young Hong Kong citizens showed preferences similar to those of older citizens just prior to the Hong Kong handover (Fung et al., 1998). Thus, consideration of both naturalistic and individualized social endings appears to be central in the ranking of social goals.

Implications for cultural psychology. In all likelihood, human appreciation of time, the need for social relatedness, and the inevitable association of age with mortality are universal. Cross-cultural investigation of the theory, however, may be fruitful in terms of both refining the theory and illuminating possible reasons for certain types of cultural differences. The ways in which time is construed, the value placed on specific goals, the meaning of relationships, and even the understanding of the afterlife may influence social preferences and goal pursuit in important and culturally distinct ways. Thus, although the essential postulate of the theory should replicate in any culture, the theoretical centrality of cognitive construals and social conditions (as opposed to intractable individual differences) are highly compatible with basic premises of cultural psychology (Markus, Kitayama, & Heiman, 1996).

The Fung et al. (1998) studies conducted in Hong Kong, for example, suggest that there may be important similarities and differences across cultures. Age differences were found in the first and third studies, but the second study conducted in the intervening period when Hong

Kong was undergoing a profound political change suggests that the approach of a broad-scale cultural ending influences social preferences in the same way that more personal endings influence preferences. Although our own exploration of cultural differences remains quite limited, the Hong Kong findings suggest that entire populations may be sensitive to time-relevant changes.

Although we can only speculate about other cultural differences that may affect time perspective and subsequent behavior, there are many. For one, religious beliefs about an afterlife may influence time perspective. Christians who believe that they will be reunited with loved ones after death may view lifetime quite differently than atheists or, for that matter, Hindus, whose beliefs in reincarnation lead to afterlife in very different forms. If, as we have shown, relatively transient social conditions alter time perspective, cultural and religious beliefs about time may exert similar influences.

Moreover, to the extent that temporal framing influences goal selection, cultures that differ in their orientation to time (Helfrich, 1996; Kluckhorn & Strodtbeck, 1961) may also differ in behavioral practices. Taken to its logical end, the theory predicts age by culture interaction effects. That is, the universal association of chronological age and closeness to death should lead to relative age differences within cultures. But cultural or religious beliefs about time may influence the degree to which younger or older people deviate from predicted life-cycle differences. Jones (1988), for example, observed that African culture and African American subcultures encourage a temporal focus on the present and that such cultures place relatively more value on pleasantness and enjoyment of life than cultures dominated by a future orientation.

Certainly the specific ways in which we have primed endings experimentally may differ across cultures. In studies conducted in the United States and Hong Kong, for example, we have instigated changes in time perspective by asking people to imagine an impending move. The identical experimental manipulation may be entirely ineffective in influencing time perspective in a nomadic culture where moves are frequent and returns are expected.

In short, socioemotional selectivity theory contends that the approach of endings directs attention to emotionally meaningful goals. To the degree that cultures vary in the meaning of endings and the relationships and actions that are considered emotionally meaningful, we anticipate considerable cultural variability in the types of stimuli that prime the attentional shift and the specific interpersonal goals that people pursue.

Implications for cognitive psychology.
For the most part, research on judgment, decision-making, and memory performance has proceeded without serious consideration of time. If, as we argue herein, time provides the structure within which people set goals, consideration of time and, by association, chronological age may yield fruitful predictions about cognitive performance. Prospect theory (Kahneman & Tversky, 1979), for example, maintains that when people make decisions, they weigh potential gains and losses. Socioemotional selectivity theory predicts that the perception of gains and losses is influenced importantly by individuals' temporal frameworks. Pursuing a relationship with a new acquaintance, for example, holds more potential gains (e.g., the possibility of developing a long-term friendship) and fewer potential losses (e.g., investing in an unsatisfying relationship) when time is expansive than when time is limited. Without a future, the promise of a new acquaintance is reduced considerably. Time will not allow potential gains to be realized. Joint consideration of prospect theory and socioemotional selectivity theory may increase the precision of theoretical predictions about social behavior.

Many aspects of cognitive functioning show clear deficits with age. None is more reliable than the decline in short- (Smith, 1996) and long-term memory (Park et al., 1996). Source memory in particular appears to deteriorate. Compared with their younger counterparts, older people recall fewer sensory, visual, and spatial details about the origins of their memories (Hashtroudi, Johnson, & Chrosniak, 1990). It is interesting to note, however, that older adults recall more than younger people about their thoughts and feelings related to the source. It remains unclear whether performance is related to motivation or disinhibition, although experimental manipulations of attentional focus do reduce age differences somewhat (Hashtroudi, Johnson, Vnek, & Ferguson, 1994). Specifically, older people perform better when instructed to focus on factual information, and younger people perform more poorly when affective focus is instructed. Hashtroudi et al. (1994) concluded that affective focus impedes source memory in younger and older people. To the extent that older adults display increased attention to emotion in everyday life, associated effects on cognitive functioning merit continued research. In addition, investigation into the specific aspects of cognitive performance most influenced by affective focus as well as identification of particular situations that heighten affective focus—such as getting feedback about a serious medical condition from a physician—may be of practical and conceptual importance for people of all ages.

Our findings fit well into the larger literature on social cognition and aging (see Hess, 1994). In a program of research on social decision-making, Blanchard-Fields and her colleagues have shown reliably that older adults weigh negative affective information about target persons more heavily than younger adults (Blanchard-Fields, 1996, 1997; Blanchard-Fields, Jahnke, & Camp, 1995). Older adults also appear to be more proficient at contextualizing formal logic and reintegrating affect into reasoning than their younger counterparts (Labouvie-Vief, 1997; Labouvie-Vief et al., 1989).

Biologically based reductions in cognitive resources and deficiencies in cognitive processing are widely believed to account for observed age-related differences in performance (Lindenberger & Baltes, 1997). We do not contest this basic influence. However, we also argue that motivational consequences of constraints on time imposed by advanced age may play a contributory role and should be given greater consideration.

Implications for clinical psychology. The ability to contemplate life constrained by mortality was considered important by early theorists, like Sigmund Freud (1920/1955), and remains central in scholarly work in psychiatry and existential psychology (e.g., Yalom, 1989). However, such emphasis has been nearly lost in empirical research on human behavior (cf. Greenberg, Simon, Pyszczynski, Solomon, & Chatel, 1992). Moreover, even though positive consequences of the awareness of death have been acknowledged over the years (Jung, 1917/1956; Yalom & Lieberman, 1991), primary emphasis, when mortality has been studied, has been placed on negative consequences rooted in death anxiety, such as social isolation (A. Freud, 1946), emotional rigidity (Banham, 1951), and social withdrawal (Cumming & Henry, 1961).

A number of dynamic and existential theorists have posited that perceptions of endings are a risk factor for depression (Yalom, 1989). Our findings suggest that endings in themselves do not increase negative affect. On average, older people—who are actually closer to the end of life than younger people—experience fewer negative emotions and more positive ones than younger people do (Gross et al., 1997). Even people approaching death due to life-threatening illnesses frequently describe life as better than ever before (Taylor, 1989; Taylor & Brown, 1988; Taylor et al., 1992). Although there are exceptions (which we address below), by and large, naturalistic "endings conditions" appear to direct attention to present-oriented goals, which subsequently holds benefits for emotional well-being.

Age differences in the incidence of psychopathology revealed by the Epidemiological Catchment Area Study (Regier et al., 1988) are certainly consistent with this general reasoning. With the exception of the dementias, findings from this national, multisite project suggest relatively low point-prevalence of virtually all psychological disorders among older adults, including major depression and anxiety disorders. Although surprising when initially reported, on reflection, these results are not so surprising. Anxiety disorders involve excessive worry about the future. The concern and dread inherent in clinical depression invoke a future in which dire scenarios will play out. Possibly, limited time focuses attention on the present, directs attention to emotional goals, and contributes to low rates of psychopathology. Value in life, for better or worse, is derived from the experience of the moment, not in what may or may not happen in the future.

Although this remains conjecture on our part, encouragement to adopt a focus on the present may help to treat depression in cases where people approaching the end of life are distressed with their lives. That is, even though mental health in general improves in old age, psychiatric settings are filled with exceptions to the rule. Some individuals do become clinically depressed when facing the end of life. Theoretically, the reframing of time could direct attention to present states and emotional goals and, in turn, entail therapeutic effects. The argument fits nicely into current models of depression. According to hopelessness theory (Abramson, Metalsky, & Alloy, 1989), for example, preoccupation with the future is a necessary precursor for the development of this depressive subtype.

Therapy termination is also relevant to time. Yalom (1989), in his discussion of psychotherapy, discusses ways in which the end of a therapeutic relationship can influence both the client and the therapist. Although therapy termination has less explicit meaning in cognitive and behavioral interventions, the general point remains that the end of therapy can loom large during the course of the therapeutic relationship. The argument we outline herein suggests that encouraging a present focus in clients may help to alleviate some of the anxiety associated with the termination of therapy.

Concluding Comments

Early theory and research on motivation attempted to describe an essential set of human motives. Only during the last two decades have researchers begun to address systematically the dynamic interplay of emotions and cognitions with particular environmental conditions that lead to the subsequent pursuit of particular goals. This article focused on a critical, yet often overlooked, element of motivation, namely the perception of time. Socioemotional selectivity theory posits that the approach of endings is related to increased investment in emotionally close social partners and increased focus on emotion regulation in everyday life. Specifically, we argue that boundaries on time provide the framework within which individuals select and prioritize goals. When time is perceived as expansive, long-term goals are chosen over others because they optimize future possibilities. Under such conditions, contact with novel social partners is prioritized over contact with familiar social partners because possible long-term payoffs have much time to be realized. When time is limited, however, short-term goals, such as social connectedness, social support, and emotional regulation assume highest priority. Under these conditions, focus shifts from the future to the present. Individuals seek out social partners with whom they experience close ties, and emotional experience is characterized by greater complexity.

Rabbi Liebman's quote, which began this article, finds support in the program of research we have described herein. Recognition of the timed fragility of the human circumstance appears to instigate motivational changes that lead to representation of the social world in emotional terms, appreciation of close emotional ties, and efforts to manage the quality of emotional experience in day-to-day life.

REFERENCES

Abramson, L. Y., Metalsky, G. I., & Alloy, L. B. (1989). Hopelessness depression: A theory-based subtype of depression. *Psychological Review, 96,* 358–372.

Antonucci, T. C. (1990). Social supports and social relationships. In R. H. Binstock & L. K. George (Eds.), *Handbook of aging and the social sciences* (pp. 205–226). San Diego, CA: Academic Press.

Antonucci, T. C. (1991). Attachment, social support, and coping with negative life events in mature adulthood. In E. M. Cummings, A. L. Greene, & K. H. Karraker (Eds.), *Life-span developmental psychology:*

Perspectives on stress and coping (pp. 261–276). Hillsdale, NJ: Erlbaum.
Antonucci, T. C., & Akiyama, H. (1997). Social support and the maintenance of competence. In S. Willis, K. W. Schaie, & M. Hayward (Eds.), *Societal mechanisms for maintaining competence in old age* (pp. 182–206). New York: Springer.
Antonucci, T. C., & Jackson, J. S. (1987). Social support, interpersonal efficacy, and health: A life course perspective. In L. L. Carstensen & B. A. Edelstein (Eds.), *Handbook of clinical gerontology* (pp. 291–311). New York: Pergamon Press.
Aveni, A. (1995). *Empires of time: Calendars, clocks and cultures*. New York: Kodansha America.
Baltes, M. M., & Carstensen, L. L. (1996). The process of successful ageing. *Ageing and Society, 16,* 397–422.
Baltes, P. B. (1997). On the incomplete architecture of human ontogeny: Selection, optimization, and compensation as foundation of developmental theory. *American Psychologist, 52,* 366–380.
Baltes, P. B., & Baltes, M. M. (1990). Psychological perspectives on successful aging: The model of selective optimization with compensation. In P. B. Baltes & M. M. Baltes (Eds.), *Successful aging: Perspectives from the behavioral sciences* (pp. 1–34). New York: Cambridge University Press.
Baltes, P. B., Mayer, K. U., Helmchen, H., & Steinhagen-Thiessen, E. (1993). The Berlin Aging Study (BASE): Overview and design. *Ageing and Society, 13,* 483–515.
Bandura, A. (1982). Self-efficacy mechanisms in human agency. *American Psychologist, 37,* 122–147.
Bandura, A. (1987). Self-regulation of motivation and action through goal systems. In V. Hamilton, G. H. Bower, & N. H. Frijda (Eds.), *Cognitive perspectives on emotion and motivation* (pp. 37–61). Dordrecht, the Netherlands: Kluwer Academic Publishers.
Bandura, A. (1991). Self-regulation of motivation through anticipatory and self-regulatory mechanisms. In R. A. Dienstbier (Ed.), *Perspectives on motivation: Nebraska symposium on motivation* (Vol. 38, pp. 69–164). Lincoln: University of Nebraska Press.
Bandura, A. (1997). *Self-efficacy: The exercise of control.* New York: Freeman.
Banham, K. M. (1951). Senescence and the emotions: A genetic theory. *Journal of Genetic Psychology, 78,* 183.
Birren, J., & Cunningham, W. (1985). Research on the psychology of aging: Principles, concepts and theory. In J. Birren & K. W. Schaie (Eds.), *Handbook of the psychology of aging* (2nd ed., pp. 3–34). New York: Van Nostrand Reinhold Company.
Blanchard-Fields, F. (1986). Reasoning on social dilemmas varying in emotional saliency: An adult developmental perspective. *Psychology and Aging, 1,* 325–333.
Blanchard-Fields, F. (1996). Social cognitive development in adulthood and aging. In F. Blanchard-Fields & T. Hess (Eds.), *Perspectives on cognitive change in adulthood and aging* (pp. 454–487). New York: McGraw-Hill.
Blanchard-Fields, F. (1997). The role of emotion in social cognition across the adult life span. *Annual Review of Geriatrics and Gerontology, 17,* 238–266.
Blanchard-Fields, F., Jahnke, H. C., & Camp, C. (1995). Age differences in problem-solving style: The role of emotional salience. *Psychology and Aging, 10,* 173–180.
Brandtstädter, J., & Greve, W. (1994). The aging self: Stabilizing and protective processes. *Developmental Review, 14,* 52–80.
Carstensen, L. L. (1991). Selectivity theory: Social activity in life-span context. *Annual Review of Gerontology and Geriatrics, 11,* 195–217.
Carstensen, L. L. (1992). Social and emotional patterns in adulthood: Support for socioemotional selectivity theory. *Psychology and Aging, 7,* 331–338.
Carstensen, L. L. (1993). Motivation for social contact across the life span: A theory of socioemotional selectivity. *Nebraska Symposium on Motivation, 40,* 209–254.
Carstensen, L. L. (1995). Evidence for a life-span theory of socioemotional selectivity. *Current Directions in Psychological Science, 4,* 151–156.
Carstensen, L. L. (1998). A life-span approach to social motivation. In J. Heckhausen & C. Dweck (Eds.), *Motivation and self-regulation across the life span* (pp. 341–364). New York: Cambridge University Press.
Carstensen, L. L., & Charles, S. T. (in press). Emotion in the second half of life. *Current Directions in Psychological Science.*
Carstensen, L. L., & Fredrickson, B. F. (1998). Socioemotional selectivity in healthy older people and younger people living with the human immunodeficiency virus: The centrality of emotion when the future is constrained. *Health Psychology, 17,* 1–10.
Carstensen, L. L., & Freund, A. (1994). The resilience of the aging self. *Developmental Review, 14,* 81–92.
Carstensen, L. L., Gottman, J. M., & Levenson, R. W. (1995). Emotional behavior in long-term marriage. *Psychology and Aging, 10,* 140–149.
Carstensen, L. L., Graff, J., Levenson, R. W., & Gottman, J. M. (1996). Affect in intimate relationships: The developmental course of marriage. In C. Magai & S. McFadden (Eds.), *Handbook of emotion, adult development and aging* (pp. 227–247). Orlando, FL: Academic Press.
Carstensen, L. L., Gross, J., & Fung, H. (1997). The social context of emotion. *Annual Review of Geriatrics and Gerontology, 17,* 325–352.
Carstensen, L. L., & Lang, F. (1997a). [Measurement of time orientation in diverse population]. Unpublished data, Stanford University, Stanford, CA.
Carstensen, L. L., & Lang, F. (1997b). Social support in context and as context: Comments on social support and the maintenance of competence in old age. In S. Willis & K. W. Schaie (Eds.), *Societal mechanisms for maintaining competence in old age* (pp. 207–222). New York: Springer.
Carstensen, L. L., Pasupathi, M., & Mayr, U. (1998). *Emotion experience in the daily lives of older and younger adults.* Manuscript submitted for publication.
Carstensen, L. L., & Turk-Charles, S. (1994). The salience of emotion across the adult life course. *Psychology and Aging, 9,* 259–264.
Cross, S., & Markus, H. (1991). Possible selves across the life span. *Human Development, 34,* 230–255.
Cumming, E., & Henry, W. E. (1961). *Growing old: The process of disengagement.* New York: Basic Books.
D'Andrade, R. G. (1981). The cultural part of cognition. *Cognitive Science, 5,* 179–195.
Deci, E. L., & Ryan, R. M. (1991). A motivational approach to self: Integration in personality. *Nebraska Symposium on Motivation, 38,* 237–288.
Elder, G., & Clipp, E. (1994). When war comes to men's lives: Life-course patterns in family, work, and health. *Psychology and Aging, 9,* 5–16.
Elder, G., Pavalko, E. K., & Hastings, T. J. (1991). Talent, history, and the fulfillment of promise. *Psychiatry, 54,* 251–267.
Field, D., & Minkler, M. (1988). Continuity and change in social support between young-old, old-old, and very-old adults. *Journal of Gerontology, 43,* P100–P106.
Fingerman, K., & Perlmutter, M. (1995). Future time perspective and life events across adulthood. *Journal of General Psychology, 122,* 95–111.
Fredrickson, B. L. (1995). Socioemotional behavior at the end of college life. *Journal of Social and Personal Relationships, 12,* 261–276.
Fredrickson, B. L., & Carstensen, L. L. (1990). Choosing social partners: How old age and anticipated endings make us more selective. *Psychology and Aging, 5,* 335–347.
Freedman, J. L., & Edwards, D. R. (1988). Time pressure, task performance, and enjoyment. In J. E. McGrath (Ed.), *The social psychology of time: New perspectives* (pp. 113–133). Newbury, CA: Sage.
Freud, A. (1946). *The ego and mechanisms of defense.* New York: International Universities Press.
Freud, S. (1955). Beyond the pleasure principle. In J. Strachey (Trans.), *The standard edition of the complete psychological works of Sigmund Freud* (Vol. 18, pp. 3–64). London: Hogarth Press. (Original work published 1920)
Fung, H. H., Carstensen, L. L., & Lutz, A. (in press). The influence of time on social preferences: Implications for life-span development. *Psychology and Aging.*
Gollwitzer, P. M. (1986). The implementation of identity intentions: A motivational-volitional perspective on symbolic self-completion. In F. Halisch & J. Kuhl (Eds.), *Motivation, intentions and volition.* Heidelberg, Germany: Springer-Verlag.
Gonzalez, A., & Zimbardo, P. G. (1985, March). Time in perspective. *Psychology Today,* 21–26.

Greenberg, J., Simon, L., Pyszczynski, T., Solomon, S., & Chatel, D. (1992). Terror management and tolerance: Does mortality salience always intensify negative reactions to others who threaten ones' worldview? *Journal of Personality and Social Psychology, 63,* 212–220.

Gross, J. J. (in press). Antecedent and response focused emotion regulation: Divergent consequences for experience, expression and physiology. *Journal of Personality and Social Psychology.*

Gross, J. J., Carstensen, L. L., Pasupathi, M., Tsai, J., Götestam Skorpen, C., & Hsu, A. (1997). Emotion and aging: Experience, expression, and control. *Psychology and Aging, 12,* 590–599.

Hashtroudi, S., Johnson, M., & Chrosniak, L. (1990). Aging and qualitative characteristics of memories for perceived and imagined complex events. *Psychology and Aging, 5,* 119–126.

Hashtroudi, S., Johnson, S. A., Vnek, N., & Ferguson, S. A. (1994). Aging and the effects of affective and factual focus on source monitoring and recall. *Psychology and Aging, 9,* 160–170.

Havighurst, R. J., & Albrecht, R. (1953). *Older people.* New York: Longmans.

Heckhausen, J., Dixon, R. A., & Baltes, P. B. (1989). Gains and losses in development throughout adulthood as perceived by different adult age groups. *Developmental Psychology, 25,* 109–121.

Helfrich, H. (1996). Psychology of time from a cross-cultural perspective. In H. Helfrich (Ed.), *Time and mind* (pp. 103–118). Seattle, WA: Hogrefe & Huber.

Hess, T. M. (1994). Social cognition in adulthood: Aging-related changes in knowledge and processing mechanisms. *Developmental Review, 14,* 373–412.

Higgins, E. T. (1987). Self-discrepancy: A theory relating self and affect. *Psychological Review, 94,* 319–340.

Higgins, E. T. (1997). Beyond pleasure and pain. *American Psychologist, 52,* 1280–1300.

Holman, E. A., & Silver, R. C. (1998). Getting "stuck" in the past: Temporal orientation and coping with trauma. *Journal of Personality and Social Psychology, 74,* 1146–1163.

James, W. (1890). *The principles of psychology* (Vols. 1 & 2). New York: Holt.

Jones, J. M. (1988). Cultural differences in temporal perspectives: Instrumental and expressive behaviors in time. In J. E. McGrath (Ed.), *The social psychology of time: New perspectives* (pp. 21–38). Newbury, CA: Sage.

Jung, C. (1956). *Two essays on analytical psychology.* R. F. C. Hull, (Trans.). New York: Meridian Books. (Original work published 1917)

Kahn, R. L., & Antonucci, T. C. (1980). Convoys over the life course: Attachment, roles and social support. In P. B. Baltes & O. G. Brim (Eds.), *Life-span development and behavior* (pp. 254–283). New York: Academic Press.

Kahneman, D., & Tversky, A. (1979). Prospect theory: An analysis of decision under risk. *Econometrica, 47,* 283–291.

Kluckhorn, F., & Strodtbeck, F. (1961). *Variations in value orientations.* Evanston, IL: Row, Peterson.

Labouvie-Vief, G. (1997). Cognitive–emotional integration in adulthood. *Annual Review of Geriatrics and Gerontology, 17,* 206–237.

Labouvie-Vief, G., DeVoe, M., & Bulka, D. (1989). Speaking about feelings: Conceptions of emotions across the life span. *Psychology and Aging, 4,* 425–437.

Labouvie-Vief, G., Hakim-Larson, J., DeVoe, M., & Schoeberlein, S. (1989). Emotions and self-regulation: A life span view. *Human Development, 32,* 279–299.

Lang, F. R., & Carstensen, L. L. (1994). Close emotional relationships in late life: Further support for proactive aging in the social domain. *Psychology and Aging, 9,* 315–324.

Lang, F. R., Staudinger, U., & Carstensen, L. L. (1998). Perspectives on socioemotional selectivity in late life: How personality and social context do (and do not) make a difference. *Journals of Gerontology: Psychological Science, 53,* P21–P30.

Lawton, M. P., Kleban, M. H., Rajagopal, D., & Dean, J. (1992). The dimensions of affective experience in three age groups. *Psychology and Aging, 7,* 171–184.

Lee, D. J., & Markides, K. S. (1990). Activity and mortality among aged persons over an eight-year period. *Journals of Gerontology: Social Sciences, 45,* S39–S42.

Levenson, R. W., Carstensen, L. L., Friesen, W. V., & Ekman, P. (1991). Emotion, physiology, and expression in old age. *Psychology and Aging, 6,* 28–35.

Levenson, R. W., Carstensen, L. L., & Gottman, J. M. (1993). Long-term marriage: Age, gender, and satisfaction. *Psychology and Aging, 8,* 301–313.

Levenson, R. W., Carstensen, L. L., & Gottman, J. M. (1994). Marital interaction in old and middle-aged long-term marriages: Physiology, affect, and their interrelations. *Journal of Personality and Social Psychology, 67,* 56–68.

Levine, R. (1997). *A geography of time: The temporal misadventures of a social psychologist.* New York: Basic Books.

Liebman, J. L. (1961). *Peace of mind.* New York: Bantam Books.

Lindenberger, U., & Baltes, P. (1997). Intellectual functioning in old and very old age: Cross-sectional results from the Berlin Aging Study. *Psychology and Aging, 12,* 410–432.

MacFarlane, J. (1938). Studies in child guidance: 1. Methodology of data collection and organization. *Monographs of the Society for Research in Child Development, 3,* 1–254.

Markus, H., Kitayama, S., & Heiman, R. (1996). Culture and "basic" psychological principles. *Social psychology: Handbook of basic principles* (pp. 857–913). New York: Guilford Press.

Markus, H., & Nurius, P. (1986). Possible selves. *American Psychologist, 41,* 954–969.

Markus, H., & Wurf, E. (1987). The dynamic self-concept: A social psychological perspective. *Annual Review of Psychology, 38,* 299–337.

Marshack, A. (1972). *The roots of civilization.* New York: McGraw-Hill.

Maslow, A. H. (1968). *Toward a psychology of being.* (2nd ed.). New York: Van Nostrand.

McGrath, J. E. (1988). The place of time in social psychology. In J. E. McGrath (Ed.), *The social psychology of time: New perspectives* (pp. 7–17). Newbury, CA: Sage.

Medina, J. J. (1996). *The clock of ages: Why we age, how we age, winding back the clock.* New York: Cambridge University Press.

Murrell, A. J., & Mingrone, M. (1994). Correlates of temporal perspective. *Perceptual and Motor Skills, 78,* 1331–1334.

Norem, J., & Cantor, N. (1986). Defensive pessimism: Harnessing anxiety as motivation. *Journal of Personality and Social Psychology, 51,* 1208–1217.

Palmore, E. (1981). *Social patterns in normal aging: Findings from the Duke Longitudinal Study.* Durham, NC: Duke University Press.

Park, D., Smith, A., Lautenschlager, G., Earles, J., Frieske, D., Zwahr, M., & Gaines, C. (1996). Mediators of long-term memory performance across the life span. *Psychology and Aging, 11,* 621–637.

Regier, D. A., Boyd, H. J., Burke, J. D., Rae, D. S., Myers, J. K., Kramer, M., Robins, L. N., George, L. K., Karno, M., & Locke, B. Z. (1988). One-month prevalence of mental disorders in the United States. *Archives of General Psychiatry, 45,* 977–986.

Rothbart, M. K. (1994). Emotional development: Changes in reactivity and self-regulation. In P. Ekman & R. J. Davidson (Eds.), *The nature of emotion: Fundamental questions* (pp. 369–372). Oxford, England: Oxford University Press.

Ryan, R. M. (1991). The nature of the self in autonomy and relatedness. In J. Strauss & G. R. Goethals (Eds.), *The self: Interdisciplinary approaches* (pp. 208–238). New York: Springer-Verlag.

Ryan, R. M. (1993). Agency and organization: Intrinsic motivation, autonomy, and the self in psychological development. *Nebraska Symposium on Motivation, 40,* 1–58.

Ryff, C. D. (1991). Possible selves in adulthood and old age: A tale of shifting horizons. *Psychology and Aging, 6,* 286–295.

Sears, D. (1981). Life stage effects on attitude change, especially among the elderly. In R. W. Fogel & J. G. March (Eds.), *Aging: Stability and change in the family* (pp. 183–204). New York: Academic Press.

Shmotkin, D. (1991). The role of time orientation in life satisfaction across the life span. *Journals of Gerontology: Psychological Sciences, 46,* P243–P250.

Shweder, R. A., & Sullivan, M. A. (1990). The semiotic subject of cultural psychology. In L. A. Pervin (Ed.), *Handbook of personality: Theory and research* (pp. 399–418). New York: Guilford Press.

Skeldon, R. (1995). Immigration and population issues. In S. Y. L. Cheung & S. M. H. Sze (Eds.), *The other Hong Kong report: 1995* (pp. 303–316). Hong Kong: The Chinese University Press.

Smith, A. D. (1996). Memory. In J. Birren, & W. Schaie (Eds.), *Handbook of the psychology of aging* (pp. 236–250). San Diego, CA: Academic Press.

Suddendorf, T., & Corballis, M. C. (1997). Mental time travel and the evolution of the human mind. *Genetic, Social, and General Psychology Monographs, 123,* 133–167.

Taylor, S. (1989). *Positive illusions: Creative self-deception and the healthy mind.* New York: Basic Books.

Taylor, S., & Brown, J. (1988). Illusion and well-being: A social psychological perspective on mental health. *Psychological Bulletin, 103,* 193–210.

Taylor, S., Kemeny, M. E., Aspinwall, L. G., Schneider, S. G., Rodriguez, R., & Herbert, M. (1992). Optimism, coping, psychological distress, and high-risk sexual behavior among men at risk for acquired immunodeficiency syndrome (AIDS). *Journal of Personality and Social Psychology, 63,* 460–473.

Tomkins, S. S. (1970). Affect as the primary motivational systems. In M. B. Arnold (Ed.), *Feelings and emotions* (pp. 101–110). New York: Academic Press.

Turk-Charles, S., Meyerowitz, B., & Gatz, M. (1997). Age differences in information-seeking among cancer patients. *International Journal of Aging and Human Development, 45,* 85–98.

White, R. W. (1959). Motivation reconsidered: The concept of competence. *Psychological Review, 66,* 297–333.

Wicklund, R. A., & Gollwitzer, P. M. (1981). Symbolic self-completion, attempted influence and self-deprecation. *Basic and Applied Social Psychology, 2,* 89–114.

Yalom, I. D. (1989). *Love's executioner and other tales of psychotherapy.* New York: Basic Books.

Yalom, I., & Lieberman, M. (1991). Bereavement and heightened existential awareness. *Psychiatry, 54,* 334–345.

Zajonc, R. (1997). Emotions. In D. Gilbert, S. T. Fiske, & G. Lindzey (Eds.), *Handbook of social psychology* (4th ed., pp. 591–631). Cambridge, MA: McGraw-Hill.

Part III
Lifestyle and Well-being in Old Age

[10]

Late-Life Engagement in Social and Leisure Activities Is Associated with a Decreased Risk of Dementia: A Longitudinal Study from the Kungsholmen Project

Hui-Xin Wang, Anita Karp, Bengt Winblad, and Laura Fratiglioni

Recent findings suggest that a rich social network may decrease the risk of developing dementia. The authors hypothesized that such a protective effect may be due to social interaction and intellectual stimulation. To test this hypothesis, data from the 1987–1996 Kungsholmen Project, a longitudinal population-based study carried out in a central area of Stockholm, Sweden, were used to examine whether engagement in different activities 6.4 years before dementia diagnosis was related to a decreased incidence of dementia. Dementia cases were diagnosed by specialists according to *Diagnostic and Statistical Manual of Mental Disorders,* Third Edition, Revised, criteria. After adjustment for age, sex, education, cognitive functioning, comorbidity, depressive symptoms, and physical functioning at the first examination, frequent (daily-weekly) engagement in mental, social, or productive activities was inversely related to dementia incidence. Adjusted relative risks for mental, social, and productive activities were 0.54 (95% confidence interval (CI): 0.34, 0.87), 0.58 (95% CI: 0.37, 0.91), and 0.58 (95% CI: 0.38, 0.91), respectively. Similar results were found when these three factors were analyzed together in the same model. Results suggest that stimulating activity, either mentally or socially oriented, may protect against dementia, indicating that both social interaction and intellectual stimulation may be relevant to preserving mental functioning in the elderly. *Am J Epidemiol* 2002;155:1081–7.

aged; dementia; incidence; leisure activities; risk factors

A positive effect of physical activities on survival has long been recognized (1–4); more recently, a similar effect was also reported for social and productive activities (5). Social disengagement has been suggested as a possible risk factor for cognitive decline in elderly persons (6–9). In a Swedish community-based study, the Kungsholmen Project, a rich social network showed a protective effect against dementia (10).

Received for publication September 10, 2001, and accepted for publication February 24, 2002.
Abbreviations: APOE, apolipoprotein E (genotype); CI, confidence interval; ICD-8, *International Classification of Diseases,* Eighth Revision; ICD-9, *International Classification of Diseases,* Ninth Revision; MMSE, Mini-Mental State Examination; RR, relative risk.
From the Aging Research Center, Division of Geriatric Epidemiology and Medicine, NEUROTEC, Karolinska Institutet, and Stockholm Gerontology Research Center, Stockholm, Sweden.
Reprint requests to Dr. Hui-Xin Wang, Stockholm Gerontology Research Center, Box 6401, 113 82 Stockholm, Sweden (e-mail: huixin.wang@phs.ki.se).

The specific effects of social and leisure activities on dementia have been investigated in only two known case-control (11, 12) and two follow-up studies (13, 14). These studies found that an inactive life was related to a higher risk of dementia. However, case-control studies have been criticized because of the presence of selection and recall biases. Follow-up studies have been hampered by the fact that subjects in the early phases of dementia could reduce their activities because of initial cognitive impairment, depressive symptoms, or other dementia-related disorders.

The present study aimed to further explore the relation between social and leisure activities and the development of dementia and to verify whether the suggested protective effect of a rich social network might be due to social interaction or intellectual stimulation. The Kungsholmen Project's database gathered information on mental, physical, social, productive, and recreational activities, collected at baseline on average 6 years before dementia diagnosis. Engagement in these activities was related to the incident dementia occurring between the first and second follow-up examinations of subjects cognitively intact at baseline and still nondemented 3 years later (first follow-up). Cognitive functioning, depressive symptoms, physical functioning, and comorbidity of the subjects when their engagement in social and leisure activities was assessed were taken into account. To explore the mechanisms underlying the reported association between social network and dementia (10), the leisure activities were divided into predominately intellectual, physical, social, productive, and recreational categories.

MATERIALS AND METHODS

Study population

All inhabitants of the Kungsholmen district of Stockholm, Sweden, aged 75 years or more in October 1987 were asked to participate in the initial examination of the Kungsholmen Project. Participants were interviewed by nurses, examined by physicians, and tested by psychologists during the baseline (1987–1989), first follow-up (1991–1993), and second follow-up (1994–1996) examinations.

Figure 1 illustrates the study population, time of detection of dementia cases, and assessment of engagement in social and leisure activities. Of the 1,810 eligible participants who underwent the baseline examination, 1,473 were diagnosed as nondemented. The detailed procedure has been described elsewhere (15, 16). Because impaired cognition or institutionalization may limit subjects' activity (8), 98 subjects whose Mini-Mental State Examination (MMSE) scores were less than 23 or who were living in an institution were excluded from the present study; 1,375 persons remained for analysis. Of these subjects, 269 died, 172 refused participation, and 934 participated in the first follow-up examination. Of these 934 subjects, 158 were diagnosed as demented. The population for the present study was composed of those 776 subjects still nondemented at the first follow-up examination. Because 44 refused to participate, a cohort of 732 nondemented subjects was followed for another 3 years (second follow-up) to detect incident dementia cases.

Incident dementia cases

The incident dementia cases examined in this study were those subjects who developed dementia during the second follow-up period. Time of dementia onset was assumed to be the midpoint between the first and second follow-up examinations or the time of death. At each examination, all cohort subjects were clinically examined following a standardized protocol, which included family and personal history collected by nurses, clinical examination conducted by physicians, and psychological tests administered by trained personnel. If a subject was unable to answer, an informant, usually the subject's next of kin, was interviewed. Details on the study design are available elsewhere (15, 16).

The diagnosis of dementia was made according to criteria specified in the *Diagnostic and Statistical Manual of Mental Disorders*, Third Edition, Revised (17) following the same three-step diagnostic procedure used during the baseline examination (18). Two physicians made the preliminary diagnoses independently. Concordant diagnoses were accepted as final diagnoses, and a third opinion was requested in case of disagreement.

If the subject had moved, he or she was traced and asked to participate in the follow-up examination. For those subjects who had died before the follow-up examination (172 died between the first and second follow-up examinations), information regarding their health status was obtained from the computerized inpatient register system, a registry of discharge diagnoses from all hospitals in Stockholm since 1969. Individual hospital records and discharge diagnoses, as well as death certificates, were collected and examined.

Assessment of social and leisure activities

Information on social and leisure activities was obtained from subjects by means of a personal interview carried out by trained nurses during the first examination. Subjects were asked 1) whether they regularly engaged in any particular activities or participated in any organizations, 2) to specify the types of activities or organizations, and 3) to report the frequency of participation.

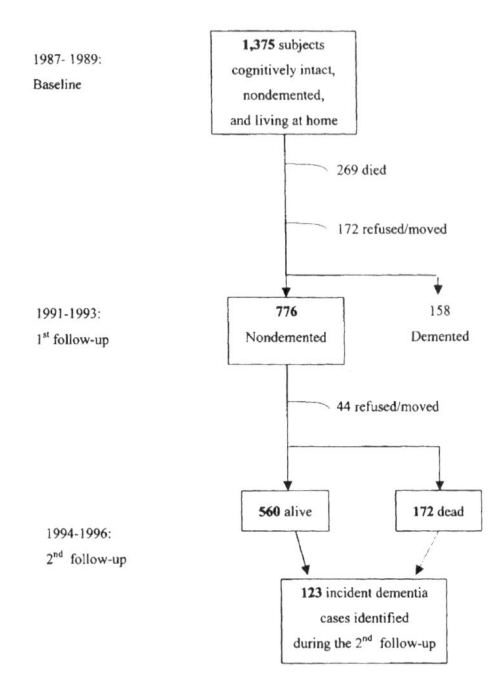

FIGURE 1. Study population, the Kungsholmen Project, Stockholm, Sweden, 1987–1996. During the baseline phase of the study, current engagement in different activities was assessed. Incident dementia cases were identified by clinical examination of the survivors and, for deceased subjects, by using clinical records and death certificates.

Social and leisure activities were grouped following the classification adopted in previous studies (5, 6, 8). Mental activity includes reading books/newspapers, writing, studying, working crossword puzzles, painting, or drawing. Physical activity encompasses swimming, walking, or gymnastics. Social activity consists of attending the theater, concerts, or art exhibitions; traveling; playing cards/games; or participating in social groups or a pension organization. Productive activity is composed of gardening, housekeeping, cooking, working for pay after retirement, doing volunteer work, or sewing, knitting, crocheting, or weaving. Recreational activity includes watching television or listening to the radio.

A subject belonged to a group if he or she participated in at least one of the group's listed activities. A person was considered to be in different groups if he or she participated in two or more groups of activities. Frequency of participation was recorded as daily, weekly, monthly, or annually.

Potential confounders

Age, sex, education, cognitive functioning, comorbidity, depressive symptoms, and physical functioning at the baseline examination were taken into account as potential confounders in the present study. Information on age and sex was obtained from the Kungsholmen Municipality. Education was assessed according to the highest level of schooling reported by the subject. Cognitive functioning was evaluated by using the MMSE (19). Depressive symptoms were assessed by using self-reported symptoms such as often feeling lonely and being in a low mood. Physical functional dependence was defined as disability regarding at least one of the basic activities of daily living: bathing, dressing, toileting, continence, feeding, or walking (20).

Previous diseases were ascertained by reviewing the hospital discharge diagnoses using the Stockholm computerized inpatient register system. Disease diagnoses were based on the *International Classification of Diseases,* Eighth Revision (ICD-8) (21), as follows: coronary heart disease (ICD-8 codes 410–414), cerebrovascular disease (ICD-8 codes 430–438), diabetes mellitus (ICD-8 code 250), malignancy (ICD-8 codes 140–208 and 230–239), and hip fracture (ICD-8 code 820). Comorbidity was considered the presence of any of these disease categories. Because this comorbidity variable took into account only those diseases that resulted in hospitalization, we repeated all analyses by using a new "comorbidity variable" derived from the data collected by the physician during the second clinical examination. The physician diagnosed diseases according to the *International Classification of Diseases,* Ninth Revision (ICD-9) (22), as follows: cardiovascular diseases (ICD-9 codes 390–398, 401–429, and 440–459), cerebrovascular diseases (ICD-9 codes 430–438), diabetes mellitus (ICD-9 code 250), malignancy (ICD-9 codes 140–208), and hip fracture (ICD-9 code 820). The new comorbidity variable was defined as the presence of any of these disease categories. Because results were similar, we used only baseline, hospital-based comorbidity data.

Social network included marital status, living arrangements, parenthood, and close social ties that defined the structure of social connections. Frequency of and satisfaction with these connections represented the perceived adequacy of the social network. Both the structure and perceived adequacy of the social network were integrated in a single index that consisted of the following four categories (10):

1. Extensive social network: a) being married and living with someone, b) having children and having daily to weekly satisfying contacts with them, and c) having relatives and/or friends and having daily to weekly satisfying contacts with them
2. Moderate social network: having any two of these three conditions
3. Limited social network: having any one of these three conditions
4. Poor social network: being single and living alone; no children and no close social ties

Statistical analysis

Logistic regression analysis was used to examine differences between participants and study dropouts. To take into account the different follow-up times, Cox proportional hazards models were used to estimate the relative risks and corresponding 95 percent confidence intervals for the social and leisure activities associated with development of dementia. All analyses were performed by using SPSS software (Statistical Package for Social Sciences; SPSS, Inc., Chicago, Illinois).

First, engagement in each type of activity was analyzed in relation to the incidence of dementia by examining participation versus no participation. Second, engagement in each type of activity was introduced into the models as a five-grade indicator variable, with no participation as the reference group and daily, weekly, monthly, and annual participation as the other categories. Finally, a reduced three-grade variable for each activity was derived from the original five-grade variable and was entered into the models as an indicator variable.

All of the associations studied were first assessed with univariate Cox proportional hazards models and then with multivariate models adjusted for all potential confounders. Age and cognitive functioning (MMSE score) were entered in the models as continuous variables (1 year/point increment). Education was entered as a categorical variable ($>$12 years, 8–12 years, and <8 years of schooling) (23). Sex (female vs. male), comorbidity (the presence of coronary heart disease, cerebrovascular disease, diabetes mellitus, malignancy, or hip fracture vs. the presence of none of them), depressive symptoms (yes vs. no), and physical functioning (dependent vs. independent) were entered as dichotomous variables.

An alternative grouping of some of the covariates was also used to assess the associations studied. For example, education was grouped according to the number of years of schooling, physical functioning was classified into seven categories—1 as most independent (requiring no personal assistance with any of the six activities of daily living) and 7 as most dependent (requiring assistance with all six of these activities)—and comorbidity was categorized as no disease, one disease, or two or more diseases.

RESULTS

The study population was composed of 776 subjects (figure 1). The mean age of participants was 81.1 (standard deviation, 4.9) years, and the mean MMSE score at baseline was 27.3 (standard deviation, 1.5). In comparison with those subjects who participated in the study, the 44 nonparticipants (4.7 percent) had less comorbidity and participated less often in mental activity and more often in social activity (odds ratios = 0.4 and 1.9, respectively; $p < 0.05$). The distributions of age, sex, education, cognitive functioning, depressive symptoms, physical functioning, and other types of activities were similar.

During the second follow-up, 123 incident cases of dementia were identified. Of these cases, one (0.8 percent) was due to Parkinson's disease and one (0.8 percent) to alcoholism. Table 1 shows the baseline characteristics of the 732 cohort subjects and the distribution of the 123 incident dementia cases. Demented subjects were older, had lower MMSE scores, had more comorbidity, had more depressive symptoms, and were more physical-functioning dependent compared with the corresponding reference group for each variable.

The adjusted relative risks of dementia associated with participation versus no participation in the following activities were 0.67 (95 percent confidence interval (CI): 0.45, 1.01) for mental activity, 0.70 (95 percent CI: 0.49, 1.01) for social activity, 0.67 (95 percent CI: 0.34, 1.33) for physical activity, 0.61 (95 percent CI: 0.40, 0.93) for productive activity, and 0.97 (95 percent CI: 0.61, 1.57) for recreational activity. Table 2 shows the adjusted relative risks of dementia in relation to social and leisure activities when frequency of participation was taken into account. Compared with those who did not, elderly subjects who participated in mental, social, or productive activity had a lower incidence of dementia. Dementia incidence decreased with increasing frequency of participation in the three types of activities.

TABLE 2. Adjusted* relative risks of dementia in relation to social and leisure activities engaged in 6.4 years prior to diagnosis, the Kungsholmen Project, Stockholm, Sweden, 1987–1996

	No. of dementia cases	RR†	95% CI†
Mental activity			
No	34	1	
Less than daily	40	0.81	0.52, 1.26
Daily	49	0.54	0.34, 0.87
Physical activity			
No	114	1	
Less than daily	6	0.97	0.42, 2.22
Daily	3	0.41	0.13, 1.31
Social activity			
No	72	1	
Less than weekly	27	0.92	0.57, 1.47
Daily-weekly	24	0.58	0.37, 0.91
Productive activity			
No	94	1	
Less than weekly	3	0.95	0.30, 3.00
Daily-weekly	26	0.58	0.38, 0.91
Recreational activity			
No	102	1	
Less than daily	6	1.06	0.46, 2.45
Daily	15	0.95	0.55, 1.63

* Adjusted for age, sex, education, baseline Mini-Mental State Examination score, comorbidity, depressive symptoms, and physical functioning.
† RR, relative risk; CI, confidence interval.

Furthermore, these associations were independent of the effects of age, sex, education, cognitive functioning, comorbidity, depressive symptoms, and physical functioning. The observed associations between frequent engagement in

TABLE 1. Baseline (1987–1989) characteristics of the cohort subjects and distribution of the incident dementia cases occurring during the second follow-up (1994–1996), the Kungsholmen Project, Stockholm, Sweden, 1987–1996

Baseline characteristics	Participants ($n = 732$)		Incident dementia cases ($n = 123$)	
	No.	%	No.	%
Age (years)				
75–79	364	49.7	36	29.3
80–84	232	31.7	55	44.7
≥85	136	18.6	32	26.1
Sex: female	543	74.2	93	75.6
Education*: >7 years	343	47.1	53	43.1
MMSE† score				
24–26	178	24.3	38	30.9
27–30	554	75.7	85	69.1
Comorbidity*	179	24.6	46	37.4
Depressive symptoms*	201	27.6	53	43.1
Physical dependence‡	132	18.2	30	24.4

* For three subjects, information was missing.
† MMSE, Mini-Mental State Examination.
‡ For eight subjects, information was missing.

activities and incidence of dementia persisted even when the effect of social network was taken into account (relative risk (RR) = 0.60, 95 percent CI: 0.37, 0.98 for mental activities; RR = 0.60, 95 percent CI: 0.38, 0.94 for social activities; and RR = 0.61, 95 percent CI: 0.39, 0.96 for productive activities).

In addition, the observed associations were independent of each other. When the three types of activities were introduced into the multivariate models simultaneously, the adjusted relative risks of dementia were 0.7 (95 percent CI: 0.5, 1.3) for mental activity, 0.7 (95 percent CI: 0.5, 1.0) for social activity, and 0.6 (95 percent CI: 0.4, 0.9) for productive activity. Table 3 shows that daily/daily-weekly participation in each activity was independently associated with a lower risk of dementia. Entering the alternative grouping of potential confounders as covariates in the models did not change the observed results substantially.

The following statistical analyses were performed to verify the results:

- Although we included only those subjects whose baseline MMSE scores were more than 23, weaker cognitive functioning (MMSE score, 24–26) may have had an impact on the studied relation. Therefore, we repeated all analyses for subjects whose MMSE scores were more than 26 at the first examination. Similar results were observed.
- To avoid biases introduced by underdiagnosis of dementia cases among deceased subjects during follow-up, further analyses were conducted for a subgroup of subjects who were survivors at the second follow-up examination. The results did not change.
- To eliminate the possibility that depression may be the cause of inactivity in elderly people, all analyses were repeated for subjects who did not have any depressive symptoms. The observed associations remained unchanged.
- We also examined the genetic influence by both introducing the apolipoprotein E (*APOE*) genotypes into the models as covariates and conducting stratified analyses for subjects with and without the *APOE*$*\varepsilon$4 allele. No substantial variations were observed.

DISCUSSION

We examined the influence of engagement in mental, physical, social, productive, and recreational activities on dementia incidence in a community-based cohort of nondemented subjects living at home, whose initial cognition level was good. Participation in these activities was assessed on average 6 years before dementia diagnosis. Our results suggest that frequent participation in mental, social, or productive activity is associated with a lower risk of dementia in the elderly. These associations are independent of the influence of age, sex, education, cognitive functioning, presence of other chronic diseases and depressive symptoms, and physical functioning.

Some possible mechanisms may be hypothesized:

- The process of mental stimulation may play a role in preserving cognition. It has been reported that continuing to engage in intellectually challenging activity may promote stability of or enhance cognitive performance (8). Mental activity involves thinking and attention control processes, which might increase or maintain brain reserve even in old age (8, 24).
- Psychosocial pathways may be involved in the beneficial effect on dementia. Participation in productive or social activities fulfills a meaningful social or economic role, which could potentially sustain a person's self-concept of usefulness and competence (25). A sense of self-efficacy has been linked to several important health outcomes in middle-aged or elderly adults (26, 27). In addition, experimental studies have shown that an enriched environment improves the plasticity and thickness of the cerebral cortex of old rats (28). Maintenance of many social connections and a high level of participation in social activities have been found to be related to a high memory performance score or to prevent cognitive decline in community-dwelling elderly persons (6, 8).

Yoshitake et al. reported that regular, moderate physical activity may preserve cognitive function (14), but we were unable to identify a significant beneficial effect of physical activity. However, only a few elderly people engaged in this type of activity, leading to limited power to detect a moderate effect.

The present findings are in line with our previous report concerning a decreased dementia risk for subjects who have a rich social network (10). The fact that a rich social network could reduce the incidence of dementia might be explained by factors other than social and emotional stimulation. For example, such subjects could have received more

TABLE 3. Independent effect of mental, social, and productive activities on dementia occurrence derived from the same Cox regression model, contrasting different frequencies of participation with nonparticipation in the activities, the Kungsholmen Project, Stockholm, Sweden, 1987–1996*

	RR	95% CI
Mental activity		
No	1	
Less than daily	0.83	0.54, 1.30
Daily	0.59	0.37, 0.96
Social activity		
No	1	
Less than weekly	0.88	0.54, 1.41
Daily-weekly	0.60	0.38, 0.94
Productive activity		
No	1	
Less than weekly	0.81	0.25, 2.58
Daily-weekly	0.61	0.39, 0.95

* Relative risks (RR) and 95% confidence intervals (CI) were derived from multiple Cox regression models and were adjusted for age, sex, education, baseline Mini-Mental State Examination score, comorbidity, depressive symptoms, physical functioning, and mental, social, or productive activities.

help with their daily needs, such as with nutrition or health care. In this study, we excluded the possible effect of social support by introducing the social network index into the models; the protective effects of mentally and socially stimulating activities were still present. The findings from our previous and present studies, taken together, suggest that a stimulating life, which includes participating in creative, educational, or interactive activities, may produce beneficial effects on dementia development.

Our findings confirmed the beneficial effect of an active life on dementia in the elderly, findings that have cautiously been suggested by a few previous reports (11–14). The caution was due to methodological limitations highlighted by the authors themselves. In our study, we overcame most of these limitations. Information on activities was collected directly from the subjects several years before dementia diagnosis. We controlled for the effects of the most relevant confounders. The possibility that depressive mood might have caused subjects' inactivity was ruled out by finding similar results for subjects without any depressive symptoms. Initial cognitive functioning was controlled for in the analysis, and similar associations were found for subjects whose cognition level was initially good. The influence of genetic variability was excluded by conducting additional stratified analyses of subjects with and without the $APOE*\varepsilon 4$ allele. Possible confounding due to the presence of other chronic diseases common in old age, as well as physical disability, was also eliminated. Finally, the effect of social support likely to be associated with an active lifestyle was excluded by adjusting for the social network index (10).

Four limitations of our study need to be discussed. First, an open question was used to obtain information on social and leisure activities; subjects were asked whether they regularly participated in any activities. Although we ascertained information regarding the frequency of participation, we do not know the extent to which subjects participated in these activities, for example, how strenuous the activity was and how long it lasted. Furthermore, because of the small number of elderly participants, we could not determine the effect of any one particular activity on dementia development.

Second, recent reports on the preclinical stages of Alzheimer's disease have shown deficits in specific cognitive domains in subjects who developed dementia 7 (29, 30) and 10 (31) years later. Although time of engagement in the activities referred to a period of life preceding by 6 years the onset of dementia, some cognitive disturbances might be present in those subjects who will later develop dementia. However, the impairment found during the preclinical phase was limited to episodic memory and clearly did not affect daily life. In addition, we found similar results when we analyzed a subgroup of subjects whose MMSE scores were high, and all of our results were adjusted for initial cognitive functioning.

Third, Berger et al. (32) reported that depressive symptoms might be part of the preclinical phase of Alzheimer's disease. In our study, the possibility that depressive symptoms might have biased the associations between these activities and dementia was ruled out because similar findings were observed for subjects without any depressive symptoms.

Finally, although we controlled for many potential confounders such as age, sex, education, cognitive functioning, chronic diseases, depressive symptoms, social network, physical functioning, and genetic variability, latent and unmeasured differences might have determined the associations between mental, physical, social, productive, and recreational activities and the incidence of dementia. Premorbid personality is one possible factor that may represent such differences. Associations between dementia and specific personality traits have been suggested by two case-control studies (33, 34). Evidence on this topic is limited by two factors. First, only two known studies have focused on this subject. Second, there are difficulties in studying this topic, which result from the retrospective assessment of personality and the presence of personality changes during the early phase of Alzheimer's disease.

In conclusion, stimulating activities that involve either mental or psychosocial components may act as stimuli to preserve cognition or hinder cognitive decline, therefore preventing elderly persons from developing dementia. We could not demonstrate a causal relation and rule out all possible confounding effects. However, because of their potential value, these results deserve to be explored further.

ACKNOWLEDGMENTS

Research grants were received from the Karolinska Institutet, the Swedish Medical Research Council, the Swedish Council for Social Research (project F0123/1999), the Swedish Municipal Pension Institute, the Torsten and Ragnar Söderbergs Foundation, the Gamla Tjänarinnor Foundation, the Groschinsky Foundation, the Gun and Bertil Stohne Foundation, and the Stiftelsen Hjälp till Medicinsk Forskning-90.

REFERENCES

1. Paffenbarger RS Jr, Hyde RT, Wing AL, et al. The association of changes in physical-activity level and other lifestyle characteristics with mortality among men. N Engl J Med 1993;328: 538–45.
2. Blair SN, Kampert JB, Kohl HW 3rd, et al. Influences of cardiorespiratory fitness and other precursors on cardiovascular disease and all-cause mortality in men and women. JAMA 1996;276:205–10.
3. Kaplan GA, Strawbridge WJ, Cohen RD, et al. Natural history of leisure-time physical activity and its correlates: associations with mortality from all causes and cardiovascular disease over 28 years. Am J Epidemiol 1996;144:793–7.
4. Kujala UM, Kaprio J, Sarna S, et al. Relationship of leisure-time physical activity and mortality: the Finnish twin cohort. JAMA 1998;279:440–4.
5. Glass TA, de Leon CM, Marottoli RA, et al. Population based study of social and productive activities as predictors of survival among elderly Americans. BMJ 1999;319:478–83.
6. Bassuk SS, Glass TA, Berkman LF. Social disengagement and incident cognitive decline in community-dwelling elderly persons. Ann Intern Med 1999;131:165–73.
7. Rogers RL, Meyer JS, Mortel KF. After reaching retirement

8. Hultsch DF, Hammer M, Small BJ. Age differences in cognitive performance in later life: relationships to self-reported health and activity life style. J Gerontol 1993;48:P1–11.
9. Freidl W, Schmidt R, Stronegger WJ, et al. Mini-Mental State Examination: influence of sociodemographic, environmental and behavioral factors and vascular risk factors. J Clin Epidemiol 1996;49:73–8.
10. Fratiglioni L, Wang HX, Ericsson K, et al. The influence of social network on the occurrence of dementia: a community-based longitudinal study. Lancet 2000;355:1315–19.
11. Broe GA, Henderson AS, Creasey H, et al. A case-control study of Alzheimer's disease in Australia. Neurology 1990;40: 1698–707.
12. Kondo K, Niino M, Shido K. A case-control study of Alzheimer's disease in Japan—significance of life-styles. Dementia 1994;5:314–26.
13. Fabrigoule C, Letenneur L, Dartigues JF, et al. Social and leisure activities and risk of dementia: a prospective longitudinal study. J Am Geriatr Soc 1995;43:485–90.
14. Yoshitake T, Kiyohara Y, Kato I, et al. Incidence and risk factors of vascular dementia and Alzheimer's disease in a defined elderly Japanese population: the Hisayama Study. Neurology 1995;45:1161–8.
15. Fratiglioni L, Grut M, Forsell Y, et al. Prevalence of Alzheimer's disease and other dementias in an elderly urban population: relationship with age, sex, and education. Neurology 1991;41:1886–92.
16. Fratiglioni L, Viitanen M, von Strauss E, et al. Very old women at highest risk of dementia and Alzheimer's disease: incidence data from the Kungsholmen Project, Stockholm. Neurology 1997;48:132–8.
17. American Psychiatric Association. Diagnostic and statistical manual of mental disorders: DSM-III-R. 3rd ed, rev. Washington, DC: American Psychiatric Association, 1987: 97–163.
18. Fratiglioni L, Grut M, Forsell Y, et al. Clinical diagnosis of Alzheimer's disease and other dementias in a population survey. Agreement and causes of disagreement in applying DSM-III-R criteria. Arch Neurol 1992;49:927–32.
19. Folstein MF, Folstein SE, McHugh PR. "Mini-Mental State": a practical method for grading the cognitive state of patients for the clinician. J Psychiatr Res 1975;12:189–98.
20. Katz S, Ford AB, Moskowitz RW, et al. The index of ADL: a standardized measure of biological and psychosocial function. JAMA 1963;185:914–19.
21. World Health Organization. International classification of diseases. Manual of the international statistical classification of diseases, injuries, and causes of death. Eighth Revision. Vol 1. Geneva, Switzerland: World Health Organization, 1967.
22. World Health Organization. International classification of diseases. Manual of the international statistical classification of diseases, injuries, and causes of death. Ninth Revision. Geneva, Switzerland: World Health Organization, 1979.
23. Qiu C, Bäckman L, Winblad B, et al. The influence of education on clinically diagnosed dementia: incidence and mortality data from the Kungsholmen Project. Arch Neurol 2001;58:2034–9.
24. Schooler C. Psychological effects of complex environments during the life span: a review and theory. Intelligence 1984;8: 259–81.
25. Herzog AR, Franks MM, Markus HR, et al. Activities and well-being in older age: effects of self-concept and educational attainment. Psychol Aging 1998;13:179–85.
26. Mendes de Leon CF, Seeman TE, Baker DI, et al. Self-efficacy, physical decline, and change in functioning in community-living elders: a prospective study. J Gerontol 1996;51: S183–90.
27. Orth-Gomér K, Rosengren A, Wilhelmsen L. Lack of social support and incidence of coronary heart disease in middle-aged Swedish men. Psychosom Med 1993;55:37–43.
28. Powell D. Profiles in cognitive aging. Cambridge, MA: Harvard University Press, 1994.
29. Bäckman L, Small BJ, Fratiglioni L. Stability of the preclinical episodic memory deficit in Alzheimer's disease. Brain 2001;124:96–102.
30. Small BJ, Fratiglioni L, Viitanen M, et al. The course of cognitive impairment in preclinical Alzheimer's disease: three- and 6-year follow-up of a population-based sample. Arch Neurol 2000;57:839–44.
31. Elias MF, Beiser A, Wolf PA, et al. The preclinical phase of Alzheimer's disease: a 22-year prospective study of the Framingham Cohort. Arch Neurol 2000;57:808–13.
32. Berger AK, Fratiglioni L, Forsell Y, et al. The occurrence of depressive symptoms in the preclinical phase of AD: a population-based study. Neurology 1999;53:1998–2002.
33. Malinchoc M, Rocca WA, Colligan RC, et al. Premorbid personality characteristics in Alzheimer's disease: an exploratory case-control study. Eur J Neurol 1997;4:227–30.
34. Meins W, Dammast J. Do personality traits predict the occurrence of Alzheimer's disease? Int J Geriatr Psychiatry 2000; 15:120–4.

[11]

Leisure Activities and the Risk of Dementia in the Elderly

Joe Verghese, M.D., Richard B. Lipton, M.D., Mindy J. Katz, M.P.H.,
Charles B. Hall, Ph.D., Carol A. Derby, Ph.D., Gail Kuslansky, Ph.D.,
Anne F. Ambrose, M.D., Martin Sliwinski, Ph.D., and Herman Buschke, M.D.

ABSTRACT

BACKGROUND
Participation in leisure activities has been associated with a lower risk of dementia. It is unclear whether increased participation in leisure activities lowers the risk of dementia or participation in leisure activities declines during the preclinical phase of dementia.

METHODS
We examined the relation between leisure activities and the risk of dementia in a prospective cohort of 469 subjects older than 75 years of age who resided in the community and did not have dementia at base line. We examined the frequency of participation in leisure activities at enrollment and derived cognitive-activity and physical-activity scales in which the units of measure were activity-days per week. Cox proportional-hazards analysis was used to evaluate the risk of dementia according to the base-line level of participation in leisure activities, with adjustment for age, sex, educational level, presence or absence of chronic medical illnesses, and base-line cognitive status.

RESULTS
Over a median follow-up period of 5.1 years, dementia developed in 124 subjects (Alzheimer's disease in 61 subjects, vascular dementia in 30, mixed dementia in 25, and other types of dementia in 8). Among leisure activities, reading, playing board games, playing musical instruments, and dancing were associated with a reduced risk of dementia. A one-point increment in the cognitive-activity score was significantly associated with a reduced risk of dementia (hazard ratio, 0.93 [95 percent confidence interval, 0.90 to 0.97]), but a one-point increment in the physical-activity score was not (hazard ratio, 1.00). The association with the cognitive-activity score persisted after the exclusion of the subjects with possible preclinical dementia at base line. Results were similar for Alzheimer's disease and vascular dementia. In linear mixed models, increased participation in cognitive activities at base line was associated with reduced rates of decline in memory.

CONCLUSIONS
Participation in leisure activities is associated with a reduced risk of dementia, even after adjustment for base-line cognitive status and after the exclusion of subjects with possible preclinical dementia. Controlled trials are needed to assess the protective effect of cognitive leisure activities on the risk of dementia.

THE INCIDENCE OF DEMENTIA INcreases with increasing age.[1,2] Although the prevention of dementia has emerged as a major public health priority, there is a paucity of potential preventive strategies.[3-5] Identifying protective factors is essential to the formulation of effective interventions for dementia. Cross-sectional studies report associations between dementia and reduced participation in leisure activities in midlife, as well as between cognitive status and participation in leisure activities in old age.[6,7] Katzman proposed that persons with higher educational levels are more resistant to the effects of dementia as a result of having greater cognitive reserve and increased complexity of neuronal synapses.[8] Like education, participation in leisure activities may lower the risk of dementia by improving cognitive reserve.[9-15]

In observational studies, elderly persons who had participated to a greater extent in leisure activities had a lower risk of dementia than those who had participated to a lesser extent.[10-15] Although these results suggest that leisure activities have a protective role, an alternative explanation is possible. In most types of dementia, there is a long period of cognitive decline preceding diagnosis.[16-18] Reduced participation in activities during this preclinical phase of dementia may be the consequence and not the cause of cognitive decline. Resolution of this issue requires a long period of observation before diagnosis to enable researchers to disentangle the potential effects of preclinical dementia. Base-line cognitive status, educational level, and level of depression may confound the relation between leisure activities and dementia.[10-15] Moreover, most studies have not assessed the associations between leisure activities and particular types of dementia.[10-14]

The Bronx Aging Study provided us with the opportunity to study the influence of leisure activities on the risk of dementia over a long period[19,20] while accounting for previously identified confounders. This community-based study has followed a cohort of persons who did not have dementia at base line, with the use of detailed clinical and neuropsychological evaluations performed at intervals for up to 21 years.[19,20] We examined the influence of individual and composite measures of cognitive and physical leisure activities on the risk of the development of dementia.

METHODS

STUDY POPULATION

The study design and recruitment methods of the Bronx Aging Study have been described previously.[19,20] Briefly, the study enrolled English-speaking subjects between 75 and 85 years of age who resided in the community. Criteria for exclusion included severe visual or hearing impairment and a previous diagnosis of idiopathic Parkinson's disease, liver disease, alcoholism, or known terminal illness. Subjects were screened to rule out the presence of dementia at base line and were included if they made eight or fewer errors on the Blessed Information–Memory–Concentration test.[19-21] This test has a high test–retest reliability (0.86), and its results correlate well with the stages of Alzheimer's disease.[22,23] At the inception of the study, the cohort was middle-class, most subjects were white (91 percent), and the majority were female (64 percent). Written informed consent was obtained at enrollment. The local institutional review board approved the study protocol.

The study enrolled 488 subjects between 1980 and 1983. Subjects underwent detailed clinical and neuropsychological evaluations at enrollment and at follow-up visits every 12 to 18 months. The potential study period consisted of the 21-year period from 1980 to 2001. We excluded 2 subjects without documented leisure activities and 17 subjects who moved or declined to return for follow-up. After these subjects had been excluded, 469 subjects (96.1 percent) were eligible. In 1992, 73 surviving subjects were still having study visits in our current project, the Einstein Aging Study.

CLINICAL EVALUATION

During the study, subjects were interviewed with the use of a structured medical-history questionnaire and were examined by study clinicians.[19,20] Functional limitations on 10 basic and instrumental activities of daily living were rated on a 3-point scale for each activity (range of total scores, 10 to 30 points), with 1 point indicating "no limitation," 2 points indicating "does activity with difficulty," and 3 points indicating "unable."[19,20] A spouse or family member accompanied most subjects or was contacted for confirmation of the history.

NEUROPSYCHOLOGICAL EVALUATION

An extensive battery of neuropsychological tests was administered at study visits.[18-20] We examined performance on the Blessed Information–Memory–Concentration test (range of scores, 0 to 33),[21] the verbal and performance IQ according to the Wechsler Adult Intelligence Scale,[24] the Fuld Object-Memory Evaluation (range of scores, 0 to 10),[25] and the Zung depression scale (range of scores, 0 to 100).[26] These tests were used to inform the diagnosis of dementia at case conferences.

LEISURE ACTIVITIES

At base line, subjects were interviewed regarding participation in 6 cognitive activities (reading books or newspapers, writing for pleasure, doing crossword puzzles, playing board games or cards, participating in organized group discussions, and playing musical instruments) and 11 physical activities (playing tennis or golf, swimming, bicycling, dancing, participating in group exercises, playing team games such as bowling, walking for exercise, climbing more than two flights of stairs, doing housework, and babysitting). Subjects reported the frequency of participation as "daily," "several days per week," "once weekly," "monthly," "occasionally," or "never." We recoded these responses to generate a scale with one point corresponding to participation in one activity for one day per week. The units of the scales are thus activity-days per week; the scales were designed to be intuitively meaningful to clinicians and elderly persons and to be useful in the design of intervention studies or public health recommendations. For each activity, subjects received seven points for daily participation; four points for participating several days per week; one point for participating once weekly; and zero points for participating monthly, occasionally, or never. We summed the activity-days for each activity to generate a cognitive-activity score, ranging from 0 to 42, and a physical-activity score, ranging from 0 to 77.

The estimates of the overall level of participation were consistent with good test–retest reliability for scores obtained on entry and at the next visit a year later on the cognitive-activity scale (Spearman $r=0.518$, $P=0.001$) and the physical-activity scales (Spearman $r=0.410$, $P=0.001$). There was no direct measurement of the time spent in activities, although participation was verified by family members or friends. The scores were not correlated with age. Scores on the cognitive-activity scale correlated with scores on the Blessed test[21] (Spearman $r=-0.286$, $P=0.001$), but not functional status (Spearman $r=-0.042$, $P=0.77$). Scores on the physical-activity scale correlated with functional status (Spearman $r=-0.293$, $P=0.001$) but not with scores on the Blessed test (Spearman $r=-0.021$, $P=0.65$).[21]

DIAGNOSIS OF DEMENTIA

At study visits, subjects in whom dementia was suspected on the basis of the observations of members of the study staff, results of neuropsychological tests, or a worsening of the scores on the Blessed test[21] by four points or a total of more than seven errors underwent a workup including computed tomographic scanning and blood tests.[19,20] A diagnosis of dementia was assigned at case conferences attended by study neurologists, a neuropsychologist, and a geriatric nurse clinician, according to the criteria of the Diagnostic and Statistical Manual of Mental Disorders, third edition (DSM-III) or, after 1986, the revised third edition (DSM-III-R).[27-29] Updated criteria for the diagnosis of dementia and particular types of dementia were introduced after the study had begun.

To ensure uniformity of diagnosis, all cases were discussed again at new diagnostic conferences held in 2001 and involving a neurologist and a neuropsychologist who had not participated in diagnostic conferences between 1980 and 1998.[29] Dementia was diagnosed according to the DSM-III-R criteria.[28] Reduced participation in leisure activities was used to assess functional decline, but the leisure-activity scales were not available to the raters assessing such decline. Disagreements between raters were resolved by consensus after the case was presented to a second neurologist, with blinding maintained. Cases of dementia were classified according to the criteria for probable or possible Alzheimer's disease published by the National Institutes of Neurological Disorders and Stroke and the Alzheimer's Disease and Related Disorders Association[30] and the criteria for probable, possible, or mixed vascular dementia published by the Alzheimer's Disease Research Centers of California.[31]

STATISTICAL ANALYSIS

Continuous variables were compared with use of either an independent-samples t-test or the Mann–Whitney U test, and categorical variables were compared with use of the Pearson chi-square test.[32] In primary analyses, we studied the association between cognitive and physical activities and the risk of dementia and specific types of dementia using Cox proportional-hazards regression analysis to estimate hazard ratios, with 95 percent confidence intervals.[33] The time to an event was defined as the time from enrollment to the date of a diagnosis of dementia or to the final contact or visit for subjects without dementia. All multivariate models reported include the following covariates unless otherwise specified: age at enrollment, sex, educational level (high school or less vs. college-level education), presence or absence of chronic medical illnesses, and base-line scores on the Blessed test. Presence of the following self-reported chronic medical illnesses was individually entered in the models: cardiac disease (angina, previous myocardial infarction, or cardiac failure), hypertension, diabetes mellitus, stroke, depression, and hypothyroidism. We also divided the study cohort into thirds on the basis of their scores on the two activity scales and determined the risk of dementia according to these groups. We examined the role of individual leisure activities by comparing subjects who participated in an activity several days or more per week (frequent participation) with subjects who participated weekly or less frequently (rare participation) and, in the full models, adjusted for participation in other leisure activities.

In secondary analyses, we examined the influence of base-line cognitive status and possible preclinical dementia. First, we sequentially excluded from the full models subjects in whom dementia developed during the first two, four, seven, and nine years of follow-up in order to avoid confounding by a possible influence of preclinical dementia on participation in leisure activities. Second, we used linear mixed models controlled for age, sex, and educational level to assess the relation between cognitive activities and base-line cognitive status and the annual rate of change in cognitive status.[34] We analyzed verbal IQ as well as specific cognitive domains, including episodic memory (with the Buschke Selective Reminding test [range of scores, 0 to 72, with lower scores indicating worse memory][35] and the Fuld Object–Memory Evaluation[25]) and executive function (with the Digit–Symbol Substitution subtest of the Wechsler Adult Intelligence Scale [range of scores, 0 to 90, with lower scores indicating worse cognition]).[24] Each model included terms for the cognitive-activity score, time, and the interaction between the two. The assumptions of the models were examined analytically and graphically and were adequately met.

RESULTS

DEMOGRAPHIC CHARACTERISTICS

During 2702 person-years of follow-up (median follow-up, 5.1 years), dementia developed in 124 subjects (Alzheimer's disease in 61, vascular dementia in 30, mixed dementia in 25, and other types of dementia in 8). By the end of the study period, 361 subjects had died, 88 subjects had dropped out (mean [±SD] follow-up, 6.6±4.9 years), and 20 subjects were still active. When the cohort was divided into thirds according to the cognitive-activity score or the physical-activity score, no significant differences in the length of follow-up were found among these subgroups.

On average, subjects in whom dementia developed were older, had lower levels of education, and had significantly lower scores on the cognitive-activity scale, but not on the physical-activity scale, than subjects in whom dementia did not develop (Table 1). Although their scores on neuropsychological tests were in the normal range (Table 1), subjects in whom dementia later developed had poorer cognition on the Blessed test (P=0.001)[21] and a lower base-line performance IQ (P=0.07).[24] The frequency of chronic medical illnesses did not differ significantly between subjects in whom dementia developed and those in whom it did not. Nineteen subjects were receiving antidepressants at enrollment. Cognitive-activity scores were inversely correlated with the Zung depression scale[26] (Spearman r=−0.215, P<0.001), as were physical-activity scores (Spearman r=−0.254, P<0.001), indicating that lower levels of participation were associated with increasing levels of depression.

A smaller proportion of the 361 subjects with a high-school education or less than of the 108 subjects who had attended college participated in reading (90 percent vs. 96 percent, P=0.05), writing (67 percent vs. 80 percent, P=0.01), doing crossword puzzles (21 percent vs. 36 percent, P=0.001), and playing musical instruments (7 percent vs. 15 percent, P=0.02). There was no difference according to educational level in the proportion of subjects who played board games or participated in group discussions.

LEISURE ACTIVITIES

Among cognitive activities, reading, playing board games, and playing musical instruments were as-

Table 1. Base-Line Characteristics of Subjects in Whom Dementia Developed and Subjects in Whom It Did Not.*			
Variable	Subjects in Whom Dementia Did Not Develop (N=345)	Subjects in Whom Dementia Developed (N=124)	P Value
Age (yr)	78.9±3.1	79.7±3.1	0.01
Female sex (%)	63	67	0.51
White race (%)	92	91	0.60
Duration of follow-up (yr)	5.6±4.1	5.9±4.1	0.52
High-school education or less (%)	74	84	0.02
Functional rating	10.9±1.9	11.5±2.1	0.01
Physical-activity score	13.6±7.6	12.8±8.2	0.31
Cognitive-activity score	10.6±5.8	7.5±5.5	<0.001
Neuropsychological tests			
Blessed Information–Memory–Concentration test	2.1±1.9	3.5±2.4	0.001
Performance IQ	105.8±12.4	97.5±13.8	0.07
Verbal IQ	111.0±15.5	103.9±15.6	0.35
Fuld Object-Memory Evaluation	7.5±1.2	6.7±1.5	0.001
Zung depression scale	46.4±10.4	48.4±10.9	0.32
Medical illnesses (%)			
Hypertension	52	45	0.12
Cardiac disease	29	23	0.72
Stroke	7	3	0.99
Diabetes	11	12	0.87
Thyroid illness	14	9	0.12
Depression	17	19	0.10

* Plus–minus values are means ±SD. P values for scales and tests were calculated by the Mann–Whitney U test. The functional rating ranges from 10 to 30, with higher scores indicating better function; scores on the physical-activity scale range from 0 to 77, with higher scores indicating greater participation; scores on the cognitive-activity scale range from 0 to 42, with higher scores indicating greater participation; the range of scores on the Blessed Information–Memory–Concentration test is 0 to 33, with higher scores indicating worse general cognitive status; the normal ranges of performance IQ and verbal IQ are 85 to 115; the range of scores on the Fuld Object-Memory Evaluation is 0 to 10, with higher scores indicating better memory; and the range of scores on the Zung depression scale is 0 to 100, with higher scores indicating a greater level of depression.

sociated with a lower risk of dementia (Table 2). Dancing was the only physical activity associated with a lower risk of dementia. Fewer than 10 subjects played golf or tennis, so the relation between these activities and dementia was not assessed.

COGNITIVE ACTIVITIES

When the cognitive-activity score was modeled as a continuous variable (Table 3), the hazard ratio for dementia for a one-point increment in this score was 0.93 (95 percent confidence interval, 0.89 to 0.96). Adjustment for the base-line score on the Blessed test in a second model (Table 3) did not attenuate the association. Participation in cognitive activities was associated with a reduced risk of Alzheimer's disease (hazard ratio, 0.93 [95 percent confidence interval, 0.88 to 0.98]), vascular dementia (hazard ratio, 0.92 [95 percent confidence interval, 0.86 to 0.99]), and mixed dementia (hazard ratio, 0.87 [95 percent confidence interval, 0.78 to 0.93]). The frequency of participation in cognitive activities was related to the risk of dementia. According to the model in which we adjusted for the base-line score on the Blessed test, the hazard ratio for subjects with scores in the highest third on the cognitive-activity scale, as compared with those with scores in the lowest third, was 0.37 (95 percent confidence interval, 0.23 to 0.61) (Table 3).

In additional analyses, adjustment for intellectual status with the use of the verbal IQ[24] did not alter the association between participation in cognitive activities and the risk of dementia (hazard ratio, 0.92 [95 percent confidence interval, 0.87 to 0.97]). Participation in cognitive activities was also associated with a reduced risk of dementia among the 361 subjects with a high-school education or less (hazard ratio, 0.94 [95 percent confidence interval, 0.91 to 0.98]). The association of cognitive activities with dementia was not affected by adjustment for functional status, the restriction of the analyses to subjects with scores of less than 5 on the Blessed test,[21] or the exclusion of subjects who died during the first year after enrollment.

PHYSICAL ACTIVITIES

The physical-activity score was not significantly associated with dementia, either when analyzed as a continuous variable or when the study cohort was divided into thirds according to this score (Table 3).

INFLUENCE OF PRECLINICAL DEMENTIA

The presence of preclinical dementia might reduce participation in leisure activities,[6,7] leading to the overestimation of its protective influence. The association between the base-line cognitive-activity score and dementia was significant even after the exclusion of 94 subjects in whom dementia was diagnosed during the first seven years after enrollment (hazard ratio, 0.94 [95 percent confidence interval, 0.88 to 0.99]) (Table 4). The association was no longer significant after the exclusion of the 105 subjects in whom dementia was diagnosed during the first nine years after enrollment. However, only 19 subjects were given a diagnosis of dementia after this point.

We used linear mixed models to examine the influence of participation in cognitive activities on the annual rate of change in cognitive function.[34] In these models (Table 5), the term for the cognitive-activity score represents the cross-sectional association between the cognitive activities and the scores on the selected tests administered at enrollment. These results indicate that subjects with increased participation in cognitive activities at entry had better overall cognitive status. Analysis with use of the term for time indicates that cognitive performance declines linearly as a function of follow-up time. The term for the interaction between the cognitive-activity score and time represents the longitudinal effect of the base-line measure of participation in cognitive activities on the annual rate of decline in

Table 2. Risk of Development of Dementia According to the Frequency of Participation in Individual Leisure Activities at Base Line.*

Leisure Activity and Frequency	Subjects with Dementia	All Subjects	Hazard Ratio for Dementia (95% CI)
	no.		
Cognitive activities			
Playing board games			
Rare	108	366	1.00
Frequent	16	103	0.26 (0.17–0.57)
Reading			
Rare	40	87	1.00
Frequent	84	382	0.65 (0.43–0.97)
Playing a musical instrument			
Rare	120	452	1.00
Frequent	4	17	0.31 (0.11–0.90)
Doing crossword puzzles			
Rare	117	407	1.00
Frequent	7	62	0.59 (0.34–1.01)
Writing			
Rare	104	382	1.00
Frequent	20	87	1.00 (0.61–1.67)
Participating in group discussions			
Rare	117	437	1.00
Frequent	7	32	1.06 (0.48–2.33)
Physical activities			
Dancing			
Rare	99	339	1.00
Frequent	25	130	0.24 (0.06–0.99)
Doing housework			
Rare	39	106	1.00
Frequent	85	363	0.88 (0.60–1.20)
Walking			
Rare	19	65	1.00
Frequent	105	404	0.67 (0.45–1.05)
Climbing stairs			
Rare	44	153	1.00
Frequent	80	316	1.55 (0.96–2.38)
Bicycling			
Rare	116	443	1.00
Frequent	8	26	2.09 (0.97–4.49)
Swimming			
Rare	108	386	1.00
Frequent	16	83	0.71 (0.22–2.29)
Playing team games			
Rare	120	450	1.00
Frequent	4	19	1.00 (0.14–7.79)
Participating in group exercise			
Rare	88	330	1.00
Frequent	36	139	1.18 (0.72–1.94)
Babysitting			
Rare	114	429	1.00
Frequent	10	40	0.81 (0.11–6.01)

*The frequency of participation in leisure activities was categorized as frequent if the subject participated at least several times per week and as rare if the subject participated once per week or less frequently. Hazard ratios were adjusted for age, sex, educational level, presence or absence of medical illnesses, score on the Blessed Information–Memory–Concentration test, and participation or nonparticipation in other leisure activities. For each activity, rare participation was used as the reference category. CI denotes confidence interval.

Table 3. Risk of Dementia According to the Base-Line Scores on the Cognitive-Activity Scale and the Physical-Activity Scale.*

Leisure Activity	No. of Subjects	Hazard Ratio for Dementia (95% CI) Model 1	Model 2
Cognitive-activity score			
1-Point increment		0.93 (0.89–0.96)	0.93 (0.90–0.97)
<8 Points	182	1.00	1.00
8–11 Points	137	0.50 (0.31–0.75)	0.48 (0.29–0.74)
>11 Points	150	0.33 (0.21–0.51)	0.37 (0.23–0.61)
Physical-activity score			
1-Point increment		0.99 (0.91–1.01)	1.00 (0.98–1.03)
<9 Points	162	1.00	1.00
9–16 Points	157	1.06 (0.67–1.65)	1.44 (0.91–2.28)
>16 Points	150	0.92 (0.58–1.45)	1.27 (0.78–2.06)

* Model 1 was adjusted for age, sex, educational level, and the presence or absence of chronic medical illnesses; model 2 includes the variables in model 1 and the base-line score on the Blessed Information–Memory–Concentration test. For each scale, scores in the lowest third were used as the reference category. CI denotes confidence interval.

Table 4. Risk of Dementia per 1-Point Increment in the Base-Line Cognitive-Activity Score, with the Sequential Exclusion of Subjects in Whom Dementia Developed during the First Nine Years of Follow-up.*

Analysis	Excluded Subjects with Dementia	Subjects in Whom Dementia Developed	Hazard Ratio (95% CI)
	no.		
Overall	0	124	0.93 (0.90–0.97)
With exclusion of subjects with a diagnosis of dementia			
Diagnosis during first 2 yr	36	88	0.94 (0.90–0.97)
Diagnosis during first 4 yr	63	61	0.94 (0.89–0.98)
Diagnosis during first 7 yr	94	30	0.94 (0.88–0.99)
Diagnosis during first 9 yr	105	19	0.96 (0.89–1.04)

* Hazard ratios are adjusted for age, sex, educational level, presence or absence of chronic medical illnesses, and score on the Blessed Information–Memory–Concentration test. CI denotes confidence interval.

performance on the selected tests; this effect was significant only for the tests of episodic memory. The estimates show that for a one-point increment in the cognitive-activity score, the annual rate of decline in scores on the Buschke Selective Reminding test is reduced by 0.043 point (P=0.02), and the annual rate of decline on the Fuld Object-Memory Evaluation is reduced by 0.006 point (P=0.04).

DISCUSSION

This prospective, 21-year study demonstrates a significant association between a higher level of participation in leisure activities at base line and a decreased risk of dementia — both for Alzheimer's disease and for vascular dementia. A one-point increment in the cognitive-activity score, which corresponds to participation in an activity for one day per week, was associated with a reduction of 7 percent in the risk of dementia. The association between cognitive activities and the risk of dementia remained robust even after adjustment for potential confounding variables such as age, sex, educational level, presence or absence of chronic medical illnesses, and base-line cognitive status. Increased participation in leisure activities was associated with a lower risk of dementia. Subjects with scores in the highest third on the cognitive-activity scale (more than 11 activity-days) had a risk of dementia that was 63 percent lower than that among subjects with scores in the lowest third.

We identified three possible explanations for the association between greater participation in leisure activities and a decreased risk of dementia. First, the presence of preclinical dementia may decrease participation in leisure activities. Second, unmeasured confounding may influence the results. Third, there may be a true causal effect of cognitive activities. We used several strategies to test the hypothesis that reduced participation in leisure activities appears to be a risk factor for, but is in fact a consequence of, preclinical dementia. Adjustment for base-line scores on cognitive tests, which predict dementia, did not alter the association between participation in cognitive activities and dementia. We have reported that an accelerated decline in memory begins seven years before dementia is diagnosed.[18] The exclusion of subjects in whom dementia was diagnosed during the first seven years after enrollment should eliminate most subjects who had preclinical dementia at enrollment. However, participation in cognitive activities predicted dementia even among those in whom it developed more than seven years after enrollment. Results from the linear mixed models that analyzed cognitive function over time corroborate the findings of previous studies[13,36] and show that increased participation in cognitive activities is associated with slower rates of cognitive decline, especially in terms of episodic memory.

Because of the observational nature of our study, there is a possibility of residual or unmeasured confounding. The observed association appears to be independent of educational level and intellectual level, which may influence the choice of leisure activities. Perhaps reduced participation in leisure activities is an early marker of dementia that precedes the declines on cognitive tests.[13] Alternatively, participation in leisure activities may be a marker of behavior that promotes health. But the specificity of our findings for cognitive activities and not physical activities argues against this hypothesis. We did not study the effect of apolipoprotein E genotype, which may influence the rates of cognitive decline.[15,36] Hence, despite the magnitude and consistency of the associations, our findings do not establish a causal relation between participation in leisure activities and dementia, and controlled trials are therefore needed.

If there is a causal role, participation in leisure activities may increase cognitive reserve, delaying the clinical or pathological onset of dementia.[8,37,38] Alternatively, participation in cognitive activities might slow the pathological processes of disease during the preclinical phase of dementia. Our findings do not imply that subjects who were less active cognitively increased their risk of dementia.

The role of individual leisure activities is not well known, since most studies have used composite measures. In a French cohort, knitting, doing odd jobs, gardening, and traveling reduced the risk of dementia.[10] In the Nun Study, low density of ideas and low levels of grammatical complexity in autobiographies written in early life were associated with low cognitive test scores in later life.[39] Reading, playing board games, playing musical instruments, and dancing were associated with a lower risk of dementia in our cohort. There was no association between physical activity and the risk of dementia. Exercise is said to have beneficial effects on the brain by promoting plasticity, increasing the levels of neurotrophic factors in the brain, and enhancing resistance to insults.[40] Cognitive and physical activities overlap, and therefore it is not surprising that previous studies have disagreed on the role of physical activities.[10-15] Although physical activities are clearly important in promoting overall health,[41] their protective effect against dementia remains uncertain.

Our study has several limitations. Ours was a cohort of volunteers who resided in the community; whites and subjects older than 75 years of age were overrepresented, as compared with the general population of those over 65 years of age, thus poten-

Table 5. Association of Participation in Cognitive Leisure Activities with Base-Line Cognitive Function and Rate of Change in Cognitive Function.*

Cognitive Test	Estimated Change in Test Score (±SE)	P Value
Buschke Selective Reminding test		
Cognitive-activity score (per 1-point increment)	0.383±0.092	<0.001
Time (per 1-year increment)	−1.578±0.211	<0.001
Interaction	0.043±0.018	0.02
Fuld Object-Memory Evaluation		
Cognitive-activity score (per 1-point increment)	0.028±0.011	0.007
Time (per 1-year increment)	0.961±0.466	0.04
Interaction	0.006±0.003	0.04
Digit–Symbol Substitution test		
Cognitive-activity score (per 1-point increment)	0.569±0.097	<0.001
Time (per 1-year increment)	−0.998±0.172	<0.001
Interaction	−0.001±0.014	>0.05
Verbal IQ		
Cognitive-activity score (per 1-point increment)	0.789±0.131	<0.001
Time (per 1-year increment)	4.472±1.980	0.02
Interaction	0.020±0.012	>0.05

* Associations were assessed by linear mixed models, controlled for age, sex, and educational level. The term for the interaction between the cognitive-activity score and time represents the longitudinal effect of the base-line measure of participation in cognitive activities on the annual rate of decline in performance on the given test.

tially limiting the generalizability of our results. Although standard criteria and well-established procedures were used to make diagnoses, some misclassification is inevitable. Time spent in each activity was not directly measured, although the history was verified by family members or other informants. Duration and cognitive demand are both important in the assessment of an activity. It is difficult to assign weights to the cognitive demands of leisure activities, since such demands vary among activities and among the persons who engage in each activity. Leisure activities were arbitrarily classified as cognitive or physical. For instance, doing housework requires not only a certain functional status but also the ability to plan, prepare, and adapt to changes in circumstances and the environment. The leisure activities we studied reflect the interests of our cohort, and it is quite likely that activities other than the ones we studied are also protective.[10-15]

Participation in leisure activities is associated with a reduced risk of development of dementia, both Alzheimer's disease and vascular dementia. The reduction in risk is related to the frequency of participation. According to our models, for example, elderly persons who did crossword puzzles four days a week (four activity-days) had a risk of dementia that was 47 percent lower than that among subjects who did puzzles once a week (one activity-day).

Clinical trials are needed to define the causal role of participation in leisure activities. A recent study reported reduced cognitive declines after cognitive training in elderly persons without dementia.[36] If confirmed, our results may support recommendations for participation in cognitive activities to lower the risk of dementia that parallel current recommendations for participation in physical activities to reduce the risk of cardiovascular diseases.[42,43]

Supported by a grant (AGO3949-15) from the National Institute on Aging.

Presented in part at the 127th annual meeting of the American Neurological Association, New York, October 12–16, 2002.

REFERENCES

1. Fratiglioni L, De Ronchi D, Aguero-Torres H. Worldwide prevalence and incidence of dementia. Drugs Aging 1999;15:365-75.
2. Jorm AF, Jolley D. The incidence of dementia: a meta-analysis. Neurology 1998; 51:728-33.
3. Seshadri S, Beiser A, Selhub J, et al. Plasma homocysteine as a risk factor for dementia and Alzheimer's disease. N Engl J Med 2002;346:476-83.
4. Engelhart MJ, Geerlings MI, Ruitenberg A, et al. Dietary intake of antioxidants and risk of Alzheimer disease. JAMA 2002;287: 3223-9.
5. Morris MC, Evans DA, Bienias JL, et al. Dietary intake of antioxidant nutrients and the risk of incident Alzheimer disease in a biracial community study. JAMA 2002;287: 3230-7.
6. Friedland RP, Fritsch T, Smyth KA, et al. Patients with Alzheimer's disease have reduced activities in midlife compared with healthy control-group members. Proc Natl Acad Sci U S A 2001;98:3440-5.
7. Kondo K, Niino M, Shido K. A case-control study of Alzheimer's disease in Japan — significance of life-styles. Dementia 1994;5: 314-26.
8. Katzman R. Education and the prevalence of dementia and Alzheimer's disease. Neurology 1993;43:13-20.
9. Rogers RL, Meyer JS, Mortel KF. After reaching retirement age physical activity sustains cerebral perfusion and cognition. J Am Geriatr Soc 1990;38:123-8.
10. Fabrigoule C, Letenneur L, Dartigues JF, Zarrouk M, Commenges D, Barberger-Gateau P. Social and leisure activities and risk of dementia: a prospective longitudinal study. J Am Geriatr Soc 1995;43:485-90.
11. Laurin D, Verreault R, Lindsay J, MacPherson K, Rockwood K. Physical activity and risk of cognitive impairment and dementia in elderly persons. Arch Neurol 2001;58:498-504.
12. Scarmeas N, Levy G, Tang MX, Manly J, Stern Y. Influence of leisure activity on the incidence of Alzheimer's disease. Neurology 2001;57:2236-42.
13. Wilson RS, Mendes De Leon CF, Barnes LL, et al. Participation in cognitively stimulating activities and risk of incident Alzheimer disease. JAMA 2002;287:742-8.
14. Wang H-X, Karp A, Winblad B, Fratiglioni L. Late-life engagement in social and leisure activities is associated with a decreased risk of dementia: a longitudinal study from the Kungsholmen project. Am J Epidemiol 2002;155:1081-7.
15. Wilson RS, Bennett DA, Bienias JL, et al. Cognitive activity and incident AD in a population-based sample of older persons. Neurology 2002;59:1910-4.
16. Small BJ, Fratiglioni L, Viitanen M, Winblad B, Backman L. The course of cognitive impairment in preclinical Alzheimer disease: three- and 6-year follow-up of a population-based sample. Arch Neurol 2000;57:839-44.
17. Elias MF, Beiser A, Wolf PA, Au R, White RF, D'Agostino RB. The preclinical phase of Alzheimer disease: a 22-year prospective study of the Framingham Cohort. Arch Neurol 2000;57:808-13.
18. Hall CB, Ying J, Kuo L, et al. Estimation of bivariate measurements having different change points, with application to cognitive ageing. Stat Med 2001;20:3695-714.
19. Katzman R, Aronson M, Fuld P, et al. Development of dementing illnesses in an 80-year-old volunteer cohort. Ann Neurol 1989;25:317-24.
20. Aronson MK, Ooi WL, Morgenstern H, et al. Women, myocardial infarction, and dementia in the very old. Neurology 1990; 40:1102-6.
21. Blessed G, Tomlinson BE, Roth M. The association between quantitative measures of dementia and of senile change in the cerebral grey matter of elderly subjects. Br J Psychiatry 1968;114:797-811.
22. Fuld PA. Psychological testing in the differential diagnosis of the dementias. In: Katzman R, Terry RD, Bick KL, eds. Alzheimer's disease: senile dementia and related disorders. Vol. 7 of Aging. New York: Raven Press, 1978:185-93.
23. Grober E, Dickson D, Sliwinski MJ, et al. Memory and mental status correlates of modified Braak staging. Neurobiol Aging 1999; 20:573-9.
24. Wechsler D. Manual for the Wechsler Adult Intelligence Scale. Washington, D.C.: Psychological Corporation, 1955.
25. Fuld PA, Masur DM, Blau AD, Crystal H, Aronson MK. Object-memory evaluation for prospective detection of dementia in normal functioning elderly: predictive and normative data. J Clin Exp Neuropsychol 1990;12:520-8.
26. Zung WWK. Depression in the normal aged. Psychosomatics 1967;8:287-92.
27. Diagnostic and statistical manual of mental disorders, 3rd ed.: DSM-III. Washington, D.C.: American Psychiatric Association, 1980.
28. Diagnostic and statistical manual of mental disorders, 3rd ed. rev.: DSM-III-R. Washington, D.C.: American Psychiatric Association, 1987.
29. Verghese J, Lipton RB, Hall CB, Kuslansky G, Katz MJ, Buschke H. Abnormality of gait as a predictor of non-Alzheimer's dementia. N Engl J Med 2002;347:1761-8.
30. McKhann G, Drachman D, Folstein M, Katzman R, Price D, Stadlan EM. Clinical diagnosis of Alzheimer's disease: report of the NINCDS-ADRDA Work Group under the auspices of Department of Health and Human Services Task Force on Alzheimer's Disease. Neurology 1984;34:939-44.
31. Chui HC, Victoroff JI, Margolin D, Jagust W, Shankle R, Katzman R. Criteria for the diagnosis of ischemic vascular dementia proposed by the State of California Alzheimer's Disease Diagnostic and Treatment Centers. Neurology 1992;42:473-80.
32. Fleiss JL. Statistical methods for rates and proportions. 2nd ed. New York: John Wiley, 1981:38-46.
33. Cox DR. Regression models and life-tables. J R Stat Soc (B) 1972;34:187-220.
34. Laird NM, Ware JH. Random-effects models for longitudinal data. Biometrics 1982;38:963-74.
35. Buschke H. Selective reminding for analysis of memory and learning. J Verbal Learn Verb Behav 1973;12:543-50.
36. Ball K, Berch DB, Helmers KF, et al. Effects of cognitive training interventions with older adults: a randomized controlled trial. JAMA 2002;288:2271-81.
37. Wilson RS, Bienias JL, Berry-Kravis E, Evans DA, Bennett DA. The apolipoprotein E varepsilon 2 allele and decline in episodic memory. J Neurol Neurosurg Psychiatry 2002; 73:672-7.
38. Stern Y, Albert S, Tang M-X, Tsai W-Y. Rate of memory decline in AD is related to education and occupation: cognitive reserve? Neurology 1999;53:1942-7.
39. Snowdon DA, Kemper SJ, Mortimer JA, Greiner LH, Wekstein DR, Markesbery WR. Linguistic ability in early life and cognitive function and Alzheimer's disease in late life: findings from the Nun Study. JAMA 1996; 275:528-32.
40. Cotman CW, Berchtold NC. Exercise: a behavioral intervention to enhance brain health and plasticity. Trends Neurosci 2002; 25:295-301.
41. Paffenbarger RS Jr, Hyde RT, Wing AL, Lee I-M, Jung DL, Kampert JB. The association of changes in physical-activity level and other lifestyle characteristics with mortality among men. N Engl J Med 1993;328:538-45.
42. American College of Sports Medicine Position Stand: exercise and physical activity for older adults. Med Sci Sports Exerc 1998; 30:992-1008.
43. Christmas C, Andersen RA. Exercise and older patients: guidelines for the clinician. J Am Geriatr Soc 2000;48:318-24.

[12]

The Efficacy of Exercise as a Long-term Antidepressant in Elderly Subjects: A Randomized, Controlled Trial

Nalin A. Singh,[1,2] Karen M. Clements,[4] and Maria A. Fiatarone Singh[1,3,4,5]

[1]Division on Aging, Harvard Medical School, Boston, Massachusetts.
[2]Brockton West Roxbury VA Medical Center, Brockton, Massachusetts.
[3]Jean Mayer United States Department of Agriculture Human Nutrition Research Center on Aging at Tufts University, Boston, Massachusetts.
[4]The Hebrew Rehabilitation Center for Aged, Roslindale, Massachusetts.
[5]The School of Exercise and Sport Science, University of Sydney, Australia.

Background. Pharmacological treatment of depression in geriatric patients is often difficult. Although unsupervised exercise has been shown to benefit younger depressed patients, there is no evidence that unsupervised exercise can be used as a maintenance treatment for depression in elderly patients. Our aim was to test the feasibility and efficacy of unsupervised exercise as a long-term treatment for clinical depression in elderly patients.

Methods. We studied 32 subjects (71.3 ± 1.2 years of age, mean ± SE) in a 20-week, randomized, controlled trial, with follow-up at 26 months. Subjects were community-dwelling patients with major or minor depression or dysthymia. Exercisers engaged in 10 weeks of supervised weight-lifting exercise followed by 10 weeks of unsupervised exercise. Controls attended lectures for 10 weeks. No contact was made with either group after 20 weeks until final follow-up. Blinded assessment was made with the Beck Depression Inventory (BDI), the Philadelphia Geriatric Morale Scale, and Ewart's Self Efficacy Scale at 20 weeks and with the BDI and physical activity questionnaire at 26 months.

Results. Patients randomized to the exercise condition completed 18 ± 2 sessions of unsupervised exercise during Weeks 10 to 20. The BDI was significantly reduced at both 20 weeks and 26 months of follow-up in exercisers compared with controls ($p < .05–.001$). At the 26-month follow-up, 33% of the exercisers were still regularly weight lifting, versus 0% of controls ($p < .05$).

Conclusions. Unsupervised weight-lifting exercise maintains its antidepressant effectiveness at 20 weeks in depressed elderly patients. Long-term changes in exercise behavior are possible in some patients even without supervision.

BOTH the World Health Organization and the National Institutes of Health Consensus Development Conference on Late Life Depression have recommended that more clinical trials be conducted in patients over the age of 70 to alleviate the personal and societal burden of depressive illness (1). Although standard treatments have been shown to be efficacious in elderly patients (2) such regimens are often unacceptable to patients or are fraught with side effects in clinical practice (3).

The efficacy of exercise as an alternative treatment in clinically depressed young or middle-aged patients has been established in at least eight randomized controlled trials of varying duration (4). In this clinical population, the efficacy of group or individual exercise is similar to psychotherapy with no direct comparison with pharmacotherapy (5). Both weight lifting and aerobic exercise (running/jogging) have been successfully utilized in these clinical trials (6,7). Although these data have been extrapolated to elderly patients as well, there are in fact only three published studies that have directly tested exercise as an intervention for clinical depression in elderly patients. McNeil and colleagues studied 30 community-dwelling individuals (mean age 73 years) who self-reported mild to moderate depressive symptoms on the Beck Depression Inventory (BDI). Subjects randomly assigned to either walking or a social contact condition for 6 weeks improved by approximately 25% to 30% compared with wait-list controls, who showed no improvement (8). This effect size is equivalent to the placebo arm of most pharmacotherapy trials for depression (9). We conducted a 10-week randomized controlled trial of supervised progressive resistance training (weight lifting) exercise in elderly patients who satisfied the Diagnostic and Statistical Manual of Mental Disorders IV (DSM-IV) criteria for clinical depression (10). We found a 60% improvement in depression in exercisers compared with a 30% improvement in controls who attended a series of health lectures. Blumenthal conducted a randomized controlled trial in 156 men and women (mean age 57 ± 7 years) with major depression comparing aerobic exercise, antidepressant medication, and a combination of medication and exercise. Results at the end of 16 weeks suggested no significant difference between the antidepressant effect of drugs versus exercise and no additive effect of the two (11). The magnitude of reduction with most pharmacotherapy trials for major depression is approximately 60% (9). Thus, to date, two published studies have found a clinically important treatment benefit associated with exercise in depressed elderly patients.

Several important questions remain to be answered in light of the above research: (i) Is the antidepressant effect of weight lifting sustainable over the long term? (ii) Is the efficacy of exercise in depression dependent upon a supervised mode of delivery or group dynamics? and (iii) Would a short period of supervised training be associated with long-term behavioral adaptations resulting in new patterns of habitual physical activity?

Such questions are extremely important to answer because depression is a chronic disorder with high rates of relapse among patients older than 70 years of age (12). In addition, there is a need to develop and test strategies in depressed elderly patients, in particular due to the paucity of data on treatment efficacy in this age group (9). In the elderly population there is a potential risk/benefit advantage to the use of exercise rather than pharmacotherapy as a treatment for depression because of the increased prevalence of medication side effects in geriatric patients as well as the other beneficial effects of exercise that have been demonstrated in this age group (3,13).

We present here Phase II (Weeks 10 through 20) and Phase III (Months 6 through 26) of our randomized controlled trial of progressive resistance training, during which the above hypotheses were tested by changing both the setting and mode of delivery of the exercise intervention. We re-assessed patients after 20 weeks and 26 months to determine the long-term effects on both depressive symptoms and physical activity habits.

METHODS

Study Design

The overall design of this randomized controlled trial is shown in Table 1. The results of Phase I have been published elsewhere (14). In Weeks 10 to 20, patients randomized to the exercise intervention continued unsupervised exercise, and both groups were monitored with a brief weekly phone call. After 20 weeks, no further instructions were given, and all subjects were re-assessed at a median of 26 months (range 22–35) after enrollment in the study. There was no significant difference in the follow-up interval between exercisers (26 ± 4 months) and controls (27 ± 4 months; $p = .70$).

Randomization was done by a computer-generated random number list. Allocations were generated by a statistician, placed in sealed envelopes, and opened after baseline assessment. The study procedures were approved by the Human Investigation Review Committee of the Jean Mayer USDA Human Nutrition Research Center on Aging (HNRC) at Tufts University in accordance with the principles of the Declaration of Helsinki as amended in Tokyo (1975) and Hong Kong (1989), and written informed consent was obtained from each subject.

Study Population

Depressed patients were recruited from the community through two volunteer databases, the HNRC and the Harvard Cooperative on Aging. Volunteers older than 60 years of age were sent a letter and a BDI to complete and return. Subjects with a score >12 on the BDI, which is the lower boundary for mild depression, were then contacted by phone. Subjects included in the study fulfilled the DSM-IV diagnostic criteria for either unipolar major or minor depression or dysthymia. Subjects were excluded if demented clinically by DSM-IV criteria; if their Folstein Mini Mental State score was <23; if they were suffering from unstable ischemic heart disease or recent myocardial infarction (<6 months), severe progressive neurological disease, symptomatic inguinal hernia, bipolar disorder, or active psychosis; if they were suicidal; if they were currently seeing a psychiatrist or had been on antidepressant drugs within the last 3 months; or if they were participating in any progressive resistance training. Subjects participating in aerobic exercise more than twice a week in the month prior to enrollment were also excluded.

Interventions

Exercise group.—Training methods during the first 10 weeks of supervised exercise have been published elsewhere (10). Briefly, we employed high-intensity progressive resistance training (PRT) of large muscle groups (both upper and lower body) 3 days a week for 10 weeks. For each machine, the resistance was set at 80% of the one-repetition maximum (1-RM), and subjects performed three sets of eight repetitions. The load was increased at each session as tolerated, and strength measures were repeated every 4 weeks to establish a new baseline. Each session lasted 45 minutes. All sessions were supervised. At the end of 10 weeks of supervised high-intensity PRT, the exercise group was offered three alternatives to continue to train during Phase II:

Table 1. Study Design

Study Phase	Exercise Group Procedures	Control Group Procedures
Phase I (Weeks 1–10)	Supervised exercise in laboratory	Health education lectures
Phase II (Weeks 11–20)	Unsupervised exercise at home, laboratory or health club setting Written exercise log Weekly phone call by investigator	Weekly phone call by investigator
Phase III (Months 6–26)[†]	No study requirements No contact with investigators	No study requirements No contact with investigators

[†]The duration of Phase III ranged from 22 to 35 months depending on the date of initial enrollment.

1. Continued training at the facility (HNRC) on the resistance-training machines (Keiser Sports Health, Fresno, CA) on which they had completed their first 10-week program. Subjects were trained in setting the machines and progressing resistance at each session by use of the Borg Scale of Perceived Exertion (15), to continue to work at approximately 80% of 1-RM. Their initial training load was estimated for them prior to beginning unsupervised exercise. The subjects had no further interaction with the research staff.
2. Home-based training with free weights. Subjects were instructed and given written materials for 10 PRT exercises for large muscle groups of upper and lower limbs. These subjects had their 1-RM on all exercises estimated prior to beginning the exercises and were instructed to progress as per the Borg Scale of Perceived Exertion at 80% of 1-RM each session.
3. Training at a community health facility that provided resistance-training equipment. The selection of machines available was discussed with the primary investigator (PI) (NAS), and a program including the large muscle groups was again chosen. Subjects were instructed on how to estimate progressive training loads of 80% of 1-RM.

For all training options, the amount of exercise prescribed was three sets of eight repetitions at 80% of the estimated 1-RM 2 to 3 days per week. All subjects were instructed to keep a written log of their strength training sessions during Phase II. One hundred percent compliance was defined as completing at least 20 sessions over the course of the unsupervised 10-week period.

Control group.—All subjects not randomly assigned to resistance training attended a series of health education lectures and videos designed as an attention control for the first 10 weeks (10). All sessions were supervised and occurred twice a week for 1 hour. During Phase II, there were no educational sessions, and subjects were given no exercise or other recommendations.

Subject Contact During Phase II

During Phase II, neither group was restricted from commencing exercise in addition to that prescribed or from seeking any treatment for depression. However, no exercise recommendations were given to the control group. All subjects were contacted weekly by telephone by the PI to monitor health status or adverse events. During this brief (5-minute) phone call, a standard set of questions was asked relating to musculoskeletal pain, total medication usage, minor illness, hospitalization, commencement of any psychiatric treatment, visits to a health professional, presence/worsening of suicidal feelings, and participation in exercise. For the exercisers only, any questions concerning their PRT exercise routine were addressed. No psychological counseling was given by phone or in person to any patients during this period.

Long-term Follow-up: Phase III

After Week 20, no further recommendations for exercise or other treatment were made to either group, and no further interactions with the research staff or facility took place. All subjects were re-assessed by mailed surveys approved by the Human Investigation Review Committee between March and September 1997, a median of 26 months (range 22–35) after beginning the study, to determine depressive symptoms using the BDI and current physical activity habits. Subjects who did not respond to the first mailed request were contacted a second time by mail and finally by telephone interview if necessary to complete the survey ($n = 3$). No subjects were lost to follow-up.

Outcome Measures

Method of collection.—All primary outcome measures of psychological symptoms were performed by a blinded assessor (KMC) at baseline, 6, 10, and 20 weeks. Baseline demographics, medical history and examination, the diagnostic testing psychiatric interview based on the *Diagnostic and Statistical Manual for Psychiatric Disorders IV (DSM-IV)* manual, and weekly monitoring for compliance and adverse events were performed by the PI (NAS). All questionnaires were administered by the interviewer except the BDI, which was self-administered at the above time points as well as at the 26-month follow-up. Physical activity habits were obtained by telephone interview during Phase II and by questionnaire or telephone interview at the 26-month follow-up in all subjects. Muscle strength was not assessed during Phases II and III.

Depression.—The primary measure of depression was the BDI (score 0–63). It was chosen because it is valid and reliable in the elderly subjects, allows comparison with the major drug and exercise treatment trials in the literature, quantifies severity of symptoms, and contains both psychological (score 0–42) and somatic (score 0–21) components, thus allowing differentiation of psychological and somatic symptom relief. Clinical symptoms and psychiatric diagnoses were assessed by structured clinician interview at 0 and 10 weeks, according to the *DSM-IV* manual.

Self-efficacy and morale.—The Philadelphia Geriatric Center Morale Scale (score 0–17) was included due to its measures of agitation (score 0–6), loneliness (score 0–6), and attitude toward aging (score 0–5), constructs not measured succinctly in the other depression scales and relevant to depressed elderly patients. Higher scores reflect better morale. An increase in self-efficacy has been proposed as one mechanism of improving mood following exercise training, and therefore Ewart's Scale of Self Efficacy (score 0–100 with higher scores indicating higher self-efficacy) was chosen for its specificity for physical self-efficacy.

Statistical Analysis

Sample size calculations were made on the basis of an 80% power to discern a 25% difference (considered clinically important) in depression outcomes between groups at $p < .05$. On the basis of previous literature for the BDI in exercise trials, we estimated that we required at least 10 subjects in each group to disprove the null hypothesis. All data were analyzed with Statview, SuperAnova (Abacus

Table 2. Baseline Subject Characteristics (n = 32)

Variable	Results	p Value
Age, y	71 (2.0)†	.34
Range	60–84	
Male, %	37	.71
Female, %	63	
Married, %	50	.76
Education, y	14.3 (0.8)†	.65
Medications per day, n	4.0 (0.6)†	.36
Chronic diseases, n	2.7 (0.3)†	.10
Mini Mental State Exam (0–30)	28 (0.3)†	.70
DSM-IV diagnosis		.40
Minor depression, n	17	
Major depression, n	13	
Dysthymia, n	2	
Duration of symptoms, mo	30 (12)†	
Previous use of antidepressant drugs, n	13	.43
Beck Depression Inventory (0–63)	20 (1)†	.84
Hamilton Rating Scale of Depression (0–52)	12 (1)†	.91

Note: DSM-IV = Diagnostic and Statistical Manual of Mental Disorders IV.
† Values are means with standard error in parentheses.

Table 3. Monitoring and Adverse Events During Phase II (Weeks 11–20)

Variable	Exercise (n = 15)	Controls (n = 14)	p Value
Hospital days	0.2 ± 0.7	0.2 ± 0.2	.37
Visits to a psychiatrist or antidepressant medication or worsening suicidal feelings	0	0	—
Visits to a health professional	2.8 ± 0.6	4.0 ± 2.0	.51
Minor illness	0.6 ± 0.2	0.6 ± 0.4	.92
Musculoskeletal pain (no. of weeks reported)	3.0 ± 0.8	6.0 ± 1.1	.05
Total no. of medications per day	3.8 ± 0.7	3.0 ± 0.5	.25

Concepts Inc., Berkeley, CA) or Systat statistical software (Systat Inc., Evanston, IL). Continuous data are described as the mean ± standard error or median and range as appropriate. Baseline differences in group characteristics were analyzed by unpaired t tests for continuous variables and chi square or Fisher's exact test for categorical data. In analyses comparing medians, a Mann Whitney U test was utilized, and analysis of categorical change was performed by chi square analysis. Outcome analysis was conducted according to the intention-to-treat principle. A repeated measures ANOVA was used to analyze the effect of time and treatment for all outcome variables. Contrasts were performed after the repeated measures ANOVA on all time points for primary depression outcomes within each treatment group. A two-sided p value <.05 was considered statistically significant.

RESULTS

Subject Characteristics

Baseline characteristics have been published in detail (10) and are summarized in Table 2. The patients (12 men, 20 women) had a mean age of 71 ± 2 years, with a duration of depressive symptoms of 30 ± 10 months. Clinical diagnoses were divided between major depression (n = 13), minor depression (n = 17), and dysthymia (n = 2), and 63% of patients had been treated in the past with pharmacotherapy, hospitalization, and/or psychotherapy for their depressive illness. Suicide attempts in the past were reported by 12% of patients. There were no significant differences at baseline in any demographic, health status, or psychological variables measured.

Compliance and Adverse Events

Subject attrition.—Two exercisers, one of whom was a control subject (hospitalization for heart failure), were unavailable for the 20-week assessment due to events unrelated to exercise (a fatal asthma attack and a pulmonary embolus secondary to a fractured hip). One exercise participant during Phase I discontinued all exercise at 6 weeks due to a flare in Paget's disease but was included in assessments at 20 weeks and 26 months. One subject in the control group began a weight-training program during Weeks 11 through 20 only but was analyzed according to randomization.

Follow-up data was available at 26 months in 30 out of 32 subjects, or 94%, of the original study group (one death, one refusal among the exercise group).

Compliance with exercise: Phase II.—Ninety-four percent of patients (16/17) initially randomized to exercise began exercise in the unsupervised period, and 14 completed the 20 weeks. These 14 subjects completed an average of 18 ± 2 sessions (range 0–30), compared with the prescribed dose of 20 sessions, and 73% met the definition of full compliance during this period (20 sessions).

Subjects trained at the HNRC (n = 9), in a health club (n = 1), or with free weights at home (n = 4). Compliance was higher (25 ± 2.3 sessions completed) in the home-based group compared with those who trained in the research lab or health club (17.9 ± 2.3 sessions; p = .09).

Long-term exercise behavior: Phase III.—One third of the group initially randomized to exercise was still weight lifting regularly (twice a week or more) at the 26-month follow-up. All of these exercise sessions took place at home or in health clubs. Although one control subject had begun resistance training during Weeks 10 through 20, at 26 months no controls were participating in weight-lifting exercise (p < .05, exercise vs control).

Adverse events.—There were no differences between groups in adverse events in the first 10 weeks. During Phase II, the number of weeks in which musculoskeletal symptoms were reported was significantly less in the exercisers compared with controls (p = .05), and there were no differences between groups in other adverse event categories (Table 3).

Primary Outcomes

Depression.—The exercise group showed significantly reduced depression compared with the control group at both 20 weeks and 26-month follow-up. At 20 weeks, the BDI

EXERCISE AS LONG-TERM ANTIDEPRESSANT

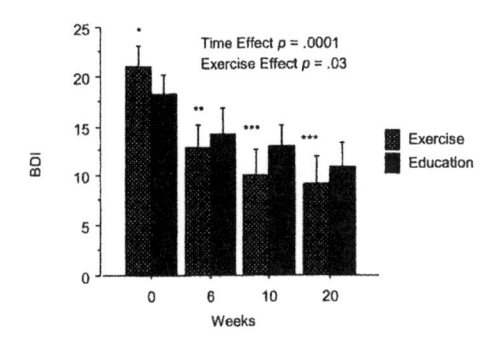

Figure 1. Change in depressive symptoms over the supervised and unsupervised phases of exercise. There was a significant effect of exercise on the reduction in depression over time. Measurements at Weeks 10 and 20 were not significantly different from each other. *Significantly different from Weeks 6, 10, and 20 ($p < .05$); **Significantly different from Weeks 0, 10, and 20 ($p < .05$); ***Significantly different from Weeks 0 and 6 ($p < .05$).

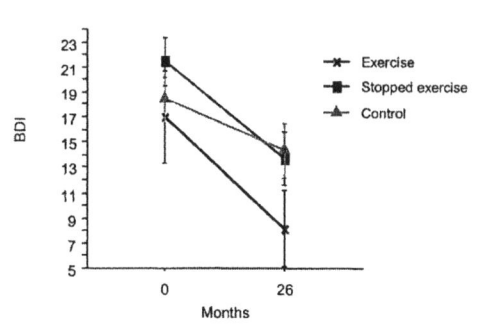

Figure 2. Comparison of relative change in depressive symptoms at 26 months in exercisers who continued to train, those who stopped training, and controls. There was no significant difference between groups at baseline. Time effect: $p < .001$; effect of group assignment: $p = .10$.

decreased from 21 ± 2.0 to 9.2 ± 2.8 in exercisers versus 18.28 ± 1.8 to 11.0 ± 2.36 in controls ($p = .036$, time × treatment interaction) (Figure 1). After 26 months, the overall changes in BDI were still significantly greater in exercisers (21 ± 2.0 to 13 ± 2.2) than in controls (18.4 ± 1.7 to 14.4 ± 2.2; $p = 0.047$ for the time × treatment interaction). Secondary analysis of actual exercise participation at 26 months showed that active exercisers demonstrated a trend toward greater long-term response than either exercisers who had stopped lifting weights or controls ($p = .1$) (Figure 2).

The relative improvements in depression scores in the exercisers were 1.5 to 2.5 times greater than those in the controls at the end of Phase II. In contrasts performed within the exercise group for the BDI, all time points were significantly different from each other ($p < .05$) except for Weeks 10 and 20 (Figure 1). Thus, the decrease in depression appeared to be gradual and greatest between 0 and 10 weeks with benefit maintained up to 20 weeks during the period of unsupervised exercise.

Both psychological and somatic subscales of the BDI significantly improved with time. Compared with the control intervention, exercise significantly improved somatic symptoms in exercisers (6.2 ± 0.6 to 3.0 ± 0.7) versus controls (6.3 ± 0.8 to 4. ± 0.7; $p = .001$) for the time × treatment interaction, with a similar trend seen in psychological symptoms ($p = .09$).

At 20 weeks, 73% (11/15) of the group randomized to exercise were classified as nondepressed versus 36% of controls ($p = .02$), using a BDI of <9 to signify no depression.

There was a trend ($r = .20$, $p = .08$) toward a direct correlation between higher baseline depressive scores and absolute reduction in depression in the exercise group at 20 weeks. This relationship was significant with the exclusion of the outlier (Figure 3). This outlying subject did no exercise after 6 weeks in Phase I of the program. This relationship was not observed among controls. During Phase I of the trial strength increased 33% (±4%) in the exercise group and −2% (±2%) in controls ($p < .001$).

Self-efficacy and morale.—Self-efficacy for jogging improved significantly in the exercise group compared with the control group at 20 weeks (Figure 4). There was no significant effect of treatment assignment on the other physical self-efficacy perceptions (walking, climbing, lifting, pushups). Total morale was significantly improved over time. Of the morale subscales, "attitude toward own aging" was significantly improved by exercise more than the control intervention, whereas the loneliness and agitation subscales were not significantly affected by group assignment (Table 4).

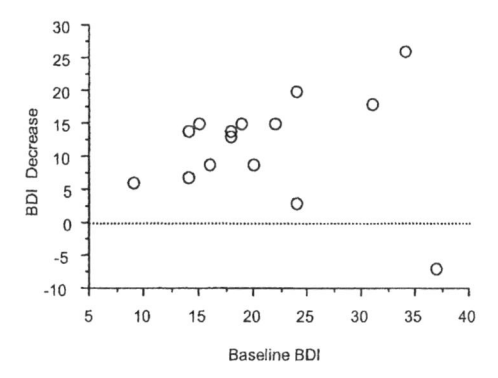

Figure 3. Decrease in the Beck Depression Inventory (BDI) score over 20 weeks related to the baseline BDI in the exercise group. With the removal of the subject who stopped training at 6 weeks (outlier), a significantly greater reduction in depressive symptoms was seen in patients with the most severe depression at baseline ($r = .64$, $p = .01$).

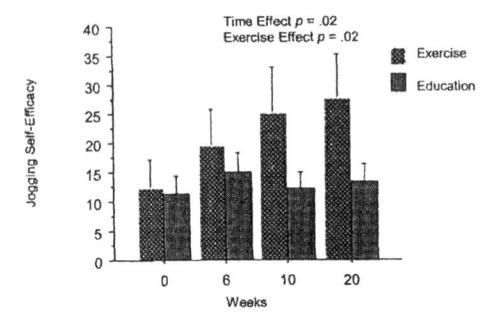

Figure 4. Changes in self-efficacy over the 20-week intervention period. Exercisers had a significant increase in self-efficacy for jogging compared with controls.

DISCUSSION

Summary of Key Findings

The primary findings of this randomized controlled trial were that (i) the antidepressant effect of exercise is maintained over 20 weeks when laboratory-based supervised exercise is changed to unsupervised patient-directed weight lifting in gym or home settings; (ii) more than 2 years after randomization, patients randomized to the exercise treatment group were still significantly different from the controls in depressive symptom response; (iii) self-efficacy and morale in depressed patients continue to improve with exercise up to 20 weeks despite the withdrawal of supervision; and (iv) 26 months after the start of the intervention, one third of the depressed patients initially assigned to the experimental group were still actively exercising at target levels.

Efficacy of treatment.—Clinical depression had resolved in 73% of exercisers after 20 weeks of treatment, as compared with 36% of controls, an efficacy rate comparable to the best trials of antidepressants with psychological counseling in young or elderly individuals (1). Whereas there is a mood-elevating effect of even a single bout of exercise, the greatest decreases in depression have been seen in programs of 17 weeks or longer (4). This is the first controlled resistance training study of greater than 8 weeks duration in a depressed population, and the only such study in elderly persons. Exercise was associated with a significant reduction in depression at both 20 weeks and after 26 months, despite the removal of supervision, transport costs, and group setting at 10 weeks.

There are only three published randomized trials of the effect of exercise on clinically depressed subjects older than 60 years of age (8,10,11). In McNiel's study, subjects (mean age 72 years) were chosen by self-reported scores of >12 on the BDI and may or may not have fulfilled diagnostic psychiatric criteria for depression (8). Over a 6-week intervention of walking versus social contact versus wait list, the BDI was reduced approximately 33% in the walking group, not significantly different from the social contact group but significantly different from wait list. In our trial of clinically depressed elderly subjects older than 60 years of age (mean age 72 years), we demonstrated a reduction of 60% in both therapist- and self-rated scales of depression in comparison to 30% in the attention control group after 10 weeks of weight training (10). Blumenthal and colleagues studied a more severely depressed group with pure major depression who were significantly younger than our subjects, with a mean age of 57 ± 7 versus 71 ± 2. The 16-week study found that aerobic exercise at high intensity (70% to 80% of heart rate reserve) resulted in 60% of subjects being classified as nondepressed (11). On the basis of this current evidence, the two forms of exercise appear to be similar in efficacy for treating depression (10,11). A direct comparison of aerobic exercise versus weight lifting in a depressed older age group is awaited. The combination of high efficacy, high compliance, and low adverse event rates we and Blumenthal observed suggests that exercise may be a viable treatment alternative for similar groups of moderately clinically depressed elderly outpatients.

Depression is generally accepted to be a chronic, relapsing disorder, frequently not completely responsive to treatment and for which maintenance therapy is required and ef-

Table 4. Philadelphia Geriatric Center Morale Scale (PGMS)

PGMS	Timepoint (wk)	Exercise ($n = 15$)	Controls ($n = 14$)	Baseline p Value	Time p Value	Exercise × Time p Value
Total PGMS	0	6.1 ± 1.0	6.9 ± 0.1	.74	<.001	.11
	6	9.3 ± 1.1	8.4 ± 1.0			
	10	10.2 ± 1.0	8.4 ± 1.1			
	20	10.6 ± 1.1	9.6 ± 1.3			
Agitation subscale	0	2.8 ± 0.5	3.2 ± 0.6	.79	<.001	.30
	6	3.9 ± 0.5	3.6 ± 0.6			
	10	4.1 ± 0.4	3.7 ± 0.5			
	20	4.4 ± 0.5	4.0 ± 0.5			
Attitude toward aging subscale	0	0.8 ± 0.2	1.0 ± 0.4	.23	<.001	.05
	6	1.9 ± 0.4	1.3 ± 0.3			
	10	2.3 ± 0.4	1.0 ± 0.3			
	20	2.4 ± 0.4	1.6 ± 0.4			
Loneliness subscale	0	2.7 ± 0.5	2.5 ± 0.5	.50	<.001	.93
	6	3.8 ± 0.5	3.3 ± 0.5			
	10	4.0 ± 0.5	3.3 ± 0.5			
	20	4.0 ± 0.5	3.7 ± 0.6			

fective in reducing relapses (12). Therefore, feasibility, compliance, and long-term adoption of any effective treatment are issues of paramount importance. In our exercise group, 94% of subjects continued, without supervision, the same type of exercise as in Phase I. Compliance was high in whatever unsupervised setting subjects chose but was highest at home. Previous work in healthy elderly subjects has also found that home-based exercise is preferred by the majority of participants and has higher compliance than center-based exercise (16). There is no available data on compliance with other forms of unsupervised exercise in a clinically depressed elderly population. The surprisingly high rate of adoption and adherence in our study despite the advanced age, initial sedentary state, and depressive symptoms in our population may be due to the initial 10-week period of supervised training they received or to the potency of the effect of exercise on their target symptoms.

Considerations of Mechanism

Efficacy of treatment.—The mechanism for the potent antidepressant effect of weight lifting exercise we observed is not yet known, but age does not appear to attenuate the response to this mode of exercise, which has also been shown to be therapeutic in younger depressed patients (17).

Exercise is postulated to exert an antidepressant effect via a variety of mechanisms including biological, cognitive, and behavioral. Distraction or social contact is one of the proposed cognitive behavioral mechanisms. The social contact of supervised exercise is an integral part of such programs, and its effect on psychological outcomes is difficult to control and quantify. However, our results clearly demonstrate that the withdrawal of staff interaction and direct supervision as well a group setting does not result in a relapse of depressive symptoms; in fact self-efficacy and morale improve even further under such conditions.

Additional support for the specificity of exercise as a treatment for depression in elderly patients is provided by the fact that there was a greater benefit of exercise in patients with more severe depression, whereas those with milder depression benefited equally from exercise or attention-control (health lecture) activities over the initial 20-week period. This finding is again contrary to a common perception that exercise acts as a "placebo" or "diversion" and by contrast suggests its potency in the realm of therapeutic options, such as combined medication and psychological counseling (12). Although weight lifting has yet to be compared directly with pharmacological management in depression in elderly persons, the recent study by Blumenthal and colleagues (11) suggests that aerobic exercise is approximately equipotent to medication management. Future studies need to address both the relative efficacy and feasibility of aerobic versus resistive exercise as well as resistive exercise versus standard therapy in depressed elderly patients.

The observed improvements in specific morale and self-efficacy subscales may shed light on some of the mechanisms associated with the antidepressant effect of exercise in elderly subjects. Exercisers developed a more positive attitude toward their own aging, in contrast to controls, yet ratings of loneliness and agitation did not differ between the groups. Depression in old age is thought to be multi-factorial, but an important etiologic factor is the multitude of losses the older person must endure. Thus a more optimistic view of the aging process may help to minimize depressive reactions to such changes and events as they occur. Increase in self-efficacy is postulated as a way of interrupting the maladaptive cognitive processes of depressed persons. Self-efficacy has been shown to increase in resistance-trained cardiac patients as well as depressed elderly patients treated with aerobic exercise or medication (11,18). Our results of improved self-efficacy in jogging in exercisers may be explained by the fact that jogging was perceived as the most difficult of the physical tasks assessed. Lifting weights is generally perceived as a novel and difficult task, especially for elderly persons. If PRT led to an increase in their perceived ability to perform tasks seen as difficult, the effect may first be generalized to the most difficult of tasks, which was jogging in our subjects. Such an increase in self-efficacy may mean that they were better equipped psychologically to face challenges. Confidence in one's physical competence induced by exercise training may then generalize to other areas of life (19). Thus, our data lend support to the self-efficacy theory of exercise and depression as well.

Limitations

There are two important limitations to our study. First, our results are applicable to clinically depressed elderly outpatients who were volunteers for a research study, which may make them different in some ways from nonresearch patients. Second, sample sizes were not estimated to allow differentiation of response rates between depressive diagnostic categories. Larger studies will need to specifically target subgroups, such as major depressives, to fully define clinical utility in various clinical settings.

Clinical and Research Implications

Direct comparisons in randomized controlled trials are needed to evaluate the potency of PRT in relation to standard care (pharmacologic and counselling), as well as other modes of exercise in depressed elderly patients.

Identification of depressive subgroups for whom exercise is most effective would be helpful for targeting and cost-effective use of resources as well as shortening the period of disability and suffering that accompanies serious depression. More information is needed on its efficacy in maintenance (prevention of recurrent episodes), treatment-resistant depression, bipolar disorder, frailty, and cognitive impairment, among others. Behavioral methods that will optimally enhance adherence to exercise over the long term in depressed patients need to be tested. It should be remembered that in antidepressant drug trials at least one third of the subjects are unable to take the medication and that little is known about compliance rates among elderly subjects (9). The overall effectiveness of therapies needs to be considered in light of both response rate and patient acceptance of treatment.

In conclusion, progressive resistance training exercise has been demonstrated in an unsupervised setting to be safe and feasible, maintaining an antidepressant effect over the long term in outpatient depressed elderly patients. The benefits of treatment were most pronounced in those with more severe depression and persisted despite the withdrawal of personal supervision and group training in the first phase of this trial. This study lays the foundation for future research, including direct comparisons with more established treatments for depression in both the acute and maintenance phases of this disabling disorder.

ACKNOWLEDGMENTS

This project was supported in part by federal funds from the U.S. Department of Agriculture and Agricultural Research Service Contract 53-3K06-5-10, grants from the U.S. Department of Agriculture, the Claude Pepper Center (AG08812), and the National Institute of Aging (UO1 AG09078), and by donations of exercise equipment by Keiser Sports Health, Inc. Any opinions, findings, conclusions, or recommendations expressed in this publication are those of the authors and do not necessarily reflect the view of the U.S. Department of Agriculture.

We thank the staff of the Exercise and Nutrition Laboratory and the Metabolic Research Unit at the HNRC for their contribution to the control intervention; the Depression Clinical and Research Program at Massachusetts General Hospital for their training in the administration of the Hamilton Rating Scale for Depression; Keiser Sports Health Equipment, Inc., for their donation of resistance training equipment; the American Association of Retired Persons for providing educational videos; Gerry Dallal, PhD, for statistical advice; and Felina-Marie Mucha-Cyr and Lori Laviolette for collection of surveys.

Address correspondence to Dr. Nalin Singh, Department of Geriatrics, Balmain Hospital, Booth Street, Balmain 2041, NSW, Australia. E-mail: singhn@email.cs.nsw.gov.au

REFERENCES

1. Lebowitz B. Diagnosis and treatment of depression in late life: an overview of the NIH consensus statement. *Am J Geriatr Psychiatry.* 1996;4(suppl 1):S3–S6.
2. Schneider L. Pharmacological considerations in the treatment of late-life depression. *Am J Geriatr Psychiatry.* 1996;51–65.
3. Thapa P, Gideon P, Cost T, Milam A, Ray W. Antidepressants and the risk of falls among nursing home residents. *N Engl J Med.* 1998;339: 875–882.
4. North TC, McCullagh P, Tran ZV. The effect of exercise on depression. *Exerc Sport Sci Rev.* 1990;18:379–415.
5. Martinsen EW. Physical activity and depression: clinical experience. *Acta Psychiatr Scand.* 1994;377(suppl):23–27.
6. Martinsen EW, Hoffart A, Solberg O. Comparing aerobic and non-aerobic forms of exercise in the treatment of clinical depression: a randomized trial. *Compr Psychiatry.* 1989;30:324–331.
7. Greist JH, Klein MH, Eischens RR, Gurman AS, Morgan WP. Running as a treatment for depression. *Compr Psychiatry.* 1979;20:41–54.
8. McNiel K, LeBlanc E, Joyce M. The effect of exercise on depressive symptoms in the moderately depressed elderly. *Psychology Aging.* 1991;3:487–488.
9. Salzman C, Schneider L, Lebowitz B. Antidepressant treatment of very old patients. *Am J Geriatr Psychiatry.* 1993;1:21–29.
10. Singh NA, Clements KM, Fiatarone MA. A randomized controlled trial of progressive resistance training in depressed elders. *J Gerontol Med Sci.* 1997;52A:M27–M35.
11. Blumenthal JA, Babyak MA, Moore KA, et al. Effects of exercise training on older patients with major depression. *Arch Intern Med.* 1999;159:2349–2356.
12. Reynolds CF, Frank E, Perel JM, et al. Nortriptyline and interpersonal psychotherapy as maintenance therapies for recurrent major depression. *JAMA.* 1999;281:39–45.
13. Ray WA, Griffen MR, Scheffner W, Baugh NK, Melton LJ. Psychotropic drug use and the risk of hip fracture. *New Engl J Med.* 1987; 316:313–319.
14. Singh N. Healthy, aging, activity and sports. In: Huber G, ed. *The Rationale for Exercise as an Antidepressant in the Elderly.* Heidelberg, Germany: Health Promotions Publications; 1997:75–80.
15. Borg G, Linderholme H. Exercise performance and perceived exertion in patients with coronary insufficiency, arterial hypertension and vasoregulatory asthenia. *Acta Med Scand.* 1970;187:17–26.
16. King A, Barr Taylor C, Haskell WL, Cramer HC, Debusk RF. Group vs. home-based exercise training in healthy older men and women. *JAMA.* 1991;266:1535–1542.
17. Doyne EJ, Ossip-Klein DJ, Bowman ED, Osborn KM, Mcdougall-Wilson IB, Neimeyer RA. Running versus weight lifting in the treatment of depression. *J Consult Clin Psychol.* 1987;55:748–754.
18. Ewart C, Stewart K, Gillian R, Keleman M. Self efficacy mediates strength gains during circuit weight training in men with coronary artery disease. *Med Sci Sports Exerc.* 1986;18:531–540.
19. Bandurra A. Toward a unifying theory of behavioural change. *Psychol Rev.* 1977;84:191–215.

Received December 18, 1999
Accepted June 6, 2000
Decision Editor: John E. Morley, MB, BCh

Part IV
Psychological Aspects of Dementia

[13]
Towards a Theory of Dementia Care: Personhood and Well-being

TOM KITWOOD and KATHLEEN BREDIN*

ABSTRACT
Some foundations are laid for a social-psychological theory of dementia care. Central to this is a conceptualisation of personhood, in which both subjectivity and intersubjectivity are fully recognised. Evidence is brought forward concerning relative well-being even in those who are, from a cognitive standpoint, severely demented. In the light of this it is argued that the key psychological task in dementia care is that of keeping the sufferer's personhood in being. This requires us to see personhood in social rather than individual terms.

Introduction

At present there is no coherent theory of the process of care for those who have a dementing illness in old age. Neither psychiatry, clinical psychology, nor any of the related disciplines has provided what is needed in this respect. In place of theory there is a considerable body of folklore and an abundance of tacit knowledge, the latter embodied often in the work of outstanding practitioners. Also there is a substantial portfolio of practical approaches, some adorned with the term 'therapy', which provide good advice drawn from everyday experience; in some of these there are the beginnings of a theory, but little more. Often it is a fairly crude pragmatism that leads to the decision to adopt one of these approaches rather than another.

Considering its great significance for gerontology, and indeed for the whole pattern of contemporary life, the absence of a theory of dementia

* Bradford Dementia Research Group, University of Bradford, England.

care is remarkable. Why should there be such a gap? One can attempt to answer this question at various levels, where each proposed explanation requires another. Most obviously, there is the fact that the psychiatry of old age has had an overwhelming tendency to make the brain rather than the personhood of the dementia sufferer its central focus of attention; the inquiry has been technical rather than personal.[1] This has been very useful for medical-scientific research, but it has delivered almost no valuable theoretical insight into the practicalities of care. Behind this lies the fact that both psychiatry and clinical psychology have been extremely reluctant to articulate and implement a clear concept of the human subject, preferring to work even at a clinical level with regularities among fairly simple observables. It might be argued that this feature has run as a great fault-line through work on mental distress ever since the days of Kraepelin, despite a succession of attempts to set matters to rights.[2] So, pressing the question further, one might ask, 'Why this flight from personhood and subjectivity?' In an obvious sense this avoidance enabled psychiatry and psychology to conform to a notion of natural science, although a rather narrow and stilted one. Less obviously and much more controversially, a stance that is mainly technical keeps distress at bay. Professionals and informal carers are vulnerable people too, bearing their own anxiety and dread concerning frailty, dependence, madness, ageing, dying and death. A supposed objectivity in a context that is, in fact, interpersonal is one way of maintaining psychological defences, and so making involvement with conditions such as dementia bearable.[3]

Whatever may be the weight of truth in these and other possible reasons, the fact is that thousands upon thousands of hours of dementia care work pass by, in which the people involved generally do not understand what they are doing. This applies, moreover, even to some who are doing excellent work. The need for a theory can hardly be doubted. A care practice, however good it might be judged to be, is relatively ineffective without a coherent theory; it is powerless at the clinical, pedagogical, and political levels. A thorough theoretisation – or, as the followers of Paulo Freire might say, a conscientisation[4] – provides awareness, a sense of value, and the basis for concerted action.

In this paper we attempt to set out the grounding for such a theory, focusing on the concept of personhood, and drawing on an observation that is gradually being recognised as crucially significant: that a dementing illness, although it often does involve a dismantling of the person, need not necessarily do so; and that a dementia sufferer can be in a state of at least relative well-being. In a subsequent paper the actual process of caregiving will be examined. Behind the view of care that we are putting forward lies a theory of dementia that has already been outlined in this journal.[5] Briefly, it suggests that the clinical presentation of dementia is far from being a direct consequence of a degenerative process in nervous tissue. Rather, the dementing process should be viewed as the outcome of a dialectical interplay between two tendencies. The first is neurological impairment, which does indeed set upper limits to how a person can perform. The second is the personal psychology an individual has accrued, together with the social psychology with which he or she is surrounded. Such a dialectical account can, in principle, rationalize the whole range of phenomena associated with dementia better than one derived simply from medical science. This does not yield a comprehensive general theory of the dementing process: that, it may be argued, is impossible. Here however, are the conceptual tools through which to construct, at least in outline, the unique course of dementia in any particular individual. Crucial to this account is a recognition of the 'malignant social psychology' which often bears down powerfully on those who are aged and confused: a psychology in which the others involved are usually well-intentioned but lacking in insight. One implication is that 'bad care' involves this malignancy to a high degree. 'Good care', conversely, is singularly free of this, and is highly respectful of personhood.

There is a problem: where is the problem?

At the very beginning of that disruption of social life which is later identified as a particular individual's dementia, a problem is developing. A person is starting to forget the shopping, or gets lost in town, or puts the electric kettle on the gas cooker. Something new and disturbing is happening in the interpersonal field. On this single point every theorist of dementia is agreed. For those who are actually involved, the problem is usually first clearly identified by others; the individual whose behaviour appears to be strange may be extremely reluctant to acknowledge that a problem exists at all.

Beyond this extremely general description – 'there is a problem' – no clear agreement exists.

How is the growing problem in the interpersonal field going to be rationalized? At the extremes, there are two main possibilities. The first is by far the most common, since it underpins the greater part of medical, nursing and social work practice, as well as the taken-for-granted world of residential care. It can be illustrated diagrammatically as shown below.

'US' | 'THEM'

Basically sound | Neurologically impaired

Damaged, derailed, deficient

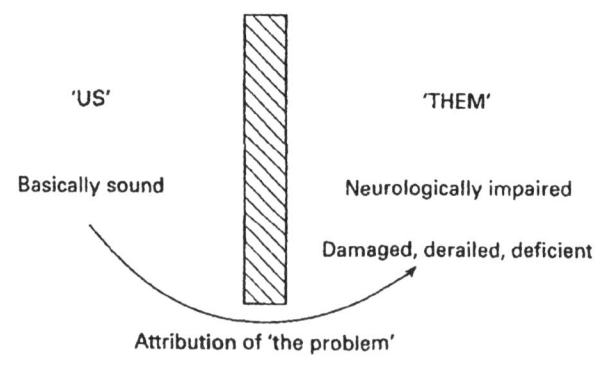

Attribution of 'the problem'

Figure 1.

Here there is a clear division between *us* (members of the 'normal' population) and *them* (the dementia sufferers). *We* are basically sound, undamaged, competent, kind. *They* are in a bad way, for they are afflicted with a primary degenerative disease in the grey matter. *They* are thus damaged, de-railed, deficient. *We* may not always be the most effective carers. So there is a need for training to give us knowledge about *their* illness; and to develop skills, especially in managing *their* 'challenging behaviours'. In the long run *they* will have to learn to accommodate themselves to the provision that *we* make for them.

This may be something of a caricature, but in one crucial respect there is certainly no exaggeration. The focus of attention is overwhelmingly on *them* as the problem, while *we* are not problematized at all. A detailed survey of all the main approaches to dementia care, for example Reality Orientation, Behaviour Modification, Reminiscence Therapy, Validation Therapy, makes this point abundantly clear.[6] The problem is to be located with *them*, while *we* bring nothing seriously problematic to the situation. Putting matters in a different way, and rather less contentiously: there is here no clear view either of relationship or of intersubjectivity. Although the subject-matter is that of caregiving, there is still an infection from the detached and supposedly objective stance that pervades psychiatry and clinical psychology.

There is, however, a different view, as illustrated below.

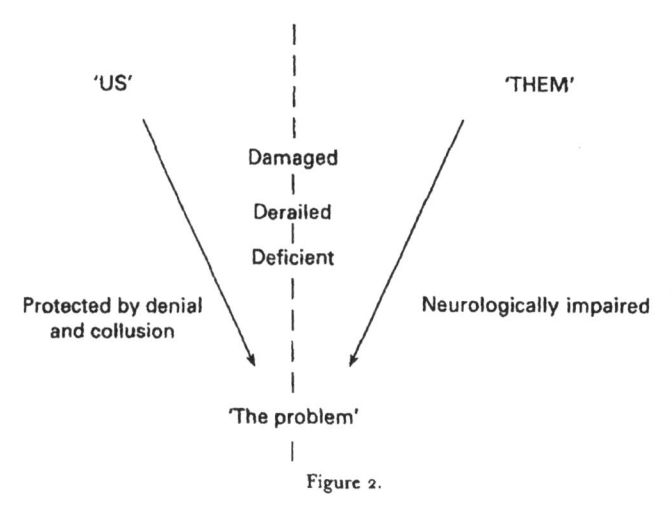

```
         |
         |
  'US'   |           'THEM'
      \  |  Damaged   /
       \ |  Derailed /
        \|  Deficient/
         |          
Protected by denial  Neurologically impaired
  and collusion   \ | /
                   \|/
                    |
                 'The problem'
                    |
```

Figure 2.

According to this, *we* are also contributors to the problem, for both *we* and *they* are human beings with our failures, limitations and suffering. In some respects, indeed, *we* might be considered more problematic than *they*. *They* are obviously damaged, derailed, deficient: a neurological process has interfered with their everyday functioning. But *we*, in our very varied ways, are damaged, derailed, deficient too. What is particularly dangerous here is that generally *we* do not acknowledge these facts. Indeed, much of our professional socialization involves a systematic training in how to avoid such a painful insight; we learn to live with very high defences against any recognition.[7] What is more, it is arguable that the general pattern of everyday life, with its hypocrisy, competitiveness and pursuit of crass materialism is, from a human standpoint, deeply pathological; those whose way of being dovetails smoothly into this pattern are the most 'normal' and well-adjusted. The truth, from this other standpoint, is that such people simply participate in an unacknowledged 'pathology of normality'.[8] Thus when the interpersonal field surrounding the beginnings of 'dementia' is looked at in this way, the problem is by no means focused on a single person whose brain is failing. Those others who have face-to-face contact are also involved; and, in the background, so also is the prevailing pattern of social relations.

This view can be taken further. For one might even suggest that in some respects *they* are rather less of a problem than *we*. *They* are generally more authentic about what they are feeling and doing; many of the polite veneers of earlier life have been stripped away. *They* are clearly dependent on others, and usually come to accept that dependence; whereas many 'normal' people, living under an ideology of extreme individualism, strenuously deny their dependency needs. *They* live very largely in the present, because certain parts of their memory function have failed. *We* often find it very difficult to live in the present, suffering constant distraction; the sense of the present is often contaminated by regrets about the past and fears concerning the future.

The view that is represented in figure 2 has never (so far as we are aware) been fully articulated in the literature on dementia and dementia care, although some of the ideas expressed in recent work do point in that direction.[9] It is in a different field – that of psychotherapy and counselling – that is it clearly recognized that *we* are, or may be, or may become part of the problem. Here it is axiomatic that any person who would help others to deal with their distress and self-defeating patterns must first get acquainted with his or her own personal difficulties, and understand his or her familiar ways of being with others. There must always be awareness, and where there are serious drawbacks growth must be allowed to take place. Without this vital preparation the would-be helper or healer may become caught up in any number of noxious interactive patterns, or get continually seduced into unproductive 'games'. We would argue strongly that a 'therapeutic' awareness of this kind could and should be a central part of caring for those who suffer from dementia. The dementing illness of one person brings to the surface a much larger problematic which challenges our commonsense and customary ways of being.

Personhood: the central issue

The presence of dementia on a large scale in contemporary society, and the dire process which it often entails, raises very deep questions about what it means to be a person. The encounter with dementia is deeply paradoxical. On the one hand, people involved in caregiving often have a strong intuitive sense that even an individual who is disastrously impaired is still recognizably a person: on the other hand the progress of a dementing illness, especially if it involves a long stay in residential or nursing care, seems to be taking personhood away.

Contradictory impressions such as these invite us to enquire closely into the nature of personhood. What is that state which we might properly call being a person? If we can engage accurately with this question, so tragically neglected in psychiatry and clinical psychology, we may come to find the proper basis for developing a theory of dementia care. Like Gilleard,[10] who has already made some very valuable suggestions on this topic, the core of our position is that personhood should be viewed as essentially social: it refers to the human being in relation to others. But also, it carries essentially ethical connotations: to be a person is to have a certain status, to be worthy of respect. In developing this view briefly here we draw on a large body of theory, much of it derived from work in counselling and psychotherapy.[11] It must be acknowledged that in this field theory often rests on rather fragmentary data, although it is a rich resource for understanding. This is somewhat in contrast to experimental psychology, where theory is often impoverished, but the fit between theory and data is relatively tight.

In the main traditions of the western world, which date from the break-up of feudalism and the theories of the Enlightenment, the term *person* has often come to be taken as having virtually the same meaning as *individual*. This idea is certainly not a cross-cultural universal. Also, it is evident that personhood is not so closely allied to individualism in the development of a single human life. The transformation of a neonate into a being who has the full range of human attributes is very clearly a social process, and not one of simple maturation. An infant exists in a kind of psychological symbiosis with the mother or other main caregiver, and comes to form definite attachments. Out of interaction, and particularly out of those occasions when the infant's gestures meet a sensitive response, selfhood emerges; the infant acquires a sense of agency and an 'inner' subjective world, progressively enriched through the acquisition of language. The greater part of infant and early child development requires the involvement of others, providing subtle support and safety, while giving the 'space' for exploration of both the interpersonal and the physical world. In an ethical sense, personhood is attributed even to the newborn infant. In an empirical sense, personhood emerges in a social context. Thus personhood is not, at first, a property of the individual; rather, it is provided or guaranteed by the presence of others. Putting it another way, relationship comes first, and with it intersubjectivity; the subjectivity of the individual is like a distillate that is collected later.

Sometime in late childhood, perhaps around the age of 8, 9 or 10, and associated with a general concretization of cognition, the basic structure of personality tends to become set. The individual has acquired by this time a set of strategies for dealing with people and situations, a view of the self, a particular array of psychological defences. There is some evidence that this structure tends to persist, being elaborated rather than radically changed as the individual moves into adolescence and adulthood.[12] What was, in the early part of life, fluid, 'held' on the individual's behalf by others, now becomes relatively fixed; or – to use a less favourable image – frozen.

So we have here one crucial parameter of personal being: the construct fluid-frozen. In adult life many people remain, more or less, in the frozen state, maintaining their defences and simply developing resources upon the same basic personality structure. Their subjectivity receives little further nourishment. The frozen state is maintained by various forms of collusion, particularly in organizations, where individuals unwittingly consent to work together in certain very restricted ways, and avoiding any deep intersubjectivity. The frozen state is fostered by extreme individualism, because this both forces a person away from the support of others and requires a reinforcement of defences against anxiety. It is ameliorated just a little by such approaches as 'humanistic management'. When a person remains frozen and unsupported but with heavy demands to deal with, he or she is liable to depression or burn-out. There is some return to fluidity, even if only very partial, in intimate friendship and in sexual love. This is also the case in counselling and psychotherapy. Jung, with his sense of an analogy between alchemy and psychology, took the term analysis in an almost literal sense. It meant a dissolving of the personality, a return to fluidity, so that new ways of being might be developed: a synthesis. Despite the variety of schools of therapy, there seems to be agreement regarding the therapist's own state of being. Those who themselves remain fixed or frozen, their subjectivity limited by highly elaborated defences, will not enable others to become fluid. It is when one person in the dyad is fluid and resourceful that the condition is provided for the other to begin to melt and change. All this may be summed up, as shown below.

```
┌─────────────────────────────────────┐
│   FROZEN                    FLUID   │
└─────────────────────────────────────┘

       Low ─────────────────▶ High
             Intersubjectivity
```

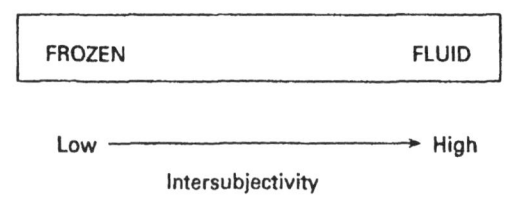

Figure 3.

This, however, is not the whole story, for there is another main state of personal being to be included. If we retain the fluid-frozen image, the third state could be described as 'shattered'. It is as if the ice block has been broken up into fragments, but without the melting that could enable a new synthesis. This approximately describes a severe psychotic breakdown. The remarkable fact here, as some of the investigators of psychosis have shown, is that an individual might be desperately alone in the sense of lacking intersubjectivity, and yet be surrounded by others. Their presence, and their contradictory meanings, are a major part of the problem.

So, condensing and simplifying a vast amount of psychological theory, the full contruct has the form shown below.

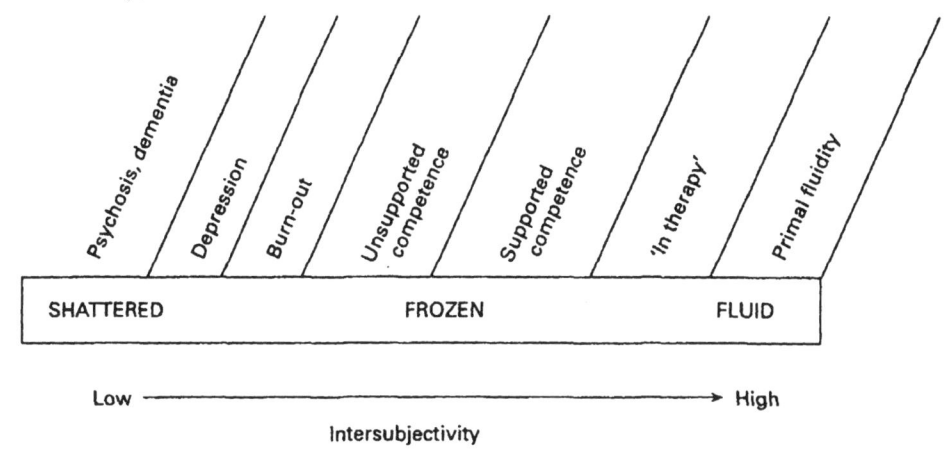

Figure 4.

Using this, severe and unattended dementia can be understood as a particular form of the 'shattered' state. With many individuals the neurological insult is resisted for a while, and some of the defences remain intact. Gradually these break down, leaving subjectivity fragmented. Here the dementia sufferer is often dreadfully isolated and unsupported. Maybe it is at this point that many of the more alarming behaviour disturbances are manifested.

Tentatively, also, a general social inference may be drawn. Everyday life continues by maintaining individuals in a relatively frozen state; its way of being positively requires it, even though the cost to personal well-being is immense. A more desirable form of life would be one in which there was vastly more intersubjectivity, and where there would be a continuing opportunity for people to be fluid; or, to alter the image, to grow and change. Our taken-for-granted world, however, is so permeated with the ideology of extreme individualism that this possibility, and the fundamental notion of personhood that underpins it, is almost totally obscured.[13]

The preservation of personhood in dementia

In the foregoing brief excursion into the nature of personhood we have, in a sense, brought the dementia sufferer and the 'other' into a single frame. This opens the way for exploring the basis for good caring; or, more broadly, for a way of meeting, of creating an intersubjectivity. Now, however, it is necessary to return specifically to the dementia sufferer, and to make a separation between personhood and cognitive ability. The two have been bound up too closely in western psychological theory, especially of late; its 'hypercognitivism' is something of a disadvantage for a humane understanding of dementia, and needs to be resisted.

Dementia is often presented as a dire condition, a terrible and progressive loss. It is easy to characterise it as a state of continuing and ever-deepening ill-being. This can hardly be disputed if attention is focused on highly developed cognitive powers to the exclusion of other human faculties. There are, however, certain lines of evidence that begin to point in more hopeful directions. Three are particularly significant for our purposes here.

The first comes directly from the care context. It is that some individuals who had seriously deteriorated in all their functioning, including some who had been written off as hopelessly demented, show considerable reversal or 'rementia' when their conditions of life, and especially their social relationships, are changed. The positive changes that are most notable are in the areas of social skill, independence and continence. As social being is recovered, so 'mind' (in some of its aspects) is restored.[14] In our own research on the evaluation of dementia care we have been given many examples of this phenomenon, and in some cases actually met the individuals concerned. There seems to be no reason to doubt the basic truthfulness of care workers' accounts, even when some allowance is made for their humanistic hopes, and their desire to convey a good impression about their work. However, it must be acknowledged that virtually all the evidence that we have on this topic is anecdotal; clearly it is very important for the understanding of dementia that this be put to the test of systematic inquiry.

The second line of evidence concerns the stabilization of some individuals who have been clearly diagnosed as suffering from one of the main degenerative dementias. We ourselves know individuals who are 5–8 years on from the first recognition of their dementia; but, who, in their present care context, are showing no signs of further deterioration, and certainly not moving towards that vegetative condition which is often held out as the inevitable end-point. Again here much of the evidence is anecdotal, but there is now one piece of research in the literature that corroborates this point with systematic data.[15] This is a study comparing two groups, each of 14 dementia sufferers, in residential care. The two groups were comparable in the degree of their dementia, and received roughly the same amount of basic nursing care. The first group, which occupied a special dementia unit, was given a programme of activities covering about 40 hours per week, whereas the second group was in a traditional form of care, with activities taking up around 3-5 hours per week. Also the first group received a medical and psychiatric check-up weekly, leading, where appropriate, to changes in the programme of care; the second group received only a monthly medical check-up. After one year only 2 of the first group showed signs of further deterioration, whereas 9 from the other group did so. This finding is strengthened by the fact that those in the first group were slightly younger, and the conventional wisdom is that personal decline proceeds more quickly with those for whom the onset of dementia is relatively early. Of course this is only a single study, the time span was short, and the numbers involved are small. The most that can be said at present is that it accords with what many experienced workers in the field of dementia care believe they have observed.

The third line of evidence comes from those experiments with 'geriatric' rats which are occasionally reported, but very rarely interpreted, in the context of writings on dementia. Diamond and her colleagues, in one such study,[16] examined a group of rats, a few right into very old age. Of these, some were put at maturity into exceedingly impoverished and solitary environments. As the rats aged, so did their brains deteriorate (as indicated by conventional post-mortem study). Some of the rats that had been subjected to the impoverished conditions were then transferred to new environments, where there were plenty of activities, and the company of other rats. After a period, their brains appeared to have undergone considerable neurological development. Putting it crudely, then, these experiments show that the brain of a declining geriatric rat can be revived solely through a change in environmental conditions. The rat, of course, is not a human being, and does not (so far as we know) have comparable problems with intersubjectivity. Yet there are great similarities in the nature of the grey matter of rats and humans. It is curious that research of this kind, which provides highly relevant direct evidence about brain structure, is almost totally ignored in the literature on dementia. There can be little doubt that comparable neurological development can occur in the ageing human brain, possibly offsetting in some cases the advance of neuropathology. There is now a little evidence from neurochemical studies with human beings, pointing directly in this direction.[17]

These three lines of evidence, inadequate though they are at present, are crucial for our understanding of dementia and for any theory of dementia care. If some degree of 'rementing' can be brought about purely through human interaction; if some sufferers do stabilize when provided with a care environment that fosters activity and cooperation; if even the ageing and damaged brain is capable of some structural regeneration, then there is ground for looking on dementia care in a very positive way. Caring is certainly much more than giving kindly oversight while witnessing the slow advance of the 'death that leaves the body behind'. Further, the idea of an inevitable progression through four or more 'stages of dementia' - the conventional wisdom that underpins a great deal of care practice and even the design of some residential and nursing homes - must be radically questioned. Of course it is possible to salvage that view by writing off all counter-examples as instances of pseudodementia or faulty diagnosis. It seems likely, though, that as expertise in dementia care advances year by year, such a position will become increasingly untenable.

Relative well-being in dementia

Evidence from the care context, then, is beginning to suggest that a dementing illness is not necessarily a process of inevitable and global deterioration. Close observation provides a far more differentiated picture. Some who have long since reached around zero score on all cognitive tests still appear to be faring well as persons. Others whose cognitive powers are only moderately impaired appear to be faring far less well. A dementing condition tends to be compounded by depression or anxiety, a sense of apathy or disencouragement. It makes good sense, then, to speak of a dementia sufferer as being in a state of relative well-being or ill-being, in a way that cuts across the dimension of cognitive impairment. On the basis of many hours of detailed observation of dementia sufferers in a variety of settings, including those which provide mainly for the very severely demented, we have drawn up a list of 12 indicators of relative well-being; each one stays close to observable behaviour. Informally we have tested the validity of the indicators by consultation with 7 experts in dementia; they have all corroborated our observations, and no further indicators that are clearly identifiable by behaviour have been proffered. The list does not, however, simply have an empirical justification, for behind it lies a conception of well-being that draws on the view of personhood we have already discussed.

The indicators are as follows. Each is illustrated by a brief vignette. Mr D or Mrs D refers to the dementia sufferer; C refers to a caregiver.

1. *The Assertion of Desire or Will*

Mrs D has had both courses of her evening meal, and has gone to sit down in an armchair. C, not realizing she has had both courses, brings the dessert to her, and tries to feed her. Mrs D says she doesn't want the food: the carer tries to coax her. Mrs D continues to refuse. C desists. Later the truth is discovered.

2. *The Ability to Experience and Express a Range of Emotions (both 'positive' and 'negative')*

Mrs D is at the day centre. Suddenly she looks exceedingly troubled. A caregiver sits next to her and puts an arm around her. Mrs D collapses into uncontrollable grief and sobbing. C continues to hold her, quietly and patiently. After a quarter of an hour or so Mrs D begins to recover her composure, and soon afterwards is sharing again in the life of the group.

3. *Initiation of Social Contact*

Mr D has a small dog, a soft toy, which he evidently treasures. He goes over to a women sitting down with her zimmer frame in front of her. He perches the dog on the zimmer frame, and tries to use it to attract her attention.

4. *Affectional Warmth*

Mrs D lives in large residential home. She often walks back and forth between wings. Whenever someone says hello to her, she stops for a moment to give them a friendly kiss on the cheek, and then continues on her way.

5. *Social Sensitivity*

C is feeling low in spirits, for reasons that have nothing to do with her work situation. Mrs D comes close to her, looks her in the face, and says 'You're not so good today, dear, are you?' C squeezes her hand, and says 'I'm feeling a bit sad, Mrs D, but I'm here.' Mrs D smiles and squeezes C's hand. Somehow Mrs D seems to understand.

6. *Self-Respect*

Mrs D has suddenly defaecated on the floor of the sitting room, in the presence of others, both men and women. She begins to wipe up the mess with her cardigan.

7. *Acceptance of Other Dementia Sufferers*

Mrs D is a vigorous wanderer; she moves fast. She catches hold of the hand of Mr D (not her spouse), who is also wandering, but much more slowly. Mr D accepts the hand and allows himself to be walked around for a while, even though the pace is so different from his own.

8. *Humour*

At the Day Care Centre a video is going to be shown about hygiene in the kitchen. There is a technical problem, and a restless atmosphere is developing. C is fumbling with the apparatus. Mr D calls out, somewhat raucously, 'Try putting a shilling in the slot'. The tension is broken by uproarious laughter.

9. *Creativity and Self-Expression*

There has been a session of singing, with accompaniment from the piano. Now the pianist is tired. Mrs D stands up and sings an old Irish song, in a trembling voice but almost perfectly in tune, and with great depth of feeling. At the end, tears are running down her cheeks.

10. Showing Evident Pleasure

It is an exercise event. About 10 people are sitting in a circle, each holding the edge of a parachute. The game is to change places beneath the parachute as it is lifted and slowly falling. Mrs D looks nervous; it is her turn. C helps her to start, and she makes it to her destination. People clap; she smiles and laughs, her face flushed.

11. Helpfulness

C, who is new to the job, enters the sitting room. She sees a group of women chatting around the fire. Mr D, who looks very stern, is wandering alone, up and down; he seems not to be showing interest in anyone. C joins the women. As there is no seats nearby, she sits on the floor. Soon afterwards, Mr D comes by with a cushion he has taken from a chair and hands it to her without saying a word.

12. Relaxation

Mrs D has a habit of lying on the floor, curled up and tense. Her arms and legs shake and her face is in a grimace. C gently takes her hands and guides her towards a sofa. He invites her to sit with him. In a few moments she has settled down, and cuddles close to him. Her body relaxes and her face becomes calm.

A justification for taking these indicators as marks of relative well-being can be made along two main lines. First, if we consult our own experience, and particularly those times when we sense ourselves to be faring well or ill, the indicators make sense. It is when we feel most discounted, oppressed, withdrawn or low in mood that we are the least likely to show signs such as these; it is when we are confident, buoyant and expansive that we are most likely to show them. There is, of course, some variation according to temperament and personality. For example, individuals differ considerably in the warmth that they generally convey to each other, and in their creative abilities; some find it relatively easy to assert their wishes, whereas others do not. Differences such as these can certainly be found also among those who are cognitively impaired. The indicators, then, are part of the common ground between those who are and who are not dementing. The crucial point is that the indicators are virtually independent of the complex cognitive skills that most adults continuously employ. Thus they are specific to, but not exclusive to, dementia sufferers. Because they are part of our shared experience, they have a face validity; that they are, or can be, present in severely demented persons is an empirical observation.

We may go some way further than this, however, in exploring the nature of well-being in dementia. Behind the observables, it is possible to suggest four apprehensions, or global sentient states, of which the indicators are, to varying degrees, an expression. (It should be noted here that the connections are not empirical, but based, rather, on the inner logic of mental states; ventures in this area are generally abhorred by main-stream psychology).

The first global state is a sense of personal worth, the 'deepest' level of self-esteem. The very fact of ageing almost always involves many losses, and consequent assaults upon an individual's well-being. The experience of beginning to lose cognitive skills, and all the social processes that ensue, is a formidable challenge over and above these common losses. Thus anyone who retains an apprehension of self-worth, and who is able to accept the process of cognitive impairment, can indeed be said to be in a state of relative well-being. Self-esteem is often, in psychological theory, attached to specific cognitions about the self; but it makes good sense to consider it also as a global feeling, of which a person has a diffuse awareness.

The second state that underlies the indicators is a sense of agency; the ability to control personal life in a meaningful way, to produce, to achieve, to make some mark upon others and the world. This is important for people in all stages of life; even, so developmental psychology now suggests, for very young babies. In traditional forms of dementia care an individual's agency tends to be continually diminished. The struggle to maintain it, even at the most rudimentary level, may be intense; perhaps this is how some of the so-called 'challenging behaviours' might be interpreted. So if a dementia sufferer keeps a sense of agency, and manifests this even in the smallest actions, there is good reason to postulate that he or she is in a state of relative well-being.

The third state is one of social confidence; that is, a feeling of being at ease with others, of being able to move towards them, of having something to offer to them. The everyday world, especially in societies that are highly technological and bureaucratic, requires the continual operation of highly-developed cognitive skills. Those in whom these are failing tend to be not only at a practical, but also at a social disadvantage. Again and again their attempts to make contact and to communicate are likely to be disregarded, and the 'malignant social psychology' to which reference has been made comes into play. Anyone who, nevertheless, maintains a sense that the social world is welcoming, and that he or she has a place within it, can be said to be faring well.

The fourth state is that of hope.[19] In other words, a person still retains a confidence that some security will remain even when so many things are changing, both outside and within. There is a freedom from the anxiety that pervades if many basic needs are not met. Hope is, pre-eminently, a sense that the future will be, in some way, 'good'. In many respects the dementia sufferer has little ground for hope; this is doubly the case in the light of the pessimism of prevailing ideology. To retain hope in the face of severe dementia is thus to have overcome huge obstacles. It is worth noting that hope, in the sense used here, need not be tied to specific scenarios about the future, and so require complex cognitive skill. It is nearer to the psychoanalytic concept of 'basic trust'.[19] When this is present a person can relax and the state of the 'free-child' (available to all of us but often kept right in the background) can prevail.

It is along lines such as these that the indicators of well-being receive a rational justification. There is additional support from consideration of ill-being, although this is not the main subject of this paper. Briefly, ill-being in dementia is very frequently observed, and is often taken to be the inevitable concomitant of advancing neuropathology. Vegetation, which according to conventional wisdom is the end-point, may be understood psychologically as a state of very severe ill-being: the individual has lost almost all that remained of self-esteem, agency, social confidence and hope, and withdrawn into terminal apathy and despair.

The 12 indicators of relative well-being, then, are both empirically demonstrable and have an underlying rationale. Some or all of them can be shown by persons who are very severely demented. Part of the relevant variability is, no doubt, neurologically based, and part is attributable to personality (in particular, to those psychological reserves that each individual brings to a dementing illness). But considering the vast differences between the behaviour of dementia sufferers in different social environments, there can be little doubt that a considerable part of the variability must be attributed to the quality of care.

The place of the other in dementia care

Persons exist in relationship; interdependence is a necessary condition of being human. Perhaps everyday life would be more fulfilling, and each individual's existence both richer and more secure, if this were widely acknowledged. A consequence would be that people would tend far more towards the psychological state characterised in this paper as fluid. As it is, many people in adulthood strive to create and maintain a sense of well-being without the deep involvement of others; in terms of our metaphor, they remain frozen. Some find fulfilment in a project: an elaborate and self-initiated plan, perhaps grasped initially at a preconscious level, and taking years to complete.

Dementia sufferers, however, are deprived of the consolation of projects, and may not even have the capacity to plan and execute the most basic tasks of daily life. The fact of dependence on others is forced upon them, whether or not it is their will. The Other is not an optional extra, but an absolute necessity. If this is true in the obvious practical matters, it is also true at the psychological level.

Everyday observation of those who are dementing, and involvement in the practicalities of care, shows how crucial it is to recognize this point. It is often the case that a dementia sufferer who is visibly withdrawing, or becoming demoralized, is transformed by a little real attention and human contact. It is as if he or she needs to be re-called to the world of persons, where a place is no longer guaranteed. At such times one or more of the indicators of well-being may be shown, only to fade quickly. Well-being, then, for dementia sufferers, often appears to be fragile and short-lived. Whereas some individuals with the full range of cognitive powers have 'inner' reserves to draw on, or at least well-developed capacities for carrying on in a 'frozen' state, those who are some way into a dementing illness do not. Often they seem to have virtually no reserves, and to be drifting towards the threshold of unbeing. Their personhood needs to be continually replenished, their selfhood continually evoked and reassured.

In some respects, then, a dementia sufferer's shattered state is like that of a very young child, who is in the primal state of fluidity. Early in life personhood is actually being created in relationship; small fragments of truly personal experience gradually coalesce, and a self, with a sense of psychological continuity, is formed. It is a process of development that absolutely needs the Other. Although the caregiver's task is demanding, in certain senses it is not difficult. It is working with a natural direction of growth, and with a given path of neurological maturation; these processes pose no dire threat. The dementia sufferer also needs the Other for personhood to be sustained. However, there are some crucial differences. Here, one might say, the natural and the social are opposing tendencies. The Other is needed, not to work with growth, but to offset degeneration and fragmentation; and the further the dementing process advances, the greater is the need for that 'person-work'. It is as if faculties which were, for a long time, the property of an individual, are now to be made over again to the interpersonal milieu from which they originated. In terms of the metaphor of states of personhood, the self that is shattered in dementia will not naturally coalesce; the Other is needed to hold the fragments together. As subjectivity breaks apart, so intersubjectivity must take over if personhood is to be maintained. At a psychological level, this may be understood as the true agenda for dementia care.

286   *Tom Kitwood and Kathleen Bredin*

At present we know dementia very largely in a context of relative deprivation. Organizational structure, the type of training and the specification of the role of careworker all tend to require people to operate, very largely, from a 'frozen' state. None of this is specific to dementia care, although it has a particular poignancy here; it simply reflects prevailing patterns of life. From time to time in the minutiae of dementia care work episodes occur which give tiny glimpses of something far better. Already there are some hospital wards, day centres and residential homes which work with a positive and personal philosophy of care, pointing to a radically different form of social being. So a picture is beginning to emerge of what dementia care might be like in a context of psychological abundance, where interdependence is openly acknowledged, and where people exist mainly in a fluid rather than a frozen state. Perhaps, if this became the norm, dementia would not turn out to be such a tragedy, and dementia care not so great a burden. To become frail in some respect is the inescapable lot of many people in later life. To take this up into care practice is simply an acknowledgment of the truth of our vulnerability and interdependence, so often strenuously denied. Thus dementia care need not be a relatively passive attendance upon an elderly man or woman's psychological undoing. Rather, it may become an exemplary model of interpersonal life, an epitome of how to be human.

NOTES

1 Kitwood, T., The technical, the personal and the framing of dementia. *Social Behaviour*, 3 (1988), 161–180.
2 See, for example, Shotter, J., *Images of Man in Psychological Research*. Methuen, London, 1975.
3 Menzies Lyth, I., *Containing Anxiety in Organizations*. Free Associations Books, London, 1989.
4 Freire, P., *Cultural Action for Freedom*. Penguin, Harmondsworth, 1972.
5 Kitwood, T., The dialectics of dementia: with particular reference to Alzheimer's disease. *Ageing and Society*, 10 (1990), 177–196.
6 Bredin, K., *A Review of Psycholosocial Interventions in Dementia*. University of Bradford, 1991. Copies available on request.
7 See, for example, Mair, M., *Between Psychology and Psychotherapy: Towards a Poetics of Experience*. Routledge, London, 1989.
8 This term, or rather 'the pathology of normalcy' was coined by Erich Fromm. See Fromm, E., *The Sane Society*. Routledge, London, 1956.
9 See, for example, Gubrium, J. *Old-timers and Alzheimer's: the Descriptive Organization of Senility*. JAI Press, London, 1986.
10 Gilleard, C. Losing One's Mind and Losing One's Place. Address to the British Society of Gerontology, 1989.
11 Kitwood, T. *Concern for Others*. Routledge, London, 1990.
12 Malerstein, A. J. and Ahern, M., *A Piagetian Model of Character Structure*. Human Sciences Press, New York, 1982.

13 Smail, D. *Illusion and Reality*. Dent, London, 1984.
14 Bell, J. and McGregor, I., Living for the moment. *Nursing Times*, 87 (1991), 18, 45–47.
15 Rovner, B., Lucas-Blanstein, J., Folstein M. F. and Smith, S. W., Stability over one year in patients admitted to a nursing home dementia unit. *International Journal of Geriatric Psychiatry*, 5 (1990), 77–82.
16 Diamond, M., The potential of the ageing brain for structural regeneration. In Arie, T. (ed.), *Recent Advances In Psychogeriatrics*, 1. Churchill, London, 1985.
17 Karlsson, I., Brane, G., Melin, E., Nyth, A-L. and Ryko, E. Effects of environmental stimulation on biochemical and psychological variables in dementia. *Acta Psychiatrica Scandinavica* (1988), 207–213.
18 We acknowledge the insight of Mr Ian Mackie, Manager of Northern View Day Hospital, Bradford, in helping to clarify this point.
19 Erik Erikson, in his theory of life-stages, sees the development of basic trust as the first task for the infant. Erikson, E., *Childhood and Society*. Penguin, Harmondsworth, 1965.

[14]

Discovering the person with Alzheimer's disease: cognitive, emotional and behavioural aspects

R. T. WOODS

Professor of Clinical Psychology of Older People, University of Wales Bangor, UK

Abstract
The person-centred approach to dementia care emerges from a new emphasis on the experience of the person with dementia. The person is seen as attempting to manage and cope with their difficulties, through a variety of coping mechanisms. Some are able to seek to maximize their cognitive capacities, and there are a number of strategies now available to assist in this process. However, the emotional aspects merit increased attention, with more awareness needed of the range of powerful emotions that may be present, and of the possibility of therapeutic interventions to alleviate symptoms of anxiety and depression. Many of the difficult behaviours seen in dementia may be understood more fully with an appreciation of their emotional underpinning, in feelings of anger, fear, insecurity and hopelessness. The interaction between caregiver strain and challenging behaviour also merits further exploration. The person-centred approach has many implications for practice, as well as for research. The perspective of the person with dementia, and outcomes reflecting that perspective, must be represented in research studies in dementia care. Caregivers, whether family members or paid workers, require additional support in order to recognize the person's needs and to meet them in ways which enable the person's identity and full human value to be upheld.

The 'discovery' of the person with dementia

The most important development in dementia care over the last decade has been a new awareness of the significance of the experience and perspective of the individual with dementia. The emphasis in the 1980's on the situation of family caregivers, the 'hidden victims of Alzheimer's disease', led to major improvements in understanding of the problems faced by families, and improved support for them. A tendency developed however, to see caregiver support as the major goal of dementia care services. At the same time, biomedical research on Alzheimer's and other dementias continued to grow apace, and served to focus attention on neurotransmitters, amyloid plaques, neurofibrillary tangles and chromosomes, rather than on the person and their reaction to the pathological changes in the brain.

In the UK, a social psychologist, the late Tom Kitwood, was the major influence in bringing the person with dementia to centre stage. In the USA, there were also calls for greater awareness of the perspective of the person with dementia (Cotrell & Schulz, 1993). Kitwood (1993) argued that the clinical presentation of dementia was not simply a manifestation of the neuropathological impairment—the damaged brain. He first drew attention to the impact of the social environment surrounding the person, suggesting that often it constituted a 'malignant social psychology', devaluing, diminishing, dehumanizing, and depersonalizing the person, leading to greater disability and dysfunction. Examples of a malignant social psychology would include infantilization, disempowerment and objectification (Kitwood, 1990). Kitwood showed how these features were everyday occurrences in most care settings, emphasizing that these were not generally the product of malicious abusive carers, but a flawed response arising from the limited skills and sensitivity most of us exhibit in the presence of cognitive impairment.

Other factors in addition to the social environment also interact with the neuropathological impairment of dementia. Amongst these would be the person's personality and life-experiences, which would together shape the person's reaction to his/her condition. The person's physical health status is another key factor interacting with neuropathological impairment. The deleterious effects of some forms of medication may be included in this category, as would the other possible causes of acute states of confusion. Kitwood (1993) expressed this understanding of the variety of influences on the presentation of dementia in a simple equation:

$$D = P + B + H + NI + SP$$

Where D = Dementia, P = Personality, B = Biography, H = Physical Health, NI = Neurological Impairment and SP = Social Psychology.

In effect, the suggestion is that the person with dementia may well appear more impaired, or to have a more severe level of dementia than is necessitated by the actual neuropathological damage that has been sustained. Potentially, there may be considerable disability, arising from these various other influences, over and above the disability directly arising from the neurological impairment. This notion of excess disability is not new (Brody et al., 1971), but merits wider currency. It emphasizes the need for holistic assessment and leads towards a more hopeful view on the potential for psychosocial interventions. Neurological impairment may not be readily modified, but certain of the other factors may be amenable to intervention, so that reductions in disability become feasible ('rementia' in Kitwood's terminology). It also makes clear that there is a need for an understanding of the person's life-story, of his/her preferences, interests, values, relationships, achievements, and disappointments. The use of life-review methods, constructing the person's life-story, perhaps in tangible form, may be especially helpful in this respect.

The experience of dementia

In recent years, several first-hand accounts of the experience of dementia have appeared (e.g. Davis, 1989; Friel-McGowin, 1993). These reinforce the long-standing view that the person with dementia is not simply a passive victim of impairment, but rather seeks actively to make sense of and cope with what is happening. From a pioneering but perhaps overlooked study, Cohen, Kennedy, & Eisdorfer (1984) described the following six phases of adaptation:

- Recognition and concern;
- Denial;
- Anger/guilt/sadness;
- Coping;
- Maturation;
- Separation from self.

The difficulty is, of course, that the person's adaptive abilities are likely themselves to be impaired by the dementia process. The variation in response style of people with dementia is now beginning to be documented. Individual differences arise from the interaction of the person's personality style with their biography and life experiences, influencing the range of coping strategies and adaptive mechanisms within the person's coping repertoire.

The coping mechanisms used in seven cases reported by Bahro, Silber, & Sunderland (1995) were described as including denial, externalization, somatization and self-blame. These patients were in the period following diagnosis. Externalization, attributing problems to others, is a mechanism frequently encountered by home care providers, who find themselves accused of stealing the person's possessions; the person defends him/herself from the possibility that he/she has mislaid the item, has forgotten where they put it, by placing the blame on the unfortunate home care worker. Some people with dementia are able to accept that their memory is not what it was, but minimize the problems arising from this. Some people attribute the difficulty to 'getting older', but see it as a minor hindrance rather than a major problem. Others deny completely that there is a difficulty. Somatization occurs where the person focuses on physical symptoms, complaining of headaches, say, or attributes changes in life-style to a physical complaint or sensory loss, rather than to cognitive changes.

Kitwood, Buckland, & Petrie (1995) report a cluster analysis of the current personality profiles of 112 people with dementia, with six clusters emerging, reflecting quite different responses to their situation, ranging from the 'happy socialite' to the person 'fighting the system', stubborn and fiercely wanting independence, through the 'vulnerable and anxiety prone'. These clusters and case descriptions raise questions as to the optimal style of coping with a dementia; self-blame is clearly likely to lead to greater distress; minimizing the importance of what has been lost—a more subtle form of denial—seems to be adaptive for some. Different styles may be effective at different stages or in different situations; denial may be adaptive, but the effort required can become unbearable. Showing sorrow and grief for what has been lost may appear the natural response, but we have as yet little understanding of whether a point of acceptance, of resolution, may be reached, or at least a lessening of grief-related distress to balance the pain of experiencing grief. The continuing losses of function, and the loss of ability to articulate clearly experiences add to the complexity of this process.

Based on in-depth qualitative interviews, Keady & Nolan have proposed a developmental model beginning in the very early stages of dementia, reflecting the uncertainty of the pre-diagnosis phase, of sensing something is not quite right (Keady & Nolan, 1995a; Keady & Nolan, 1995b). The stages are described as:

- Slipping
- Suspecting
- Covering up
- Revealing
- Confirming
- Surviving/Maximizing
- Disorganization
- Decline & death

Keady and Nolan were struck by the efforts made by a number of those interviewed to cope and optimize their function in the 'surviving/maximizing' phase, before the disorganization stage took hold. This phase reflects some adjustment and acceptance; it is important to distinguish this active strategy from a passive resignation and withdrawal. It is noteworthy that the person and their family will probably not receive any external help or input until the 'Confirming' stage, where a diagnostic assessment is sought, and the importance of increasing understanding of the pre-diagnostic phase is clear.

Insight, the person's awareness of their condition, is now being addressed (e.g. Mullen et al., 1996) but raises complex issues. What is the person aware of? Is Alzheimer's a memory problem or a loss of capacity in everyday life? As measured in most studies, it reflects the extent to which the person with dementia is in agreement with the caregiver's perspective. This is not ideal, given the potential impact of relationship dynamics and caregiver mood on caregiver reports. To what extent does denial, as a defence mechanism, contribute to apparent lack of insight? Indeed, are insight and denial simply two-sides of the same coin, as implied by Cheston & Bender (1999)? Or is lack of insight another result of neuropathological damage—an example of anosognosia perhaps? It would not be surprising, for example, if patients with frontal lobe type dementia had problems of insight and awareness. There is agreement that insight and cognitive status are related, although the relationship with the score on a measure such as the Mini-Mental State Examination (MMSE; Folstein et al., 1975) is probably not linear (Zanetti et al., 1999), perhaps reflecting the multiple abilities being assessed by this apparently simple and certainly crude assessment of cognitive abilities. It would appear that depression in dementia is not strongly related to the presence of insight regarding cognitive impairment (Verhey et al., 1993). In this study, it was the presence of psychic anxiety that showed a significant relationship with insight.

Given that people with dementia are often not informed of the diagnosis (Rice & Warner, 1994), a lack of formal insight is perhaps to be expected. Opinions are divided as to what people with dementia should be told, or indeed whether they should be told at all (Gilliard & Gwilliam, 1996). Caregivers are now nearly always told the diagnosis and are reported to want to protect the person with dementia, whilst acknowledging that if in the same position themselves they would want to be told (Maguire et al., 1996). The debate is reminiscent of the situation with cancer 20 years ago; to tell or not to tell? In the future will we likewise look back and wonder what all the concern was about, that of course people with dementia should be informed of their diagnosis? Part of the difficulty clinically at present is what to tell: diagnosing the specific dementia is not yet straightforward; the prognosis in the individual case remains uncertain, for example, in terms of speed of progression and areas of function likely to be impaired. Tackling sensitively the specific practical implications of the diagnosis, for example, in terms of ability to drive and competence to make financial decisions may help the broader discussion of an uncertain future. Husband (1999) describes using Cognitive Behaviour Therapy (CBT) with three patients to assist in adaptation to the diagnosis, beginning with a focus on the person's beliefs and knowledge regarding dementia and going on to develop coping strategies.

Holding on cognitively

There is increasing interest in applying cognitive rehabilitation techniques with people with dementia (e.g. Arkin, 1997; Camp et al., 1996; Clare et al., 1999). These approaches are proving helpful with people who have experienced other forms of brain trauma (Wilson, 1989), and aim to apply principles and methods from cognitive psychology to the problems being experienced. The major strategies may be summarized as follows (Woods, 1996):

Use of internalized mnemonics: Here the person is taught to use strategies to aid learning and retrieval e.g. visual imagery to remember a person's name or a list of items. Although less generally applicable than other strategies, in view of the cognitive ability and effort required in order to use the mnemonics, some successful cases have been reported (Clare et al., 1999; Hill et al., 1987).

Reducing cognitive load: If cognitive demands can be reduced on the person, their retained abilities may be used more effectively. This may be achieved through environmental adaptations, simplifying the locating of important rooms and places through careful and clear sign-posting, reducing the number of irrelevant and distracting sources of stimuli, making use of familiar, well-learned associations wherever possible. A small homely unit, with a few, consistent staff, and many familiar items and possessions in the person's own room, will be much less inherently cognitively demanding than a large institution, with long corridors, many other residents and a frequently changing staff group. External memory aids also assist in reducing the cognitive load, obviating the need for effortful, self-initiated cognitive processes. Memory aids shown to be helpful in single case studies include watches, diaries and specially made booklets/wallets containing relevant pictures and information (Bourgeois, 1990; Bourgeois, 1992; Hanley & Lusty, 1984; Woods, 1983). Some aids act as retrieval cues; to be effective they need to be salient and placed so that the person will encounter the cue at the relevant time. It is important to recognize that in most of these studies, specific training was needed for the cues to be used by the person with dementia; this has also been shown in several studies where people with dementia have been trained to find locations in a hospital ward or nursing home; sign-posting alone had less impact than training to use the sign-posts and other landmarks in the environment (Gilleard, Mitchell, & Riordan, 1981; Hanley, 1981; Lam & Woods, 1986). Such a use of cues fits well with the conclusion of Bäckman (1992), that people with dementia require support at both the time of learning and at the time of retrieval for optimal performance.

Enhancing learning: Although learning is of course almost universally impaired in dementia, it is by no means impossible (see Miller & Morris, 1993, pp. 113–115, for a summary of the relevant research). It is encouraging that rates of forgetting are relatively unimpaired after the first ten minutes or so, so that if material can be adequately registered, retention is feasible. Several methods for facilitating acquisition have been described. Spaced retrieval involves the learning of one item at a time, with the retrieval period being increased gradually each time the person correctly retrieves the item (Camp & Schaller, 1989; McKitrick, Camp, & Black, 1992). The active process of retrieval is thought to be important in consolidating the memory for the item. If the person is unable to retrieve the item, they are prompted, and the retrieval interval is then reduced, before being built up once again. Camp et al., (1996) report the successful use of the spaced retrieval procedure in order to teach the person with dementia to make use of a memory aid (a calendar). Recently, attention has been drawn to the benefits of ensuring, as far as possible, that the learning proceeds without the person making errors; such errors often serve to interfere with effective learning, in that the person is likely to remember the error in competition with the correct response. Clare et al., (1999) describe the errorless learning procedure, where prompts are used to guide the person into giving the correct response, and guessing is discouraged. Procedural learning, where encoding proceeds through a motor act, or practice of a sequence of movements, has also been shown to be relatively intact (Bird & Kinsella, 1996), and has been applied to enhancing the performance of everyday skills in several studies (Josephsson et al., 1993; Zanetti et al., 1997).

There are several procedures and techniques that may be used to enhance and maximize cognitive function in people with dementia, but how helpful are these techniques in practice? Given that the person's cognitive abilities would be expected to continue to decline, are these approaches encouraging dementia care workers to make heroic, but ultimately hopeless, efforts to swim against the tide? There can be little question that efforts to generally reduce the cognitive load, to target the person's resources on areas of importance to him/her, to provide an environment where intact memory function is less important, will be of benefit to most people with dementia. How much effort is justified in relation to the more intensive memory programmes described, for example, by Arkin (1997) or Clare et al., (1999)? By their very nature, these programmes draw attention to the memory deficit, and require a shared understanding that such a problem exists, and that the person wishes to work to improve their memory function. Even in the early stages of dementia, it is not yet clear what proportion of patients would be able and willing to focus on their memory difficulties in this way.

Anxiety regarding the difficulties experienced may indeed interfere with the learning process—the failure of one of the four people with dementia in the study reported by Josephsson et al., (1993) to show learning was attributed to high levels of anxiety. Even where the person is keen to proceed with memory exercises, this may serve as a way of coping with intense fears and anxieties, which, in the author's clinical experience, may surface in the midst of a spaced-retrieval exercise. The American Psychiatric Association's Practice Guideline for the treatment of patients with dementia (American Psychiatric Association, 1997), draws attention to case reports of anger, frustration and depression, and concludes 'Cognition-oriented treatments... are unlikely to be beneficial' and 'do not appear to warrant the risk of adverse events'. Some of the concerns arise from the well-documented misuse of Reality Orientation (RO) (Dietch, Hewett, & Jones, 1989), and do serve to reinforce the importance of a sensitive, individualized, person-centred approach to cognitive rehabilitation (Holden & Woods, 1995). In fact, the evidence for the effectiveness of RO group sessions, in relation to benefits on verbal orientation and on behavioural function, is relatively well established (Spector et al., 2000). Such sessions, where perhaps five or six people with dementia would meet several times a week with members of staff around an orientation board, carrying out a variety of cognitive activities focused on 'current reality' were ubiquitous in dementia care settings in the early 1980's. The fall from favour of RO related more to attempts to apply it in a standardized (and too often patronizing) way to all patients, without individualizing its application, in terms of the relevance and importance to the person of the goals of intervention.

The emotional response of the person with dementia

It is well established that substantial numbers of people with dementia also have symptoms of depression and/or anxiety. Depression co-existing with dementia has received much less attention over the years than is due, probably because of an over-emphasis on distinguishing the two conditions, rather than recognizing depression as a common concomitant of dementia. Reifler & Larson (1990) report a prevalence of between a quarter and a third of dementia patients with a co-existing depression in their outpatient studies. These mood disorders were seen as a major source of 'excess disability' in dementia. In an attempt to reduce the level of disability, depressed patients were randomly allocated to receive either anti-depressant medication or a placebo; both groups showed reduced depression, with the placebo group's improvement attributed to increased support and attention during the treatment trial. Several studies have suggested that depressed mood may be more common than the presence of an actual depressive disorder (see Cotrell & Schulz, 1993), and prevalence figures will vary according to the diagnostic criteria used (Cheston & Bender, 1999).

In relation to anxiety, Ballard et al., (1996) reported that, in a memory clinic sample, 30% of patients diagnosed as having dementia had one or more anxiety symptoms, with 38% reporting tension. Three subgroups were identified: those whose anxiety arose in the context of depression; those who also suffered hallucinations or delusions; and finally a group who showed some insight into their problems, who were anxious they would be embarrassed in particular situations because of their cognitive lapses. Different treatment strategies might be indicated in different case-profiles, and there is increasing interest in offering psychological therapies for anxiety, depression and adjustment to loss to people with dementia.

An early report (Welden & Yesavage, 1982) described the successful application of a relaxation therapy; more recently, Suhr, Anderson, & Tranel (1999) demonstrated the benefits of progressive muscle relaxation (which can be learned through procedural learning) in this population. Thompson et al., (1990) and Teri & Gallagher-Thompson (1991), describe the applicability of CBT to depression in dementia. Scholey & Woods (in press) report six case studies using CBT in patients with early dementia, with some improvement in five of the cases. Teri & Uomoto (1991) report training family caregivers to manage depression in the person with dementia, by increasing involvement and engagement in pleasurable activities, following a more behavioural model of depression as a lack of social reinforcement, and emphasizing less the cognitive aspects, which may be difficult to work with as the person's impairment level increases. A clinical trial of this approach, (Teri et al., 1997), suggested that improvements in mood were apparent in both the person with dementia and the family caregiver. Groups for people with memory difficulties, offering opportunities for peer support as well as development of problem-solving coping strategies have also been described, particularly for early-stage patients (Allen, 1996; Birnie, 1997; Yale, 1995).

Cheston (1998) reviews the growing literature on psychotherapeutic work with people with dementia, which mainly consists of clinical accounts (e.g. Hausman, 1992; Sinason, 1992). Hausman recommends beginning the therapeutic relationship as early as possible in the course of the dementia, and ideally continuing until the person dies, so that the therapist does not become another of the person's losses. The goals of psychotherapy in this context require careful consideration. The issue of insight is important here; to what extent should lack of insight be seen as arising from defence mechanisms of denial and repression, and become an appropriate goal for psychotherapeutic intervention? Or, should the psychotherapist only work with those who have awareness and insight, in order to assist the person to come to terms with, and adjust to the losses of ability and function? Cheston makes the helpful point that rather than thinking in terms of 'doing psychotherapy' with people with dementia, we might think of 'being psychotherapeutic' with the person. Good psychotherapeutic listening skills, open to hearing the emotional significance of what the person says, able to tune into symbolic and metaphoric communication, able to be reflective with the person, will be invaluable in understanding more fully the emotional world of the person and his/her response to their experience of dementia (Mills, 1997; Cheston, 1996). This short-term goal of facilitating communication at the level of emotions, might ultimately contribute to longer-term goals of insight or acceptance, but may be valuable in itself.

Validation Therapy (Feil, 1993) has been widely used in the dementia care field, and similarly has as its focus the emotional communication of the person with dementia, in contrast to the more cognitive emphasis of Reality Orientation. As a therapy 'package', the preliminary evidence for its effectiveness is mixed (Toseland et al., 1997). However, as an approach to communication, it has much to commend it, enabling care-staff to listen respectfully and sensitively to the feelings expressed, without becoming embroiled in fruitless confrontations regarding dates and times and chronology, recognizing the importance of tailoring responses to the individual's characteristics. Feil draws attention to unresolved conflicts and trauma emerging in the midst of the dementia, and perhaps pays rather less heed to more immediate causes of frustration and distress in the current environment. There is a danger that distress is then seen as inevitably located in the individual, and the care environment's contribution may escape scrutiny, despite perhaps being more immediately amenable to intervention. However, it is likely that some people with dementia will have had difficult and upsetting experiences many years previously, which may surface in ways that are difficult to interpret and understand. Sometimes knowledge of the person's life-story helps to piece together the drama being re-enacted—the motivation of the patient agitatedly searching the ward for 'John', calling out in distress and anguish, became clearer when we discovered her youngest son had been killed in an accident in the sea in his early twenties; or the ex-prisoner-of-war who become angry and aggressive whenever he encountered a locked door. The importance of providing a safe, containing environment where strong emotions can be expressed and validated cannot be over-emphasized if such individuals are to be helped.

Feil suggests that in the context of dementia, universal needs and longings emerge—the need for safety, to feel loved, to have purposeful activity, to have others to love and care for, for example. Miesen (Miesen, 1992; Miesen, 1993) has likened dementia to the 'strange situation' in developmental research on attachment behaviour in children, where the infant is observed during a brief separation from, and then a reunion, with a parent. He describes 'parent fixation', where the person is frequently searching for a parent, talking about them as if alive, in terms of the person's need for a safe, secure attachment figure, in the midst of the puzzling, perplexing world of dementia. Bender & Cheston (1997) identify four 'discrete states' of emotional response in dementia: anxiety; depression; grief and despair/terror. Solomon & Szwarbo (1992) have similarly drawn attention to issues of loss, anxiety, fear and even terror, but also highlight the high prevalence of anger and suspiciousness in the 86 patients they interviewed (58% and 35% respectively). The range of powerful emotions present, and the lessened availability of socially acceptable means of expressing them, may be an important factor in the challenging behaviour seen in dementia. However, as Kitwood (1997) argues, when the person's needs are more fully met the potential for positive emotional states, such as satisfaction, humour, affection and pleasure remains.

Understanding difficult behaviour in dementia

It has become increasingly clear that for families and care-staff, it is the non-cognitive features of dementia that are most taxing and experienced as stressful (Donaldson, Tarrier, & Burns, 1998). A number of these are clearly related to the person's emotional state, mood and anxiety. Hope et al., (1997) suggest there are three distinct behavioural syndromes in dementia: over-activity (including aimless walking); aggressive behaviour; and psychosis (hallucinations, persecutory ideas and extreme anxiety). However, the elaboration of typologies of, say, wandering (Hope & Fairburn, 1990), aggression (Stokes, 1989; Ware, Fairburn, & Hope, 1990) and sexual problems (Haddad & Benbow, 1993) support the need for a multi-factorial understanding of such difficulties. Two people may both be said to 'wander', but the actual behaviour and its function may be quite different.

Challenging behaviour is seen psychologically as an expression of an unmet, or poorly communicated need (Stokes, 1996). The person's learned, sophisticated means of meeting basic needs are damaged by the dementia, exposing a 'dysfunctional and at times grotesque distortion of goal-directed communication and conduct' (Stokes, 1996, pp 676). Thus aggression occurs most often during intimate care, when plausibly the person feels most vulnerable and threatened; shouting out may reflect a physical pain that cannot be adequately communicated, or a need for contact for a person who feels abandoned and desolate when familiar others are not in view; wandering may, for some, reflect a search for something or someone familiar and safe, in a place that appears strange and frightening. Magai & Cohen (1998) have shown an association between the person with dementia having been rated (by a family carer) as having had a long-standing insecure attachment style and behavioural disturbance, providing further support for the notion that in dementia we see the person's raw attempts to remain safe and secure, stripped of the layers of socialization which normally surrounds all of our attempts at 'attention seeking'.

There remains a tendency for difficult behaviour to be seen as a property of the person with dementia, rather than as arising in interaction with the care environment. Thus, difficult behaviour is seen as leading to increased carer strain (e.g. Donaldson et al., 1998). The inter-relationship between carer strain and challenging behaviour might better be seen as a dynamic process; a carer under strain may be much more critical of the person with dementia (Bledin et al., 1990), and have less adaptive coping mechanisms; the person with dementia may respond to negative interactions with greater anxiety or agitation; this may lead to further strain in the caregiver and so the cycle continues. In a recent study where daughter caregivers were video-taped in two structured tasks with their dementing mothers, daughters reporting higher levels of stress tended to depersonalize their mothers more, independent of the level of severity of their dementia (Woods, Phibbs & Steele, 2000). Carer strain changes the emotional climate for the person with dementia too, and they may well respond to a negative atmosphere with behaviour that is viewed as challenging.

In the residential context, interventions for challenging behaviour may be viewed as successful where staff perceive the behaviour as less difficult to manage, even if its frequency does not change (Moniz-Cook et al., 1998). The factors leading to staff finding behaviour more challenging include their own anxiety as well as features of the home environment (Moniz-Cook, Woods, & Gardiner, 2000). Again, challenging behaviour is in part related to the perception, appraisal and approach of the caregiver.

Implications for practice

The person-centred approach to care, which underlies this paper, has a number of implications for services and for caregivers. Perhaps the most important relates to the role of the caregiver, whether family member or paid staff member. The role that is required of the front-line carer then places demands on the training and support made available by service providers.

The role of the carer

Kitwood sees personhood as "a standing or status that is bestowed upon one human being, by others, in the context of relationship and social being" (Kitwood, 1997, p. 8). His definition recognizes the interdependence of human beings and their interconnectedness. Carers accordingly make a major contribution to the extent of personhood enjoyed by the person with dementia. Personhood is created (or diminished) in the social relationships around the person with dementia; it is a product of the caregiving relationship. Carers require both skill and ease in relating warmly to others in order to be able to facilitate personhood. It is important to recognize that the interaction is not between one party who is 'damaged' and another who is whole and perfect. The person with dementia may be more vulnerable in some ways, but the caregiver is also 'damaged' in at least some areas of function—perhaps on an interpersonal level, or with specific fears and uncertainties regarding impairment and death.

A key area of potential loss relates to the person's sense of identity. The person's autobiographical memory may decline to the extent that whilst some early memories remain, the gap in the middle years is such that the person finds it hard to account for how they have reached their current situation, leading to a sense of discontinuity and disconnection (Morris, 1996). Mills (1997) has shown how the person's identity as revealed through their narratives, may fragment with continued cognitive decline, but that it may still be understood by those who have heard the story earlier. Families have the advantage of knowing the person for many years, but all can assist in holding and supporting the person's autobiographical memory (Cheston, 1998). A life-story book provides a tangible reminder of some important aspects of the person's life, and offers an opportunity for others to communicate to the person with dementia that he/she remains valued and worthy of attention and interest.

The role of service providers

The carer needs support as well as training, in order to recognize his/her own vulnerabilities, and to be able to identify their contribution to his/her relationships with people with dementia. A carer alone will, despite excellent intentions, struggle to put into practice person-centred care. Kitwood has called for a change of culture in dementia care, away from the old culture, imbued with its malignant social psychology, to a new culture where person-centred care is developed and practiced. Staff need to be valued in the new culture; they cannot deliver person-centred care, if they are not themselves treated as valued individuals. Where staff job satisfaction is higher, quality of care is also better (Gilloran et al., 1995). If staff are to be receptive to the emotional response of people with dementia, they will need access to support and supervision where the emotional impact on themselves is addressed (Berg, Hansson, & Hallberg, 1994).

Attitude to the person with dementia

To deliver person-centred care, services need to ensure that they have not implicitly taken on board the 'living death' model of dementia. This model is based on the extent of the loss experienced by many family carers:

"It is as if my husband/wife/mother/father is dead, but his/her body is still here…"

Such a model only requires services to warehouse and maintain the body until physical death joins the social death implicit within it. The major therapeutic effort is then directed at the family and their grief and strain. In contrast, person-centred care requires skilled input for the person with dementia and his/her family; input that provides the best physical, psychological and social care for all concerned. The needs of the person with dementia for support before, during and after the diagnostic process must be more widely recognized. Pre-diagnostic assessment counselling would be the expectation in other potentially devastating disorders, and should be offered routinely in dementia assessment clinics.

Conclusion

The inter-relationship of cognitive, behavioural and emotional aspects of the person with dementia deserves wider recognition. The person's emotional response may well underlie challenging behaviour and/or reduce cognitive function; cognitive re-training may be used to reduce behavioural problems (e.g. Bird, Alexopoulos, & Adamowicz, 1995). Looking at these aspects in isolation will not be helpful.

This approach requires a fresh look at outcomes; whether the person is institutionalized or not can no longer be seen as an adequate reflection of outcome for the person with dementia. The recent development of a number of quality of life scales is welcome in this respect (e.g. Brod et al., 1999). Measuring quality of life and related mood states such as anxiety and depression, is progressing—largely driven by the requirements of pharmacological research. Bond (1999) suggests that there are however a number of radically different meanings of the concept 'quality of life' emerging in the field, and some caution is required in taking at face value new assessment measures.

It is nevertheless encouraging that when we need to know what the person with dementia thinks or feels, there is now more of a tendency to actually first ask the person with dementia, before asking a proxy, who, if a family carer, may find it difficult to give an objective view (cf. Teri & Truax, 1994). The use of detailed observational methods, such as that devised by Kitwood, 1997 (Dementia Care Mapping), may be helpful where the person is less able to express him or herself. However, the study by Mozley et al., (1999) reporting that 77.5% of residents of homes with an MMSE score of 10 or more were "interviewable" reminds us that we should first ask the person him/herself, before moving to proxy and observational measures. The type and profile of impairment will be as important as a simple rating of severity. More generally, people with dementia require advocacy so that their voice is heard, at the individual and group levels. With the earlier recognition of dementia, self-advocacy is becoming feasible, but appropriate support will be needed for the person to be able to speak out on behalf of other people with dementia and themselves.

The goals that are set in order to evaluate approaches to dementia care must be realistic, but based on changes of importance and relevance to the individual with dementia. "We need to break away from our pre-occupation with treatment in the sense of cure and recovery, and be aware of the different types of goal that are feasible, and the value of some of the more limited goals in improving the patient's quality of life" (Woods & Britton, 1985, p. 217). For example, reminiscence work need not be abandoned if participants' MMSE scores do not improve after ten sessions or so—a more relevant and important outcome might be a measure of mood or of social interaction within the session. What is important to the individual may well change as their disabilities change; early on, a person may wish to engage cognitively, and successes in everyday memory may be significant; later, being able to talk to an interested listener about past experiences may be more rewarding; later still, sensory stimulation—perhaps a hand massage or some favourite music—may be the channel for communication. The onus falls increasingly on the carer to respond flexibly in supporting personhood as the person's capacities lessen. There is certainly a need for more sensitive and appropriate measurement tools that would enable the benefits of such a response to be evaluated.

However, the expectation of decline and loss of function must not prevent us being aware that in some instances there might be more positive long-term changes, the person even showing indications of growth and development. Kitwood reports a number of such instances (Kitwood, 1995), with growth for example in areas of creativity and in previously hidden areas of personality. Freedom of expression and a release from previous constraints and concerns may present new sources of pleasure and satisfaction for the person with dementia. In our concern for the tragedy of Alzheimer's disease and the suffering endured, we must not lose sight of the opportunities for the human spirit to emerge in the midst of undeniably difficult circumstances.

References

ALLEN, C. (1996). The effectiveness of memory aid groups. *PSIGE Newsletter, 56,* 15–19.
AMERICAN PSYCHIATRIC ASSOCIATION. (1997). Practice guideline for the treatment of patients with Alzheimer's disease and other dementias of late life. *American Journal of Psychiatry, 154, 5 (Supplement),* 1–39.
ARKIN, S. M. (1997). Alzheimer memory training: quizzes beat repetition, especially with more impaired. *American Journal of Alzheimer's Disease, 12,* 147–158.
BÄCKMAN, L. (1992). Memory training and memory improvement in Alzheimer's disease: rules and exceptions. *Acta Neurologia Scandinavica, Supplement 139,* 84–89.
BAHRO, M., SILBER, E. & SUNDERLAND, T. (1995). How do patients with Alzheimer's disease cope with their illness? A clinical experience report. *Journal of American Geriatrics Society, 43,* 41–46.
BALLARD, C., BOYLE, A., BOWLER, C. & LINDESAY, J. (1996). Anxiety disorders in dementia sufferers. *International Journal of Geriatric Psychiatry, 11,* 987–990.
BENDER, M. P. & CHESTON, R. (1997). Inhabitants of a lost kingdom: a model for the subjective experiences of dementia. *Ageing & Society, 17,* 513–532.
BERG, A., HANSSON, U. W. & HALLBERG, I. R. (1994). Nurses' creativity, tedium and burnout during 1 year of clinical supervision and implementation of individually planned nursing care: comparisons between a ward for severely demented patients and a similar control ward. *Journal of Advanced Nursing, 20,* 742–749.
BIRD, M., ALEXOPOULOS, P. & ADAMOWICZ, J. (1995). Success and failure in five case studies: use of cued recall to ameliorate behaviour problems in senile dementia. *International Journal of Geriatric Psychiatry, 10,* 305–311.
BIRD, M., & KINSELLA, G. (1996). Long-term cued recall of tasks in senile dementia. *Psychology & Aging, 11,* 45–56.
BIRNIE, J. (1997). A memory group for older adults. *PSIGE Newsletter, 59,* 30–33.
BLEDIN, K., MACCARTHY, B., KUIPERS, L. & WOODS, R. T. (1990). Daughters of people with dementia: expressed emotion, strain and coping. *British Journal of Psychiatry, 157,* 221–227.
BOND, J. (1999). Quality of life for people with dementia: approaches to the challenge of measurement. *Ageing & Society, 19,* 561–579.
BOURGEOIS, M. S. (1990). Enhancing conversation skills in patients with Alzheimer's disease using a prosthetic memory aid. *Journal of Applied Behavior Analysis, 23,* 29–42.
BOURGEOIS, M. S. (1992). *Conversing with memory impaired individuals using memory aids: a memory aid workbook.* Bicester: Winslow Press.
BROD, M., STEWART, A. L., SANDS, L. & WALTON, P. (1999). Conceptualization and measurement of quality of life in dementia: the dementia quality of life instrument (DQoL). *Gerontologist, 39,* 25–35.
BRODY, E. M., KLEBAN, M. H., LAWTON, M. P. & SILVERMAN, H. A. (1971). Excess disabilities of mentally impaired aged: impact of individualized treatment. *Gerontologist, 11,* 124–133.
CAMP, C. J., FOSS, J. W., O'HANLON, A. M., & STEVENS, A. B. (1996). Memory interventions for persons with dementia. *Applied Cognitive Psychology, 10,* 193–210.
CAMP, C. J. & SCHALLER, J. R. (1989). Epilogue: spaced-retrieval memory training in an adult day-care center. *Educational Gerontology, 15,* 641–648.
CHESTON, R. (1996). Stories and metaphors: talking about the past in a psychotherapy group for people with dementia. *Ageing & Society, 16,* 579–602.
CHESTON, R. (1998). Psychotherapeutic work with people with dementia: a review of the literature. *British Journal of Medical Psychology, 71,* 211–231.
CHESTON, R. & BENDER, M. (1999). Brains, minds and selves: changing conceptions of the losses involved in dementia. *Ageing & Society, 72,* 203–216.

CLARE, L., WILSON, B. A., BREEN, K. & HODGES, J. R. (1999). Errorless learning of face-name associations in early Alzheimer's disease. *Neurocase, 5,* 37–46.

COHEN, D., KENNEDY, G. & EISDORFER, C. (1984). Phases of change in the patient with Alzheimer's dementia. *Journal of American Geriatrics Society, 32,* 11–15.

COTRELL, V., & SCHULZ, R. (1993). The perspective of the patient with Alzheimer's disease: a neglected dimension of dementia research. *Gerontologist, 33,* 205–211.

DAVIS, R. (1989). *My journey into Alzheimer's disease.* Wheaton, Illinois: Tyndale.

DIETCH, J. T., HEWETT, L. J. & JONES, S. (1989). Adverse effects of reality orientation. *Journal of American Geriatrics Society, 37,* 974–976.

DONALDSON, C., TARRIER, N. & BURNS, A. (1998). Determinants of carer stress in Alzheimer's disease. *International Journal of Geriatric Psychiatry, 13, (4),* 248–256.

FEIL, N. (1993). *The Validation breakthrough: simple techniques for communicating with people with "Alzheimer's type dementia".* Baltimore: Health Professions Press.

FRIEL-MCGOWIN, D. F. (1993). *Living in the labyrinth: a personal journey through the maze of Alzheimer's.* San Francisco: Elder.

FOLSTEIN, M. F., FOLSTEIN, S. E. & MCHUGH, P. R. (1975). Mini-Mental State: a practical method for grading the cognitive state of patients for the clinician. *Journal of Psychiatric Research, 12,* 189–198.

GILLEARD, C., MITCHELL, R. G. & RIORDAN, J. (1981). Ward orientation training with psychogeriatric patients. *Journal of Advanced Nursing, 6,* 95–98.

GILLIARD, J. & GWILLIAM, C. (1996). Sharing the diagnosis: a survey of memory clinics, their policies on informing people with dementia and their families, and the support they offer. *International Journal of Geriatric Psychiatry, 11,* 1001–1003.

GILLORAN, A., ROBERTSON, A., MCGLEW, T., & MCKEE, K. (1995). Improving work satisfaction amongst nursing staff and quality of care for elderly patients with dementia: some policy implications. *Ageing & Society, 15,* 375–391.

HADDAD, P. M. & BENBOW, S. M. (1993). Sexual problems associated with dementia: Part 1: problems and their consequences. *International Journal of Geriatric Psychiatry, 8,* 547–551.

HANLEY, I. G. (1981). The use of signposts and active training to modify ward disorientation in elderly patients. *Journal of Behaviour Therapy & Experimental Psychiatry, 12,* 241–247.

HANLEY, I. G., & LUSTY, K. (1984). Memory aids in reality orientation: a single-case study. *Behaviour Research & Therapy, 22,* 709–712.

HAUSMAN, C. (1992). Dynamic psychotherapy with elderly demented patients. In G. JONES & B. M. L. MIESEN (Eds.), *Care-giving in dementia: research and applications* (pp. 181–198). London: Routledge.

HILL, R. D., EVANKOVICH, K. D., SHEIKH, J. I. & YESAVAGE, J. A. (1987). Imagery mnemonic training in a patient with primary degenerative dementia. *Psychology & Aging, 2,* 204–205.

HOLDEN, U. P. & WOODS, R. T. (1995). *Positive approaches to dementia care (Third Edition).* Edinburgh: Churchill Livingstone.

HOPE, R. A., & FAIRBURN, C. G. (1990). The nature of wandering in dementia: a community-based study. *International Journal of Geriatric Psychiatry, 5,* 239–245.

HOPE, T., KEENE, J., FAIRBURN, C., MCSHANE, R., & JACOBY, R. (1997). Behaviour changes in dementia 2: are there behavioural syndromes? *International Journal of Geriatric Psychiatry, 12, (11),* 1074–1078.

HUSBAND, H. J. (1999). The psychological consequences of learning a diagnosis of dementia: three case examples. *Aging & Mental Health, 3, (2),* 179–183.

JOSEPHSSON, S., BÄCKMAN, L., BORELL, L., BERNSPANG, B., NYGARD, L. & RONNBERG, L. (1993). Supporting everyday activities in dementia: an intervention study. *International Journal of Geriatric Psychiatry, 8,* 395–400.

KEADY, J. & NOLAN, M. (1995a). IMMEL: assessing coping responses in the early stages of dementia. *British Journal of Nursing, 4, (6),* 309–314.

KEADY, J. & NOLAN, M. (1995b). IMMEL 2: working to augment coping responses in early dementia. *British Journal of Nursing, 4, (7),* 377–381.

KITWOOD, T. (1990). The dialectics of dementia: with particular reference to Alzheimer's disease. *Ageing & Society, 10,* 177–196.

KITWOOD, T. (1993). Towards a theory of dementia care: the interpersonal process. *Ageing & Society, 13,* 51–67.

KITWOOD, T. (1995). Positive long-term changes in dementia: some preliminary observations. *Journal of Mental Health, 4,* 133–144.

KITWOOD, T. (1997). *Dementia reconsidered: the person comes first.* Buckingham: Open University Press.

KITWOOD, T., BUCKLAND, S. & PETRIE, T. (1995). *Brighter futures: a report on research into provision for persons with dementia in residential homes, nursing homes and sheltered housing.* Kidlington: Anchor Housing Association.

LAM, D. H. & WOODS, R. T. (1986). Ward orientation training in dementia: a single-case study. *International Journal of Geriatric Psychiatry, 1,* 145–147.

MAGAI, C. & COHEN, C. I. (1998). Attachment style and emotion regulation in dementia patients and their relation to caregiver burden. *Journal of Gerontology, 53B, (3),* 147–154.

MAGUIRE, C. P., KIRBY, M., COEN, R., COAKLEY, D., LAWLOR, B. A. & O'NEILL, D. (1996). Family members' attitudes toward telling the patient with Alzheimer's disease their diagnosis. *British Medical Journal, 313,* 529–530.

MCKITRICK, L. A., CAMP, C. J. & BLACK, F. W. (1992). Prospective memory intervention in Alzheimer's disease. *Journal of Gerontology, 47,* 337–343.

MIESEN, B. M. L. (1992). Attachment theory and dementia. In G. JONES & B. M. L. MIESEN (Eds.), *Care-giving in dementia* (pp. 38–56). London: Routledge.

MIESEN, B. M. L. (1993). Alzheimer's disease, the phenomenon of parent fixation and Bowlby's attachment theory. *International Journal of Geriatric Psychiatry, 8,* 147–153.

MILLER, F. & MORRIS, R. (1993). *The psychology of dementia.* Chichester: Wiley.

MILLS, M. A. (1997). Narrative identity and dementia: a study of emotion and narrative in older people with dementia. *Ageing & Society, 17,* 673–698.

MONIZ-COOK, E., AGAR, S., SILVER, M., WOODS, R., WANG, M., ELSTON, C. & WIN, T. (1998). Can staff training reduce behavioural problems in residential care for the elderly mentally ill? *International Journal of Geriatric Psychiatry, 13,* 149–158.

MONIZ-COOK, E., WOODS, R. & GARDINER, E. (2000). Staff factors associated with perception of behaviour as 'challenging' in residential and nursing homes. *Aging & Mental Health, 4, (1),* 48–55.

MORRIS, R. G. (1996). The neuropsychology of Alzheimer's disease and related dementia. In R. T. WOODS (Ed.), *Handbook of the clinical psychology of ageing* (pp. 219–242). Chichester: Wiley.

MOZLEY, C. G., HUXLEY, P., SUTCLIFFE, C., BAGLEY, H., BURNS, A., CHALLIS, D. & CORDINGLEY, L. (1999). 'Not knowing where I am doesn't mean I don't know what I like': cognitive impairment and quality of life responses in elderly people. *International Journal of Geriatric Psychiatry, 14,* 776–783.

S16 R.T. Woods

Mullen, R., Howard, R., David, A. & Levy, R. (1996). Insight in Alzheimer's disease. *International Journal of Geriatric Psychiatry, 11,* 645–651.

Reifler, B. V. & Larson, E. (1990). Excess disability in dementia of the Alzheimer's type. In E. Light & B. D. Lebowitz (Eds.), *Alzheimer's disease treatment and family stress* (pp. 363–382). New York: Hemisphere.

Rice, K. & Warner, N. (1994). Breaking the bad news: what do psychiatrists tell patients with dementia about their illness? *International Journal of Geriatric Psychiatry, 9,* 467–471.

Scholey, K. & Woods, R.T. (in press) Cognitive behaviour therapy for depression in dementia. *Clinical Psychology & Psychotherapy.*

Sinason, V. (1992). The man who was losing his brain. In V. Sinason (Ed.), *Mental handicap and the human condition: new approaches from the Tavistock* (pp. 87–110). London: Free Association Books.

Solomon, K. & Szwarbo, P. (1992). Psychotherapy for patients with dementia. In J. E. Morley, R. M. Coe, R. Strong, & G. T. Grossberg (Eds.), *Memory function and aging-related disorders.* New York: Springer.

Spector, A., Orrell, M., Davies, S. & Woods, B. (2000). Reality orientation for dementia: a systematic review of the evidence for its effectiveness. *Gerontologist, 40,* 206–212.

Stokes, G. (1989). Managing aggression in dementia: the do's and don'ts. *Geriatric Medicine (April),* 35–40.

Stokes, G. (1996). Challenging behaviour in dementia: a psychological approach. In R. T. Woods (Ed.), *Handbook of the clinical psychology of ageing.* (pp. 601–628). Chichester: Wiley.

Suhr, J., Anderson, S. & Tranel, D. (1999). Progressive muscle relaxation in the management of behavioural disturbance in Alzheimer's disease. *Neuropsychological Rehabilitation, 9,* 31–44.

Teri, L. & Gallagher-Thompson, D. (1991). Cognitive-behavioural interventions for treatment of depression in Alzheimer's disease. *Gerontologist, 31,* 413–416.

Teri, L., Logsdon, R. G., Uomoto, J., & McCurry, S. M. (1997). Behavioral treatment of depression in dementia patients: a controlled clinical trial. *Journal of Gerontology, 52B,* 159–166.

Teri, L. & Truax, P. (1994). Assessment of depression in dementia patients: association of caregiver mood with depression ratings. *Gerontologist, 34,* 231–234.

Teri, L. & Uomoto, J. M. (1991). Reducing excess disability in dementia patients: training caregivers to manage patient depression. *Clinical Gerontologist, 10, (4),* 49–63.

Thompson, L. W., Wagner, B., Zeiss, A. & Gallagher, D. (1990). Cognitive/behavioural therapy with early stage Alzheimer's patients: an exploratory view of the utility of this approach. In E. Light & B. D. Lebowitz (Eds.), *Alzheimer's disease: treatment and family stress* (pp. 383–397). New York: Hemisphere.

Toseland, R. W., Diehl, M., Freeman, K., Manzanares, T. & McCallion, P. (1997). The impact of validation group therapy on nursing home residents with dementia. *Journal of Applied Gerontology, 16, (1),* 31–50.

Verhey, F. R. J., Rozendaal, N., Ponds, R. W. H. M. & Jolles, J. (1993). Dementia, awareness and depression. *International Journal of Geriatric Psychiatry, 8,* 851–856.

Ware, C. J. G., Fairburn, C. G. & Hope, R. A. (1990). A community based study of aggressive behaviour in dementia. *International Journal of Geriatric Psychiatry, 5,* 337–342.

Welden, S. & Yesavage, J. A. (1982). Behavioral improvement with relaxation training in senile dementia. *Clinical Gerontologist, 1,* 45–49.

Wilson, B. A. (1989). Designing memory-therapy programmes. In L. W. Poon, D. C. Rubin, & B. A. Wilson (Eds.), *Everyday cognition in adulthood and late life* (pp. 615–638). Cambridge: Cambridge University Press.

Woods, R. T. (1983). Specificity of learning in reality orientation sessions: a single-case study. *Behaviour Research & Therapy, 21,* 173 - 175.

Woods, R. T. (1996). Cognitive approaches to the management of dementia. In R. G. Morris (Ed.), *The cognitive neuropsychology of Alzheimer-type dementia* (pp. 310–326). Oxford: Oxford University Press.

Woods, R. T. & Britton, P. G. (1985). *Clinical psychology with the elderly.* London: Croom Helm / Chapman Hall.

Woods, R. T., Phibbs, E. & Steele, H. (2000). Attachment and care-giving in dementia. Paper presented at BPS PSIGE Annual Conference, Birmingham.

Yale, R. (1995). *Developing support groups for individuals with early stage Alzheimer's disease: planning, implementation and evaluation.* Baltimore: Health Profession Press.

Zanetti, O., Binetti, G., Magni, E., Rozzini, L., Bianchetti, A. & Trabucchi, M. (1997). Procedural memory stimulation in Alzheimer's disease: impact of a training programme. *Acta Neurologica Scandinavica, 95,* 152–157.

Zanetti, O., Vallotti, B., Frisoni, G. B., Geroldi, C., Bianchetti, A., Pasqualetti, P. & Trabucchi, M. (1999). Insight in dementia: when does it occur? Evidence for a non-linear relationship between insight and cognitive status. *Journal of Gerontology, 54B,* 100–106.

[15]
Reality Orientation for Geriatric Patients

LUCILLE R. TAULBEE, R.N., B.S., *Clinical Supervisor*
JAMES C. FOLSOM, M.D., *Acting Director*
Veterans Administration Hospital
Tuscaloosa, Alabama

IN OUR geriatric unit we have 180 psychiatric, medically infirm patients, most of whom are ambulatory. They were sent to the unit because they were confused, disoriented, and lost to themselves and their families. Some younger men who suffered brain damage as the result of accidents are included. When they arrived, they all were frightened, unhappy, and uncomfortable people, but their look of hopelessness soon changed to hopefulness when we told them their names, where they were, and what date and day of the week it was. Thus we launched our unit program of reality orientation.

In planning this program, we benefited from the experiences of other hospitals that had developed similar programs through trial and error. One of the earliest reality-orientation programs was called the "aide-centered activity program for elderly patients" and was initiated in 1958 at Winter Veterans Administration Hospital in Topeka, Kansas. The nursing assistants, who spent more time with patients than anyone else did, took on responsibilities that extended far beyond the daily physical care of their charges. They became members of the rehabilitation team, which met frequently to plan individual treatment for the patients.

In 1961 a similar program was established at the Mental Health Institute, Mount Pleasant, Iowa, where the personnel were dedicated to the belief that elderly mentally ill patients can be treated with some success. Team members set about proving this on the active-treatment geriatrics ward. They learned that, above all, the staff must not give up hope and must not let the patients give up hope. In addition they learned that no patient behavior is too minor to be significant, and that they should share all their observations with one another. They learned to look at their own behavior and see how it affected others. Most important, they learned how to work together to help bring patients back to reality.

Our present reality-orientation program is a modification of these two programs and of our own first reality-orientation project, which was established in 1963. We learned that confused patients are not ready for remotivation until after they have graduated from reality orientation; as a result we keep the two programs separate. We have added half-hour classroom sessions to reinforce the 24-hour orientation process. The patients are divided into basic and advanced classes: the basic group attends twice a day, seven days a week; the advanced group attends only one class a day, Monday through Friday. When the patient's progress report and staff observations show he is ready, he is promoted from the basic to the advanced class. Consistency is emphasized: the same two nursing assistants are regularly assigned to instruct the classes, and the same personnel relieve them on their days off.

During the classes, which have four patients each, the instructor presents basic personal and current information over and over to each patient, beginning with the patient's name, where he is, and the date. Only when he has relearned these basic facts is the patient presented with other facts, such as his age, hometown, and former occupation.

Classroom materials include individual calendars, word-letter games, blackboard, felt board, mock-up clock, unit building blocks for coordination and color matching, plastic numbers, and large-piece puzzles. A prominent classroom feature is the reality-orientation board, which lists the name of the hospital and its location; the current year, month, and day of the week; the name of the next meal; the weather; and other details.

The teaching process goes on continually, in the classroom, individually on the unit, and in reality-orientation groups. Throughout the program each patient wears a name plate, his bed bears a name tape, and there is a name card at his place at the dining room table.

Reality orientation is ideally suited for the patient with a moderate to severe degree of organic

---

The authors express their appreciation to all members of the treatment team who participated in developing this program, especially to Margaret Keller, R.N., the unit head nurse.

The reality-orientation board and some other equipment used in the classes are displayed by one of the nursing assistants, Robert A. Mitchell, who serves as an instructor for most of the reality-orientation classes. The content of the program is kept simple, personal, and repetitive; it is designed to help confused geriatric or brain-damaged patients to relearn the basic facts about themselves, their homes, and their daily environment.

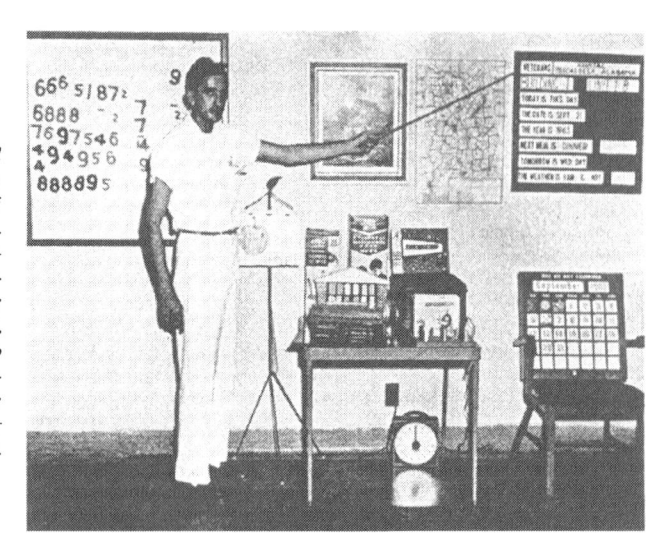

cerebral deficit, usually the result of arteriosclerosis. His first symptom may have been absent-mindedness. His friends began to avoid him. His family began to show anxiety and became worried about his loss of recent memory and his aimless wanderings about town. Frequently, partial or complete loss of vision, hearing, or speech accelerated the downhill process.

Our objective is to reverse this process. After a psychological evaluation has been completed, the members of the treatment team interview each patient; they prescribe the reality-orientation program if they feel he can benefit from it. We then attempt to correct as far as possible any loss of hearing, sight, or speech.

We begin the patient's re-education by helping him use the part of his cerebral function that is still intact. The team approach is the most effective, because a consistent attitude can be maintained by everyone dealing with a particular patient. The attitude adopted is one of active or passive friendliness; it is supportive and makes the patient feel that he is worth something after all, that he can still accomplish something, that life has not passed him by, and that there are still people in the world who care about him. The therapeutic atmosphere is quiet and calm. The demands are minimal; the patient progresses slowly in the treatment program. When he masters one simple task, his accomplishment is made known to the entire team. This is important, because nursing personnel on the day, evening, and night shifts may see the patient in different ways.

We keep detailed individual records that reflect progress. These records have sometimes shown that a patient has regressed; on review, we have found that either his medication has been changed or the dosage adjusted. The records also help his family understand the problems involved, so that they can deal with them later without anxiety or anger. Short home visits can be planned as the patient progresses; family members can also take him outside the hospital to restaurants, clothing stores, or the barber shop, provided they keep in mind how much anxiety he can tolerate.

Mr. A is one of our favorite success stories. He came to us in a state of utter confusion. He is 72 years old, and his family reported that he had suddenly become a problem at home because he was totally unaware of his surroundings. After being interviewed in a treatment planning conference, he was placed on the reality-orientation program. We soon learned that he could neither read nor write his name. He would mark an X to indicate his signature.

After four weeks in the program, Mr. A could print his name and other simple words. His confusion lifted, perhaps in part because his medication had been reduced. He was so enthusiastic about his progress in learning to write that he asked if he could continue to go to school after he returned home. He discussed this idea with his brother, who also was unable to read or write; plans were made for both of them to attend adult training classes in a nearby community.

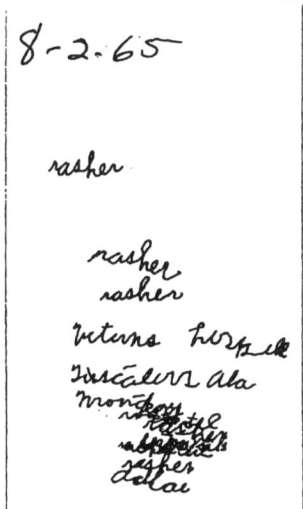

One patient's progress in the reality-orientation program is shown in his attempts to sign his name. On the sheet of paper reproduced at left, the instructor printed the patient's name; the patient's efforts to copy it produced only a black scribble. Four months later he was able to write his name and other data in a legible, if tremulous, fashion. He used capitals properly. The first letters of his name have been deleted here.

Mr. R, 73, is a psychiatric patient who has been hospitalized since 1923. When he came into the program, he had not spoken a word for 15 years. He is ambulatory and was placed in the program in the hope that he could learn enough about time and place to obtain privileges and go to off-ward activities unescorted. We hoped also that the classes might induce him to talk again. Accordingly, he was given the same opportunity as his classmates to recite individually. His progress was very slow. At the beginning his only response was to print his name if the instructor guided his hand and pencil. After three and a half months, however, he would go to the blackboard when his name was called and write his own name and the names of the other class members. He would go up to the reality-orientation board when he was asked to do so, but would merely stand while the instructor read the lines for him. Now, after seven and a half months, Mr. R reads aloud the entire reality-orientation board to the class. He talks with personnel outside the classroom and goes to off-unit activities, including trips to the canteen to enjoy a coffee break with the other patients in the program.

Mr. G, 75, has organic brain damage and so far has made only minimal progress in the reality-orientation program. He made only one response to any question: "Jasper, as quick as I can." These seemed to be the only words he knew. After three weeks in the class, he knows his name, but usually starts to count the letters instead of spelling them. He seems to enjoy the classwork, and although he is making little progress, he has been kept in the program. We plan to work with him more intensively, using picture recognition and word/picture association.

The program has now been in effect for one year, and 64 patients have been assigned to it. Seventeen have completed basic and advanced courses. Five of these have been discharged from the hospital; one is on a trial visit at home; one is in the community placement program; two have been transferred to facilities requiring self-care; and eight are in remotivation groups and have privilege cards.

We have recently selected patients to take part in a research project to evaluate the effectiveness of the program. Three groups of disoriented patients are being compared. One group is assigned to the orientation program in its present form. The progress of this group will be compared with that of another group scheduled only in the usual hospital activities. The third group is in the orientation program and also receives money for correct answers, to determine whether or not such rewards can speed up the orientation process.

Although the study is not completed, we believe that the benefits derived from our reality-orientation program demonstrate its potential value for general medical and surgical patients, such as those suffering from postoperative confusion, and those disoriented through cerebral vascular accident. If reality orientation were made part of an established program in preventive nursing for such patients, we believe that fewer of them would have to be sent to psychiatric units.

(25)

Efficacy of an evidence-based cognitive stimulation therapy programme for people with dementia

Randomised controlled trial

AIMEE SPECTOR, LENE THORGRIMSEN, BOB WOODS, LINDSAY ROYAN, STEVE DAVIES, MARGARET BUTTERWORTH and MARTIN ORRELL

Background A recent Cochrane review of reality orientation therapy identified the need for large, well-designed, multi-centre trials.

Aims To test the hypothesis that cognitive stimulation therapy (CST) for older people with dementia would benefit cognition and quality of life.

Method A single-blind, multi-centre, randomised controlled trial recruited 201 older people with dementia. The main outcome measures were change in cognitive function and quality of life. An intention-to-treat analysis used analysis of covariance to control for potential variability in baseline measures.

Results One hundred and fifteen people were randomised within centres to the intervention group and 86 to the control group. At follow-up the intervention group had significantly improved relative to the control group on the Mini-Mental State Examination ($P=0.044$), the Alzheimer's Disease Assessment Scale – Cognition (ADAS–Cog) ($P=0.014$) and Quality of Life – Alzheimer's Disease scales ($P=0.028$). Using criteria of 4 points or more improvement on the ADAS–Cog the number needed to treat was 6 for the intervention group.

Conclusion The results compare favourably with trials of drugs for dementia. CST groups may have worthwhile benefits for many people with dementia.

Declaration of interest None. Funding detailed in Acknowledgements.

Psychological treatments for dementia, such as reality orientation, have been in use for nearly half a century (Taulbee & Folsom, 1966). Despite their longevity, their effects remain open to question and many studies have been either small, of poor methodological quality, or both (Orrell & Woods, 1996). Reality orientation operates through the presentation and repetition of orientation information, either throughout the day ('24-hour') or in groups meeting on a regular basis to engage in orientation-related activities ('classroom') (Brook et al, 1975). A recent Cochrane review found that reality orientation was associated with significant improvements in both cognition and behaviour, but also identified a need for large, well-designed, multi-centre trials (Spector et al, 1998, 2000). The results of the Cochrane review were used to develop a programme of evidence-based therapy focused on cognitive stimulation (Spector et al, 2001). The cognitive stimulation therapy was piloted in three care homes and one day centre, leading to improvements in cognition and depression for people participating in the programme compared with the control group (Spector et al, 2001). The aim of the study reported here was to evaluate the effects of cognitive stimulation therapy groups on cognition and quality of life for people with dementia, in a single-blind, multi-centre, randomised controlled trial (RCT).

METHOD

Participants

A total of 169 day centres and residential homes with a minimum of 15 residents each (to maximise numbers of suitable participants) were contacted in the participating areas (the National Health Service Trusts for Barking, Havering and Brentwood, Tower Hamlets, Enfield, and Camden and Islington, as well as Quantum Care, a voluntary organisation in Hertfordshire). The researchers investigated all interested centres (day centres and residential homes) to determine whether there were adequate numbers of potential participants with dementia, by using an inclusion criteria flow chart. A minimum of eight or more eligible people were required in each centre, because five were needed for the group, leaving three or more control participants.

Inclusion criteria

People were considered suitable for full assessment and participation if they:

(a) met the DSM–IV criteria for dementia (American Psychiatric Association, 1994);

(b) scored between 10 and 24 on the Mini-Mental State Examination (MMSE; Folstein et al, 1975);

(c) had some ability to communicate and understand communication – a score of 1 or 0 in questions 12 and 13 of the Clifton Assessment Procedures for the Elderly – Behaviour Rating Scale (CAPE–BRS; Pattie & Gilleard, 1979);

(d) were able to see and hear well enough to participate in the group and make use of most of the material in the programme, as determined by the researcher;

(e) did not have major physical illness or disability which could affect participation;

(f) did not have a diagnosis of a learning disability.

Design and process of randomisation

In residential homes and day centres with at least eight suitable participants, full assessments were conducted in the week prior to, and the week following, the intervention by a researcher masked to group membership. Groups were established in 23 centres (18 residential homes and 5 day centres). Of 292 people screened, 201 participants (115 treatment, 86 control) entered the study (Fig. 1). There were more people in the intervention group because frequently centres had only eight or nine suitable participants, and five of these had to be randomised to the intervention group. Control group participants from each centre continued with usual activities while the group therapy was in progress. For most residential homes 'usual activities' consisted of doing nothing. For the other centres, usual activities included games such as bingo, music and singing, arts and crafts, and activity groups. Within each centre, one researcher (the therapist) ran the group and the other (the assessor) conducted initial and follow-up assessments, ensuring masking. Participants were randomly allocated into treatment and control groups. The assessor ordered the names of the selected participants for each centre alphabetically and allocated numbers in sequence according to the total number to be randomised (8–10). The therapist independently placed identical numbered discs into a sealed container and the first five numbers to be drawn out formed the treatment group. The appropriate multi-centre and local research ethics committees granted ethical approval. Informed consent was obtained from participants. After an explanation of the study, those who agreed to participate were asked to sign the consent form in the presence of a witness (usually a member of staff). People whom the staff felt were too impaired to understand the nature of the study were excluded, and it usually followed that they were too impaired to participate in the groups. Using the results from our pilot study, we estimated that a sample size of 64 in each group was required to achieve 80% power to detect a difference in means of 2 points (MMSE). This assumed that the common standard deviation was 4.0, using a two-group t-test with a 0.05 (two-sided) significance level.

The programme

The 14-session programme ran twice a week for 45 min per session over 7 weeks. It was designed using the theoretical concepts of reality orientation and cognitive stimulation. It largely focused on a trial of cognitive stimulation (Breuil et al, 1994), which was identified through the systematic reviews as having the most significant results. Topics included using money, word games, the present day and famous faces. The programme included a 'reality orientation board', displaying both personal and orientation information, including the group name (chosen by participants). The board was to provide a focus, reminding people of the name and nature of the group, and creating continuity. Each session began with a warm-up activity, typically a softball game. This was a gentle, non-cognitive exercise, aiming to provide continuity and orientation by beginning all sessions in the same way. Sessions focusing on themes (such as childhood and food) allowed the natural process of reminiscence but had an additional focus on the current day. Multisensory stimulation was introduced when possible. Sessions encouraged the use of information processing rather than factual knowledge. For example, in the 'faces' activity, people were asked, 'Who looks the youngest?' 'What do these people have in common?', with factual information as an optional extra. A range of activities for each session enabled the facilitator to adapt the level of difficulty of the activities to take into account the group's cognitive capabilities, interests and gender mix. The 14-session programme has been previously described in depth (Spector et al, 2001).

Assessment measures

Cognition

The primary outcome variable was the MMSE (Folstein et al, 1975). This is a brief, widely used test of cognitive function, with good reliability and validity. The secondary outcome variable was the Alzheimer's Disease Assessment Scale – Cognition (ADAS–Cog; Rosen et al, 1984); this is a more sensitive scale measuring cognitive function and including more items that assess short-term memory. It is frequently used in drug trials as the principal cognitive measure, allowing the effects of cognitive stimulation therapy to be compared with antidementia drugs.

Quality of life

The Quality of Life – Alzheimer's Disease scale (QoL–AD; Logsdon et al, 1999) was used as a secondary outcome variable; it has 13 items covering the domains of physical health, energy, mood, living situation, memory, family, marriage, friends, chores, fun, money, self, and life as a whole. This brief, self-report questionnaire has good internal consistency, validity and reliability (Thorgrimsen et al, 2003).

Communication

The Holden Communication Scale (Holden & Woods, 1995), which is completed by staff, covers a range of social behaviour and communication variables, including conversation, awareness, pleasure, humour and responsiveness.

Behaviour

The Clifton Assessment Procedures for the Elderly – Behaviour Rating Scale (CAPE–BRS; Pattie & Gilleard, 1979) covers general behaviour, personal care and behaviour towards others. It has good reliability and validity, and was included to assess the overall level of functional impairment and dependency.

Global functioning

The Clinical Dementia Rating scale (CDR; Hughes et al, 1982), completed by the researcher, provided a global rating of dementia severity at baseline.

Depression

The Cornell Scale for Depression in Dementia (Alexopoulos et al, 1988) rates depression in five broad categories (mood-related signs, behavioural disturbance, physical signs, biological functions and ideational disturbance) using information from interviews with staff and participants. Good reliability and validity have been demonstrated.

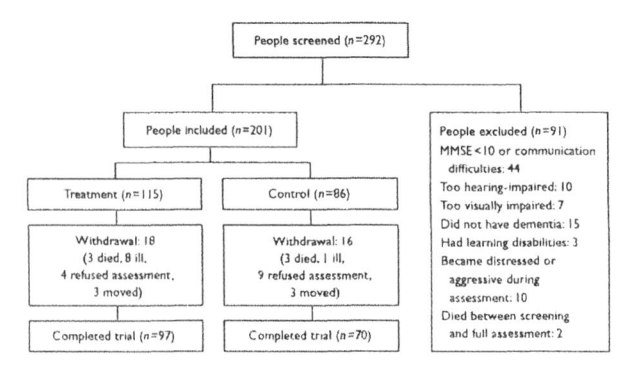

Fig. 1 Profile of trial and attrition. MMSE, Mini-Mental State Examination.

People screened (n=292)
People included (n=201)
Treatment (n=115)
Control (n=86)
Withdrawal: 18 (3 died, 8 ill, 4 refused assessment, 3 moved)
Withdrawal: 16 (3 died, 1 ill, 9 refused assessment, 3 moved)
Completed trial (n=97)
Completed trial (n=70)
People excluded (n=91)
MMSE <10 or communication difficulties: 44
Too hearing-impaired: 10
Too visually impaired: 7
Did not have dementia: 15
Had learning disabilities: 3
Became distressed or aggressive during assessment: 10
Died between screening and full assessment: 2

Table 1 Characteristics and scores of participants at baseline assessment

Characteristics	Treatment group (n=115)	Control group (n=86)	All (n=201)
Age (years): mean (s.d.)	85.7 (6.2)	84.7 (7.9)	85.3 (7.0)
Female:male ratio[1]	4.0:1 (96, 24)	3.3:1 (62, 19)	3.7:1 (158, 43)
MMSE score: mean (s.d.)	14.2 (3.9)	14.8 (3.8)	14.4 (3.8)
ADAS–Cog score: mean (s.d.)	27.4 (7.2)	26.8 (7.9)	27.0 (7.5)
CDR score: mean (s.d.)	1.4 (0.5)	1.4 (0.5)	1.4 (0.5)
QoL–AD score: mean (s.d.)	33.2 (5.9)	33.3 (5.7)	33.3 (5.8)
Cornell score: mean (s.d.)	5.2 (5.0)	6.9 (4.7)	5.5 (4.9)
RAID score: mean (s.d.)	8.4 (8.0)	10.1 (8.5)	9.1 (8.2)
CAPE–BRS score: mean (s.d.)	11.3 (4.7)	11.5 (5.1)	11.4 (4.8)
Holden score: mean (s.d.)	11.1 (5.9)	9.9 (5.5)	10.6 (5.7)

ADAS–Cog, Alzheimer's Disease Assessment Scale – Cognition; CAPE–BRS, Clifton Assessment Procedures for the Elderly – Behaviour Rating Scale; CDR, Clinical Dementia Rating; Cornell, Cornell Scale for Depression in Dementia; Holden, Holden Communication Scale; MMSE, Mini-Mental State Examination; QoL–AD, Quality of Life – Alzheimer's Disease; RAID, Rating Anxiety in Dementia.
1. Actual n in parentheses.

Anxiety

Anxiety was assessed using the scale Rating Anxiety in Dementia (RAID; Shankar et al, 1999); this rates anxiety in four main categories (worry, apprehension and vigilance, motor tension, and automatic hypersensitivity) using interviews with staff and participants. It has good validity and reliability.

Analysis

Data were entered into the Statistical Package for the Social Sciences, version 10 for Windows (SPSS, 2001). An intention-to-treat analysis was conducted and analysis of covariance (ANCOVA) was chosen as the method of analysis because it controls for variability in pre-test scores (the 'covariate'; Vickers & Altman, 2001). Age, gender and baseline score on the scale being examined were entered as covariates, together with 'centre' entered as a random factor, because treatment was defined as participation in the group programme within the confines of one of the 23 centres.

RESULTS

Of the 115 participants in the treatment group 97 were assessed at follow-up, as were 70 of the 86 control participants (Fig. 1). The mean attendance was 11.6 sessions (s.d.=3.2, range 2–14) and 89% of people attended seven or more sessions. Table 1 compares treatment and control participants' characteristics in terms of age, gender and baseline scores and provides information about the total participant group. We attempted to collect data on years of education but in the vast majority of instances this was not available. None of the participants had been prescribed an acetylcholinesterase inhibitor.

Difference between groups at follow-up

In Table 2, significance levels set at 5% are presented from the ANCOVA comparing groups (treatment and control) in all instances. Significant results for covariates (centre and/or gender) are included when they occurred. At follow-up, the treatment group had significantly higher scores on MMSE and ADAS–Cog and rated their quality of life (QoL–AD) more positively than the control group did, and the confidence intervals for the differences between groups were above zero for all three measures. There was a trend towards an improvement in communication in the treatment group (P=0.09) but no difference between the groups in terms of functional ability (CAPE–BRS), anxiety or depression. Centre emerged as a significant covariate in relation to ADAS–Cog, Holden Communication Scale, Cornell and RAID scales,

Table 2 Change from baseline in measures of efficacy at follow-up: intention-to-treat analysis

Efficacy measure[1]	Change from baseline Treatment Mean (s.d.)	Change from baseline Control Mean (s.d.)	Group difference Mean (s.e.)	Group difference 95% CI	ANCOVA: between-group difference	ANCOVA: other significant differences[1]
MMSE	+0.9 (3.5)	−0.4 (3.5)	+1.14 (0.09)	0.57 to 2.27	F=4.14, P=0.044	None
ADAS–Cog	+1.9 (6.2)[3]	−0.3 (5.5)[4]	+2.37 (0.87)	0.64 to 4.09	F=6.18, P=0.014	C: P=0.006
QoL–AD	+1.3 (5.1)	−0.8 (5.6)	+1.64 (0.78)	0.09 to 3.18	F=4.95, P=0.028	G: P=0.010
Holden	+0.2 (6.1)	−3.2 (6.3)	+2.3 (0.93)	−0.45 to 4.15	F=2.92, P=0.090	C: P=0.009; G: P=0.001
CAPE–BRS	−0.2 (6.1)	−0.7 (5.5)	+0.40 (0.65)	−0.9 to 1.69	F=0.58, P=0.449	C: P<0.001; G: P=0.001
RAID	−0.5 (10.2)	−0.7 (10.3)	−1.30 (1.10)	−3.48 to 0.87	P=0.200	C: P<0.001
Cornell	0 (6.2)	−0.5 (7.0)	+0.12 (0.72)	−1.56 to 1.31	P=0.648	C: P<0.001

ADAS–Cog, Alzheimer's Disease Assessment Scale – Cognition; ANCOVA, analysis of covariance; CAPE–BRS, Clifton Assessment Procedures for the Elderly – Behaviour Rating Scale; Cornell, Cornell Scale for Depression in Dementia; Holden, Holden Communication Scale; QoL–AD, Quality of Life – Alzheimer's Disease; RAID, Rating Anxiety in Dementia.
1. Primary outcome measure: MMSE; secondary outcome measures: ADAS–Cog and QoL–AD.
2. C, difference between centres; G, difference between genders.
3. Zero or more points improvement: n=58 (50%); 4 or more points improvement: n=34 (30%).
4. Zero or more points improvement: n=32 (37%); 4 or more points improvement: n=11 (13%).

Table 3 Numbers needed to treat: comparison of cognitive stimulation therapy with antidementia drug trials

Treatment	Analysis 1[1] NNT (95% CI)	Analysis 2[1] NNT (95% CI)
CST programme	8 (4–144)	6 (4–17)
Rivastigmine, 6–12 mg (Corey-Bloom et al, 1998; Rösler et al, 1999)	4 (3–6)	13 (7–11)
Donepezil, 5 mg	5 (4–9)	10 (5–180)
Donepezil, 10 mg (Rogers et al, 1998)	5 (3–8)	4 (3–7)
Galantamine, 32 mg (Wilcock et al, 2000)	5 (4–8)	6 (4–9)
Tacrine,[2] 160 mg (Knapp et al, 1994)		7 (3–10)

CST, cognitive stimulation therapy; NNT, number needed to treat.
1. Analysis 1 – Alzheimer's Disease Assessment Scale – Cognition score with no deterioration as improvement; analysis 2 – same score with increase of 4 or more as improvement.
2. Tacrine is not licensed for use in the UK.

and CAPE–BRS score. A number of gender differences emerged. Quality of life for women in the treatment group improved more than that for the men, whereas the quality of life for men in the control group deteriorated significantly more than it did for the women. Dependency levels (CAPE–BRS) and communication (Holden) also deteriorated for men in the treatment group (though less than for the men in the control group). In contrast, women in the treatment group improved on both measures whereas women in the control group deteriorated (though less than the men in the control group).

Numbers needed to treat

The number needed to treat (NNT) is a calculation of the number of people who needed to be treated in a particular intervention in order to achieve one favourable outcome. It is calculated as the reciprocal of the 'absolute risk reduction': the difference in the proportion experiencing a specified adverse outcome between the control and treatment groups. Using the formulae and framework provided in a previous study (Livingston & Katona, 2000) including acetylcholinesterase inhibitors, two NNT analyses using the ADAS–Cog scores were performed in this study (Table 3):

(a) when calculating no deterioration (score ≥0) as improvement and any deterioration (<0) as adverse, 50% of the treatment group improved compared with 37% of the control group: thus eight people needed to be treated in order for one to benefit (95% CI 4–144);

(b) when calculating an increase in score of 4 or over as improvement and 3 or below as adverse, 30% of the treatment group improved compared with 13% of the control group: thus six people needed to be treated in order for one to benefit (95% CI 4–17).

DISCUSSION

Major findings

This evidence-based programme of cognitive stimulation therapy showed significant improvements in two measures of cognition, including the MMSE (the primary outcome measure), and also in the QoL–AD (a secondary outcome measure). The improvements in cognition are consistent with the findings of earlier studies (Woods, 1979; Breuil et al, 1994). The overall ADAS–Cog (a secondary outcome measure) change indicated improvement in a number of factors. With the exception of explicit rehearsal in place orientation, which is directly questioned, there was no obvious reason why participation in groups should have had a direct practice effect on any other tasks in the ADAS–Cog, such as word recall or recognition. This suggests that generalised cognitive benefits resulted from inclusion in the programme. Nevertheless, such groups probably need to be ongoing, at least weekly, to increase the chance of the relative benefits being sustained.

Contrary to the Cochrane review (Spector et al, 1998) we found no change in behaviour in this study (and the former review found only one individual trial that demonstrated a significant difference in behaviour (Baines et al, 1987)). Changes in cognition might be unlikely to have any impact on areas of functional dependence described in the CAPE–BRS, such as feeding and dressing (Woods, 1996). Other authors (Zanetti et al, 1995) have suggested that behavioural outcome measures are often not sensitive enough to detect the functional impact of cognitive stimulation programmes. There were positive trends in communication, which had not been shown empirically in any of the earlier reality orientation trials. Communication is a factor that is likely to deteriorate in individuals moving into residential care, yet the small-group context was probably novel for many of the participants, perhaps exercising long unused communication skills. It is not known why women reacted more favourably to the programme. For men, being in the minority in most groups could have created discomfort and a reluctance to communicate.

Variation between centres

There was a significant variation between centres from baseline to follow-up in measures of cognition (ADAS–Cog), behaviour, mood and communication. Some centres appeared more institutionalised, and in these there were poor staff–patient relationships and functioning was not optimised. Thus, it might have been the case that the effects of groups were not strong enough to combat the effects of a negative environment. Moreover, in some centres with a better quality of social environment, perhaps including a local programme of activities, residents might have been functioning near their optimum, leaving little scope for improvement. Groups including people at different stages of dementia were sometimes difficult to run. People with milder dementia could become irritated by people with more severe cognitive impairment, and observing their confusion might have been off-putting and hence detrimental to the group process. Pitching the sessions at an appropriate level was clearly important. It is possible that the social interaction provided by the groups could have been of benefit, but our Cochrane review (Spector et al, 1998) found that in RCTs social groups appeared to be of no benefit to cognition.

Limitations

Rigorous inclusion criteria were necessary to ensure a reasonably homogeneous participant group, and were aimed at recruiting people who were able to participate and less likely to leave the study. This meant many centres were excluded because of insufficient numbers. Cluster randomisation might have been useful in allowing centres with five to seven suitable candidates to be included, but would have had the disadvantage that large numbers of clusters would be needed to ensure statistical power and external validity (Bowling, 1997). More importantly, the significant difference between centres on many scales in this study shows that it would have been difficult to ensure the comparability of clusters. Outside the context of a research trial, groups would probably be selected through clinical judgement, considering how people would mix; and people with poorer vision or hearing, or with greater communication difficulties, might be included to make up numbers.

There were a number of other limitations. In the randomisation procedure ideally the generation of the allocation sequence, enrolment into the trial and allocation to group should be separate and performed by different, independent staff. Differences in control conditions between centres meant that the 'control group' was not homogeneous; however, 'usual activities' generally meant doing nothing. Last, in contrast to the results on the primary and secondary outcome measures which were rated directly with the participants, none of the scales rated by staff (e.g. mood, communication, behaviour) showed significant improvements for the cognitive stimulation therapy group. Staff perceptions about the therapy groups might have introduced a bias into the ratings of the scales. We took precautions to avoid this by ensuring that the local member of staff who acted as co-therapist was not involved in completion of the rating scales. However, it is likely that other staff could have been aware of which people were in the groups and this might have influenced their ratings.

Comparison with acetylcholinesterase inhibitors

Number-needed-to-treat analyses were previously performed for three acetylcholinesterase inhibitors: tacrine, rivastigmine and donepezil (Livingston & Katona, 2000). Analyses were performed identically in this study, considering two levels of change as improvement, so that a direct comparison could be made (Table 3). Calculations were also included for galantamine, using the results from another trial (Wilcock et al, 2000). These comparisons show that for small improvements or no deterioration, the programme was not quite as effective as rivastigmine, donepezil and galantamine. For greater improvements (4 or more points), cognitive stimulation therapy did as well as galantamine or tacrine and substantially better than rivastigmine or the lower dosage of donepezil (5 mg). Only the higher dosage of donepezil (10 mg) had a smaller NNT. These results are particularly interesting considering that the drug programmes lasted for 24 weeks, 26 weeks or 30 weeks compared with only 7 weeks of cognitive stimulation therapy. However, since these drug studies applied only to Alzheimer's disease, and since drug therapy and psychological therapy are different forms of treatment, some caution is required when interpreting these comparisons.

Mechanisms for change

There are a number of possible mechanisms of change. The learning environment during sessions was designed to be optimal for people with dementia, for example by focusing on implicit memory and integrating reminiscence and multi-sensory stimulation throughout the programme. Stimulation in the group could improve cognition and might make participants feel more able to communicate. The groups could work against the excess disability due to the 'malignant social psychology' of a negative social environment (Kitwood, 1997) by improving self-esteem through social stimulation and encouragement. Finally, groups positively reinforced questioning, thinking and interacting with other people, objects and the environment. This effect might have extended beyond the groups, with people communicating more effectively and responding to the environment and to others.

Recent research has highlighted strategies that can involve memory training and cognitive stimulation programmes. Providing participants with 'didactic training' (forming mental images of words) and 'problem solving' (practical steps to manage daily problems, such as using notebooks and calendars) has been shown to result in small but short-lived changes in memory performance (Zarit et al, 1982). The use of external memory aids, such as diaries, calendars, large clocks and clear signposting, is becoming increasingly common for people with dementia. Research is also identifying ways of creating an optimal learning environment: for example, 'errorless learning' involves encouraging people, when learning new information, only to respond when they are sure that they are correct, thus avoiding interference effects; and 'spaced retrieval' involves learning and retaining information by recalling information over increasingly long periods (Clare & Woods, 2001).

Implications

This study found improvements in both the primary (MMSE) and secondary (ADAS–Cog and QoL–AD) outcome measures for people in the cognitive stimulation therapy group. Although there is a body of research on the various psychological interventions for dementia, much of it lacks methodological rigour and might not be considered 'evidence-based'. The previous RCTs were small, with the largest having 56 participants (Breuil et al, 1994), and could be criticised for weaknesses such as lack of standardisation of groups, selection and detection biases, and absence of intention-to-treat analyses. Our study is the only major evidence-based trial examining the effectiveness of cognitive stimulation therapy for dementia. Some guidelines counsel against the use of cognitive stimulation programmes because of the possibility of adverse reactions such as frustration (American Psychiatric Association, 1997). This study has shown that cognitive improvements are associated with benefits to quality of life rather than deterioration. Indeed, this is the first study to show improvements in quality of life of people with dementia participating in such a programme. The findings suggest that reality orientation groups, which are widely used both throughout the UK and internationally, are likely to be beneficial for many people with dementia and should be regarded more positively by staff, carers and service providers. Future research needs to identify the most effective ways of teaching care staff to implement this programme, the possible benefits of a longer-term cognitive stimulation therapy programme, and the potential effects of combining cognitive stimulation therapy with drug therapy.

ACKNOWLEDGEMENTS

This paper is dedicated to the memory of Margaret Butterworth, who died in December 2002 having worked tirelessly for the needs of carers and people with dementia over many years. The work was led by Dr Martin Orrell, who received funding from the NHS London Regional Office, Research and Development Programme, and Barking, Havering and Brentwood Community NHS Trusts. The views expressed in the publication are those of the authors and not necessarily those of the NHS or the Department of Health. We thank all the residents and staff of the residential homes and day centres who participated in the study. We also thank Professor Stephen Senn, and Pasco Fearon for statistical advice.

REFERENCES

Alexopoulos, G. S., Abrams, P. C., Young, R. C., et al (1988) Cornell Scale for depression in dementia. *Biological Psychiatry*, 23, 271–284.

American Psychiatric Association (1994) *Diagnostic and Statistical Manual of Mental Disorders* (4th edn) (DSM–IV). Washington, DC: APA.

__ (1997) Practice guidelines for the treatment of Alzheimer's disease and other dementias of late life. *American Journal of Psychiatry*, 154 (suppl.), 1–39.

Baines, S., Saxby, P. & Ehlert, K. (1987) Reality orientation and reminiscence therapy. A controlled cross-over study of elderly confused people. *British Journal of Psychiatry*, 151, 222–231.

Bowling, A. (1997) *Research Methods in Health: Investigating Health and Health Services*. Milton Keynes: Open University Press.

Breuil, V., De Rotrou, J., Forette, F., et al (1994) Cognitive stimulation of patients with dementia: preliminary results. *International Journal of Geriatric Psychiatry*, 9, 211–217.

Brook, P., Degun, G. & Maher, M. (1975) Reality orientation, a therapy for psychogeriatric patients: a controlled study. *British Journal of Psychiatry*, 127, 42–45.

Clare, L. & Woods, R. T. (2001) *Cognitive Rehabilitation in Dementia*. Hove: Psychology Press.

Corey-Bloom, J., Anand, R. & Veach, J. (1998) A randomized trial evaluating the efficacy and safety of ENA 713 (rivastigmine tartrate) in patients with mild to moderately severe Alzheimer's disease. ENA 713 B352 Study Group. *International Journal of Geriatric Psychopharmacology*, 1, 55–65.

Folstein, M. F., Folstein, S. E. & McHugh, P. R. (1975) Mini-mental state: a practical method for grading the cognitive state of patients for the clinician. *Journal of Psychiatric Research*, 12, 189–198.

Holden, U. P. & Woods, R. T. (1995) *Positive Approaches to Dementia Care* (3rd edn). Edinburgh: Churchill Livingstone.

Hughes, C. P., Berg, L., Danziger, W. L., et al (1982) A new clinical scale for the staging of dementia. *British Journal of Psychiatry*, 140, 566–572.

Kitwood, T. (1997) *Dementia Reconsidered*. Milton Keynes: Open University Press.

Knapp, M. J., Knopman, D. S., Soloman, P. R., et al (1994) A 30-week randomized controlled trial of high-dose tacrine in patients with Alzheimer's disease. *JAMA*, 271, 985–991.

Livingston, G. & Katona, C. (2000) How useful are cholinesterase inhibitors in the treatment of Alzheimer's disease? A number needed to treat analysis. *International Journal of Geriatric Psychiatry*, 15, 203–207.

Logsdon, R., Gibbons, L. E., McCurry, S. M., et al (1999) Quality of life in Alzheimer's disease: patient and caregiver reports. *Journal of Mental Health and Aging*, 5, 21–32.

Orrell, M. & Woods, B. (1996) Tacrine and psychological therapies in dementia – no contest? Editorial comment. *International Journal of Geriatric Psychiatry*, 11, 189–192.

Pattie, A. H. & Gilleard, C. J. (1979) *Clifton Assessment Procedures for the Elderly (CAPE)*. Sevenoaks: Hodder & Stoughton.

Rogers, S. L., Farlow, M. R., Doody, R. S., et al (1998) A 24-week, double-blind, placebo-controlled trial of donepezil in patients with Alzheimer's disease. Donepezil Study Group. *Neurology*, 50, 136–145.

Rosen, W. G., Mohs, R. C. & Davis, K. L. (1984) A new rating scale for Alzheimer's disease. *American Journal of Psychiatry*, 141, 1356–1364.

Rösler, M., Amand, R., Cicin-Sain, A., et al (1999) Efficacy and safety of rivastigmine in patients with Alzheimer's disease: international randomised controlled trial. *BMJ*, 318, 633–638.

Shankar, K., Walker, M., Frost, D., et al (1999) The development of a valid and reliable scale for anxiety in dementia. *Aging and Mental Health*, 3, 39–49.

Spector, A., Orrell, M., Davies, S., et al (1998) Reality orientation for dementia: a review of the evidence for its effectiveness. *Cochrane Library*, issue 4. Oxford: Update Software.

__, __, __, et al (2000) Reality orientation for dementia: a systematic review of the evidence of effectiveness from randomised controlled trials. *Gerontologist*, 40, 206–212.

__, __, __, et al (2001) Can reality orientation be rehabilitated? Development and piloting of an evidence-based programme of cognition-based therapies for people with dementia. *Neuropsychological Rehabilitation*, 11, 377–397.

SPSS (2001) *SPSS for Windows, Version 10*. Chicago, IL: SPSS.

Taulbee, L. R. & Folsom, J. C. (1966) Reality orientation for geriatric patients. *Hospital and Community Psychiatry*, 17, 133–135.

CLINICAL IMPLICATIONS

■ Cognitive stimulation therapy groups appear to improve both cognitive function and quality of life for people with dementia.

■ The degree of benefit for cognitive function appears similar to that attributable to acetylcholinesterase inhibitors.

■ The groups were popular with the participants, and can be conducted in a variety of settings.

LIMITATIONS

■ To maintain the benefits relative to the control group, it is likely that cognitive stimulation therapy would need to be continued on a regular basis long after the end of the 14-session programme.

■ Staff ratings might have included an element of bias despite efforts to reduce this.

■ Many centres were excluded because they had insufficient numbers or residents fitting the inclusion criteria.

AIMEE SPECTOR, PhD, LENE THORGRIMSEN, BA, Department of Psychiatry and Behavioural Sciences, University College London; BOB WOODS, MSc, Dementia Services Development Centre, University of Wales, Bangor; LINDSAY ROYAN, BA, Department of Clinical Psychology, Petersfield Centre, Harold Hill, London; STEVE DAVIES, MSc, Department of Psychology, Derwent Unit, Princess Alexandra Hospital, Harlow, Essex; MARGARET BUTTERWORTH (deceased), BA, MARTIN ORRELL, PhD, Department of Psychiatry and Behavioural Sciences, University College London, UK

Correspondence: Dr Martin Orrell, Department of Psychiatry and Behavioural Sciences, UCL, Wolfson Building, 48 Riding House Street, London WIN 8AA, UK. Tel: 020 7679 9452; fax: 020 7679 9426; e-mail: m.orrell@ucl.ac.uk

(First received 13 January 2003, final revision 13 May 2003, accepted 13 May 2003)

Thorgrimsen, L., Selwood, A., Spector, A., et al (2003) Whose quality of life is it anyway? The validity and reliability of the Quality of Life – Alzheimer's Disease (QOL–AD) scale. *Alzheimer's Disease and Associated Disorders*, in press.

Vickers, A. J. & Altman, D. G. (2001) Analysing controlled trials with baseline and follow up measurements. *BMJ*, **323**, 1123–1124.

Wilcock, G. K., Lilienfeld, S. & Gaens, E. (2000) Efficacy and safety of galantamine in patients with mild to moderate Alzheimer's disease: multicentre randomised controlled trial. Galantamine International Study Group. *BMJ*, **321**, 1445–1449.

Woods, R. T. (1979) Reality orientation and staff attention: a controlled study. *British Journal of Psychiatry*, **134**, 502–507.

___ (1996) Psychological 'therapies' in dementia. *Handbook of the Clinical Psychology of Ageing* (ed. R. T. Woods), pp. 575–600. Chichester: John Wiley & Sons.

Zanetti, O., Frisoni, G. B., De Leo, D., et al (1995) Reality orientation therapy in Alzheimer's disease: useful or not? A controlled study. *Alzheimer's Disease and Associated Disorders*, **9**, 132–138.

Zarit, S. H., Zarit, J. M. & Reever, K. E. (1982) Memory training for severe memory loss: effects on senile dementia patients and their families. *Gerontologist*, **22**, 373–377.

[17]

Nonpharmacologic Interventions for Inappropriate Behaviors in Dementia

A Review, Summary, and Critique

Jiska Cohen-Mansfield, Ph.D.

Inappropriate behaviors are very common in dementia and impose an enormous toll both emotionally and financially. Three main psychosocial theoretical models have generally been utilized to explain inappropriate behaviors in dementia: the "unmet needs" model, a behavioral/learning model, and an environmental vulnerability/ reduced stress-threshold model. A literature search yielded 83 nonpharmacological intervention studies, which utilized the following categories of interventions: sensory, social contact (real or simulated), behavior therapy, staff training, structured activities, environmental interventions, medical/nursing care interventions, and combination therapies. The majority are reported to have a positive, albeit not always significant, impact. Better matching of the available interventions to patients' needs and capabilities may result in greater benefits to patients and their caregivers. (Am J Geriatr Psychiatry 2001; 9:361–381)

Inappropriate behaviors are very common in dementia and impose an enormous toll both emotionally and financially. These behaviors increase suffering for the person with dementia and burden for caregivers; they prompt utilization of more restrictive care, and result in the application of both pharmacologic and nonpharmacologic treatments. For the purpose of this article, inappropriate behaviors will be defined as "inappropriate verbal, vocal, or motor activity that is not judged by an outside observer to be an obvious outcome of the needs or confusion of the individual."[1] These behaviors have been labeled problem behaviors, disruptive behaviors, disturbing behaviors, behavioral problems, and agitation, all of which are used interchangeably in this article. Inappropriate behaviors may result from depressed affect, but the term refers specifically to observable behavior, rather than internal states. Similarly, delusions and hallucinations are only included to the extent that these are manifested as inappropriate behavior; the core manifestation (i.e., the misinterpretation of reality) is not. Inappropriate behaviors have been divided into four main subtypes:[2] 1) physically aggressive behaviors, such as hitting, kicking or biting; 2) physically nonaggressive behaviors, such as pacing or inappropriately handling objects; 3) verbally nonaggressive agitation, such as constant repetition of sentences or requests; and 4) verbal aggression, such as cursing or screaming. In the past, inappropriate behaviors have been handled with psychotropic drugs or physical restraints, or ignored. Research and clinical observations

Review of Nonpharmacologic Interventions

have questioned these practices, leading to the OBRA '87 mandate to reduce physical and chemical restraints. In response to these developments, a plethora of nonpharmacologic interventions have been initiated. However, our understanding of these interventions, their effects, and their feasibility is limited. This article addresses these issues along the following lines: the underlying assumptions and the importance of nonpharmacologic interventions; results of a literature search on the impact of nonpharmacologic interventions; and barriers to knowledge and implementation of nonpharmacologic interventions.

The Underlying Assumptions and the Importance of Nonpharmacologic Interventions

In order to understand the rationale for the different nonpharmacologic interventions utilized in the research literature, it is important to understand the theoretical framework they embrace in conceptualizing inappropriate behaviors in dementia. Three theoretical models have generally been applied: 1) the "unmet needs" model; 2) a behavioral/learning model; and 3) an environmental vulnerability/reduced stress-threshold model.

Unmet needs. Nonpharmacologic interventions generally aim to address the underlying needs that are causing the inappropriate behavior. As can be surmised from the definition of inappropriate behaviors, these needs are frequently not apparent to the observer or the caregiver, or else caregivers do not feel able to fulfill these needs. Significant proportions of nursing home residents who present inappropriate behaviors suffer from sensory deprivation, boredom, and loneliness. Therefore, providing sensory stimulation, activities, and social contacts are among the most commonly described interventions. A more insightful approach would be to prevent the patients from reaching the point of unmet need and to assist these persons in fulfilling their own needs. The provision of hearing aids may decrease isolation due to sensory deprivation; the provision of an easily accessible outdoor area can provide both activity and sensory stimulation.

Another type of need relates to the quality of care: reduced levels of restraints, sufficient levels of light, good toileting procedures, better communication, proper treatment of pain, etc. Some of the interventions explored, especially those related to staff training, focus on these needs.

Learning/behavioral models. The behavioral model assumes that a connection between antecedents, behavior, and reinforcement has been learned, and that a different learning experience is needed to change the relationship between antecedents and behavior (the ABC model = Antecedents → Behavior → Consequences; where antecedents operate through stimulus control, and the consequences reinforce behavior, or reinforce certain behavior related to specific antecedent stimuli). Many problem behaviors are learned through reinforcement by staff members, who provide attention when problem behavior is displayed. A modification of reinforcement contingencies is needed to change the behavior.

Environmental vulnerability/reduced stress-threshold model. Treatments of reduced stimulation levels or provision of relaxation techniques (e.g., massage) are based on the assumption that the dementia process results in greater vulnerability to the environment and a lower threshold at which stimuli affect behavior. Therefore, a stimulus that may be appropriate for a cognitively intact person may result in overreaction in the cognitively impaired person. According to the concept of progressively lowered stress threshold,[3,4] persons with dementia progressively lose their coping abilities and therefore perceive their environment as more and more stressful. At the same time, their threshold for encountering this stress decreases, resulting in anxiety and inappropriate behavior when the environmental stimuli exceed the threshold for stress. An environment of reduced stimulation is supposed to limit the stress experienced and thereby reduce the level of inappropriate behavior. Similarly, relaxation will reduce the stress and thereby decrease the manifestation of undesirable behavior.

The different models are not mutually exclusive and may be complementary. An environmental vulnerability may make the person who suffers from dementia more susceptible to environmental antecedents and consequences. The environmental vulnerability may produce an unmet need when normal levels of stimulation are perceived as overstimulation. Furthermore, different models may account for different behaviors in different people. As will be seen below, the different models provided the basis for different interventions, and in turn, the relative efficacy of these interventions may be used to indicate the usefulness of the different models.

Advantages of Nonpharmacologic Interventions

The reasons for using a nonpharmacologic interventions approach to treating inappropriate behaviors in dementia include the following: 1) it aims at addressing the psychosocial/environmental underlying reason for the behavior, as documented in previous research; 2) it avoids the limitations of pharmacological interventions, namely, adverse side effects, drug-drug interactions, and limited efficacy;[5,6] and 3) when medication is efficacious, it may mask the actual need by eliminating the behavior that serves as a signal for the need, thereby reducing the already-compromised communication by the elderly person and limiting the caregiver's ability to properly care for him or her.

LITERATURE SURVEY OF EFFICACY OF NONPHARMACOLOGIC INTERVENTIONS

Methods

Literature searches were conducted on PsycLIT, MEDLINE, and a nursing subset of MEDLINE. Articles were chosen that fulfilled the following criteria: 1) published as an article in a scientific book or journal (i.e., excluding presentations, abstracts, and reports); 2) participants were at least 60 years old and suffered from dementia or cognitive impairment; and 3) a measure of the behavior or of change was obtained.

The articles were organized by type of intervention. The categorization is based on the main intervention as presented in the article, but the decision is sometimes arbitrary, such as the differentiation between sensory enhancement and activities, or between outdoor walks and physical activities, which is equivocal. A coding system was developed to describe the studies along the following dimensions: behavior, participants, setting, design, intervention, and findings.

Search Results

Eighty-three articles were identified that met the above criteria. The following categories of interventions were identified (number of articles for each type is listed in parentheses):

- Sensory intervention (for stimulation or relaxation), including: music (11), massage/touch (6), white noise (2), and sensory stimulation (4)
- Social contact (real or simulated), including one-on-one interaction (2), pet visits (3), and simulated presence therapy and videos (4)
- Behavior therapy, including differential reinforcement (7), cognitive (1), and stimulus control (8)
- Staff training (6)
- Activities, including structured activities (3), outdoor walks (2), and physical activities (2)
- Environmental interventions, including wandering areas (2), natural or enhanced environments (2), and reduced-stimulation environments (2)
- Medical/nursing care interventions, including light or sleep therapy (8), pain management (1), hearing aids (1), and removal of restraints (2)
- Combination therapies, including individualized (3) and group treatments (2); (See Table 1)

The largest number of articles was found in the area of sensory enhancement, especially for the provision of music for either stimulation or relaxation. Behavioral interventions had the second-highest number of papers; however, this is the only category where the majority of the articles are case studies or include only small sample sizes (see Figure 1). The vast majority of these articles were published in the 1990s, the exception being articles describing behavioral interventions that were published as early as 1978.[7] Most of the interventions fit within the framework of the unmet-needs model; the behavioral interventions generally coming from a behavioral-theoretical framework, and the reduced-stimulation environments, as well as some of the relaxing sensory interventions, originating with the reduced stress-threshold framework.

Research studies characteristics. The majority of the studies were conducted in residential facilities, primarily in nursing homes (76%, including special care units), with the rest in hospitals (24%), the community, or other types of residential arrangements. Most of the studies examined inappropriate behaviors as a whole and did not examine subtypes of behavior. The assessment methods varied across studies, with some using systematic observations, others utilizing standardized scales of caregivers' ratings or an item from such a scale, and some developing a rating assessment tool for the study. These methods yielded a great variation in what

Review of Nonpharmacologic Interventions

TABLE 1. Intervention articles

Reference	Subjects	Intervention	Findings
Sensory Enhancement/Relaxation			
I. Massage/Touch			
Kilstoff and Chenoweth[61]	N = 16; NHR; clients of a multicultural daycare center in Australia	Gentle hand treatment with three essential oils for 10–15 min.	Analysis of family carers recording showed a decrease of over 20% in wandering and agitation/anxiety
Kim and Buschmann[56]	N = 30; NHR; mean age = 76.58	Hand massage of each hand for 2.5 min., with verbalization	Sig. decrease on E-BEHAVE-AD during treatment time
Rowe and Alfred[62]	N = 14; mean age = 76.77 (68–90), residing in the community	Slow-stroke massage for 5 days	Trend (NS) toward reduction of agitation (BSRS)
Scherder et al.[57]	N = 16; mean age, 85.7 (78–92), residing in a private residence	Massage (rubbing, brushing, kneading, mostly on the back)	No sig. reduction in aggressiveness (BOP)
Snyder et al.[55]	N = 26; AUR; age 60–97	Nurses administered hand massages to residents before care activity	Sig. decrease during the morning only
Snyder et al.[59]	N = 18; AUR; mean age = 77.7 (66–90)	Hand massage, therapeutic touch, administered for 10 days each in the afternoon; (presence used as control condition)	No effect on targeted agitated behavior; sig. effect on anxious (fidgety) behaviors for 3 of the 4- to 5-day intervention periods (not for Presence/Control).
II. Music (during meals, bathing, general)			
Denney[11]	N = 9; NHR; (MMSE: 0–5) mean age = 74.8	"Quiet music" during lunchtime	Sig. decrease in agitation (CMAI-GA)
Goddaer and Abraham[12]	N = 29; NHR; mean age = 81.3 (67–93)	Relaxing music during lunchtime	Sig. decrease in overall agitation (CMAI-GA); no sig. difference in aggressive behaviors
Ragneskog et al.[13]	N = 5; NHR; mean age = 80 (69–94)	Music (soothing, '20s and '30s pop) played during dinnertime	No effect
Clark et al.[9]	N = 18; NHR; mean age = 82 (55–95)	Music during bathing; total of 20 bathing episodes (10 treatment; 10 control)	Sig. decrease in total number of behaviors and hitting behavior
Thomas et al.[10]	N = 14; NHR; ages 69–86	Individualized music played before and during bathing	Sig. reduced aggressive behavior (CMAI-a) during music time
Brotons and Pickett-Cooper[18]	N = 30 in 4 NH; mean age = 82 (70–96)	Music therapy twice per week for 30 min. (singing, playing instruments, music game)	Sig. reduced agitation (DBRS) during music therapy sessions and after music therapy
Cohen-Mansfield and Werner[14]	N = 32; NHR; mean age = 87.8, 97% with dementia	1: videotape of a family member talking to elderly person 2: one-to-one social interaction with research assistant (RA) 3: individualized music tapes, 30 min.	Greatest decrease of VDB during one-to-one interaction, followed by exposure to family video, and then music
Gerdner[63]	N = 39; mean age = 82 years, in a long-term care facility	Individualized music and classical "relaxation" music	Sig. decrease in agitation during individualized music (vs. classical); Sig. decrease during classical music after 20 min. of intervention
Tabloski et al.[17]	N = 20; NHR; mean age = 78.4 (68–74)	Listening to soft music with headphones for 15 min.	Sig. decrease in agitation (ABS) from 24.15 to a mean of 18.45 during intervention
Casby and Holm[64]	1: 87-year-old woman, verbally agitated 2: 77-year-old, verbally agitated 3: 69-year-old man, verbally agitated	A: No intervention B: Relaxing classical music C: Favorite music	Decrease in vocalizations during intervention phase
Gerdner and Swanson[16]	1: 89-year-old woman; MMSE: 0 2: 87-year-old woman; MMSE: 7; exhibiting pacing/wandering 3: 87-year-old woman; MMSE: 5 4: 94-yea-old woman; MMSE: 0	Individually selected music presented on an audio cassette player	1: Trend in decrease of agitation (CMAI-a) and continued after the intervention 2: Decreased agitation on 4 out of 5 days 3: Decreased agitation 4: Decreased agitation

(continued)

TABLE 1. Intervention articles *(continued)*

Reference	Subjects	Intervention	Findings
III. White Noise			
Burgio et al.[19]	N = 13; NHR; mean age = 83.08 (67-99); MMSE: 1.66; verbally agitated	"White noise" audiotapes (environmental sounds)	Sig. decrease (23%) in the 9 responders; (treatment tapes were used in only 51% of the observations)
Young et al.[20]	N = 8; mean age = 70 (60-82); wandering behavior in a geriatric hospital	Modified white noise (slow surf rate) at bedside	No effect overall; two patients individually analyzed showed improvement
IV. Sensory Stimulation			
Holtkamp et al.[65]	N = 17; NHR	Activities in the "snoezelen" room	Decrease of behavioral problems in residents with "snoezelen" activities
Witucki and Twibell[66]	N = 15; mean age = 81.13 (60-95); MMSE: 0-2, in a long-term care facility	Sensory stimulation (music, touch, smell)	Sig. decrease in DS-DAT, particularly in fidgety body language, with each of the sensory stimulation types
Snyder and Olson[67]	N = 5; NHR; mean age = 92	Hand massage or music, each for 10 days	Trend toward decrease in aggressive behavior in each
Brooker et al.[68]	N = 4; NHR; ages: 74, 77, 79, 91	Aromatherapy and/or massage for 10 sessions	Clinical staff impression of benefit to all, but observational data and comparison to control condition show benefit for 2, and sig. decrease in only 1 participant; no advantage of combining massage and aromatherapy; 2 participants manifested increased agitation during treatment
Social Contact: Real or Simulated			
I. Pets			
Churchill et al.[23]	N = 28; AUR; mean age = 83.3	Certified therapy dog for two 30-min. sessions	Sig. decrease in agitation (ABMI) with the dog present
Fritz et al.[24]	N = 64; mean age = 74.6 (53-92), in a private residence	Companion animals	Sig. lower prevalence of verbal aggression and anxiety in pet-exposed patients
Zisselman et al.[22]	n = 33, pets intervention; N = 58 total; only 22% w/ dementia, in a hospital	5 days for 1 hour; pets (dog)	Trend (NS) decrease in irritable behavior (MOSES); no sig. difference between pet and exercise
II. One-to-One Interaction			
Cohen-Mansfield and Werner[41]	N = 41; NHR; verbally agitated	One-on-one social interaction with research assistants (RAs)	Decrease in verbal agitation (five did not complete 10 sessions)
Runci et al.[25]	81-year-old verbally agitated woman in a long-term care facility	1: Music therapy with interaction in English 2: Music therapy with interaction in Italian	Italian interaction sig. reduced noise-making, vs. English interaction
III. Simulated Interaction/Family Videos			
Camberg et al.[69]	N = 54; mean age = 82.7; MMSE: 5.1, in a long-term care facility	Simulated presence: interactive audiotape containing one side of a conversation	Sig. decrease in problem behaviors (SCMAI and observations)
Hall and Hare[70]	N = 36; NHR; mean age = 76.3 (65-98)	Video Respite™, 21-min.-long interactive videotape of music and reminiscence	No effect
Werner et al.[71]	N = 30; NHR; verbally agitated	Family-generated videotapes, 30 min. for 10 consecutive days	46% (sig.) decrease in disruptive behaviors during videotape exposure
Woods and Ashley[72]	N = 27; NHR; age 76-94	Simulated presence: telephone audio recording of caregiver	Sig. decrease of problem behavior 91% of the time

(continued)

Review of Nonpharmacologic Interventions

TABLE 1. Intervention articles *(continued)*

Reference	Subjects	Intervention	Findings
Behavior Therapy			
I. Differential Reinforcement			
Doyle et al.[73]	$N=12$ verbally agitated Ss in a long-term care facility	Reinforcement of quiet behavior and environmental stimulation based on individual preferences	Decrease in noise-making (CMAI) in 3 cases; 4 cases w/ no effect (7 of 12 completed study)
Heard and Watson[74]	$N=4$; NHR; age 79–83; exhibiting wandering	Differential reinforcement = tangible reinforcers (food) Extinction = attention given in the absence of the behavior	Decrease in wandering (from 50% to 80% reduction)
Mishara[7]	$N=80$; mean age = 68.8 ($\pm$ SD 5.1) in a chronic geriatric mental hospital	Token economy: rewards(tokens) for desirable behavior, could then be exchanged for secondary reinforcers General milieu: all secondary reinforcers were available for anyone who wanted them; activities were offered for participation but not rewarded	Sig. decreased behavior in general milieu; trend (NS) decrease in token economy
Rogers et al.[75]	$N=84$; NHR; mean age = 82; mean MMSE: 6.07	Skill elicitation: identify and elicit retained ADL skills; habit training: reinforce and solidify skills	Sig. decrease in disruptive behavior
Birchmore and Clague[76]	70-year-old female NHR; verbally agitated	Stroking back as reward for quiet behavior	Decrease in vocalizations
Boehm et al.[77]	1: 87-year-old woman 2: 55-year-old man	Behavioral plan that prompted calm, cooperative behavior by reinforcing (food, toys, and praise) for each small step toward the desired behavior	1: Decrease of disruptive behavior during bathing 2: Nearly eliminated disruptive behavior during shaving and bathing
Lewin and Lundervold[78]	1: 73-year-old woman, verbally aggressive, in a foster home 2: 76-year-old AU NHR; physically aggressive woman, in a foster home	1: Communication/problem-solving strategy and record keeping record of subject's yelling episodes 2: Implementation of a new routine incompatible with aggression (e.g., supporting herself by holding towel bar)	1: Yelling behavior stopped, even at 1 month follow-up 2: Sig. decrease in aggressive behavior, but variable
II. Stimulus Control			
Chafetz[79]	$N=30$; AUR; mean age = 81; exit-seeking	Placement of two-dimensional grid in front of glass exit doors	No effect
Hussian[80]	$N=5$; mean age = 71.2; inappropriate toileting, bed misidentification, exit-seeking in a long-term care facility	B_1: Verbal and /or physical prompts were given to attend to enhancing stimuli (yellow restroom doors)B_2: stimulus-enhancement alone	Sig. decrease of problem behavior for each resident
Hussian and Brown[81]	$N=8$; mean age = 78.5; hazardous ambulation in a public mental hospital	Various two-dimensional grid patterns placed on floor in front of exit door	Sig. decrease of hazardous ambulation; horizontal superior to vertical configuration
Mayer and Darby[82]	$N=9$; mean age = 77.8; MMSE: ≤ 12; exhibiting wandering behavior in a psychiatric ward	Mirrors in front of exit doors to prevent exiting	Sig. decrease in successful exiting
Bird et al.[83]	1: 73-year-old woman 2: 62-year-old man with frequent visits to bathroom, residing in a private home 3: 83-year-old woman in a hostel w/ anxiety about medication 4: 88-year-old woman, verbally aggressive 5: 83-year-old man; MMSE: 9; urination in corners, residing in a private home	1: Stimulus control (taught to associate stop sign with stopping and walking away) 2: Stimulus control(beeper signal associated with toileting demand) 3: Spaced retrieval with fading cues 4: Spaced retrieval and fading cues 5: Spaced retrieval; taught to associate cue with location of toilet	1: Decrease in inappropriate entries (mean of 43.6 to 2) 2: Decrease in anxiety while wearing beeper, but retained fear of soiling himself 3: Decrease in verbal demands for medication 4: No effect 5: Decrease in inappropriate toileting, although prompting needed at night

(continued)

TABLE 1. Intervention articles (continued)

Reference	Subjects	Intervention	Findings
Hussian[84]	$N = 3$; mean age = 73.4; pacing/wandering in a long-term care facility	First, stimuli (orange arrows, blue circles) were linked to positive and negative consequences (food, loud noise); then, stimuli were placed in areas where participants were encouraged or discouraged to walk, respectively	Decrease of entries into potentially hazardous areas
(Study 2)	$N = 3$; mean age = 74.67; in a long-term care facility	Trained to respond to two stimuli differently; attention to desirable stimulus resulted in reinforcement	Differential reinforcement with stimulus control resulted in reduction of behavior
(Study 3)	64-year-old male NHR; genital exposure and masturbation in lounge areas	1 = rules; 2 = differential reinforcement; 3 = 2 + antecedent enhancement	Decrease in inappropriate behavior in public area and continued at follow-up
III. Cognitive			
Hanley et al.[26]	$N = 57$, in a psychogeriatric hospital and home for elderly	Reality-orientation (RO): cognitive retraining where orientation information is rehearsed	No effect with RO class (GRS)
Staff Training			
Cohen-Mansfield et al.[33]	All NHR in the participating units	In-service training for nursing staff	No effect
Matteson et al.[32]	Original sample: $n = 63$, in a VA nursing home, for treatment group; $N = 30$, in a community nursing home, for control; mean age = 77; mean MMSE: 12.5; Completers: 43 Treatment, 14 Control	Staff training based on adapting ADL activities to resident's level on Piaget's stages; also, environmental modification included cues of colors, symbols, pictures, music, etc.; psychotropic drug withdrawal was also undertaken	No sig. decrease from pre-test to 3 mo., but sig. decreases to 12 and 18 months post-test (NHBPS) for treatment group; control group decreased at 3 and 12 months, but increased to pre-test level at 18 months
McCallion et al.[30]	$N = 105$; NHR	Nursing Aides Communication Skills Program (NACSP)	Sig. reduction in agitated behavior (MOSES and CMAI) for at least 3 months
Mentes and Ferrario[28]	$N = 8$; NHR; physically aggressive	Calming Aggressive Reactions in the Elderly (C.A.R.E): education program for nurse aides	Decrease in agitation from 11 to 9 incidents of staff abuse after the intervention
Wells et al.[31]	$N = 40$; NHR	Educational program on delivering activities; focused monitoring care	Decreased level of agitation (MIBM and PAS)
Williams et al.[29]	$N = 2$; residents of VA special-care unit responsible for many staff injuries	Staff training in small groups, including empathy training, theory training, and skill training	Sig. decrease, from 0.19 to 0.04 incidents per day, according to patient record review
Structured Activities			
I. Structured Activities			
Aronstein et al.[34]	$N = 15$; NHR; mean age = 81 (68–94)	Recreational interventions (manipulatives, nurturing, sorting, sewing, and music)	Decrease in agitation (CMAI) 57% of the time
Groene[53]	$N = 30$; mean age = 77.5 (60–91); pacing/wandering in an Alzheimer unit	Mostly music (playing instruments, singing, dancing) or mostly reading for 7 days	Decreased wandering in music sessions vs. reading sessions
Sival et al.[35]	1: 76-year-old, verbally aggressive woman; 2: 82-year-old, physically agitated woman; 3: 81-year-old man. All in private residences	Activities program outside their units (musical activities, social activities, games, creative works, singing)	Inconclusive (SDAS-9)
II. Outdoor Walks			
Cohen-Mansfield and Werner[37]	$N = 12$; NHR	Escorting residents to an outdoor garden (one-to-one supervision)	Sig. decrease in physically aggressive and nonaggressive behaviors (CMAI)

(continued)

Review of Nonpharmacologic Interventions

TABLE 1. Intervention articles *(continued)*

Reference	Subjects	Intervention	Findings
Holmberg[85]	$N=11$; NHR; wandering and physically aggressive agitation	Group walk through common areas or outside, singing and holding hands	Sig. decrease in agitation on group days vs. non-group days

III. Physical Activities

Buettner et al.[54]	$N=36$; NHR; mean age: 82.4; MMSE: 6.5	Sensorimotor program to improve strength and flexibility vs. a traditional program	Decreased agitation during the sensorimotor vs. the traditional program
Zisselman et al.[22]	$n=25$ in exercise group; $N=58$ total in a hospital; only 22% had dementia	Exercise 5 days for 1 hour	NS trend of decrease in agitation (MOSES)

Environmental Interventions

I. Wandering Areas

McMinn and Hinton[38]	$N=13$ participants in a psychiatric facility	Released from mandatory confinement indoors	Decrease in verbal and physical aggression, especially among men
Namazi and Johnson[39]	$N=22$; AUR; mean age = 80 (69-98)	Unlocking exit door to outside walking paths	Decrease in agitated behaviors (CMAI and DBDS) when door was unlocked

II. Natural/Enhanced Environments

Cohen-Mansfield and Werner[41]	$N=27$; NHR; mean age = 84.4 (75-93)	Enhanced environment (corridors decorated to depict nature and/or family environment)	Decrease in most types of agitation (CMAI) vs. No Scenes
Whall et al.[40]	$N=31$ in five NH	Natural environment (e.g., bird sounds, pictures, food) during bathing	Sig. decrease from baseline to T_1 and T_2 and in treatment group vs. control (CMAI-W)

III. Reduced Stimulation

Cleary et al.[86]	$N=11$; NHR; mean age = 87.2 (81-94)	Reduced Stimulation Unit	Decrease in agitation from 1.7 to 0.8 (4-point scale)
Meyer et al.[42]	$N=11$, residing in an Alzheimer's boarding home	Quiet Week, including no TV/radio; staff used quiet voices and reduced fast movements	Sig. decrease in non-calm behaviors

Medical/Nursing Care Interventions

I. Light Therapy/Sleep

Koss and Gilmore[44]	$N=18$; NHR	Increased light intensity during dinnertime	Sig. decrease in agitated behaviors
Lovell et al.[87]	$N=6$; NHR; mean age = 89.2	Bright light (2,500 Lx) in the morning for 10 days	Sig. decrease in agitation (ABRS)
Lyketsos et al.[88]	$N=15$, in a chronic care facility	Bright-light therapy	No effect (BEHAVE-AD) vs. a control group
Mishima et al.[89]	$N=24$; mean age = 75 in an acute-care hospital	Morning-light therapy	Sig. decrease in problem behaviors from an average of 23.9 to 11.6; also, an increase in nocturnal sleep
Okawa et al.[90]	$N=24$; mean age = 76.6; $n=8$ (controls), in a geriatric ward w/ sleep-wake disorders	Phototherapy with illumination of 3,000 lux in the morning	Effective for sleep-wake rhythm disorder in 50%; behavioral disorders decreased
Satlin et al.[91]	$N=10$; mean age = 70.1, in a VA hospital, with sundowning (MMSE: 0.6)	2-hour exposure to light (1,500–2,000 lux) while seated in a geri-chair	No effect on agitation, but a decline in severity of sundowning and sleep-wake problem patterns
Thorpe et al.[92]	$N=16$; ages 60-89 in a long-term care facility	Light administered using the Day-Light Box 1,000	Trend to decreased agitation (CMAI and EBIC) vs. baseline in post-treatment week
Alessi et al.[45]	$N=29$; NHR; mean age = 88.3	Increased daytime activities and a nighttime program to reduce sleep-disruptive noise	22% decrease in agitation vs. baseline (sig. difference from control group); increase in nighttime sleep from 51.7% to 62.5% vs. controls

(continued)

TABLE 1. Intervention articles (continued)

Reference	Subjects	Intervention	Findings
II. Pain Management			
Douzjian et al.[48]	N = 8; long-term residents of skilled nursing facility; >70 years old	650 mg acetaminophen tid	Five residents (63%) showed decrease in behavior measured; four orders for antipsychotic drugs and one for antidepressant drugs successfully discontinued
III. Hearing Aids			
Palmer et al.[48]	N = 8; 5 men, 3 women, ages 71–89; MMSE: 5–18; community-dwelling	Hearing aids provided	Decrease in problem behavior as reported by caregiver
IV. Removal of Restraints			
Middleton et al.[93]	N = 4; age 69–82, in a long-term care facility	Pain management, restraint management, and beta-blockers	Decrease in the amount and intensity of aggressive behaviors (OAS)
Werner et al.[46]	N = 172; NHR, no Restraints: n = 30; mean age: 86.9; Restrained: n = 142; mean age: 86.1	Educational program for nursing staff, then removal of restraints	Sig. decrease in all types of agitation (SCMAI; only those exhibiting agitation while restrained included for analysis)
Combination Therapies			
I. Individualized Treatments			
Hinchliffe et al.[94]	N = 40; mean age = 81 (65–93); MMSE≥8 in the community	Individualized treatments: combination of pharmacologic and nonpharmacological interventions (activities, if understimulated)	Sig. decrease in problem behaviors in first treatment group, but not in the delayed-treatment condition
Holm et al.[95]	N = 250; mean age = 81 (SD = 8) in an acute-care hospital	Individualized inpatient program plan; pharmacologic and nonpharmacologic	Sig. decrease in agitation (RAGE); problem behaviors eliminated in 38% of patients
Matthews et al.[96]	N = 33; mean age = 84.2 (67-98) in a dementia unit	Client-oriented care, residents' wishes respected; scheduled events adjusted for individual residents	Sig. decrease in verbal agitation (CMAI) 6–8 weeks after the change
II. Intervention Programs			
Rovner et al.[8]	N = 81; NHR; mean age = 81.6	Activity program (music, exercise crafts, relaxation, reminiscences, word games), reevaluation of psychotropic medication, and educational rounds	Sig. decrease in agitation vs. control group (at 6 months, behavior disorder exhibited by 28.6% vs. 51.3%)
Wimo et al.[97]	N = 31; median age = 82 (62-96), residing in a psychogeriatric ward	Program developed including team care, enhanced environment, flexibility in daily routine, evaluations	No effect on irritability; worsening in restlessness vs. controls

Note: NS = not statistically significant; sig. = statistically significant; SD = standard deviation; S = subject; NHR = nursing home residents; AUR = Alzheimer disease unit residents; NH = nursing home; VDB = verbally disruptive behavior; ABMI = Agitation Behavior Mapping Instrument;[1] ABRS = Agitation Behavior Rating Scale;[98] ABS = Agitated Behavior Scale;[99] BOP = Beoordelingsschaal Voor Oudere Patienten;[100] BSRS = Brief Behavior Symptom Rating Scale;[101] CMAI = Cohen-Mansfield Agitation Inventory;[102] CMAI-a = Adaptation of Cohen-Mansfield Agitation Inventory;[103] CMAI-GA Cohen-Mansfield Agitation Inventory,[102] as modified by Goddaer and Abraham;[12] CMAI-W = Cohen-Mansfield Agitation Inventory,[102] as modified by Chrisman et al.;[104] DBDS = Dementia Behavior Disturbance Scale;[105] DBRS = Disruptive Behavior Rating Scales;[106] DS-DAT = Discomfort Scale for Dementia of the Alzheimer's Type;[107] E-BEHAVE-AD adaptation by Auer et al.[108] of the Behavioral Pathology in Alzheimer's Disease Rating Scale (BEHAVE-AD);[109] EBIC = Environment Behavior Interaction Code;[110] GRS = Geriatric Rating Scale;[111] MIBM = Modified Interaction Behaviour Measure;[112] MOSES = Multidimensional Observation Scale for Elderly Subjects;[113] NHBPS = Nursing Home Behavior Problem Scale;[114] OAS = Overt Aggression Scale;[115] PAS = Pittsburgh Agitation Scale;[116] PGDRS = Psychogeriatric Dependency Rating Scale;[117] RAGE = Rating Scale for Aggressive Behavior in the Elderly;[118] SCMAI = Short Form of the Cohen-Mansfield Agitation Inventory;[119] SDAS-9 = Social Dysfunction and Aggression Scale.[120]

is actually measured, with some including an average of ratings of different constructs such as delusions, hallucinations, suspiciousness, violence, etc., and others concentrating on specific behaviors, such as aggressive behaviors or disruptive vocalizations. The studies also vary greatly in the time period for which the impact is examined—during the actual intervention, during the period after the intervention, or a global period that

Review of Nonpharmacologic Interventions

included the intervention and a time following it. The duration of treatment varied by the type of treatment. Massage therapy was usually conducted for 5 minutes once or twice per day; listening to music frequently lasted 15 or 30 minutes. Use of hearing aids was much longer, and total environmental change encompassed a total period of weeks or longer. The design used most often was either a comparison of baseline with intervention or a comparison of baseline, intervention, and a post-intervention period. Very few studies used a control group or a control condition.

Treatment efficacy. For every major category of intervention type, most of the studies (91% of all studies) report a benefit concerning inappropriate behaviors, and some (53% of all studies) report a significant improvement from baseline to the treatment condition. For each category, there are also studies that either find no statistically significant difference, or do not use statistical analysis to examine the change from baseline to treatment, or show mixed results. The differences in intervention procedures and in methods among the studies do not allow direct comparison between their findings. A more detailed examination of the findings and their significance is included in Table 1 and in the following summary of results for each type of intervention.

The vast majority of studies did not estimate the cost of intervention. One exception is Rovner et al.,[8] where the intervention rounds, which combined structured activities, psychiatric consultation, and educational activities, cost $8.94 per patient per day. However, the calculation of the cost is complex; for example, how much nursing staff time can be saved by having the activity staff occupy participants? Adjustments based on reduction in use of psychotropic medication, use of physical restraints, and reduction in the levels of drug side effects would be needed for a complete estimate.

Sensory Enhancement/Relaxation Methods

Massage/Touch. Six articles report studies of massage or therapeutic touch. Usually, the procedure took about

FIGURE 1. Number of articles by types of intervention and number of participants (Case Studies defined as studies with ≤9 participants).

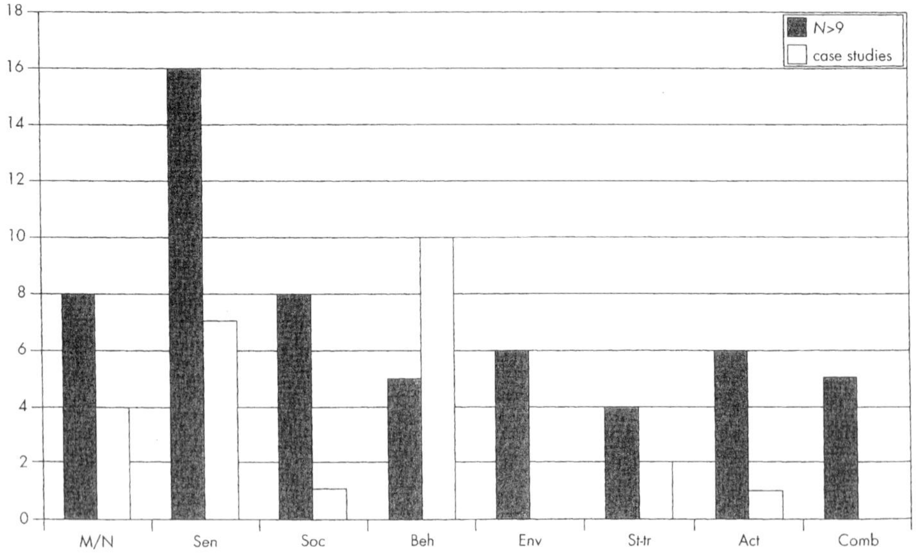

Note: M/N = medical/nursing care interventions; Sen = sensory; Soc = social contact (real or simulated); Beh = behavior therapy; Env = environmental interventions; St-tr = staff training; Act = structured activities; Comb = combination therapies.

5 minutes and was performed once or twice per day. One study reported unequivocal success (using a combination of massage and verbalizations). The other studies reported either a positive trend, partial effects (on physical and verbal behaviors) or no effect of the intervention (on aggression).

Music. Music intervention was used for two general purposes: as a relaxation during meals or bathing, or to provide sensory stimulation. The music intervention therefore ranged from listening to a music tape (in some studies, with headphones) to a music therapy session, which included musical games, dancing, movement, and singing. In using music for relaxation during bathing, two studies found that music was effective in reducing aggressive behaviors during bathing procedures and that there was a trend for decreasing other problem behaviors.[9,10] Of the three studies that examined the relaxing impact of quiet music during mealtimes, two reported a significant decline in agitation during lunchtime,[11,12] and the third did not demonstrate an effect during dinner.[13] Several studies reported a reduction in verbal agitation or agitation in general while patients listened to music on a tape or a CD player.[14-17] In about half of these studies, the music was individualized to match the person's preferences, whereas other studies used soft or classical music. The effect of music was reported to occur primarily during the listening sessions, and to be reduced after the conclusion of the session. Finally, music therapy, which included singing, playing instruments, and dancing, was reported to result in a significant decrease in agitation.[18]

White noise. The use of white noise is believed to induce relaxation and sleep and thereby decrease nocturnal restlessness. Positive results have been reported in some, but not all, cases.[19,20]

Sensory stimulation. This refers to a combination of stimuli delivered to different sensory modalities, including hearing, touch, and smell.[21] One Dutch article described the benefits of the "snoezelen" sensory stimulation. Most of the studies report improvement, although it is not necessarily statistically significant. One study showed no benefit of combining aromatherapy with massage; however, that study did not find a significant impact of each separately, either.

Social Contact: Real or Simulated

Pet therapy. Three studies suggest a beneficial effect of pet therapy. An intervention of 1-hour daily visits with a dog for 5 days showed a trend toward improvement ($P<0.07$) on the Irritable Behavior scale of the MOSES (Multidimensional Observation Scale for Elderly Subjects) rated for the week of treatment for 33 hospital patients on a geriatric psychiatry unit. Some, but not all, of the patients suffered from dementia.[22] These results may underestimate the impact of the intervention such that a greater effect might have been seen with ratings taken immediately after treatment; ½-hour sessions with a dog resulted in significantly lower levels of agitation than ½-hour sessions with only the researcher present in 28 special-care unit residents.[23] Finally, the presence of a pet at home was related to a lower prevalence of verbal aggression[24] in a study of 65 persons suffering from dementia.

One-on-one interaction. We found[14] that one-on-one interaction for ½ hour per day for 10 days was effective in decreasing verbally disruptive behaviors by 54%, a reduction that was significantly larger than the control condition of the same duration in 41 nursing home residents. The importance of interaction was also demonstrated by the Runci et al.[25] finding that interaction in Italian was superior to interaction in English when each was combined with music therapy to reduce vocal agitation in an 81-year-old Italian woman suffering from dementia.

Simulated interaction. Two studies report a significant positive impact of Simulated Presence Therapy, an audiotape that contains a relative's portion of a telephone conversation, and leaves pauses that allow the older person to respond to the relative's questions. A different type of simulated social contact, videotapes of family members talking to nursing home residents, was reported to result in an average decrease of 46% in verbally disruptive behavior during exposure to the videotape. In contrast, a generic videotape of reminiscence and relaxation did not result in reduction in agitation. (See Table 1.)

Behavioral Interventions

Most articles presenting behavioral techniques are case reports. The methods used include extinction (i.e.,

Review of Nonpharmacologic Interventions

withholding of positive reinforcement during inappropriate behavior), differential reinforcement (i.e., reinforcing either quiet behavior or behavior that is incompatible with the inappropriate behavior, or successive approximations to desired behavior), and stimulus control (teaching an association between a stimulus/cue and behavior). Reinforcements include social reinforcement, food, touch, going outside, etc. The majority of the studies reported a reduction in problem behavior. However, some of the studies reported no effect,[26] and others required an additional procedure (instruction in positive statements in addition to extinction) to produce an effect.[27] One behavioral study actually supports the provision of stimulation or environmental enhancement (noncontingent reinforcement) over the use of contingent reinforcement.[7]

Staff Training

Most staff training programs focus on understanding inappropriate behaviors, improving verbal and nonverbal communications with persons suffering from dementia, and improving methods of addressing their needs. Findings suggest that repeated ongoing training is needed to affect staff behavior. The CARE program (Calming Aggressive Reactions in the Elderly)[28] involved six staff-training sessions that emphasized risk factors for aggression, preventive and calming techniques, and protective intervention. Sessions utilized videotaped vignettes, discussions, and role-play, and they emphasized nonverbal communications. The authors reported a decline from 11 to 9 incident reports of staff abuse over the 3-month period of the intervention.[29] The NACSP (Nursing Assistant Communication Skill Program)[30] included five group-training sessions and four individual conferences with nursing assistants. The program emphasized enhancing residents' ability to use sensory input, effective and ineffective communication styles, utilization of memory aids, and addressing residents' needs. The program resulted in a significant decrease in verbal agitation and in physically nonaggressive behaviors at the end of 3 months, relative to a control group. Results were less compelling at 6 months, suggesting that additional ongoing training may be needed. Another training program, an abilities-focused program of morning care,[31] included a five-session educational program about the impact of dementia on social and self-care abilities, methods of assessing abilities, and interventions to maintain or compensate for those abilities. Agitation was significantly decreased after intervention from baseline in comparison with the same timeframe-related changes in a control group. An emphasis on Activities of Daily Living (ADLs) is also a major focus in Matteson et al.'s[32] program of staff training, emphasizing adaptation of ADLs to the person's level of functioning, based on Piaget's stages. Finally, a one-session training program on understanding and treating physically non-aggressive behaviors yielded no improvement in staff or resident behavior.[33]

Structured Activities

Surprisingly, relatively little research was found concerning the impact of structured activities per se (though some combination therapies and music therapy include structured activities). A positive impact of activities is reported by Aronstein et al.,[34] who presented 15 nursing home residents with recreational interventions, including: manipulative (e.g., bead maze), nurturing (e.g., doll), sorting (e.g., puzzles), tactile (e.g., fabric book), sewing (lacing cards), and sound/music (e.g., melody bells). Fourteen episodes of agitation were observed in five residents, and the interventions were judged as helpful in alleviating agitation in 57% of these episodes. Another study of group activities that was provided to three patients[35] yielded inconclusive results.

Outdoor walks. Two studies used outdoor walks for wanderers, and both found that this intervention led to decreases in inappropriate behavior.[36,37] Both studies involved interpersonal contact during the walk, though that was more pronounced in Holmberg's[36] study, which also included singing and holding hands.

Environmental Design

Access to an outdoor area. Two studies showed that free access to an outdoor area result in decreased agitation.[38,39] When the person has control over the ability to go outdoors, that control is expected to be of additional therapeutic benefit beyond that of the outdoor walk experience.

Natural environments. A natural environment, consisting of recorded songs of birds, babbling brooks, or small animals, together with large, bright pictures matching the audiotapes and offering of foods such as pudding, were presented during shower time. This resulted in significant reductions in agitation in the treatment group of 15 nursing home residents, in comparison with the control group of 16 residents who received usual care.[40] A simulated home environment and a nature environment, each composed of visual, auditory, and olfactory stimuli, were compared in a study of nursing home residents who wander. Results showed a trend toward less trespassing, exit-seeking, and other agitated behaviors in the altered environments, as compared with the unit's usual decor.[41]

Reduced-stimulation units. Two articles describe a reduction in agitation after the initiation of a reduced-stimulation environment. The first study involved camouflaged doors; small tables for eating; small-group activities; neutral colors on pictures and walls; no televisions, radios, or telephones (except one for emergencies); a consistent daily routine; and an educational program for staff and visitors concerning use of touch, eye contact, slow and soft speech, and allowing residents to make choices. As a result, both agitation and use of restraints declined (no statistical test is presented for agitation). The second study[42] included elimination of television/radio/stereo or piano-playing; use of quiet voices by staff at all times; relocation of the public entrance to an area that was out of sight of the residents; and reduced use of telephone. Observation of 11 residents before and after the changes showed a statistically significant decrease in agitated behaviors.

Medical/Nursing Interventions

Bright-light therapy and sleep interventions. Bright-light therapy has been used to improve sleep and reduce agitation, which can result from fatigue or circadian rhythm disturbances. The results of the seven studies using light therapy for this purpose are inconclusive in that some report no effect, some report a significant decrease, and some report a trend (see Table 1). These differences may stem from differences in design and measurement or from differences in population. For example, Van Someren et al.[43] noted that the impact of bright-light therapy was evident in persons with intact vision but not in those who were significantly visually impaired. Light has also been used differently in a study by Koss and Gilmore,[44] who reported that increased light intensity and enhanced visual contrast (achieved by the colors of tablecloths, napkins, etc.) during evening meals resulted in a significant increase of food intake and a significant decrease in agitation during the intervention periods, compared with pre-intervention and post-intervention periods.

Increasing sleep to reduce agitation without use of bright light was the approach taken by Alessi et al.[45] They found that increased daytime physical activity, decreased nighttime noise, and decreased sleep disruptions by nursing care staff resulted in a decrease in inappropriate behaviors during the day.

Restraint removal. Two uncontrolled, small studies suggest that removal of physical restraints reduced inappropriate behaviors;[46,47] the article by Middleton et al.[47] also described another resident for whom pain management resulted in a decrease in aggression.

Pain management. A trial of pain medication for eight nursing home residents with difficult behaviors showed that behavioral symptoms decreased, and psychotropic medication was successfully discontinued in 63%.[48]

Hearing aids. Addressing the hearing impairment of eight community-dwelling persons suffering from dementia by fitting them with hearing aids resulted in a significant decrease in inappropriate behaviors.[49] Similarly, a case study that does not have a specific measurement of behavior reports a decrease in yelling behavior with the introduction of an amplification device.[50]

Combination Interventions

Combination interventions usually combine pharmacological and nonpharmacological treatments, as well as structured activities and nursing care interventions (e.g., reduction in physical restraints). Some of those have used an individualized approach, where a treatment plan is fitted for each participant on the basis of his or her previous treatment, abilities, and type of problem behaviors; others have used a general group-treatment approach. Most, but not all, of the combination approaches report significant improvement of behavior with the program, although one of the studies reported worsening.

In addition to providing information concerning the impact of specific interventions, the literature examines the issues of the usefulness of individualization of treatments and of comparison across treatments.

Individualization of Treatment

The best support for the notion that intervention needs to be individualized to the person's past preferences comes from a study conducted by Gerdner.[15] She found that music based on participants' past preferences had a greater beneficial impact on behavior than non-individualized music. Several other studies have addressed the issue of individualization. In a study comparing different interventions, Cohen-Mansfield et al.[33] found that persons manifesting different types of verbally disruptive behaviors tended to benefit more from different interventions. For example, those with hallucinations benefited more from the videotape of family members talking to them, whereas those who were requesting attention benefited most from the one-on-one social interaction. Several articles describe individualized approaches to treating behavioral problems.[51-53]

The delineation of the parameters to be addressed in individualization may be assisted by a model of examining the heterogeneity in dementia.[52] This model describes inter-person differences as stemming from variation in the domains of biological/medical, psychosocial, and environmental, each of which is examined across the time-points of initial predisposition, lifelong influences, and current conditions. This framework may be useful in classifying the issues that need to be taken into account in the individualization of treatment. Obviously, issues of cognitive level, sensory deficits, mobility, social abilities, and environmental resources all have an effect on the tailoring of a specific nonpharmacologic treatment for a given behavior.

Comparison Across Treatments

Whereas a valid comparison of treatments used in different studies is currently impossible because of the heterogeneity in methods and treatment applications across studies, several studies used specific comparisons within each study that can help clarify the principles needed for maximizing the impact of intervention. A comparison of sensory stimulation (individualized music tape) to simulated social contact (videotape of family member) to actual social contact (one-on-one interaction) revealed that actual social contact had the highest impact in reducing verbal/vocal inappropriate behaviors.[14] Another study, of 30 Alzheimer-unit residents who wandered, found that music therapy activities (listening, playing percussion instruments, singing, and movement or dance) promoted more seating behavior than reading aloud to the resident. Both types of intervention were conducted in one-on-one sessions with the therapist, and, whenever possible, the content of the session was individualized to match the resident's past preferences.[54] Another study[55] compared two complex treatment modules: a traditional activity program, which included sensory stimulation, sewing club, ceramics group, adapted bingo, chair exercise, arts and crafts, sing-a-longs, etc., with the Neuro-Developmental Sequencing Program (NDSP), which included sensory air-mat therapy, sensory stimulation box program, geri-exercise to music, sensory cooking groups, build-your-own games, special-event preparation program, and sensory special events. In a crossover design controlling for order effects, of 32 nursing home residents, the NDSP group showed significant decreases in agitation as well as improvement in grip-strength. These studies present a first step and highlight the necessity for additional research that compares interventions and their "fit" with individual needs.

DISCUSSION

The Nature of the Interventions: The Interconnections Between Domains of Functioning

Nonpharmacologic interventions address a wide range of underlying problems: hearing problems, sleep difficulties (light therapy), communication problems, inactivity, and loneliness. These difficulties in life experience are closely interlinked among themselves. The approach to reducing inappropriate behavior in dementia is therefore identical to addressing those difficulties and improving quality of life for this population. As such, these interventions may provide an initial guide to a needed reform in the care of persons with dementia. The required care would better address their needs and thereby decrease rates of inappropriate behaviors.

The research reviewed shows that despite the many difficulties (described below) of conducting research in this population, a wide variety of approaches have been tried successfully. Many nonpharmacological approaches resulted in a statistically and clinically meaningful improvement in the manifestation of behavior problems. Even when no statistical results are presented, the combination of several studies showing the same trend lends support to the approaches described. Furthermore, many nonpharmacologic interventions result in an improvement in the quality of life of the older person, above and beyond the benefit shown in reduction of inappropriate behavior. Nonpharmacologic interventions, therefore, essentially address improvements in quality of care and the ensuing quality of life.

The principles listed below, which received consistent support in the research described here, should be considered primary targets for future nonpharmacologic interventions:

- Medical and nursing care that effectively address limitations in functioning, including pain, sensory limitations, sleep problems, and limitations on autonomy, such as physical restraints
- Provision of social contact
- Provision of meaningful stimuli or activity
- Tailoring the intervention to the individual
- Staff training to improve care
- Reduction in stressful stimuli or increasing relaxation during care activities

The Relationship Between Pharmacologic and Nonpharmacologic Interventions

This relationship has not been addressed in the literature. Many of the nonpharmacologic intervention studies include participants who are already receiving psychotropic medication that has not alleviated the problem. For some of these, the pharmacologic treatment was kept constant during the interventions, and in others the researcher had no control over the medications the participants were taking.

The comparison of pharmacologic and nonpharmacologic studies that are independently conducted is difficult. Many of the pharmacologic studies investigate new drugs for FDA approval, utilizing a double-blind, placebo-controlled design, which is not feasible in nonpharmacologic studies. In our experience, these pharmacologic studies have different inclusion criteria, so that many more of the frail patients and those with extreme dementia are excluded from these studies, in comparison with nonpharmacologic studies. The placebo condition in pharmacologic studies frequently has a significant impact in reducing inappropriate behaviors. Whereas such an outcome could be attributed to a Hawthorne effect and observer bias, the large size of the effect, compared with the inability of many of the studies reviewed here to achieve a significant effect, prompts me to interpret this effect as a result of one-on-one interaction, which is a potent and expensive nonpharmacologic intervention. Finally, pharmacologic studies are performed within the framework of the FDA guidelines of "burden of proof," which are different from what is needed to convince the caregiver audience of the efficacy of nonpharmacologic interventions.

The comparison of pharmacologic with nonpharmacologic interventions and the role these should and could play goes beyond the scope of this article and deserves a public debate. In our opinion, the nonpharmacologic interventions described in this article generally address the basic needs of the person with dementia and provide humane care—and therefore should precede pharmacologic interventions.

Limitations of Existing Knowledge

Despite a substantial number of articles describing the impact of nonpharmacologic interventions for persons with dementia, the understanding of the efficacy of these interventions is quite limited. Many questions remain unanswered, such as: What is the size of the effect? What percent of participants show improvement? How consistent is the effect over time? Many of the articles provide only partial answers, at best. The ambiguity in the understanding of efficacy in the studies is due to multiple limitations, some of which are methodological and others, conceptual.

Methodological issues limiting the understanding of efficacy: diverse measurement methods. Different studies utilize various measurements, including standardized informant ratings (see footnote to Table 1), systematic observations, and other informant ratings developed specifically for the study. Different instruments target different behaviors and different attributes of the behaviors, such as occurrence, frequency, or severity. Similarly, there is variation in the time-frame in which the impact of intervention is measured. Frequently, data are attained during the intervention, sometimes immediately after the intervention, and, on other occasions, during the period around the intervention (e.g., the day or week in which the intervention took place).

Criteria for success. The method by which results are reported varies greatly, so that some researchers report

Review of Nonpharmacologic Interventions

an improvement when any of the participants manifest any improvement, whereas others require statistical significance or a clinically meaningful improvement, as well as statistical significance. Even when results are reported in detail, they sometimes represent partial success, which is difficult to interpret. For example, in a well-designed study by Snyder et al.,[56] a significant effect of hand massage on the main agitated behavior was found in the morning; however, there was no effect on the second agitated behavior, nor was there an effect when the intervention was carried out in the evening. The efficacy of the intervention therefore remains ambiguous. When success of the intervention is established, the magnitude of the effect may vary, depending on other variables, such as the duration of the intervention.[57]

Screening procedures. When calculating the percentage of persons who benefited from treatment, the criteria for determining eligible study participants vary across studies. Some studies utilize screening procedures that test the feasibility of conducting the intervention prior to implementation,[19] and, in these cases, the treatment-effect size reported is therefore larger than if all those eligible for treatment were considered. Screening criteria often vary among studies and may exclude a variety of medical disorders. For instance, Scherder et al.[58] excluded persons with a history of psychiatric disorder, alcoholism, cerebral trauma, cerebrovascular disease, hydrocephalus, neoplasm, infection, epilepsy, kidney or lung diseases, disturbances of consciousness, or focal brain abnormalities, which would be expected to affect the generalizability of results. Other studies screened out those who did not attend treatment sessions.[18] Screening may be essential to the treatment procedures, as in the case of selecting participants who do not have severe hearing impairment for music therapy.

Control procedures. Many (about half) of the studies examine change from baseline to intervention, and do not use any control procedures. Therefore, in these studies, it is difficult to determine whether the effect is that of the intervention, the passage of time, or changes that tend to occur in the population studied. It can be argued that when participants are chosen because of significant levels of inappropriate behavior, their behavior may improve over time simply by "regression towards the mean," or, in other words, because the initial screening caught them at the time at which they were most agitated. On the other hand, the institution of a control group or a control condition is not always feasible for ethical or financial reasons; for example, not providing hearing aids or not reducing physical restraints, or alternatively, removing hearing aids that had been provided or re-instituting physical restraints would all be questionable practices. The optimal utilization of control procedures is also a matter of debate. The great heterogeneity among dementia sufferers would dictate a within-person control condition; however, given that these persons are in a state of decline regardless of intervention procedures, it can be argued that a parallel-group control is needed to control for that impact.

Treatment of failures. The incidence of treatment failures is greatly underreported. Reports of treatment failures tend not to be submitted or accepted for publication. Therefore, the results of such studies would not be available to the public. This is especially true of case studies. We chose to include case studies despite this limitation because some studies are extremely difficult to conduct, and case studies may offer the only opportunity to examine innovative ideas for intervention. Even when studies use larger sample sizes, the issue of failures may be neglected by describing only the successes and not examining the possibility of worsening behavior.

The Relationship Between Target Symptom and Type of Intervention

The vast majority of studies reviewed used a group of inappropriate behaviors as the dependent variable. There was usually no attempt to analyze the impact of the intervention on specific types of inappropriate behaviors.

The lack of differentiation of the target symptom is a problem for two reasons. First, there is evidence that the etiology of the different subtypes of behavior tends to be different, and it therefore stands to reason that certain interventions would be appropriate for some types of behavior and not for others. Second, the goal of intervention for aggressive and verbally agitated behaviors is generally to reduce this occurrence, whereas for physical nonaggressive behaviors, which provide exercise and stimulation for the residents, the goal is frequently to accommodate the behavior or to channel it into avenues that do not disturb others. For example, the study outcome may not be a decrease in the rate of walking, but rather a change in location, decreased trespassing, or decreased disturbance to other residents or caregivers. Indeed, the focus of several articles on wanderers was to enhance the well-being of wanderers, rather than decrease their wandering behaviors.[37,59]

Intrinsic and Conceptual Issues Limiting the Understanding of Efficacy

Variation of treatment parameters. Each type of nonpharmacologic intervention applies one instance of the infinite variations possible for that type of intervention. Variation can occur in duration, timing, level (e.g., brightness of light), or size (e.g., objects to be manipulated), to name a few. Treatment failure or success may depend on these specifics, rather than on the inherent applicability of the genre of intervention. For example, one critique of a bright-light therapy study, which resulted in no effect, suggested that different hours should have been used; or a music therapy may have not been effective because of the specific type of music chosen, the volume at which it was played, etc.

The active ingredient in the intervention. Even with convincing evidence that an intervention has been beneficial, the actual procedure responsible for this success is usually less clear. The reason for this ambiguity is that most intervention studies actually use several procedures in the treatment. For example, being taken for a walk outdoors involves social contact with the person who is accompanying the patient outdoors, a change in environment, outdoor light and air, etc; being read to involves some additional social contact with the person who is the reader; behavioral interventions frequently provide food and attention that were not otherwise available, etc. The question is, therefore: What is the important component of the intervention? Is it the treatment as titled—"reading," "differential reinforcement," and the like, or is it an unacknowledged component? One study that attempted to address this question compared hand massage to the mere presence of the nursing staff.[60] In that case, mere presence had no effect, and the effect of the intervention was somewhat questionable. The potent role of social contact, which is involved in many of the interventions, is seen in a study that found social interaction to be a more successful intervention than individualized music or a videotaped family member for persons with verbal agitation.[14] Its probable role is also seen in the significant placebo effect found in pharmacology studies. Some of the difficulties in clarifying the cause of effects in complex intervention trials are discussed in Cook and Campbell.[61]

Effectiveness and Implementation in Practice

The utilization of nonpharmacologic interventions in practice is limited. The biggest barrier is the lack of financial resources, or, stated otherwise, the lack of reimbursement. Whereas the use of psychotropic drugs is directly reimbursed, utilization of nonpharmacologic approaches is not. Furthermore, many of the more "medical" preventive treatments of inappropriate behaviors are not reimbursed, such as hearing aids or dental evaluations and treatment. Additional barriers include lack of knowledge by caregivers as to how to care for persons who suffer from complex cognitive and medical disabilities, habits established in residential facilities over the years, the perception that medication is easier to administer, and a system that does not address the quality of living with dementia from a holistic point of view.

Reasons for Limitations in Available Research

The limited understanding of the usefulness of nonpharmacologic treatments stems not only from the limitations in current research, but also from the difficulties in conducting such research, with regard to inherent barriers—participants' limitations, system and caregiver issues, and external barriers.

Inherent barriers: participants' limitations. These involve the frailty of participants, where a significant proportion must be excluded during a study because of death or acute illness. Furthermore, the participants' limitations make the research process extremely dependent on the cooperation of the caregivers and the research setting. Such research calls for involving family caregivers in obtaining consent, requiring the assistance of formal caregivers for information and behavior ratings, and acquiring the collaboration of the nursing home, all of which make conducting research cumbersome. The barriers to communication and to implementation of interventions are numerous, and include participant disabilities in vision, hearing, language, or mobility. Finally, another hurdle in conducting this research lies in the inter- and intra-person variability in the manifestation of behavior. Indeed, the comments from several of the reviewed studies, which stated that baseline levels of inappropriate behaviors were probably too low to detect an effect as a result of an intervention, may be attributed to fluctuations in levels of agitation.

System and caregiver barriers. Relatives of potential participants frequently feel that their relative is too frail to participate in research, even when the research offers potential benefits and negligible risks. Many relatives feel the situation is hopeless and do not believe that any relief can be offered. The willingness to consent is even lower if the participant is assigned to a control condition. Nursing homes are also sometimes reluctant to involve themselves in the research process, either from fear of criticism or because they are wary of additional demands on over-burdened personnel. The nursing home's design, practices, schedule, and other system characteristics can also impede the implementation of nonpharmacologic interventions, even when the intervention would be more cost-effective in the long run. For instance, interventions with pet therapy would be much easier and more widely utilized if a pet lived on the premises, rather than having staff constantly schedule pets to be brought to the facility. However, implementing an on-site pet therapy program would require a system change. Many other interventions can be maximized via a system rather than a topical change. Finally, ethical considerations also limit the types of interventions and controls that can be performed.

External limitations. These stem from limited sources of funding (in comparison with drug research), resulting in utilization of only one or two sites and a limited number of participants. Indeed, much of the research in this area tends to be clinical research performed in the effort to improve care within a facility. Also, the combination of inherent and system difficulties in conducting this type of research is unfamiliar to many review committees, so that inappropriate expectations cause realistic studies to be rejected.

RECOMMENDATIONS: FUTURE DIRECTIONS

The results of the literature review show that many nonpharmacologic interventions show promise for treating inappropriate behaviors in dementia. The field needs to be expanded in a number of ways in order to have clinical usefulness. There is a need to address 1) the issue of individualization and proper selection of treatment: Which interventions are appropriate for which persons manifesting which behaviors? When is the goal enhanced stimulation and social contact, and when is it relaxation? Are some interventions always superior to others? 2) the specifics of the interventions: what characteristics of interventions optimize their impact? such characteristics include timing, duration, location, and intensity; 3) the issue of costs: When are lower-cost interventions comparable in effectiveness to higher-cost interventions? Which system issues need to be considered in order to make a quality approach fiscally viable? 4) the basic understanding of quality care in dementia: What is the best way to provide ADL care, sleep care, and mobility care that incorporates prevention and minimization of patient discomfort, and takes into account the interrelationship between system issues (e.g., waking the resident up for incontinence care may be important for skin care but may compromise sleep care)? What methods will best address the multiple interrelated aspects of functioning in a holistic fashion? and 5) system change: What types of training are needed, what changes in staffing roles and structure and ongoing feedback mechanisms are needed to translate the research from efficacy to practice? More funding for research is needed to allow for larger and better-designed studies that can address some of the research methodology limitations described above. Finally, as such knowledge is gained, concomitant changes in reimbursement and the structure of system-of-care need to take place in order to improve the practice of dementia care.

References

1. Cohen-Mansfield J, Billig N: Agitated behaviors in the elderly, I: a conceptual review. J Am Geriatr Soc 1986; 34:711–721
2. Cohen-Mansfield J, Werner P, Watson V, et al: Agitation among elderly persons at adult day-care centers: the experiences of relatives and staff members. Int Psychogeriatr 1995; 7:447–458
3. Hall GR: Caring for people with Alzheimer's disease using the conceptual model of progressively lowered stress threshold in the clinical setting. Nurs Clin North Am 1994; 29:129–141
4. Hall GR, Buckwalter KC: Progressively lowered stress threshold: a conceptual model for care of adults with Alzheimer's disease. Arch Psychiatr Nurs 1987; 1:399–406
5. Cohen-Mansfield J, Lipson S, Werner P, et al: Withdrawal of haloperidol, thioridazine, and lorazepam in the nursing home. Arch Intern Med 1999; 159:1733–1740
6. Schneider LS: Meta-analysis of controlled pharmacologic trials. Int Psychogeriatr 1996; 8:375–379

7. Mishara BL: Geriatric patients who improve in token economy and general milieu treatment programs: a multivariate analysis. J Consult Clin Psychol 1978; 46:1340-1348
8. Rovner BW, Steele CD, Shmuely Y, et al: A randomized trial of dementia care in nursing homes. J Am Geriatr Soc 1996; 44:7-13
9. Clark ME, Lipe AW, Bilbrey M: Use of music to decrease aggressive behaviors in people with dementia. J Gerontol Nurs 1998; 24:10-17
10. Thomas DW, Heitman RJ, Alexander T: The effects of music on bathing cooperation for residents with dementia. J Music Ther 1997; 34:246-259
11. Denney A: Quiet music: an intervention for mealtime agitation. J Gerontol Nurs 1997; Jul:16-23
12. Goddaer J, Abraham IL: Effects of relaxing music on agitation during meals among nursing home residents with severe cognitive impairment. Arch Psychiatr Nurs 1994; 8:150-158
13. Ragneskog H, Branc G, Karlson I, et al: Influence of dinner music on food intake and symptoms common in dementia. Scand J Caring Sci 1996; 10:11-17
14. Cohen-Mansfield J, Werner P: Management of verbally disruptive behaviors in nursing home residents. J Gerontol Med Sci 1997; 52A:M369-M377
15. Gerdner LA: Effects of individualized vs. classical "relaxation" music on the frequency of agitation in elderly persons with Alzheimer's disease and related disorders. Int Psychogeriatr 2000; 12:49-65
16. Gerdner LA, Swanson EA: Effects of individualized music on confused and agitated elderly patients. Arch Psychiatr Nurs 1993; 7:284-291
17. Tabloski PA, McKinnon-Howe L, Remington R: Effects of calming music on the level of agitation in cognitively impaired nursing home residents. Am J Alzheimer Care Rel Disord Res 1995; 10:10-15
18. Brotons M, Pickett-Cooper PK: The effects of music therapy intervention on agitation behaviors of Alzheimer's disease patients. J Music Ther 1996; 33:3-18
19. Burgio L, Scilley K, Hardin JM, et al: Environmental "white noise": an intervention for verbally agitated nursing home residents. J Gerontol Psychol Sci Soc Sci 1996; 51B:364-373
20. Young SH, Muir-Nash J, Ninos M: Managing nocturnal wandering behavior. J Gerontol Nurs 1988; 14:6-12
21. Bower H: Sensory stimulation and the treatment of senile dementia. Med J Aust 1967; 1:1113-1119
22. Zisselman MH, Rovner BW, Shmuely Y, et al: A pet therapy intervention with geriatric psychiatric inpatients. Am J Occup Ther 1996; 50:47-51
23. Churchill M, Safaoui J, McCabe B, et al: Using a therapy dog to alleviate the agitation and desocialization of people with Alzheimer's disease. J Psychosoc Nurs Ment Health Serv 1999; 37:16-24
24. Fritz C, Farver T, Kass P, et al: Association with companion animals and the expression of noncognitive symptoms in Alzheimer's patients. J Nerv Ment Dis 1995; 183:459-463
25. Runci S, Doyle C, Redman J: An empirical test of language-relevant interventions for dementia. Int Psychogeriatr 1999; 11:301-311
26. Hanley IG, McGuire RJ, Boyd WD: Reality orientation and dementia: a controlled trial of two approaches. Br J Psychiatry 1981; 138:10-14
27. Hussian RA: A combination of operant and cognitive therapy with geriatric patients. Int J Behav Geriatr 1983; 1:57-60
28. Mentes JC, Ferrario J: Calming aggressive reactions: a preventive program. J Gerontol Nurs 1989; 15:22-27
29. Williams DP, Wood EC, Moorleghen F: An in-service workshop for nursing personnel on the management of catastrophic reactions in dementia victims. Clin Gerontologist 1994; 14:47-53
30. McCallion P, Toseland RW, Lacey D, et al: Educating nursing assistants to communicate more effectively with nursing home residents with dementia. Gerontologist 1999; 39:546-558
31. Wells DL, Dawson P, Sidani S, et al: Effect of an abilities-focused program of morning care on residents who have dementia and on caregivers. J Am Gerontol Soc 2000; 48:442-449
32. Matteson MA, Linton AD, Barnes SJ, et al: Management of problematic behavioral symptoms associated with dementia: a cognitive developmental approach. Aging Clin Exp Res 1997; 9:342-355
33. Cohen-Mansfield J, Werner P, Culpepper WJ, et al: Evaluation of an in-service training program on dementia and wandering. J Gerontol Nurs 1997; 23:40-47
34. Aronstein Z, Olsen R, Schulman E: The nursing assistant's use of recreational interventions for behavioral management of residents with Alzheimer's disease. Am J Alzheimers Dis Other Demen 1996; 11:26-31
35. Sival RC, Vingerhoets RW, Haffmans PM, et al: Effect of a program of diverse activities on disturbed behavior in three severely demented patients. Int Psychogeriatr 1997; 9:423-430
36. Holmberg SK: Evaluation of a clinical intervention for wanderers on a geriatric nursing unit. Arch Psychiatr Nurs 1997; 11:21-28
37. Cohen-Mansfield J, Werner P: Visits to an outdoor garden: impact on behavior and mood of nursing home residents who pace, in Research and Practice in Alzheimer's Disease. Edited by Vellas B, Fitten J, Frisoni G. Paris, France, Serdi, 1998, pp 419-436
38. McMinn BG, Hinton L: Confined to barracks: the effects of indoor confinement on aggressive behavior among inpatients of an acute psychogeriatric unit. Am J Alzheimers Dis Other Demen 2000; 15:36-41
39. Namazi KH, Johnson BD: Pertinent autonomy for residents with dementias: modification of the physical environment to enhance independence. Am J Alzheimer Dis Rel Dis Res 1992; 7:16-21
40. Whall A, Black M, Groh C, et al: The effect of natural environments upon agitation and aggression in late-stage dementia patients. Am J Alzheimers Dis Other Demen 1997; Sep/Oct:216-220
41. Cohen-Mansfield J, Werner P: The effects of an enhanced environment on nursing home residents who pace. Gerontologist 1998; 38:199-208
42. Meyer DL, Dorbacker B, O'Rourke J, et al: Effects of a "quiet week" intervention on behavior in an Alzheimer boarding home. Am J Alzheimer Care Rel Dis Res 1992; 7:2-6
43. Van Someren E, Kessler A, Mirmiran M, et al: Indirect bright light improves circadian rest-activity rhythm disturbances in demented patients. Biol Psychiatry 1997; 41:955-963
44. Koss E, Gilmore GC: Environmental interventions and functional ability of AD patients, in Research and Practice in Alzheimer's Disease. Edited by Vellas B, Fritten J, Frisoni G. Paris, France, Serdi, 1998, pp 185-192
45. Alessi CA, Yoon EJ, Schnelle JF, et al: A randomized trial of a combined physical activity and environmental intervention in nursing home residents: do sleep and agitation improve? J Am Geriatr Soc 1999; 47:784-791
46. Perla W, Cohen-Mansfield J, Koroknay V, et al: The Impact of a restraint-reduction program on nursing home residents. Geriatr Nurs 1994; 15:142-146
47. Middleton J, Knezecek S, Robinson L, et al: An exploratory study

Review of Nonpharmacologic Interventions

47. of pain in the institutionalized elderly. Am J Alzheimers Dis Other Demen 1997; 12:159–166
48. Douzjian M, Wilson C, Shultz M, et al: A program to use pain control medication to reduce psychotropic drug use in residents with difficult behavior. Ann Long-Term Care 1998; 6:174–179
49. Palmer CV, Adams SW, Bourgeois M, et al: Reduction in caregiver-identified problem behavior in patients with Alzheimer disease post- hearing-aid fitting. J Speech Lang Hear Res 1999; 42:312–328
50. Leverett M: Approaches to Problem Behaviors in Dementia. (The Mentally Impaired Elderly). Binghamton, NY, Haworth, 1991, pp 93–105
51. Mintzer JE, Lewis L, Pennypaker L: Behavioral Intensive Care Unit (BICU): a new concept in the management of acute agitated behavior in elderly demented patients. Gerontologist 1993; 33:801–806
52. Cohen-Mansfield J, Golander H, Arnheim G: Self-identity in older persons suffering from dementia: preliminary results. Soc Sci Med 2000; 51:381–394
53. Williams DP, Wood EC, Moorleghen F, et al: A decision model for guiding the management of disruptive behaviors in demented residents of institutionalized settings. Am J Alzheimers Dis Other Demen 1995; 10:22–29
54. Groene RW: Effectiveness of music therapy, I: intervention with individuals having senile dementia of the Alzheimer's type. J Music Ther 1993; 30:138–157
55. Buettner L, Lundegren HLD, Farrell P, et al: Therapeutic recreation as an intervention for persons with dementia and agitation: an efficacy study. Am J Alzheimers Dis Other Demen 1996; 11:4–12
56. Snyder M, Egan EC, Burns KR: Interventions for decreasing agitation behaviors in persons with dementia. Journal of Gerontological Nursing 1995; 21:34–40
57. Kim EJ, Buschmann MT: The effect of expressive physical touch on patients with dementia. Int J Nurs Stud 1999; 36:235–243
58. Scherder E, Bouma A, Steen L: Effects of peripheral tactile nerve stimulation on affective behavior of patients with probable Alzheimer's disease. Am J Alzheimers Dis Other Demen 1998; 13:61–68
59. Arno S, Frank D: A group for "wandering" institutionalized clients with primary degenerative dementia. Perspectives in Psychiatric Care 1994; 30:13–16
60. Snyder M, Egan EC, Burns KR: Efficacy of hand massage in decreasing agitation behaviors associated with care activities in persons with dementia. Geriatric Nursing 1995; Mar/Apr:60–63
61. Cook TD, Campbell DT: Quasi-Experimentation Design and Analysis Issues for Field Settings. New York, Houghton-Mifflin, 1979
62. Kilstoff K, Chenoweth L: New approaches to health and well-being for dementia day-care clients, family carers, and day-care staff. International Journal of Nursing Practice 1998; 4:70–83
63. Rowe M, Alfred D: The effectiveness of slow-stroke massage in diffusing agitated behaviors in individuals with Alzheimer's disease. Journal of Gerontological Nursing 1999; 25:22–34
64. Gerdner LA: Effects of individualized vs. classical "relaxation" music on the frequency of agitation in elderly persons with Alzheimer's disease and related disorders. Int Psychogeriatr 2000; 12:49–65
65. Casby JA, Holm MB: The effect of music on repetitive disruptive vocalizations of persons with dementia. Am J Occup Ther 1994; 48:883–889
66. Holtkamp CC, Kragt K, van Dongen MC, et al: Effect of snoezelen on the behavior of demented elderly. Tijdschr Gerontol Geriatr 1997; 28:124–128
67. Witucki JM, Twibell RS: The effect of sensory stimulation activities on the psychological well-being of patients with advanced Alzheimer's disease. Am J Alzheimer Dis Other Demen 1997; 9:10–15
68. Snyder M, Olson J: Music and hand massage interventions to produce relaxation and reduce aggressive behaviors in cognitively impaired elders: a pilot study. Clinical Gerontologist 1996; 17:64–69
69. Brooker DJ, Snape M, Johnson E, et al: Single case evaluation of the effects of aromatherapy and massage on disturbed behavior in severe dementia. Br J Clin Psychol 1997; 36:287–296
70. Camberg L, Woods P, Ooi WL, et al: Evaluation of Simulated Presence: a personalized approach to enhance well-being in persons with Alzheimer's disease. J Am Geriatr Soc 1999; 47:446–452; Notes: Comment in: J Am Geriatr Soc 1999; 47:492–493
71. Hall L, Hare J: Video respite for cognitively impaired persons in nursing homes. Am J Alzheimers Dis Other Demen 1997; May/June 117-121
72. Werner P, Cohen-Mansfield J, Fischer J, et al: Characterization of family-generated videotapes for the management of verbally disruptive behaviors. J Appl Gerontol 2000; 19:42–57
73. Woods P, Ashley J: Simulated Presence Therapy: using selected memories to manage problem behaviors in Alzheimer's disease patients. Geriatr Nurs 1995; 16:9–14
74. Doyle C, Zapparoni T, O'Connor D, et al: Efficacy of psychosocial treatments for noise-making in severe dementia. Int Psychogeriatr 1997; 9:405–422
75. Heard K, Watson TS: Reducing wandering by persons with dementia using differential reinforcement. J Appl Behav Anal 1999; 32:381–384
76. Rogers JC, Holm MB, Burgio LD, et al: Improving care routines of nursing home residents with dementia. J Am Geriatr Soc 1999; 47:1049–1057
77. Birchmore T, Clague S: A behavioral approach to reduce shouting. Nurs Times 1983; 79:37–39
78. Boehm S, Whall AL, Cosgrove KL, et al: Behavioral analysis and nursing interventions for reducing disruptive behaviors of patients with dementia. Appl Nurs Res 1995; 8:118–122
79. Lewin LM, Lundervold D: Behavioral treatment of elderly in foster care homes. Adult Foster Care J 1987; 1:238–249
80. Chafetz PK: Two-dimensional grid is ineffective against demented patients' exiting through glass doors. Psychol Aging 1990; 5:146–147
81. Hussian RA: Modification of behaviors in dementia via stimulus manipulation. Clin Gerontologist 1988; 8:37–43
82. Hussian RA, Brown DC: Use of two-dimensional grid patterns to limit hazardous ambulation in demented patients. J Gerontol 1987; 42:558–560
83. Mayer R, Darby SJ: Does a mirror deter wandering in demented older people? Int J Geriatr Psychiatry 1991; 6:607–609
84. Bird M, Alexopoulos P, Adamowicz J: Success and failure in five case studies: use of cued recall to ameliorate behaviour problems in senile dementia. Int J Geriatr Psychiatry 1995; 10:305–311
85. Hussian RA: Stimulus control in the modification of problematic behavior in elderly institutionalized patients. Int J Behav Geriatr 1982; 1:33–46
86. Holmberg SK: Evaluation of a clinical intervention for wanderers on a geriatric nursing unit. Arch Psychiatr Nurs 1997; 11:21–28
87. Cleary TA, Clamon C, Price M, et al: A reduced-stimulation unit: effects on patients with Alzheimer's disease and related disorders. Gerontologist 1988; 28:511–514
88. Lovell BB, Ancoli-Israel S, Gevirtz R: Effect of bright-light treat-

ment on agitated behavior in institutionalized elderly subjects. Psychiatry Res 1995; 57:7-12

89. Lyketsos C, Veiel L, Baker A, et al: A randomized, controlled trial of bright-light therapy for agitated behaviors in dementia patients residing in long-term care. Int J Geriatr Psychiatry 1999; 14:520-525

90. Mishima M, Okawa M, Hishikawa Y, et al: Morning bright-light therapy for sleep and behavior disorders in elderly patients with dementia. Acta Psychiatr Scand 1994; 89:1-7

91. Okawa M, Mishima K, Hishikawa Y, et al: Circadian rhythm disorders in sleep–waking and body temperature in elderly patients with dementia and their treatment. Sleep 1991; 14:478-485

92. Satlin A, Volicer L, Ross V, et al: Bright-light treatment of behavioral and sleep disturbances in patients with Alzheimer's disease. Am J Psychiatry 1992; 149:1028-1032

93. Thorpe L, Middleton J, Russell G, et al: Bright-light therapy for demented nursing home patients with behavioral disturbance. Am J Alzheimers Dis Other Demen 2000; 15:18-26

94. Middleton M, Richardson JS, Berman E: An assessment and intervention study of aggressive behavior in cognitively impaired institutionalized elderly. Am J Alzheimers Dis Other Demen 1997; 12:24-29

95. Hinchliffe AC, Hyman IL, Blizard B, et al: Behavioural complications of dementia: can they be treated? Int J Geriatr Psychiatry 1995; 10:839-847

96. Holm A, Michel M, Stern GA, et al: The outcomes of an inpatient treatment program for geriatric patients with dementia and dysfunctional behaviors. Gerontologist 1999; 39:668-676

97. Matthews EA, Farrell GA, Blackmore AM: Effects of an environmental manipulation emphasizing client-centred care on agitation and sleep in dementia sufferers in a nursing home. J Adv Nurs 1996; 24:439-447

98. Wimo A, Nelvig A, Nelvig J, et al: Can changes in ward routines affect the severity of dementia? a controlled, prospective study. Int Psychogeriatr 1993; 5:169-178

99. Bliwise DL, Ingham RH, Date ES, et al: Nerve conduction and creatinine clearance in aged subjects with periodic movements in sleep. J Gerontol 1989; 44:M164-M167

100. Corrigan JD: Development of a scale for assessment of agitation following traumatic injury. J Clin Exp Neuropsychol 1989; 11:261-277

101. Van der Kam P, Mol F, Wimmers M: Beoordelingsschaal voor Oudere Patienten. Deventer, The Netherlands, Van Loghum Slaterus, 1971

102. Rabins P: The validity of a caregiver-rated brief behavior symptom rating scale for use in the cognitively impaired. Int J Geriatr Psychiatry 1994; 9:205-210

103. Cohen-Mansfield J, Marx MS, Rosenthal AS: A description of agitation in a nursing home. J Gerontol 1989; 44:M77-M84

104. Cohen-Mansfield J: Agitated behaviors in the elderly, II: preliminary results in the cognitively deteriorated. J Am Geriatr Soc 1986; 34:722-727

105. Chrisman M, Tabar D, Whall AL, et al: Agitated behavior in the cognitively impaired elderly. J Gerontol Nurs 1991; 17:9-13

106. Baumgarten M, Becker R, Gauthier S: Validity and reliability of the Dementia Behavior Disturbance Scale. J Am Geriatr Soc 1990; 38:221-226

107. Mungas D, Weiler P, Franzi C, et al: Assessment of disruptive behavior associated with dementia: the Disruptive Behavior Rating Scales. J Geriatr Psychiatry Neurol 1989; 2:196-202

108. Hurley AC, Volicer BJ, Hanrahan PA, et al: Assessment of discomfort in advanced Alzheimer patients. Res Nurs Health 1992; 15:369-377

109. Auer SR, Monteiro IM, Reisberg B: The empirical behavioral pathology in an Alzheimer's disease rating scale (E-BEHAVE-AD). Int Psychogeriatr 1996; 8:247-266

110. Reisberg B, Borenstein J, Salob SP, et al: BEHAVE-AD: a clinical rating scale for the assessment of pharmacologically remediable behavioral symptomatology in Alzheimer's disease, in Alzheimer's Disease: Problems, Prospects, and Perspectives. Edited by Altman JJ. New York, Plenum, 1987

111. Stewart NJ, Hiscock M, Morgan DG, et al: Development and psychometric evaluation of the Environment-Behavior Interaction Code (EBIC). Nurs Res 1999; 48:260-268

112. Plutchik R, Conte H, Lieberman M, et al: Reliability and validity of a scale for assessing the functioning of geriatric patients. J Am Geriatr Soc 1970; 18:491-500

113. Burgener SC, Jirovec M, Murrell L, et al: Caregiver and environmental variables related to difficult behaviors in institutionalized, demented elderly persons. J Gerontol 1992; 47:P242-P249

114. Helmes E, Caspo KG, Short JA: Standardization and validation of the Multidimensional Observation Scale for Elderly Subjects (MOSES). J Gerontol 1987; 42:395-405

115. Ray WA, Taylor JA, Lichtenstein MJ, et al: The Nursing Home Behavior Problem Scale. J Gerontol 1992; 47i:M9-M16

116. Yudofsky SC, Silver JM, Jackson W, et al: The Overt Aggression Scale for the Objective Rating of Verbal and Physical Aggression. Am J Psychiatry 1986; 143:35-39

117. Rosen J, Burgio L, Kollar M, et al: The Pittsburgh Agitation Scale. Am J Geriatr Psychiatry 1994; 2:52-59

118. Wilkinson IM, Graham-White J: Psychogeriatric Dependency Rating Scales (PGDRS): a method of assessment for use by nurses. Br J Psychiatry 1980; 137:558-565

119. Patel V, Hope RA: A rating scale for aggressive behaviour in the elderly: the RAGE. Psychol Med 1992; 22:211-221

120. Cohen-Mansfield J: Instruction Manual for the Cohen-Mansfield Agitation Inventory (CMAI). Manual of The Research Institute of the Hebrew Home of Greater Washington, 1991

121. European Rating Aggression Group: Social Dysfunction and Aggression Scale (SDAS-21) in generalized aggression and in aggressive attacks: a validity and reliability study. Int J Meth Psychiatr Res 1992; 43:485-490

Early diagnosis of dementia: neuropsychology

Florence Pasquier

Received: 20 July 1998
Accepted: 23 July 1998

F. Pasquier
Department of Neurology
Memory Clinic
Centre Hospitalier Régional
et Universitaire
F-59037 Lille, France
Tel.: +33-320-445785
Fax: +33-320-446028
e-mail: pasquier@chru-lille.fr

Abstract Neuropsychology contributes greatly to the diagnosis of dementia. Cognitive deficits can be detected several years before the clinical diagnosis of dementia. The neuropsychological profile may indicate the underlying neuropathology. Neuropsychological assessment at an early stage of dementia has two goals: (a) to determine a memory disorder, not always associated with a memory complaint, and (b) to characterize the memory disorder in light of the cognitive neuropsychology and to assess other cognitive (and noncognitive) functions toward integrating the memory disorder in a syndrome. We review the global tools, the memory tests that describe the memory profile and indicate the underlying pathology, the assessment of other cognitive functions, and the neuropsychological patterns of typical Alzheimer's disease, frontotemporal dementia, primary progressive aphasia, semantic dementia, Lewy body dementia, subcortical dementia, and vascular dementia. These patterns must be interpreted in the light of the history, rate of progression, imaging results, and nature of existing behavioral disturbances. Moreover, there may be overlap between two or more pathologies, which complicates the diagnostic process. Follow-up of patients is necessary to improve diagnostic accuracy.

Key words Dementia · Diagnosis · Neuropsychology · Alzheimer's disease

Introduction

Neuropsychology contributes greatly to the diagnosis of dementia: it documents significant cognitive decline and reveals patterns of cognitive dysfunction that suggest the cause of the dementia. Cognitive deficits can be detected several years before the clinical diagnosis of dementia [49]. Establishing the neuropsychological profile often indicates the underlying neuropathology. Although Alzheimer's disease (AD) is the most frequent disorder, it is not the only cause of dementia in adults. Therefore carrying out the neuropsychological assessment at an early stage of dementia has two goals: (a) revealing memory disorders, which are not always associated with memory complaints (memory impairment is a core feature of dementia, while memory complaints are not always due to a memory disorder, e.g., in anxiety disorders), and (b) characterizing the memory disorder in the context of cognitive neuropsychology, thus allowing other cognitive (and noncognitive) functions to be integrated with the memory disorder into a broader syndrome.

Here we concentrate on the conditions in which dementia is relatively isolated, in the absence of major motor symptoms.

Neuropsychological tools

Global tools: comprehensive assessment of dementia

The multi-item rating scales and batteries of brief cognitive tests evaluate the various cognitive functions that are typically impaired in dementia. Scores on various separate items or tests are summed to provide a total score representing overall cognitive status. These comprehensive assessments are typically used in the diagnosis to confirm the presence of cognitive impairment. The major problem of these cognitive tests in short formats is that their sensitivity is not uniform but varies by age, education, social class, and living situation (e.g., at home, independent of family members, in a geriatric institution, in hospital) [5, 10, 44, 61, 97]. However, they are useful in grading the severity of dementia and assessing the rate of cognitive decline.

One of the simplest and most universal tests is the Mini-Mental State Examination (MMS) [20]. An MMS score of 27 or higher is usually taken as excluding mental impairment [21], while one of 23 or lower generally indicates sufficient cognitive decline for the diagnosis of dementia to be made in epidemiological studies. MMS has disadvantages for the screening of vascular dementia (VaD) [80]: it emphasizes language and verbal memory, it lacks the recognition part of memory, it has no timed elements, and it is not sensitive to impairments in executive functions or mental slowing.

One of the most useful instruments is the Mattis Dementia Rating Scale (DRS) [52]. This was designed as a screening instrument to detect the presence of brain pathology in impaired geriatric patients. It evaluates a broad array of cognitive functions and includes subtests for attention, initiation, perseveration, construction, conceptualization, verbal and nonverbal memory. Thus it is sensitive to frontal and fronto-subcortical dysfunctions. High test-retest reliability has been reported [52], and normative data have been published [89].

Some of the most well-known tests are not designed for diagnosis and are used principally for longitudinal studies. For example, the Alzheimer's Disease Assessment Scale (ADAS) [81] was designed to provide a composite assessment of longitudinal investigations and clinical trials including patients with AD, Also, the Blessed rating instrument does not seem ideal for evaluating the severity of dementia in AD [77].

Some interview schedules explore the cognitive functioning of the suspected demented, his/her daily living adaptation, and the presence of psychiatrically relevant symptoms (provided by a close relative or informant). Among the few standardized interview schedules currently available, the Cambridge Mental Disorders of the Elderly Examination (CAMDEX) [82, 83], which contains a cognitive section (CAMCOG), offers high psychometric quality due to its sensitivity to different levels of severity of dementia, rated on the basis of internationally established criteria [65, 66]. In particular, the CAMDEX reliably detects cases of minimal and mild dementia [64] and is independent of cultural factors [15, 36, 48, 63]. However, the generalized employment of CAMDEX in dementia is made difficult by its length (its administration requires 60–90 min). A short version has been designed which requires about 30 min to administer and consists of 106 of the 340 items of the full form [64].

The Consortium to Establish a Registry for Alzheimer's Disease (CERAD) was developed in the United States to standardize assessment of the presenting neurological manifestations, cognitive impairment, and neuropathological abnormalities in patients with AD [38, 60]. The neuropsychological part may be used to detect and to stage dementia [101]. The normative data of the neuropsychological battery are available [102].

These global tools are useful for documenting dementia but not appropriate for detecting subtle cognitive impairment or discriminating cognitive profiles. The etiological diagnosis of dementia requires a more detailed analysis. Assessing neuropsychological functions should include tests of each major cognitive domain. A qualitative analysis of the errors or types of failures in individual tasks is also required to distinguish between different diseases.

Assessment of memory

In diagnosing the cause of dementia it is important to distinguish between failures of (a) storage (or retention), associated with damage to limbic and especially hippocampal structures, (b) retrieval associated with frontal-subcortical dysfunctions, and (c) short-term memory associated with temporo-parietal lesions:

- Storage disorders are characterized on testing by deficits in both recall and recognition and rapid loss of information at delayed recall. The patient shows little benefit from cues and provision of multiple choice alternatives.
- Retrieval disorders are characterized by a difficulty in accessing information. Free recall is low, perhaps because of lack of active or efficient search strategies, but cues and multiple-choice alternatives enhance performance. Recognition is better than recall, and delayed recall is not impaired.
- Short-term memory disorders are characterized on testing by reduced memory span and rapid loss of information measured by the Brown-Peterson paradigm [68].

The Wechsler Memory Scale-Revised (WMS-R), contains nine subtests and has excellent age norms. It may distinguish amnesic from demented patients [6], but it was not designed for this purpose, and the overall score submerges potential differences in reasons for failure. Moreover, it does not assess specifically the various components of memory.

The best instrument for assessing memory disorders in early dementia is probably the Free and Cued Selective Reminding Test (FCSRT) [31, 32]. Unlike most clinical memory tests which do not control cognitive processing, this test includes a study procedure in which subjects search for items (e.g., grapes) in response to cues (e.g., fruit) that are later used to elicit recall of items not retrieved by free recall. Including a study procedure is particularly important for identifying early dementia. Other pathological or physiological conditions which limit learning when study conditions are not controlled are otherwise confused with dementia-associated memory impairment in preclinical and early stage disease. Furthermore, cued recall is considered the most useful test among a large neuropsychological battery in making diagnosis decision by neuropsychologists [96]. Performance on the FCSRT distinguishes dementia from normal aging with accuracy. Moreover, the test (immediate recall, free and cued recall, learning slope, recognition, delayed free and cued recall) provides a characterization of the memory impairment which distinguishes AD from subcortical dementia [76] and from frontotemporal dementia (FTD) [69]. This test is sensitive to early neuropathological changes in AD, in comparison to global status tests [33], with a correspondence with the Braak and Braak histological stages.

Short-term memory, assessed by the digit span, is not very sensitive to dementia [18, 49] but may be particularly impaired in progressive aphasia. The Corsi test [92], a spatial span measure, may be more sensitive to dementia. The performance on dual tasks is impaired early in dementia, but the specificity of this impairment according to the required tasks is not yet known.

Assessment of other cognitive functions

Language (production and comprehension), motor/praxis, perceptual and visuospatial, attention and concentration, and "frontal lobe" function must be assessed to integrate the memory impairment into a neuropsychological syndrome. A number of tests are discussed here, but the purpose of this section is not to review psychometric tests in general since each neuropsychologist is accustomed to using his/her own battery. The most important thing in clinical practice is to use pertinent tools to detect and characterize a dysfunction. In addition, the choice of tests depends on the purpose of the study, and, in particular, good tools for early diagnosis are not necessary the best for the follow-up.

Language

The various components of language may be assessed by confrontation naming: the short version of the Token test [13], reading, writing, and word fluency. Word fluency (letter and category fluency tests) is very sensitive to dementia but is not specific regarding cause. The value of language assessment (type of paraphasia/paragraphia, syntax, phonology, fluency) for differential diagnosis in patients visiting a memory clinic has recently been assessed [93].

Visuospatial ability

Several tests are available for assessing perceptual and particularly visuospatial functions, such as the "embedded" figures tests, the Wechsler Adult Intelligence Scale (WAIS) block design subtests, and the clock drawing test. Disturbances of visual function are not uncommon in AD, and several cases with complex impairment of visuospatial abilities have been described, while these functions are preserved in other dementias.

Apraxia

Constructional praxis (spontaneous drawing, copying geometrical figures) and gestural praxis (imitation and command, uni- and bimanual, object utilization), should be assessed. The nature of the production suggest impairment of the frontal lobe or the subcortical-frontal structures as a difficulty in control and temporal sequencing. It indicates damage of the superior parietal regions as a consequence of spatial dysfunction.

Frontal lobe tests

So-called frontal lobe tests, those evaluating abstraction, planning, and mental flexibility such as the Stroop test [94] and the Trail Making test [78], the Wisconsin card-sorting test, and set-shifting are useful but are not actually specific or sensitive to frontal lobe impairment per se. Divided attention and dual tasks are impaired early in dementia but do not seem to differ between the various types of dementia.

Abstract thinking, concept formation, and problem solving are not the first functions to be impaired in AD [28]. Measures include the WAIS similarities subtest of abstract verbal reasoning, concept formation, and language comprehension. Raven's Progressive Matrices examine problem-solving ability and are frequently used in place of the WAIS to estimate general intelligence in the elderly and to detect cognitive impairment [9].

Neuropsychological profiles of the main dementia syndromes at early stage

The typical AD syndrome is the most common condition. However, patients may present with a different neuropsychological profile. Some of these are likely to be related to AD but others are certainly not. The differential diagnosis between AD and non-AD is of major importance for treatment and research purposes.

Weintraub and Mesulam [99] identified four behaviorally related neuropsychological profiles, based on their experience: (a) progressive amnestic dementia, (b) primary progressive aphasia, (c) progressive visuospatial dysfunction, and (d) progressive comportment dysfunction. Progressive amnestic dementia and progressive visuospatial dysfunction are likely to involve AD [4, 41] while primary progressive aphasia and progressive behavioral disorders are not. In asymmetric cortical degeneration syndromes, neuropathological study usually shows mild nonspecific degenerative changes [8].

We focus on the most frequent syndromes that may pose differential diagnostic problems with AD.

Typical Alzheimer's disease

The first symptom of typical AD [57] is impairment of recent memory: poor learning and retention of information over time. Patients with AD show poor learning over repeated trials and may make intrusion errors [7]. This is a disorder of storage, retrieval, and later of short-term memory. The test for delayed recall has been found to be the best overall discriminative measure to differentiate patients with early AD from cognitively normal elderly controls with the CERAD battery [100, 101], and this is confirmed by other studies [1, 50]. Patients with AD lose more information after a brief delay than patients with amnesic or dementing disorder. Albert [1] found that the first delayed recall trial from the California verbal learning test, the immediate recall of figures from the Wechsler memory scale, and the time to completion on trail B of the trail making test to be the most significant predictors of progression of cognitive difficulties in subjects followed up for several years. Digit span may be in the normal range at early stages.

Comparison of the relative prevalence of different cognitive deficits indicates that the disorder of lexical-semantic language is second [42], while syntactic and phonological abilities are relatively preserved. Multivariate procedures to determine the efficacy of various measures in distinguishing between early AD and controls have found that the only nonmemory factor that assists delayed recall (the best discriminator) is confrontation naming [101]. The typical pattern of language impairment at an early stage is one resembling anomic aphasia but with few neologistic paraphasia, progressing through patterns resembling transcortical sensory aphasia but with relatively good performance on tasks such as sentence repetition. It is manifested by word-finding pauses in conversational speech. In formal testing, patients are impaired on reading comprehension and verbal reasoning. Verbal fluency tests are impaired in the early stage, especially the category fluency, but this is not specific to AD [73].

Visuospatial skills are often impaired relatively early in the disease. Patients with AD suffer from disorientation and are unable to copy three-dimensional figures accurately [11]. On the WAIS they obtain their lowest scores on Block Design and have difficulty copying the designs of the Benton visual retention test [67]. Facial recognition is generally impaired early in AD, with deficit attributable to both perceptual and memory dysfunction.

Frontotemporal dementia

Most of the patients with FTD meet the criteria for AD. Standard tests and many tasks traditionally thought to be sensitive to frontal dysfunction are ineffective in discriminating between AD and FTD [30]. Nevertheless, the diagnosis of FTD is clinically possible on the basis of history (personality and behavioral changes precede and remain prominent during the course of the disease), the nature of the behavioral disorder, normality on EEG, predominance of frontal or anterior temporal abnormalities on brain imaging, and neuropsychology [17, 69, 91].

At the beginning of the disease, scores on global scales such as the WAIS may be within the normal range. There is no systematic dissociation between verbal and performance IQ, in contrast to AD [59], although it is sometimes observed [45]. It highlights the dissociation between the profound alteration in personality and behavior and breakdown in social competence, and relative preservation of cognitive skills [91]. It contributes to the misdiagnosis of FTD. The MMS score may remain high for a long time [19]. Counting backwards may be the most sensitive subtest in FTD. Thus this tool does not seem suitable as a screening tool for differentiating FTD from AD. The Mattis DRS [52] is more reliable, as it is in subcortical dementia [86].

At early stages, patients are typically oriented in time and place and provide correct current autobiographical information. Family members notice a memory impairment but considers it less important than the behavioral disorder [69] and regard it as due to the behavioral difficulties [34]. Some memory tests are normal [43]. Patients may obtain normal scores on the logical memory subtest of the Wechsler Memory Scale with disjoined account [69]. Thus the choice of the test is important for showing the memory deficit. On the FCSRT [31, 32], free recall is as poor as in AD at the same degree of severity of dementia, but recall performance is more enhanced by the use of specific, directed questions rather than open-ended questions and by the use of cues and provision of multiple-choice alternative responses in FTD than in AD [62, 69, 91]. Table 1 compares AD and FTD on cognitive testing.

The pattern of memory breakdown is consistent with a "frontal-type" amnesia, with memory failures arising sec-

Table 1 Major differences between AD and FTD on cognitive testing (from [73])

	FTD vs AD
Short-term memory	
Digit span	=
Brown-Petterson paradigm	
Verbal	=
Visuospatial	>
Verbal explicit long-term memory	
Immediate recall	>
Free recall	=
Benefit of cueing	>
Recognition	>
Delayed cued recall	>
Implicit memory	
Verbal priming	>
Perceptual priming	>
Verbal fluency	=
Attention	
Selective attention (cancellation task)	
False alarms	>
Sustained attention	>
Alert	<
Stroop test	
Time	<
Errors	=
Trail Making Test (part B)	
Time	<
Errors	>

ondary to failures of attentional, retrieval strategies, organizational, and regulatory factors rather than a primary impairment of storage. The variability and unpredictability of memory performance support this hypothesis.

Spontaneous speech is usually reduced. Language utterances are typically grammatically correct without paraphasias and are sometimes of the semantic type [62, 69, 91]. There may be stereotyped remarks. Comprehension typically remains well preserved except for complex syntactic sentences which requires mental manipulation and sequencing of information. Naming skills are usually well preserved, although responses of the "don't know" variety are not rare. Reading aloud is preserved. Verbal fluency is impaired early [59, 73].

Patients have no difficulties in the perceptual recognition of objects and the appropriate use of objects. The main feature is that spatial skills are notably preserved [69, 91]. Although during the early part of the disease patients may perform poorly on constructional tasks such as drawing and block constructions, qualitative examination of the pattern of impaired performance suggests that this does not have a primarily spatial basis but arises secondary to organizational failure. This feature distinguishes FTD from AD. Upon testing, gestural praxis may be more easily evoked by imitation than by verbal command, and long remain normal, which is also a differential trait from AD.

Frontal lobe tests may be impaired, but surprisingly not always, at early stages of the disease.

FTD is associated with a primary degeneration of the frontal and anterior temporal lobes that may correspond with several histological syndromes, including Pick's disease and nonspecific degeneration, but not with AD. It is not yet possible to distinguish Pick's disease neuropsychologically from nonspecific frontal lobe degeneration.

Primary progressive aphasia

If the language disorder remains isolated for more than 2 years without behavioral abnormalities, the syndrome of "primary progressive aphasia" should be considered [91, 99]. It is characterized by difficult speech output, phonemic paraphasias, and relative preservation of comprehension, different from the pattern of AD. Calculation disorders may be contemporary, as well as some orofacial dyspraxia. Nonlanguage tasks are performed well, although praxic difficulties may be present on testing [58, 91, 99].

It is unlikely to find Alzheimer pathology at autopsy of patients with this syndrome. Nonspecific frontotemporal lobe degeneration or Lewy body disease and even corticobasal degeneration are more likely.

Semantic dementia

Some patients present with a progressive fluent aphasia on testing, in which the "aphasia" appears to reflect a severe loss of the semantic components of language with a preservation of other linguistic abilities. This syndrome is termed "semantic dementia" [90] (see below). It is characterized by profound loss of meaning for both words and objects. The loss of knowledge in semantic dementia is not confined to tests for understanding word meaning and word production. They are also grossly impaired on nonverbally based tasks requiring the matching of semantically related pictures of objects. This is in contrast to well-preserved memory for day-to-day events, such as remembering recent personal events and appointments [29, 39, 40, 90, 98]. Patients perform visuospatial and praxis tasks normally, and memory is not impaired at an early stage.

Relatively few patients with semantic dementia undergo postmortem histological study, but all show either classic Pick's disease or nonspecific temporal more than frontal degeneration [29, 40, 91].

Lewy body dementia

There are still only few neuropsychological data available on patients with Lewy body dementia. This dementia is characterized by cortical and subcortical-frontal dysfunctions [54–56]. In a retrospective study, Salmon et al. [87] compared patients with Lewy body disease with equally demented patients with "pure" AD and found that they have severe deficits in visuospatial and visuoconstructive abilities. Differences in the impairment of visual memory and attention have been described between patients with Lewy body disease and those with AD [84, 88]. Studies have demonstrated that Lewy body dementia without concomitant AD can produce a global dementia characterized by particularly pronounced deficits in memory (i.e., retrieval), attention, visuospatial abilities, and psychomotor speed [85]. A recent study has shown severe but similar degrees of impaired performances in tests of attention/short-term memory (digit span) frontal lobe function (verbal fluency, category, and Nelson card-sort test) and motor sequencing in both Lewy body dementia and AD groups as in Parkinson's disease patients and controls [26]. In the clock face test improved performance was noted in the "copy" compared to "draw" part of the test in controls, patients with AD and those with Parkinson's disease but not in the patients with Lewy body dementia, who achieved equally poor scores in both part of the test. This feature could help to distinguish between patients with Lewy body dementia and patients with AD. The clock face test assesses executive and visuospatial functioning, which may be greatly impaired in Lewy body dementia [26]. Fluctuations in performance from one testing to another is a striking feature in Lewy body disease [53].

Subcortical dementia

The clinical concept of subcortical dementia was introduced by Albert et al. [2] to describe the mental deterioration in Huntington's disease and progressive supranuclear palsy. This concept has been extended to other extrapyramidal syndromes. Its cardinal features are: forgetfulness, i.e., difficulty in retrieving learned material; slowing of mental and motor processes; intellectual deterioration characterized by impaired ability to manipulate acquired knowledge to generate problem solving; impairment of arousal, attention, and motivation and affective changes (depression); and impairment of set-shifting [12]. Freedman and Albert [22] have suggested that the term frontotemporal system dementia would be more accurate since it is better correlated with anatomical and functional disturbances of the frontal lobe and the deep white matter.

This syndrome is encountered in VaD and in extrapyramidal diseases (progressive supranuclear palsy, Huntington's disease, and Parkinson's disease (for review see [16]). It obviously has common features with FTD, but motor and mental slowing (in absence of adverse medications such as neuroleptics) is very late in FTD and suggests a dysfunction of basal ganglia, as well as an apathetic state; magnetic resonance imaging is thus needed to detect lacunae in the thalamus caudate or lenticular nuclei [72, 74].

Corticobasal degeneration

This is characterized by a severe asymmetric apraxia, which may or may not be accompanied by spatial dysfunction. It may also be associated with a mild subcortical dementia [51].

Vascular dementia

A wide variety of neuropsychological changes may be observed in VaD. Clinical features depend on the location, number, size, and cause of vascular lesions [80]. Among neuropsychological deficits, the presence of cognitive and behavioral disorders resembling those in patients with lesions of the prefrontal cortex is frequently underlined [27]. The first description of qualitative neuropsychological aspects in the subcortical type of VaD (small vessels, in contrast to the cortical form due to large vessel disease) was published by Cummings and Benson [11]. This form of VaD may lack an abrupt onset and show a progressive course; it is therefore sometimes confused with AD. The neuropsychological profile is of subcortical dementia with mental slowing and problems in retrieval more than of storage.

The MMS has disadvantages for VaD screening [80]. The Mattis DRS is preferable. However, no specific pattern has been found to distinguish between VaD and AD, except for a greater impairment of conceptualization in Bingswanger's disease than in AD [3]. A list is available of the tests that are sensitive to the disturbances in VaD [71, 79, 95].

Differences between AD and VaD have been reported in executive and motor functions, language, speech, attention, fluency, and episodic memory. VaD patients are better at naming and commit fewer intrusion errors than AD patients in confrontation naming. Lexical-semantic abilities are better preserved, but syntax and motor aspects of speech are more impaired [42]. The motor speech abnormalities include dysarthria, reduced rate, and disruption of melody and pitch. There is a slight difference in favor of AD for executive functions, in agreement with studies emphasizing the importance of frontal lobe dysfunction in VaD. Moreover, patients with VaD are more helped by semantic cues in retrieving information than are patients with AD [14], again in agreement with a frontal-subcortical dysfunction rather than a hippocampal impairment. Some patterns of behavior, such as the closing-in phe-

Table 2 Suggested neuropsychological assessment of dementia at early stage (from [74])

Cognitive function assessed	Suggested tests
Overall severity of dementia	Mattis Dementia Rating Scale [52]
Short-term memory	Digit span (Wechsler Memory Scale)
	Block tapping test [92]
Verbal long-term memory	FCSRT [32, 33]
Organized information (+/−)	Logical memory (Wechsler Memory Scale)
Visual long-term memory	Subtest of the Wechsler Memory Scale revised
Intelligence	Subtest of the WAIS
Frontal lobe test	Stroop test [94]
	Digit Cancellation test [92]
	Go–No Go test
Motor speed	Finger tapping
Constructional abilities	
Spontaneous speech	
Confrontation naming	
Comprehension	Token test, short version [13]
Verbal fluency	
Behavioral changes	Questionnaire de dyscontrole comportemental [46]
	Frontotemporal behavioral scale [47]

nomenon and the tendency to globalistic and odd responses on the Raven's Colored Matrices are considered to be a better indicator of a degenerative than for a vascular form of dementia [24]. VaD patients are helped by the cueing of geometrical figures if they fail to draw it, in contrast to AD patients [23].

Conclusion

There are qualitative differences in the cognitive impairment of patients with AD and patients with other types of dementia that contribute to the clinical differential diagnosis between neurodegenerative dementias. Neuropsychological assessment is of help for the early diagnosis of dementia to determine a profile that suggests its cause. We suggest a set of tests to assess dementia at early stage (Table 2). However, the results must be interpreted in the light of the patient's history, rate of progression, imaging, and nature of any behavioral disturbances. There may be some overlap between two or more pathologies such as AD plus vascular changes [37, 70] or AD plus Lewy bodies [35] that complicates the diagnostic processing. Follow-up of patients is necessary to improve diagnostic accuracy.

References

1. Albert MS (1996) Cognitive and neurobiologic markers of early Alzheimer's disease. Proc Natl Acad Sci USA 93:13547–13551
2. Albert ML, Feldman RG, Willis AL (1974) The subcortical dementia of subcortical palsy. J Neurol Neurosurg Psychiatry 37:121–130
3. Bernard BA, Wilson RS, Gilley DW, Fleischman DA, Whalen ME, Bennet DA (1994) The dementia of Binswanger's disease and Alzheimer's disease: cognitive, affective and behavioral aspects. Neuropsychiatr Neuropsychol Behav Neurol 7:30–35
4. Berthier ML, Leiguarda R, Starkstein SE, Sevlever G, Taratuto AL (1991) Alzheimer's disease in a patient with posterior cortical atrophy. J Neurol Neurosurg Psychiatry 54:1110–1111
5. Bleecker ML, Bolla-Wilson K, Karvas C. Agnew J (1988) Age specific norms for Mini Mental State Examination. Neurology 38.1565 1568
6. Butters N, Salmon DP, Cullum CM, et al (1988) Differentiation of amnesic and demented patients with the memory Wechsler memory scale–revised. Clin Neuropsychol 2:133
7. Butters N, Delis DC, Lucas JA (1995) Clinical assessment of memory disorders in amnesia and dementia. Annu Rev Psychol 46:493–523
8. Caselli RJ, Jack CR (1992) Asymmertric cortical degeneration syndromes. A proposed clinical classification. Arch Neurol 49:770–780
9. Cohn JB, Wilcox CS, Lerer BE (1991) Development of an "early" detection battery for dementia of the Alzheimer type. Prog Neuropsychopharmacol Biol Psychiatry 15:433–479
10. Cummings JL (1993) Mini-Mental State Examination. Norms, normals and numbers. JAMA 269:2420–2421
11. Cummings JL, Benson DF (1983) Dementia: a clinical approach. Butterworth, Boston
12. Cummings JL, Benson DF (1984) Subcortical dementia review of an emerging concept. Arch Neurol 41:874–879
13. De Renzi E, Faglioni P (1978) Normative data and screening power of a shortened version of the Token test. Cortex 14:41–49

14. Delre ML, Pennesse F, Ciurlino P, Abate G (1993) Analysis of verbal memory and learning by means of selective reminding procedure in Alzheimer and multi-infact dementias. Aging Clin Exp Res 5:185–193
15. Derix MM, Hofstede AB, Teunisse S. Hidjdra A, Walstra GJ, Weinstein HC, van Gool WA (1991) CAMDEX-N: the Dutch version of the the Cambridge Examination for Mental Disorders of the Elderly with automatic data processing. Tijdschr Gerontol Geriatr 22:143–150
16. Dubois B, Pillon B (1997) Cognitive deficits in Parkinson's disease. J Neurol 244:2–8
17. Elfgren C, Brun A, Gustafson L, Johansen A, Minthon L, Passant U, Risberg J (1994) Neuropsychological tests as discriminators between dementia of Alzheimer type and frontotemporal dementia. Int J Geriatr Psychiatry 9:635–642
18. Flicker C, Ferris S, Reisberg B (1991) Mild cognitive impairment in the elderly: predictors of dementia. Neurology 41:1006–1009
19. Filley CM, Kleinschmidt-De Masters BK, Gross KF (1994) Non-Alzheimer fronto-temporal degenerative dementia. A neurobehavioral and pathologic study. Clin Neuropathol 13:109–116
20. Folstein MF, Folstein SE, McHugh PR (1975) "Mini Mental State": a practical method for grading the cognitive state of patients for the clinician. J Psychiatr Res 12:189–198
21. Folstein MF, Anthony C, Perhed I, Duffy B, Gruenberg EM (1985) The meaning of cognitive impairment in the elderly. J Am Geriatr Soc 33:228–235
22. Freedman M, Albert ML (1985) Subcortical dementia. In: Vinken PJ, Bruyn GW, Klawans HL (eds) Handbook of clinical neurology, vol 46. Amsterdam, Elsevier, pp 311–316
23. Gainotti G, Carlomagno S, Monteleone D, Parlato V, Bonavita V (1991) Le rôle de quelques indices neuropsychologiques dans le diagnostic différentiel entre maladie d'Alzheimer et formes vasculaires de démences. Rev Neuropsychol 1:347–365
24. Gainotti G, Parlato V, Monteleone D, Carlomagno S (1992) Neuropsychological markers of dementia on visuaspatial tasks: a comparison between Alzheimer's type and vascular forms of dementia. J Clin Exp Neuropsychol 14:239–252

25. Galloway P, Sahgal A, McKeith IG, Lloyd S, Cook JH, Ferrier NI, Edwardson JA (1992) Visual pattern recognition memory and learning deficits in senile dementias of Alzheimer and Lewy body types. Dementia 3:101–107
26. Gnanalingham KK, Byrne EJ, Thornton A, Sambrooks MA, Bannister P. (1997) Motor and cognitive function in Lewy body dementia: comparison with Alzheimer's and Parkinson's disease. J Neurol Neurosurg Psychiatry 6 2:243–252
27. Godefroy O (1994) Frontal lobe dysfunction in vascular dementia. In: Leys D, Scheltens P (eds) Vascular dementia. ICG, Dordrecht, pp 53–67
28. Grady CL, Haxby JV, Horwitz B, et al (1988) Longitudinal study of the early neuropsychological and cerebral metabolic changes in dementia of the Alzheimer type. J Clin Exp Neuropsychol 10:576–596
29. Graff-Radford NR, Damasio AR, Hyman BT, et al (1990) Progressive aphasia in a patient wiht Pick's disease. Neurology 40:620–626
30. Gregory CA, Orrell M, Sahakian B, Hodges JR (1997) Can frontotemporal dementia and Alzheimer's disease be differentiated using a brief battery of tests? Int J Geriat Psychiatry 12:375–383
31. Grober E, Buschke H (1987) Genuine memory deficits in dementia. Dev Neuropsychol 3:13–36
32. Grober E, Buschke H, Crystal H, Bang S, Dresner R (1988) Screening for dementia by memory testing. Neurology 38:900–903
33. Grober E, Dickson DW, Sliwinski M, et al (1997) Free and cued selective reminding is sensitive to neuropathology of early Alzheimer's disease. Neurology 48; A338
34. Gustafson L, Brun A, Risberg J (1990) Frontal dementia of non-Alzheimer type. Adv Neurol 51:65–71
35. Hansen L, Salmon D, Galasko D, Masliah E, Katzman R, DeTeresa R, et al (1990) The Lewy body variant of Alzheimer's disease: a clinical and pathologic entity. Neurology 40:1–8
36. Hendrie HC, Hall KS, Brittain HM, Austrom MG, Farlow M, Parker J, Kane M (1988) The CAMDEX: a standardized instrument for the diagnosis of mental disorders in the elderly: a replication with a US sample. J Am Geriatr Soc 36:402–408
37. Hénon H, Durieu I, Hamon M, Lucas C, Godefroy O, Pasquier F, Leys D (1997) Prevalence of preexisting dementia in consecutive unselected stroke patients. Stroke 428:2429–2436

38. Heyman A, Fillenbaum GG, Mirra SS (1990) Consortium to Establish a Registry for Alzheimer's Disease (CERAD): clinical, neuropsychological, and neuropathological components. Aging 2:415–424
39. Hodges JR, Patterson K, Oxburry S. Funnell E (1992) Semantic dementia. Progressive fluent aphasia with temporal lobe atrophy. Brain 115:1783–1806
40. Hodges JR, Patterson KE, Tyler LK (1994) Loss of semantic memory: implications for the modularity of mind. Cogn Neuropsychol 11:505–543
41. Hoff PR, Archin N, Osmand AP, Dougherty JH, Wells C, Bouras C, Morrison JH (1993) Posterior cortical atrophy in Alzheimer's disease: analysis of a new case and re-evaluation of a historical report. Acta Neuropathol 86:215–223
42. Huff FJ (1990) Language in normal aging and age-related neurological diseases. In: Boller F, Grafman J (eds) Handbook of neuropsychology. vol 4. Elsevier, Amsterdam, pp 251–264
43. Johanson A, Hagberg B (1989) Psychometric characteristics in patients with frontal lobe degeneration of non-Alzheimer type. Arch Gerontol Geriatr 8:129–137
44. Jorm AF, Scott R, Henderson AS, Woods T, Harris SJ (1988) Educational level differences on the Mini-Mental State: the role of test bias. Psychol Med 18:727–731
45. Knopman DS, Christensen KJ, Schut LJ, et al (1989) The spectrum of imaging and neuropsychological findings in Pick's disease. Neurology 9:362–368
46. Lebert F, Pasquier F, Petit H (1996) Evaluation comportementale dans la DTA par le questionnaire de dyscontrôle comportemental (QDC) Presse Med 25:665–667
47. Lebert F, Pasquier F, Souliez L, Petit H (1998) Frontotemporal behavioural scale. Alzheimer Dis Assoc Disord (in press)
48. Linas J, Vilalta J, Lopez PS, Amiel J, Vidal C (1990) The Cambridge Mental Disorder of the Elderly Examination. Validation of the Spanish adaptation. Neurologia 5:117–120
49. Linn RT, Wolf PA, Bachman DL, et al (1995) The "preclinical phase" of probable Alzheimer's disease. A 13-year prospective study of the Framingham Cohort. Arch Neurol 52:485–490
50. Locascio JJ, Growdon JH. Corkin S (1995) Cognitive test performance in detecting, staging and tracking Alzheimer's disease. Arch Neurol 52:1087–1099

51. Massman PJ, Kreiter KT, Jankovic J, Doody RS (1996) Neuropsychological functioning in cortico-basal ganglionic degeneration: differentiation from Alzheimer's disease. Neurology 46:720–726
52. Mattis S (1976) Mental status examination for organic mental syndrome in the elderly patients. In: Bellak L, Karasu TB (eds) Geriatric psychiatry: a handbook for psychiatrists and primary care physicians. Grune & Stratton, New York, p 77–121
53. Mega MS, Masterman DL, Benson F, et al (1996) Dementia with Lewy bodies: reliability and validity of clinical and pathologic criteria. Neurology 47:1403–1409
54. McKeith IG, Fairbairn AF, Perry RH (1992) Clinical diagnostic criteria for Lewy body dementia. Dementia 3:251–252
55. McKeith IG, Perry R, Fairbairn AF, et al (1992) Operational criteria for senile dementia of Lewy body type (SDLT). Psychol Med 22:911–922
56. McKeith IG, Galasko D, Kosaka K, et al (1996) Consensus guidelines for the clinical and pathological diagnosis of dementia with Lewy bodies (DLB): report of the consortium on DLB international workshop. Neurology 47:113–1124
57. McKhann G, Drachman D, Folstein M, et al (1984) Clinical diagnosis of Alzheimer's disease: report of the NINCDS-ADRDA work group under the auspices of Department of Health and Human Services Task Force on Alzheimer's disease. Neurology 34:939–944
58. Mesulam MM (1987) Primary progressive aphasia. Differentiation from Alzheimer's disease. Ann Neurol 22:533–534
59. Miller BL, Cummings JL, Villanueva-Meyer J, et al (1991) Frontal lobe degeneration: clinical neuropsychological, and SPECT characteristics. Neurology 41:1374–1382
60. Morris JC, Heyman A, Mohs RC, et al (1989) The Consortium to Establish a Registry for Alzheimer's Disease (CERAD). I. Clinical and neuropsychological assessment of Alzheimer's disease. Neurology 39:1159–1165
61. Murden RA, McRae TD, Kaner S, Bucknam M (1991) Mini-Mental Exam scores vary with education in Blacks and Whites. J Am Geriatr Soc 39:149–155
62. Neary D, Snowden JS (1996) Clinical features of frontotemporal dementia. In: Pasquier F, Lebert F, Scheltens P (eds) Frontotemporal dementia. ICG, Dordrecht, pp 31–47

63. Neri M, Andermarcher E, Spano A, Salvioli G, Cipolli C (1992) Validation study of the Italian version of the Cambridge Mental Disorders of the Elderly Examination: preliminary findings. Dementia 3:70–77
64. O'Connor DW (1990) The contribution of CAMDEX to the diagnosis of mild dementia in community surveys. Psychiatr J University Ottawa 15:216–220
65. O'Connor DW, Pollit PA, Hyde JB, Fellows JL, Miller ND, Brook CP, Reiss BB, Roth M (1989) The prevalence of dementia as measured by the Cambridge Mental Disorders of the Elderly Examination. Acta Psychiatr Scand 79:190–198
66. O'Connor DW, Pollit PA, Hyde JB, Fellows JL, Miller ND, Roth M (1990) A follow-up study of dementia diagnosed in the community using the CAMDEX. Acta Psychiatr Scand 81:78–82
67. Ogden JA (1990) Spatial abilities and deficits in aging and age-related disorders. In: Boller F, Grafman J (eds) Handbook of neuropsychology, vol 4. Elsevier, Amsterdam, pp 265–278
68. Peterson LR, Petersen MJ (1959) Short term retention of individual items. J Exp Psychol 91:341–343
69. Pasquier F (1996) Neuropsychological features and cognitive assessment in frontotemporal dementia. In: Pasquier F, Lebert F, Scheltens P (eds) Frontotemporal dementia. ICG, Dordrecht, pp 49–69
70. Pasquier F, Leys D (1997) Why stroke patients are prone to develop dementia? J Neurol 244:135–142
71. Pasquier F, Jacob B, Lefebvre C, Grymonprez L, Debachy B, Petit H (1994) How to evaluate cognitive dysfunction in patients with vascular dementia. In: Leys D, Scheltens P (eds) Vascular dementia. ICG, Dordrecht, pp 47–53
72. Pasquier F, Lebert F, Petit H (1994) Pseudo progressive dementia and "strategic" infarcts. In: Leys D, Scheltens P (eds) Vascular dementia. ICG, Dordrecht, pp 99–103
73. Pasquier F, Lebert F, Grymonprez L, Petit H (1995) Verbal fluency in dementia of frontal lobe type and dementia of Alzheimer type. J Neurol Neurosurg Psychiatry 58:81–84
74. Pasquier F, Lebert F, Petit H (1995) Dementia, apathy, and thalamic infarct. Neuropsychiatr Neuropsychol Behav Neurology 8:208–214
75. Pasquier F, Lebert F, Petit H (1997) Consultations et Centre de la Mémoire. Solal, Marseille
76. Pillon B, Deweer B, Agid Y, Dubois B (1993) Explicit memory in Alzheimer's, Huntington's, and Parkinson's disease. Arch Neurol 50:374–379

77. Reisberg B, Ferris SH, de Leon MJ, et al (1988) Stage-specific behavioral, cognitive, and in vivo changes in age-associated memory impairment (AAMI) and primary degenerative dementia of the Alzheimer type. Drug Dev Res 15:101
78. Reitan RM (1958) Validity of trail making test as an indicator of organic brain damage. Percept Mot Skills 271–276
79. Roman GC (1992) Vascular dementia: proceedings of the NINDS-AIREN International Workshop on Vascular Dementia; NIH, Bethesda, MD, April 19–21, 1991. New Issues Neurosci 4:79–183
80. Roman G, Tateichi TK, Erkinjuntti T, et al (1993) Vascular dementia: diagnostic criteria for research studies. Report of the NINDS-AIREN International Workshop. Neurology 43:250–260
81. Rosen WG, Mohs RC, Davis KL (1984) A new rating scale for Alzheimer's disease. Am J Psychiatry 141:1356
82. Roth M, Tym E, Mountjoy CP, Huppert F, Hendrie H, Verma S, Goddard R (1986) CAMDEX: a standardized instrument for the diagnosis of mental disorders in the elderly with special reference to the early detection of dementia. Br J Psychiatry 149:698–709
83. Roth M, Huppert FH, Tym E, Mountjoy CQ (1988) CAMDEX, the Cambridge Examination for Mental Disorders of the Elderly. Cambridge University Press, Cambridge
84. Sahgal A, Galloway P, McKeith IG, Edwardson JA, Lloyd S (1992) A comparative study of attentional deficits in senile dementias of Alzheimer and Lewy body types. Dementia 3:350–354
85. Salmon DP, Galasko D (1997) Neuropsychological aspects of Lewy body dementia. In: Perry R, McKeith I, Perry E (eds) Dementia with Lewy bodies. Clinical, pathological, and treatment issues. Cambridge University Press
86. Salmon DP, Kwo-on-Yuen PF, Heindel WC, Butters N, Thal LJ (1989) Differentiation of Alzheimer's disease and Huntington's disease with the Dementia Rating Scale. Arch Neurol 46:1204–1208
87. Salmon DP, Galasko D, Hansen LA, Masliah E, Butters N, Thal LJ, Katzman R (1996) Neuropsychological deficits associated with diffuse Lewy body disease. Brain Cogn 31:148–165

88. Sahgal A, Galloway P, McKeith IG, Lloyd S, Cook JH, Ferrier NI, Edwardson JA (1992) Matching-to-sample deficits in patients with senile dementias of Alzheimer and Lewy body types. Arch Neurol 49:1043–1046

89. Schmidt R, Freidl W, Fazekas F, et al (1994) Mattis dementia rating scale: normative data from 1001 healthy volunteers. Neurology 44:964–966

90. Snowden JS, Goulding PJ, Neary D (1989) Semantic dementia: a form of circumscribed atrophy. Behav Neurol 2:167–182

91. Snowden JS, Neary D, Mann DMA (1996) Fronto-temporal lobar degeneration, fronto-temporal dementia, progressive aphasia, semantic dementia. Churchill-Livingstone, New York

92. Spinnler H, Tognoni G (1987) Standardizzazione e taratura italiana di test neuopsicologici. Ital J Neurol Sci [Suppl 8]

93. Stevens SJ, Harvey RJ, Kelly CA, Nicholl CG, Pitt BMN (1996) Characteristics of language performance in four groups of patients attending a memory clinic. Int J Geriat Psychiatry 11:973–982

94. Stroop JR (1935) Studies of interference in serial verbal reactions. J Exp Psychol 18:643–662

95. Tatemichi TK, Desmonds DW, Mayeux R, et al (1992) Dementia after stroke: baseline frequency, risks and clinical features in a hospitalized cohort. Neurology 42:1185–1193

96. Tuokko H, Kristjansson E, Miller J (1995) Neuropsychological detection of dementia: an overview of the neuropsychological component of the Canadian study of Health and Aging. J Clin Exp Neuropsychol 17:352–373

97. Uhlmann RF, Larson EB (1991) Effect of education on the Mini-Mental State Examination as a screening test for dementia. J Am Geriatr Soc 39:876–880

98. Warrington EK (1975) The selective impairment of semantic memory. Q J Exp Psychol 27:635–637

99. Weintraub S, Mesulam M-M (1993) Four neuropsychological profiles in dementia. In: Boller F, Grafman J (eds) Handbook of neuropsychology, vol 8, sect 11. Elsevier, Amsterdam, pp 253–282

100. Welsh K, Butters N, Hughes J, Mohs R, Heyman A (1991) Detection of abnormal memory decline in mild cases of Alzheimer's disease using CERAD neuropsychological measures. Arch Neurol 48:278–281

101. Welsh K, Butters N, Hughes J, Mohs R, Heyman A (1992) Detection and staging of dementia in Alzheimer's disease. Use of the neuropsychological measures developed for the Consortium to Establish a Registry for Alzheimer's Disease. Arch Neurol 49:448–452

102. Welsch KA, Butters N, Mohs RC, et al (1994) The consortium to establish a registry for Alzheimer's disease (CERAD). V. A normative study of the neuropsychological battery Neurology 44:609–614

[19]

Staff factors associated with perception of behaviour as 'challenging' in residential and nursing homes

E. MONIZ-COOK,[1] R. WOODS[2] & E. GARDINER[3]

[1]*Department of Clinical Psychology, School of Medicine, University of Hull, Hull,* [2]*Institute of Medical & Social Care Research, University of Wales, Bangor &* [3]*Department of Mathematics, University of Hull, Hull, UK*

Abstract
Three hundred and twenty-six staff, working in 14 residential and nursing homes across England, were asked to rate their 'ease of management' on 14 vignettes of challenging resident behaviour. Multiple regression was used to examine the correlates of staff appraisal of their management of challenging behaviour, using over 30 staff variables. These included demographics, experience, stress, burnout, job satisfaction, knowledge of dementia and management practices in the home. Only staff anxiety, supervisor support and the potential to relate to residents as individuals predicted 'perceived management difficulty'. In any given home, there was great variation in staff perception, and overall, qualified staff appear to have greater difficulty in managing challenging behaviour, as compared with care assistants. The clinical significance of these results for psychogeriatric interventions that focus on advising care staff on the management of resident behaviour is discussed.

Introduction

The extensive literature on stress and caregiving in dementia focused, until the mid-1990s, on the experiences of family carers. Since then, studies in North America have suggested that the factors that contribute to stress and burnout in staff working in residential and day care settings include the shift (Novak & Chappell, 1996), working conditions (Wilber & Specht, 1994), social support (Chappell & Novak, 1992), staff appraisal (Novak & Chappell, 1994) and uncooperative or difficult behaviour (Chappell & Novak, 1994). In the UK, staff stress and/or burnout have been linked with resident aggression (MacPherson et al., 1994), organisational aspects of the work setting (Baillon et al., 1996) and the quality of staff interactions with the residents that they care for (Jenkins & Allen, 1998). The contribution of difficult, uncooperative or aggressive resident behaviour to staff distress parallels the family caregiving literature, where some studies argue strongly that behaviour disturbance or 'non-cognitive features', which we refer to as 'challenging behaviour,' predict carer stress (see, for example, Donaldson et al., 1998). However, the relationship between resident behaviour and staff distress is complex, since the majority of difficult and uncooperative behaviour is predictable, not necessarily intrinsic to the resident, appears to occur during a self-care activity such as dressing or bathing (Beck et al., 1990; Burgener et al., 1992) and can be minimised if the caregiver remains relaxed and smiling (Burgener et al.,1992). Of perhaps more interest is the observation that problematic behaviour in a given resident is often perceived differently by different staff and its impact on different staff can also differ widely (Everitt et al., 1991). The emerging opinion is that the training of care staff is important (Baillon et al., 1996) and should be aimed at helping them work with residents (Chappell & Novak, 1994) or at altering their appraisal of the residents' behaviour (Novak & Chappell, 1994). Indeed, Monahan (1993) found that following an educational intervention, staff perceived behavioural symptoms as less problematic and were thus able to respond more effectively to specific behavioural problems of the resident. Another recent staff training intervention noted significant reductions in staff reports of residents' challenging behaviour, although the actual behaviours did not reduce (Moniz-Cook et al., 1998). Given that challenging behaviour can result in a reduced quality of life for both staff and resident, and that staff perception of the resident is probably as important to the psychogeriatric clinician as the resident's actual behaviour, we were interested in whether staff variables in themselves had an influence on their reports of difficult resident behaviour.

Thus one aim of this study was to assess whether staff stress, burnout, knowledge of dementia, job satisfaction, aspects of the work environment or demographic variables predicted their perceived difficulty in the management of challenging resident behaviour.

We were also interested in whether staff appraisal of their management of challenging behaviour differed across the different types of homes available to older people in the UK. This interest arose from two observations: first, that nursing homes, for example, have a requirement for specified numbers of qualified nurses as compared with residential homes and that the cost per resident is greater; and second, that following policy changes reflected in the National Health Service and Community Care Act (1990), local authorities were required to place the majority of residents requiring residential care, within the private sector. Many of the local authority homes therefore became private enterprises, where pay and conditions usually, but not always, matched those of the original local authority. This compared with a growing number of private residential homes, where, on the whole, care assistant pay was lower (i.e. £2.80 per hour on average). The present survey occurred at the time when much of the 1990 Act was in the process of implementation across the country and we were interested in whether, as a consequence of this, staff in some settings felt that they had greater difficulty in managing challenging behaviour.

Method

Procedure

All 435 staff who had frequent contact with residents in 14 'volunteer' residential and nursing homes were surveyed in a 'quality of life' study . Homes were selected as 'quality homes' because of their documented interest in, or programme of, staff training in the management of dementia and challenging behaviour. Questionnaire packs were delivered and collected 2 weeks later, by the researcher, with a covering note to assure confidentiality. Three hundred and twenty-six staff (75%) returned completed questionnaires with reasons for non-return as follows: absence due to short-term sickness (9%; $n=39$), long-term sickness (2%; $n=8$), annual leave (5%; $n=22$) and refusals/packs mislaid/no reason (9%; $n=40$).

Sample

The sample consisted of two private nursing homes, four private residential homes, five ex-local authority (now privately funded) residential homes and three local authority residential homes in Kent, the Midlands and Yorkshire. There was a range of 16–50 care staff working in each home. Staff in the sample were 74.4% care assistants, 9.0% officers or matrons, 8.7% managers and administrators, 6.7% qualified nurses and 1.3% domestics. Overall, 6.6% of staff were less than 20 years of age, 19.2% were aged 20–30, 18.3% were aged 30–40, 34.1% were aged 40–50 and 21.8% were more than 50 years old. The average number of hours worked per week was 27.9 (standard deviation (SD)=8.4) and the average length of experience caring for older people was 7.0 years (SD=5.8).

There was a range of 16–60 residents in each home with an average mean age of 82.7 years (SD=8.14, range 41–103). Twenty-seven per cent of these were male and 52% were described by staff as having dementia.

Measures

The self-report questionnaire pack consisted of the following.

(1) Demographics sheet (age band, grade of post, hours worked per week, duration of time working at home, experience of working with older people in months/years).

(2) Maslach Burnout Inventory (MBI) (Maslach & Jackson, 1981). A 22-item measure of the three facets of burnout: emotional exhaustion (EE) (feeling drained by the emotional nature of the work); depersonalisation (DP) (no longer treating residents as individuals); and reduced personal accomplishment (PA) (a reduced sense of satisfaction from doing a worthwhile job).

(3) General Health Questionnaire (GHQ-28) (Goldberg, 1978). A measure of general psychological well-being which has been used extensively with occupational samples including health professionals (Firth-Cozens & Hardy, 1992). This version has four subscales measuring depression (Scale A), anxiety (Scale B), somatic disturbance (Scale C) and social dysfunction (Scale D). Likert scoring (0123) was used for subscale scores and the GHQ scoring system 0011 was used with a cut off >5 to identify psychiatric 'cases'.

(4) Job Satisfaction Index (JS) (Firth-Cozens & Hardy, 1992). An 18-item compound Likert scale in which respondents rate their satisfaction with different aspects of their job on a scale from extremely dissatisfied (1) to extremely satisfied (7).

(5) Dementia Knowledge Quiz. A 17-item multiple choice quiz about dementia with items from Gilleard & Groom (1994) and Deickmann et al. (1988). Correct answers are scored as +1, 'don't know' responses as 0 and incorrect answers as –1/3, to compensate for the effect of guessing. The total score ranges from –5.66 to +17, with positive scores indicating knowledge above chance.

(6) Perceived difficulty in managing challenging behaviour: the Challenging Behaviour Vignettes (Silver, 1998). These consist of 14 hypothetical

vignettes of challenging behaviour in a residential setting. Staff rate their ease of management of a given vignette, on a four-point Likert scale (1234), i.e. 'easy to cope with or manage' to 'very difficult to cope with or manage'. They also rate one of four management styles, for each vignette, but we did not use these data for the present analysis and details are therefore not described here.

(7) Work Environment Scale (WES) and Sheltered Care Environment Scale (SCES) (Moos, 1991; Moos & Lemke, 1992). These are two measures of organisational variables or the 'environment' of a home, commonly referred to as work milieu or social climate scales. The WES is a 90-item scale measuring 10 aspects of the work milieu. These are: involvement (staff commitment to their job); peer cohesion (staff support of one another); supervisor support (management support of staff); autonomy (staff encouraged to make their own decisions); task orientation (emphasis on efficiency and getting a job done); work pressure (time urgency dominates the work environment); clarity (staff are clear about what to expect in their job); control (management uses rules to control staff); innovation (emphasis on change and new approaches); and physical comfort (pleasant physical surroundings). The SCES is a 63-item scale of seven subscales, designed to measure what a care environment may be like, for residents. It can be completed by residents, staff or both. Here, staff reported their perceptions of the environment from the perspective of a resident. The subscales are: cohesion (staff support of residents and residents' support of each other); conflict (residents' criticism of each other and the home); independence (residents encouraged to be responsible and self-directed); self-disclosure (residents openly express their concerns); organisation (importance of order, routines, clarity of rules and procedures in the home); resident influence (residents can influence regulations and can be free from restriction); and physical comfort (comfort, privacy, pleasant decor and sensory satisfaction are provided).

Statistical analysis

Average scores over the items were calculated for some questionnaires (for example, the Challenging Behaviour Vignettes) and total scores for others, for use in the modelling. The data collected included variables measured at two levels in a hierarchy: home (the first level); and staff within each home (the second level).

Our aims were as follows.

(1) To assess the contribution of a range of staff variables to the prediction of staff reports of the difficulty of managing challenging resident behaviour. These staff variables include staff perceptions of the environment and social climate as well as intra-personal measures.

(2) To assess whether staff reports differ across the different types of homes available to older people in the UK.

To do this, we used a multiple regression analysis at two levels. Multi-level modelling is now the accepted statistical method for analysing the effect of variables measured at more than one level on an outcome variable. An introduction to this technique can be found in Goldstein (1987). The first level included the differences between homes and between types of homes. At this level it was anticipated that there could be substantial between-home variation in the perception of challenging behaviour, since different home types receive differential funding, depending on whether they are residential or nursing, public or private (profit-making) homes. Also, there may have been substantial between-home variation in perception as a result of other, unmeasured differences between homes. The second level included the various staff measures. The statistical program Genstat, version 5 release 4.1 for Unix, was used because of its flexibility in multi-level modelling.

Missing values (89 staff out of 326 had one or more missing values) were imputed using the MULT-MISS procedure in Genstat. This gave some non-integer values for the ordinal variables, which were rounded to the nearest integer. Since staff grade was not an ordinal variable, the MULTMISS procedure could not be applied, and staff with unknown grades were therefore omitted, giving a final sample size of 311 for the regression analysis.

A two-level model was fitted to the vignette 'perceived management difficulty' mean scores by residual maximum likelihood, using the REML directive in Genstat. In the initial model, the home was considered as a random first-level factor and the type of home as a fixed first-level factor. The homes were considered as a random rather than a fixed factor, because differences between the actual homes in the study were not of interest but the degree of random variation of staff perception between homes more generally, was. At the second (staff) level, age band, hours worked, experience with older people, burnout (MBI-EE, MBI-DP and MBI-PA), depression (GHQ-A), anxiety (GHQ-B), somatization (GHQ-C) and social disturbance (GHQ-D), job satisfaction, knowledge (Dementia Knowledge Quiz), grade, all the WES subscales and all the SCES subscale scores were included with fixed (i.e. non-random) coefficients. Backward elimination was performed to simplify the model. Additionally, tests were made to examine whether the predictor variables GHQ-A, GHQ-B, GHQ-C and GHQ-D could be replaced by either the variable GHQ-0011, or the psychiatric 'case' binary variable. For the final model selected, checks were made by plotting residuals against fitted values and producing a normal probability plot of the residuals.

Results

Differences between homes and home-type in ease of coping with challenging behaviour

As illustrated in Fig. 1, there is no evidence that staff in some homes have greater difficulty in managing challenging behaviour than staff in other homes. However, the within-home variation appears to differ between homes; in particular, there is a large range in 'perceived management difficulty' scores for home 12.

The variance component corresponding to the random home effect for between-home variation was not statistically significant. Furthermore, the type of home did not have a statistically significant effect.

Predictors of 'perceived management difficulty'

Since there was no statistically significant random variation between homes and no statistically significant differences between home types, these terms were removed and the model was therefore reduced to an ordinary (single-level) multiple regression model. Using backward elimination, the model simplified to that containing terms GHQ-B (anxiety), grade, WES-SS (supervisor support), SCES-Coh (cohesion) and SCES-Inf (resident influence). These variables accounted for 16.1% of the variance. The parameter estimates (partial regression coefficients), standard errors and significance levels are shown in Table 1.

Thus, if all other variables are held constant, for an increase of 1 point in GHQ-B (anxiety), a small increase of 0.018 is expected on the 'perceived management difficulty' mean score; for an increase of 1 point in the WES-SS (supervisor support), an increase of 0.028 is expected; for an increase of 1 point in SCES-Coh (cohesion), a decrease of 0.042 is expected; and for an increase of 1 point in SCES-Inf (resident influence), a decrease of 0.030 is expected on the 'perceived management difficulty' mean. Interestingly, the bivariate correlation for the WES-SS subscale was essentially zero, although WES-SS accounted for moderate variability within the regression model.

As compared with care assistants (who comprised the majority of the sample) the 'perceived management difficulty' mean score is 0.19 higher for staff in charge of homes (officers or matrons), 0.15 higher for qualified nurses and 0.13 higher for domestics, if all other variables are held constant. However only 1.3% (n=4) of the sample were domestics, so any comparisons involving this category have large standard errors, i.e. the difference in the predicted 'perceived management difficulty' mean between care assistants and domestics has a large standard error and is not statistically significant. The 'perceived management difficulty' means for managers of the homes and for care assistants are about the same, if all other factors are held constant.

Residual plots did not reveal any patterns, apart from three outliers whose 'perceived management difficulty' mean scores are considerably higher than those predicted by the model. These were cases 22 and 23 (home 12) and 155 (home 3): see Fig. 1.

Discussion

First, we set out to examine whether staff in the different types of residential settings varied in their

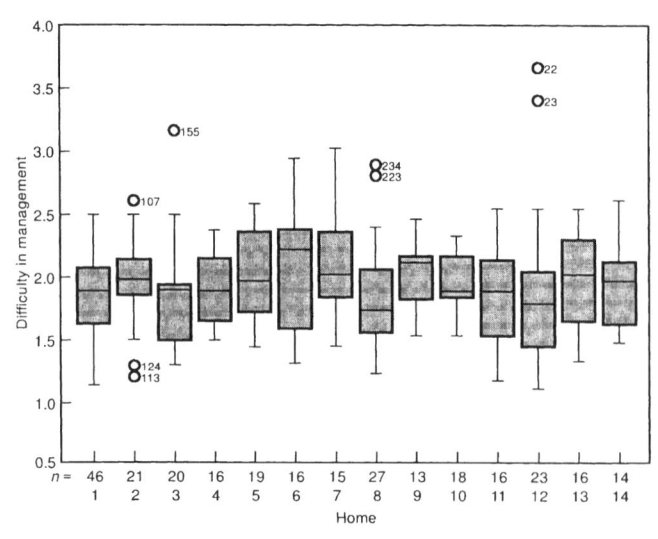

FIG. 1. Differences between homes in perceived management difficulty.

TABLE 1. Multiple regression showing the predictors of perceived difficulty in the management of challenging behaviour

	Estimate[1]	Standard error	t value	p value
Constant	2.0817	0.0935	22.26	0.0001
GHQ-B (anxiety and insomnia)	0.01774	0.00487	3.64	0.0004
Officers/matron[2]	0.1919	0.0706	2.72	0.0007
Managers[2]	−0.0044	0.0736	−0.06	0.9522
Qualified nurses[2]	0.1462	0.0792	1.85	0.0652
Domestics[2]	0.132	0.174	0.76	0.4478
WES-SS (supervisor support)	0.0278	0.0106	2.63	0.0009
SCES-Coh (cohesion)	−0.0420	0.0115	−3.66	0.0002
SCES-Inf (resident influence)	−0.0299	0.0118	−2.54	0.0116

[1] Parameter 'estimate' refers to the partial regression coefficients.
[2] Statistical significance assessed by F-test (not t-test) as grade is a categorical variable.

perception of the ease of management of challenging behaviour. Although there was no difference between types of home, our finding that there is greater within-home variation is of clinical value with regard to the training and support of staff who care for residents who might challenge them. Psychogeriatric National Health Services that offer advice, support or 'consultation clinics' (Jackson & Lyons, 1996) to staff in homes need to recognise that individual staff can vary in their management of difficult resident behaviour. Otherwise there is the risk of offering specialist advice which one set of staff who may have relative ease in managing a given challenging ('aggressive') resident can implement, whilst others in the same establishment, who have difficulty in managing aggressive behaviour, remain unable to implement the advice, resulting in an assault by the 'aggressive resident' and a crisis referral to psychogeriatric services. Our data did not allow us to properly examine the outliers (care assistants 22, 23 and 155) as we did not collect personal data about staff. For example, family and social support can alleviate stress in nursing assistants (Chappell & Novak, 1992) and, given that anxiety predicts 'perceived management difficulty', we may conclude that personal variables might account for the perceptions of these staff. Interestingly, in both homes 3 and 12, where these 'outliers' worked, there was a high level of noise and upheaval due to building and refurbishment, which may have affected tolerance and perception of the ability to manage challenging behaviour.

The finding that qualified staff (matrons, officers and nurses) appear to have more perceived difficulty in managing challenging behaviour confirms the Australian study (Snowden et al., 1996) where variations in reports of challenging behaviour between qualified and unqualified staff in residential settings were noted. This finding is also of clinical significance, since qualified staff in charge of a home are often the point of contact between the home and the psychogeriatric team. Thus, one might envisage the situation where one or two care staff within a home continue to have difficulty in the management of a challenging resident (when in reality other staff are coping) and report this to the qualified person in charge, who also also perceives the resident as difficult and requests an increase in psychotropic medication or an unnecessary 'crisis' referral to a psychiatric hospital. Although there is a widespread call for the training of unqualified care staff in the management of problem behaviour in care settings (see, for example, Moniz-Cook et al., 1998), our data suggest that qualified staff may also lack the skills or experience to manage the changing ageing population in care settings.

Second, we examined the predictors of perceived difficulty in managing challenging behaviour. A total of 30 staff variables were examined, including age, hours worked per week, experience of working with older people, three aspects of burnout (MBI), four aspects of psychiatric morbidity (GHQ A–D), knowledge of dementia, job satisfaction, 10 aspects of how the home is organised to support staff (WES) and seven aspects of how the home is organised to support residents (SCES). Only staff anxiety, supervisor support and the potential for a person-centred, individualised approach to resident care (four variables in total) related to staff perceptions of behaviour as challenging. Surprisingly, the knowledge of dementia did not have a significant effect on perceived difficulty in the management of challenging behaviour. The relationship between GHQ anxiety (but not depression, somatic complaints, social dysfunction or any of the burnout subscales) and 'perceived management difficulty' is important. Jackson & Lyons (1997, p. 682), in a letter about their routine roving psychogeriatric clinics for residential care, note that the number of 'crisis, domiciliary visits and inpatient hospital admissions' fell dramatically and that this was accompanied by the care staff perceiving that hospital admission was actually easier to facilitate! It may be that routine reassurance from a psychiatrist, including the knowledge that the hospital was available for an emergency, reduced staff anxiety and improved their efficacy in implementing the management advice offered. Empirical support is seen in a recent British study, where at 6-month follow-up, a programme of in-service staff training followed by the development of individualised resident care plans had a positive impact on psychiatric morbidity in care staff working in residential and nursing homes (Proctor et al., 1998). Other empirical support comes from a series of

Swedish studies which focused on clinical supervision followed by implementation of individualized patient care plans in dementia wards: over a 1-year period nurse creativity and the nurse–patient relationship improved, whilst staff strain, tedium and burnout reduced (Berg et al., 1994; Hallberg & Norberg, 1993). The relationship between the two SCES subscales and 'perceived management difficulty' suggests that the more staff are able to relate to the residents as individuals (resident influence) and are able to offer them help and support (cohesion), the less they perceive difficult behaviour as challenging. In the family caregiving literature, Johnson (1996) notes that when the care-receiver was made to feel more like an object (i.e. less of an individual), this was associated with increased conflict in the relationship and higher levels of upset. In hospital settings, there is also an indication that where the dignity and autonomy of dependent care-receivers are not preserved, there are acrimonious relations (Drew, 1986). The Scandinavian studies also confirm that staff attitude, i.e viewing the patient's life as meaningful and developing a cooperative nurse–patient relationship, is important in reducing strain and burnout (Astrom et al., 1991; Hallberg & Norberg, 1995). Pietrukowicz & Johnson (1991) found that access to a resident's life history resulted in staff rating the resident as more instrumental, autonomous and personally acceptable. Therefore, if care staff have a better understanding of the premorbid personality, individuality and experience of the resident with dementia, they may find it easier to adopt a person-centred style to resident care, which may in turn enhance the staff–resident relationship and result in staff perceptions of difficult behaviour as less challenging. This may also explain why a person-centred staff training programme showed improvements in staff perceptions of their difficulty in the management of challenging behaviour, but not in the actual reported resident behaviour (Moniz-Cook et al., 1998). The relationship between the WES-SS (supervisor support) subscale and 'perceived management difficulty' was unexpected. Where supervisor support is high, staff appear to have increased perceived difficulty in the management of challenging behaviour. One explanation for this is that if staff feel properly supported by their supervisor, they may be more willing to admit to the difficulties they experience in managing challenging behaviour. Alternatively, it may be that the quality of supervisor support is inadequate, that the involvement of the supervisor reduces staff efficacy, or that staff only rely on increased support from their supervisor when they perceive a resident as difficult. The statistical significance of the WES-SS subscale is difficult to interpret, since the pairwise correlation between the 'perceived difficulty in management' mean score and WES-SS was essentially 0, although WES-SS appears to have a statistically significant effect on the 'perceived difficulty in management' score when adjusted for other variables in the regression model. It must also be borne in mind that the correlations between the predictor variables identified within our model and the outcome variable, although statistically significant, were weak.

The amount of variance explained by the regression model was modest, as has been shown in other studies (Beck et al., 1998; Chappell & Novak, 1994). As in the family caregiving literature (see Grafstrom et al., 1994; Morris & Morris, 1993), the relationships between problem behaviour, burden, stress, coping and outcome may be complex. For example, we examined proximal work-related variables as correlates of perceived difficulty in the management of challenging behaviour (i.e. age, experience). Background variables, such as personal circumstances and life events (for example, family problems) or a staff member's idiosyncratic response to environmental circumstances (for example, the weather, or noise) might also contribute to perceptions of management difficulty. Examples of 'self-related' (personal) characteristics which may influence how well care staff may cope with work are documented by Benjamin & Spector (1990) and include staff beliefs about their qualifications, their personal abilities and skills, their interaction with their own family and their personal accommodation situation. The psychometric structure of the actual predictor measure (the 'perceived management difficulty' scale) may be another reason for the low variance explained by our model. Although this scale has good internal consistency and test–retest reliability (Silver, 1998), its four-point Likert rating scale may be an inadequate measure of the range of staff appraisal of ease of management of challenging behaviour. There was a tendency for staff to use Likert categories 1 and 2, perhaps because they were unwilling to be viewed as a 'failure' in resident care. Thus, a wider range of options within a Likert scale might improve our understanding of the predictors of difficulty in the management of challenging behaviour.

The strength of this study is its sample size, which exceeds other British research into formal carer stress in residential and nursing homes (for example, Baillon et al., 1996; Benjamin & Spector, 1990; Dunn et al., 1994; Jenkins & Allen, 1998; MacPherson et al., 1994; Moniz-Cook et al., 1997). Second, its sample was derived from a spread of homes across England, enhancing its generalizability. Third, it begins to unravel the complex area of staff efficacy in the management of challenging behaviour in residential and nursing homes. It has four limitations. First, its cross-sectional data hamper our understanding of the time-related process of the perception of difficulty in the management of challenging behaviour, i.e causality cannot be imputed. Second, our sample consisted of 'volunteer' homes which had in-service staff training in dementia and challenging behaviour planned or in place. Thus, generalizability may be compromised. Third, we relied on self-report of staff appraisal despite the observation that the measurement of challenging behaviour in surveys is in itself imperfect (see Hope & Patel, 1993). However, our results confirm that should such survey data be necessary, it is important to rely on the reports of a variety of staff and staff grades, if the reality of staff or resident experience is to be captured. Fourth, the vignette methodology may not measure the actual difficulties that staff might experience, since they are hypothetical and do not necessarily reflect the relationship between staff and an actual resident (although many vignettes closely approximated challenging residents).

This paper reports on one phase of a search for meaningful correlates of staff appraisal of their management of challenging behaviour. The high prevalence of challenging behaviour has an impact on both staff and the resident and studies that overlook one group (either resident or staff) fail to acknowledge the dynamic resident–staff relationship and the potential for alleviation of both resident and staff distress. A future paper will explore the correlates of both actual resident behaviour and staff perception of this. Exploration of the correlates of staff perception of the ease of management of challenging behaviour suggests that this is related to staff distress and that, in any given home, training support and advice should take into account the wide variation in staff perception and target both qualified staff-in-charge and care assistants, and developing person-centred approaches in dementia care (Kitwood, 1997) may help staff to manage residents who are perceived as 'difficult' or challenging.

Acknowledgements

The authors wish to acknowledge the contribution of Miriam Silver for data collection and Dr M. Wang for initial methodological advice. This study was funded by the National Health Service Executive (Northern & Yorkshire research and development programme). The views expressed are attributed solely to the authors.

References

ASTROM, S., NILSSON, M., NORBERG, A., SANDMAN, P. & WINBLAD, B. (1991). Staff burnout in dementia care—relations to empathy and attitudes. *Nursing Studies, 28,* 65–71.

BAILLON, S., SCOTHERN, G., NEVILLE, P.G. & BOYLE, A. (1996). Factors that contribute to stress in care staff in residential homes for the elderly. *International Journal of Geriatric Psychiatry, 11,* 219–226.

BECK, C., BALDWIN, B., MODLIN, T. & LEWIS, S. (1990). Caregivers' perception of aggressive behaviour in cognitively impaired nursing home residents. *Journal of Neuroscience Nursing, 22,* 169–172.

BECK, C., FRANK, L., CHUMBLER, N.R., O'SULLIVAN, P., VOGELPOHL, T.S., RASIN, J., WALLS, R. & BALDWIN, B. (1998). Correlates of disruptive behaviour in severely cognitively impaired nursing home residents. *The Gerontologist, 38,* 189–198.

BENJAMIN, L.C. & SPECTOR, J. (1990). The relationship of staff, resident and environmental characteristics to stress experienced by staff caring for the dementing. *International Journal of Geriatric Psychiatry, 5,* 25–31.

BERG, A., HANSSON, U.W. & HALLBERG, I.R. (1994). Nurses' creativity, tedium and burnout during 1 year of clinical supervision and implementation of individually planned nursing care: comparisons between a ward for severely demented patients and a similar control ward. *Journal of Advanced Nursing, 20,* 742–749.

BURGENER, S.C., JIROVEC, M., MURRELL, L. & BARTON, D. (1992). Caregiver and environmental variables related to difficult behaviors in institutionalised demented elderly persons. *Journal of Gerontology: Psychological Sciences, 47,* 242–249.

CHAPPELL, N.L. & NOVAK, M. (1992). The role of support in alleviating stress among nursing assistants. *The Gerontologist, 32,* 351–359.

CHAPPELL, N.L. & NOVAK, M. (1994). Caring for institutionalised elders: stress among nursing assistants. *Journal of Applied Gerontology, 13,* 299–315.

DEICKMANN, L., ZARIT, S.H., ZARIT, J.M. & GATZ, M. (1988). The Alzheimer's disease knowledge test. *The Gerontologist, 28,* 402–407.

DONALDSON, C., TARRIER, N. & BURNS, A. (1998). Determinants of carer stress in Alzheimer's disease. *International Journal of Geriatric Psychiatry, 13,* 248–256.

DREW, N. (1986). Exclusion and confirmation: a phenomenology of patients' experiences with caregivers. *Image: Journal of Nursing Scholarship, 18,* 39–43.

DUNN, L.A., ROUT, U., CARSON, J. & RITTER, S.A. (1994). Occupational stress amongst care staff working in nursing homes: an empirical investigation. *Journal of Clinical Nursing, 3,* 177–183.

EVERITT, D.E., FIELDS, D.R., SOUMERAI, S.S. & AVORN, J. (1991). Resident behaviour and staff distress in the nursing home. *Journal of the American Geriatric Society, 39,* 792–798.

FIRTH-COZENS, J. & HARDY, G.E. (1992). Occupational stress, clinical treatment and changes in job perceptions. *Journal of Occupational and Organisational Psychology, 65,* 81–88.

GILLEARD, C. & GROOM, F. (1994). A study of two dementia quizzes. *British Journal of Clinical Psychology, 33,* 529–534.

GOLDBERG, D. (1978). *Manual of the General Health Questionnaire.* Windsor: NFER-NELSON.

GOLDSTEIN, H. (1987). *Multi-level models in educational and social research.* London: Griffin.

GRAFSTROM, M., FRATIGLIONI, L. & WINBLAD, B. (1994). Caring for an elderly person: predictors of burden in dementia care. *International Journal of Geriatric Psychiatry, 9,* 373–379.

HALLBERG, I.R. & NORBERG, A. (1993). Strain among nurses and their emotional reactions during 1 year of systematic clinical supervision combined with the implementation of individualised care in dementia nursing. *Journal of Advanced Nursing, 18,* 1860–1875.

HALLBERG, I.R. & NORBERG, A. (1995). Nurses' experiences of strain and their reactions in the care of severely demented patients. *International Journal of Geriatric Psychiatry, 10,* 757–766.

HOPE, T. & PATEL, V. (1993). Assessment of behavioural phenomena in dementia. In A. BURNS (Ed.), *Ageing in dementia; a methodological approach* (pp. 221–236). London: Edward Arnold.

JACKSON, G.A. & LYONS, D. (1996). Psychiatric clinics in

residential homes for the elderly. *Psychiatric Bulletin*, *20*, 518-520.

JACKSON, G.A. & LYONS, D. (1997). A roving clinic for residential homes: letter to the editor. *International Journal of Geriatric Psychiatry*, *12*, 682.

JENKINS, H. & ALLEN, C. (1998). The relationship between staff burnout/distress and interactions with residents in two residential homes for older people. *International Journal of Geriatric Psychiatry*, *13*, 466-472.

JOHNSON, J.R. (1996). Risk factors associated with negative interactions between family caregivers and elderly care-receivers. *International Journal of Aging and Human Development*, *43*, 7-20.

KITWOOD, T. (1997). *Dementia reconsidered: the person comes first.* Oxford: Oxford University Press.

MACPHERSON, R., EASTLEY, R.J., RICHARDS, H. & MIAN, I.H. (1994). Psychosocial distress among workers caring for the elderly. *International Journal of Geriatric Psychiatry*, *9*, 381-386.

MASLACH, C. & JACKSON, S.E. (1981). *Burnout inventory manual.* Palo Alto, CA: Consulting Psychologists Press.

MONAHAN, D.J. (1993). Staff perceptions of behavioural problems in nursing home residents with dementia: the role of training. *Educational Gerontology*, *19*, 683-694.

MONIZ-COOK, E., MILLINGTON, D. & SILVER, M. (1997). Residential care for older people: job satisfaction and psychological health in care staff. *Health and Social Care in the Community*, *5*, 124-133.

MONIZ-COOK, E., AGAR, S., SILVER, M., WOODS, R., WANG, M., ELSTON, C. & WIN, T. (1998). Can staff training reduce behavioural problems in residential care for the elderly mentally ill? *International Journal of Geriatric Psychiatry*, *13*, 149-158.

MOOS, R.H. (1991). *Manual of the Work Environment Scale.* Palo Alto, CA: Consultant Psychologists Press.

MOOS, R.H. & LEMKE, S. (1992). *Manual of the Sheltered Care Environment Scale.* Palo Alto, CA: Center for Health Care Evaluation, Department of Veterans' Affairs and Stanford University Medical Centers.

MORRIS, R.G. & MORRIS, L. (1993). Psychosocial aspects of caring for people with dementia: conceptual and methodological issues. In A. BURNS (Ed.), *Ageing in dementia: a methodological approach* (pp. 251-279). London: Edward Arnold.

NOVAK, M. & CHAPPELL, N.L. (1994). Nursing assistant burnout and the cognitively impaired elderly. *International Journal of Aging and Human Development*, *39*, 105-120.

NOVAK, M. & CHAPPELL, N.L. (1996). The impact of cognitively impaired patients and shift on nursing assistant stress. *International Journal of Aging and Human Development*, *43*, 235-248.

PIETRUKOWICZ, M.E. & JOHNSON, M.M.S. (1991). Using life histories to individualise nursing home staff attitudes toward residents. *The Gerontologist*, *31*, 102-106.

PROCTOR, R., STRATTON-POWELL, H., TARRIER, N. & BURNS, A. (1998). The impact of training and support on stress among care staff in nursing and residential homes for the elderly. *Journal of Mental Health*, *7*, 59-70.

SILVER, M. (1998). The challenging behaviour vignettes: assessing the management styles care staff use to deal with challenging behaviour in residential and nursing homes for older people. MSc thesis, University of Hull, UK.

SNOWDEN, J., MILLER, R. & VAUGHAN, R. (1996). Behavioural problems in Sydney nursing homes. *International Journal of Geriatric Psychiatry*, *11*, 535-541.

WILBER, K.H. & SPECHT, V.C. (1994). Prevalence and predictors of burnout among adult day care providers. *Journal of Applied Gerontology*, *13*, 282-298.

Part V
Families and Carers in Old Age

[20]

Factors Affecting the Emotional Wellbeing of the Caregivers of Dementia Sufferers

ROBIN G. MORRIS, LORNA W. MORRIS and PETER G. BRITTON

Recent research on the factors that mediate the emotional wellbeing of the caregivers of dementia sufferers is reviewed. The roles of such factors as the caregiver's attributional style and coping strategies, the caregiver's relationship with the dementia sufferer, and levels of formal and informal support are discussed with reference to identifying those caregivers who are particularly vulnerable to emotional disorder or strain.

One of the main concerns of psychogeriatric practice is to provide treatment and rehabilitation for dementia sufferers. With the present emphasis on community-based programmes, the clinician aims to achieve this goal by mobilising and maintaining the effectiveness of informal support systems (Bergmann et al, 1978; Kahn & Tobin, 1981; Jones & Munbodh, 1982; MacDonald et al, 1982). Indeed, there is evidence that the maintenance of an elderly dementia sufferer in the community is closely related to the degree of family support (Bergmann et al, 1978; Poulshock & Deimling, 1984), and that institutionalisation may have more to do with the attitudes and wellbeing of the caregiver than the impairment of the dementia sufferer (Greene & Timbury, 1979; Gilhooly, 1986; Zarit et al, 1986; Gilleard, 1987). In the current climate of developing more community-orientated services, the needs of the caregiver are likely to assume a greater priority.

The primary burden of support for a dementia sufferer usually falls on one person who takes on the role of caregiver and, as a result, often experiences considerable hardship in terms of the physical and emotional burden (Grad & Sainsbury, 1965; Johnson, 1983; Gilleard, 1984). There are several descriptive accounts of the experiences of caregivers, including *The 36-Hour Day* (Mace & Rabins, 1981) and *Alzheimer's Disease: a Guide for Families* (Powell & Courtice, 1983), that give information of immediate clinical relevance. The research reviewed in this paper is an attempt to investigate some of these problems, bringing together research from related disciplines, including old age psychiatry and clinical and social psychology. It is concerned with quantitative indices of emotional disorder, burden or strain which are related to the caregiver's response to his or her situation and social or familial context. One of the aims of this research is to identify the types of caregiver who are particularly vulnerable to strain or depression - those who are more 'at risk' in terms of their emotional wellbeing.

Many of the recent studies have been influenced by the seminal work of Grad and Sainsbury (Grad & Sainsbury, 1965; Sainsbury & Grad de Alarcon, 1970), who evaluated the burden of community care of elderly psychiatric patients following the desegregation of a sample of psychiatric patients into the community. They applied the distinction between '*objective*' and '*subjective*' burden. The former is used in reference to the behavioural changes of the dementia sufferer and the practical problems that follow; for example, the physical burden of nursing care and changes in the caregiver's daily routine (Fatheringham et al, 1972). Stemming from this idea is Gilleard's (1984) use of the term 'daily hassles', which concern the day-to-day stressors that impinge on the caregiver, such as the irritating and frustrating demands of the dementia sufferer. 'Objective' burden also encompasses Poulshock & Deimling's (1984) notion of 'caregiving impact' - the social effect on the caregiver's daily life, such as changes in family relations, employment and health (Rabins et al, 1982).

'Subjective' burden refers to the emotional reaction of the caregiver, including perception of the strain, reduced morale, anxiety, and depression (Machin, 1980; Rabins et al, 1982; Gilhooly, 1984a; Morris et al, 1988). Table I summarises recent studies which have used quantitative indices of 'subjective' burden specifically in caregivers of dementia sufferers. The number of studies that quote the *degree* of 'subjective' burden are relatively few: the majority are concerned with correlating measures of emotional wellbeing or strain against other variables, such as the degree of dementia (e.g. Zarit et al, 1980). These few studies indicate the diversity in responses among different samples of caregivers.

TABLE I
Summary of studies investigating the mental health of the caregivers of dementia sufferers

	Measures	Outcome
Global ratings		
Bergmann & Jacoby (1983)	General Health Questionnaire	High prevalence of psychiatric illness
Eagles et al (1987a,b)	General Health Questionnaire	Prevalence of psychiatric illness no higher than among other caregivers
Gilhooly (1984a, 1986) ($n = 37$, same sample in both studies)	OARS Multidimensional Functional Assessment Questionnaire	Good mental health
	Kutner morale scale	Slightly low morale
Gilleard et al (1984) (three samples, $n = 53, 129, 42$)	Goldberg Health Questionnaire	High prevalence of psychiatric illness
Depression		
Fitting et al (1986)	Wiggins Depression Scale	Slightly high depression
George & Gwyther (1986)	Bradburn Affect Balance	Moderately high negative affect
Morris et al (1988)	Beck Depression Scale	Slightly high depression
Pagel et al (1985), Coppel et al (1985) ($n = 68$, same sample in both studies)	Beck Depression Scale, Hamilton Rating Scale	Moderately high depression; 28 currently met RDC criteria, 27 met criteria previously
Anxiety/stress		
George & Gwyther (1986)	Short Psychiatric Evaluation Schedule	Stress symptoms 3 times normal

For example, Gilhooly (1984a; 1986) reports that her mixed sample of mainly spouse and sibling caregivers are in 'good' mental health, although she acknowledges that she may have selected a sample of caregivers who are well adjusted to their situation. In contrast, a high number of reported stress symptoms and negative affect were found by George & Gwyther (1986), using the Short Psychiatric Evaluation Schedule (Pfeiffer, 1979) and Affect Balance Scale (Bradburn, 1969).

Many studies report a level of depression higher than that expected for a community sample. Morris et al (1988) report depression slightly higher than normal: 14% of their sample could be classified as clinically depressed (using the Beck Depression Inventory criterion of scores greater than 13). This is consistent with Fitting et al's (1986) finding of a moderately high rate of depression, measured using the Wiggins depression scale. Pagel et al (1985) and Coppel et al (1985) found a much higher incidence of clinical depression in their sample: 40% were clinically depressed, according to the Research Diagnostic Criteria (RDC; Endicott et al, 1981) and a further 41% had at some stage been depressed in the course of caregiving.

As an index of emotional disorder, the prevalence of probable psychiatric 'caseness' in caregivers has been measured, using the General Health Questionnaire (GHQ). Two studies have found high rates. Bergmann & Jacoby (1983) estimated that 33% of caregivers have psychiatric disorder. Gilleard et al (1984) arrived at a much higher estimate: 68% exceeded the threshold value of 4/5 on the GHQ, a figure that is considerably larger than the GHQ prevalence rates in other community samples (Goldberg, 1978; Tarnopolsky et al, 1979; Benjamin et al, 1982). In contrast to these two studies, Eagles et al (1987a,b) report no difference in GHQ scores between co-resident 'supporters' of demented and non-demented elderly relatives.

The discrepancies between the studies may reflect the sampling characteristics. The study by Eagles et al drew upon a community sample rather than psychiatric referrals – raising the possibility that the high prevalence of 'caseness' in the other studies is due to the fact that families better able to cope are less likely to come into contact with psychiatric services.

Another reason for discrepancies between studies may be the diversity of responses to caregiving, which should be considered within a social context (Eagles et al, 1987a,b). As will be shown below, the 'subjective' burden of caregiving must be considered in a broader context than merely as reactive to the behavioural changes of the dementia sufferer. There are a range of mediating variables that might influence a person's emotional response to caregiving; for example, the meaning a person attributes to his or her situation, the quality of the carer's relationship with the dementia sufferer, the coping strategies of the carer, and the availability of formal and informal support. Before discussing these issues, the review focuses on the problems that arise more directly from the behaviour of the dementia sufferer.

Problems arising from the behaviour of the dementia sufferer

It is commonly held that caring for an elderly person who is mentally impaired is more of an emotional burden than caring for someone with physical disabilities (Isaacs, 1971; Poulshock & Deimling, 1984). This is perhaps a consequence of the fact that the disabilities of the dementia sufferer have more far-reaching consequences in terms of changes in the supporter's lifestyle (Horowitz, 1985), and also because of the disruption of the relationship (Morris et al, 1988). As indicated above, it is not simply the degree of impairment or disability that causes distress to the caregiver. Despite this, recent studies have helped to establish which *features* of dementia are most burdensome for the caregivers, irrespective of mediating factors.

Typically, these problems have been elicited from caregivers using a behavioural checklist. An intriguing method, developed by Sanford (1975), is to ask the caregiver to indicate the incidence of behavioural alterations listed on a checklist and then require the caregiver to state which problems would need to be alleviated to establish a tolerable situation in the home. Using this method, Sanford found that sleep disturbance, faecal incontinence, general immobility and dangerous behaviour were the least well tolerated. Subsequent studies using problem checklists have produced similar findings. Hirschfield (1978) and Machin (1980) also found nocturnal wandering and incontinence to be problems, together with the patient's refusal to wash, which was elicited as a further important problem in both studies. Gilleard et al (1982) and Greene et al (1982) factor-analysed the data from their studies in an attempt to classify the behavioural problems. Gilleard et al (1982) established five problem dimensions, which they labelled 'dependency', 'disturbance', 'disability', 'demand' and 'wandering'. Using a different scale, Greene et al (1982) derived just three factors: 'apathy/withdrawal', 'behavioural disturbance' and 'mood disturbance'. The differences between the two studies indicate the potential difficulties of establishing common factors between problems even when using factor-analytical methodology.

In a subsequent study, Gilleard (1984) investigated the extent to which the elicited behavioural alterations were perceived as problems by the caregivers. Instead of using Sanford's method for assessing tolerance, he required the caregiver to rate the severity of elicited problems. Using a large sample of caregivers ($n = 214$), he found that the perceived major problems were the need for constant supervision, proneness to falls, incontinence, night-time wandering, and the inability of the dementia sufferer to engage in meaningful activities on his or her own initiative.

There is broad agreement between studies concerning what behavioural alterations are more likely to be reported as problems: in summary, the main factors appear to be incontinence, overdemanding behaviour and the need for constant supervision. These may represent two aspects of caregiving that are particularly stressful: firstly, the aversive and intolerable behaviour of the dementia sufferer, and secondly, the 'daily grind', in which the caregiver experiences no respite from the heavy burden of caregiving (Gilhooly, 1984b).

To what extent are these problems linked to distress in the caregiver? Some studies show a weak association between dementia disability and emotional disturbance or strain. Notably, Zarit et al (1980) report no correlation between memory and behaviour problems and the caregiver's 'subjective' burden, a finding replicated by Zarit et al (1981) and Fitting et al (1986). Clearly, these problems were distressing to the caregiver, but not sufficiently so to be related to the experience of burden. Pagel et al (1985) found that, despite the relatively high incidence of depression, this was not correlated with dementia disability, assessed using the Sickness Impact Scale. Similarly, Gilhooly (1984a) reported only a marginally significant correlation between general mental health and the dementia sufferer's rating on a modified version of the Clinical Sensorium. There was no correlation with the supporter's reports of impairment.

Other studies report significant associations, but these tend to be relatively weak and do not apply to all aspects. For example, Newbigging (1981) found that loss of morale was significantly associated with the duration of dementia, while depression was not. George & Gwyther (1986) report a small but significant correlation between the patient's symptoms and the caregiver's level of stress symptoms. Further research may be needed to determine more closely what types of behavioural problem are associated with emotional disorder. Machin (1980) and Greene et al (1982) found that the degree of strain, assessed using a 'strain scale', was related to levels of apathy and withdrawal in the dementia sufferer. This result differs from that of Gilleard et al (1982), who report the strongest association between strain and 'demand' problems, which included demanding attention, disrupting social life, and interpersonal conflicts.

There is an obvious problem in comparing studies which use different measures and have different sampling characteristics. However, some of the discrepancies observed between the studies reviewed above may reflect the complex relationship between problem behaviour and strain or emotional disturbance in the caregiver. One aspect of this complexity encompasses the multifaceted changes in the dementia sufferer, which interact with the needs of the caregiver. For example, Gilleard (1984) proposed that apathy and withdrawal may be related to caregiver strain because they result in an increasingly one-sided and unrewarding relationship. In contrast, demanding behaviour produces strain because of the constant harrassment of the caregiver and the manner in which it generates interpersonal conflict. It may be necessary to take into account other aspects, such as the social context of caregiving, and the relationship between the caregiver and the dementia sufferer. These factors are considered below.

The caregiving relationship

As indicated above, qualitative aspects of the caregiver's relationship with the dementia sufferer may play an important role in mediating the degree of 'subjective' burden. This is a complex issue, given that caregivers are not a homogeneous group; several studies report significant differences in the way caregivers respond, depending on their familial relationship (Cantor, 1983). In part this may relate to the impact that caregiving has on the various aspects of the caregiver's daily life (Poulshock & Deimling, 1984). For example, the experience of a non-resident daughter caregiver who expects to be substantially involved with parenting her own children is likely to be very different from that of an elderly spouse caregiver.

The general finding is a negative correlation between the 'distance' in the blood/role relationship and the mental health of the caregiver: the greater the familial distance, the better the caregiver's mental health (Cantor, 1983; Gilhooly, 1984*a*; George & Gwyther, 1986). There is some evidence that this is true even if the age differences among spouse caregivers and other caregivers are statistically controlled (George & Gwyther, 1986). Gilhooly (1984*a*) explains this finding in terms of the degree of emotional and practical involvement of the caregiver. Consistent with this idea, Cantor (1983) found that spouses reported the greatest degree of physical and financial strain and were most concerned about the morale of the dementia sufferer. Despite the increased burden, spouse caregivers are less willing to consider long term institutional care for their relatives, and more likely to feel able to continue in the caregiving role (Gilhooly, 1986). George & Gwyther (1986) have referred to the fact that 'distance' in blood/role relationship is often confounded with living arrangements. Spouse caregivers are more often co-resident with the dementia sufferer and thus are more likely to play a greater part in day-to-day caregiving.

Several investigators have suggested that gender differences exist in response to caregiving. Among spouse caregivers, wives tend to experience a higher degree of subjective burden or distress (Fitting *et al*, 1986; George & Gwyther, 1986; Zarit *et al*, 1986). Horowitz (1985) found that, out of adult children supporters, daughters are usually more closely emotionally involved and experience a higher degree of strain. Horowitz (1985) relates this to gender expectations, suggesting that women were traditionally expected to be more involved in household work than men, bringing them into greater contact with the dementia sufferer. It has also been suggested that, for women, the caregiving role conflicts with a desire to achieve more autonomy (Fitting *et al*, 1986). Many women have changed their role in middle age from the traditional role as mother and homemaker, so the caregiving role threatens their effort towards more personal fulfilment (Brody, 1981).

Men may also have a different approach to caregiving, as indicated by Zarit *et al* (1986). They suggest that men may have different strategies for dealing with the dementia sufferer, which enable them to distance themselves from the everyday problems. In their study they found that husbands were often observed to take a more instrumental approach to daily problems. Interestingly, they found that on a two-year follow-up the difference between subjective burden reported by husbands and wives had disappeared. They relate this to a possible change in coping styles, as the wives adopt a similar coping style to husband caregivers. There is also some suggestion that formal and informal support is not so beneficial in alleviating burden for female caregivers (Zarit *et al*, 1981), possibly because they are less able to hand over the responsibility of caregiving and feel guilty about not providing care themselves.

The quality of the relationship between caregiver and dementia sufferer may also be an important factor in mediating emotional distress (Isaacs *et al*, 1972; Zarit *et al*, 1980). It seems that, paradoxically, *within* the relationship, the closer the emotional bond, the *less* is the strain for the caregiver (Horowitz & Shindelman, 1983; Tobin & Kulys, 1981). For example, there is evidence that caregivers of frail elderly relatives who maintain positive feelings towards their relative have a greater level of commitment to caring and a lower level of perceived strain (Horowitz & Shindelman, 1983). This also appears to be true for caregivers of dementia sufferers, for Gilleard *et al* (1984) report that the quality of the 'past' relationship, measured using a rating scale, accounted for a significant proportion of the variance in predicting mental health in the caregiver.

Morris *et al* (1988) studied the association between 'past' and 'present' levels of marital intimacy in spouse caregivers. Marital intimacy was measured using an intimacy scale, derived from Waring *et al* (1980), which investigated eight different facets of intimacy: affection, cohesion, expressiveness, compatibility, conflict resolution, sexuality, autonomy, and identity. Morris *et al* (1988) found that a low 'past' level of intimacy was associated with an increased level of both perceived strain and depression in the spouse caregiver. They speculate that this is because a poor previous relationship results in extra tension, resentments, and hostility when the impaired partner becomes dependent on the caregiver. It is also possible that those people who experienced high levels of intimacy before the onset of dementia in their spouse undertook the caregiving role because they felt a deep affection and a desire to care for their partner, rather than out of a sense of obligation.

Morris *et al* (1988) used their measures of 'past' and 'present' intimacy to study the effect of loss of intimacy. Here it was predicted that the mental deterioration of the partner would lead to negative changes in the relationship. For example, the apathy and withdrawal referred to by Machin (1980) and Greene *et al* (1982) would lead to a reduction in such aspects of intimacy as the sharing of private thoughts, the capacity to communicate about the relationship, and the ability to resolve differences of opinion. Indeed, the increasing self-centredness of the dementia sufferer is likely to transform the relationship into one that is increasingly one-sided. Morris *et al* (1988) found that loss of intimacy was correlated with increased levels of depression, but not strain. This was despite the finding that the levels of reported strain were higher than those of depression.

This finding agrees with research concerning loss (Parkes, 1972; Bowlby, 1980): depression is a common response to loss of any description, with the person 'mourning' for that which has been taken away. Many caregivers experience anticipatory grief as they observe the deterioration of their relative. In addition, the loss of a previously close relationship and the social isolation which can accompany caregiving may make the person especially vulnerable to depression (Brown *et al*, 1987).

Attributional factors and coping strategies

The quality of the relationship between caregiver and dementia sufferer may also depend on the ability of the caregiver to find meaning from the caregiving situation (Hirschfield, 1981). It seems plausible that those people who experienced high levels of intimacy will be more ready to accept their caregiving role. Some caregivers may more easily adopt the caregiving role because they wish to repay care given to themselves in the past. The manner in which caregivers interpret their situation may also influence their vulnerability to stress and psychiatric disorder.

Part of the caregiver's difficulty in coming to terms with his or her situation stems from the time-course of the disorder. Due to the insidious onset of the disorder, the caregiver attributes the behaviour of the dementia sufferer to something other than dementia, sometimes leading to guilt and self-blame. At the same time, as the disorder progresses, caregivers may experience a loss of control over different aspects of their lives, for which they are unprepared (Mace & Rabins, 1981). Recently, the context of caring for a dementing spouse has been used to test predictions derived from research relating attributional theories to depression (Coppel *et al*, 1985; Pagel *et al*, 1985; Morris, 1986).

According to early formulations of attributional theory and depression, people are more prone to depression if they make causal attributions for important negative outcomes which are internal, stable and global (Abramson *et al*, 1978). Research with caregivers has also taken into account more recent formulations which are concerned with people's concept of causality and control over their responses to specific negative events (Wortman & Dintzer, 1978; Hammen & deMayo, 1982; Brewin, 1984). In line with this approach, Pagel *et al* (1985) investigated loss of control, self-blame and depression in their sample of 68 spouse caregivers of Alzheimer-type dementia patients (21 hospitalised and 47 co-resident). Caregivers were asked to rate their perception of control and causal attributions for changes in the behaviour of the Alzheimer patient prior to diagnosis and their perceived control over the patient's current behaviour. In line with research that considers attributions in the context of specific *events* (Cutrona, 1983), the questions referred to the attributions for the particular aversive stimulus itself rather than the perceived causes. For example, a question relating to perceived current control was 'how much control do you feel you have over your spouse's (upsetting behaviour) in terms of being able to influence it within a certain range?'

Perceived loss of control was consistently associated with a higher level of depression, but not of anxiety or hostility. Caregivers tended to be more depressed if they thought that their spouse's behaviour was caused by themselves. The tendency for self-blame was associated with higher levels of anxiety and hostility, suggesting that it was more broadly related to generalised demoralisation and conflict. This pattern of results held when follow-up measures of depression, anxiety and hostility were taken.

Using the same sample, Coppel et al (1985) explored the issue of whether different coping reactions predisposed the caregivers to depression. They drew a distinction between the caregiver's perceived ability to cope with the dementia sufferer's unpredictable and upsetting behaviour, and changes in the caregiver's own life situation – the 'caregiving impact' (Poulshock & Deimling, 1984). Their results highlight the complex associations between attributions and depression in relation to this issue. For example, when upsetting behaviour was taken to be the situational context, the caregiver was more likely to be depressed if this behaviour was seen to be something that affected everything. In the context of caregiving impact, caregivers were more depressed if they thought that the changes affected everything and had become a permanent feature of their everyday lives.

There is some evidence that if caregivers feel unable to cope with the changes in their lives brought about by their spouse's disorder, this predisposes them to depression (Coppel et al, 1985). Caregivers were more depressed if they were dissatisfied with their ability to cope with changes in their daily lives and if they thought they were unable to cope in the present or future. This contrasts with the caregivers' reaction to their spouse's unpredictable behaviour. In this case, lack of control, unpreparedness and high expectations in handling the dementia sufferer were related to depression.

Using a sample of purely co-resident spouse caregivers of Alzheimer-type dementia sufferers, Morris (1986) confirmed some of the above findings. She reports significant correlations between the level of depression and the degree to which caregivers perceived the strain and distress they were experiencing to be longlasting, and also the degree to which the behaviour of the dementia sufferers affected all aspects of their daily lives. In agreement with Coppel et al (1985), she found a relatively high correlation between the level of depression and the ability of the caregiver to cope with his or her spouse's upsetting behaviour. There was also a significant association between depression and the ability of the caregivers to cope with their *own* emotional reactions. An interesting aspect of this study was that these associations extended beyond depression to the level of strain experienced by the caregiver.

These studies indicate that the manner in which caregivers respond to their situation may be important in determining the level of emotional disorder. Despite this, it may be difficult to establish causal links between these factors, given the lack of success in this direction in other areas of research (Lewinsohn et al, 1981). In summary, the studies reviewed above indicate that caregivers are most likely to be depressed if they feel a loss of control over their spouse's behaviour, if they feel unable to cope with the impact of caregiving, and if their situation is perceived to be stable and to affect everything.

Formal and informal support

The perceived ability to cope with the impact of caregiving may depend in part on the amount and quality of formal and informal support that the caregiver receives. Intuitively, it might appear that the formal support received, such as visits from a community nurse, home help and day care should alleviate the degree of subjective burden. However, the relationship between formal support and burden is not quite so straightforward.

A social work study by Levin et al (1986) suggests that the build-up of strain over a two-year period is less when caregivers are receiving more formal support, although a significant proportion of caregivers in this study did not feel that the services they received were entirely relevant or sufficient. Gilhooly (1984a) reports an association between the extent of home-help services and the morale and mental health of caregivers. The number of visits from community nurses was also associated with increased morale. However, in Gilhooly's study there appeared to be no relationship between the level of day hospital care or provision of meals on wheels and the caregiver's emotional wellbeing. Gilleard et al (1984) found no association between scores on the General Health Questionnaire and level of professional support. Indeed, Morris (1986) reports a paradoxical *positive* relationship between the amount of caregiver strain and formal support. These discrepant findings can be accommodated if it is assumed that in some cases formal support serves to alleviate distress, while in other cases caregivers who are distressed elicit further formal support.

The level of informal support is frequently considered by people working with caregivers. It has been argued that service providers should work towards promoting the caregivers' natural support system, such as their social network or family, rather than attempting to replace it with formal care (Zarit & Zarit, 1982). One approach to this issue has been to reorganise services around the community and to promote voluntary support for caregivers. Davies & Challis (1986) implemented a pilot scheme in which a team of social workers co-ordinated professional and voluntary support to interweave with the elderly clients' existing social support network, and recruited volunteers who could provide practical help and ease the social isolation of caregivers. Although this scheme was primarily intended for frail elderly people, it has been used to improve the quality of care for dementia sufferers (Challis & Davies, 1986). In this scheme, the network of professional and volunteer support was successful in maintaining 50% of dementia sufferers in the community within a year, in contrast to 23% of a control population. An advantage of such a scheme is that by using volunteers the services are more tailored to individual needs, which increases the quality of community care and distributes the load of caregiving within the community. Also, the care provided in this pilot study was more cost-effective than residential provision. Levin et al (1986) similarly recommend a 'care attendant' scheme to improve service provision within the community.

The importance of promoting voluntary or informal support is underlined by evidence that caregivers who have a larger network of social support tend to feel less need of formal support (Fitting et al, 1986), and indeed, make less demand on community services (Caserta et al, 1987). The dynamics of informal support have not been extensively studied, but it is clearly a complex issue, because the caregiver is usually part of a family or social network system which is not divorced from the caregiving process (Zarit & Zarit, 1982; Niederehe & Fruge, 1984). A negative aspect of caregiving is the restriction of social activities and consequent social isolation (Poulshock & Deimling, 1984). To some extent this may be offset by the degree of social and family support; for example, Zarit et al (1980) found that feelings of burden were decreased in caregivers who had more family visits.

In contrast, there are studies, such as that of Gilhooly (1984a), suggesting that the level of mental health is not related to the level of social resources, or to contact with friends or non-resident relatives. Also, Gilleard et al (1984) reported no association between the level of mental health and the supporter's rating of the amount of family help received and the number of visits per week. These contrary findings may reflect the fluctuating relationship between emotional wellbeing and support, according to whether one is reactive to the other. It is also possible that the measures of family or social support used are not sufficiently reliable. For example, measuring the number of visits per week may indicate little about how effective the family contact is in providing support. In an attempt to deal with these problems, Morris (1986) administered a measure of social support derived from the Californian Human Population Laboratory Questionnaire (Berkman, 1983). This measure enabled her to look at the emotional, instrumental and financial help received, and at the web of social relationships that surrounded the caregiver. For example, caregivers would be asked whether they could count on extra help from somebody if they needed help with daily tasks such as shopping or cleaning.

Using this measure, Morris (1986) found that caregivers were less depressed and felt less strain when they received more informal social support (this contrasts with the finding that strain and depression were positively correlated with formal support). Interestingly, the caregivers' satisfaction with the amount of formal services received was positively related to the amount of social support, indicating that those caregivers who have a good social network are more satisfied with the formal services they receive.

A further indication of the importance of informal social support has been the success of relative support groups in helping caregivers. The efficacy of these groups has rarely been investigated, but those studies that have been made appear to show positive results (Barnes et al, 1981; Steuer & Clark, 1982; Glosser & Wexler, 1985; Kahan et al, 1985). For example, in one study, by Kahan et al (1985), caregivers who had participated in support groups reported a reduction in burden and level of depression, whereas people who received no intervention reported increased burden after four months of study. The reduced burden appeared to result from the relatives feeling they had increased control over their lives and more certainty about their ability to continue caregiving – an observation that merits further investigation within the framework of recent research on attributional style and coping strategies. Related to this, Glosser & Wexler (1985) report that caregivers participating in a relative support group rated very highly the provision of information about behavioural management of dementia sufferers. Another evaluative study, by Barnes et al (1981), indicates that relative support groups are successful in helping spouse caregivers to feel more supported and less isolated, and also helped to resolve some of the feelings created by their partner's illness. It helped some of the spouses to become more aware of their own needs and to regain some self-identity in relation to the dementia sufferers.

Discussion

The studies reviewed above indicate that recent research has gone beyond the demonstration that caregivers experience burden and emotional disorder. There are many factors that affect the emotional wellbeing of the caregiver, including his or her attributions and coping strategies, the quality of the caregiver's relationship with the dementia sufferer, and the family and social context. All of these factors have been investigated in at least a preliminary fashion, yielding knowledge that might be useful for those providing support and counselling to caregivers. The study carried out by the National Institute of Social Work (Levin et al, 1986) indicated that caregivers gave high praise to professionals who helped them to come to terms with the changes in their relatives and with their feelings of sadness, loss and loneliness.

It might be argued that the level of emotional disorder is not particularly high in caregivers (Gilhooly, 1984a) and that psychiatrists may not need to become involved with caregivers (Eagles et al, 1987a,b). Even if this proves to be the case, it would surely be acknowledged that some caregivers do not easily adapt to the stresses of caregiving and are at risk in terms of their ability to continue in their role. Isaacs (1971) suggests that approximately one-third of admissions of dementia sufferers to a particular geriatric unit were to relieve families who had become exhausted or demoralised by caregiving, and there is also evidence that the main reason for referral to a day hospital is the degree of strain on family caregivers (Greene & Timbury, 1979; Zarit et al, 1986). Some services have been experimenting with the provision of intermittent relief schemes, to deal with this problem (Argyle et al, 1985). The research reviewed above may help to indicate those caregivers who are most at risk: for example, those who have a poor premorbid relationship with the dementia sufferer, a poor sense of being able to control their own reactions, and weak social support.

The dominant research strategy has been to correlate different measures to establish associative links between the different factors. This approach should be regarded as preliminary even if it is supplemented with multivariate statistics, giving some insight into the causative factors determining the caregiver's emotional wellbeing. In this respect, longitudinal studies should be regarded with more certainty, such as the finding by Levin et al (1986) that over a two-year period the build-up of strain for caregivers is less when they are receiving more social support. Information yielded from intervention studies, such as the evaluation of relative support groups or of the effect of day care and hospital respite services on the caregiver, can also be more readily applied to make decisions about clinical practice.

In conclusion, the present review indicates that some progress has been made in determining what factors are influencing the ability of caregivers of dementia sufferers to cope with their role. In the context of a growing number of dementia sufferers living in the community, this information may be useful in furthering our understanding of the caregiver and directing resources most effectively.

References

ABRAMSON, L. Y., SELIGMAN, M. E. P. & TEASDALE, J. (1978) Learned helplessness in humans: critique and reformulation. *Journal of Abnormal Psychology*, 87, 49–79.

ARGYLE, N., JESTICE, S. & BROOK, P. (1985) Psychogeriatric patients: their supporter's problems. *Age and Ageing*, 14, 355–360.

BARNES, R. F., RASKIND, M. A., SCOTT, M. & MURPHY, C. (1981) Problems of families caring for Alzheimer patients: the use of a support group. *Journal of the American Geriatrics Association*, 29, 80–85.

BENJAMIN, S., DECALMER, P. & HARAN, D. (1982) Community screening for mental illness: a validity study of the General Health Questionnaire. *British Journal of Psychiatry*, 140, 174–180.

BERGMANN, K. & JACOBY, R. (1983) The limitation and possibilities of community care for the elderly demented. In *Elderly People in the Community: Their Service Needs*. London: Her Majesty's Stationery Office.

——, FOSTER, E. M., JUSTICE, A. W. & MATHEWS, V. (1978) Management of the demented elderly patient in the community. *British Journal of Psychiatry*, 132, 441–449.

BERKMAN, L. F. (1983) The assessment of social networks and social support in the elderly. *Journal of the American Geriatrics Society*, 31, 743–749.

BOWLBY, J. (1980) *Attachment and loss*, vol. 3. New York: Basic Books.

BRADBURN, N. M. (1969) *The Structure of Psychological Wellbeing*. Chicago: Aldine.

BREWIN, C. R. (1984) Attributions for industrial accidents: their relationship to rehabilitation outcome. *Journal of Social and Clinical Psychology*, 2, 156–164.

BRODY, I. M. (1981) "Women in the middle" and family help to older people. *Gerontologist*, 21, 471-480.
BROWN, G. W., BIFULCO, A. & HARRIS, T. O. (1987) Life events, vulnerability and the onset of depression: some refinements. *British Journal of Psychiatry*, 150, 30-42.
CANTOR, M. H. (1983) Strain among caregivers: a study of experience in the United States. *Gerontologist*, 23, 597-604.
CASERTA, M. S., LUND, D. A., WRIGHT, S. D. & REDBURN, D. E. (1987) Caregivers of dementia patients: the utilization of community services. *Gerontologist*, 27, 209-214.
CHALLIS, D. & DAVIES, B. (1986) *Case Management in Community Care: an Evaluated Experiment in the Home Care of the Elderly*. Aldershot: Gower.
COPPEL, D. B., BURTON, C., BECKER, J. & FIORE, J. (1985) Relationships of cognitions associated with coping reactions to depression in spousal caregivers of Alzheimer's disease patients. *Cognitive Therapy and Research*, 9, 253-266.
CUTRONA, C. E. (1983) Causal attributions and perinatal depression. *Journal of Abnormal Psychology*, 92, 161-172.
DAVIES, B. & CHALLIS, D. (1986) *Matching Resources to Needs in Community Care: an Evaluated Demonstration of a Long-term Model*. Aldershot: Gower.
EAGLES, J. M., BEATTIE, J. A. G., BLACKWOOD, G. W., RESTALL, D. B. & ASHCROFT, G. W. (1987a) The mental health of elderly couples - I: The effects of the cognitively impaired spouse. *British Journal of Psychiatry*, 150, 299-308.
——, CRAIG, A., RAWLINSON, F., RESTALL, D. B., BEATTIE, J. A. G. & BESSON, J. A. O. (1987b) The psychological well-being of supporters of the demented elderly. *British Journal of Psychiatry*, 150, 293-298.
ENDICOTT, J., COHEN, J., NEE, J., FLEISS, J. & SARANTAKOS, S. (1981) Hamilton Depression Rating Scale. *Archives of General Psychiatry*, 38, 98-103.
FATHERINGHAM, J., SKELTON, M. & HODDINOTT, B. (1972) The effects on the families of the presence of a mentally retarded child. *Canadian Psychiatric Association Journal*, 17, 283-289.
FITTING, M., RABINS, P., LUCAS, J. M. & EASTHAM, J. (1986) Caregivers for dementia patients: a comparison of husbands and wives. *Gerontologist*, 26, 248-252.
GEORGE, L. K. & GWYTHER, L. P. (1986) Caregiver well-being: a multidimensional examination of family caregivers of demented adults. *Gerontologist*, 26, 253-259.
GILHOOLY, M. L. M. (1984a) The impact of caregiving on caregivers: factors associated with the psychological well-being of people supporting a dementing relative in the community. *British Journal of Medical Psychology*, 57, 35-44.
—— (1984b) The social origins of senile dementia. In *Psychological Approaches to the Care of the Elderly* (eds I. Hanley & J. Hodge). London: Croom Helm.
—— (1986) Senile dementia: factors associated with caregiver's preference for institutional care. *British Journal of Medical Psychology*, 59, 165-171.
GILLEARD, C. J. (1984) *Living with Dementia: Community Care of the Elderly Mentally Infirm*. London: Croom Helm.
—— (1987) Influence of emotional distress among supporters on the outcome of psychogeriatric day care. *British Journal of Psychiatry*, 150, 219-223.
——, BOYD, W. D. & WATT, G. (1982) Problems in caring for the elderly mentally infirm at home. *Archives of Gerontology and Geriatrics*, 1, 151-158.
——, BELFORD, H., GILLEARD, E., WHITTICK, J. E. & GLEDHILL, K. (1984) Emotional distress among the supporters of the elderly mentally infirm. *British Journal of Psychiatry*, 145, 172-177.

GLOSSER, G. & WEXLER, D. (1985) Participants' evaluation of educational/support groups for families of patients with Alzheimer's disease and other dementias. *Gerontologist*, 25, 232-236.
GOLDBERG, D. P. (1978) *Manual for the General Health Questionnaire*. Windsor: NFER-Nelson.
GRAD, J. & SAINSBURY, P. (1965) An evaluation of the effects of caring for the aged at home. In *Psychiatric Disorders in the Aged*. WPA symposium. Manchester: Geigy.
GREENE, J. G., SMITH, R., GARDINER, M. & TIMBURY, G. C. (1982) Measuring behavioural disturbance of elderly demented patients in the community and its effects on relatives: a factor analytic study. *Age and Ageing*, 11, 121-126.
—— & TIMBURY, G. C. (1979) A geriatric psychiatry day hospital service: a five year review. *Age and Ageing*, 8, 49-53.
HAMMEN, C. L. & DEMAYO, R. (1982) Cognitive correlates of teacher stress and depressive symptoms: implications for attributional models of depression. *Journal of Abnormal Psychology*, 91, 96-101.
HIRSCHFIELD, M. J. (1978) *Families Living with Senile Brain Disease*. Doctor of Nursing Science dissertation, University of California, San Francisco.
—— (1981) Families living and coping with the cognitively impaired. In *Recent Advances in Nursing - Vol. 2: Care of the Ageing* (ed. L. Archer Copp). Edinburgh: Churchill Livingstone.
HOROWITZ, A. (1985) Sons and daughters as caregivers to older parents: differences in role performance and consequences. *The Gerontologist*, 25, 612-617.
—— & SHINDELMAN, L. W. (1983) Reciprocity and affection: past influences on current caregiving. *Journal of Gerontological Social Work*, 5, 5-20.
ISAACS, B. (1971) Geriatric patients: do their families care? *British Medical Journal*, 4, 282-285.
——, LIVINGSTONE, M. & NEVILLE, Y. (1972) *Survival of the Unfittest: a Study of Geriatric Patients in the East End of Glasgow*. London: Routledge & Kegan Paul.
JOHNSON, C. L. (1983) Dyadic family relations and social support. *Gerontologist*, 23, 377-383.
JONES, I. G. & MUNBODH, R. (1982) An evaluation of a day hospital for the demented elderly. *Health Bulletin (Edinburgh)*, 40, 10-15.
KAHAN, J., KEMP, B., STAPLES, F. R. & BRUMMEL-SMITH, K. (1985) Decreasing the burden in families caring for a relative with a dementing illness: a controlled study. *Journal of the American Geriatrics Association*, 33, 664-670.
KAHN, R. L. & TOBIN, S. S. (1981) Community treatment for aged persons with altered brain function. In *Clinical Aspects of Alzheimer's Disease and Senile Dementia* (eds E. Miller & G. D. Cohen). New York: Raven Press.
LEVIN, E., SINCLAIR, I. & GORBACH, P. (1986) *The Supporters of Confused Elderly Persons at Home*. London: National Institute of Social Work.
LEWINSOHN, P. M., STEINMETZ, J. L., LARSON, D. W. & FRANKLIN, J. (1981) Depression-related cognitions: antecedents or consequences? *Journal of Abnormal Psychology*, 90, 213-219.
MACDONALD, A. J. D., MANN, A. H., JENKINS, R., GODLOVE, C. & RODWELL, G. (1982) An attempt to determine the impact of four types of care upon the elderly. *Psychological Medicine*, 12, 193-200.
MACE, N. L. & RABINS, P. V. (1981) *The 36-Hour Day*. Baltimore: Johns Hopkins University Press.
MACHIN, E. (1980) *A Survey of the Behaviour of the Elderly and their Supporters at Home*. MSc thesis, University of Birmingham.
MORRIS, L. W. (1986) *The Psychological Factors Affecting Emotional Wellbeing of the Spouse Caregivers of Dementia Sufferers*. MSc thesis, University of Newcastle-upon-Tyne.

——, Morris, R. G. & Britton, P. G. (1988) The relationship between marital intimacy, perceived strain and depression in spouse caregivers of dementia sufferers. *British Journal of Medical Psychology* (in press).

Newbigging, K. (1981) *'A Ripe Old Age': an Investigation of Relatives of Elderly Dependants with Dementia*. Inquiry report, British Psychological Society Diploma in Clinical Psychology.

Niederehe, G. & Fruge, E. (1984) Dementia and family dynamics: clinical research issues. *Journal of Geriatric Psychiatry*, 17, 21-56.

Pagel, M. D., Becker, J. & Coppel, D. B. (1985) Loss of control, self-blame and depression: an investigation of spouse caregivers of Alzheimer's disease patients. *Journal of Abnormal Psychology*, 94, 169-182.

Parkes, C. M. (1972) *Bereavement: Studies of Grief in Adult Life*. London: Tavistock Publications.

Pfeiffer, E. (1979) A short psychiatric evaluation schedule: a new 15-item monotonic scale indicative of functional psychiatric disorder. In *Brain Function in Old Age* (proceedings of Bayer symposium VII). New York: Springer.

Poulshock, S. W. & Deimling, G. T. (1984) Families caring for elders in residence: issues in the measurement of burden. *Journal of Gerontology*, 39, 230-239.

Powell, L. S. & Courtice, K. (1983) *Alzheimer's Disease: a Guide for Families*. Don Mills, Ontario: Addison-Wesley.

Rabins, P. V., Mace, H. L. & Lucas, M. J. (1982) The impact of dementia on the family. *Journal of the American Medical Association*, 248, 333-335.

Sainsbury, P. & Grad de Alarcon, J. (1970) The psychiatrist and the geriatric patient: the effects of community care on the family of the geriatric patient. *Journal of Geriatric Psychiatry*, 4, 23-41.

Sanford, J. R. A. (1975) Tolerance of debility in elderly dependants by supporters at home: its significance for hospital practice. *British Medical Journal*, iii, 471-475.

Steuer, J. & Clark, E. (1982) Family support groups within a research project on dementia. *Clinical Gerontologist*, 1, 87-95.

Tarnopolsky, A., Hand, D. J., McLean, E. K., Roberts, N. & Wiggins, R. D. (1979) Validity and uses of a screening questionnaire (GHQ) in the community. *British Journal of Psychiatry*, 134, 508-515.

Tobin, S. & Kulys, R. (1981) The family in the institutionalization of the elderly. *Journal of Social Issues*, 37, 145-157.

Waring, E. M., Tillman, M. P., Frelick, L., Russell, L. & Weisz, G. (1980) Concepts of intimacy in the general population. *Journal of Nervous and Mental Disease*, 168, 471-474.

Wortman, C. B. & Dintzer, L. (1978) Is an attributional analysis of the learned helplessness phenomenon viable? A critique of the Abramson-Seligman-Teasdale reformulation. *Journal of Abnormal Psychology*, 87, 75-90.

Zarit, J. M., Gatz, M. & Zarit, S. H. (1981) Family relationships and burden in long-term care. Paper presented at 34th Annual Scientific Meeting of Gerontological Society of America, Toronto, Canada. *The Gerontologist*, 21, 286.

Zarit, S. H. & Zarit, J. M. (1982) Families under stress: interventions for caregivers of senile dementia patients. *Psychotherapy: Theory, Research and Practice*, 19, 461-471.

——, Reever, K. E. & Bach-Peterson, J. (1980) Relatives of the impaired elderly: correlates of feeling of burden. *Gerontologist*, 20, 649-655.

——, Todd, P. A. & Zarit, J. M. (1986) Subjective burden of husbands and wives as caregivers: a longitudinal study. *Gerontologist*, 26, 260-266.

*R. G. Morris, MA, MSc, PhD, *Lecturer in Clinical Psychology*; L. W. Morris, BSc, MSc, *Research Associate*; P. G. Britton, BSc, PhD, *Senior Lecturer in Clinical Psychology; Department of Psychiatry, Royal Victoria Infirmary, Newcastle-upon-Tyne, NE1 4LP*

*Correspondence

This paper views caregiver stress as a consequence of a process comprising a number of interrelated conditions, including the socioeconomic characteristics and resources of caregivers and the primary and secondary stressors to which they are exposed. Primary stressors are hardships and problems anchored directly in caregiving. Secondary stressors fall into two categories: the strains experienced in roles and activities outside of caregiving, and intrapsychic strains, involving the diminishment of self-concepts. Coping and social support can potentially intervene at multiple points along the stress process.
Key Words: Caregiver strains; Role strains; Loss; Self-concept; Stress mediators

Caregiving and the Stress Process: An Overview of Concepts and Their Measures[1]

Leonard I. Pearlin, PhD,[2] Joseph T. Mullan, PhD,[2] Shirley J. Semple, MA,[2] and Marilyn M. Skaff, MA[2]

It can hardly go unnoticed that research into caregiving has become a flourishing enterprise. Several reasons explain this striking growth of interest. One concerns the changing demographic landscape of contemporary societies: people live longer; the longer they live, the more at risk they are for chronic ailments that impair their ability to care for themselves; and, because of medical advances, impaired people survive for longer periods of time despite their health problems. It is also clear, painfully so to many, that as the need for care for the chronically impaired grows, so do its costs and the elusiveness of its quality. We know that most families are committed to caring for impaired relatives at home (Shanas, 1979; Brody, 1985). It is likely that because of the formidable barriers to suitable institutional care, however, many families continue to keep their relatives at home even after their resolve has been worn down.

Given that these kinds of changes have made informal family caregiving a typical experience, it is understandable that its economic, social, and psychological impacts would become areas of intense research concern. The research, of course, has been driven by several disciplinary perspectives and theoretical orientations. Probably none is more prominent in current research into caregiving than that concerned, either explicitly or implicitly, with stress and its mediation. Indeed, caregiving is potentially a fertile ground for persistent stress. A brief consideration of caregiving will help to reveal why this is so.

Caregiving and Stress

Informal caregiving simply refers to activities and experiences involved in providing help and assistance to relatives or friends who are unable to provide for themselves. Whereas caring is the *affective* component of one's commitment to the welfare of another, caregiving is the *behavioral* expression of this commitment. Giving care to someone is an extension of caring about that person. Looked at this way, caring and caregiving are intrinsic to any close relationship; that is, they are present in all relationships where people attempt to protect or enhance each other's well-being. Caring and caregiving are the *sine qua non* of what Cooley (1915) described as primary relationships. Indeed, because caregiving is embedded in ordinary relationships, it is, strictly speaking, not accurate to treat it as though it were itself a role. Instead, caregiving refers to particular kinds of actions that are found in the context of established roles, such as wife-husband, child-parent.

Considering how quotidian caregiving is, it hardly seems the stuff out of which severe stress springs. Under some circumstances, however, caregiving is transformed from the ordinary exchange of assistance among people standing in close relationship to one another to an extraordinary and unequally distributed burden. The emergence of a serious and prolonged impairment, such as Alzheimer's disease, is such a circumstance. Where impairment leads to increasing dependency on others for the satisfaction of basic needs, a profound restructuring of the established relationship can occur. Caregiving, which previously might have been but one fleeting component of an encompassing relationship, can now come to be the dominant, overriding component. Under conditions of chronic and progressive impairment, therefore, caregiving may imperialistically expand to the point where it occupies virtually the entirety of the relationship.

As the capabilities of parties to the relationship

---

[1]Support for this work was provided by the National Institute of Mental Health, under grant #MH42122. We thank our co-investigators, Drs. Carol Aneshensel, William Jagust, and David Lindeman, as well as Lisa Hoffman and Jane Karp for their collaboration on this work. We are also grateful for the generous help and encouragement of William Fisher and Peter Braun. Address correspondence to Dr. Leonard I. Pearlin, Human Development and Aging Program, 1350 7th Ave., CSBS 237, University of California, San Francisco, CA 94143-0848.

[2]Human Development and Aging Program, University of California, San Francisco.

become increasingly imbalanced, the reciprocities and give and take that had existed fade into the past. This is especially the case where the disability involves cognitive deterioration, as in Alzheimer's disease and other dementias. Help, assistance, and affection become unidirectional, eventually going only from the caregiver to the recipient. We shall later spell out some of the specific ingredients of caregiving that can exert a stressful impact. Whatever these specific ingredients are, the sheer dramatic and involuntary transformation of a cherished relationship is itself a major source of stress (Pearlin, 1983). It is altogether understandable, then, that scholars who study caregiving would be interested in the stress that befalls the caregiver. There are caregivers, of course, who manage to find some inner enrichment and growth even as they contend with mounting burdens. Nevertheless, it is difficult to imagine many situations that equal — let alone surpass — the stressfulness of caregiving to relatives and friends with severe chronic impairments.

Although caregiving has acted as a magnet in attracting the interests of stress researchers, those drawn to it don't necessarily view it through the same theoretical or methodological lens. The confusing diversity and the shortcomings found generally in psychosocial stress research certainly find their way into research that deals specifically with caregiving. Diversity and confusion are not necessarily to be abhorred; perhaps these are the unavoidable byproducts of any field that has rapidly generated intense research activity. But these by-products have their costs, primarily in the sprouting of inconsistent or seemingly discontinuous knowledge. There have been recent calls to move caregiving research toward greater sophistication (Zarit, 1989; Romeis, 1989). And there have also been efforts to bring sound measurement closer to the many aspects of caregiving and its impact (Lawton et al., 1989). The aim of this paper is to join in these efforts.

Procedures

To implement our aim, we do two things. First, we lay out a conceptual scheme for the study of caregiver stress and, second, we present a number of the measures we have developed to assess the multiple components of the scheme. Because the utility of measures depends on how well they reflect the concepts they are intended to assess, the measures we introduce here were developed after our conceptual framework. This framework is a product both of many years of research into the stress process and of considerable exploratory research among spouses and adult children who care for relatives with Alzheimer's disease. Much of our general understanding of the stress process usefully applies to the study of caregivers, and what we have learned from the study of caregivers has usefully informed our general understanding of the stress process.

The measures that are presented were constructed from our current multiwave study of 555 caregivers in the San Francisco Bay Area and Los Angeles, probably the largest such study undertaken to date. The caregivers were recruited primarily from the pool of people who contacted local Alzheimer's Associations (ADRDA) in the San Francisco Bay Area and in Los Angeles County. We attempted to contact everyone who was a self-described primary caregiver of a noninstitutionalized spouse or parent (or parent-in-law) with Alzheimer's or a similar dementia. In a subsequent screening call, we verified that these criteria were met. In those instances in which the person was not the primary caregiver, we asked for the identification and location of the family member who was primarily responsible for caregiving. When the caregiving was shared, we chose the spouse whenever possible. Three interviews will be conducted over a 2-year period, providing an opportunity to chart changes brought on by the institutionalization and death of patients, as well as changes that occur within the household caregiving situation. Two interviews have been completed, but only the framework guiding the first is presented here.

In Table 1 the distributions of key characteristics of the sample are shown separately for spousal and adult children caregivers. It can be noted that the proportions who are husbands, wives, daughters, or sons are almost the same as in a national study of caregivers (Stone, Cafferata, & Sangl, 1987). The sample is tilted toward the middle class, as indicated by educational status. In this respect, too, it is similar to other caregiver studies. By no means can this sample be thought of as representative of all caregivers. Indeed, even if it were, we would not know it because the universe it would represent is unknown. What is important to recognize is that the distribution of characteristics is sufficiently broad to permit the analysis of their associations with other attributes of the caregivers.

The measures are presented as appendices rather than as part of the text; this better allows for their separate and detailed examination. Not all of the measures and scales used in our research are included in the appendices. Essentially, only newly created measures of key experiences or dispositions are included. Several others are described in the text but not appended. Although most of the measures presented in the appendices are based on the factor analyses of data gathered from the 555 participants, the construction of these measures began with the open-ended exploratory interviews. In these interviews, caregivers were asked about the problems they faced, the actions, feelings, and sentiments evoked by these problems, and their attempts to manage their difficulties. From the transcripts of the interviews, conceptual themes were identified and structured questions formed. These questions were then put through a series of pretests and revisions before being incorporated into the final scheduled interview. The manner in which the measures were developed as well as their psychometric properties provide us with an overall sense of confidence that they are serviceable and reliable indicators of our concepts.

A final introductory comment. The conceptual

framework we shall outline and the measures of its components are not presented as footsteps to be followed by others engaged in caregiver research. Fortunately, there is more than one way to think about the issues we address and more than one way to measure constructs. Our hope is to provoke critical thinking about issues that deserve attention and to bring choices into clearer awareness as future research is planned. In this way, perhaps, these materials will contribute to the coherence of a field of research that is somewhat fragmented and not as substantial as is warranted by the importance of its subject matter.

The Conceptual Components of Caregiver Stress

One will find that a number of the elements of caregiver stress in which we are interested are also to be found in the research of others. However, areas of overlapping interest are likely to have different conceptual underpinnings. Basically, we approach the study of caregiver stress from the perspective of what has come to be referred to as the stress process. The very notion of process forces attention on the relationships among the many conditions leading to personal stress and the ways these relationships develop and change over time. From this perspective, we are not interested in simply identifying conditions that might be associated with stress as much as in knowing how these conditions arise and how they come to be related to each other. Four domains make up this process, each comprising multiple components. The domains are: the background and context of stress; the stressors; the mediators of stress; and the outcomes or manifestations of stress. As we describe each of these, the notion of a stress process in caregiving will become clearer. Figure 1 is presented as a graphic guide to our discussion.

The Background and Contexts of the Stress Process

Virtually everything we are interested in learning about caregiving and its consequences is potentially influenced by key characteristics of the caregiver. The effects of ascribed statuses, such as age, gender, and ethnicity, along with educational, occupational, and economic attainments are expected to be threaded throughout the entire stress process. These characteristics signify where people stand within stratified orders having unequal distributions of rewards, privileges, opportunities, and responsibilities. The kinds and intensities of stressors to which people are exposed, the personal and social resources available to deal with the stressors, and the ways stress is expressed are all subject to the effects of these statuses.

Links between social and economic characteristics of caregivers and other components of the stress process in which they are caught up are of utmost importance. They demonstrate that even seemingly random exigencies, such as the occurrence of Alzheimer's disease, can set in motion processes that to some extent are regulated and directed by the larger

Table 1. Distributions of Sample Characteristics of Alzheimer's Caregivers

Variable	Spousal caregivers (N = 326)	Children caregivers (N = 229)
City		
San Francisco	56%	52%
Los Angeles	44	48
Caregiver relationship		
Wife	58	—
Husband	42	—
Daughter	—	76
Son	—	16
Daughter-in-law	—	8
Son-in-law	—	—
Marital status		
Married	100	58
Divorced/separated	—	19
Widowed	—	8
Never married	—	15
Living with AD person		
Yes	99	61
No	1	39
Race		
White	87	80
Black	7	15
Asian	2	3
Hispanic	4	2
Respondent education		
Less than high school	18	6
High school	29	25
Some college	22	32
College graduate	14	18
College +	17	19
Employment status		
Employed	17	57
Not employed	83	43
Respondent age[a]		
Less than 44	1	27
45–54	5	39
55–64	17	28
65–74	45	6
75–88	32	—
AD person age[b]		
Less than 44	1	—
45–54	2	—
55–64	14	2
65–74	39	18
75–84	39	54
85–94	5	26
Years caregiving		
Less than 1	27	21
1–2	37	36
3–5	30	33
6 or more	6	10

[a]Spousal mean age = 70; child mean age = 51.
[b]Spousal mean age = 72; child mean age = 80.

social orders of the society and the statuses of people within them. Caregivers may come to feel cut off from the larger society, but they are still very much influenced by its organization. Although these kinds of linkages have had some analytic attention in studies of caregiver stress, particularly with regard to gender (e.g., Zarit, Todd, & Zarit, 1986; Young & Kahana, 1989), they deserve much more. As we have

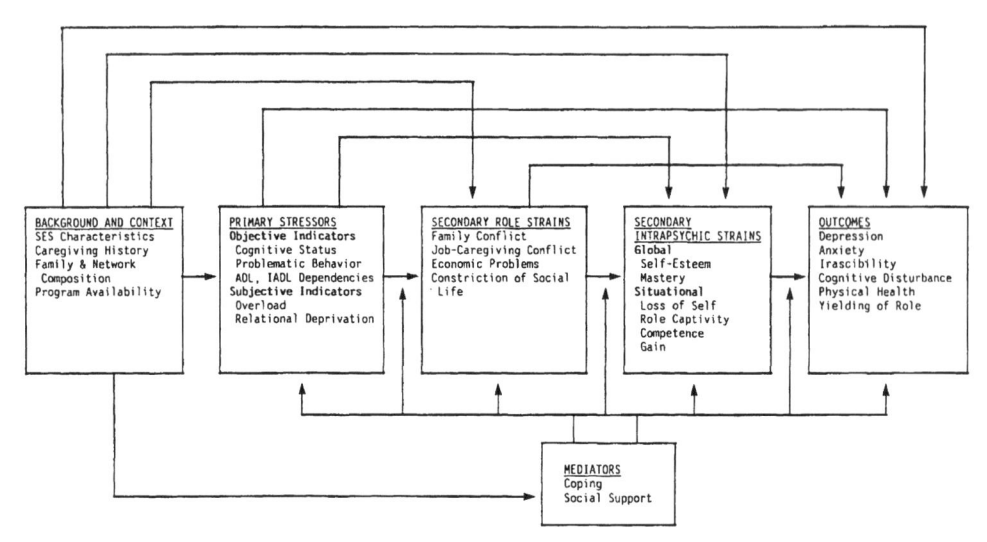

Figure 1. A conceptual model of Alzheimer's caregivers' stress. The stress process is made up of four domains: the background and context of stress; the stressors; the mediators of stress; and the outcomes or manifestations of stress.

observed elsewhere (Pearlin, 1989), information about people's statuses is too frequently gathered and then used only as statistical controls while looking at relationships among other conditions.

Aspects of the caregiving history are also taken into account. A number of items of information make up this history. Among them is the relationship of the caregiver to the patient, whether a husband or wife, son or daughter (or daughter-in-law). Information is also gathered about conflict and distance that might have existed in the past caregiver-patient relationship. Additional questions are asked about a range of physical health problems of the patient that could bear on caregiving demands. Finally, the length of time that the patient has required care is established. The duration of caregiving activities is, of course, a marker of the chronicity of the stressors that the caregiver experiences.

As can be seen in Figure 1, we also consider access to and use of resources and programs as important contextual elements of the stress process. We refer here to networks (including family) to which caregivers have attachments, the composition of the networks, and the nature and frequency of contacts with their members. It can be noted that the notion of network is different from that of social support. Network represents the totality of one's relationships, whereas support, which we treat as a mediator, pertains to the assistance one may derive from but a portion of the network (Pearlin, 1985). Although one cannot have social support without having a network, one may conceivably have a network without support.

Another type of resource is represented by community-based formal programs created to benefit patients, caregivers, or both. There are many programs that are designed to provide specialized services for patients or caregivers. However, the availability of such programs varies considerably from one community to another. They also vary in cost (and their affordability by caregivers), the availability of transportation to the programs, the hours of the day they function, and, of course, their proximity to the caregiver. Consequently, the actual use of programs by caregivers may be limited by a number of extraneous factors. To the extent that one can and does draw upon these kinds of resources, one can escape some of the vicissitudes and hardships of caregiving one might otherwise experience. From a structural perspective, many of these programs link the caregiver to the larger community. This linkage itself might help to reduce the isolation and alienation that many caregivers experience.

Primary and Secondary Stressors

We turn next to *stressors*, which are at the heart of the stress process in which caregiving may be embedded. These are the conditions, experiences, and activities that are problematic for people; that is, that threaten them, thwart their efforts, fatigue them, and defeat their dreams. Giving care to the seriously impaired can produce a variety of stressors. In earlier investigations of caregiving, especially those borrowing from the ground-breaking work of Zarit, Reeves, and Bach-Peterson (1980), multiple stressors were usually aggregated into unitary measures. Although these measures were discovered to be related to depression and other outcomes, their composite characters made it difficult to discern the particular stressors that contribute most to these outcomes. Although it is useful to know that global burden contributes to depression, eventually we need to know which specific burdens are most likely to result in depression and the conditions under which these burdens are most likely to be present. In this paper, we seek to identify and disaggregate some of the more salient stressors subsumed by the global notion of burden.

As seen in Figure 1, we divide stressors into those that are *primary* and *secondary*. We view primary stressors as driving the process that follows. By and large, they stem directly from the needs of the patient and the nature and magnitude of the care demanded by these needs. It is almost axiomatic that serious stressors, especially those that are chronic, generate other stressors. We conceive of the demands of caregiving as encompassing primary stressors that in turn lead to other problems and hardships, which we refer to as secondary. The labels of primary and secondary are not intended to suggest that one is more important than the other but only to point up that a configuration of interrelated stressors can and often does emerge as individuals are immersed in the long-term care of an impaired relative.

Primary stressors. — One indicator of a primary stressor is the *cognitive status* of the Alzheimer's patient. The range and difficulty of caregiving activities and the ability of caregivers to manage their relationships with their impaired relatives grow out of the patient's memory loss, communication deficits, and recognition failures. The evaluation of cognitive status, although made by the caregiver, is based on standard tests typically used in the clinic (Folstein, Folstein, & McHugh, 1975). The questions asking about cognitive status can be found in Appendix A. Questions about the validity of caregivers' judgments of patients' cognitive functioning may understandably arise. In this regard, it can be noted that about 75 of our participants care for relatives who are clients of the Northern California Alzheimer's Disease Center, where independent clinical tests were administered to the patients. There is a strong correlation ($r = .65$) between the ratings caregivers give their relatives on our scale of cognitive functioning and the ratings of the same relatives made by clinical workers using the Mini-Mental Test. It would appear that caregivers are quite able to evaluate the cognitive abilities of their relatives with a high degree of accuracy.

A second and somewhat related indicator of a primary stressor entails the problematic behavior of the patient and the surveillance, control, and work such behaviors require on the part of the caregiver (Appendix B). The level of vigilance that must be maintained and the "damage control" that must be exercised to ensure that the patient harms neither himself nor others constitute, from all indications, a formidable stressor (Pruchno & Resch, 1989). Moreover, the special kind of attention required by such behavior serves as a constant and painful reminder of the changed persona of the patient.

A third indicator of a primary stressor is familiar to many studies of caregivers. It consists of the number of activities for which the impaired person is dependent on the caregiver and the extent of dependency for each activity. Activities for which this information is gathered are fairly standard (and, therefore, not appended) and include both those involved in satisfying daily needs (ADL) and instrumental logistical needs (IADL) (Katz et al., 1963; Lawton & Brody, 1969). It can be assumed that the more dependent impaired persons are, the greater is the sheer amount and difficulty of work caregivers must perform for them. Although it is entirely reasonable to treat daily dependencies as an indicator of hardship, research results do not show that the condition of the patient has a strong or consistent relationship to caregiver stress (e.g., George & Gwyther, 1986). It would seem that the magnitude of the workload by itself is not a potent stressor. We have learned, however, that when the efforts of the caregiver to satisfy daily and instrumental needs are met by resistance on the part of the recipient, then stress is more likely to result. Having to satisfy dependencies is by itself less difficult than having to do it with a recalcitrant relative. Consequently, we added to the assessment of daily dependencies a single question regarding the patient's overall resistance to help.

Daily dependencies, problematic behaviors, and cognitive status are objective indicators of stressors in the sense that they are based on the health, behavior, and functional capabilities of the impaired relative. From this kind of information about patients, inferences can be drawn about the custodial care and attention the patient needs and the demands and hardships caregivers presumably encounter. It is also likely that the scope and difficulty of caregiving activities come to symbolize the changes that have overtaken the life and the self of the caregiver. Thus, these objective assessments of the patients' behaviors and capabilities serve two purposes in our model: as indicators of the current demands of caregiving and as benchmarks of transformations that have already occurred and those that are expected.

Two additional indicators of primary stressors bypass the condition of the patient and inquire directly about hardships subjectively experienced by caregivers. One of these taps the overload or burnout felt by caregivers (Appendix C). The items constituting the measure bespeak not only the level of fatigue felt by caregivers but also the relentlessness and uncompromising nature of its source. The other we refer to as relational deprivation. As we have emphasized, Alzheimer's disease and other dementias have a transforming effect on the patient and this, then, unavoidably restructures the caregiver-patient relationship, stripping it of its former reciprocities. As the impairment progresses, caregivers may come to feel increasingly separated from the parts of their lives that have been supported by or shared with their relatives.

The items making up the measure of relational

deprivation are found in Appendix D. It can be noted that this measure is divided into two subscales. One involves the exchange of intimacy, seen in items A, B, and C. The second pertains more to goals and social activities that were once shared with the patient but that are no longer attainable. This is tapped by items D, E, and F. Although each subscale forms a distinct factor, these two aspects of relational deprivation are related to each other ($r = .52$).

Secondary stressors: Role strains and intrapsychic strains. — The stressors identified thus far are anchored either in the needs and demands of the patient and the caregiving required to satisfy them or in the restructured relationship between caregiver and patient. Although they may plateau or even recede, we assume that the natural history of these kinds of stressors is in the general direction of greater severity. Thus, the primary stressors are likely to be both durable and intensified over time. These conditions are productive of other stressors, those we call secondary. As seen in Figure 1, we distinguish two types of secondary stressors. One type, comprising *role strains*, is found in roles and activities outside the caregiving situation. The second is made up of a variety of *intrapsychic strains*. It should be reemphasized that neither type is secondary in terms of their potency. Once established, there is reason to believe that secondary stressors are every bit as powerful as those that are primary in producing stress outcomes.

The family, of course, is a central arena for secondary role strains (e.g., Rabins, Mace, & Lucas, 1982), and having a close relative who needs care can certainly reawaken old family grievances and create new ones as well. Three dimensions of conflict were identified in exploratory interviews and developed as scales for use in our survey (Appendix E). As seen in Appendix E, the sheer level of conflict along these dimensions is modest. However, because people typically have a strong stake in family relations, any threat to them can have a strong impact (Pearlin & Turner, 1987). One type of conflict between caregivers and other family members arises out of differences around *issues* of impairment: beliefs about the disability of the patient, its seriousness, and appropriate strategies for dealing with it. A second conflict, also between the caregiver and other relatives of the disabled person, is rooted in disagreements over both the amount and quality of attention given to the *patient* by the other family members. The third dimension of conflict is around the attention and acknowledgment accorded the *caregiver* for the care that person gives to the relative. The intercorrelations between these three dimensions are quite high: between the issues and patient scales $r = .55$; between issues and caregivers $r = .51$; and for the measures of conflicts involving the patient and the caregiver $r = .71$. Despite their close interrelationships, they appear to be quite different in their effects, with conflicts directly involving the caregiver most likely to arouse distress.

Occupation is another institution in which problems and conflicts are likely to have serious consequences. It is entirely possible that occupation, along with incumbency in other outside roles, may have some beneficial effects for caregivers (Stoller & Pugliesi, 1989). However, our exploratory interviews have confirmed earlier studies (e.g., Scharlach & Boyd, 1989) showing that caregivers who are employed outside the home frequently experience cross-pressures and dilemmas at the junctures of caregiving and occupation. Our measure of job-caregiving conflicts appears in Appendix F.

Economic strains, too, can be formidable. These strains are appraised by three indicators: reductions in household income, increases in expenditures related to the care and treatment of the patient, and whether there is enough money to make ends meet month to month (Appendix G). The answer to these three queries can be independent of one another, and therefore, there is no basis for scaling the items. Furthermore, it can be recognized that economic hardships might have existed prior to and independently of the impairment of the relative and of the caregiving situation. Therefore, the causal links of impairment and caregiving to economic strains are best established by observing changes in the economic circumstances of the household at the multiple points of the interviewing.

A final secondary role strain involves informal rather than institutional roles and statuses. There is often a marked constriction of social and recreational life as caregiving responsibilities escalate. These social activities, in which one no longer engages at previous levels, can be longingly missed. To evaluate the constriction of social life we rely on the extensive information we have gathered about contacts and activities with friends and relatives and their changes over time.

An underlying premise of our conceptual scheme is that one set of stressors can lead to another. As noted earlier, we refer to role strains as secondary stressors because they are viewed as an outgrowth of the ongoing caregiving situation. Another type of stressor is distinctly different from the role strains but, because it is under the influence of other stressors, is also considered to be secondary. These are what we refer to as *intrapsychic strains*, which, for the most part, involve dimensions of self-concept and kindred psychological states. Past research has indicated that under conditions of enduring hardships, self-concepts may be damaged (Pearlin et al., 1981), and when this happens, people are more likely to suffer symptoms of depression. Caregiving to chronically disabled relatives fits this scenario. The relentless and progressively expanding demands of caregiving, together with ensuing secondary role strains, are capable of diminishing positive elements of self; this, in turn, leaves people increasingly vulnerable to stress outcomes. In the conceptual framework portrayed by Figure 1, the intrapsychic strains represent the final but crucial step in an antecedent process.

Some of the self-concepts in which we are interested have traditionally been labeled in positive terms. These positive labels might appear discrepant with our references to stressful intrapsychic strains; however, what is regarded as strainful is not the presence of a positive self-concept but either its diminishment or barriers to its development. This is certainly the case with *self-esteem and mastery*, two elements of self-concept that have been closely studied in earlier stress research (Pearlin et al., 1981). Self-esteem, which simply refers to the regard in which one holds oneself, is measured by the Rosenberg (1965) scale. Mastery, or the control that individuals feel they are able to exercise over forces importantly affecting their lives, is measured by a scale previously developed by Pearlin (Pearlin & Schooler, 1978).

Self-esteem and mastery represent rather global and overarching elements of self. That is, they are constructs whose assessment is not tied to a particular context. In our current study of caregivers, we sought to expand our understanding of the place of the self in the stress process by including dimensions of self-concept that are anchored specifically in the caregiving situation and whose measurement reflects this context. There are four of these, one of which is *role captivity* (Appendix H). This is an intrapsychic strain that refers to being an unwilling, involuntary incumbent of a caregiver role. Essentially, the sense of being a captive exists when one wants to be and to do something other than that in which they feel compelled to engage. It is a concept that first emerged in a study of gender and depression (Pearlin, 1975) and was identified as an underlying theme in some of our exploratory interviews with caregivers. The *loss of self* is yet another theme that emerged from these exploratory interviews. To the extent that the identity and life of the caregiver has been closely bound to that of the patient, the caregiver may experience a loss of his or her own identity as the patient's persona becomes fragmented and blurred. This loss may also be exacerbated when caregiving comes to exclude other activities and roles in which the caregiver previously found self-validation. Self-loss is measured by a simple two-item scale (Appendix I).

Two additional measures of intrapsychic strain, each phrased in positive terms, are *competence and gain*. Competence is measured by a four-item scale that essentially asks people to rate the adequacy of their performance as caregivers (see Appendix J). The measure of personal gain or enrichment (Appendix K) is testimony to the fact that many people manage to find some inner growth as they face the severe challenges of caregiving. Competence and gain were included partly out of interest in whether the enhancement of self is negatively related to stress outcomes, just as we knew the diminishment of self to be positively related to stress. They were also included to determine if the enhancement of some elements of self counterbalanced or compensated for the diminishment of others. This issue awaits further analysis.

These four measures of situational intrapsychic strain involve closely kindred constructs whose independence might be in question. In this regard, it is useful to note that the intercorrelations among the measures are not strikingly high. The strongest relationship ($r = .35$) is between role captivity and self-loss, and next in magnitude is the correlation between role competence and role gain ($r = .32$). The correlation between captivity and competence is $-.17$; between self-loss and competence it is $-.13$; and, finally, there is no correlation between self-loss and gain.

The differentiation in our conceptual model of primary and secondary stressors and the distinction between role and intrapsychic strains are heuristically important. This conceptualization is useful in revealing the dynamic character of caregiver stress, especially in multiwave studies extending over a broad time span. It treats stress not as stemming from a happening or from a circumscribed problem, but, rather, from the way caregivers' lives become organized and the effects of this organization on their self-judgments. This perspective is particularly pertinent to caregiving, an activity that can result in far-reaching and enduring repercussions in the life of the caregiver and of every other family member in close contact with the situation. As we shall discuss, the distinction and specification of primary and secondary stressors also provides a more detailed picture of how and where the mediators may potentially intervene in the stress process.

Mediating Conditions

It is virtually always observed in stress research that people exposed to seemingly similar stressors are affected by them in dissimilar ways. This is certainly the case in studies of caregivers. It is the mediators that are usually called upon to provide the explanation for this outcome variability. *Coping and social support* are generally regarded as the two principal mediators. Analytic interest in these mediators in the study of caregivers is essentially the same as in stress research in general. That is, we seek to learn if differences in coping responses or in the use of social support can account for the fact that caregivers confronting equivalent life problems are unequally damaged by the problems. Why is it that some caregivers seem to fare better than others, though their life circumstances might not be easier? As we have argued elsewhere (Pearlin, 1990), the answer to this question probably cannot be answered solely by the mediators. Yet there is no doubt that they can have a major explanatory role.

Indeed, stress research may typically underestimate the power of the mediators. The usual mode of analysis is to determine if the strength of the relationship between a stressor and an outcome is reinforced or attenuated under different mediating conditions (see Wheaton, 1985, for detailed discussion). Buffering is assumed to take place when the cushioning effect of the mediator increases with the severity of the stressor. Buffering is a direct effect in the sense that its effects can be judged by looking directly at the outcome. However, the specification of primary and secondary stressors in Figure 1 suggests that there might also be indirect effects, which, if not observed, would lead to an underestimation of mediating effects. We refer specifically to the capacity of the mediators to limit the proliferation of secondary stressors. Thus, as suggested by the arrows in Figure 1, the mediators may serve both to lessen the intensity of stressors and to block their contagion at the junctures between the primary and secondary stressors. To the extent that these kinds of interventions occur, the mediators would indirectly be limiting deleterious outcomes. Obviously, these interventions need to be examined along with those that more directly reduce stressors and buffer the outcomes.

Coping. — Turning to the assessment of the mediators, we consider coping first. Coping represents behaviors and practices of individuals as they act on their own behalf. In keeping with our past research (Pearlin & Aneshensel, 1986), we conceive of coping in response to life problems as having three possible functions: management of the situation giving rise to stress; management of the meaning of the situation such that its threat is reduced; and management of the stress symptoms that result from the situation. We believe that it is strategically useful to measure these three functional aspects of coping separately and, more difficult, to measure each major life exigency with instruments specific to that exigency (Pearlin, Turner, & Semple, 1989). As others have also recognized (e.g., Quayhagen & Quayhagen, 1988), coping with caregiving cannot adequately be assessed with general-duty instruments or with instruments developed to measure how people cope with other life problems. Our measures meet these criteria: they assess the different functions of coping and are specific to the study of caregivers.

The items used to measure management of the situation (Appendix L) are not factored because there is no theoretical reason to suppose that the items are correlated in any structured order and, therefore, they will be analyzed as single items. The items that measure management of the meaning of the situation form three distinct factors (Appendix M). One involves the reduction of expectations (items A, B, & C), a second the use of positive comparisons (items D, E, & F), and the third a search for a larger sense of the illness (items G, H, & I). It can be seen that these subscales do not have robust reliability coefficients. Because of their instability, the measures assessing the management of meaning should be used with caution. Finally, we have a number of items that tap individuals' efforts to lessen awareness of the situation or to decrease the symptoms of stress that result from it. These items, shown in Appendix N, are not scaled but will be analyzed separately. Note that the efficacy of coping cannot be judged solely by the manifest content of questions asking about coping, no matter how reasonable the content might appear to be. As we have described in detail elsewhere (Pearlin, 1990; Pearlin & Aneshensel, 1986; Pearlin & Schooler, 1978) the efficacy of coping can be evaluated only through the analysis of its mediating effects at various junctures of the stress process.

Social support. — Our observations concerning the direct and indirect interventions are as applicable to social support as to coping. Thus, it should be determined if, in addition to its direct buffering effects, social support prevents or inhibits the development of secondary stressors. There is, of course, a sizeable literature on the role of social support in the stress process and the various ways to measure it (House & Kahn, 1985; Lin, Dean, & Ensel, 1986). We rely on assessments of two types of support that are central to the construct: instrumental and expressive support. The availability of instrumental support is measured by discrete items asking, for example, whether there is someone who assists the caregiver in the care of the relative or who helps with household chores. Expressive support is scaled (Appendix O), with its items tapping the perceived availability of a person who is caring, trustworthy, uplifting, and a confidant.

Outcomes

Social scientists are interested in the stress process because it helps to highlight the structural arrangements of the society and its institutional forces that affect people's lives. The effects — or outcomes — that are usually observed in social research involve the well-being of people, their physical and mental health, and their ability to sustain themselves in their social roles. These are precisely the kinds of outcomes we have taken for study. On the mental health side, they include standard symptom measures of depression, anxiety, irascibility, and cognitive disruptions. These measures (which are not appended) are primarily drawn from the Hopkins Checklist (Lipman et al., 1969; Derogatis et al., 1971). We also inquire fairly extensively about caregivers' physical health, limitations in their ability to engage in usual activities, and the occurrence of injuries. Still another pivotal outcome is the yielding of caregiver activities. This can be gradual or abrupt, and it may entail either the transfer of responsibilities to others or the institutional placement of the disabled relative. These kinds of changes will be observed over the multiple waves of interviewing.

The various outcomes should not necessarily be treated as interchangeable ways to assess the stressful impact of the antecedent process. It may be more fruitful to consider the different types and levels of outcomes as interrelated. Our own view is that elements of emotional distress are likely to surface first and, if they persist, they may be eventually inimical to physical well-being. In instances where there is a deterioration in both the mental and physical health of the caregiver, it can be assumed that a reduction or reluctant yielding of caregiving becomes more likely to occur. Whether disengagement from active caregiving helps to promote recovery from its negative emotional and physical effects remains to be seen. In any event, it is evident that these kinds of long-term relationships among outcomes are forged only under sustained, chronic conditions of stress.

Discussion

This is a very brief sketch of a complex process whose components each merit a much more detailed discussion than provided in this paper. However brief, the paper is intended to convey some of the conceptual specification and elaboration needed to understand the web of conditions joined together as the lives of caregivers move forward over time. It also provides an array of newly created measures of the various concepts. Although the development of measures is time consuming and painstaking, it is frequently necessary if we are to have a close union between concepts and their measures.

We believe that it is useful to think of caregiver stress not as an event or as a unitary phenomenon. It is, instead, a mix of circumstances, experiences, responses, and resources that vary considerably among caregivers and that, consequently, vary in their impact on caregivers' health and behavior. The mix is not stable; a change in one of its components can result in the change of others. A great deal has been learned in previous research about these components of the stress process and how they are best measured and evaluated. Obviously, however, much remains to be learned of how they enter into and shape the directions of caregivers' lives.

Certain caveats are in order pertaining to our conceptual model — or, for that matter, any model. The constructs that are included and the hypothesized relationships among them provide only general guidelines for research. The model should be regarded as an heuristic device rather than as a literal reflection of realities and the pathways that join them, many of which are still unclear. In the case of the conceptual framework described here, our past work provides a level of confidence about its utility. Yet we are just as confident that as studies of caregiver stress advance and provide opportunities for the empirical testing of the model, it will need to be further modified and extended. Most certainly, some of the relationships among constructs that we have treated here as being unidirectional will prove to be reciprocal. The model, consequently, should be regarded as something to be built upon rather than something to be followed or perpetuated. The result, we believe, will be a keener appreciation of informal caregiving, what it entails and what it costs.

References

Brody, E. M. (1985). Patient care as a normative family stress. *The Gerontologist, 25,* 19–29.
Cooley, C. N. (1915). *Social organization.* New York: Scribner.
Derogatis, L. R., Lipman, R. S., Covi, L., & Rickles, K. (1971). Neurotic symptom dimensions. *Archives of General Psychiatry, 24,* 454–464.
Folstein, M. F., Folstein, S. E., & McHugh, P. R. (1975). Mini-mental state: A practical method for grading the cognitive state of patients for the clinician. *Journal of Psychiatric Research, 12,* 189–198.
George, L. K., & Gwyther, L. P. (1986). Caregiver well-being: A multidimensional examination of family caregivers of demented adults. *The Gerontologist, 26,* 253–259.
House, J. S., & Kahn, R. L. (1985). Measures and concepts of social support. In S. Cohen and S. L. Syme (Eds.), *Social support and health.* Orlando, FL: Academic Press.
Katz, S., Ford, R. W., Moskowitz, R. W., Jackson, B. A., & Jaffe, M. W. (1963). Studies of illness in the aged: The index of ADL, a standardized measure of biological and psychological function. *Journal of the American Medical Association, 186,* 914–919.
Lawton, M. P., & Brody, E. M. (1969). Assessment of older people: Self-maintaining and instrumental activities of daily living. *The Gerontologist, 9,* 179–186.
Lawton, M. P., Kleban, M. H., Moss, M., Ravine, M., & Glicksman, A. (1989). Measuring caregiving appraisal. *Journal of Gerontology, 44,* P61–P71.
Lin, N., Dean, A., & Ensel, W. (1986). *Social support, life events, and depression.* Orlando, FL: Academic Press.
Lipman, R. S., Rickles, K., Covi, L., Derogatis, L., & Uhlenhuth, E. H. (1969). Factors of symptom distress. *Archives of General Psychiatry, 21,* 328–338.
Pearlin, L. I. (1975). Sex roles and depression. In N. Datan and L. Ginsberg (Eds.), *Life-span developmental psychology: Normative life crises.* New York: Academic Press.
Pearlin, L. I. (1983). Role strains and personal stress. In H. B. Kaplan (Ed.), *Psychosocial stress: Trends in theory and research.* New York: Academic Press.
Pearlin, L. I. (1985). Social process and social supports. In S. Cohen and S. L. Syme (Eds.), *Social support and health.* New York: Academic Press.
Pearlin, L. I. (1989). The sociological study of stress. *Journal of Health and Social Behavior, 30,* 241–256.
Pearlin, L. I. (1990). The study of coping: An overview of problems and directions. In J. Eckenrode (Ed.), *The social context of coping.* New York: Plenum Press.
Pearlin, L. I., & Aneshensel, C. (1986). Coping and social supports: Their functions and applications. In L. H. Aiken and D. Mechanic (Eds.), *Applications of social science to clinical medicine and health.* New Brunswick, NJ: Rutgers University Press.
Pearlin, L. I., & Schooler, C. (1978). The structure of coping. *Journal of Health and Social Behavior, 19,* 2–21.
Pearlin, L. I., & Turner, H. A. (1987). The family as a context of the stress process. In S. V. Kasl and C. L. Cooper (Eds.), *Stress and health: Issues in research methodology.* New York: John Wiley and Sons.
Pearlin, L. I., Turner, H. A., & Semple, S. J. (1989). Coping and the mediation of caregiver stress. In E. Light and B. Lebowitz (Eds.), *Alzheimer's disease treatment and family stress: Directions for research.* Washington, DC: National Institute of Mental Health.
Pearlin, L. I., Lieberman, M. A., Menaghan, E. G., & Mullan, J. T. (1981). The stress process. *Journal of Health and Social Behavior, 22,* 337–356.
Pruchno, R. A., & Resch, N. L. (1989). Aberrant behaviors and Alzheimer's disease: Mental health effects of spouse caregivers. *Journal of Gerontology, 44,* S177–S182.
Quayhagen, M. P., & Quayhagen, M. (1988). Alzheimer's stress: Coping with the caregiving role. *The Gerontologist, 28,* 391–396.
Rabins, P., Mace, N., & Lucas, M. J. (1982). The impact of dementia on the family. *Journal of the American Medical Association, 248,* 333–335.
Romeis, J. C. (1989). Caregiving strain: Toward an enlarged perspective. *Journal of Aging and Health, 1,* 188–208.
Rosenberg, M. (1965). *Society and the adolescent self-image.* Princeton, NJ: Princeton University Press.
Scharlach, A. E., & Boyd, S. L. (1989). Caregiving and employment: Results of an employee survey. *The Gerontologist, 29,* 382–387.
Shanas, E. (1979). The family as a support system in old age. *The Gerontologist, 19,* 169–174.
Stoller, E. P., & Pugliesi, K. L. (1989). Other roles of caregivers: Competing responsibilities or supportive resources. *Journal of Gerontology, 44,* S231–S230.
Stone, R., Cafferata, G. L., & Sangl, J. (1987). Caregivers of the frail elderly: A national profile. *The Gerontologist, 27,* 616–626.
Wheaton, B. (1985). Models for the stress-buffering functions of coping. *Journal of Health and Social Behavior, 26,* 352–364.
Young, R. F., & Kahana, E. (1989). Specifying caregiver outcomes: Gender and relationship aspects of caregiving strain. *The Gerontologist, 29,* 660–666.
Zarit, S. H. (1989). Do we need another "stress and caregiving" study? *The Gerontologist, 29,* 147.
Zarit, S. H., Reeves, K. E., & Bach-Peterson, J. (1980). Relatives of the impaired elderly: Correlates of feelings of burden. *The Gerontologist, 20,* 649–655.
Zarit, S. H., Todd, P., & Zarit, J. (1986). Subjective burden of husbands and wives as caregivers. *The Gerontologist, 26,* 260–266.

APPENDICES

Note: The reliability (alpha) of each scale is parenthetically noted next to the name of the scale. Next to each item is the mean value of responses to the item.

A. Cognitive Status (alpha = .86)
Now, I'd like to ask you some questions about your (relative's) memory and the difficulty (he/she) may have doing some things. How difficult is it for your (relative) to:

A. Remember recent events (2.8)
B. Know what day of the week it is (3.0)
C. Remember (his/her) home address (2.4)
D. Remember words (2.0)
E. Understand simple instructions (2.2)
F. Find (his/her) way around the house (1.3)
G. Speak sentences (1.7)
H. Recognize people that (he/she) knows (1.5)

Response categories: (4) Can't do at all; (3) Very difficult; (2) Fairly difficult; (1) Just a little difficult; (0) Not at all difficult.

B. Problematic Behavior (alpha = .79)
In the *past week*, on how many days did you *personally* have to deal with the following behavior of your (relative)? On how many days did (she/he):

A. Keep you up at night (1.8)
B. Repeat questions/stories (2.6)
C. Try to dress the wrong way (2.1)
D. Have a bowel or bladder "accident" (1.9)
E. Hide belongings and forget about them (2.3)
F. Cry easily (1.6)
G. Act depressed or downhearted (2.1)
H. Cling to you or follow you around (2.4)
I. Become restless or agitated (2.6)
J. Become irritable or angry (2.3)
K. Swear or use foul language (1.6)
L. Become suspicious, or believe someone is going to harm (him/her) (1.8)
M. Threaten people (1.3)
N. Show sexual behavior or interests at wrong time/place (1.1)

Response categories: (4) 5/more days; (3) 3–4 days; (2) 1–2 days; (1) No days.

C. Overload (alpha = .80)
Here are some statements about your energy level and the time it takes to do the things you have to do. How much does each statement describe you?

A. You are exhausted when you go to bed at night (2.6)
B. You have more things to do than you can handle (2.6)
C. You don't have time just for yourself (2.6)
D. You work hard as a caregiver but never seem to make any progress (2.4)

Response categories: (4) Completely; (3) Quite a bit; (2) Somewhat; (1) Not at all.

D. Relational Deprivation
Caregivers sometimes feel that they lose important things in life because of their relative's illness. To what extent do you feel that you personally have lost the following? How much have you lost:

Deprivation of Intimate Exchange: (alpha = .77)
A. Being able to confide in your (relative) (3.1)
B. The person that you used to know (3.3)
C. Having someone who really knew you well (2.6)

Deprivation of Goals and Activities: (alpha = .67)
D. The practical things (he/she) used to do for you (2.0)
E. A chance to do some of the things you planned (2.9)
F. Contact with other people (2.3)

Response categories: (4) Completely; (3) Quite a bit; (2) Somewhat; (1) Not at all.

E. Family Conflict (Scales created by Shirley J. Semple)
Issues of Seriousness/Safety of AD Patient (alpha = .80)
Family members don't always see eye to eye when it comes to their relative who is ill. How much disagreement have you had with anyone in your family concerning any of the following issues?

A. The seriousness of your (relative's) memory problem (1.67)
B. The need to watch out for your (relative's) safety (1.41)
C. What things your (relative) is able to do for (him/herself) (1.46)
D. Whether your (relative) should be placed in a nursing home (1.49)

Attitudes and Actions Toward Patient (alpha = .86)
Family members may differ among themselves in the way they deal with a relative who is ill. Thinking of all your relatives, how much disagreement have you had with anyone in your family because of the following issues? How much disagreement have you had with anyone in your family because they:

E. Don't spend enough time with your (relative) (1.65)
F. Don't do their share in caring for your (relative) (1.61)
G. Don't show enough respect for your (relative) (1.37)
H. Lack patience with your (relative) (1.46)

Attitudes and Actions Toward Caregiver (alpha = .84)
I've just asked you how your relatives act toward your (relative). Now I'd like to ask how they act toward you, the caregiver. Again, thinking of all your relatives, how much disagreement have you had with anyone in your family because of the following issues? How much disagreement have you had with anyone in your family because they:

I. Don't visit or telephone you enough (1.39)
J. Don't give you enough help (1.48)
K. Don't show enough appreciation for your work as a caregiver (1.35)
L. Give you unwanted advice (1.49)

Response categories: (4) Quite a bit of disagreement; (3) Some disagreement; (2) Just a little disagreement; (1) No disagreement.

F. Job-Caregiving Conflict (alpha = .75)
From your own personal experience, how much do you agree or disagree with the following statements about your present work situation? In the last 2 months or so:

A. You have had less energy for your work (2.4)
B. You have missed too many days (1.8)
C. You've been dissatisfied with the quality of your work (2.0)
D. You worry about your (relative) while you're at work (2.6)
E. Phone calls about or from your (relative) interrupt you at work (2.0)

Response categories: (4) Strongly agree; (3) Agree; (2) Disagree; (1) Strongly disagree.

G. Economic Strains (To be assessed by separate items)
These questions ask about your household expenses and your standard of living. Think back over your financial situation as it was *just before* you began to take care of your (relative).

A. Compared to that time, how would you describe your *total* household income from all sources? (3.4)
B. Compared to that time, how would you describe your monthly expenses? (2.4)

Response categories: (5) Much less now; (4) Somewhat less now; (3) About the same; (2) Somewhat more now; (1) Much more now.

C. In general how do your family finances work out at the end of the month? (1.6)

Response categories: (3) Not enough to make ends meet; (2) Just enough to make ends meet; (1) Some money left over.

H. Role Captivity (alpha = .83)
Here are some thoughts and feelings that people sometimes have about themselves as caregivers. How much does each statement describe your thoughts about your caregiving? How much do you:

A. Wish you were free to lead a life of your own (2.5)
B. Feel trapped by your (relative's) illness (2.6)
C. Wish you could just run away (1.9)

Response categories: (4) Very much; (3) Somewhat; (2) Just a little; (1) Not at all.

I. Loss of Self (alpha = .76)
Caregivers sometimes feel that they lose important things in life because of their relative's illness. To what extent do you feel that you personally have lost the following? How much have you lost:

A. A sense of who you are (1.6)
B. An important part of yourself (2.0)

Response categories: (4) Completely; (3) Quite a bit; (2) Somewhat; (1) Not at all.

J. Caregiving Competence (Scale created by Marilyn M. Skaff) (alpha = .74)
Here are some thoughts and feelings that people sometimes have about themselves as caregivers. How much does each statement describe your thoughts about your caregiving? How much do you:

A. Believe that you've learned how to deal with a very difficult situation (3.3)
B. Feel that all in all, you're a good caregiver (3.6)

Response categories: (4) Very much; (3) Somewhat; (2) Just a little; (1) Not at all.

Think now of all the things we've been talking about: the daily ups and downs that you face as a caregiver; the job you are doing; and the ways you deal with the difficulties. Putting all these things together, how (WORD) do you feel?

C. Competent (3.3)
D. Self-confident (3.3)

Response categories: (4) Very; (3) Fairly; (2) Just a little; (1) Not at all.

K. Personal Gain (alpha = .76)
Sometimes people can also learn things about themselves from taking care of a close relative. What about you? How much have you:

A. Become more aware of your inner strengths (3.3)
B. Become more self-confident (2.7)
C. Grown as a person (2.9)
D. Learned to do things you didn't do before (3.1)

Response categories: (4) Very much; (3) Somewhat; (2) Just a little; (1) Not at all.

L. Management of Situation (To be assessed by separate items)
Here are some things that people do to make caregiving easier for themselves. How often do you:

A. Try to be firm in directing your (relative's) behavior (2.9)
B. Do the things you really have to do and let the other things slide (2.9)
C. Try to find ways to keep your (relative) busy (2.5)
D. Try to learn as much as you can about the illness (e.g., read books, talk to doctors, go to lectures) (3.2)

Response categories: (4) Very often; (3) Fairly often; (2) Once in a while; (1) Never.

Have you done anything to try to prevent your (relative) from having accidents or from wandering? If so, could you give me one or two examples of something you've done?

M. Management of Meaning
Here are ways that some people think about caregiving, and about their relative with memory problems. How often do you think in these ways? How often do you:

Reduction of Expectations (alpha = .48)
A. Try to accept your (relative) as (he/she) is, not as you wish (he/she) could be (3.4)
B. Try to think about the present rather than the future (3.3)
C. Try to keep your sense of humor (3.5)

Making Positive Comparisons (alpha = .63)
D. Remind yourself that others are worse off (3.2)
E. Try to think about the good times you had in the past (2.9)
F. Look for the things that you always liked and admired in your (relative) (2.9)

Construction of Larger Sense of Illness (alpha = .49)
G. Try to make sense of the illness (2.6)
H. Pray for strength to keep going (3.2)
I. Remind yourself that this is something to expect as people get older (2.3)

Response categories: (4) Very often; (3) Fairly often; (2) Once in a while; (1) Never.

N. Management of Distress (To be assessed by separate items)
Here are things that some people do when they are under stress from caregiving. How often do you do them?

A. Spend time alone (2.3)
B. Eat (2.0)
C. Smoke (1.4)
D. Get some exercise (2.3)
E. Watch TV (2.6)
F. Read (2.6)
G. Take some medication to calm yourself (1.3)
H. Drink some alcohol (1.4)

Response categories: (4) Very often; (3) Fairly often; (2) Once in a while; (1) Never.

O. Expressive Support (alpha = .87)

Let's turn now to the help and support you get from your friends and relatives. Thinking about your friends and family, *other than your (relative)*, please indicate the extent to which you agree or disagree with the following statements.

A. There is really no one who understands what you are going through (*Reversed*) (2.8)
B. The people close to you let you know that they care about you (3.4)
C. You have a friend or relative in whose opinions you have confidence (3.4)
D. You have someone who you feel you can trust (3.6)
E. You have people around you who help you to keep your spirits up (3.3)
F. There are people in your life who make you feel good about yourself (3.4)
G. You have at least one friend or relative you can really confide in (3.5)
H. You have at least one friend or relative you want to be with when you are feeling down or discouraged (3.2)

Response categories: (4) Strongly agree; (3) Agree; (2) Disagree; (1) Strongly disagree.

Factors contributing to feelings of burden of caregivers of elderly persons with senile dementia were studied. The amount of burden of caregivers was found to be less when more visits were paid to the dementia patient by other relatives. Severity of behavioral problems was not associated with higher levels of burden. The results suggest the importance of providing support to caregivers as a critical step in the community care of elderly persons with dementia.

Relatives of the Impaired Elderly: Correlates of Feelings of Burden[1]

Steven H. Zarit, PhD,[2] Karen E. Reever, MPA/MSG,[3]
Julie Bach-Peterson, MSG[4]

Senile dementia, which affects 5 to 10% of the older population, results in cognitive impairments and memory loss that generally leave the afflicted person in need of supportive care. While placement is often made into nursing homes or other protective settings, the majority of older people with senile dementia live in the community rather than an institution (Bergmann, 1975; Kay et al. 1964). Family members are the main caregivers, providing most of the assistance or supervision that is needed (Bergmann et al., 1978). Community care of persons with senile dementia and other chronic illnesses has many advantages (see Kahn, 1975; Kahn & Zarit, 1974), but often places a major burden on family members or other caregivers. The present research investigates factors related to the amount of burden experienced by the principal caregivers of older persons with senile dementia. The purpose of this study is to identify sources of that burden, thereby facilitating the development of interventions to reduce the caregiver's burden.

Senile Dementia in the Community

Epidemiological evidence indicates that most older persons with senile dementia can and do remain in the community. Bergmann (1975) has estimated that the average finding of community surveys is that 4.2% of the over-65 community population have senile dementia. Kay et al. (1964) found severe mental deterioration to be present in 4.9% of their older British community sample and mild mental deterioration to be present in an additional 5.2% of those 65 and over. Approximately 90% of the organically impaired older people in that study lived in the community rather than institutions.

Home care is often provided at great cost to families in terms of psychological, physical and financial resources (Lowenthal, et al., 1967). Institutionalization of an ill elder is frequently used to relieve burden on families or other caregivers.

At the same time the gerontological literature has stressed the importance of finding alternatives to institutionalization because of its negative effects especially on elderly with dementia. Some studies, for example, have reported especially high rates of mortality among relocated dementia patients compared to those remaining In the community (Blenkner, 1967). Furthermore, because of their inability to retain new information, dementia patients may show greater impairment in unfamiliar settings, while in their own homes familiar cues can often trigger well established habits (Plutzky, 1974).

Alternative ways to reduce burden of home care have not been given sufficient attention. One exception is a comprehensive study by Sainsbury and Grad de Alarcon (1970) which examined the impact of community versus hospital care on the burden of caregivers of dementia patients. They found that burden was reduced an equal amount for both groups.

Several studies have pointed to specific behaviors that are troublesome to family members.

[1]This research was supported in part by Grant No. 5 R01 MH 31129-02, NIMH. A version of this paper was presented at the meetings of the Gerontological Society, Washington, DC, Nov., 1979.
[2]Asst. Prof., Andrus Gerontology Ctr., Univ. of Southern California, Los Angeles, CA 90007.
[3]Project Coordinator, Memory Project, Andrus Gerontology Ctr.
[4]Gerontological Specialist, Didi Hersch Community Mental Health Ctr.

In the study by Sainsbury and Grad de Alarcon (1970) behaviors found to be particularly worrisome to caregivers included potentially harmful behavior to self or other, behaving oddly, restlessness, and being troublesome at night. Several of these worrisome behaviors are the same as those identified by Lowenthal (1964) to predict institutionalization. Sanford (1975) measured the tolerance of caregivers toward problems encountered in giving care to mentally impaired older people. Caregivers found the lack of time for themselves and sleep disturbances the most difficult to tolerate.

While pinpointing problem behaviors, these studies have not clarified how specific behaviors contribute to the burden of home care. Other factors that need to be considered are the relationship of the caregiver to the older person with dementia and the support available from other family members.

The Community Study of Caregivers

Because of the importance of family to maintain persons with senile dementia in the community, the present investigation examines how caregivers feelings of burden are affected by the impairments manifested by the dementia patient and by various aspects of the home care situation. An interview to assess the level of burden experienced by caregivers was developed and has been studied in relation to the behaviors affected by senile dementia, including the occurrence of behavior and memory problems and the degree of functional and cognitive impairment. The burden of caregivers has also been examined in terms of social factors affecting care of the dementia patient, such as the amount of formal and informal support the caregiver receives and other situational characteristics.

Older people with senile dementia ($N = 29$) and their primary caregivers ($N = 29$) were interviewed. The mean age of the subjects with dementia was 76 years. This group consisted of 16 white males and 13 white females. All but four of the caregivers interviewed were female, 18 being spouses and 11 daughters. Persons were designated as the primary caregiver if they were principally responsible for providing or coordinating the resources required by the person with dementia, such as housekeeping, financial help and shopping. The age range of the caregivers was 42 to 82 years with a mean age of 65. Subjects were recruited from a research and training center offering counseling and memory training to older persons.

Interviews took place in the home of the dementia subject. The home setting was chosen because it was felt that familiar surroundings were less stressful and provided a more accurate picture of the older person's ability to function. Each interview took about 1½ hours to administer.

The presence of senile dementia was determined by pre-screening subjects with the Kahn Mental Status Questionnaire (MSQ) and the Face-Hand Test (FHT). These tests, when administered together, have shown good validity with psychiatric diagnosis of senile dementia (Kahn et al. 1960). While sometimes criticized as insensitive to mild degrees of dementia, these tests have the advantage of yielding few false positive results, thus reducing the likelihood of including older people without senile dementia in the sample (Kahn & Miller, 1978). Two or more mistakes on the MSQ and any mistakes on the FHT after four learning trials were considered an indication of dementia. Possible causes of intellectual impairment other than senile dementia were ruled out by obtaining a clinical history and in most cases corroborating medical findings.

The level of cognitive impairment of the dementia patient was indicated by scores on the two screening measures (MSQ and FHT) and by the 30-item mental status test developed by Jacobs et al. (1977). While containing items of orientation that are identical with the MSQ, this test also includes 20 other questions that tap mental speed, reasoning, learning, calculations and the ability to maintain and shift sets. This test thereby samples more areas of cognitive functioning that can be impaired with dementia than the Kahn MSQ. Higher scores indicate more errors on these mental status measures. A combined Mental Status score is also used.

The Memory and Behavior Problems Checklist determined the type and frequency of memory and behavior problems exhibited by the impaired older person. Caregivers were asked to read through a list of 16 common memory and behavior problems, such as "wandering or getting lost" and "having embarrassing, rude or objectionable behavior," and then to indicate how often this behavior occurred in the past month. Total memory and behavior problem scores were generated for the number of different problems occurring and their frequency.

It was expected that caregiver's burden would increase as functional abilities of the caregiver and older person with senile dementia decrease. To determine the level of functional ability of the subject with dementia, Lawton's (1971) Physical and Instrumental Activity of Daily Living scales (PADL and IADL) were used. These tools assess the levels of assistance required by the older person with senile dementia to do physical activities such as dressing and walking as well as instrumental activities such as using the telephone. A short version of the IADL was used to determine the caregiver's difficulty in performing daily activities. Higher scores reflect more impairment.

The measurement of the degree of burden was made with a 29-item self-report inventory, which was administered to the primary caregiver during the assessment interview. The questions were selected based on clinical experience with caregivers and prior studies (e.g., Lowenthal, et al., 1967). They covered the areas most frequently mentioned by caregivers as problems, including caregiver's health, psychological well-being, finances, social life and the relationship between the caregiver and the impaired person. Examples of statements used are "I feel my spouse tries to manipulate me" and "I feel that I am contributing to the well-being of my spouse." The caregiver indicated how much discomfort this concern caused by choosing the most appropriate phrase from "not at all" to "extremely." It was assumed that discomfort caused by these situations places burden upon the caregiver. A total burden score was calculated and used in the analysis. (Four of the 29 items were scored in the opposite direction and subtracted from the total). The complete interview appears in Table 1.

Demographic data, including age, sex, education, income and relationship of the caregiver to the subject with dementia, was gathered on all subjects. The duration of the illness was determined from a history obtained from the caregiver. In addition, caregivers were asked about the frequency of visits of other family members to the dementia patient, and if any formal social or health services were being provided.

Factors Associated with Feelings of Burden

An examination of the interview and test results indicated that the sample of 29 subjects with senile dementia had considerable cognitive and behavioral impairment (Table 2).

Table 1. The Burden Interview.

1. I feel resentful of other relatives who could but who do not do things for my spouse.
2. I feel that my spouse makes requests which I perceive to be over and above what s/he needs.
3. Because of my involvement with my spouse, I don't have enough time for myself.
4. I feel stressed between trying to give to my spouse as well as to other family responsibilies, job, etc.
5. I feel embarrassed over my spouse's behavior.
6. I feel guilty about my interactions with my spouse.
7. I feel that I don't do as much for my spouse as I could or should.
8. I feel angry about my interactions with my spouse.
9. I feel that in the past, I haven't done as much for my spouse as I could have or should have.
10. I feel nervous or depressed about my interactions with my spouse.
11. I feel that my spouse currently affects my relationships with other family members and friends in a negative way.
12. I feel resentful about my interactions with my spouse.
13. I am afraid of what the future holds for my spouse.
14. I feel pleased about my interactions with my spouse.
15. It's painful to watch my spouse age.
16. I feel useful in my interactions with my spouse.
17. I feel my spouse is dependent.
18. I feel strained in my interactions with my spouse.
19. I feel that my health has suffered because of my involvement with my spouse.
20. I feel that I am contributing to the well-being of my spouse.
21. I feel that the present situation with my spouse doesn't allow me as much privacy as I'd like.
22. I feel that my social life has suffered because of my involvement with my spouse.
23. I wish that my spouse and I had a better relationship.
24. I feel that my spouse doesn't appreciate what I do for him/her as much as I would like.
25. I feel uncomfortable when I have friends over.
26. I feel that my spouse tries to manipulate me.
27. I feel that my spouse seems to expect me to take care of him/her as if I were the only one s/he could depend on.
28. I feel that I don't have enough money to support my spouse in addition to the rest of our expenses.
29. I feel that I would like to be able to provide more money to support my spouse than I am able to now.

Scores on mental status tests generally indicated major deficits. There was a range of 1 to 10 errors on the Kahn MSQ, with a mean score of 6.4 out of 10 possible incorrect responses. Subjects made an average of 8.3 incorrect trials out of a possible 16 on the Face-Hand Test. The Jacob's MSQ scores were similar with a range of 8 to 30 errors and an average score of 18.6 incorrect. The average duration of symptoms of dementia was reported to be 3.1 years, with a range from 6 months to 10 years.

Scores on measures of functional ability and frequency of memory and behavioral problems associated with senile dementia also indicate

Table 2. Mean Scores and Standard Deviations of Characteristics of the Dementia Sample for All Subjects and Two Subsamples.

Variable	Total Sample (N = 29)	Daughters as Caregivers (N = 11)	Spouses as Caregivers (N = 18)
Mental Status Errors			
Kahn MSQ	6.4 (2.8)	6.6 (3.6)	6.3 (3.1)
Face Hand Test	8.3 (6.9)	8.8 (6.3)	8.0 (7.4)
Jacobs Questionnaire	18.6 (7.3)	18.7 (8.1)	18.6 (7.1)
Duration of Illness (yrs.)	3.1 (2.2)	3.8 (3.2)	2.7 (1.3)
Frequency of Memory Problems (per month)	96.1 (38.7)	118.5 (36.2)	82.4 (34.2)
Frequency of Behavior Problems (per month)	30.2 (39.9)	44.3 (39.0)	21.7 (39.0)
Physical ADL	2.4 (3.0)	2.5 (3.4)	2.3 (2.8)
Instrumental ADL	10.0 (4.7)	9.9 (3.4)	10.1 (5.4)
Frequency of Family Visits (per month)	9.3 (9.8)	14.4 (13.4)	6.1 (5.0)
Caregiver's Level of Burden	30.8 (13.8)	28.3 (14.6)	32.5 (13.4)

that this sample is substantially impaired in many areas. From a list of eight possible memory problems, 62% of the caregivers indicated four or five of these problems occurred within the past month. The most frequent memory problems included asking repetitive questions, losing things and forgetting what day it is. Behavior problems occurred less frequently, with only 18% of the sample reporting three or more problems in the past month from the checklist of eight items. Neglecting self care and restlessness were the most frequent behavior problems, and were reported by 34% of the sample.

Of the measures of functional ability of the impaired subject, instrumental activities of daily living required the most attention from caregivers. Two-thirds of the impaired persons needed at least some help with most of these activities. Physical activities, such as eating, walking and toileting, were less affected by dementia, with most subjects independent in these areas. Mean scores were 10.0 out of 24 on the IADL scale and 2.4 out of 21 on the PADL scale (higher scores indicate more dependence).

About nine visits per month from family other than the primary caregiver to the older person with dementia were reported by our sample. Frequency of visits ranged from as few as no visits to as often as daily visits. For this study family includes children, grandchildren and siblings. Children were the most frequent visitors (five visits per month) when compared to grandchildren (2.9 visits per month) and siblings (1.3 visits per month).

The level of burden measured was less than expected considering the complexity of many of the cases. The mean score was 31 (range 1 to 66; $SD = 13.3$) out of a possible 84 on the burden interview. Items on which the most burden was reported involved the caregiver's lack of time for oneself, the excessive dependency of the patient on the caregiver, and caregiver's fears about further deterioration in the patient's behavior.

It was expected that feelings of burden would be related to the extent of behavior impairment manifested by the person with senile dementia. Table 3 shows correlations between various measures of functioning (with higher scores indicating more impairment) and the burden interview. Contrary to expectations, none of the behavior variables, including the frequency of memory and behavior problems, the extent of cognitive impairment on the mental status tests, and the level of functional impairment on the IADL and PADL scales, were correlated with the level of burden. Similarly, duration of the illness was not related to burden. Of the remaining measures, only the frequency of family visits was significantly related to level of burden ($r = -0.48, p < .01$). The negative correlation indicates that subjects receiving more visits from children (other than the primary caregiver), grandchildren and siblings had caregivers who reported less burden. Other significant relations in Table 3 were among measures of mental status, duration of illness, memory and behavior problems and functional impairment (PADL and IADL). Family visits were not correlated to measures other than burden.

Since some caregivers were spouses and others were daughters of the impaired person, it was decided to test whether the relationship of the caregiver to the impaired person affected the findings. A preliminary step compared the scores of husbands and wives as caregivers. Though husbands had fewer family visits than wives, this did not significantly lower the frequency of family visits for all spouses. Other variables, including burden, were similar for husbands and wives as caregivers.

Table 3. Correlations between Characteristics of the Dementia Sample.

Variables	Mental Status	Duration of Illness	Memory Problems	Behavior Problems	Physical ADL	Instrumental ADL	Family Visits
Duration of Illness	0.30						
Memory Problems	0.17	0.40*					
Behavior Problems	0.30	0.46*	0.45*				
Physical ADL	0.19	0.51*	0.46*	0.76*			
Instrumental ADL	0.51*	0.46*	0.48*	0.44*	0.59*		
Family Visits	−0.05	−0.27	−0.20	0.00	0.22	0.27	
Caregiver's Burden	−0.06	0.02	0.16	−0.07	−0.06	−0.20	−0.48*

* = $p < 0.05$; N = 29.

Separate analyses were carried out for subjects whose caregivers were spouses and for those whose daughters provided the assistance. As shown in Table 2, there was no difference in the feelings of burden reported by daughters compared to spouses, or in the level of impairment of persons with dementia in the two subgroups. Correlations were also made on the relation of burden to the other variables within each subsample. As with the whole sample, burden was inversely related to number of family visits to the impaired person's household for both daughters ($r = -0.66$) and spouses ($r = -0.47$). No other variable was significantly associated with feelings of burden.

Feelings of Burden and Community Care

The surprising aspect of this study is that extent of burden reported by primary caregivers of persons with senile dementia was not related to the behavior problems caused by the illness, but was associated with the social supports available, specifically the number of visitors to the household. Previous research on the impaired elderly has stressed that specific behaviors are troublesome to family members, for example, wandering and insomnia, but the frequency of these problems was not found to contribute to the amount of feelings of burden. Clearly, such things as severe memory loss and the problems associated with it are distressing to family members, but the ability of caregivers to cope with that situation may depend on the other supports available to them. No information was elicited on what visitors were doing or the quality of the visits, which undoubtedly affect the degree of relief caregivers receive. Nonetheless, the sheer quantity of visits from other family members was important.

A limitation of this study is that caregivers did not report what could be considered high levels of burden. All of the caregivers had decided, at least for the present, not to institutionalize the person with senile dementia. They may, therefore, not be representative of all families caring for individuals with this disorder. On the other hand, the extent of behavioral impairments found in the dementia patients indicates they had a fairly extensive degree of difficulty and were not mildly impaired or in the early stages of the illness. In a few cases the duration of the disorder was as long as 10 years. Hence, though the sample may not have been representative, problems resulting from dementia which were faced by these caregivers covered a wide range of severity and duration.

One implication of these findings is that an intervention program that increases informal social supports may be effective with a caregiver who reports excessive feelings of burden. Professionals can provide this service directly, by forming a supportive counseling relationship with involved family members. Other types of professional interventions are described below. Though these interventions are assumed to support caregivers, none have looked at what caused burden on caregivers nor have they attempted to measure the supportive impact of their intervention on caregivers. Given the above findings about burden, however, these projects describe promising approaches for families caring for someone with senile dementia.

Pasamanick and his associates (1967) reported that home visits made by public health nurses to families of schizophrenics had a beneficial effect on patient outcome. The supported home group of schizophrenics showed less hospitalization and a greater percentage of time at home than controls not receiving the visiting program. The main role of the public health nurse was to listen to clients and their families and to offer some counseling. This listening was felt to be the crucial element in the success of the home care group.

Another means of delivering support is through group meetings for the caregivers of older people with senile dementia. Hudis (1977) has found that such group meetings give members an opportunity to share concerns, clarify problems and roles, and develop skills for problem solving and coping. It is also an efficient means of educating caregivers about senile dementia and community resources that may be useful. The mutual support among group members may generate self-help groups run by members themselves.

It is also possible to work with the entire natural support network of the person with dementia to provide assistance to the primary caregiver. Garrison and Howe (1976) describe how network therapy can be used with those with senile dementia. The goal of network therapy is to use affective and instrumental resources present within the natural support network to promote coping with problem behaviors. By helping the entire natural support network to share in the supportive care of the older person, the responsibilities on the primary caregiver are reduced and, hence, burden may be lessened. The results of family meetings held by the authors have been encouraging, increasing the amount of help given to the primary caregiver and increasing the understanding of the situation by everyone involved.

For those older people who have no natural support network or need additional network members, the use of a natural neighbor has been demonstrated in the literature. A natural neighbor has been defined as someone to whom people turn to for assistance on an informal basis (Patterson, 1977). Collins and Pancoast (1976) describe how to find, build and maintain a consulting relationship with a natural neighbor. Community volunteers can also be used to fortify the natural support network of the impaired older person. With one or a combination of these interventions one can attempt to enhance the supportive function of a natural support system and relieve excessive burden on the primary caregiver.

Each of these approaches have in common a major focus on the caregiver's well-being, rather than seeking solutions to specific behavior and memory problems of the dementia patient. While it is sometimes possible to alter a troublesome behavior pattern, there will be some deficits in functioning that cannot be modified through any interventions currently available. Because of the intractable nature of many problems associated with senile dementia, interventions which focus principly on control of specific memory or behavior deficits have a low probability of success. An approach that includes support to caregivers as well as attention to any modifiable aspects of the patient's behavior may contribute the most to making the situation more manageable.

Summary and Conclusion

In summary, this research looks at the possible factors contributing to feelings of burden of those caring for older people with senile dementia. Caregivers and older persons with senile dementia living in the community were interviewed in their homes. Of the variables considered, including the extent of cognitive impairment, memory and behavior problems, functional abilities, and the duration of illness, only the frequency of family visits had a significant effect upon the degree of caregiver's feelings of burden. In situations where more visits were paid to the impaired older person from family other than the primary caregiver, burden was less.

The strong relation between visits from family and caregiver's burden is important to service providers focusing on the needs of the older person with senile dementia. It suggests that primary caregivers would be best served by interventions that involve other members of the impaired older person's natural support system and make use of the resources within this network. Several methods of intervention with a natural support system have been described including network sessions, discussion groups, the use of home visitors and natural neighbors.

The present study suggests that enhancing the informal support network of the older person with dementia may also prevent overwhelming burden on the primary caregiver and the breakdown of the family system, thereby reducing the rate of institutionalization.

References
Bergmann, K. The epidemiology of senile dementia. *British Journal of Psychiatry*, special publication, 1975, 9, 100-109.
Bergmann, K., Foster, E. M., Justice, A. W., & Mathews, V. Management of the demented elderly patient in the community. *British Journal of Psychiatry*, 1978, 132, 441-449.
Blenkner, M. Environmental change and the aging individual. *Journal of Gerontology*, 1967, 7, 101-105.

Collins, A. H., & Pancoast, D. L. *Natural helping networks: A strategy for prevention,* National Association of Social Workers, Washington, DC, 1976.

Garrison, J., & Howe, A. Community intervention with elderly: A social network approach. *Journal of the American Geriatrics Society,* 1976, 24, 329-333.

Hudis, I. E. A group program for families of the aging: A service strategy for strengthening natural supports. Paper presented at the 30th Annual Meeting of the Gerontological Society, San Francisco, CA, Nov. 20, 1977.

Jacobs, J. W., Bernhard, J. R., Delgado, A., & Strain, J. J. Screening for organic mental syndromes in the medically ill. *Annals of Internal Medicine,* 1977, 86, 40-46.

Kahn, R. L. The mental health system and the future aged. *Gerontologist,* 1975, 15, 24-31.

Kahn, R. L., & Miller, N. E. Assessment of altered brain function in the aged. In M. Storandt, I. C. Siegler & M. Elias (Eds.), *The clinical psychology of aging.* Plenum Press, New York, 1978.

Kahn, R. L., & Zarit, S. H. Evaluation of mental health programs for the aged. In P. O. Davidson, F. W. Clark & L. A. Hamerlynck (Eds.), *Evaluation of behavioral programs: In community, residential and school settings.* Research Press, Champaign, IL, 1974.

Kahn, R. L., Goldfarb, A. I., Pollack, J., & Peck, A. A brief objective measure for the determination of mental status of the aged. *American Journal of Psychiatry,* 1960, 117, 326-328.

Kay, D.W. K., Beamish, P., & Roth, M. Old age mental disorders in Newcastle upon Tyne: Part I. A study of prevalence. *British Journal of Psychiatry,* 1964, 110, 146-158.

Lawton, M. P. The functional assessment of elderly people. *Journal of the American Geriatrics Society,* 1971, 19 465-480.

Lowenthal, M. F. *Lives in distress.* Basic Books, Inc., New York, 1964.

Lowenthal, M. F., Berkman, P., & Associates. *Aging and mental disorder in San Francisco.* Jossey-Bass, San Francisco, 1967.

Pasamanick, B., Scarpitti, R. P., & Dinitz, S. *Schizophrenics in the community: An experimental study in the prevention of hospitalization.* Appleton-Century Crofts, New York, 1967.

Patterson, S. L. Toward a conceptualization of natural helping, *ARETE,* 1977, 4(3), 162-171.

Plutzky, M. Principles of psychiatric management of chronic brain syndrome. *Geriatrics,* 1974, 29, 120-127.

Sainsbury, P., & Grad de Alarcon, J. The psychiatrist and the geriatric patient: The effects of community care on the family of the geriatric patient. *Journal of Geriatric Psychiatry,* 1970, 1, 23-41.

Sanford, J. F. A. Tolerance of debility in elderly dependents by supporters at home: Its significance for hospital practice. *British Medical Journal,* 1975, 3, 471-473.

[23]

Meta-Analysis of Psychosocial Interventions for Caregivers of People with Dementia

Henry Brodaty, MD, FRANZCP, FRACP,[*†] *Alisa Green, B. Sc (Psychol). Hons,*[†] *and Annette Koschera, PhD*[†]

OBJECTIVES: To review published reports of interventions for caregivers (CGs) of persons with dementia, excluding respite care, and provide recommendations to clinicians.

DESIGN: Meta-analytical review. Electronic databases and key articles were searched for controlled trials, preferably randomized, published in English from 1985 to 2001 inclusive. Thirty studies were located and scored according to set criteria, and the interventions' research quality and clinical significance were judged.

SETTING: Home or noninstitutional environment.

PARTICIPANTS: Informal CGs—persons providing unpaid care at home or in a noninstitutional setting.

MEASUREMENTS: The primary measures were psychological morbidity and burden. Other varied outcome measures such as CG coping skills and social support were combined with measures of psychological distress and burden to form a main outcome measure.

RESULTS: The quality of research increased over the 17 years. Results from 30 studies (34 interventions) indicated, at most-current follow-up, significant benefits in caregiver psychological distress (random effect size (ES) = 0.31; 95% confidence interval (CI) = 0.13–0.50), caregiver knowledge (ES = 0.51; CI = 0.05–0.98), any main caregiver outcome measure (ES = 0.32; CI = 0.15–0.48), and patient mood (ES = 0.68; CI = 0.30–1.06), but not caregiver burden (ES = 0.09; CI = −0.09–0.26). There was considerable variability in outcome, partly because of differences in methodology and intervention technique. Elements of successful interventions could be identified. Success was more likely if, in addition to CGs, patients were involved. Four of seven studies indicated delayed nursing home admission.

CONCLUSION: Some CG interventions can reduce CG psychological morbidity and help people with dementia stay at home longer. Programs that involve the patients and their families and are more intensive and modified to CGs' needs may be more successful. Future research should try to improve clinicians' abilities to prescribe interventions. **J Am Geriatr Soc 51:657–664, 2003.**

Key words: meta-analysis; family caregivers; dementia; interventions

Most people with dementia have at least one supporter or caregiver (CG), usually a spouse or relative. CGs experience adverse psychological, physical, social, and financial consequences,[1,2] such as higher rates of depression,[3,4] poorer physical health than non-CG controls,[5] social isolation,[6] and direct (e.g., medications) and indirect (e.g., loss of earnings due to relinquishing of paid work) financial costs. CGs are crucial for maintaining people affected with dementia in the community. When there is no CG, or when the CG is stressed, the likelihood of nursing home admission rises sharply.[7]

Clinicians and researchers have devised many methods of trying to help CGs such as education and training programs, support groups, and counseling. Successful interventions have been reported to reduce CG distress, depression, and psychological morbidity; to delay nursing home admission of patients; and to improve patients' psychological well-being. The aim of this study was to review the evidence for the outcome of CG interventions (excluding respite care, which is a patient-targeted intervention—see Gottlieb et al. for a review)[8] and to provide recommendations for clinicians. The review has been restricted to studies involving informal CGs (persons providing unpaid care, at home or in a noninstitutional environment).

METHOD

Key words (caregiver, carer, self-help groups, support groups, education, training, skills training, counseling, psychotherapy, intervention, and therapy) were used to search published literature in English for controlled studies of interventions for CGs of people with dementia and were each combined with the search terms "random allocation" and/or "control group" and "dementia" or "Alz-

From the *School of Psychiatry, University of New South Wales, Sydney, Australia; and †Academic Department for Old Age Psychiatry, Prince of Wales Hospital, Randwick, New South Wales, Australia
Address correspondence to Professor Henry Brodaty, Academic Department for Old Age Psychiatry, The Euroa Center, Prince of Wales Hospital, Avoca Street, Randwick, Sydney, NSW 2031, Australia. E-mail: h.brodaty@unsw.edu.au

heimer's disease." The following electronic databases were searched: Medline (1985–Week 4, December 2000), PsychInfo (1984–Week 2, December 2000), Ageline (1985–2000/12), CINAL (1985–2000), Cochrane Library 1998 (Issue 3 Database), EBM Reviews—Best Evidence (1991—November/December 2000), EBM Reviews—Cochrane Database of Systematic Reviews (4th Quarter 2000), EMBASE (1988–Week 51, 2000).

All randomized or quasi-experimental trials in which CGs were allocated to intervention or nonintervention (control) groups were selected. Participants in the selected studies were informal CGs of people diagnosed with Alzheimer's disease.

One of the investigators (AG) scrutinized the resulting abstracts, and papers judged relevant were obtained. If doubt existed regarding an article's relevance, a second investigator (HB) reviewed the abstract. References of obtained papers were reviewed to locate any additional papers. Fifty-two articles met criteria for inclusion, seven of which, as shown in brackets in Table 2, were excluded because they were descriptions of earlier studies published by the same research group and added no new information.

The primary outcome measures were psychological morbidity and burden. Measures of psychological morbidity included the General Health Questionnaire, Hamilton Depression Rating Scale, Brief Symptom Inventory, Self-Rating Depression Scale, Hopkins Symptom Checklist, Center for Epidemiological Studies Depression Scale, and the Positive and Negative Affect Scale. Burden was measured using the Burden Interview, Rankin Scale, Caregiver Hassles Scale, Screen for Caregiver Burden, or other objective burden scales.

For those studies that did not include a measure of psychological morbidity or burden, the varied outcome measures used were combined with measures of psychological distress and burden to form "any main outcome measure." These included measures of CG coping skills (Health Specific Family Coping Index) and social support (Instrumental and Expressive Social Support Scale). Knowledge of Alzheimer's disease was examined separately and was measured using the Alzheimer's Disease Knowledge Test, Dementia Quiz, Dementia Knowledge Test, and other individual knowledge measures. "Study success," categorized as a dichotomous dependent variable, was defined as significant change in one of the main outcome measures or an effect size (ES) of 0.5 or greater.

A small number of studies looked at patient mood as an outcome, measured using the Cornell Scale for Depression in Dementia and the Geriatric Depression Scale. Finally, the effects of CG interventions on nursing home placements were examined.

Follow-up points were classified as posttest, 3- to 6-month follow-up, more than 6-month follow-up, and most-current follow-up of each study. For the statistical analyses of study characteristics (see below) the most-current follow-up was the dependent variable.

Both reviewers (AG and HB) independently rated the methodological quality of the included studies according to criteria based upon Cochrane Collaboration Guidelines[9] (Table 1). Characteristics of the design, subjects, outcomes, statistics, and results were used to evaluate the quality of studies (Table 2, quality scores).

Interventions were also rated in terms of their "dosage" or the "strength" of the intervention (Table 2), where the number of sessions/occasions of contact were rated as a minimal (1–2 sessions), moderate (3–5 sessions), medium-high (6–10 sessions), or high/intensive (>10 sessions).

Meta-analysis was performed using MetaView version 4.0 (Cochrane Collaboration, Oxford, England). ES for continuous data was calculated as standardized mean difference (SMD (Cohen's d) with 95% confidence intervals (CIs)) between treatment and control group.[48,50,51] An ES of 0.2 may be statistically significant but is considered weak, 0.5 is considered moderate, and 0.8 or above as strong.[52] ESs for dichotomous outcome data were reported as odds ratios (ORs).[53] Weighted average ESs were calculated weighting each individual ES by the inverse of its variance.[53] All pooled calculations included a test of homogeneity of means. Results were compared for fixed-effects and random-effects models.[54]

In most cases, there was no substantial difference between fixed-effects and random-effects models. Results for random-effects models are displayed because tests for homogeneity and heterogeneity of studies under examination in terms of methods, type of intervention, sample characteristics, and outcome measures support the use of a random-effects model for most of the pooled estimates.[48,49,54] Sensitivity analyses were conducted using various combinations of trials and estimates.

SPSS version 10.0 (SPSS Inc., Chicago, IL) was used to analyze predictors of ES. Chi-square (χ^2) analysis was employed for dichotomous data and Mann-Whitney U tests (two-tailed; denoted as U) for continuous data. Spearman rank correlation coefficient (Spearman rho) was used as a measure of association.

Where studies contained more than one intervention

Table 1. Criteria for Rating Quality of Studies

Criterion	Score
Design	
Randomized	1
Controlled (or comparison group used)	1
Subjects	
Use of standardized diagnostic criteria	1
All subjects accounted for/withdrawals noted	1
Outcomes	
Well-validated, reliable measures (caregiver and/or patient)	1
Objective outcome (e.g., institutionalization or death)	1
Questionable/unreliable outcome measures	0
Statistics	
Statistical significance considered	1
Adjustment for multiple comparisons	1
Evidence of sufficient power	1
Results	
Blind ratings	1
Follow-up assessment 6 months or beyond	1
Good quality	>7
Poor quality	<5

Table 2. Characteristics of Included Studies

Study	Design	Outcome Measure*	Instrument	Number of Subjects Randomized†	Intervention Type	Quality	Dosage
Brennan et al. 1995[10] (same sample as Bass et al. 1998)[11]	RCT	Any main outcome measure	IESS	102 (51 each group) Withdrawals = 6	S	6	4
Brodaty & Gresham, 1989[12] (same sample as Brodaty et al. 1991, 1997)[13,14]	RCT	Psychological morbidity Delay to nursing home admission‡	GHQ	100 (tmt group 1 = 33, tmt group 2, = 31, control = 32)	E, S, C, F, SM, P	7	4
Brodaty et al. 1994[15]	NR	Psychological morbidity Burden Knowledge	GHQ BI Knowledge measure	81 (completed = 33, partially completed = 22, control = 26)	E, S, SM	6	3
Chang et al. 1999[16]	RCT	Psychological morbidity Burden	BSI CAT	87 (65 completed: tmt = 31, control = 34)	P	6	3
Chiverton & Caine, 1989[17]	NR	Any main outcome measure Knowledge	HSFCI HSFCI	47 (40 completed: 20 each group)	E, S	5	2
Chu et al. 2000[18]	RCT	Delay to nursing home admission‡		75 (tmt = 37, control = 38) withdrawals = 6	T	7	4
Dröes et al. 1999[19]	NR	Patient mood	CDS	56 (tmt = 33,control = 23) withdrawals = 14	E, S, P	6	4
Eloniema-Sulkava et al. 1999[20]	RCT	Delay to nursing home admission‡		100 (tmt = 53, control = 47)	E, C, P	7	4
Gendron et al. 1996[21]	RCT	Psychological morbidity Burden	HSC BI	35 (tmt = 17, control = 18) withdrawals = 9	S, T	7	3
Hebert et al. 1994[22] (same sample as Herbert et al. 1995)[23]	RCT	Psychological morbidity Burden Knowledge Delay to nursing home admission‡	BSI BI ADKT	45 (tmt = 24, control = 21) withdrawals = 7	S, SM	8	3
Hinchliffe et al. 1995[24]	RCT	Psychological morbidity	GHQ	40 (tmt = 22, control = 18) withdrawals = 14	E, S, C, SM, P	8	4
Kahan et al. 1985[25]	NR	Psychological morbidity Burden Knowledge	SDS BI Dementia Quiz	40 (tmt = 22, control = 18)	S	3	3
LoGiuodice et al. 1999[26]	RCT	Psychological morbidity Burden Knowledge	GHQ BI DKT	50 (25 each group) withdrawals = 5	C, F, P	7	1
Marriot et al. 2000[27]	RCT	Psychological morbidity Patient mood	GHQ CSDD	42 (3 groups of 14) withdrawals = 1	E, S, SM, T	9	4

(Continued)

Table 2. (Continued)

Study	Design	Outcome Measure*	Instrument	Number of Subjects Randomized†	Intervention Type	Quality	Dosage
McCallion et al. 1999[28]	RCT	Burden Patient mood	CHS CSDD	66 (tmt = 32, control = 34) withdrawals = 9	E, P	10	3
McCurry et al. 1998[29]	RCT	Psychological morbidity Burden	CES-D SCB	36 (tmt1 = 7, tmt2 = 15, control = 15) withdrawals = 2	S, T, SM	6	3
Mittelman et al. 1996[30] (same sample as Mittelman et al. 1993, 1995)[31,32]	RCT	Delay to nursing home admission‡		206 (103 each group) withdrawals = 15	S, C, F	7	4
Mittelman et al. 1995[32]	RCT	Psychological morbidity	GDS	206 (withdrawals = 9)	S, C, F	7	4
Mohide et al. 1990[33] (same sample as Drummond et al. 1991)[34]	RCT	Psychological morbidity Delay to nursing home admission‡	CES-D	60 (30 each group)	E, S, F	7	4
Moniz-Cook et al. 1998[35]	NR	Psychological morbidity	GHQ	30 (15 each group) withdrawals = 5	P	8	3
Morris et al. 1992[36]	NR	Psychological morbidity Knowledge	BDI Knowledge questionnaire	39 (tmt = 13, control = 18) withdrawals = 8	SM	4	2
Ostwald et al. 1999[37]	RCT	Psychological morbidity Burden	CES-D BI	117 (tmt = 72, control = 45) withdrawals = 23	E, F	5	3
Quayhagen et al. 1989[38]	NR	Psychological morbidity Burden	HSC BI	16 (tmt = 10, control = 6) withdrawals = 4	T, P	6	4
Quayhagen et al. 2000[39] – Day care – Dyadic counseling – Cognitive stimulation	RCT	Psychological morbidity Burden	BSI MBPC-B	103 (group n's = 21, 29, 22, 16, 15)	C, P, S S, P C P	7	Day care = 4 Dyad counsel = 3 Cog stim = 3
Riordan et al. 1998[40]	NR	Delay to nursing home admission‡		38 (19 each group) withdrawals = 15	S	5	4
Ripich et al. 1998[41]	NR	Psychological morbidity Burden Knowledge	PANAS CHS Knowledge questionnaire	37 (tmt = 19, control = 18)	E	5	2
Roberts et al. 1999[42]	RCT	Psychological morbidity	PAIS	77 (tmt = 38, control = 39) withdrawals = 19	C	7	3
Robinson et al. 1988[43] (same sample as Robinson & Yates, 1994)[44]	RCT	Burden	Objective burden scale	20 (tmt = 11, control = 9)	S, T	4	2

(Continued)

Table 2. (Continued)

Study	Design	Outcome Measure*	Instrument	Number of Subjects Randomized†	Intervention Type	Quality	Dosage
Teri et al. 1997[45] Problem solving Pleasant events	RCT	Psychological morbidity Burden Patient mood	HDRS BI CDS	88 withdrawals = 16	T, P	7	Problem solving = 3 Pleasant events = 3
Zanetti et al. 1998[46]	NR	Psychological morbidity Burden Knowledge	BSI Rankin scale ADKT	23 (tmt = 12, control = 11) withdrawals = 2	S, T	4	3
Zarit et al. 1987[47] Counseling Support group	RCT	Psychological morbidity Burden	BSI BI	184 (group n's = 44, 36, 39) withdrawals = 65	E, F SM S	7	Counseling = 3 Support = 3

* Category of outcome in which this measure was included.
† Intention-to-treat figures.
‡ Time/delay to nursing home admission was a separate analysis, not part of meta-analysis.
ADKT = Alzheimer's Disease Knowledge Test; BDI = Beck Depression Inventory; BI = Burden Interview; BSI = Brief Symptom Inventory; C = counseling of carer; CAT = Caregiver Appraisal Tool; CES-D = Center for Epidemiological Studies—Depression Scale; CDS = Cornell Depression Scale; CHS = Caregiving Hassles Scale; CSDD = Cornell Scale for Depression in Dementia; DKT = Dementia Knowledge Test; E = education; F = family counseling; extended family involvement; GDS = Geriatric Depression Scale; GHQ = General Health Questionnaire; HDRS = Hamilton Depression Rating Scale; HSC = Hopkins Symptom Checklist; HSFCI = Health Specific Family Coping Index for Non-Institutional Care; IESS = Instrumental and Expressive Social Support Scale; MBPC-B = Memory and Behavior Problem Checklist, Part B; NR = nonrandomized (Quasi-experimental); P = patient involvement; PAIS = Psychosocial Adjustment to Relative's Illness; PANAS = Positive and Negative Affect Scale; RCT = randomized controlled trial; S = support group/program; SCB = Screen for Caregiver Burden; SDS = Self-Rating Depression Scale; SM = stress management; T = training; tmt = treatment.

---

group (e.g., support group compared with counseling group vs control), each intervention group was entered into the analysis separately. The following studies were excluded: (1) two studies[55,56] with a sample size of five or fewer in treatment or control group, (2) 11 studies[57–67] with insufficient outcome information to calculate ES or nursing home delay, and (3) two interventions with extreme values (values more than three times the interquartile range; dual seminar intervention (SMD for Brief System Inventory depression = −1.86);[39] the other three interventions for this study were included in the analysis), and Perkins et al. 1990[68] (SMD for caregiver morale = 3.09).[51] Therefore, of the 45 studies that met criteria for inclusion, 30 (34 interventions) were included in at least one analysis.

RESULTS

The 30 controlled studies involved 2,040 CGs (intention-to-treat; range 16–206, median = 53), who were predominantly spouses (of persons with dementia), female, and aged 55 and older (see Table 2 for included studies).

Quality ratings, which ranged from 3 to 10 (mean ± standard deviation = 6.4 ± 1.5), tended to improve over time (Spearman rho = 0.3; P = .07). There was no significant correlation of quality of research on ES (any outcome, distress, burden) using nonparametric measures (Spearman rho = 0.2, 0.3, and 0.2, respectively).

The ESs for psychological morbidity are shown in Table 3. Although 77% of the studies showed a positive ES for psychological morbidity (range −0.59–1.81), this was only statistically significant in five of the 20 positive interventions. The ES for burden ranged from –0.6 (95% CI = −1.33–0.14) to 1.07 (95% CI = 0.12–2.03). Only one intervention of 20 (a social skills training program)[43] showed a statistically significant effect on burden. Overall, 23 of 34 (68%) interventions met the criteria for study success.

Weighted average ESs (95% CI; number of studies) were calculated for CG psychological morbidity, 0.31 (0.13–0.50; n = 26); CG burden, 0.09 (−0.09–0.26; n = 20); changes in patient mood, 0.68 (0.30–1.06; n = 5); CG knowledge, 0.51 (0.05–0.98; n = 8); and overall effect on "any main outcome measure," 0.32 (0.15–0.48; n = 30). The weight used here was the inverse of its variance (i.e., larger studies are given more weight).[53,69] Low but significant ESs on most outcome measures (apart from burden) suggest a low but positive overall effect of these CG interventions, but the variability between studies is substantial. The pooled estimates displayed were calculated for the most-current follow-up assessment, which was posttest for most studies. Eight studies reported results for additional follow-up assessments (mean = 27 weeks; range = 12–48 weeks). Pooled estimates for time intervals of 3 to 6 months and more than 6 months are available upon request.

Sensitivity analyses for the most-current assessment point were performed, excluding extreme values (see above), dropping one study at a time and obtaining CIs for the remaining studies.[51] Certain studies proved more influential than others, yet discrepancies in CIs for pooled calculations were small and did not result in a change of significance when compared with the overall result. An

Table 3. Effect Size for Psychological Morbidity at Most Current Follow-Up Assessment

Study	Standardized Mean Difference* (95% Confidence Interval)
Moniz-Cook et al. 1998 (GHQ)	1.81 (0.94–2.67)
Marriot et al. 2000 (GHQ)	1.57 (0.69–2.45)
Hinchliffe et al. 1995 (GHQ)	1.42 (0.64–2.21)
Teri et al. 1997; problem solving (HDRS)	1.10 (0.27–1.92)
Quayhagen et al. 1989 (HSC)	0.92 (−0.16–2.00)
Brodaty and Gresham 1989 (GHQ)	0.77 (0.27–1.28)
Quayhagen et al. 2000; cog. stimulation (BSI)	0.59 (−0.09–1.27)
Teri et al. 1997; pleasant events (HDRS)	0.53 (−0.23–1.29)
Zanetti et al. 1998 (BSI)	0.46 (−0.42–1.34)
Chang et al. 1999 (BSI)	0.45 (−0.04–0.95)
Mittelman et al. 1995 (GDS)	0.29 (0.02–0.60)
Mohide et al. 1990 (CES-D)	0.26 (−0.35–0.87)
Ostwald et al. 1999 (CES-D)	0.25 (−0.20–0.70)
McCurry et al. 1998 (CES-D)	0.21 (−0.58–1.00)
Hebert et al. 1994 (BSI)	0.20 (−0.47–0.86)
Ripich et al. 1998 (PANAS)	0.15 (−0.50–0.81)
Quayhagen et al. 2000; day care (BSI)	0.12 (−0.58–0.83)
Kahan et al. 1985 (SDS)	0.09 (−0.53–0.72)
Gendron et al. 1996 (HSC)	0.07 (−0.60–0.73)
Zarit et al. 1987; counseling (BSI)	0.02 (−0.43–0.48)
Morris et al. 1992 (BDI)	−0.09 (−0.80–0.63)
Brodaty et al. 1994 (GHQ)	−0.16 (−0.71–0.38)
Zarit et al. 1987; support group (BSI)	−0.17 (−0.60–0.27)
Logiudice et al. 1999 (GHQ)	−0.18 (−0.87–0.52)
Roberts et al. 1999 (PAIS)	−0.24 (−0.75–0.28)
Quayhagen et al. 2000; dyadic counseling (BSI)	−0.59 (−1.23–0.05)

* Effect size measured as standardized mean difference between treatment and control group.
GHQ = General Health Questionnaire (Goldberg & Williams, 1988); BSI = brief symptom inventory (Derogatis et al. 1983); SDS = Self-rating Depression Scale (Zung, 1965); HSC = Hopkins Symptom Checklist (Derogatis et al. 1974); CES-D = Center for Epidemiological Studies Depression Scale (Radloff, 1977); PANAS = Positive and Negative Affect Scale (modified version; Watson et al. 1988); PAIS = Psychosocial Adjustment to Illness Scale.

exception was the sensitivity analysis for knowledge, for which the overall SMD for random effect models was significant, whereas removal of any of the more successful studies led to nonsignificant results.

A post hoc analysis of study characteristics was used to test possible predictors of positive ES. The following predictor variables were examined: whether the intervention involved support/help from extended family; counseling of the CG; and involvement of CG and patient in intervention (e.g., teaching the caregiver skills applicable to the patient such as pleasant event planning, cognitive stimulation), support group, and stress management. Continuous dependent variables were the ES (SMD for random effect models) for CG psychological morbidity and the ES on any main outcome measure.

Using univariate analyses, the study characteristic "involvement of CG and patient in the intervention" showed an effect on any outcome measure (U = 43.0; P = .01), on CG psychological morbidity (U = 28; P = .01) and on study success (χ^2 = 4.0; df = 1; continuity correction: P = .05). No other study characteristic showed a significant effect.

The dosage of interventions ranged from minimal (n = 1), to moderate (n = 4), medium-high (n = 17), and high/intensive (n = 12). Higher dosage was associated with decreased psychological distress (Spearman rho = 0.6; P = .003), but there was a nonlinear tendency with interventions with a dosage of greater than 3.5 being less effective than interventions around 3.5.

Seven studies used time until nursing home placement as an outcome measure.[12,18,20,22,30,33,40] Two of these showed significant ESs (Brodaty et al.[12] OR = 5.0, 95% CI = 1.72–14.70; Mittelman et al.[30] SMD = 3.21, 95% CI = 2.80–3.63), and two reported a longer median time of home care until institutionalization in the intervention group than in the control group (Eloniemi-Sulkava et al.[20] 2-year follow-up: median time of home care in those patients who were institutionalized 473 vs 240 days, respectively; P = .02; Riordan et al.[40] 326 vs 160 days, respectively). Chu et al.[18] divided patients into very mildly and mildly to moderately impaired. Those in the latter class who received treatment remained in the community an average of 52.53 days longer than control group patients. Delays in nursing home admission of between 53 and 329 days were reported.[12,18,20,30,40] Two studies[35,40] reported that significantly more control patients received permanent residential care at follow-up assessment. Qualitatively, a continuing relationship between helper and CG, flexibility of the intervention, and a variety of interven-

DISCUSSION

CG interventions have modest but significant benefits on CG knowledge, psychological morbidity, and other main outcome measures (such as coping skills and social support). At the most-current follow-up, there was a mean ES of 0.3 for all CG outcomes and for CG psychological morbidity in particular, meaning that the average patient in the treatment group was less depressed than about 62% of patients in the control group. There was an even stronger ES (0.7 for posttest and 0.5 for most-current follow-up) in the increase in CG knowledge (about dementia and how to cope with it). There was also a strong ES for patient mood, but interventions did not appear to influence CG burden.

The findings regarding the predictors of positive ES are based on small numbers and should be interpreted with caution. The heterogeneity of sample characteristics and study design contribute a considerable amount of variance but cannot be controlled because of lack of information and the small number of studies. Additionally, the power of the analyses to detect small to medium ESs with a t-test was less than 0.5 ($\alpha = .05$).[52]

Despite these modest findings, CGs were frequently satisfied or very satisfied with the their interventions,[15,21,22,25,36,40,42] appraised their own coping skills as improved,[17] reported that their relationship with the patient had improved,[28] identified helpful training elements,[39] and mostly (71%) reported that they would use training again.[43] CG interventions can have effects on delaying nursing home admission, which for many is desirable. Unsuccessful interventions are short educational programs (beyond enhancement of knowledge);[14,27] support groups alone, single interviews, and brief interventions or courses that were not supplemented with long-term contact do not work.

The variability in outcomes is attributable to many factors. Patients were heterogeneous with regard to age, sex, and living arrangements; type and severity of dementia; and prevalence of behavioral and psychological symptoms associated with dementia. CGs also differed significantly with regard to demographic variables, relationship to patient (e.g., spouse vs adult child vs other), other demands on their time (working, other family members to care for), and practical and social supports. The different methods of recruitment (volunteers, clinics, advertisements, and Alzheimer's associations) may have introduced bias. Whether the different follow-up periods influenced the results was considered. Eleven studies had more than one posttest assessment. In these studies, the average ES for psychological distress improved, whereas the ES for burden decreased, but these findings would have to be corrected for many covariates and could not be considered representative of all 30 studies. Finally, the number of subjects in trials was small; there was limited power, statistical comparisons were multiple (corrections for these were few), and intention-to-treat analyses were largely not performed.

Despite these limitations, it is clear that some interventions can make a difference. What are the important elements? Statistically, the only feature that emerged as significant was involvement of the patient in addition to the CG in a structured program, such as teaching the CG problem-solving skills in the care of the patient.[45] The small numbers of subjects in a large number of trials may have militated against the emergence of other features that appear qualitatively important: practical support for the CG, involvement of the extended family, structured individual counseling, and a flexible provision of a consistent professional to provide long-term support. Ceiling and floor effects prevented the realization of beneficial effects. For example if only a minority of CGs were significantly depressed before intervention, this limited the possibility of demonstrating a significant reduction in depression score. The difficulty in recruiting and treating sufficient numbers of subjects precluded the examination of interactions between which intervention for which CG supporting which patient with what dementia at what time in the course of the condition.

The implications from this meta-analysis are that CG interventions have the potential to benefit patients and CGs. The quality of research is advancing, but there is considerable room for methodological improvement. Future research should be conducted with more rigor: randomized, controlled, blind outcome assessments, followups for at least 6 months, and use of well-validated and reliable outcome criteria measuring outcomes proximally (burden, knowledge) and distally (depression, quality of life). The next steps include evaluation of more-intensive interventions and interactions with drug therapies.

ACKNOWLEDGMENTS

Many thanks to Dusan Hadzi-Pavlovic for invaluable statistical advice.

REFERENCES

1. Max W, Webber PA, Fox PJ. Alzheimer's disease. The unpaid burden of caring. J Aging Health 1995;7:179–199.
2. Brodaty H, Green A. Family caregivers for people with dementia. In: O'Brien J, Ames D, Burns A, eds. Dementia, 2nd Ed. London: Arnold, 2000, pp. 193–205.
3. Baumgarten M, Battista RN, Infante-Rivard C et al. The psychological and physical health of family members caring for an elderly person with dementia. J Clin Epidemiol 1992;45:61–70.
4. Rosenthal CJ, Sulman J, Marshall VW. Depressive symptoms in family caregivers of long stay patients. Gerontologist 1993;33:249–257.
5. Schulz R, Vistainer P, Williamson GM. Psychiatric and physical morbidity effects of caregiving. J Gerontol 1990;45:P181–P191.
6. Brodaty H, Hadzi-Pavlovic D. Psychosocial effects on carers of living with persons with dementia. Aust N Z J Psychiatry 1990;24:351–361.
7. Brodaty H, McGilchrist C, Harris L et al. Time until institutionalization and death in patients with dementia: Role of caregiver training and risk factors. Arch Neurol 1993;50:643–650.
8. Gottlieb BH, Johnson J. Respite programs for caregivers of persons with dementia: A review with practice implications. Aging Ment Health 2000;4:119–129.
9. Clarke M, Oxman AD, eds. Cochrane Reviewers Handbook 4.1.1 In: The Cochrane Library, Oxford: Update Software. 2000.
10. Brennan FP, Moore SM, Smyth KA. The effects of a special computer network on caregivers of persons with Alzheimer's disease. Nurs Res 1995;44:166–172.
11. Bass DM, McClendon MJ, Flatley Brennan P et al. The buffering effect of a computer support network on caregiver strain. J Aging Health 1998;10:20–43.
12. Brodaty H, Gresham M. Effect of a training programme to reduce stress in carers of patients with dementia. BMJ 1989;299:1375–1379.
13. Brodaty H, Gresham M, Luscombe G. The Prince Henry Hospital dementia caregivers training programme. Int J Geriatr Psychiatry 1997;12:183–192.

14. Brodaty H, Peters KE. Cost effectiveness of a training program for dementia carers. Int Psychogeriatr 1991;3:11–21.
15. Brodaty H, Roberts K, Peters K. Quasi-experimental evaluation of an educational model for dementia caregivers. Int J Geriatr Psychiatry 1994;9:195–204.
16. Chang BL. Cognitive-behavioural intervention for homebound caregivers of persons with dementia. Nurs Res 1999;48:173–182.
17. Chiverton P, Caine ED. Education to assist spouses in coping with Alzheimer's disease. A controlled trial. J Am Geriatr Soc 1989;37:593–598.
18. Chu P, Edwards J, Levin R et al. The use of clinical case management for early stage Alzheimer's patients and their families. Am J Alzheimers Dis Other Demen 2000;15:284–290.
19. Dröes RM, Breebaart E, Ettema TP et al. Effect of integrated family support versus day care only on behaviour and mood of patients with dementia. Int Psychogeriatr 1999;12:99–115.
20. Eloniemi-Sulkava U, Sivenius J et al. Support program for demented patients and their carers: The role of dementia family care coordinator is crucial. In: Iqbal K, Swaab DF, Winblad B et al, eds. Alzheimer's Disease and Related Disorders. West Sussex: John Wiley & Sons, 1999, pp. 795–802.
21. Gendron C, Poitras L, Dastoor DP et al. Cognitive-behavioural group intervention for spousal caregivers. Findings and clinical considerations. Clin Gerontol 1996;17:3–19.
22. Hébert R, Leclerc G, Bravo G et al. Efficacy of a support programme for caregivers of demented patients in the community: A randomized controlled trial. Arch Gerontol Geriatr 1994;18:1–14.
23. Hébert R, Girouard D, Leclerc G et al. The impact of a support programme for care-givers on the institutionalisation of demented patients. Arch Gerontol Geriatr 1995;20:129–134.
24. Hinchliffe AC, Hyman IL, Blizard B et al. Behavioural complications of dementia—Can they be treated? Int J Geriatr Psychiatry 1995;10:839–847.
25. Kahan J, Kemp B, Staples FR et al. Decreasing the burden in families caring for a relative with a dementing illness: A controlled study. J Am Geriatr Soc 1985;33:664–670.
26. LoGiudice D, Waltrowicz W, Brown K et al. Do memory clinics improve the quality of life of carers? A randomized pilot trial. Int J Geriatr Psychiatry 1999;14:626–632.
27. Marriott A, Donaldson C, Tarrier N et al. Effectiveness of cognitive-behavioural family intervention in reducing the burden of care in carers of patients with Alzheimer's disease. Br J Psychiatr 2000;176:557–562.
28. McCallion P, Toseland RW, Freeman K. An evaluation of a family visit education program. J Am Geriatr Soc 1999;47:203–214.
29. McCurry SM, Logsdon RG, Vitiello M et al. Successful behavioural treatment for reported sleep problems in elderly caregivers of dementia patients: A controlled study. J Gerontol B Psychol Sci Soc Sci 1998;53B:P122–P129.
30. Mittelman MS, Ferris SH, Shulman E et al. A family intervention to delay nursing home placements of patients with Alzheimer's disease. A randomized controlled trial. JAMA 1996;276:1725–1731.
31. Mittelman MS, Ferris SH, Shulman E et al. A comprehensive support program. Effect on depression in spouse-caregivers of AD patients. Gerontologist 1995;35:792–802.
32. Mittelman MS, Ferris SH, Steinberg G et al. An intervention that delays institutionalisation of Alzheimer's disease patients: Treatment of spouse-caregivers. Gerontologist 1993;33:730–740.
33. Mohide EA, Pringle DM, Streiner DL et al. A randomized trial of family caregiver support in the home management of dementia. J Am Geriatr Soc 1990;38:446–454.
34. Drummond M, Mohide EA, Tew M et al. Economic evaluation of a support programme for demented elderly. Int J Technol Assess Health Care 1991;7:209–219.
35. Moniz Cook E, Agar S, Gibson GD et al. A preliminary study of the effects of early intervention with people with dementia and their families in a memory clinic. Aging Ment Health 1998;2:199–211.
36. Morris RG, Woods RT, Davies KS et al. The use of a coping strategy focused support group for carers of dementia sufferers. Counselling Psychol Q 1992;5:337–348.
37. Ostwald SK, Hepburn KW, Caron W et al. Reducing caregiver burden. A randomized psychoeducational intervention for caregivers of persons with dementia. Gerontologist 1999;39:299–309.
38. Quayhagen MP, Quayhagen M. Differential effects of family-based strategies on Alzheimer's disease. Gerontologist 1989;29:150–155.
39. Quayhagen MP, Quayhagen M, Corbeil RR et al. Coping with dementia. Evaluation of four nonpharmacologic interventions. Int Psychogeriatr 2000;12:249–265.
40. Riordan J, Bennett A. An evaluation of an augmented domiciliary service to older people with dementia and their carers. Aging Ment Health 1998;2:137–143.
41. Ripich DN, Ziol E, Lee MM. Longitudinal effects of communication training on caregivers of persons with Alzheimer's disease. Clin Gerontologist 1998;19:37–53.
42. Roberts J, Browne G, Milne C et al. Problem-solving counseling for caregivers of the cognitively impaired: Effective for whom? Nurs Res 1999;48:162–172.
43. Robinson KM. A social skills training program for adult caregivers. Adv Nurs Sci 1988;10:59–72.
44. Robinson K, Yates K. Effects of two caregiver-training programs on burden and attitude toward help. Arch Psychiatr Nurs 1994;8:312–319.
45. Teri L, Logsdon RG, Uomoto J et al. Behavioral treatment of depression in dementia patients: A controlled clinical trial. J Gerontol B Psychol Sci Soc Sci 1997;52B:P159–P166.
46. Zanetti O, Metitieri T, Bianchetti A et al. Effectiveness of an educational program for demented person's relatives. Arch Gerontol Geriatr Suppl 1998;6:531–538.
47. Zarit SH, Anthony CR, Boutselis M. Interventions with care givers of dementia patients: Comparison of two approaches. Psychol Aging 1987;2:225–232.
48. Normand SL. Tutorial in biostatistics. Meta-analysis. Formulating, evaluating, combining, and reporting. Stat Med 1999;18:321–359.
49. Engels EA, Schmid CH, Terrin N et al. Heterogeneity and statistical significance in meta-analysis: An empirical study of 125 meta-analyses. Stat Med 2000;19:1707–1728.
50. Hunter JE, Schmidt FL. Methods of Meta-Analysis. Correcting Error and Bias in Research Findings. London: Sage, 1990.
51. Olkin I. Diagnostic statistical procedures in medical meta-analyses. Stat Med 1999;18:2331–2341.
52. Cohen J. Statistical Power Analysis for the Behavioural Sciences. London: Lawrence Erlbaum, 1988.
53. Clarke M, Oxman AD, eds. Cochrane Reviewers' Handbook 4.0. Review Manager, Version 4.0. Oxford: The Cochrane Collaboration, 1999.
54. Hardy R, Thompson SG. Detecting and describing heterogeneity in meta-analysis. Stat Med 1998;17:841–856.
55. Gendron CE, Poitras LR, Engels ML et al. Skills training with supporters of the demented. J Am Geriatr Soc 1986;34:875–880.
56. Sutcliffe C, Larner S. Counselling carers of the elderly at home: A preliminary study. Br J Clin Psychol 1988;27:177–178.
57. Haley WE, Brown L, Levine EG. Experimental evaluation of the effectiveness of group intervention for dementia caregivers. Gerontologist 1987;27:376–382.
58. Baldwin BA, Kleeman KM, Stevens GL et al. Family caregiver stress. Clinical assessment and management. Int Psychogeriatr 1989;1:185–194.
59. Dellasega C. Coping with care-giving. Stress management for caregivers of the elderly. J Psychosoc Nurs Ment Health Serv 1990;28:15–22.
60. Goodman CC, Pynoos J. A model telephone information and support program for caregivers of Alzheimer's patients. Gerontologist 1990;30:399–404.
61. Seltzer MM, Litchfield LC, Kapust LR et al. Professional and family collaboration in case management: A hospital-based replication of a community-based study. Soc Work Health Care 1992;17:1–22.
62. Weinberger M, Gold DT, Divine GW et al. Social service interventions for caregivers of patients with dementia: Impact on health care utilization and expenditures. J Am Geriatr Soc 1993;41:153–156.
63. Farran CJ, Keane-Hagarty E. Multi-modal intervention strategies for caregivers of persons with dementia. In: Light E, ed. Stress Effects on Family Caregivers of Alzheimer's Patient's: Research and Interventions. New York: Springer Publishing, 1994, pp. 242–259.
64. Challis D, Von Abendorff R, Brown P et al. Care management and dementia: An evaluation of the Lewisham Intensive Case Management Scheme. In: Hunter S, ed. Dementia: Challenges and New Directions. London: Jessica Kingsley, 1997, pp. 139–164.
65. Burgener SC, Bakas T, Murray C et al. Effective caregiving approaches for patients with Alzheimer's disease. Geriatr Nurs 1998;19:121–126.
66. Buckwalter KC, Gerdner L, Kohout F et al. A nursing intervention to decrease depression in family caregivers of persons with dementia. Arch Psychiatr Nurs 1999;13:80–88.
67. Corbeil RR, Quayhagen MP, Quayhagen M. Intervention effects of dementia caregiving interaction. A stress-adaptation modeling approach. J Aging Health 1999;11:9–95.
68. Perkins RE, Poynton CF. Group counselling for relatives of hospitalized presenile dementia patients: A controlled study. Br J Clin Psychol 1990;29:287–295.
69. Laird NM, Mosteller F. Some statistical methods for combining experimental results. Int J Tech Assess Health Care 1990;6:5–30.

[24]

Sustained Benefit of Supportive Intervention for Depressive Symptoms in Caregivers of Patients With Alzheimer's Disease

Mary S. Mittelman, Dr.P.H.

David L. Roth, Ph.D.

David W. Coon, Ph.D.

William E. Haley, Ph.D.

Objective: The long-term effect of counseling and support on symptoms of depression was examined in spouse-caregivers of patients with Alzheimer's disease.

Method: The participants were 406 spouse-caregivers of Alzheimer's disease patients who lived at home at baseline. The caregivers were randomly assigned to either a group receiving enhanced counseling and support treatment or a group receiving usual care (control group). Caregivers in the enhanced treatment group were provided with six sessions of individual and family counseling, agreed to join support groups 4 months after enrollment, and received ongoing ad hoc counseling. The Geriatric Depression Scale was administered at baseline and at regular follow-up intervals for as long as the caregiver participated in the study.

Results: After baseline differences were controlled for, caregivers in the enhanced treatment group had significantly fewer depressive symptoms after the intervention than did the control subjects. These effects were sustained for 3.1 years after baseline, similar across gender and patient severity level, and sustained after nursing home placement or death of the patient.

Conclusions: Counseling and support lead to sustained benefits in reducing depressive symptoms in spouse-caregivers of Alzheimer's disease patients and should be widely available to provide effective, evidence-based intervention for family caregivers.

(Am J Psychiatry 2004; 161:850–856)

Family members, often at great personal cost, provide much of the care for older adults with Alzheimer's disease and other dementias in the community (1). Family caregivers of relatives with Alzheimer's disease are at high risk for psychological distress, with rates of clinical depression and depressive symptoms far in excess of those for age-matched comparison subjects (2). This risk persists over the many years of caregiving (3) and even after caregiving ends with the death of the care recipient (4).

Carefully designed psychosocial interventions have been shown to be effective in reducing caregiver depressive symptoms (5, 6). Little is known about the long-term impact of caregiver interventions in reducing depressive symptoms. Caregiver intervention studies rarely follow participants for longer than a year or after potentially stressful transitions in caregiving, such as the nursing home placement or death of the care recipient. The New York University Spouse-Caregiver Intervention Study provided an ideal context in which to study the long-term impact of caregiver intervention on depressive symptoms. Over 9.5 years, 406 spouse-caregivers, enrolled in two successive cohorts, were randomly assigned to either enhanced counseling and support intervention or to usual care, which served as a control condition. The project is unique in that it has followed caregivers for a long period of time, with little attrition. Results from the first 206 subjects enrolled in the project have been reported previously (6, 7) and indicate that the intervention had an increasingly stronger effect on depressive symptoms in the first year after enrollment (6). Analyses of the entire study group of 406 caregivers and of the long-term effects of the intervention on depressive symptoms beyond the first year have not heretofore been reported.

Because the intervention was designed to improve caregiving skills, mobilize the support of naturally existing family networks, and provide the opportunity for counseling as needed over the entire course of caregiving, we hypothesized that the intervention would yield sustained benefits in reducing depressive symptoms, regardless of gender or level of dementia severity, not only while the family member continued to provide care at home but also after potentially stressful events such as nursing home placement and death of the patient. A secondary hypothesis was that the demonstrated effectiveness of the caregiver intervention in comparison to usual care for symptoms of depression 1 year after enrollment for the first cohort would be replicated in the second cohort, even though educational material and community supports have become increasingly available for caregivers since the study began. Finally, we were interested in exploring whether the intervention was of similar effectiveness for caregiving husbands and wives and for caregivers of patients at all levels of dementia severity.

Method

Subjects

Each study subject was the spouse of a patient with a clinical diagnosis of Alzheimer's disease and had the primary responsibility for the patient's care. All patients were living at home with their spouses at baseline. In each family, the patient or the caregiver had to have at least one other relative living in the New York City metropolitan area.

Subjects were recruited through the New York University Alzheimer's Disease Center, the local chapters of the Alzheimer's Association, media announcements, and referrals from physicians, social workers, lawyers, Alzheimer's disease day care centers, and social service agencies. The institutional review board of the New York University School of Medicine reviewed and approved this project. Written consent to participate in the project was obtained from each caregiver, as well as from any other participating family members.

The total study group consisted of 406 caregivers. The study had two enrollment phases, resulting in two cohorts of subjects. In the first phase, 206 subjects were recruited over a 3.5-year period beginning in August 1987. In the second phase, an additional 200 subjects were recruited over a 5.5-year period beginning in June 1991.

Study Design

After a comprehensive baseline assessment, study subjects were randomly assigned by lottery to one of two groups—a treatment group that received enhanced counseling and support or a control group that received the usual care offered family members of patients at the New York University Alzheimer's Disease Center. Participants were free to seek additional assistance and support elsewhere at any time throughout the study.

All caregivers were interviewed every 4 months during the first year and every 6 months thereafter, by telephone or in person, with the comprehensive battery of structured questionnaires first administered at baseline.

All caregivers were followed until 2 years after the death of the patient or until they refused or were no longer able to participate in the study. The analysis for this report is confined to the first 5 years after enrollment, the time period for which we have follow-up interviews for the most recently enrolled subjects. Thus, the analyses include the results of up to 12 interviews: intake, every 4 months for the first year, and every 6 months for years 2 to 5. Of the original 406 subjects, we assessed 380 (93.6%) at 1 year, 328 (80.8%) at 3 years, and 223 (54.9%) at 5 years of follow-up.

Treatment

The enhanced counseling and support treatment was delivered by counselors with advanced degrees in social work or allied professions and has been described in detail in a recent publication (8). The first component consisted of two individual and four family counseling sessions that included relatives suggested by the caregiver but never included the patient. The content of these sessions was determined by the needs of each caregiver (e.g., learning techniques for management of troublesome patient behavior, promoting communication among family members). Counselors also provided education about Alzheimer's disease and community resources.

The second component of the intervention was participation in a support group, beginning after the first follow-up interview. Caregivers in the group receiving enhanced treatment agreed at baseline that they would join support groups that met weekly and provided a venue for continuous emotional support and education. The third component of the treatment was ad hoc counseling—the continuous availability of counselors to caregivers and families to help them deal with crises and with the changing nature and severity of their relatives' symptoms over the course of the disease. The emergence of new psychiatric and behavioral problems of patients, which are generally more stressful than the need for assistance with activities of daily living or physical limitations (2), often precipitated ad hoc calls from caregivers. Ad hoc counseling made it possible for caregivers and families to determine the amount of contact they had with the counselors beyond the scheduled structured sessions. Each caregiver in the enhanced treatment group was offered all of the treatment components. Caregivers in the usual care group received the services provided to all families of patients at the New York University Alzheimer's Disease Center, which included information about resources and advice upon request, but they did not have formal counseling sessions and their family members did not have contact with the counselors. They were free to participate in the same support groups and ad hoc counseling used by caregivers in the enhanced treatment group if they so chose. Because the same highly skilled and trained counselors at the New York University Alzheimer's Disease Center were available to participants in both the intervention and control groups, caregivers in the control group undoubtedly received more information and support than is generally available in typical medical and community settings.

One counselor was assigned to each caregiver because we felt that counseling and support would be most effective if each caregiver had an ongoing relationship with someone who was familiar with his or her situation. Anecdotal evidence suggests that the follow-up assessments, conducted by the same counselors, were viewed as helpful by the caregivers receiving usual care, as well as by those receiving enhanced treatment.

The study had a low dropout rate; in the first 5 years after enrolling, 28 (6.9%) of the caregivers dropped out, of whom 13 (3.2%) were caring for patients at home at the time of refusal. An additional 55 caregivers dropped out because they became too ill to participate (N=20, 4.9%), entered nursing homes (N=4, 1.0%), or died (N=31, 7.6%). These retention rates are a major strength of the study and suggest that caregivers in both groups valued the contacts and assistance they received through the project.

Measures Used in the Analysis

Caregiver depression was assessed at baseline and at every follow-up assessment with the Geriatric Depression Scale (9), a 30-item self-report questionnaire with a yes/no format that was specially developed for use with the elderly; possible scores range from 0 to 30 (alpha=0.94). A cutoff score of 11 yields a sensitivity of 84% and a specificity of 95% (10). At baseline, 42.9% of the caregivers in this study (52.0% of the women and 29.0% of the men) had scores above the cutoff, indicative of possible clinical depression.

The severity of the patient's dementia was determined at baseline and at each follow-up interview by using the Global Deterioration Scale (11) (alpha=0.83), a semistructured rating of patient functioning by the interviewer based on information provided by the caregiver. Patients with dementia have scores ranging from 4 to 7 on this scale, with 4 representing mild dementia and 7 representing severe dementia.

Statistical Methods

Changes in depression over the first year of the clinical trial were examined by using an intent-to-treat analysis, with the last value carried forward for the 26 participants (6.4%) who did not provide complete data through the 1-year follow-up assessment. In addition, mixed-model growth curve analyses were conducted by using SAS Proc Mixed (12) to examine the longitudinal trajec-

TABLE 1. Baseline Characteristics of Patients With Alzheimer's Disease and Their Spouse-Caregivers in Two Cohorts of a Caregiver Intervention Study

Variable	Caregiver Cohort 1 (1987–1991) (N=206) Mean	SD	Caregiver Cohort 2 (1991–1996) (N=200) Mean	SD	Total Group (N=406) Mean	SD
Age of caregiver (years)	70.9	8.9	71.8	9.1	71.3	9.0
Age of patient (years)	73.6	8.2	75.1	8.5	74.3	8.4
Caregiver's baseline score on Geriatric Depression Scale (9) (possible scores=0–30)	9.8	6.5	9.8	6.7	9.8	6.6

	N	%	N	%	N	%
Gender of caregiver						
Female	119	57.8	125	62.5	244	60.1
Male	87	42.2	75	37.5	162	39.9
Race/ethnicity of caregiver						
White	186	90.3	183	91.5	369	90.9
Black	15	7.3	11	5.5	26	6.4
Hispanic	4	1.9	6	3.0	10	2.5
Asian	1	0.5	0	0.0	1	0.2
Patient's baseline score on Global Deterioration Scale (11)						
4 (mild dementia)	65	31.6	71	35.5	136	33.5
5	83	40.3	85	42.5	168	41.4
6	58	28.2	43	21.5	101	24.9
7 (severe dementia)	0	0.0	1	0.5	1	0.2

tories of depression. These growth curve models offer important advantages over more traditional repeated-measures analyses, especially in handling missing data (13). Growth curves were fit for each individual subject on the basis of the number of data this person provided, allowing subjects who discontinued or completed the study before the 5-year assessment to be included in the longitudinal analyses without imputation of data for the missing observations. Imputing the last observed value and carrying it forward was considered acceptable for the relatively few missing data in the first year, but it would have led to considerable bias if applied for the increasing number of missing data through 5 years after randomization.

Variability in the actual time of the assessments was explicitly included in the growth curve models by analyzing time as a random effect. Individual growth curve parameters were modeled as a function of group (enhanced treatment versus usual care) and other predictors of interest. Restricted maximum likelihood estimation was used, and an unstructured covariance structure was specified. The depression scores obtained after treatment onset (i.e., 4-month follow-up, 8-month follow-up, etc.) were analyzed as repeated observations of the dependent variable, with "mean-centered" baseline depression scores serving as a covariate. These "mean-centered" scores consisted of deviation scores; the mean baseline depression score across all caregivers (9.64) was subtracted from each individual caregiver's baseline depression score. Other predictor variables included gender (female versus male), group (enhanced treatment versus usual care), the amount of time from baseline to when each follow-up depression score was obtained, the status of the patient at the time of the interview (living at home, in a nursing home, or dead), the interaction of group and time, and the interaction of baseline depression and time. The status of the patient was analyzed as a time-dependent covariate, whereas baseline caregiver depression, gender, and group were analyzed as time-invariant covariates.

Linear, quadratic, and logarithmic growth models were examined for two different time periods. First, we analyzed changes over the first year of the study only (4-month, 8-month, and 12-month follow-ups); the group main effect and group-by-time interaction effect from these analyses addressed hypotheses similar to those tested by the intent-to-treat analyses. Second, we analyzed effects from the end of year 1 to the end of year 5 (12-month, 18-month, 24-month,.... 60-month follow-ups).

Additional growth curve analyses were conducted to determine whether depression varied as a function of cohort (enrollment phase 1 versus enrollment phase 2, time-invariant) or patient Global Deterioration Scale score (time-dependent). For all growth curve models, the Akaike information criterion (14) was used to evaluate overall model fit and to select the best-fitting longitudinal change pattern (i.e., linear, quadratic, or logarithmic).

Results

The 203 caregivers assigned to enhanced counseling and support treatment had a mean age of 71.5 years (range= 40–93) and consisted of 111 wives and 92 husbands. Caregivers in the usual care control group had a mean age of 71.1 years (range=47–95), and this group comprised 133 wives and 70 husbands. Table 1 shows demographic and clinical characteristics of the caregivers and patients at baseline. Even though the caregivers were randomly assigned to the intervention and control groups, the difference in the gender composition of the two groups was statistically significant (χ^2=4.65, df=1, p=0.03). Baseline depression scores were also significantly lower for the caregivers receiving enhanced treatment (mean=8.9, SD=5.7) than for the caregivers in the control group (mean=10.6, SD=7.2) (F=6.59, df=1, 404, p=0.01), mostly because wives (of whom there were more in the control group) had higher baseline depression scores (mean=11.1, SD=6.7) on average than husbands (mean=7.7, SD=5.7) (F=28.93, df=1, 404, p<0.0001). These baseline differences indicated that baseline depressive symptoms and gender should be included as covariates in the longitudinal models.

Effects of Intervention Over First Year

In the first year after baseline, there was a gradual decrease in symptoms of depression among caregivers in the group receiving enhanced treatment and an increase among the group receiving usual care. At the 1-year follow-

TABLE 2. Logarithmic Model of Depression Changes From Baseline Through Year 1 Among 406 Spouse-Caregivers of Patients With Alzheimer's Disease Who Received Enhanced Caregiver Treatment or Usual Care[a]

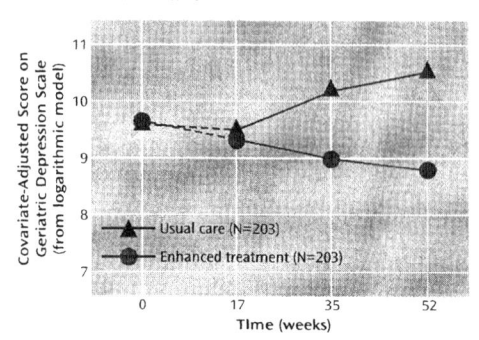

Predictor	Effect on Caregiver's Score on Geriatric Depression Scale From Baseline Through Year 1				
	Estimate	SE	t	df	p
Intercept	9.696	0.445	21.78	387	<0.0001
Baseline depression score (minus 9.64 [group mean])	0.737	0.324	22.75	331	<0.0001
Caregiver gender: female (1) versus male (0)	0.104	0.413	0.25	331	0.81
Caregiver group: enhanced treatment (1) versus usual care (0)	–1.141	0.409	–2.79	331	0.006
Time (log weeks since baseline minus 3.49 [mean])	0.925	0.314	2.95	359	0.004
Patient placement: nursing home (1) versus community (–1)	–0.468	0.281	–1.66	331	0.10
Patient death: death (1) versus nursing home or community (0)	–2.012	1.374	–1.46	331	0.15
Interaction of caregiver group and time	–1.378	0.438	–3.15	331	0.002
Interaction of caregiver's baseline depression score and time	0.153	0.034	–4.54	331	<0.0001

[a] Enhanced treatment included individual and family counseling, a regular support group, and access to additional ad hoc counseling. Usual care consisted of information and access to support groups and counseling.

up, the difference in the change on the Geriatric Depression Scale score between the enhanced treatment group (mean=–1.1, SD=5.0) and the usual care group (mean=0.3, SD=6.0) was statistically significant (F=6.40, df=1, 404, p=0.02) according to the intent-to-treat approach. For the growth curve analyses examining changes over the first year after randomization, the logarithmic growth curve model was found to provide better fit than either the linear or quadratic model, as indicated by the lowest Akaike information criterion score (logarithmic=5985, linear=6002, quadratic=6016). This means that better fit was obtained when the rate of change in depression was allowed to gradually decrease over time (the logarithmic model) than when this rate of change was constrained to be constant over time (the linear model). Table 2 presents the results for the logarithmic growth model during the first year after baseline for participants in both intervention groups from both cohorts. The predictor labeled "time" was obtained by calculating the natural logarithm of the number of weeks from baseline to an assessment and "centering" this value by subtracting its mean of 3.49.

The significant predictors of depressive symptoms over the first year after randomization were the baseline depression score, intervention group, time since baseline, the group-by-time interaction effect, and the baseline-by-time interaction effect. The predicted effects for group,

FIGURE 1. Covariate-Adjusted Depression Scores From Baseline Through Year 1 Among Spouse-Caregivers of Patients With Alzheimer's Disease Who Received Enhanced Caregiver Treatment or Usual Care[a]

[a] Enhanced treatment included individual and family counseling, a regular support group, and access to additional ad hoc counseling. Usual care consisted of information and access to support groups and counseling. The dashed lines represent the baseline covariate adjustment, that is, the equating of groups at baseline, with the actual covariate-adjusted curves beginning at the 4-month assessment point.

time, and the group-by-time interaction are depicted in Figure 1. The model-predicted values indicate that depression scores decreased during the first year for caregivers in the enhanced treatment group but increased slightly during the first year for those in the control group. As in the intent-to-treat analyses, the treatment and control groups were significantly different on covariate-adjusted depression scores at 1 year (p=0.0005) but not at 4 months (p=0.58) after randomization. In contrast to the intent-to-treat analyses, the covariate-adjusted growth curve models also revealed significant group differences at 8 months (p=0.004). The analysis also revealed that 39.9% of the caregivers in the group receiving enhanced treatment were above the threshold for clinically significant depression at baseline, while only 29.8% of these caregivers exceeded the cutoff after 1 year of intervention. The corresponding percentages for the caregivers in the control group were 45.8% and 45.1% for baseline and 1 year, respectively.

We investigated whether the previously published findings on the first cohort 12 months after randomization (6) could be replicated by using mixed-model growth curve analyses. Traditional regression analyses of data from the first cohort had shown a steadily increasing difference between the enhanced treatment and usual care caregivers in the change from baseline in the number of depressive symptoms. In the present study, we investigated the replicability of this longitudinal pattern by fitting growth models for the first year for the two cohorts separately. Consistent effects were found across both cohorts, with the group-by-time interaction effect from the logarithmic model significant for both cohort 1 (t=–2.38, df=167, p=0.02) and cohort 2 (t=–2.13, df=161, p=0.04).

TABLE 3. Linear Model of Depression Changes From Year 1 Through Year 5 Among 406 Spouse-Caregivers of Patients With Alzheimer's Disease Who Received Enhanced Caregiver Treatment or Usual Care[a]

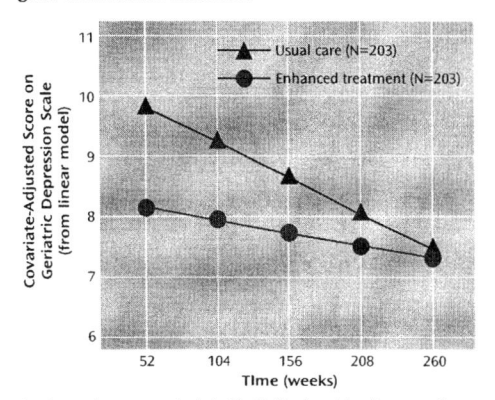

Predictor	Effect on Caregiver's Score on Geriatric Depression Scale From Year 1 Through Year 5			
	Estimate	SE	t	df	p
Intercept	9.010	0.469	19.22	388	<0.0001
Baseline depression score (minus 9.64 [group mean])	0.527	0.037	14.19	1725	<0.0001
Caregiver gender: female (1) versus male (0)	−0.065	0.499	−0.13	1725	0.90
Caregiver group: enhanced treatment (1) versus usual care (0)	−1.047	0.473	−2.22	1725	0.03
Time (log weeks since baseline minus 142.16 [mean])	−0.012	0.003	−4.29	368	<0.0001
Patient placement: nursing home (1) versus community (−1)	−0.696	0.141	−4.93	1725	<0.0001
Patient death: death (1) versus nursing home or community (0)	−2.472	0.361	−6.84	1725	<0.0001
Interaction of caregiver group and time	0.007	0.004	2.01	1725	0.05
Interaction of caregiver's baseline depression score and time	−0.001	0.000	−4.75	1725	<0.0001

[a] Enhanced treatment included individual and family counseling, a regular support group, and access to additional ad hoc counseling. Usual care consisted of information and access to support groups and counseling.

Sustainability of Intervention Effects in Years 1–5

For the growth curve analyses examining long-term effects from the end of year 1 through year 5 after baseline, a linear growth model was found to provide better fit than either a quadratic or logarithmic model (Akaike information criterion: linear=13,848, quadratic=13,867, logarithmic=13,877). This suggests that the rate of change in depression was fairly constant across time for both groups. Table 3 presents the results for the linear growth model for the two cohorts combined. Significant effects were found for all predictors except gender. The baseline-by-time interaction effect reflects the finding that depression scores were less correlated with baseline depression scores as the time from baseline increased. Figure 2 shows the significant group main effect, time main effect, and group-by-time interaction effect from this linear model. The caregivers receiving enhanced treatment averaged 1.05 depression points lower than the caregivers receiving usual care over this time period. While the difference between groups decreased in magnitude as time went on, post hoc analysis of the least squares means indicated that, after baseline differences were controlled for, caregivers in the enhanced treatment group had significantly lower depression scores (p<0.05) than caregivers in the control group through 161 weeks (3.1 years) after enrollment.

FIGURE 2. Covariate-Adjusted Depression Scores From Year 1 Through Year 5 Among Spouse-Caregivers of Patients With Alzheimer's Disease Who Received Enhanced Caregiver Treatment or Usual Care[a]

[a] Enhanced treatment included individual and family counseling, a regular support group, and access to additional ad hoc counseling. Usual care consisted of information and access to support groups and counseling.

The proportion of subjects above the threshold for clinically significant depression remained higher in the control group throughout the 5 years of the analysis. Among caregivers in the enhanced treatment group, 29.8% exceeded this threshold after 1 year of intervention, 26.2% exceeded the threshold after 3 years, and 27.0% exceeded the threshold after 5 years. The corresponding rates for caregivers in the control group were 45.1%, 31.9%, and 30.0% for 1, 3, and 5 years after baseline, respectively.

Additional models were run to examine the effects of caregiver gender and of patient severity of dementia, nursing home placement, and death on depressive symptoms and treatment-related changes. The patient's Global Deterioration Scale score was added to the growth models as a time-dependent categorical covariate with four levels. Significant main effects were found for dementia severity both for the first year (F=3.69, df=3, 327, p=0.02) and for years 1–5 (F=3.94, df=3, 1548, p=0.009), indicating that caregiver depression was higher when the patient's dementia was more severe. However, neither severity of dementia nor caregiver gender had a significant interaction with treatment group in either the analysis for the first year or the analysis for years 1–5, indicating that the intervention was equally effective in reducing symptoms of depression across dementia severity level and gender. While the analyses showed that caregiver depressive symptoms decreased significantly after nursing home placement or death of the care recipient (Table 3), the interactions between treatment group and these patient outcomes were not significant, suggesting that the intervention continued to have an impact even after these highly stressful transitional events.

Discussion

The results indicate that the enhanced counseling and support intervention is an effective treatment for caregiver distress. Spouse-caregivers who received this intervention showed fewer depressive symptoms than participants receiving usual care at the 1-year follow-up, and sustained improvements were detectable more than 3 years after enrollment. The effects were replicated across cohort, caregiver gender, dementia severity level, and even nursing home placement or death of the patient.

These intervention effects were detected despite comparison with a control group that was likely to have received much more assistance than the typical care available in community and medical settings. In contrast to longitudinal studies following family caregivers of dementia patients without providing intervention, which have shown stable levels of depressive symptoms over time (3, 4), this study provided benefits to caregivers in the usual care control group. They, as well as caregivers in the enhanced treatment group, showed significant decreases in depression from years 1 through 5, suggesting benefit from study participation. Thus, our results may actually underestimate the full impact of the intervention.

Few caregiver intervention studies have demonstrated effects on symptoms of depression beyond 12 months of follow-up, and we are aware of none that has shown results beyond 18 months. In our study, while no group differences were evident at the first follow-up (4 months after baseline), there were increasing differences apparent at 8 and 12 months, suggesting that the benefit of treatment was fully realized only after the caregivers received all three components of the intervention. The sustained effects demonstrated by the intervention may be due to its flexibility and the opportunity to learn skills or develop psychosocial coping resources useful over the long course of providing care for a patient with Alzheimer's disease.

Although the present project has attained a large number of subjects, long follow-up, and low rate of attrition that we believe are unique in the caregiving intervention literature, several limitations should be noted. The counselors who provided the enhanced treatment or usual care, and therefore were not blinded to treatment condition, conducted the follow-up interviews. However, the Geriatric Depression Scale consists of yes/no self-report questions, which are less subject to interviewer bias than interviewer rating measures. Previous research has shown that even when interviewers are blinded, 86% can accurately guess which participants have received active psychotherapy in a randomized trial, but only interviewer rating measures (not used as outcomes in our project) are typically affected by interviewer knowledge of group assignment (15). In studies of psychosocial intervention, it is not possible for the subjects themselves to be blinded to treatment condition. However, the subjects in this study completed the Geriatric Depression Scale, a symptom inventory, without reference to the treatment they received. Moreover, the subjects in the usual care group also received a considerable amount of support and counseling. Consequently, the lack of blinding in our study is unlikely to explain the observed differences in scores on the Geriatric Depression Scale. Another limitation is that we have studied the impact of this intervention only on spouses in an urban setting, and our subjects were predominantly Caucasian. Future studies should investigate whether similar interventions are as effective with more diverse groups of caregivers.

In summary, our results suggest that a short course of intensive counseling and readily available supportive maintenance can have long-lasting effects in reducing symptoms of depression among caregivers of dementia patients. Caregivers generally do not have access to such intense, individualized, multifaceted, and carefully planned interventions. In most clinical settings, caregivers may be referred to support groups and advised to use informative self-help materials, such as *The 36-Hour Day* (16). Our results, and those of previous studies (5), suggest that support and information alone are helpful but are not optimal interventions for caregivers.

The New York University Alzheimer's Disease Center counseling and support intervention, if widely available, could have a major impact on health care costs, on the emotional distress associated with caregiving, and perhaps on factors related to depressive symptoms, including health, disability, and related health care utilization and costs (17). Since family caregiving affects about 25 million American families (1), providing effective interventions for caregivers should become a high priority. With the increasing emphasis on providing patients with evidence-based treatment, caregivers should have access to interventions that have demonstrated effectiveness.

Received Nov. 25, 2002; revisions received May 6 and Sept. 15, 2003; accepted Sept. 18, 2003. From the Silberstein Aging and Dementia Research Center, New York University School of Medicine; the Department of Biostatistics, School of Public Health, University of Alabama at Birmingham; the Institute on Aging, San Francisco; and the School of Aging Studies, University of South Florida, Tampa. Address reprint requests to Dr. Mittelman, Silberstein Institute for Aging and Dementia, Department of Psychiatry, New York University School of Medicine, 550 First Ave., New York, NY 10016; mary.mittelman@med.nyu.edu (e-mail).

Supported by grants from NIMH (R01 MH-42216) and the National Institute on Aging (R01 AG-14634). Additional resources were provided by the New York University Alzheimer's Disease Center (supported by grant P30 AG-08051 from the National Institute on Aging).

The authors thank the New York University Counseling Team, especially Emma Shulman, C.S.W., and Gertrude Steinberg, M.A., for inspiring the New York University Spouse-Caregiver Intervention Study and Olivio Clay, who assisted with the data analysis.

References

1. Ory MG, Yee JL, Tennstedt SL, Schulz R: The extent and impact of dementia care: unique challenges experienced by family caregivers, in Handbook on Dementia Caregiving: Evidence-

CAREGIVERS OF ALZHEIMER'S PATIENTS

Based Interventions for Family Caregivers. Edited by Schulz R. New York, Springer Publishing, 2000, pp 1–32
2. Schulz R, O'Brien AT, Bookwala J, Fleissner K: Psychiatric and physical morbidity effects of dementia caregiving: prevalence, correlates, and causes. Gerontologist 1995; 35:771–791
3. Roth DL, Haley WE, Owen JE, Clay OJ, Goode KT: Latent growth models of the longitudinal effects of dementia caregiving: a comparison of African American and White family caregivers. Psychol Aging 2001; 16:427–436
4. Robinson-Whelen S, Tada Y, MacCallum RC, McGuire L, Kiecolt-Glaser JK: Long-term caregiving: what happens when it ends? J Abnorm Psychol 2001; 110:573–584
5. Sorensen S, Pinquart M, Duberstein P: How effective are interventions with caregivers? an updated meta-analysis. Gerontologist 2002; 42:356–372
6. Mittelman MS, Ferris SH, Shulman E, Steinberg G, Ambinder A, Mackell J, Cohen J: A comprehensive support program: effect on depression in spouse-caregivers of AD patients. Gerontologist 1995; 35:792–802
7. Mittelman MS, Ferris SH, Shulman E, Steinberg G, Levin B: A family intervention to delay nursing home placement of patients with Alzheimer disease: a randomized controlled trial. JAMA 1996; 276:1725–1731
8. Mittelman MS, Epstein C, Pierzchala A: Counseling the Alzheimer's Caregiver: A Resource for Health Care Professionals. Chicago, AMA Press, 2002
9. Sheikh JI, Yesavage JA: Geriatric Depression Scale (GDS): recent evidence and development of a shorter version, in Clinical Gerontology: A Guide to Assessment and Intervention. Edited by Brink TL, Brink T. New York, Haworth Press, 1986, pp 165–173
10. Brink TL, Yesavage JA, Owen L, Heersema PH, Adey M, Rose TL: Screening tests for geriatric depression. Clin Gerontol 1982; 1:37–44
11. Reisberg B, Ferris SH, De Leon MJ, Crook T: The Global Deterioration Scale for assessment of primary degenerative dementia. Am J Psychiatry 1982; 139:1136–1139
12. Littell RC, Milliken GA, Stroup WW, Wolfinger RD: SAS System for Mixed Models. Cary, NC, SAS Institute, 1996
13. Francis DJ, Fletcher JM, Stuebing KK, Davidson KC, Thompson NM: Analysis of change: modeling individual growth. J Consult Clin Psychol 1991; 59:27–37
14. Akaike H: A new look at statistical model identification. IEEE Transactions on Automatic Control 1974; 19:716–723
15. Carroll KM, Rounsaville BJ, Nich C: Blind man's bluff: effectiveness and significance of psychotherapy and pharmacotherapy blinding procedures in a clinical trial. J Consult Clin Psychol 1994; 62:276–280
16. Mace NL, Rabins PV: The 36-Hour Day: A Family Guide to Caring for a Person With Alzheimer's Disease, Related Dementing Illnesses, and Memory Loss in Later Life, 3rd ed. Baltimore, Johns Hopkins University Press, 1999
17. Unutzer J, Patrick DL, Simon G, Grembowski D, Walker E, Rutter C, Katon W: Depressive symptoms and the cost of health services in HMO patients aged 65 years and older: a 4-year prospective study. JAMA 1997; 277:1618–1623

[25]

Long-Term Effects of a Control-Relevant Intervention With the Institutionalized Aged

Judith Rodin
Yale University

Ellen J. Langer
Harvard University

Elderly nursing home residents who were tested as part of an intervention designed to increase feelings of choice and personal responsibility over daily events were reevaluated 18 months later. Nurses' ratings and health and mortality indicators suggest that the experimental treatment and/or the processes that it set in motion had sustained beneficial effects.

In a field study (Langer & Rodin, 1976), we assessed the effects of an intervention designed to encourage elderly nursing home residents to make a greater number of choices and to feel more control and responsibility for day-to-day events. The study was intended to determine whether the decline in health, alertness, and activity that generally occurs in the aged in nursing home settings could be slowed or reversed by choice and control manipulations that have been shown to have beneficial effects in other contexts (Lefcourt, 1973; Seligman, 1975; Zimbardo & Ruch, 1975). This also allowed us to extend the domain of the control conception by using a new population and a new set of response variables.

The hospital administrator gave a talk to residents in the experimental group emphasizing their responsibility for themselves, whereas the communication given to a second, comparison group stressed the staff's responsibility for them as patients. To bolster the communication, residents in the experimental group were offered plants to care for, whereas residents in the comparison group were given plants that were watered by the staff. In reality, the choices and potential for responsibility that we enumerated in the treatment condition were options that were already available; the administrator simply stated them clearly as possibilities. Thus the institutional readiness was already there, and the experimental induction was intended to bolster individual predispositions for increased choice and self-control.

The data indicated that residents in the responsibility-induced group became more active and reported feeling happier than the comparison group of residents, who were encouraged to feel that the staff would care for them and try to make them happy. Patients in the responsibility-induced group also showed a significant improvement in alertness and increased behavioral involvement in many different kinds of activities, such as movie attendance, active socializing with staff and friends, and contest participation. In addition to collecting these multiple questionnaire and behavioral measures at the time, we have now been able to collect long-term follow-up data on several variables, including mortality. As in Langer and Rodin (1976), our intent was to gather as many measures as were accessible for this population with the goal of increasing accuracy with increased heterogeneity of methodology (Campbell & Fiske, 1959).

Method

Subjects

There were 91 subjects given the original experimental treatment. The analyses in Langer and

---

The research was supported by National Science Foundation Grant BNS76-10939. We are grateful to Thomas V. Tolisano and the entire staff of Arden House for allowing us continued access to conduct this research. We appreciate the comments of Barry Collins on an earlier version of this manuscript.

Requests for reprints should be sent to Judith Rodin, Department of Psychology, Box 11A Yale Station, New Haven, Connecticut 06510, or to Ellen Langer, Department of Psychology and Social Relations, Harvard University, Cambridge, Massachusetts 02138.

Table 1
Number of Subjects in Test Samples

Condition	Responsibility induced	Comparison	Control
Received original induction	47	44	—
Included in Langer & Rodin (1976) analyses	24	28	—
In follow-up and included in Langer & Rodin (1976) analyses	14	12	—
Total in follow-up	20	14	9

Rodin (1976) were based on 52 of these subjects. These were all the people for whom two nurses' ratings (for reliability assessment) were available. Table 1 indicates which subjects are included in the follow-up analyses. Twenty-six of the 52 were still in the nursing home and were retested. Twelve had died, and 14 had been transferred to other facilities or had been discharged. The differences between treatment conditions in mortality are considered in a subsequent section. The groups did not differ in transfer or discharge rate. Only 9 other persons from the original sample of 91 were available for retesting. Since they had incomplete nurses' ratings in the first study, they are only included in follow-up analyses not involving change scores in nurses' evaluations. Almost all of the participants now lived in different rooms, since the facility had completed a more modern addition 13 months after the experimental treatment.[1]

We also evaluated a small control group of patients who had not participated in the first study due to a variety of scheduling problems. Five had previously lived on the same floor as subjects in the responsibility-induced condition, and 4 lived on the same floor as the comparison group. All were now living in the new wing. The average length of time in the nursing home was 3.9 years, which was not reliably different for the three groups.

Measures

Nurses' ratings. Two nurses on different shifts evaluated each patient along 9-point verbally anchored semantic differential scales for mood, awareness, sociability, mental attitude, and physical activity. Nurses were unaware of a relationship between prior experimental treatments and the purpose of these particular ratings.

Physician's ratings. A doctor on the nursing home staff evaluated the medical records of each patient for two periods. The first period represented the 6 months prior to the first study in 1974, and the second period represented the 6 months that immediately preceded the follow-up. On the basis of the medical data reported on the charts, he assigned the person an overall health score (1 = very good to 5 = poor) for each period. The physician's health ratings were independent of the nurses' evaluations, which did not appear on the medical charts that he used. Like the nurses, he was unaware of the nature of the study and how his ratings would be used. Further, the physician was not employed by the nursing home when the original intervention occurred.

Behavioral indices. After all the questionnaire measures had been taken, one of us (JR) gave a talk at the nursing home on psychology and aging. This was advertised widely among the residents, and they were encouraged to come and ask questions. The number of people in each condition who attended and the frequency and type of questions they asked were recorded.

Mortality. A frequency count of deaths occurring during the 18-month period was made, and the cause of death was noted.

Results

Nurses' Ratings

Since the interrater reliability coefficient between nurses who rated the same patient was high ($r = .76$), the ratings were averaged, and the resulting means were used for subsequent analysis.[2] First, a composite score was developed representing the total of the individual evaluative items. A one-way analysis of variance comparing the responsibility-induced ($M = 25.03$), comparison ($M = 18.71$), and no-treatment ($M = 17.60$) groups was significant, $F(2, 40) = 7.04$, $p < .01$. A

---

[1] All patients were given the option to move, and all did so. Those who wished to remain with their roommates were kept together, although people previously on the same floor were not all moved together to the same floor in the new wing. Interestingly, 33% of the patients in the responsibility-induced group, as compared to 21% in the comparison group, spontaneously requested to move even before they were given the choice.

[2] Two nurses on each floor rated all relevant patients on their floor, regardless of condition. Six nurses participated as raters. Since the patients no longer all lived together, residents formerly in the same group and thus rated by the same nurses were now rated by different nurses. Thus it is unlikely that the means for each treatment group were due to differences in the nurses who did the rating rather than to the patients themselves.

Scheffé test indicated that the responsibility-induced group was rated reliably higher than the comparison group, $F(1, 40) = 6.31$, $p < .05$.

The means for each individual item are presented in Table 2. On the average, the patients in the responsibility-induced group were judged to be significantly more actively interested in their environment, more sociable and self-initiating, and more vigorous than residents in the comparison group. The mean ratings also show the similarity between the comparison group given the "happiness" induction and the no-treatment group.

Composite scores for all the evaluative items were also available from the questionnaire, which the nurses completed prior to the original intervention and at the 3-week posttest. The means presented in Table 3 include all residents for whom these two scores and follow-up data were available ($n = 14$ for the responsibility-induced group, and $n = 12$ for the comparison group). Change scores between the preintervention means and the 18-month follow-up data indicate that the decline was significantly smaller for the responsibility-induced group ($M = 58.21$) than for the comparison condition ($M = 175.42$), $t(24) = 2.68$, $p < .02$. Change scores calculated between the 3-week postintervention ratings and the 18-month follow-up showed

Table 2
Mean Ratings for Residents 18 Months Following Experimental Interventions

Nurses' rating	Responsibility induced (20)[a]	Comparison (14)[a]	No treatment control (9)[b]
Happy	4.35	3.68	3.28
Actively interested	5.15	3.96	3.95
Sociable	5.00	3.78	3.40
Self-initiating	5.15	3.90	4.18
Vigorous	4.75	3.39	3.33

Note. The difference between the responsibility-induced and comparison groups was reliable at $p < .05$ for all ratings but happy. Numbers in parentheses are *n*s.
[a] Received experimental treatment in Langer and Rodin (1976).
[b] Not previously tested.

Table 3
Mean Composite Nurses' Evaluation Scores Taken at Three Different Time Periods Relative to the Intervention

Time period	Responsibility induced	Comparison
Preintervention	402.38	442.93
Postintervention (3 weeks)	436.50	413.03
Follow-up (18 months)	352.33	262.00

Note. There were seven 10-point items on the scales used by Langer and Rodin (1976), making a total of 70 points possible. There were five items in the follow-up questionnaire, and the ratings were made on 9-point scales making a total of 45 possible points. The Langer and Rodin totals were multiplied by 9 and the follow-up totals by 14 to make the scores comparable.

marginally reliable differences in the same direction, $t(24) = 1.82$, $p < .10$.

Health Ratings

Change scores were calculated between the preintervention (1974) and follow-up (1976) health evaluation ratings. Health ratings were retrospective, based on the medical records, so change scores could be calculated for all 43 follow-up subjects. There was no significant difference among the three groups in the preintervention health evaluations, $F(2, 40) = 1.77$. The responsibility-induced group showed a mean increase in general health of .55 on a 5-point scale, which was reliably greater than means for the comparison group ($M = -.29$) and the no-treatment group ($M = -.33$), $F(2, 40) = 3.73$, $p < .05$.

Mortality

The most striking data were obtained in death rate differences between the two treatment groups. Taking the 18 months prior to the original intervention as an arbitrary comparison period, we found that the average death rate during that period was 25% for the entire nursing home. In the subsequent 18-month period following the intervention,

Table 4
Mean Ratings Prior to Intervention Grouped by Subsequent Mortality Outcome

	Responsibility induced		Comparison	
Variable	Dead	Living	Dead	Living
Time institutionalized	2.40 (7)	2.70 (40)	2.80 (13)	2.20 (31)
Health ratings	3.57 (7)	3.85 (40)	3.69 (13)	3.64 (31)
Nurses' evaluations	36.20 (5)	44.79 (19)	31.69 (8)	47.39 (20)

Note. The numbers in parentheses represent the number of residents on whom each mean is based.

only 7 of the 47 subjects (15%) in the responsibility-induced group died, whereas 13 of 44 subjects (30%) in the comparison group had died. Using the arcsine transformation for frequencies, this difference is reliable ($z = 3.14$, $p < .01$).

Because these results were so startling, we assessed other factors that might have accounted for the differences. Unfortunately, we simply cannot know everything about the equivalency of these subjects prior to the intervention. We do know that those who died did not differ reliably in the length of time that they had been institutionalized or in their overall health status when the study began. These means are presented in Table 4, which also presents the nurses' evaluations prior to the intervention. From these ratings it is clear that the nurses had given lower evaluations prior to the intervention to those patients who subsequently died than to those who were still living, $F(1, 48) = 7.73$, $p < .01$. The interaction between treatment group and the life–death variable was not significant, however.

The actual causes of death that appeared on the medical record varied greatly among individuals and did not appear to be systematic within conditions. For example, deaths in the responsibility-induced group were listed as due to factors such as cardiovascular disease, congestive heart failure, gastrointestinal bleeding, lymphoma, and cerebral hemorrhage. Similarly there were patients in the comparison group whose cause of death was also listed as congestive heart failure and cardiac arrest, as well as those dying from problems like gangrene foot and polynephritis.

Behavioral Measures

There were no reliable differences among the three conditions in lecture attendance. Thirty-three percent of the responsibility-induced group attended, as compared to 30% of the comparison group and 20% of the no-treatment group. However, these groups did differ in the number and type of questions that they asked. Of the 14 questions that were asked, 10 came from residents in the responsibility-induced condition. The lecture and questions were taped, and subsequent content analysis by a coder who was blind to the experimental treatments indicated that 4 of the 10 questions had themes of autonomy and independence. For example, one female inquired whether intelligence really did decline with age, and if so, did that necessarily mean that older people should be taken care of? Another asked how to make her children feel less guilty about putting her in the nursing home. No questions from the comparison or no-treatment group dealt with these themes, but 2 of their 4 questions dealt with death. For example, one man asked whether senility could cause death. A woman who had obviously read the self-reported experiences of people who had a close brush with death asked whether this euphoric feeling was a universal experience or whether it differed as one got older. No one in the responsibility-induced group asked a death-relevant question.

Discussion

The intervention described by Langer and Rodin (1976) was stimulated, in part, by our theoretical interest in control. We attempted to capture these theoretical concerns in a manipulation that suggested how elderly residents might increase choice and self-control in the nursing home. The manipulation did indeed produce strong effects that lasted as long as 18 months later. Compared to the staff-support comparison group, and to the no-treatment group where relevant, residents in the responsibility-induced condition showed higher health and activity patterns, mood and sociability which did not decline as greatly, and they had mortality rates that were lower. We would like to interpret these effects as suggesting that decline can be slowed or, with a stronger intervention, perhaps can even be reversed by manipulations that provide an increased sense of effectance in the institutionalized elderly. Krantz (Note 1) and Schulz (1976) also recently found that experimental manipulations involving increased or diminished prediction and control have a significant impact on the elderly. Moreover, adjustment to relocation for older people appears more related to whether or not they have had a choice regarding the new setting than to specific features of the setting itself (Sherman, 1975).

Since the original intervention (Langer & Rodin, 1976) encouraged residents to create or utilize opportunities for control over ongoing daily events rather than over momentary, experimentally created tasks, it seemed reasonable to assume that the effects of this induction would continue after the study itself was completed. However, despite our intent in designing this particular set of interventions to extend the domain of the control conception, we have no real way of knowing without direct on-line observation exactly what the process was that generated the obtained improvements. As is often the case in any field study, we were unable to control some important features of the setting due to both ethical and practical constraints.

First, it would certainly have been more desirable to randomly assign residents to conditions within a floor rather than between floors. A manipulation aimed at changing the behavior of any individual resident could have interacted with changes occurring in his or her neighbors, who were also exposed to the same manipulation. However, we believed that at least some of the residents might discuss the administrator's communication if they saw themselves divided into different groups and that we would be unable to know whether and for whom this had occurred. Once having decided to assign by floor, we would also have chosen to have a third floor as a no-treatment control group. Although we simply lacked this option, data from the control group formed for the follow-up suggest that the responsibility group improved, rather than that the comparison group worsened, relative to "no-treatment" controls.

Second, the nurses could undoubtedly have made a great deal of difference in a variety of ways. Although they were unaware of the nature of the original intervention and did not attend the meeting where the communication was given, simply recording data about the residents and perhaps feeling observed themselves may have changed their awareness and behavior. In addition, once the patients began to change, the nurses must have responded favorably to improved behavior, sociability, and self-reliance. We can only take the administrator's word that he did not change his own behavior differentially toward the patients as a result of delivering the communications. The differences in nurses' ratings between conditions were maintained, however, even with changes in the nursing personnel, staff rotations, a move, and relocation of some residents to different floors. Nonetheless, it is striking to note that the nurses' evaluations of the patients and not the overall health ratings were more closely related to subsequent life and death. Either the psychological variables that the nurses were rating are better predictors of later mortality than medical symptom evaluations or the nurses' views of the residents are significant factors in their potential longevity. One clear area for further study is the patient–nurse interaction to assess if and how this factor is related to patient health.

Finally, it is especially true that this particular nursing home was open and primed to be responsive. When the options for increased patient involvement do not already exist, simple interventions of the sort used by Langer and Rodin (1976) may have to be elaborated over repeated trials and bolstered by changing the setting enough to allow the manipulations to have a sustainable outcome.

This is not an exhaustive list; it is simply provided to illustrate some of the most plausible ways in which the results could have been obtained without being due to increased choice and responsibility per se. Whatever the actual mediating process, it seems clear that decline is not inevitable. Indeed, the strength of the data suggests the value of further investigation into the context-specific social–psychological factors that influence aging. In these studies, process measures must now be taken to assess how the manipulations actually produce their effects.

If the improvements are due to greater control, it must surely be the case that potential benefits are nonmonotonically related to increasing control. For example, one can conceive of circumstances in which a great amount of choice and responsibility would have negative effects for both the patients themselves and on the setting too. In addition, it should be clear that interventions that increase control-relevant features of one's life, including increased predictability, decision-making, and outcome control, should be those that are not withdrawn by the termination of the study. The long-term beneficial effects observed in the present study probably were obtained because the original treatment was not directed toward a single behavior or stimulus condition. They instead fostered generalized feelings of increased competence in day-to-day decision making where it was potentially available. To the extent that a treatment is successful in providing these kinds of control, its termination could serve to make salient the loss of control and, as such, might lead to even greater debilitation than was first encountered.

Reference Note

1. Krantz, D. Data presented at an invited discussion on *New directions in control research*. Presented at the annual meeting of the American Psychological Association, Washington, D.C., September 1976.

References

Campbell, D. T., & Fiske, D. W. Convergent and discriminant validation by the multitrait-multimethod matrix. *Psychological Bulletin,* 1959, *56,* 81–105.

Langer, E. J., & Rodin, J. The effects of choice and enhanced personal responsibility for the aged: A field experiment in an institutional setting. *Journal of Personality and Social Psychology,* 1976, *34,* 191–198.

Lefcourt, H. The function of the illusion of control and freedom. *American Psychologist,* 1973, *28,* 417–425.

Schulz, R. Effects of control and predictability on the psychological well-being of the institutionalized aged. *Journal of Personality and Social Psychology,* 1976, *33,* 563–573.

Seligman, M. E. P. *Helplessness.* San Francisco: Freeman, 1975.

Sherman, S. Patterns of contacts for residents of age-segregated and age-integrated housing. *Journal of Gerontology,* 1975, *30,* 103–107.

Zimbardo, P. G., & Ruch, F. L. *Psychology and life* (9th ed.). Glenview, Ill.: Scott, Foresman, 1975.

Received February 16, 1977 ▪

[26]

Dementia Care and Quality of Life in Assisted Living and Nursing Homes

Sheryl Zimmerman, PhD,[1] Philip D. Sloane, MD, MPH,[2] Christianna S. Williams, PhD,[3] Peter S. Reed, PhD, MPH,[4] John S. Preisser, PhD,[5] J. Kevin Eckert PhD,[6] Malaz Boustani, MD, MPH,[7] and Debra Dobbs, PhD[8]

Purpose: There are few empirical studies relating components of long-term care to quality of life for residents with dementia. This study relates elements of dementia care in residential care/assisted living (RC/AL) facilities and nursing homes to resident quality of life and considers the guidance this information provides for practice and policy. **Design and Methods:** We used a variety of report and observational measures of the structure and process of care and 11 standardized measures of quality of life to evaluate the care for and quality of life of 421 residents with dementia in 35 RC/AL facilities and 10 nursing homes in four states. Data were collected cross sectionally on-site, and we conducted a 6-month follow-up by telephone. **Results:** Change in quality of life was better in facilities that used a specialized worker approach, trained more staff in more domains central to dementia care, and encouraged activity participation. Residents perceived their quality of life as better when staff was more involved in care planning and when staff attitudes were more favorable. Better resident–staff communication was related to higher quality of life as observed and reported by care providers. Also, more stable resident–staff assignment was related to care providers' lower quality-of-life ratings. **Implications:** Improvement in resident quality of life may be achieved by improved training and deployment of staff.

Key Words: Long-term care, Residential care, Staff practices, Training, Observation

---

Between 23% and 42% of residents in residential care/assisted living (RC/AL) settings have moderate or severe cognitive impairment, as do more than one half of nursing home residents (Zimmerman et al., 2003). While attention has been focused on the quality of long-term care for decades, remarkably little has focused on how care in both of these settings relates to quality of life for persons with dementia—in part because dementia-focused quality-of-life measures are comparatively new, and in part because RC/AL as a site of long-term care has only recently come under study (Ready & Ou, 2003; Wunderlich & Kohler, 2001). Such information is critically needed to guide policy and the development of best practices.

This article focuses on care and quality-of-life issues that have practice and policy relevance. It characterizes the current state of dementia care in RC/AL and nursing homes (based on report and observation); describes the characteristics and quality of life of residents with dementia in RC/AL and nursing homes (examining quality of life both cross sectionally and longitudinally, using multiple quality-of-life measures from the perspectives of residents and staff, and from observation); determines how dementia care (including special care units for residents with dementia) relates to resident quality

---

This research was supported by grants from the National Alzheimer's Association Program and Community Services Division and Medical and Scientific Division (Grant Nos. IIRG-00-2222 and IIRG-01-3019). The authors express appreciation for the cooperation of the staff, residents, and families participating in the Collaborative Studies of Long-Term Care (CS LTC). Gratitude also is extended to the data collectors, as well as to Jane Darter and Karminder Gill, for their expert data collection and management.

Address correspondence to Sheryl Zimmerman, PhD, Cecil G. Sheps Center for Health Services Research and the School of Social Work, University of North Carolina, 725 Martin Luther King Jr. Blvd., Chapel Hill, NC 27514. E-mail: Sheryl_Zimmerman@unc.edu

[1] Cecil G. Sheps Center for Health Services Research and the School of Social Work, University of North Carolina at Chapel Hill.
[2] Cecil G. Sheps Center for Health Services Research and the Department of Family Medicine, University of North Carolina at Chapel Hill.
[3] Cecil G. Sheps Center for Health Services Research and the School of Public Health, University of North Carolina at Chapel Hill.
[4] Alzheimer's Association, National Office, Chicago, IL.
[5] Department of Biostatistics, School of Public Health, University of North Carolina at Chapel Hill.
[6] Department of Sociology and Anthropology, University of Maryland–Baltimore County.
[7] Regenstrief Institute, Inc. and Center for Aging Research, Indiana University, Indianapolis.
[8] Cecil G. Sheps Center for Health Services Research, University of North Carolina at Chapel Hill.

of life; and considers the guidance this information provides for practice and policy.

Design and Methods

Sample and Recruitment

The Dementia Care project recruited individuals with a diagnosis of dementia living in a diverse set of facilities in four states that have different yet well-developed RC/AL industries (Florida, Maryland, New Jersey, and North Carolina). RC/AL included those facilities licensed by states at a nonnursing home level of care that provide room and board; assistance with activities of daily living (ADLs), personal care, and medication administration; and 24-hour oversight. Using the typology developed for the Collaborative Studies of Long-Term Care (CS-LTC), the study stratified RC/AL facilities to include: (a) facilities with < 16 beds; (b) facilities with ≥ 16 beds of the "new-model" type (those proliferating under the recent surge of assisted living that provide nursing care and cater to an impaired population); and (c) "traditional" facilities with ≥ 16 beds, not meeting new-model criteria. Details of the CS-LTC and the facility typology can be found elsewhere (Zimmerman et al., 2001).

The Dementia Care project enrolled a purposive sample of 45 facilities. For efficiency, facilities with fewer than 2 eligible residents (in smaller facilities) or 13 eligible residents (in other facilities) were excluded from study. Facilities were enrolled in a manner that maintained stratification across states and by facility type and that maximized the number of residents from smaller facilities. Twenty-two facilities (33%) declined to participate. These facilities did not differ from participating facilities in reference to type, size, or state. The final sample included 14 (31%) RC/AL facilities with < 16 beds; 11 (24%) traditional facilities; 10 (22%) new-model facilities; and 10 (22%) nursing homes. Twelve facilities were from North Carolina, and all other study states had 11 facilities. Given the purposive nature of facility selection, the descriptive data presented in this study are best used to formulate hypotheses.

Residents were randomly selected in each facility from among those aged 65 years or older who had a diagnosis of dementia. They were ineligible if they had a primary diagnosis of Huntington's disease, alcohol-related dementia, schizophrenia, manic-depressive disorder, or mental retardation. To provide similar representation across facility types, a maximum of 4 residents per smaller facility and 19 per larger facility were enrolled. A total of 575 eligible residents or their families were approached for consent. Of these, 421 (73%) agreed to participate, 66 (11%) declined, and 88 (15%) were unable to provide consent and had family who were unreachable. Additional information about the design is provided in the introduction to this issue (Zimmerman, Sloane, Heck, Maslow, & Schulz, 2005).

Data Collection

Data collection was conducted between September 2001 and February 2003. Data collectors observed the physical environment of all facilities and characteristics of a random sample of participating residents in each facility (79%) and conducted interviews with each resident participant (95% response rate), his or her most involved family member (84% response rate), the direct care provider who knew the resident best (98% response rate), the supervisor (position above a direct care provider) who knew the most about the resident (89% response rate), and the facility administrator (to obtain facility-level data; 100% response rate). In 4% of cases—usually in smaller facilities—the direct care provider and supervisor were the same individual. Ninety-four percent of direct care providers were nurse or personal care aides, and 78% of supervisors were registered nurses (RNs) or licensed practical nurses (LPNs).

Measures

Data were collected to assess care provision (facility-level and resident-level) and resident quality of life.

Facility-Level Care Provision.—Dementia care measured at the facility level applied to all participants within a facility (or unit, if the facility included both an area designated for dementia care and an area not so designated). Administrators provided information about facility demographics (facility type, age, profit status, affiliation with another level of care or a chain of facilities, number of beds, presence of dementia-specific unit) and case-mix related to dementia diagnosis and each of six ADL impairments (eating, dressing, walking, transferring, bathing, and continence). The administrator also reported on several aspects of staffing, including the stability of care provider–resident assignments, whether the facility provided care based on a universal worker perspective (where staff fill multiple roles) and/or a specialized worker perspective (where staff have specialized roles), the number of nurses and nursing or personal care aides (overall and contract), staff turnover (at the administrator, nursing, and aide level), and the extent to which the facility sought to hire workers with experience in dementia care. Four measures of facility policies and practices were obtained, based on the Policy and Program Information Form (POLIF; Moos & Lemke, 1996): policy choice (7 items), leniency of admissions (24) and discharge policies (24), and acceptance of problem behavior (16). The latter three measures were assessed separately for dementia-specific and non-dementia-specific areas when applicable, and all were scored from 0 to 100, reflecting the percentage of items endorsed. Involvement in formal care planning of professional staff (averaged across administrator, physician, nurse, activity specialist, social service worker, mental health specialist, clergy, and dietician) and aides was scored from never to weekly.

Facility-level items regarding formal staff training, resident assessment, and treatment practices were ascertained for each of the following six domains of care: depression, pain, behavioral symptoms, ambulation, nutrition, and hydration. (The brief reports included in this issue further detail these measures.) Reports of the proportion of supervisory and direct care staff who received formal training in each domain within the past year were categorized as 0 (none), 1 (some; 1–74%), or 2 (most; $\geq$ 75%); scores were then summed across the six domains to yield a 0 through 12 summary score. Similarly, an assessment variable was created, consisting of the sum of domains for which the facility used professional assessment (e.g., mental health professionals for depression) and written, standardized assessment. A professional treatment variable was created as the average across the six areas of the percent of residents receiving ongoing, professional treatment for impairment in that area; "other/informal treatment" was created to be the number of areas for which the facility used other treatments; and perceived treatment success was the number of areas in which the administrator felt the facility did "quite a bit" or "extremely well" treating their residents. Except for perceived success, assessment and treatment were obtained separately for dementia-specific and non-dementia-specific areas. Three additional measures of treatment included the proportion of study participants who had received an antipsychotic or sedative hypnotic medication at least 4 out of the last 7 days (reported by the supervisor), the extent to which the facility provided and encouraged activity participation in 10 domains, separately by care area (e.g., exercise, personal care, social, meal preparation, work-oriented; Zgola, 1987), and the use of stimuli in seven areas (e.g., craft or household items).

Finally, data collectors systematically observed the environment, using the Therapeutic Environment Screening Survey for RC/AL (TESS–RC/AL), a measure derived from the Therapeutic Environment Screening Survey for Nursing Homes (TESS-NH; Sloane et al., 2002). Observations were used to compute two scales (separately for dementia-specific and non-dementia-specific areas): the Special Care Unit–Environmental Quality Score (SCU-EQS), which ranges from 0 to 38 and assesses 18 components relevant for individuals with dementia (e.g., orientation and memory cues); and the Assisted Living–Environmental Quality Score (AL-EQS), which ranges from 0 to 30 and assesses 15 components (some of which are in the SCU-EQS) more characteristic of assisted living environments (e.g., resident autonomy and homelikeness).

Resident-Level Care Provision. —Dementia care measured at the resident level referred specifically to the study participants or their staff care providers, using data from interviews with staff and family members, and direct observation. The supervisor reported whether the resident had received cholinesterase inhibitors at least 4 of the past 7 days. Direct care providers reported their approaches to dementia care, their work satisfaction, and their work stress. The Approaches to Dementia measure was used to assess staff attitudes; it contains 19 items, summed to form a total score as well as person-centered and hope subscores (Lintern, Woods, & Phair, 2000b). The Work Stress Inventory was used to assess the frequency of 45 staff stressors related to work events, resident care, relationships with coworkers and supervisors, workload and scheduling, and physical design (Schaefer & Moos, 1993). Work satisfaction was measured using the 21-item Staff Experience Working with Demented Residents measure, which assesses satisfaction of one's own expectations, coworkers and supervisors, work environment, and resident care (Åström, Nilsson, Norberg, Sandman, & Winblad, 1991). These measures are described in detail elsewhere in this issue (Zimmerman, Williams, et al., 2005). In addition, family members reported the amount of time they spent each week visiting or talking on the phone with the resident.

Direct observations of study residents were conducted at 5-min intervals during three 1-hr observation periods (chosen to exclude mealtimes), from which four measures of resident care were derived. Communication was measured as the percent of observations during which the resident received any verbal communication from a staff member, physical contact was the percent of observations during which the resident had any physical contact with another person, and personal detractors and positive person work were similarly measured as the percent of observations in which any personal detractors (staff behaviors that demean or depersonalize) or positive person work (positive interactions between staff and resident) were noted (Bradford Dementia Group, 1997). Whether the resident was ever observed in restraints (full or partial bedrails, trunk, wrist, ankle, or chair restraints) also was noted, and during the first observation each hour, residents were assessed to determine if they appeared ungroomed, unkempt, or unclean and whether appearance was ever inappropriate with respect to time of day, season, or place.

Resident Characteristics. —The supervisor provided information on several resident characteristics, including demographics (age, gender, race, marital status) and length of stay. The presence of behavioral symptoms of dementia during the past 2 weeks was measured using the Cohen-Mansfield Agitation Inventory (CMAI; Cohen-Mansfield, 1986), functional status was measured as the number of activities in which the resident needed supervision or assistance using the seven items from the Minimum Data Set Activities of Daily Living (MDS-ADL) scale (Morris, Fries, & Morris, 1999), residents were classified as being depressed if they scored ≥ 7 on the Cornell Scale for Depression in Dementia (CSDD; Alexopoulos, Abrams, Young, & Shamoian, 1988), and comorbidity was the number of chronic conditions (out of 11) reported by the supervisor. Finally, cognitive deficit was categorized based on the Mini-Mental State Exam (MMSE; Folstein, Folstein, & McHugh, 1975) score administered to the resident, or (if the MMSE was not available) the Minimum Data Set–Cognition Scale (MDS-COGS; Hartmaier, Sloane, Guess, & Koch, 1994) reported by the supervisor. Cognition was scored as follows: mild (MMSE 17–30 or MDS-COGS 0–1), moderate (MMSE 10–16 or MDS-COGS 2–4), severe (MMSE 3–9 or MDS-COGS 5–6), or very severe (MMSE 0–2 or MDS-COGS 7–10).

Quality of Life.—Quality of life was assessed by the resident (three measures), direct care provider (six measures, one of which was longitudinal), and through observation (three measures); measures are described in detail elsewhere (Sloane et al., 2005, this issue). Unless otherwise noted, higher scores indicate better quality of life. Residents with a MMSE of 10 or greater completed the Dementia Quality of Life (DQOL; Brod, Stewart, Sands, & Walton, 1999), the Quality of Life in Alzheimer's Disease Activity measure (QOL in AD–Activity; Albert et al., 1996), and the Quality of Life–Alzheimer's Disease (QOL-AD; Logsdon, Gibbons, McCurry, & Teri, 2000), as modified by Edelman, Fulton, Kuhn, and Change (2005, this issue) for use in long-term care settings.

Care providers completed proxy versions of the QOL in AD–Activity, and the QOL-AD, as well as the positive and negative affect portions of the QOL in AD (higher negative affect scores indicate poorer quality of life), and the Alzheimer Disease Related Quality of Life (ADRQL; Rabins, Kasper, Kleinman, Black, & Patrick, 2000). Additionally, the proxy version of the QOL-AD was readministered 6 months after initial data collection. We computed raw change as the difference between baseline and 6 months, with positive scores indicating improvement in quality of life; to account for regression to the mean, we estimated adjusted change as the residual from regression of raw change on the baseline value, which therefore has a sample mean of exactly zero (Cronbach & Furby, 1970). Because change is influenced by baseline status, we based all statistical comparisons on adjusted values.

Using the observational procedures described above, we recorded behaviors in accordance with the Dementia Care Mapping (DCM) protocol (Bradford Dementia Group, 1997) and a modification of the Philadelphia Geriatric Center Affect Rating Scale (PGC-ARS; Lawton, Van Haitsma, & Klapper, 1996). DCM-derived measures included the percent of observations with a Type I Behavior Category Code (DCM % BCC Type I), considered to be "good" behaviors such as conversation or creative expression, and the mean Well- and Ill-Being (WIB) score, with anchors of +5 and −5, indicating the state of well-being. (See Brooker, 2005, and Sloane et al., 2005, this issue, for a more in-depth discussion). The PGC-ARS was coded to record the predominant emotion at each observation (scored from 0 for anxiety, fear, or sadness, to 3 for high pleasure) and summarized at the resident level as the percent of the highest possible score.

Analyses

We used simple descriptive methods (means and standard deviations for continuous measures, percentages for categorical measures) to describe the components of dementia care. For measures assessed separately in dementia-specific and non-dementia-specific care areas, comparisons used generalized estimating equations (GEE: Diggle, Heagerty, Liang, & Zeger, 2002) applied to linear (continuous) or logistic (dichotomous) models, specifying an exchangeable correlation matrix to account for resident clustering within facility.

We estimated means and standard errors of the quality-of-life measures according to facility type and resident characteristics, dichotomized at the sample median or at commonly accepted cutpoints; we adjusted the standard errors for clustering using Taylor series expansion methods (Woodruff, 1971). We tested the statistical significance of these associations using linear mixed models with random effects specified as follows: for care provider reported quality-of-life measures, models included random effects for facility and care provider (nested within facility); for resident-reported measures, models include a random effect for facility; and for directly observed measures, models include random effects for facility and observer.

We estimated the association between care and quality of life using partial Pearson correlation coefficients, adjusting for facility type; resident age, gender, race, marital status, length of stay; and cognitive, ADL, number of comorbid conditions, depressive, and behavioral symptoms. To maximize the sample size for resident-reported quality-of-life analyses in the presence of covariate missingness, we did not adjust associations for age, race, marital status, or length of stay (none of which was significantly related to quality of life). We tested the statistical significance of these associations using linear mixed models, controlling for these

Results

The mean values shown in Table 1 indicate that, on average, almost one third of beds were dementia specific, and slightly more than one half of the facility residents were reported to have dementia or at least one ADL impairment. In the average facility, staff tended to be reassigned to new residents monthly or less frequently, and 58% and 38% of facilities used a universal worker and specialized worker philosophy, respectively. Approximately 11% of nursing care and 2% of personal care was provided by contract workers, with 46% of nurses turning over annually. Care planning practices included the involvement of professional staff and aides 1 to 3 times a month. On average, less than 75% of staff were trained in the six care areas (the figure corresponding to a score of 8), but facilities provided professional assessment in more than five of the areas and written or standardized assessment in approximately three. Almost one third of residents were reported to have received professional care in the six care areas, with the administrator perceiving success in five areas. In the average facility, nearly one half (48%) of study residents were taking antipsychotic or sedative hypnotic drugs.

Variables for which two figures are provided refer to dementia specific versus non-dementia-specific care areas. While the environmental AL-EQS was scored statistically significantly higher in non-dementia-specific areas (13.4 vs 11.9), dementia-specific areas were more accepting of problem behaviors (23% vs 13%) and encouraged activities slightly more frequently (score 2.4 vs 2.2; all $p < .05$).

Table 2 separates care by dementia-specific area for all resident-level variables. It shows that supervisors (of the residents enrolled in this study) who worked in non-dementia-specific areas had slightly more experience but that positive person work and physical contact were witnessed more often in dementia-specific areas (22% vs 17%, and 9% vs 6% of observations, respectively). Overall, 13% and 20% of resident participants were in restraints and ungroomed during at least one observation, and 29% were taking a cholinesterase inhibitor. On average, families spent almost 7 hr per week visiting or talking with the resident.

As rated by care providers and observation (in unadjusted analyses), quality of life was related to facility type (see Table 3). Care providers in RC/AL rated quality of life higher than those in nursing homes using three different measures (ADRQL, QOL in AD–positive affect, QOL-AD); two measures did not differentiate facility type (QOL in AD–activity, QOL in AD–negative affect), nor did change in quality of life. The remainder of Table 3 provides the distributions of quality of life by resident characteristics. Change in quality of life (9th and 10th QOL columns) was related only to level of cognitive impairment (more impaired residents had greater reductions in QOL-AD compared to less impaired residents; raw change of −2.6 vs −2.1, $p < .01$) and depression (depressed individuals had greater reductions in QOL-AD compared to the nondepressed; change of −2.7 vs −2.2, $p < .05$). Cross sectionally, based on resident report, only fewer comorbidities were related to better quality of life. Based on care provider report and observation, less cognitive and functional impairment and no behavioral symptoms or depression were associated with better quality of life.

Tables 4 and 5 indicate statistically significant covariate adjusted associations between facility-level (Table 4) and resident-level (Table 5) components of care and quality of life. Looking first at change in quality of life over 6 months, adjusted quality of life was better (declined less) in facilities with specialized workers, with more staff training in more areas (supervisor and direct care staff), and that encouraged activity participation more frequently (all $p < .05$). No resident-level components of care were associated with change in quality of life at this statistical level, nor were the many other facility-level components under study.

Further, while facility type and many other facility characteristics were not significantly related to cross-sectional quality of life in adjusted analyses (facility size, age, affiliation, percent dementia beds, and dementia and ADL impairment case-mix), a better environment was related to worse quality of life reported by care providers (QOL in AD–negative affect, and QOL-AD) but better observed quality of life on the DCM BCC Type I codes (SCU-EQS $p < .05$ for all). Similarly, while many staff variables were not significantly related to quality of life (universal worker, RN, LPN, and aide FTEs; administrator and aide turnover; and extent hire for experience), more stability in staff-resident assignment was related to worse quality of life as reported by the care provider. Larger numbers of contract workers on staff were related to better quality of life as reported by residents and care providers, and higher RN and LPN turnover was related to worse quality of life on the observation of DCM well-being.

The remaining rows on Table 4 indicate the diversity with which policies and practices relate to quality of life. While virtually all policies and practices under study related to quality of life, they did so inconsistently across different measures. For example, having more flexible admission, discharge, and acceptance of problem behavior policies related positively to care provider report of QOL in AD–positive affect, and involving professional staff in care planning related positively to resident reported QOL-AD and observed affect (PGC-ARS). The

Table 1. Distribution of Facility-Level Components of Dementia Care in the Study Sample

Facility-Level Characteristic[a]	M (SD) or %[b]
Demographics	
Type	
RC/AL	
< 16 bed	31.1%
Traditional	24.4%
New-model	22.2%
Nursing home	22.2%
Size (no. of beds)	61.8 (52.2)
Age (years)	19.8 (20.7)
For profit	75.6%
Affiliated	22.2%
Chain	44.4%
Dementia-specific beds (%)	29.9 (40.4)
Case-mix (all facility residents)	
Percent with dementia	55.7 (24.4)
Average percent with ADL impairment (of 6)[c]	56.5 (24.1)
Physical environment (observed)[c]	
SCU-EQS (0–38)	23.6 (5.6); 25.2 (5.2)
AL-EQS (0–30)	11.9 (4.0); 13.4 (4.3)*
Staffing	
Stability of staff-resident assignment (0–5)[c]	3.6 (1.8); 3.1 (1.8)
Universal worker philosophy	58.3%; 58.8%
Specialized worker philosophy	37.5%; 38.2%
Nursing (FTE, RN or LPN, per 10 residents)	1.2 (1.3)
Aide (FTE per 10 residents)	4.1 (2.2)
Extent hire for experience (1–5)[c]	3.0 (1.1)
Contract workers	
Percent of nursing (RN, LPN) by contract workers	11.3 (24.5)
Percent of personal care by contract workers	2.1 (6.5)
Annual turnover (%)	
Administrator	9.3 (34.4)
RN and LPN	46.4 (59.9)
Nurse aide	72.1 (92.3)
Policies and Practices	
Permissive admission policies (of 24, %)	88.3 (9.2); 83.9 (11.5)
Permissive discharge policies (of 24, %)	89.1 (7.8); 86.8 (9.6)
Acceptance of problem behaviors (of 16, %)	23.1 (15.6); 13.1 (11.5)*
Policy choice (of 7, %)	56.5 (28.5)
Care planning[c]	
Professional staff involvement (0–3)	2.1 (1.1)
Aide involvement (0–3)	1.9 (1.2)
Formal training, last year (in 6 areas)[c]	
Supervisors (0–12)	8.3 (4.0)
Direct care staff (0–12)	8.0 (3.9)
Assessment[c]	
Professional (of 6 areas)	5.5 (0.8); 5.3 (1.4)
Written, standardized (of 6 areas)	3.0 (2.0); 2.7 (2.2)
Treatment	
Professional (average percent across 6 areas)[c]	30.3 (16.7); 28.0 (14.3)
Other or informal (of 6 areas)[c]	4.6 (1.7); 4.7 (1.7)
Perceived success (of 6 areas)[c]	4.9 (1.4)

Table 1. (Continued)

Facility-Level Characteristic[a]	M (SD) or %[b]
Percent on antipsychotic or sedative hypnotic	47.7 (27.6)
Encouragement of activities (0–4)[c]	2.4 (0.7); 2.2 (0.5)*
Use of stimuli by residents with dementia (0–4)[c]	2.1 (0.8)

Notes: RC/AL = residential care/assisted living; ADL = activity of daily living; SCU-EQS = Special Care Unit–Environmental Quality Scale; AL-EQS = Assisted Living–Environmental Quality Scale; RN = registered nurse; LPN = licensed practical nurse. For the table, N = 45 facilities.
[a]All data are from administrator interview, except physical environment (which was based on direct observation) and medication use (which was aggregated from supervisor reports of residents enrolled in this study). The sample size for facilities varied from 41–45 because of missing data.
[b]Characteristics with two values shown were measured separately for dementia-specific and non-dementia-specific care areas within facilities. The first value is for the dementia-specific portion (n = 24); the second is for the non-dementia-specific portion (n = 35). Ten facilities were entirely dementia specific, 14 were partially dementia specific, and the remaining 21 had no area designated for dementia-specific care.
[c]ADLs include eating, dressing, walking, transferring, bathing, and continence; SCU-EQS and AL-EQS are explained in the text; staffing stability was scored from 0 = changes more than once a week to 5 = never changes (average between 3 and 4 indicates changes between monthly and less than once a month); extent hire for experience is the extent to which the facility tries to hire workers with training and/or experience in dementia care, scored from 1 = not at all to 5 = extremely (3 corresponds to moderately); policies are explained in the text; care planning is frequency of involvement in formal care plan meetings, scored from 0 = never to 3 = weekly and (for professional staff) was averaged across eight types of staff (2 corresponds to 1–3 times a month); formal training is a summary score for the proportion of supervisory and direct care staff with formal training in detection and treatment of problems in each of six care areas (pain, depression, ambulation, eating, drinking, behavioral symptoms), scored as 0 = none, 1 = 1–74%, 2 = 75% or more; assessment is the number of six care areas in which the facility or unit uses professional assessment by medical personnel or written, standardized assessment; professional treatment is the average percent of residents who received ongoing professional treatment for problems in each of the six care areas during the past year; other, informal treatment is the number of six care areas in which the facility uses such treatment; perceived success is the number of these six care areas for which the administrator felt the facility was "quite a bit" or "extremely" successful in treating residents; encouragement of activities is for 10 activities, and was the average frequency (scored as 0 = never to 4 = several times a day) that the activity was provided and resident participation encouraged (2 corresponds to between one and 6 days per week); and use of stimuli is for seven types of stimuli, and was the average frequency (scored as 0 = never to 4 = several times a day) that the stimuli were available and used by at least 1 resident with dementia (2 corresponds to between 1 and 6 days per week).
*p < .05 for difference between dementia-specific care area and non-dementia-specific care area, based on resident-level analysis in which residents are assigned a value based on area of residence, using GEE applied to linear or logistic regression for continuous and dichotomous characteristics, respectively, to account for clustering within facilities.

strongest association for resident-reported quality of life was witnessed for facility use of antipsychotic and sedative hypnotic medications (negatively associated with QOL-AD, p < .01). The one facility-level

Table 2. Distribution of Resident-Level Components of Dementia Care, Overall and by Residence in Dementia Specific Care Area or Facility

Resident-Level Characteristic[a]	Overall (N = 421)	In Dementia Specific Care Area or Facility (N = 170)	In Nondementia Specific Care Area or Facility (N = 239)
Reported and observed care (%)			
Use of cholinesterase inhibitor	29.2	35.3	26.0
Observation (ever observed)			
In restraints	13.2	12.4	12.8
Ungroomed appearance	19.8	18.8	19.8
Unsuitable appearance	7.6	6.3	7.9
Staff experience, perceptions and observed behaviors			
Experience in current position[b]			
Supervisor (1–5)	4.3 (1.0)	4.1 (1.0)	4.5 (0.9)*
Direct care provider (1–5)	4.4 (0.9)	4.4 (0.9)	4.3 (1.0)
Perceptions of direct care provider[b]			
Approaches to care, total (19–95)	71.1 (7.0)	71.9 (6.5)	70.7 (7.3)
Hope (8–40)	24.2 (4.5)	24.3 (4.5)	24.2 (4.7)
Person-centered (11–55)	46.9 (4.2)	47.6 (4.4)	46.4 (4.1)
Work stress (1–5)	1.8 (0.5)	1.8 (0.6)	1.8 (0.5)
Work satisfaction (0–84)	62.2 (10.3)	62.7 (9.8)	62.1 (10.7)
Observation (0–100%)[c]			
Percent, communication	19.7 (18.3)	21.9 (17.3)	18.0 (19.1)
Percent, personal detractors	3.4 (6.5)	3.2 (4.8)	3.6 (7.8)
Percent, positive person work	19.2 (16.3)	22.0 (15.4)	17.2 (16.9)*
Percent, physical contact	7.6 (9.0)	9.2 (9.1)	6.2 (8.8)*
Family involvement (hr/week)	6.8 (7.2)	6.2 (6.7)	7.3 (7.5)

Notes: For the table, N = 421 residents.
[a] Data are from supervisor, direct care provider, and family interview, or direct observation (36 observations, conducted every 5 minutes over three nonmealtime hours for restraint use, communication, personal detractors, positive person work, and physical contact; and on three observations conducted during the first 5 minutes of each hour for appearance). Direct observations were completed for 333 residents (138 in dementia-specific care areas or facilities and 187 in non-dementia-specific care areas or facilities). For measures derived from interviews, the sample size varies from 343–379 for the overall sample, from 129 to 154 for residents of dementia-specific care areas or facilities, and from 196 to 228 for residents of non-dementia-specific care areas or facilities, because of missing data. Location of residence (special care area vs not) was unknown for 12 residents of one facility; these residents were included in the overall estimates but excluded from the area-specific estimates.
[b] Experience was scored as: 1 = < 1 month; 2 = 1–5 months; 3 = 6–11 months; 4 = 1–2 years; 5 = > 2 years. Approaches to care (Lintern, Woods, & Phair, 2000a, 2000b) was based on the sum of responses to 19 items (each scored from 1 = strongly agree to 5 = strongly disagree) regarding approaches to dementia and attitudes towards individuals with dementia; the hope subscale included 8 items, and the person-centered subscale included 11 items, with higher scores indicating more positive attitudes. Work stress was the Work Stress Inventory (Schaefer & Moos, 1993), the average of the frequency (each scored 1 = never to 5 = often) for 45 work stressors, with higher scores indicating greater stress. Work satisfaction was the Experience of Work with Demented Residents measure (Aström et al., 1991) and was the sum of 21 items, each scored 0 = not at all to 4 = extremely, with higher scores indicating greater satisfaction.
[c] Each of the observational items was the percent of observations (out of up to 36 per resident) during which the item was observed. Communication refers to communication from staff. Personal detractors and positive person work are explained in the text. Physical contact refers to observed contact with staff or other residents.
*p < .05 for difference between dementia-specific care area and non-dementia-specific care area, based on resident-level analysis in which residents were assigned a value based on area of residence, using GEE applied to linear or logistic regression for continuous and dichotomous characteristics, respectively, to account for clustering within facilities.

component of care that related to quality of life as assessed by residents, care providers, and observation was the provision of professional treatment for the six care areas under study; it was negatively related to quality of life as reported by residents (DQOL) and observed (DCM BCC Type I codes), but positively related to care provider reports (QOL in AD–positive affect).

In addition, one component of resident-level care related to quality of life across all three sources (see Table 5). Residents who were observed to be ungroomed reported their own quality of life to be worse (QOL-AD), as did care providers (QOL in AD–activity) and observation (DCM BCC Type I codes). Residents who had staff who espoused more dementia-sensitive attitudes (especially hope) rated their quality of life higher on two measures (DQOL and QOL in AD–activity). Observed interactional style (more communication, positive person work, and physical contact, fewer personal detractors) was

Table 3. Distribution of Quality of Life Score, by Facility Type and Resident Characteristics

		Resident Report[a]				Direct Care Provider Report[a]						Observation[a]	
Characteristic	N	DQOL (n = 100)	QOL in AD–Activity (n = 110)	QOL-AD (n = 120)	ADRQL (n = 410)	QOL in AD–Activity (n = 400)	QOL in AD–Positive Affect (n = 403)	QOL in AD–Negative Affect (n = 383)	QOL-AD (n = 410)	QOL-AD, Raw Change[a] (n = 402)	QOL-AD, Adjusted Change (n = 402)	PGC-ARS (n = 333)	DCM, % BCC Type I (n = 333)	DCM, WIB (n = 333)
Overall	421	17.5 (0.4)	9.5 (0.6)	42.8 (1.0)	75.2 (0.9)	9.3 (0.4)	11.9 (0.2)	6.7 (0.2)	36.9 (0.5)	−2.4 (0.5)***	0.00 (0.47)	33.6 (0.5)	35.4 (1.9)	.74 (.04)
Facility type														
Nursing home (reference)	137	18.3 (0.7)	10.1 (1.2)	42.1 (1.0)	71.3 (1.8)	8.3 (0.5)	11.0 (0.3)	7.2 (0.4)	34.6 (1.0)	−1.8 (0.7)	−0.18 (0.73)	32.0 (0.8)	29.1 (3.2)	.54 (.07)
< 16 beds	48	16.0 (1.3)†	7.2 (1.2)	39.0 (3.2)	76.6 (2.5)†	9.3 (1.1)	11.8 (0.6)	6.2 (0.5)	37.7 (1.3)†	−2.2 (1.1)	0.54 (1.12)	32.9 (0.6)	45.2 (5.0)*	.80 (.06)*
Traditional	101	17.7 (0.5)	9.8 (1.0)	44.7 (1.4)	79.9 (1.8)**	9.9 (0.8)	12.7 (0.3)**	6.3 (0.4)	38.9 (1.0)**	−2.7 (1.3)	0.48 (1.07)	34.6 (1.1)*	40.9 (4.9)†	.90 (.06)***
New-model	135	17.3 (0.7)	9.8 (1.4)	42.8 (1.7)	75.2 (1.2)†	10.0 (0.7)	12.1 (0.3)†	6.5 (0.3)	37.6 (0.9)†	−3.0 (0.9)	−0.38 (0.91)	35.0 (0.8)*	33.9 (2.7)	.81 (.06)**
Length of stay														
< 12 months	94	17.2 (0.6)	9.8 (0.8)	42.3 (1.3)	78.5 (2.2)†	10.3 (0.7)*	12.0 (0.3)	6.4 (0.4)	39.4 (1.1)***	−3.7 (1.0)	−0.39 (0.86)	34.7 (1.1)	38.7 (3.7)	.84 (.06)†
≥ 1 year	276	17.4 (0.6)	9.1 (0.9)	42.3 (1.4)	73.8 (1.1)	9.1 (0.4)	11.8 (0.2)	6.7 (0.2)	36.1 (0.6)	−2.0 (0.6)	0.03 (0.56)	33.4 (0.4)	35.5 (2.2)	.72 (.04)
Age														
< 85 years	203	17.5 (0.5)	9.5 (0.8)	43.1 (1.2)	74.1 (1.3)	9.6 (0.5)	11.7 (0.3)	6.9 (0.3)†	36.6 (0.7)	−1.7 (0.6)	0.61 (0.58)†	34.1 (0.6)	36.8 (2.4)	.79 (.04)†
≥ 85 years	206	17.5 (0.7)	9.5 (0.9)	42.2 (1.5)	75.9 (1.2)	9.1 (0.4)	12.0 (0.2)	6.4 (0.2)	37.3 (0.6)	−3.4 (0.6)	−0.86 (0.62)	33.3 (0.6)	34.1 (2.4)	.70 (.05)
Gender														
Male	88	18.1 (0.6)	10.8 (1.4)	43.6 (1.5)	75.8 (1.8)	8.9 (0.5)	11.9 (0.4)	6.4 (0.4)	37.0 (0.8)	−2.7 (0.9)	−0.36 (0.86)	32.8 (0.6)	33.1 (3.2)	.72 (.05)
Female	333	17.3 (0.5)	9.1 (0.6)	42.5 (1.0)	75.0 (1.0)	9.5 (0.4)	11.9 (0.2)	6.7 (0.2)	36.9 (0.6)	−2.3 (0.5)	0.09 (0.49)	33.8 (0.5)	36.0 (2.2)	.75 (.04)
Race														
White	338	17.3 (0.4)	9.1 (0.7)	42.2 (1.0)	74.4 (1.0)	9.3 (0.4)	11.8 (0.2)	6.8 (0.2)†	36.8 (0.6)	−2.5 (0.6)	−0.18 (0.52)	33.5 (0.5)	34.8 (2.0)†	.75 (.04)
Non-White	35	17.8 (1.6)	10.2 (1.7)	44.1 (3.0)	78.9 (2.8)	10.4 (1.2)	12.2 (0.5)	5.6 (0.5)	38.4 (1.5)	−2.1 (1.6)	0.85 (1.60)	35.2 (1.6)	49.3 (5.2)	.70 (.15)
Married														
Yes	52	18.3 (0.9)	11.0 (2.1)	43.7 (2.0)	72.1 (2.5)	9.0 (0.8)	11.2 (0.4)	7.4 (0.5)†	36.5 (1.3)	−3.9 (1.0)	−1.65 (0.92)	31.2 (0.9)**	32.8 (4.2)	.68 (.09)
No	279	17.1 (0.4)	9.2 (0.7)	42.1 (1.1)	75.2 (1.2)	9.6 (0.4)	12.0 (0.2)	6.6 (0.2)	36.9 (0.6)	−2.1 (0.6)	0.25 (0.55)	34.3 (0.6)	37.7 (2.5)	.75 (.04)
Cognitive impairment														
Mild to moderate	152	17.5 (0.4)	9.5 (0.6)	42.8 (1.0)	82.4 (1.1)***	11.1 (0.6)***	12.5 (0.3)**	5.8 (0.3)***	40.6 (0.7)**	−2.1 (0.8)	1.65 (0.73)**	36.1 (0.8)***	44.3 (3.2)***	.92 (.05)***
Severe to very severe	259	—	—	—	71.1 (1.1)	8.4 (0.4)	11.5 (0.2)	7.1 (0.2)	34.9 (0.6)	−2.6 (0.6)	−0.93 (0.54)	32.3 (0.5)	31.6 (1.8)	.66 (.05)
Behavioral symptom														
None	141	16.9 (0.5)	9.0 (0.8)	41.3 (1.3)	79.1 (1.2)***	10.1 (0.6)**	12.1 (0.3)*	5.9 (0.3)***	38.2 (0.7)*	−2.5 (0.9)	0.33 (0.85)	34.7 (0.7)*	41.3 (3.2)*	.87 (.04)***
≥ 1	206	17.8 (0.5)	9.9 (0.8)	43.5 (1.3)	71.9 (1.4)	8.9 (0.5)	11.6 (0.3)	7.2 (0.3)	35.9 (0.7)	−2.3 (0.7)	−0.22 (0.60)	33.1 (0.6)	33.6 (2.4)	.66 (.06)
Functional impairment														
0–4 ADLs	198	17.4 (0.4)	9.3 (0.7)	42.1 (1.1)	78.3 (1.3)***	10.5 (0.6)***	12.1 (0.2)	6.3 (0.3)	39.6 (0.7)***	−3.2 (0.8)	0.22 (0.71)	35.0 (0.6)***	39.2 (2.7)†	.87 (.03)***
5–7 ADLs	164	17.1 (0.8)	9.1 (1.5)	42.2 (1.8)	70.6 (1.3)	8.3 (0.4)	11.5 (0.3)	7.1 (0.3)	33.7 (0.6)	−1.5 (0.6)	−0.29 (0.58)	31.9 (0.6)	32.5 (2.3)	.59 (.06)
Comorbidity														
0–2	230	17.6 (0.4)	9.1 (0.7)	43.6 (1.1)*	75.2 (1.2)	9.3 (0.5)†	11.9 (0.2)	6.5 (0.3)	37.0 (0.6)	−2.6 (0.6)	−0.20 (0.60)	34.2 (0.5)	37.5 (2.5)	.81 (.03)*

(Table continues on next page)

positively related to care provider-rated and observed quality of life. Finally, family involvement was related to higher QOL in AD–activity, as rated by care providers.

Discussion

Just as the measurement of quality of life is complex and multifaceted (Sloane et al., 2005, this issue), so too is the study of how care relates to quality of life. On the one hand, some argue that such study requires longitudinal assessment, assessing care at baseline, and quality of life at baseline and follow-up, and then relating care to change in quality of life (Gonzalez-Salvador et al., 2000; Ready & Ott, 2003). Only one other study has completed a longitudinal assessment of dementia quality of life in long-term care (using the ADRQL), finding a small (5 percentage points) and potentially clinically inconsequential decline in quality of life over 2 years (with some residents showing improved quality of life over time); further, there was no association between change and resident status at baseline (Lyketsos et al., 2003). Using a different measure, the 15-item QOL-AD (ranging from 15 to 60, with a baseline mean of 36.9, SE 0.5), the current study similarly found little (albeit significant) change over time (raw change −2.4, SE 0.05, $p < .0001$), and for 36% of the residents, improvement of at least one point over the 6-month study interval. The authors of the ADRQL study postulated that the lack of decline in their sample might reflect the high quality of care in the one facility in which their study was conducted—which hypothetically moderated the expected decline—and called for a comparative study to tease out such relationships.

The present study of care provided to 421 residents in 45 facilities was designed to do just that. At follow-up, residents fared better in facilities with specialized workers, with more staff training in more areas (supervisor and direct care staff), and that encouraged activity participation more frequently. Specifically, mean raw change was −1.3 (SD 7.4) versus −3.0 (SD 8.2) in facilities with specialized workers compared to those without. In facilities in which 75% or more of supervisors were trained in at least five of the six domains, raw mean change was −1.0 (SD 8.3) versus −3.4 (SD 7.5); comparable figures for care provider training were −0.4 (SD 7.6) vs −3.5 (SD 7.9). In facilities that encouraged activities once a day or more, it was −1.9 (SD 7.8) versus −2.6 (SD 8.0). Interestingly, these are all facility-level variables, and none of the resident-level components of care related to change in quality of life. On the one hand, such findings are promising because they imply that facility-wide change can impact resident well-being; on the other, they call into question the degree to which individualized care is benefiting residents with dementia. It must be acknowledged, however, that this study may not

Table 4. Statistically Significant Covariate Adjusted HLM-Based Tests of Association Between Facility-Level Components of Care and Quality of Life

	Resident Report			Direct Care Provider Report						Observation		
Facility-Level Component of Care	DQOL (n = 84)	QOL in AD–Activity (n = 92)	QOL-AD (n = 101)	ADRQL (n = 302)	QOL in AD–Activity (n = 296)	QOL in AD–Positive Affect (n = 296)	QOL in AD–Negative Affect (n = 281)	QOL-AD (n = 301)	QOL-AD, Raw Change (n = 295)	QOL-AD, Adjusted Change (n = 295)	PGC-ARS (n = 245)	DCM, % BCC Type I (n = 245)	DCM, WIB (n = 245)
Demographics													
For profit						+*		+*				−*	
Chain											−*		
SCU-EQS			+*				+**	−**				+**	
AL-EQS			+*					−***				+**	
Staffing													
Stability													
Specialized worker	−*			−**	−**		+**	−*	+*	+**	+**		
RN or LPN (contract)		+**	−*	+**	+*								
Aide (contract)													
RN and LPN turnover													−**
Policies and practices													
Admission policies	−*					+**		+*					
Discharge policies						+**							
Accept problematic behavior				+**		+**							
Policy choice											+**		+*
Care planning													
Professional staff			+**						+***	+**	+**		
Aide			+*					+*	+***	+**	+**		
Training													
Supervisor												−**	
Care staff													
Assess													
Professional												−*	−*
Standardized													
Treat													
Professional	−**		−*			+**		+*				−*	
Other, informal	−*												
Perceived success												+**	
Use of antipsychotic or sedative hypnotic	−*		−***		−**				+**	+**			
Encourage activities			+*						+*	+*		−*	
Use of stimuli													

Notes: HLM = hierarchical linear model; DQOL = Dementia Quality of Life; QOL in AD = Quality of Life in Alzheimer's Disease; QOL-AD = Quality of Life–Alzheimer's Disease; ADRQL = Alzheimer Disease Related Quality of Life; PGC-ARS = Philadelphia Geriatric Center Affect Rating Scale; DCM % BCC = Dementia Care Mapping Behavior Category Code (percent of Type I observations); WIB = well- or ill-being; SCU-EQS = Special Care Unit Environmental Quality Scale; AL-EQS = Assisted Living Environmental Quality Scale; RN = registered nurse; LPN = licensed practical nurse. The sample size at the top of each column is the number of residents with data on that quality-of-life measure and all the covariates. Sample sizes vary among the rows from 71 to 101 for resident-reported quality of life, 241 to 302 for care-provider-reported quality of life, and 211 to 245 for observed quality of life. Columns with a "+" or "−" indicate positive and negative associations, respectively, based on hierarchical linear models with the specified quality-of-life measure as the dependent variable. For resident-reported measures, models included a random effect for facility. For care-provider-reported measures, models included random effects for facility and care provider (nested within facility). For observed measures, models included random effects for facility and observer. Associations were additionally adjusted for facility type (RC/AL vs nursing home) and resident gender, cognitive deficit, behavioral symptoms, ADL impairment, comorbidity, and depressive symptoms; associations with care provider report and observed measures were further adjusted for resident tenure, age, race and marital status. Facility type; size; age; affiliation; percent dementia beds; dementia and ADL impairment case-mix; universal worker; RN, LPN, and aide FTEs; administrator and aide turnover; and extent hire for experience were not significantly associated with any quality-of-life measures (p > .10).

*p < .10; **p < .05; ***p < .01.

Table 5. Statistically Significant Covariate Adjusted HLM-Based Tests of Association Between Resident-Level Components of Care and Quality of Life

	Resident Report					Direct Care Provider Report					Observation		
Resident-Level Component of Care	DQOL ($n = 84$)	QOL in AD-Activity ($n = 92$)	QOL-AD ($n = 101$)	ADRQL ($n = 302$)	QOL in AD-Activity ($n = 296$)	QOL in AD-Positive Affect ($n = 296$)	QOL in AD-Negative Affect ($n = 281$)	QOL-AD ($n = 301$)	QOL-AD Raw Change ($n = 295$)	QOL-AD, Adjusted Change ($n = 295$)	PGC-ARS ($n = 245$)	DCM, % BCC Type I ($n = 245$)	DCM, WIB ($n = 245$)
Reported and observed care													
Dementia area									—*				
Cholinesterase inhibitor											+*		
Restraints, ever[a]	NA	NA	NA								—*	—***	—***
Ungroomed appearance			—**		—**							—***	
Staff experience, perceptions, and observed behavior													
Approaches													
Total	+**			+**		+**							
Hope	+***	+*											+**
Person-centered		+**				+**							
Work stress				—*									
Work satisfaction					+*						+***	+***	+***
Communication					+***						—***	—***	—***
Personal detractors							—*						
Positive person work			+***			+**					+**	+***	+***
Physical contact			+*									+***	+**
Family involvement				+***									

Notes: HLM = hierarchical linear model; DQOL = Dementia Quality of Life; QOL in AD = Quality of Life in Alzheimer's Disease; QOL-AD = Quality of Life-Alzheimer's Disease; ADRQL = Alzheimer Disease Related Quality of Life; PGC-ARS = Philadelphia Geriatric Center Affect Rating Scale; DCM BCC = Dementia Care Mapping Behavior Category Code (percent of Type I observations); WIB = well- or ill-being. The sample size at the top of each column is the number of residents with data on that quality-of-life measure and all the covariates. Sample sizes vary among the rows from 63 to 101 for resident-reported quality of life, 220 to 302 for care-provider-reported quality of life, and 198 to 245 for observed quality of life. Columns with a "+" or "—" indicate positive and negative associations, respectively, based on hierarchical linear models with the specified quality-of-life measure as the dependent variable. For resident-reported quality-of-life measures, models included a random effect for facility. For care-provider-reported quality-of-life measures, models included random effects for facility and care provider (nested within facility). For observed measures, models included random effects for facility and observer. Associations were additionally adjusted for facility type (RC/AL vs nursing home) and resident gender, cognitive deficit, behavioral symptoms, ADL impairment, comorbidity, and depressive symptoms; associations with care provider report and observed measures were further adjusted for resident tenure, age, race and marital status. Unsuitable appearance and experience of supervisor and direct care staff were not significantly associated with any quality-of-life measures ($p > .10$).
[a] Association of restraint use with resident-reported quality of life cannot be estimated, as those residents reporting quality of life were never observed in restraints.
*$p < .10$; **$p < .05$; ***$p < .01$.

have had sufficient power to detect some of these associations—but even if it did, they likely would have been small, and, similar to the ADRQL study, of questionable clinical relevance. Nonetheless, considering this acknowledged limitation, the fact that three components of care related to change over time may highlight the utility of turning attention to the areas of specialized workers, staff training, and encouragement of activity participation. In one area this attention may spark debate, as many states promote the practice of universal workers (Mollica, 2002), and the expanded use of specialized workers may change demands for care.

The authors of the ADRQL study concluded that the ADRQL is sensitive to change over time (although noted that such sensitivity might be limited) and appropriate for use as an outcome measure in intervention studies. In the current study, change in quality of life measured with the QOL-AD was significantly different over an even shorter period of time (6 months as opposed to 2 years); also, it detected a significant relationship with cognitive and affective status (such that a more favorable status at baseline related to relatively better quality of life at follow-up) and was markedly lower for residents immediately before the time of discharge or death compared to those who remained in the facility through 6 months (raw change −4.7 [SD 7.7] vs −1.7 [SD 7.9]). Finally, the fact that the QOL-AD detected differences among components of care further merits its consideration as an outcome measure. It might be a particularly useful measure if interest was in how the resident rated his or her quality of life, as the patient version of the QOL-AD can be reliably and validly completed by those with a MMSE score as low as 10; the degree to which this version is sensitive to change is unknown, however (Logsdon, Gibbons, McCurry, & Teri, 2002).

If one were of a different mindset, one would recognize that a longitudinal study comparing care to quality of life in a cohort of current residents (as opposed to a new admissions cohort) may be insensitive to the effects the care environment had exerted since the time of admission. In such a case, a cross-sectional comparison of care to quality of life, adjusting for resident status, might best indicate this relationship. In making those comparisons, this study found many associations of care to outcomes; given the multiple comparisons, it is best to focus on the detected patterns.

The 11 measures used in this study define quality of life differently and from three different vantage points. None constitutes a gold standard, although many suggest that the resident's point of view should take priority (Brod et al., 1999). In this study, we could conduct analyses for at most 120 resident reports, and significant associations with so modest a sample are worthy of discussion. From the resident's perspective, quality of life was higher for those in facilities that more frequently involved more staff in care planning and whose care providers felt more hope (e.g., that residents can make decisions, that they will not inevitably go "down hill," and that feeling attached to residents need not be avoided). Also, quality of life was lower in facilities that provided more treatment, including antipsychotic and sedative hypnotic medications, and when residents themselves were ungroomed. Other authors have found a relationship between anxiolytic treatment and reduced quality of life, and the likely explanation is that more intense treatment is used (not entirely successfully) for residents who are more impaired (a relationship that persisted despite controlling for resident status in these analyses; Gonzalez-Slavador et al., 2000).

A limitation of relating care provider assessments of quality of life to outcomes is that such assessments are influenced by caregiver factors (Gonzalez-Slavador et al., 2000; Karlawish, Casarett, Klocinski, & Clark, 2001; Winzelberg, Williams, Preisser, Zimmerman, & Sloane, 2005, this issue). Thus, it may come as no surprise that residents with whom workers communicate more and toward whom they display positive person work (e.g., enable the resident to do what he or she couldn't otherwise do) tend to be rated more highly. One finding to note is that these same interpersonal components are related to observational indicators of quality of life, such that these residents display more positive affect, behaviors, and general well-being. Thus, to the extent that workers have the time and can feel and act positively toward residents, quality of life is likely to be improved. Further, these attitudes relate to worker satisfaction as well, and so all parties may benefit when positive interactions are maximized (Zimmerman, Williams, et al., 2005, this issue). Finally, contrary to conventional wisdom, more stability in staff–resident assignment was related to worse staff ratings of quality of life (but not to resident or observer ratings of quality of life). Whether stability is affecting care provider attitudes (and hence ratings), or whether it is actually affecting resident quality of life is not known. A recent study showed no clear superiority of permanent versus rotating staffing, and so this area merits further attention (Burgio, Fisher, Fairchild, Scilley, & Hardin, 2004).

Finally, it would be remiss to not stress the fact that (a) resident appearance was related to at least one measure of quality of life as rated by residents, care providers, and observation, and (b) facility type (RC/AL vs nursing home) and number of dementia beds were not related to any quality-of-life measures. Grooming may be an inherent indicator of dignity and, as such, may be an implicit marker of poor quality of life. As far as setting of care, there is increasing evidence that the quality of care in nursing homes has been improving (Feldman & Kane, 2003) and no overwhelming indication that special dementia care is related to better outcomes (Phillips et al., 1997). Thus, while RC/AL developed in part so that older adults could avoid nursing home placement, the tide may have turned, and these settings may be less different than some consider—and equally suitable (although perhaps not equally affordable) for the care of residents with dementia (Kane & Wilson, 2001; Zimmerman et al., 2003). At minimum, it is likely that such gross categorizations of care (RC/AL, nursing home) do not relate to differences in care that are affecting resident quality of life.

What then do these myriad findings suggest? They certainly suggest directions for hypothesis generation and further exploration and evaluation. While causal attribution is not possible, the findings suggest that facilities should consider (and studies should evaluate) using a specialized worker perspective, train all staff in domains central to dementia (depression, pain, behavioral symptoms, ambulation, nutrition, and hydration), and encourage activity participation (related to change in quality of life over time). They suggest that attention be paid to resident grooming (related to quality-of-life ratings by residents, staff, and observation). They suggest that facilities should involve staff in care planning, encourage care providers to feel more hope, and avoid antipsychotic and sedative hypnotic medications, if possible (related to resident perceptions of quality of life). They suggest that staff should communicate more, and positively, with residents (related to care provider rating and observed quality of life) and that rotating worker assignment be further explored (related to care provider rating). To the extent that all of these areas are under the control of the facility, and can be implemented with few new resources, all are worth consideration and evaluation to improve the quality of life of long-term care residents with dementia. In fact, the Alzheimer's Association is undertaking a national educational campaign, the Campaign for Quality in Residential Care, to implement and evaluate many of these components of care. Thus, the growth of evidence-based practice to improve the quality of life for residents with dementia in long-term care is evident, and promising.

References

Albert, S. M., Del Castillo-Castaneda, C., Sano, M., Jacobs, D. M., Marder, K., Bell, K., et al. (1996). Quality of life in patients with Alzheimer's disease as reported by patient proxies. *Journal of the American Geriatrics Society, 44*, 1342–1347.

Alexopoulos, G. S., Abrams, R. C., Young, R. C., & Shamoian, C. A. (1988). Cornell Scale for Depression in Dementia. *Biological Psychiatry, 23*, 271–284.

Åström, S., Nilsson, M., Norberg, A., Sandman, P. O., & Winblad, B. (1991). Staff burnout in dementia care: Relations to empathy and attitudes. *International Journal of Nursing Studies, 28*, 65–75.

Bradford Dementia Group (1997). *Evaluating dementia care: The DCM method (7th ed.).* Bradford, UK: Author.

Brod, M., Stewart, A. L., Sands, L., & Walton, P. (1999). Conceptualization and measurement of quality of life in dementia: The dementia quality of life instrument (DQoL). *The Gerontologist, 39*, 25–35.

Brooker, D. (2005). Dementia Care Mapping: A review of the research literature. *The Gerontologist, 45*(Special Issue I), 11–18.

Burgio, L. D., Fisher, S. E., Fairchild, J. K., Scilley, K., & Hardin, J. M. (2004). Quality of care in the nursing home: Effects of staff assignment and work shift. *The Gerontologist, 44*, 368–377.

Cohen-Mansfield, J. (1986). Agitated behaviors in the elderly. II. Preliminary results in the cognitively deteriorated. *Journal of the American Geriatrics Society, 34*, 722–727.

Cronbach, J. L., & Furby, L. (1970). How we should measure "change"—Or should we? *Psychological Bulletin, 74*, 68–80.

Diggle, P. J., Heagerty, P., Liang, K.-Y., & Zeger, S. L. (2002). *The analysis of longitudinal data* (2nd ed.). Oxford, UK: Oxford University Press.

Edelman, P., Fulton, B. R., Kuhn, D., & Change, C.-H. (2005). A comparison of three methods of measuring dementia-specific quality of life: Perspectives of residents, staff and observers. *The Gerontologist, 45*(Special Issue I), 27–36.

Feldman, P. H., & Kane, R. L. (2003). Strengthening research to improve the practice and management of long-term care. *Milbank Quarterly, 81*, 179–220.

Folstein, M. F., Folstein, S. E., & McHugh, P. R. (1975). "Mini-mental state." A practical method for grading the cognitive state of patients for the clinician. *Journal of Psychiatric Research, 12*, 189–198.

Gonzalez-Salvador, T., Lyketsos, C. G., Baker, A., Hovanec, L., Roques, C., Brandt, J., et al. (2000). Quality of life in dementia patients in long-term care. *International Journal of Geriatric Psychiatry, 15*, 181–189.

Hartmaier, S. L., Sloane, P. D., Guess, H. A., & Koch, G. G. (1994). The MDS Cognition Scale: A valid instrument for identifying and staging nursing home residents with dementia using the Minimum Data Set. *Journal of the American Geriatrics Society, 42*, 1173–1179.

Kane, R., & Wilson, K. B. (2001). *Assisted living at the crossroads: Principles for its future.* Portland, OR: The Jessie F. Richardson Foundation.

Karlawish, J. H. T., Casarett, D., Klocinski, J., & Clark, C. (2001). The relationship between caregivers' global ratings of Alzheimer's disease patient's quality of life, disease severity, and the caregiving experience. *Journal of the American Geriatrics Society, 49*, 1066–1070.

Lawton, M. P., Van Haitsma, K., & Klapper, J. (1996). Observed affect in nursing home residents with Alzheimer's disease. *Journal of Gerontology: Psychological Sciences, 51B*, P3–P14.

Lintern, T., Woods, B., & Phair, L. (2000a). Before and after training: A case study of intervention. *Journal of Dementia Care, 8*(1), 15–17.

Lintern, T., Woods, B., & Phair, L. (2000b). Training is not enough to change care practice. *Journal of Dementia Care, 8*(2), 15–17.

Logsdon, R. G., Gibbons, L. E., McCurry, S. M., & Teri, L. (2000). Quality of life in Alzheimer's disease: Patient and caregiver reports. In S. M. Albert & R. G. Logsdon (Eds.), *Assessing quality of life in Alzheimer's disease* (pp. 17–30). New York: Springer Publishing Company.

Logsdon, R. G., Gibbons, L. E., McCurry, S. M., & Teri, L. (2002). Assessing quality of life in older adults with cognitive impairment. *Psychosom Med, 64*, 510–519.

Lyketsos, C. G., Gonzales-Salvador, T., Chin, J. J., Baker, A., Black, B., & Rabins, P. (2003). A follow-up study of change in quality of life among persons with dementia residing in a long-term care facility. *International Journal of Geriatric Psychiatry, 18*, 275–281.

Mollica, R. (2002). State assisted living policy, 2002. Retrieved June 10, 2004, from http://www.nashp.org/_docdisp_page.cfm?LID=24F0A0A1-2066-4E84-B113F4B919FC006C2002

Morris, J. N., Fries, B. E., & Morris, S. A. (1999). Scaling ADLs within the MDS. *Journal of Gerontology: Medical Sciences, 54B*, M546–M553.

Moos, R. H., & Lemke, J. H. (1996). *Evaluating residential facilities.* Thousand Oaks, CA: SAGE Publications, Inc.

Phillips, C. D., Sloane, P. D., Hawes, C., Koch, G., Han, J., Spry, K., et al. (1997). Effect of residence in Alzheimer disease special care units on functional outcomes. *Journal of the American Medical Association, 278*, 1340–1344.

Rabins, P. V., Kasper, J. D., Kleinman, L., Black, B. S., & Patrick, D. L. (2000). Concepts and methods in the development of the ADRQL: An instrument for assessing health-related quality of life in person's with Alzheimer's disease. In S. M. Albert & R. G. Logsdon (Eds.), *Assessing quality of life in Alzheimer's disease* (pp. 51–68). New York: Springer Publishing Company.

Ready, R. E., & Ott, B. R. (2003). Quality of life measures for dementia. *Health and Quality of Life Outcomes, 1*(1), 11.

Schaefer, J. A., & Moos, R. H. (1993). Work stressors in health care: Context and outcomes. *Journal of Community and Applied Social Psychology, 3*, 235–242.

Sloane, P. D., Mitchell, C. M., Weisman, G., Zimmerman, S., Long, K. M., Lynn, M., et al. (2002). The Therapeutic Environment Screening Survey for Nursing Homes (TESS-NH): An observational instrument for assessing the physical environment of institutional settings or persons with dementia. *Journal of Gerontology: Social Sciences, 57B*, S69–S78.

Sloane, P. D., Zimmerman, S., Williams, C. S., Reed, P. S., Gill, K. S., & Preisser, J. S. (2005). Evaluating the quality of life of long-term care residents with dementia. *The Gerontologist, 45*(Special Issue I), 37–49.

Winzelberg, G. S., Williams, C. S., Preisser, J. S., Zimmerman, S., & Sloane, P. D. (2005). Factors associated with direct care providers quality of life ratings for residents with dementia in long-term care facilities. *The Gerontologist, 45*(Special Issue I), 107–115.

Woodruff, R. S. (1971). A simple method for approximating the variance of a complicated estimate. *Journal of the American Statistical Association, 66*, 411–414.

Wunderlich, G. S., & Kohler, P. O. (2001). *Improving the quality of long-term care*. Washington, DC: National Academy Press.

Zgola, J. M. (1987). *Doing things: A guide to programming activities for persons with Alzheimer's disease and related disorders*. Baltimore, MD: The Johns Hopkins University Press.

Zimmerman, S., Gruber-Baldini, A. L., Sloane, P. D., Eckert, J. K., Hebel, J. R., Morgan, L. A., et al. (2003). Assisted living and nursing homes: Apples and oranges? *The Gerontologist, 43*, 107–117.

Zimmerman, S., Sloane, P. D., Eckert, J. K., Buie, V. C., Walsh, J. F., Hebel, J. R., et al. (2001). An overview of the Collaborative Studies of Long-term Care. In S. Zimmerman, P. D. Sloane, & J. K. Eckert (Eds.), *Assisted living: Needs, practices, and policies in residential care for the elderly* (pp. 117–143). Baltimore, MD: The Johns Hopkins University Press.

Zimmerman, S., Sloane, P. D., Heck, E., Maslow, K., & Schulz, R. (2005). Introduction: Dementia care and quality of life in assisted living and nursing homes. *The Gerontologist, 45*(Special Issue 1), 5–7.

Zimmerman, S., Williams, C. S., Reed, P. S., Boustani, M., Preisser, J. S., Heck, E., et al. (2005). Attitudes, stress, and satisfaction of staff who care for residents with dementia. *The Gerontologist, 45*(Special Issue I), 97–106.

Received September 20, 2004
Accepted March 3, 2005
Decision Editor: Richard Schulz, PhD

Part VI
Psychological Aspects of Mental Health Problems in Old Age

[27]

Depression in Late Life: Review and Commentary

Dan G. Blazer

Department of Psychiatry and Behavioral Sciences and Center for the Study of Aging,
Duke University Medical Center, Durham, North Carolina.

Depression is perhaps the most frequent cause of emotional suffering in later life and significantly decreases quality of life in older adults. In recent years, the literature on late-life depression has exploded. Many gaps in our understanding of the outcome of late-life depression have been filled. Intriguing findings have emerged regarding the etiology of late-onset depression. The number of studies documenting the evidence base for therapy has increased dramatically. Here, I first address case definition, and then I review the current community- and clinic-based epidemiological studies. Next I address the outcome of late-life depression, including morbidity and mortality studies. Then I present the extant evidence regarding the etiology of depression in late life from a biopsychosocial perspective. Finally, I present evidence for the current therapies prescribed for depressed elders, ranging from medications to group therapy.

Depression ... so mysteriously painful and elusive ... remains nearly incomprehensible to those who have not experienced it in its extreme mood, although the ... "blues" which people go through occasionally ... are of such prevalence that they do give many individuals a hint of the illness in its catastrophic form.

William Styron,
from his book *Darkness Visible* (1, p. 7)

DEPRESSION is perhaps the most frequent cause of emotional suffering in later life and significantly decreases quality of life in older adults (2–7). In recent years, the literature on late-life depression has exploded. Excellent North American epidemiological studies from the 1980s and early 1990s have been complemented by more recent reports from other countries (2,4,8–12). Many gaps in our understanding of the outcome of late-life depression have been filled (13–15). Intriguing findings have emerged regarding the etiology of late-onset depression (16–18). The number of studies documenting the evidence base for therapy has increased dramatically (19,20). In this review, I first address case definition, and then I review the current community- and clinic-based epidemiological studies. Next I address the outcome of late-life depression, including morbidity and mortality studies. Then I present the extant evidence regarding the etiology of depression in late life from a biopsychosocial perspective (6,21). Finally, I present evidence for the current therapies prescribed for depressed elders, ranging from medications to group therapy. Given the plethora of literature, important (though on my view not critical) studies have necessarily been omitted, yet the current review reflects the astounding advance of our database since I reviewed the subject in 1989 (22).

CASE DEFINITION

Clinicians and clinical investigators do not agree as to what constitutes clinically significant depression, regardless of age, nor is there universal agreement about how depression should be disaggregated into its component subtypes. The subtypes most cogent to late-life depression are reviewed in the paragraphs that follow. (Because of space limitations, bereavement and bipolar disorder have been omitted from this review.) There is considerable overlap across these subtypes, as the differentiations often reflect particular orientations toward dissecting the syndrome, that is, different ways of "slicing the pie." When the factor structure for the range of depressive symptoms is examined across the life cycle, there are no major differences between Caucasians and African Americans (23), between men and women (4,23), or between older and younger adults (4,24).

Major depression is diagnosed in the *Diagnostic and Statistical Manual*, Fourth Edition (DSM-IV), when the older adult exhibits one or both of two core symptoms (depressed mood and lack of interest) along with four or more of the following symptoms for at least 2 weeks: feelings of worthlessness or inappropriate guilt; diminished ability to concentrate or make decisions; fatigue; psychomotor agitation or retardation; insomnia or hypersomnia; significant decrease or increase in weight or appetite; and recurrent thoughts of death or suicidal ideation (25). The symptoms of moderate to severe depression presented to the clinician are similar across older adults and persons in midlife if there are no comorbid conditions (26). However, there may be subtle differences by age. For example, melancholia (symptoms of noninteractiveness and psychomotor retardation or agitation) appears to have a later age of onset than nonmelancholic depression in clinical populations, with psychomotor disturbances being more distinct in older persons (27,28).

Minor, subsyndromal, or subthreshold depression is diagnosed according to the Appendix of DSM-IV when one of the core symptoms just listed is present along with one to three additional symptoms (25). Other operational definitions of these less severe variants of depression include a score of 16+ on the Center for Epidemiologic Studies Depression Scale (CES-D) (29) but not meeting criteria for major depression (10), a primarily biogenic depression not meeting criteria for major depression yet responding to antidepressant medication (30), or a score of 11–15 on the CES-D (31) and therefore not meeting the CES-D criteria for clinically significant depression, that is, subthreshold depression. Minor depression variously defined has been associated with impairment similar to that of major depression, including impaired physical functioning, disability days, poorer self-rated health, use of psychotropic medications, perceived low social support, female gender, and being unmarried (10,31).

Other investigators have suggested a syndrome of *depression without sadness*, thought to be more common in older adults (32,33), or a depletion syndrome manifested by withdrawal, apathy, and lack of vigor (34–36). *Dysthymic disorder* is a long-lasting chronic disturbance of mood, less severe than major depression, that lasts for 2 years or longer (25). It rarely begins in late life but may persist from midlife into late life (37,38). The aforementioned list is actually truncated from all the different potential subtypes of depression that have been suggested, both past and present. Modern psychiatry has been criticized for its tendency to split syndromes into so many different subtypes without adequate empirical (especially biological) data to justify such splitting (39). One investigator has suggested that the only meaningful split of the depressive spectrum is a split between the more physical symptoms of depression (such as anhedonia, agitation, and perhaps some of the symptoms of executive dysfunction, see the paragraphs that follow) and the more psychological symptoms (40).

Depression in late life is frequently *comorbid* with other physical and psychiatric conditions, especially in the oldest old (41). For example, depression is common in older patients recovering from myocardial infarction and other heart conditions (41,42), and in those suffering from diabetes (43), hip fracture (44), and stroke (45). In community-dwelling Mexican American elders, depression was associated with diabetes, arthritis, urinary incontinence, bowel incontinence, kidney disease, and ulcers (a profile different from Caucasians, who exhibit comorbidities such as hip fracture and stroke) (46). Major depression is generally thought to be present in approximately 20% of Alzheimer's patients (47–49). In some studies, however, the rates are much lower (1–5%) (50). Depressive symptoms may be common even in elders with mild dementia of the Alzheimer's type (51).

Some differences have been reported between *early onset* (first episode before the age of 60) and *late onset* (first episode after the age of 60) depression. Personality abnormalities, a family history of psychiatric illness, and dysfunctional past marital relationships were significantly more common in early onset depression (52). However, when severity, phenomenology, history of previous episode, and neuropsychological performance were compared, there were no differences between early onset and late onset depression in elderly people (52).

Interest in differentiating early- versus late-onset depression in late life has arisen in large part because some people have speculated that contributors to etiology may vary by age of onset. For example, *vascular depression* (depression proposed to be due to vascular lesions in the brain) may be much more common with late-onset depression, and the clinical presentation may differ, even if only in subtle ways (16,47,53). Severely depressed older adults exhibit impairment in set shifting, verbal fluency, psychomotor speed, recognition memory, and planning (executive cognitive function) (54). The clinical presentation of elderly patients with this "depression–executive dysfunction syndrome" is characterized by psychomotor retardation and reduced interest in activities but a less pronounced vegetative syndrome than is seen in the depressed without executive dysfunction. The dysfunction consists of impaired verbal fluency, impaired visual naming, and poor performance on tasks of initiation and perseveration (55,56). Vascular depression is associated with absence of psychotic features, less likelihood of a family history, more anhedonia, and greater functional disability when compared with nonvascular depression (16,47,53,57).

Psychotic depression, when contrasted with nonpsychotic depression, occurs in 20–45% of hospitalized elderly depressed patients (58) and 3.6% of persons in the community with depression (59). Recently a group of investigators proposed a *depression of Alzheimer's disease*. In persons who meet criteria for dementia of the Alzheimer's type (25), three of a series of symptoms that includes depressed mood, anhedonia, social isolation, poor appetite, poor sleep, psychomotor changes, irritability, fatigue or loss of energy, feelings of worthlessness, and suicidal thoughts must be present for the diagnosis to be made (60).

EPIDEMIOLOGY OF LATE-LIFE DEPRESSION

Depressive symptoms are less frequent (or no more frequent) in late life than in midlife (2,61,62), though some suggest these estimates are biased secondary to "censoring" of population studies of older adults by means of increased mortality among the depressed and difficulty in case finding (63) (see Table 1). In a recent study, the lower frequency of depressive symptoms in elderly people compared with people in midlife was associated with fewer economic hardships and fewer experiences of negative interpersonal exchanges among both older disabled and nondisabled respondents. In addition, religiosity among older disabled adults also accounted for part of the lower frequency (64).

Reports of the prevalence of clinically significant depressive symptoms among community-dwelling older adults range from approximately 8% to 16% (2,4,9,62,65). Some suggest that depression may be more frequent among Mexican Americans than among non-Hispanic Caucasians and African Americans. In one study, 25% of older Mexican Americans scored 16+ on the CES-D (66). In studies of samples of mixed Caucasians and African Americans, rates are similar (2,4). Nevertheless, African Americans are generally seen by psychiatrists to have fewer depressive symptoms and are much less likely to be treated with antidepressant medications (67,68).

Depressive symptoms are more frequent among the oldest old, but the higher frequency is explained by factors associated with aging, such as a higher proportion of women, more physical disability, more cognitive impairment, and lower socioeconomic status (41,69). When these factors are controlled, there is no relationship between depressive symptoms and age (2). The 1-year incidence of clinically significant depressive symptoms is high in the oldest old, reaching 13% in those aged 85 years or older (70).

The prevalence estimates of major depression in community samples of elderly people have been quite low,

Table 1. Representative Studies of the Prevalence and Incidence of Depression in Older Adults

Author (Ref.)	Sample and Instrument	Prevalence–Incidence Estimate	Comments
Berkman et al. (4)	Community sample of adults 65+ y of age in New Haven, using the CES-D	1-wk prevalence estimate of 16% w/ clinically significant depressive symptoms	
Blazer et al. (2)	Community sample of adults 65+ y of of age in urban and rural NC, using the CES-D	1-wk prevalence estimate of 9% w/ clinically significant depressive symptoms	No differences with increasing age when confounding variables such as gender and functional status were controlled. No racial differences
Weissman et al. (8) Eaton et al. (74)	Community sample of adults 65+ y of age in 5 U.S. communities, both urban and rural, using the DIS	Overall estimate of the prevalence of major depression was 1.4% in women and 0.4% in men; estimate of incidence 0.15% overall	
Steffens et al. (12)	Community sample of adults 65+ y of age in Cache County, UT, using modified DIS	Overall estimate of the prevalence of major depression was 4.4% in women and 2.7% in men	
Beekman et al. (10)	Community sample of adults 65+ y of age in The Netherlands	Overall estimate of the prevalence of major depression was 2% and of minor depression was 12.9%	
Koenig et al. (76)	Hospitalized sample of VA subjects, using the DIS	Overall estimate of the prevalence of major depression was 11.5%, w/ an additional 23% experiencing significant depressive symptoms	
Parmelee et al. (80)	LTC residents, using a DSM-IIIR checklist	Overall estimate of the prevalence of major depression was 12.4%, w/ an additional 35% experiencing significant depressive symptoms	

Notes: CES-D = Center for Epidemiologic Studies Depression Scale; DIS = Diagnostic Interview Schedule; VA = Veterans Administration; DSM = Diagnostic and Statistical Manual; LTC = long-term care.

ranging from 1% to 4% overall, with higher prevalence among women yet with no significant racial or ethnic differences (3,9,11,12). Estimates for dysthymia and minor depression are somewhat higher, with the same pattern of distribution across sex and race or ethnicity. In the North Carolina Epidemiologic Catchment Area (ECA) Study, in which the Diagnostic Interview Schedule (DIS) was used (71), the prevalence estimate was 0.8% for major depression, 2% for dysthymia, and 4% for minor depression (3). Prevalence in the ECA studies overall in the elderly population was 1.4% in women and 0.4% in men (8). The prevalence of major depression in the Cache County, Utah, study of community-dwelling elderly persons was 4.4% in women and 2.7% in men (12). In Liverpool, investigators estimated 2.9% of elders with major depression and 8.3% with minor depression (72). In The Netherlands, investigators found 2.0% of older persons with major depression and 12.9% with minor depression (10). In Sweden, prevalence of major depression in the community was higher among the oldest old, from 5.6% at the age of 70 to 13% at the age of 85 (73).

In the United States, the estimate of incidence (new cases over a year) of major depression from the ECA overall was 3 per 1000, with a peak in subjects in their fifties (74). The incidence of major depression in elderly people was 0.15%, similar to the rate in younger age groups (70,74,75). In a study from Sweden, the incidence of major depression was 12 per 1000 person-years in men and 30 per 1000 person-years in women between the ages of 70 and 85. The incidence increased from 17 per 1000 person-years between the ages of 70 and 79 to 44 per 1000 person-years between 79 and 85.

The prevalence estimates for major depression among older adults hospitalized for medical and surgical services is 10–12%, with an additional 23% experiencing significant depressive symptoms (76). Major depression affects 5–10% of older adults who visit a primary care provider (77–79). For example, in one study among 247 subjects in a primary care setting, 9% were diagnosed with major depression, 6% with minor depression, and 10% with subsyndromal depression. Fifty-seven percent of these depressed patients experienced active depression at 1-year follow-up (77).

In one large study of a long-term care (LTC) facility, 12.4% experienced major depression and 35% experienced significant depressive symptoms (80). In another study, depression was found in 20% of patients admitted to a LTC facility. Incidence of major depression at 1 year was 6.4% (81). In another study of an LTC facility, prevalence of major depressive disorder among testable subjects was 14.4% (15% could not be tested) and prevalence of minor depression was 17%. Less than 50% of cases were recognized by nursing and social work staff (82). Recognition and treatment in LTC facilities for depression is consistently poor across studies. For example, only 55% of depressed patients in one LTC facility received antidepressant therapy, and 32% of those received inadequate doses (83). Screening LTC patients for depression, such as by using the Geriatric Depression Scale (84), can increase the frequency of treatment or referral by primary care physicians in LTC (85).

OUTCOME OF LATE-LIFE DEPRESSION

Course of Late-Life Depression

A 6-year follow-up of community dwelling older adults in The Netherlands illustrates the chronicity of late-life depression. Among those with clinically significant depressive symptoms, 23% remitted, 44% tracked an unfavorable but fluctuating course, and 33% tracked a severe chronic course. In the subthreshold group, 25% experienced a chronic course. Thirty-five percent of the major depressives and 52% of the dysthymics experienced a chronic course (13).

Major depression in older persons over longer follow-up periods exhibits a chronic remitting course in most clinical studies (86–91). In a 6-year follow-up of elderly depressives, 31% recovered and remained well, 28% suffered at least one relapse but recovered, 23% only partially recovered, and 17% remained depressed throughout the follow-up (86). In another study, among a group of elderly depressed patients (many of whom were medically ill) followed for 1 year, 35% had good outcome, 48% had either remittance and recurrence or remained continuously ill, 3% developed dementia, and 14% died (87). In a follow-up of younger subjects who experienced early-onset severe depression and survived into late life (follow-up for 25 years), only 12% remained continuously well in one study, with neurotic and endogenous depression exhibiting similar outcomes (92). These findings are similar to those in studies of persons in young adulthood and midlife (93,94). Elderly depressed outpatients without significant comorbid medical illness or dementia and who are treated optimally may exhibit a much better outcome, with over 80% recovering and remaining well throughout follow-up (90). In contrast, elders with a lack of instrumental and social support and poor self-rated health experience a longer time to remission (95).

The Impact of Medical Comorbidity, Functional Impairment, and Cognitive Impairment

Medical comorbidity, functional impairment, and comorbid dementing disorders all adversely influence outcome of depression. Depression, in turn, adversely affects the outcome of the comorbid problems. Depression is a major cause of weight loss in late life (96). Depression is frequently associated with chronic medical illnesses such as cardiovascular disease, and it can complicate the course of these illnesses (97). In one study, older patients with depression following a myocardial infarction were much more likely to die in the first 4 months after the event (26% vs 7%) (98). Depression in late life was an independent risk factor for heart failure among elderly women but not among elderly men in another study (99,100). In another study, depression was associated with a decrease in bone mineral density in controlled analyses in people aged 65 years or older (risk factors for osteoporosis) (101,102). Finally, late-life depression has been found to be a risk for poor self-rated health over time (103).

Few mechanisms for these associations have been identified at present, yet some have been theorized and explored. Platelet activation is increased in elderly depressed patients, especially those with the serotonin-transporter-linked promotor region 5-HTTLPR polymorphism (this group had significantly higher platelet factor 4 and beta-thromboglobulin levels). This finding suggests how some depressed patients may be at greater biological risk for morbidity and mortality with ischemic heart disease (104). Poor appetite can lead to low body mass index associated with late-life depression and subsequent frailty and failure to thrive (41,105,106). In an 18-month prospective study of community-dwelling older adults (including both spousal caregivers of dementia patients and noncaregiving controls), those with chronic, mild depressive symptoms had poorer T-cell responses to two mitogens from baseline to follow-up. In addition, among those with depression, older age was associated with the poorest blastogenic response to mitogens at follow-up. The stress of caregiving may have augmented this response. Older patients with depression have higher levels of the cytokine interleukin 6, indicating increased inflammatory activity, which may be linked to increased bone resorption (or depressed patients may be more sedentary, leading to increased resorption rates), thus increasing the risk for hip fracture (107,108).

Depression is clearly associated with functional impairment (2,109,110) and effects disability status over time (55,111,112). In one study, depression increased the risk for activities of daily living disability and mobility disability over 6 years by 67% and 73%, respectively (113). Even less severe symptoms of depression are associated with functional decline, such as "depression without sadness" (32). Disability is also a risk factor for depression (114,115). A number of explanations have been proposed. Physical disability appears to lead to higher numbers of negative life events. In addition, physical disability can lead to restriction of valued social or leisure activities, isolation, and reduced quality of social support (116). If disability can be improved, then depression may be relieved. Yet another explanation is that depression as a state is disabling. For example, executive-type cognitive impairments caused by depression may explain why depressed persons are more disabled (55,117). When depression accompanies stroke, functional outcome is compromised as well (118).

Functional decline is not inevitable following depression, however. A diagnosis of depression in older primary care patients in one study led to poorer self-reported role functioning but not to poorer self-reported physical functioning (119). Instrumental support provided to elders (such as helping with tasks) was generally protective against worsening performance on instrumental abilities of daily living among elderly patients with recurrent unipolar depression. Subjective and structural dimensions of social support protected the most severely depressed elderly patients against the loss of basic maintenance abilities (a clinical sample) (120).

Severe depression with cognitive impairment, even when the cognitive impairment remits, is a risk for Alzheimer's disease (AD) over 5 years (14). Early depressive symptoms among subjects with minimal cognitive impairment (MCI) may represent a preclinical sign and should be considered a risk factor for impending AD or vascular dementia (121). Depression further complicates the course of AD by increasing disability and physical aggression and leading to greater caregiver depression and burden (122–124). However, in a follow-up study, depressive symptoms among AD patients have higher rates of spontaneous resolution without requiring intensive drug treatment than among vascular dementia patients, in whom depressive symptoms are more persistent and refractory to drug treatment (121).

Nonsuicide Mortality

Nonsuicide mortality is a significant adverse outcome resulting from late-life depression. In a review of 61 reports from 1997 to 2001, 72% demonstrated a positive association between depression and mortality in elderly people (15). Another reviewer reported that, in 23 mortality studies of depression (subjects 65+ years of age), the pooled odds of dying if subjects were depressed were 1.75. A longer follow-up predicted smaller effect size. Both severity and duration of depressive symptoms predict mortality in the elderly population in these studies (125). Representative extant studies include summary data from the ECA study, in which the investigators found a fourfold increase in the odds of dying over a follow-up of 15 months if persons 55+ years of age experienced a mood disorder (111). Other cross-national studies of a positive association were found in Australia and Japan (126,127). Among community-dwelling persons in The Netherlands, both major and minor depression increased the risk for cardiac mortality in subjects with and without baseline cardiac disease (128). The association between depression and mortality holds in many of these studies, despite the addition of potentially confounding variables. For example, in one study, high levels of depressive symptoms independently predicted mortality in a study where demographics, medical comorbidity, smoking, and body mass index were controlled (129). In studies from North Carolina and New York, however, investigators failed to find an association (130,131). One reason for the lack of association in some studies may be the selection of control variables to be included, especially chronic disease and functional impairment. For example, in a study of the North Carolina Established Populations for Epidemiologic Study of the Elderly (EPESE) cohort, the unadjusted relative odds of mortality among depressed subjects at baseline was 1.98. These odds moved toward unity as other risk factors were controlled, such as chronic disease, and health habits, cognitive impairment, functional impairment, and social support were added to the model (132). Therefore, the specific variables controlled in mortality studies may determine the association between depression and mortality.

The effect of depression on mortality may vary by sex. In elderly Japanese American men but not women, depressive symptoms were a risk for mortality in the physically healthy (133). In another study, depressive symptoms were a significant risk factor for cardiovascular but not cancer mortality in older women (134,135). In a controversial report, investigators found that subthreshold depression (CES-D scores of 12–16) was not associated with mortality in men but was negatively related to 3-year mortality in women (odds ratio = .6) (136). In other words, mild depressive symptoms were protective in this highly controlled analysis of community-based data.

Suicide

Suicide frequency in the 65+ age group in the United States was 16.9/100,000 per year in 1998 (137,138). The frequency for white men increased with age, reaching 62/100,000 in the 65+ age range. Frequency among nonwhite men was highest in young adulthood and was slightly higher in midlife among women. The association of depression and suicide has been well established in the literature across the life cycle (138–143). Elderly persons attempting suicide are also more likely to be widow(er)s, live alone, perceive their health status to be poor, experience poor sleep quality, lack a confidant, and experience stressful life events, such as financial discord and interpersonal discord (138,143). The most common means of committing suicide is the use of voluntary drug ingestion. Whereas completed suicides increase with age, suicidal behaviors do not increase (144). There are approximately four attempts for each completed suicide in late life compared with 10 or more attempts per completed suicide earlier in life (145). Suicidal ideation is high among older adults, ranging from 5% to 10% of the population of older adults (138,140).

Health Services Utilization

Late-life depression leads to increased use of hospital and outpatient medical services (146–148). For example, having depressive symptoms was associated with a 19% increase in the number of outpatient encounters and a 30% increase in total outpatient charges in a Minnesota health maintenance organization. Taking antidepressant medications was associated with a 32% increase in total outpatient charges but was not significantly associated with number of outpatient encounters. Depressive symptoms and antidepressant therapy were not significantly associated with inpatient utilization or charges (149). Older persons are quite likely to use antidepressant medications, most of which are prescribed for depression (68). In a community sample in North Carolina, 14.3% of Caucasians and 5% of African Americans used antidepressants in 1996 (in controlled analyses, Caucasians were 3.8 times more likely to use antidepressants than African Americans).

ETIOLOGY

Biological

Any discussion of the biological etiology of depression must begin with *medical illness,* for depression among the medically ill in late life is almost ubiquitous, as just documented. In addition to the association of depression with dementing disorders, cardiovascular disease, and hip fractures, among patients with Parkinson's disease, 20% meet criteria for major depression and 21% meet it for minor depression (150). Depression has been associated with pain in institutionalized elderly people (151) and is also common among homebound elders with urinary incontinence (152). Both alcohol dependence and major depression pose significant risk for the development of the other disorder at 1-year follow-up (153). In a series of recently reported studies, diastolic hypotension was associated with low positive affect, whereas systolic hypertension was associated with a positive affect. Use of antihypertensive medication was independently associated with lower positive affect in elderly people (154). Male veterans who were hospitalized during World War II for head injury were more likely to report major depression in subsequent years (155).

Great interest has arisen in recent years to search for *genetic susceptibility* to mood disorders across the life cycle (156). In a community sample of elderly twins, genetic influences accounted for 16% of the variance in total depression scores on the CES-D and 19% of psychosomatic and somatic complaints. In contrast, genetics contributed a minimal amount to the variance in reports of depressed mood and psychological well-being (157). Yet the likelihood of identifying a family history of mood disorder in a clinically depressed older adult is lower than for persons in midlife. In a clinical study, the risk for immediate relatives of patients with depression whose onset occurred after age 50 was 8.3% compared with 20.1% for relatives of patients whose onset occurred at a younger age (158).

Attention has been directed to specific genetic markers for late-life depression. Given the great interest in the ε4 allele of the apolipoprotein E gene, a number of studies have focused on this susceptibility gene for Alzheimer's disease. No association was found in a community sample between ε4 and depression (159). In another study, hyperintensities in deep white matter but not in the periventricular white matter were associated with depressive symptoms, especially in elders carrying the ε4 allele (160). Other investigators have concentrated on genes possibly associated with vascular lesions in the central nervous system. In one study, patients with late onset depression had an increased rate of the C677T mutation of the MTHFR (methylene tetrahydrofolate reductase) enzyme. This mutation may place older persons at risk for vascular depression (57). CADASIL (cerebral autosomal dominant arteriopathy with subcortical infarcts and leukoencephalopathy) is a disease of the notch 3 gene. Depression is one of the initial symptoms in this condition, suggesting that genetic polymorphisms or mutations may predispose older adults to vascular depression. This genotype, however, is rare (161,162).

Much attention has been directed to *vascular risk* for late-life depression, and this attention dates back at least 40 years, although the advent of magnetic resonance imaging boosted interest considerably (86,163–166). Recent studies suggest that vascular lesions in selected regions of the brain may contribute to a unique variety of late-life depression—hence the interest in vascular depression as just discussed. The vascular depression impairments resemble impairments exhibited in frontal lobe syndromes. Magnetic resonance imaging of depressed patients has revealed structural abnormalities in areas related to the cortical–striatal–pallidal–thalamus–cortical pathway (167), including the frontal lobes (168), caudate (169), and putamen (170). These circuits are strongly implicated in the development of spontaneous performance strategies demanded by executive tasks. Recent interest has also focused on a smaller size of the orbital frontal cortex in late-life depression (171). In addition, left hippocampal volume has been found to be smaller in depressed elders who develop dementia over time (172). The frontal white matter (not gray matter) lesions in late-life depression are associated with increased myoinositol–creatinine and choline–creatinine ratios. These changes may reflect biological changes in nonneural (glial) tissue, which in turn affects synaptic activity (166).

Serotonin activity, specifically, $5\ HT_{2A}$ receptor binding, decreases dramatically in a variety of brain regions through midlife, but there is less decrease from midlife to late life. These $5\ HT_{2A}$ receptors in normal healthy subjects decreased markedly from young adulthood to midlife (70% from the levels at age 20 through the fifth decade), and then leveled off as age advanced. Receptor loss occurred across widely scattered regions of the brain (anterior cingulated, occipital cortex, and hippocampus) (18). The relationship of serotonin depletion can also be studied indirectly by the study of radioisotope-labeled or tritiated imipramine binding (TIB) sites. There is a significant decrease in the number of platelet-TIB sites in elderly depressed patients, compared with elderly controls and individuals suffering from Alzheimer's disease (173).

In aged monkeys (*Macaca mulatta*), significant age-related decreases in $5\ HT_{1A}$ receptor binding were observed only in the frontal and temporal cortices. In the hippocampus, although $5\ HT_{1A}$ receptor binding indicated nonsignificant age-related changes, the degree of displacement when binding to a receptor agonist was decreased in the aged monkeys. This finding suggests that age-related impairment of $5\ HT_{1A}$ receptor response might be related to the reduced efficacy of antidepressant therapy in elderly patients with depression (174).

Endocrine changes have also been associated with late-life depression. Although the dexamethasone suppression test was long ago ruled out as a diagnostic test for depression, nonsuppression of cortisol is associated with late-life depression compared with age-matched controls (175). Depression is associated with hypersecretion of corticotropin-releasing factor (CRF), which is thought to mediate sleep and appetite disturbances, reduced libido, and psychomotor changes (176). Aging is associated with an increased responsiveness of adrenocorticotropic hormone (ACTH), cortisol, and dehydroepiandrosterone sulfate (DHEA-S) to CRF (177). Low levels of DHEA have been associated with higher rates of depression and a greater number of depressive symptoms in community-dwelling older women (178). Total testosterone levels were lower in elderly men with dysthymic disorder than in men with major depressive disorder and men without depressive symptoms in another study (179). However, the efficacy of testosterone in treating depression has not been established (180). Depression has also been associated with postprandial systolic hypotension (181). Hormone replacement in women has been associated with improvements in mood (182).

Psychological

Behavioral, psychodynamic, and cognitive aberrations have all been suggested as causes of late-life depression. Three examples will illustrate these proposed etiologies. The *behavior* of learned helplessness, originally used to described the increasingly passive behavior of dogs produced by inescapable shock, has been expanded to explain depressive symptoms across the life cycle, suggesting that the cause of depression is the expectation that initiating action in a continually stressful environment is futile (6,183, 184). The association of depression with severe or frequent adverse life events could be interpreted in part as a behavioral response to continued adverse stressors. Depression in old age has been associated with emotional abuse and neglect during childhood, as well as relational stress and problem behavior of significant others during late adulthood (especially high when many events reported during adulthood and late adulthood) (185). In a meta-analysis, the number of total negative life events and daily hassles was associated with depression in elderly people (186). Severe events show the largest relative risk, but ongoing difficulties account for the most episodes. The association of severe events with onset tends to be stronger in first than in recurrent episodes. Mild events can trigger a recurrence but not a first episode, suggesting that once the development of the behavior of "depression" follows a stressor, the triggers for subsequent episodes of depression need not be severe thereafter (187).

According to one *psychodynamic* theory, the search for restitution secondary to the inevitable losses in late life is a major developmental task for aging individuals and a depression-like syndrome may appear, a "depletion syndrome," when this task is not accomplished successfully. If one lives long enough, the inevitable object loss, body change, and disease lead to a state of both internal and external depletion (6,188). A more recent yet controversial theory complements the depletion theory, suggesting that successful aging is associated with "selective optimization with compensation" (189). This model is based on a recognition by the elder of the realities of aging, especially the losses. Such recognition leads to selection of realistic activities, optimization of those activities, and compensation for lost activities, which in turn leads to a reduced and transformed life.

Perhaps the most dominant psychological model of depression is the model of *cognitive distortions* (190). In a case-control study, patients with major depression perceived greater negative impact of life events than patients with dysthymic disorder and healthy controls (191). The interpretation of life events is the key to understanding depression under this theory. Cognitions may be distorted such that the elder has unrealistic expectations, overgeneralizes certain adverse events, overreacts to events, and personalizes events. Perceived negative interpersonal events are associated with depression in elders, particularly in those who demonstrate a high need for approval and reassurance in the context of interpersonal relationships. In contrast, negative achievement events are associated with depression in those who placed a heavy emphasis on personal success and control. This conceptualization is consistent with the diathesis-stress model, namely that negative experience best predicts depression when a specific type of event affects a personal vulnerability (192,193).

Social

The association between late-life depression and impaired social support has been established for many years. In a community study in Hong Kong (194), impaired social support and depression were associated (including network size, network composition, social contact frequency, satisfaction of social support, and instrumental–emotional support). Impaired social support is associated with poorer outcome of depression in older men but not older women (195). In female caregivers of demented elderly people, the prevalence rate of depressive disorders reaches 45–47%, and these women are twice as likely to use psychotropic drugs (196,197). Loneliness may be a key factor in depression among caregivers (198). Some have attempted to couple the theory of social disengagement with aging (much debated in the literature) with depression, suggesting that some symptoms of depression, such as lack of social interest and greater self-involvement, mirror attributes of older adults according to Disengagement Theory (199,200). Other factors being equal, it is probable that elders who are less socially engaged are more depressed. For example, elders who stopped driving had a greater risk of worsening depressive symptoms (201).

Spiritual and Existential

Religious practice is associated with less depression in elderly Europeans (EURODEP), both on the individual and the national level. This is especially true when religious practice is embedded within a traditional value orientation (202). Some investigators have proposed that "religious coping" (subjects perceiving that religion is the most important factor in coping) is associated with improved emotional and physical health (203,204). They found that religious coping was associated with a decrease in certain types of depressive symptoms, including loss of interest, feelings of worthlessness, withdrawal from social interactions, loss of hope, and other cognitive symptoms of depression. Religious coping was not associated with a reduction in somatic symptoms.

DIAGNOSTIC EVALUATION

Much of the diagnostic workup of late-life depression derives from what we know about symptom presentation and etiology (see Table 2). Basically, the diagnosis is made on the basis of a history augmented with a physical and fine-tuned by laboratory studies. There is no biological marker or test that makes the diagnosis, though for some subtypes of depression, such as vascular depression, the presence of subcortical white matter hyperintensities on magnetic resonance imaging scanning are critical to the diagnosis (6,185).

Screening is beneficial when standardized screening scales such as the Geriatric Depression Scale (GDS) or the CES-D are used (29,84,205). Screening in primary care is critical. Not only is the frequency of depression high, but suicidal ideation is high as well. The prevalence of serious suicidal ideation in one primary care setting was 1% and the prevalence approaches 5% among older adults who report significant symptoms of depression (206,207). However, the documented success of screening has been mixed in extant studies. Internists tend to accept responsibility for treating late-life depression but perceive their clinical skills as inadequate and are frustrated with their practice environment (207). Nearly all studies of treatment efficacy with pharmacotherapy or psychotherapy focus on older adults with uncomplicated major depression, which may apply to less than 15% of the depressed people in primary care (208). Primary care physicians were informed of patient-specific treatment recommendations for depressed patients 60+ years of age in one controlled study. The patients of physicians in the intervention group were more likely to be diagnosed with depression and prescribed antidepressant medications,

Table 2. Diagnostic Workup of the Depressed Older Adult

Routine	Elective
Screening for significant depressive symptoms (using a standardized screening scale such as the CES-D or GDS)*	MRI to establish the diagnosis of vascular depression
Present and past history, including history from a family member—include assessment of nutritional status and functional status and current medications[†]	Vitamin B_{12} and folate assays when vitamin deficiency is suspected
Screen for cognitive functioning[‡]	Polysomnography if significant sleep abnormalities cannot be explained
Routine laboratory tests, esp. chemistry screen and electrocardiogram if antidepressants are to be prescribed[§]	T_3 and T_4 TSH to screen for undiagnosed thyroid dysfunction

Notes: CES-D = Center for Epidemiologic Studies Depression Scale; GDS = Geriatric Depression Scale; MRI = magnetic resonance imaging; TSH = thyroid-stimulating hormone.
* See Refs. 29 and 84; [†] Ref. 6; [‡] Ref. 210; [§] Refs. 41 and 244.

though the outcome of the depression was no better for the intervention group than for the control group (209).

Cognitive status should be assessed with the Mini-Mental State Examination (MMSE), given the high likelihood of comorbid depression and cognitive dysfunction (210). Nutritional status is most important to evaluate in the depressed elder, including height, weight, history of recent weight loss, lab tests for hypoalbuminemia, and cholesterol, given the risk for frailty and failure to thrive in depressed elders, especially the oldest old (41,106). General health perceptions (211) as well as functional status (activities of daily living) should be assessed for all depressed elderly patients (212,213). Other factors critical to assess in the diagnostic workup include social functioning (214), medications (many prescribed drugs can precipitate symptoms of depression), mobility and balance, sitting and standing blood pressure, blood screen, urinalysis, chemical screen (e.g., electrolytes, which may signal dehydration) and an electrocardiogram if cardiac disease is present (especially if antidepressant medications are indicated) (41).

TREATMENT

Biological

Antidepressant medications have become the foundation for the treatment of moderate to severe depression in older adults. Virtually all antidepressant medications are equally effective for treating serious major depression across the life cycle (19,215,216). Studies that compare tricyclic antidepressants (TCAs) and selective serotonin reuptake inhibitors (SSRIs) usually find equal efficacy, yet there are fewer side effects with SSRIs (217). Therefore, SSRIs are the treatment of choice (203,206). The antidepressants even appear to be efficacious in subjects with subcortical hyperintensities (vascular depression) (218,219). Although subjects with depression and smaller frontotemporal volumes on magnetic resonance imaging were more treatment resistant in one study (220), a number of studies document the efficacy of antidepressant therapy for treating depression in dementia (221–223).

Antidepressants appear less efficacious in treating less severe depression (224). A large study in a primary care setting found that paroxetine showed moderate benefits for depressive symptoms and mental health functioning in elderly patients with dysthymia and more severely impaired elderly patients with minor depression (compared with problem-solving therapy) (225). The overall evidence suggests that antidepressants and counseling have relatively small benefit in these less severe conditions (226). The use of St. John's wort (Hypericum perforatum) has been recommended for less severe depression and, given that it is available over the counter, it is used by mildly depressed older adults (and perhaps some who are more severely depressed). A recent study did not find that St. John's wort was as effective as sertraline in moderately severe major depression (mostly persons in midlife) (227). Nevertheless, this study has been criticized for not focusing on the mildly depressed.

Most of the SSRIs have been demonstrated to be efficacious in elderly people, including the drugs fluoxetine (228), sertraline (229), paroxetine (217,230), citalopram (231), and fluvoxamine (232). (Escitalipram, recently entering the antidepressant market, has not been shown to be specifically efficacious in the elderly population.) Other new-generation antidepressants that have been shown to be efficacious include venlafaxine (233), mirtazapine (234, 235), nefazodone (in a general study of depression), and buproprion (236,237). Nefazodone (238) has not been shown to be specifically efficacious in elderly people, because to date there has been no study of the drug in the elderly population.

In a recent consensus of practicing geriatric psychiatrists, the SSRIs along with psychotherapy are the treatments of choice for late-life depression, along with venlafaxine XR. Buproprion and mirtazapine are alternates (as was electroconvulsive therapy, or ECT, in severe depression). Medication (SSRI plus an antipsychotic, with risperidone and olanzapine being the antipsychotics most commonly recommended) and (or) ECT are the preferred treatments of unipolar psychotic major depression. Medications plus psychotherapy are recommended for dysthymic disorder. Education plus watchful waiting are recommended for minor depression that lasts for less than 2 weeks (antidepressant medication plus psychotherapy are recommended for minor depression if symptoms persist). The preferred antidepressant for treating both major and minor depression is citalopram (20–30 mg) followed by sertraline (50–100 mg) and paroxetine (20–30 mg), with fluoxetine (20 mg) as an alternate. Nortriptyline (40–100 mg) is the preferred tricyclic agent, with desipramine (50–100 mg) as the alternate. The consensus recommendation is to continue an antidepressant 3–6 weeks before a change in medications is made. If little or no response is observed, the consensus is to switch to venlafaxine (75–200 mg). For a first episode of depression with recovery following antidepressant therapy, 1 year of continual therapy is recommended. For two episodes, 2+ years of continual therapy and for three or more episodes,

3+ years of continual therapy are recommended (239), as shown in Table 3.

Many factors may alter the efficacy or the side effects of the antidepressant drugs in late life. For example, estrogen therapy and DHEA have been demonstrated to augment sertraline treatment (240,241). A number of the cytochrome P450 enzymes that metabolize most medications are inhibited by antidepressants, such as CYP3A, CYP2D6, DYP2C, CYP1A2, and CYP2E1. The CYP3A enzymes metabolize 60% of the medications used today. Fluoxetine is a moderate inhibitor of CYP3A4. Approximately 8–10% of adults lack the CYP2dD6 enzyme, and paroxetine is a potent inhibitor of this enzyme (which may explain, among some patients treated with paroxetine, the lack of efficacy of analgesics such as codeine that are metabolized by this enzyme). Citalopram and venlafaxine are the "cleanest" of the medications in terms of inhibition of the cytochrome P450 enzymes (242,243).

Elderly inpatients on SSRIs or venlafaxine are at definite risk for developing hyponatremia (39% in one study) and should have sodium levels checked before and after commencement of antidepressant medications (244). This hyponatremia is due to the syndrome of inappropriate secretion of antidiuretic hormone. Other serious side effects reported with the SSRIs include the risk of falls (no less risk than with the tricyclics in one study) (245), the serotonin syndrome (lethargy, restlessness, hypertonicity, rhabdomyolysis, renal failure, and possible death) (246), and gastrointestinal bleeding (247). Less serious side effects include weight loss, sexual dysfunction, anticholinergic effects (most pronounced with paroxetine), agitation, and difficulty sleeping.

Subjects with psychotic depression respond poorly to antidepressants but well to ECT (248). Many studies have documented the effectiveness of ECT in older adults (249–251). Some investigators report the response as good in elderly as in young people (252), whereas others suggest that the response is less optimal in the oldest old (253). In one study using bilateral ECT versus pharmacotherapy, the 65+ age group had a better response to ECT than younger age groups (254). Memory problems remain the major adverse effect from ECT that affects quality of life. Memory problems are usually transient and clear within weeks following treatment. A relatively new procedure that could replace ECT in some situations is repetitive transcranial magnetic stimulation (rTMS) (255). TMS does not require anesthesia and seizure induction is avoided. Though not studied specifically in elderly people, in one outcome study, patients treated with rTMS compared with ECT responded equally well and their clinical gains lasted at least as long as those with ECT (256). In another study, executive function improved in both middle-aged and elderly depressed subjects with rTMS compared with sham treatments (257).

Investigators with the Alameda County Study explored the association of exercise and depression, controlling for functional status. Among subjects who were not depressed at baseline, those who reported a low activity level were at significantly greater risk for depression at follow-up (258). On the basis of controlled trials, an aerobic exercise training program may be considered an alternative to antidepressants for treatment of depression in older persons (259). However, the advantages of exercise are not limited to aerobic activities. Unsupervised weight lifting has been found to decrease depressive symptoms up to 20 weeks after induction (260). Light therapy may also be beneficial, especially if the depression follows a seasonal pattern. Thirty minutes of bright light a day improved depression among institutionalized elders in one controlled study (261).

Table 3. Consensus Treatments of Late-Life Depression

Diagnosis	Treatment
Major depression	SSRIs plus psychotherapy. Citalopram (20–30 mg) first choice, followed by sertraline (50–100 mg) and paroxetine (20–30 mg); 1-y continued therapy if treatment successful; ECT if the depression is severe and unresponsive to antidepressant medications
Unipolar psychotic major depression	SSRIs plus an antipsychotic agent (risperidone and olanzapine); move quickly to ECT if therapy not effective
Dysthymic disorder	SSRIs plus psychotherapy
Minor depression	Education plus watchful waiting for depression lasting <2 wk; SSRIs plus psychotherapy if symptoms persist

Note: From Alexopoulos et al. (239). SSRI = selective serotonin reuptake inhibitor; ECT = electroconvulsive therapy.

Psychological

Psychotherapy has received much attention and study as a treatment modality for depressed older adults over the past 20 years. This attention results from the development of "manualized" therapies, such as cognitive behavioral therapy (CBT) and interpersonal therapy (IPT). These therapies can be taught clearly and easily to Masters-level clinicians and can be monitored for accuracy in following the procedures of the therapy. Most of these therapies are short term (12–20 sessions) and therefore much more attractive to third-party payers. In addition, the educational (as opposed to a reflective) posture of the therapist employing manualized therapies is attractive to elders. In one study comparing range of referrals, outcomes, attendance rates, and length of time in therapy between older and younger adults participating in cognitive therapy, there was no significant differences in therapy outcome apart from home adjustment measures where older adults showed greater improvement. Younger adults showed significantly higher rates of nonattendance and had higher dropout rates (262).

Nevertheless, psychotherapy remains an infrequently prescribed therapy for depressed older adults. In a study of general internists, only 27% said they would refer a depressed older adult for psychotherapy (263). In a sample of primary care elderly patients in Quebec, the acceptability of a therapy was dependent on the severity of symptoms. CBT and cognitive bibliotherapy were rated more acceptable than antidepressants when the symptoms were less severe. Antidepressants were more acceptable than either CBT or bibliotherapy when the patient's symptoms were severe (264).

CBT and IPT have been the most frequently studied of the manualized therapies (20,262–266). Exact mechanisms that render CBT and IPT effective, however, remain unclear (267). CBT focuses on thoughts that may perpetuate depression. The therapeutic goal of the therapist is to teach the patient to change these thought patterns or adapt to them. By changing thoughts, people change dysfunctional attitudes as well, and these attitudes are hypothesized to precipitate and perpetuate depressive thoughts (192). Studies increasingly suggest that the more central mechanism for changing thought patterns is the development of metacognition, that is, "stepping back" and responding to negative thoughts as transitory events rather than as inherent aspects of the self (268). In one study comparing CBT and brief psychodynamic therapy to a wait-list control group, all of the treatment modalities led to a comparable and clinically significant reduction of depression (265). Twelve months after the treatment, 58% of the sample population was depression free, and at 24 months, 70% was depression free. In another study, older depressed patients were assigned to CBT alone, medication alone, or a combination of medication and CBT (269). Although all groups showed improvement, the combined group showed the greatest improvement.

IPT is a manualized treatment that focuses on four components hypothesized to lead to or maintain depression: grief (e.g., death of a loved one); interpersonal disputes (e.g., conflict with adult children); role transitions (e.g., retirement); and interpersonal deficits (e.g., lack of assertiveness skills). The treatment has been adapted specifically for older adults (270,271). In combination with nortriptyline, IPT has been shown to be an effective treatment for elderly depressed subjects (90,272,273). In one study, investigators achieved an excellent initial response (74%) with only 15% recurrence at the end of 1 year (90). Subjects who respond do not tend to relapse over fairly extensive periods (272).

More reflective therapies include psychodynamic therapy, life review therapy, and reminiscence therapy. Cases of successful psychodynamic therapy have been presented in the literature among older adults (274), and in one study psychodynamic therapy was as effective as CBT (275). Given its very nature, however, psychodynamic psychotherapy is most difficult to investigate empirically. In life review therapy, subjects are encouraged to acknowledge past conflicts and consider their meaning. In reminiscence therapy, the focus is more on positive memories in group settings. Both structured and unstructured reminiscence therapy lead to improvement compared with controls, and the structured group did even better (276). In contrast, another study found no improvement over wait-list controls (277). Bibliotherapy emphasizes a skills acquisition approach through select readings from books. For example, subjects may read *Feeling Good* (278), a self-help book that emphasizes employing cognitive skills to overcome depression. In a series of controlled randomized studies for mild to moderate depression in older adults, bibliotherapy was shown to be efficacious (279–282). Bibliotherapy has advantages for older adults. Elders can read and process the material at their own pace. Fears of stigmatization can be avoided and, for elders with impaired activities of daily living, this intervention does not require as many visits to a therapist (267).

Group therapy is used frequently with older adults, though it is less often studied compared with individual therapy (283). Self-management therapy and education groups were equally effective and superior to wait-list controls in one study (284). CBT and psychodynamic group therapy were more effective than placebo but less effective than tricyclics in other studies (285,286). In a recent study, investigators found that antidepressant medication plus clinical management, either alone or with addition of group-administered dialectical behavior therapy (skills training and scheduled coaching sessions), found that the medication–dialectical behavior therapy groups had a higher continued remission rate than medications alone (267,287).

Combined Medication and Psychotherapy

In geriatric patients with recurrent major depression, maintenance treatment with nortriptyline or IPT is superior to placebo in preventing or delaying recurrence. Combined treatment using both appears to be the optimal clinical strategy in preserving recovery (272). Combined treatment with nortriptyline and IPT is also more likely to maintain social adjustment (performance–impaired or not, interpersonal behavior–hypersensitivity, friction–quarreling, satisfaction–loneliness) than treatment with either alone (288).

The PROSPECT (Prevention of Suicide in Primary Care Elderly-Collaborative Trial) is testing whether a trained clinician (a "health specialist") can work in close collaboration with a primary care physician to implement a comprehensive depressive management program including pharmacotherapy and IPT. The goal is to reduce suicidal ideation (289). Older patients with suicidal ideation in the midst of a recurrent episode of major depression respond as well as nonsuicidal patients, yet those with ideation have higher relapse rates during continuation treatment and were more likely to receive augmentation pharmacotherapy (290).

CAN LATE-LIFE DEPRESSION BE PREVENTED?

The extant psychiatric literature suggests virtually no empirical evidence of psychosocial primary prevention. A MEDLINE review of the *American Journal of Psychiatry* from 1990 to 2001 and the *American Journal of Geriatric Psychiatry* from 1997 to 2001 did not yield a single empirical study of the primary prevention of depression in the elderly population (or of an intervention strategy that might be considered universal) (291). The few references to primary prevention of late-life depression focused on blood pressure control to prevent cerebrovascular disease as a means of preventing vascular depression (292). In contrast, these journals are replete with articles regarding secondary prevention, that is, the early treatment of depression with medications and psychotherapy to remit depression and prevent its serious consequences as already described (19,272). As already described regarding the PROSPECT study, tertiary prevention (prevention of the serious consequences of late-life depression such as suicide) has received attention as well. The biological emphasis of today's psychiatry coupled with the paucity of empirical studies that document the benefit of primary (or universal) prevention undoubtedly have influenced recent contributions to the literature.

A recent study among elderly people is directly relevant to primary prevention (293). Elderly subjects who experienced chronic illness were randomly assigned to a classroom intervention, a home study program, and a wait list. Both interventions provided instruction on mind–body relationships, relaxation training, cognitive restructuring, problem solving, communication, behavioral treatment for insomnia, nutrition, and exercise (a multimodal intervention strategy that integrates many approaches to enhancing self-efficacy in elderly people). The home version was delivered by class videotapes and readings. Compared with the control condition, both interventions led to significant decreases in self-reports of pain, sleep difficulties, and symptoms of depression and anxiety. Such nonpharmacological interventions among vulnerable older adults may become increasingly important in our efforts to decrease the burden of depression among older adults.

FUTURE DIRECTIONS

In a recent editorial derived from a conference devoted to the diagnosis and treatment of late-life depression, the authors concluded, "Treatment works, but mood disorders in old age remain a big public health issue. Disability, decline, diminished quality of life, demands on care givers and discriminatory reimbursement policies [persist] ... partnerships among researchers, clinicians, governmental agencies, third payers, patients and family members will be essential to further progress in the next 10 years" (294, p. 146). No one can reasonably argue with this conclusion. I would add that perhaps some slight paradigm shifts may be called for as well. For example, we must consider more carefully the boundaries between "true" clinical depression and less severe (perhaps adaptive) depressive symptoms among elders. In addition, the efficacy of antidepressants (which are now used widely) has been amply demonstrated in clinical trials, yet we have not verified the effectiveness of these medications in reducing the burden of depressive symptoms among the populace of older adults and in decreasing the frequency of suicide. Effectiveness studies are critical lest we falsely equate use of medications with adequate treatment of depressed elders. Finally, the lives of older adults in the United States over the past 20 years have been more healthy, happy, and economically viable than at any time during the twentieth century. Unfortunately, current government policies, especially the erosion of retirement plans, increasingly evasive universal health care, and the erosion of more meaningful and long-lasting social ties (295) may place older adults at much greater vulnerability over the next 20 years.

ACKNOWLEDGMENT

Address correspondence to Dan G. Blazer, Department of Psychiatry and Behavioral Sciences and Center for the Study of Aging, Box 3003, Duke University Medical Center, Durham, NC 27710. E-mail: blaze001@mc.duke.edu

REFERENCES

1. Styron W. *Darkness Visible: A Memoir of Madness.* New York: Random House; 1990.
2. Blazer D, Burchett B, Service C, George L. The association of age and depression among the elderly: an epidemiologic exploration. *J Gerontol Med Sci.* 1991;46:M210–M215.
3. Blazer D, Hughes D, George L. The epidemiology of depression in an elderly community population. *Gerontologist* 1987;27:281–287.
4. Berkman L, Berkman C, Kasl S, et al. Depressive symptoms in relation to physical health and functioning in the elderly. *Am J Epidemiol.* 1986;124:372–388.
5. Doraiswamy P, Khan Z, Donahue R, Richard NE. The spectrum of quality-of-life impairments in recurrent geriatric depression. *J Gerontol Med Sci.* 2002;57A:M134–M137.
6. Blazer D. *Depression in Late Life.* New York: Springer; 2002.
7. Schneider L, Reynolds C, Lebowitz B, Friedhoff A. *Diagnosis and Treatment of Depression in Late Life.* Washington, DC: American Psychiatric Press; 1994.
8. Weissman M, Bruce M, Leaf P, Florio L, Holzer III C. Affective disorders. In: Regier DA, Robins LN, eds. *Psychiatric Disorders in America.* New York: The Free Press; 1991:53–80.
9. Blazer D, Williams C. The epidemiology of dysphoria and depression in an elderly population. *Am J Psychiatr.* 1980;137:439–444.
10. Beekman A, Deeg D, van Tilberg T, Smit J, Hooijer C, van Tilberg W. Major and minor depression in later life: a study of prevalence and risk factors. *J Affect Disord.* 1995;36:65–75.
11. Beekman A, Copeland J, Prince M. Review of community prevalence of depression in later life. *Br J Psychiatr.* 1999;174:307–311.
12. Steffens D, Skook I, Norton MC. Prevalence of depression and its treatment in an elderly population: the Cache County study. *Arch Gen Psychiatr.* 2000;57:601–607.
13. Beekman A, Geerlings S, Deeg D, et al. The natural history of late-life depression. *Arch Gen Psychiatr.* 2002;59:605–611.
14. Alexopoulos G, Meyers B, Young R, Mattis S, Kakuma T. The course of geriatric depression with "reversible dementia": a controlled study. *Am J Psychiatr.* 1993;150:1693–1699.
15. Schulz R, Drayer R, Rollman B. Depression as a risk factor for non-suicide mortality in the elderly. *Biol Psychiatr.* 2002;52:205–225.
16. Alexopoulos G, Meyers B, Young R, Campbell S, Silbersweig D, Charlson M. 'Vascular depression' hypothesis. *Arch Gen Psychiatr.* 1997;54:915–922.
17. Kumar A, Zhisong J, Bilker W, Udupa J, Gottlieb G. Late-onset minor and major depression: early evidence for common neuroanatomical substrates detected by using MRI. *Proc Nat Acad Sci.* 1998;95:7654–7658.
18. Sheline Y, Mintun M, Moerlein S, Snyder A. Greater loss of 5-HT(2A) receptors in midlife than in late life. *Am J Psychiatr.* 2002;159:430–435.
19. Salzman C, Wong E, Wright B. Drug and ECT treatment of depression in the elderly, 1996–2001: a literature review. *Biol Psychiatr.* 2002;52:265–284.
20. Arean P, Cook B. Psychotherapy and combined psychotherapy/pharmacotherapy for late life depression. *Biol Psychiatr.* 2002;52:293–303.
21. Engel G. The clinical application of the biopsychosocial model. *Am J Psychiatr.* 1980;137:535–544.
22. Blazer D. Depression in the elderly. *N Engl J Med.* 1989;320:164–166.
23. Blazer D, Landerman L, Hays J, Simonsick E, Saunders W. Symptoms of depression among community-dwelling elderly African-American and White older adults. *Psychol Med.* 1998;28:1311–1320.
24. Ross C, Mirowsky J. Components of depressed mood in married men and women: The Center for Epidemiological Studies, Depression Scale. *Am J Epidemiol.* 1984;122:997–1004.
25. APA. DSM-IV: Diagnostic and Statistical Manual of Mental Disorders. Washington, DC: American Psychological Association; 1994.
26. Blazer D, Bachar J, Hughes D. Major depression with melancholia: a comparison of middle-aged and elderly adults. *J Am Geriatr Soc.* 1987;35:927–932.
27. Parker G, Roy K, Hadzi-Pavlovic D, Wilhelm K, Mitchell P. The differential impact of age on the phenomenology of melancholia. *Psychol Med.* 2001;31:1231–1236.
28. Parker G. Classifying depression: should paradigms lost be regained? *Am J Psychiatr.* 2000;157:1195–1203.
29. Radloff L. The CES-D Scale: a self-report depression scale for research in the general population. *Appl Psychol Meas.* 1977;1:385–401.

30. Snaith R. The concepts of mild depression. *Br J Psychiatr.* 1987;150: 387–393.
31. Hybels C, Blazer D, Pieper C. Toward a threshold for subthreshold depression: an analysis of correlates of depression by severity of symptoms using data from an elderly community survey. *Gerontologist.* 2001;41:357–365.
32. Gallo J, Rabins P, Lyketsos C. Depression without sadness: functional outcomes of nondysphoric depression in later life. *J Am Geriatr Soc.* 1997;45:570–578.
33. Gallo J, Rabins P, Anthony J. Sadness in older persons: 13-year follow-up of a community sample in Baltimore, Maryland. *Psychol Med.* 1999;29:341–350.
34. Adams K. Depressive symptoms, depletion, or developmental change? Withdrawal, apathy, or lack of vigor in the Geriatric Depression Scale. *Gerontologist.* 2001;41:768–777.
35. Newman J. Aging and depression. *Psychol Aging.* 1989;4:150–165.
36. Newman J, Engel R, Jensen J. Age differences in depressive symptom experiences. *J Gerontol.* 1991;46:224–235.
37. Devenand D, Noble M, Singer T, et al. Is dysthymia a different disorder in the elderly? *Am J Psychiatr.* 1994;151:1592–1599.
38. Blazer D. Dysthymia in community and clinical samples of older adults. *Am J Psychiatr.* 1994;151:1567–1569.
39. Horowitz A. *Creating Mental Illness.* Chicago: University of Chicago Press; 2002.
40. Parker G, Hadzi-Pavlovic D. *Melancholia: A Disorder of Movement and Mood.* New York: Cambridge University Press; 1996.
41. Blazer D. Psychiatry and the oldest old. *Am J Psychiatr.* 2000;157: 1915–1924.
42. Sullivan M, LaCroix A, Baum C. Functional status in coronary artery disease: a one year prospective study of the role of anxiety and depression. *Am J Med.* 1997;103:348–356.
43. Blazer D, Moody-Ayers S, Craft-Morgan J, Burchett B. Depression in diabetes and obesity: racial/ethnic/gender issues in older adults. *J Psychosom Res.* 2002;52:1–4.
44. Magaziner J, Simonsick E, Kashner M. Predictors of functional recovery in the years following hospital discharge for hip fracture. *J Gerontol Med Sci.* 1990;45:M110–M107.
45. Robinson R, Price T. Post-stroke depressive disorders: a follow-up study of 103 patients. *Stroke.* 1982;13:635–641.
46. Black S, Goodwin J, Markides K. The association between chronic diseases and depressive symptomology in older Mexican Americans. *J Gerontol Med Sci.* 1998;53A:M118–M194.
47. Krishnan K, Hays J, Blazer D. MRI-defined vascular depression. *Am J Psychiatr.* 1997;154:497–501.
48. Reifler B, Larson E, Henley R. Coexistence of cognitive impairment and depression in geriatric outpatients. *Am J Psychiatr.* 1982;139:623–626.
49. Patterson M, Schnell A, Martin R, Mendez M, Smyth K. Assessment of behavioral and affective symptoms in Alzheimer's disease. *J Geriatr Psychiatr Neurol.* 1990;3:21–30.
50. Weiner M, Edland S, Luszczynska H. Prevalence and incidence of major depression in Alzheimer's Disease. *Am J Psychiatr.* 1994;151: 1006–1009.
51. Rubin E, Veiel L, Kinscherf D, Morris J, Storandt M. Clinically significant depressive symptoms and very mild to mild dementia of the Alzheimer type. *Int J Geriatr Psychiatr.* 2001;16:694–701.
52. Brodarty H, Luscombe G, Parker G, et al. Early and late onset depression in old age: different aetologies, same phenomenology. *J Affect Disord.* 2001;66:225–236.
53. Salloway S, Malloy P, Kohn R, et al. MRI and neuropsychological differences in early- and late-life-onset geriatric depression. *Neurology.* 1996;46:1567–1574.
54. Beats B, Sahakian B, Levy R. Cognitive performance in tests sensitive to frontal lobe dysfunction in the elderly depressed. *Psychol Med.* 1996;26:591–603.
55. Alexopoulos G, Vrontou C, Kakuma T, et al. Disability in geriatric depression. *Am J Psychiatr.* 1996;153:877–885.
56. Lockwood K, Alexopoulos G, vanGorp W. Executive dysfunction in geriatric depression. *Am J Psychiatr.* 2002;159:1119–1126.
57. Hickie I, Scott E, Naismith S, et al. Late-onset depression: genetic, vascular and clinical contributions. *Psychol Med.* 2001;31:1403–1412.
58. Meyers B. Geriatric delusional depression. *Clin Geriatr Med.* 1992;8: 299–308.
59. Kivela S, Pahkala K, Laippala P. Prevalence of depression in an elderly Finnish population. *Acta Psychiatr Scand.* 1988;78:401–413.
60. Olin J, Schneider L, Katz I, et al. Provisional diagnostic criteria for depression of Alzheimer Disease. *Am J Geriatr Psychiatr.* 2002;10: 125–128.
61. Charles S, Reynolds C, Gatz M. Age-related differences and changes in positive and negative affect over 23 years. *J Personal Social Psychol.* 2001;80:136–151.
62. Murrell S, Himmelfarb S, Wright K. Prevalence of depression and its correlates in older adults. *Am J Epidemiol.* 1983;117:173–185.
63. Mirowsky J, Reynolds J. Age, depression, and attrition in the National Survey of Families and Households. *Sociolog Methods Res.* 2000;28: 476–504.
64. Schieman S, van Gundy K, Taylor J. The relationship between age and depressive symptoms: a test of competing explanatory and suppression influences. *J Aging Health.* 2002;14:260–285.
65. Blazer D, Swartz M, Woodbury M, Manton K, Hughes D, George L. Depressive symptoms and depressive diagnoses in a community population. *Arch Gen Psychiatr.* 1988;45:1078–1084.
66. Gonzalez H, Haan M, Hinton L. Acculturation and the prevalence of depression in older Mexican Americans: baseline results from the Sacramento Area Latino Study on Aging. *J Am Geriatr Soc.* 2001; 49:948–953.
67. Teresi J, Abrams R, Holmes D, Ramirez M, Shapiro C, Eimicke J. Influence of cognitive impairment, illness, gender, and African-American status on psychiatric ratings and staff recognition of depression. *Am J Geriatr Psychiatr.* 2002;10:506–514.
68. Blazer D, Hybels C, Simonsick E, Hanlon J. Marked differences in antidepressant use by race in an elderly community sample: 1986–1996. *Am J Psychiatr.* 2000;157:1089–1094.
69. White L, Blazer D, Fillenbaum G. Related health problems. In: Cornoni-Huntley J, Blazer D, Lafferty M, Everett D, Brock D, Farmer M, eds. *Established Populations for Epidemiologic Studies of the Elderly.* Bethesda, MD: National Institute on Aging; 1990:70–85.
70. Meller I, Fichter M, Schroppel H. Incidence of depression in octo- and nonagenerarians: results of an epidemiological follow-up community study. *Europ Arch Psychiatr Clin Neurosci.* 1996;246:93–99.
71. Robins L, Helzer J, Croughan J. Diagnostic Interview Schedule: its history, characteristics and validity. *Arch Gen Psychiatr.* 1981;38: 381–389.
72. Copeland J, Dewey M, Wood N, Searle R, Davidson I, McWilliam C. Range of mental illness among the elderly in the community: prevalence in the Liverpool area using the GMS-AGECAT package. *Br J Psychiatr.* 1987;150:815–823.
73. Palsson S, Ostling S, Skoog I. The incidence of first-onset depression in a population followed from the age of 70 to 85. *Psychol Med.* 2001; 31:1159–1168.
74. Eaton W, Kramer M, Anthony J, Dryman A, Shapiro S, Locke B. The incidence of specific DIS/DSM-III mental disorders: data from the NIMH epidemiologic catchment area program. *Acta Psychiatr Scand.* 1989;79:109–125.
75. Forsell V, Winblad B. Incidence of major depression in a very elderly population. *Intl J Geriatr Psychiatr.* 1999;14:368–372.
76. Koenig H, Meador K, Cohen H, Blazer DG. Depression in elderly hospitalized patients with medical illness. *Arch Intern Med.* 1988;148: 1929–1936.
77. Lyness J, Caine E, King D, Conwell Y, Duberstein P, Cox C. Depressive disorders and symptoms in older primary care patients. *Am J Geriatr Psychiatr.* 2002;10:275–282.
78. Oxman T, Barrett J, Barrett J, Gerber P. Symptomology of late-life minor depression among primary care patients. *Psychosomatics.* 1990; 31:174–180.
79. Schulberg H, Mulsant B, Schulz R, Rollman B, Houck P, Reynolds C. Characteristics and course of major depression in older primary care patients. *Intl J Psychiatr Med.* 1998;28:421–436.
80. Parmelee P, Katz I, Lawton M. Depression among institutionalized aged: assessment and prevalence estimation. *J Gerontol Med Sci.* 1989;44:M22–M29.
81. Payne J, Sheppard J, Steinberg M, et al. Incidence, prevalence and outcomes of depression in residents of a long-term care facility with dementia. *Intl J Geriatr Psychiatr.* 2002;17:247–253.

82. Teresi J, Abrams R, Holmes D, Ramirez M, Eimicke J. Prevalence of depression and depression recognition in nursing homes. *Soc Psychiatr Psychiatr Epidemiol.* 2001;36:613–629.
83. Brown M, Lapane K, Luisi A. The management of depression in older nursing home patients. *J Am Geriatr Soc.* 2002;50:69–76.
84. Yesavage J, Brink T, Rose T. Development and validation of a geriatric depression screening scale: a preliminary report. *J Psychiatr Res.* 1983;17:37–49.
85. Soon J, Levine M. Screening for depression in patients in long-term care facilities: a randomized controlled trial of physician response. *J Am Geriatr Soc.* 2002;50:1092–1099.
86. Post F. *The Significance of Affective Symptoms at Old Age.* London: Oxford University Press; 1962.
87. Murphy E. The prognosis of depression in old age. *Br J Psychiatr.* 1983;142:111–119.
88. Baldwin R, Jolley D. The prognosis of depression in old age. *Br J Psychiatr.* 1986;149:574–583.
89. Alexopoulos G, Meyers B, Young R, et al. Recovery in geriatric depression. *Arch Gen Psychiatr.* 1996;53:305–312.
90. Reynolds C, Frank E, Pereil J. Combined pharmacotherapy and psychotherapy in the acute and continuation treatment of elderly patients with recurrent major depression: a preliminary report. *Am J Psychiatr.* 1992;149:1687–1692.
91. Blazer D, Hughes D, George L. Age and impaired subjective support: predictors of depressive symptoms at one-year follow-up. *J Nervous Mental Dis.* 1992;180:172–178.
92. Brodaty J, Luscombe G, Peisah C, Anstey K, Andrews G. A 25-year longitudinal, comparison study of the outcome of depression. *Psychol Med.* 2001;31:1347–1359.
93. Keller M, Shapiro R, Lavori P, Wolfe N. Recovery in major depressive disorder: analyses with the life table. *Arch Gen Psychiatr.* 1982; 39:905–910.
94. Keller M, Shapiro R, Lavori P, Wolfe N. Relapse in major depressive disorder: analysis with the life table. *Arch Gen Psychiatr.* 1982;39: 911–915.
95. Bosworth H, McQuoid D, George L, Steffens D. Time-to-remission from geriatric depression. *Am J Geriatr Psychiatr.* 2002;10:551–559.
96. Morley J, Kraenzle D. Causes of weight loss in a community nursing home. *J Am Geriatr Soc.* 1994;42:583–585.
97. Frasure-Smith N, Lesperance F, Talajic M. Depression following myocardial infarction. Impact on 6-month survival. *JAMA.* 1993;270: 1819–1825.
98. Romanelli J, Fauerbach J, Buch D, Ziegelstein R. The significance of depression in older patients after myocardial infarction. *J Am Geriatr Soc.* 2002;50:817–822.
99. Williams S, Kasl S, Heiat A, Abramson J, Krumholz H, Vaccarino V. Depression and risk of heart failure among the elderly: a prospective community-based study. *Psychosomatic Med.* 2002;64:6–12.
100. McGuire L, Kiecolt-Glaser J, Glaser R. Depressive symptoms and lymphocyte proliferation in older adults. *J Abnorm Psychol.* 2002;111: 192–197.
101. Robbins J, Hirsch C, Whitmer R, Cauley J, Harris T. The association of bone mineral density and depression in an older population. *J Am Geriatr Soc.* 2001;49:732–736.
102. Lyles K. Osteoporosis and depression: shedding more light upon a complex relationship. *J Am Geriatr Soc.* 2001;49:827–828.
103. Han B. Depressive symptoms and self-rated health in community-dwelling older adults: a longitudinal study. *J Am Geriatr Soc.* 2002; 50:1549–1556.
104. Whyte E, Pollock BG, Wagner W, et al. Influence of serotonin transporter-linked region polymorphism on platelet activation in geriatric depression. *Am J Psychiatr.* 2001;158:2074–2076.
105. Galanos A, Pieper C, Cornoni-Huntley J. Nutrition and function: is there a relationship between body mass index and the functional capabilities of community-dwelling elderly? *J Am Geriatr Soc.* 1994; 42:368–373.
106. Fried L, Walston J. Frailty and failure to thrive. In: Hazzard W, Blass J, Ettinger W, Halter J, Ouslander J, eds. *Principles of Geriatric Medicine and Gerontology.* New York: McGraw-Hill; 1999:1387–1402.
107. Michelson D, Stratakis C, Hill L. Bone mineral density in women with depression. *N Engl J Med.* 1996;335:1176–1181.
108. Schweiger U, Deuschle M, Korner A. Low lumbar bone mineral density in patients with major depression. *Am J Psychiatr.* 1994;151: 1691–1695.
109. Hays J, Saunders W, Flint E, Blazer D. Social support and depression as risk factors for loss of physical function in late life. *Aging Mental Health.* 1997;1:209–220.
110. Bruce M. Depression and disability in late life: directions for future research. *Am J Geriatr Psychiatr.* 2001;9:102–112.
111. Bruce M, Leaf P. Psychiatric disorders and 15-month mortality in a community sample of older adults. *Am J Publ Health.* 1989;79:727–730.
112. Zeiss A, Lewinsohn P, Rohde P. Relationship of physical disease and functional impairment to depression in older people. *Psychol Aging.* 1996;11:572–581.
113. Penninx B, Leveille S, Ferrucci L, van Eijk J, Guralnik J. Exploring the effect of depression on physical disability: longitudinal evidence from the Established Populations for Epidemiologic Studies of the Elderly. *Am J Publ Health.* 1999;89:1346–1352.
114. Kennedy G, Kelman H, Thomas C. The emergence of depressive symptoms in late life: the importance of declining health and increasing disability. *J Commun Health.* 1990;15:93–104.
115. Roberts R, Kaplan G, Shema S. Does growing old increase the risk for depression? *Am J Psychiatr.* 1997;154:1384–1390.
116. Blazer D. Impact of late-life depression on the social network. *Am J Psychiatr.* 1983;140:162–166.
117. Lenze E, Rogers J, Martire L, et al. The association of late-life depression and anxiety with physical disability. *Am J Geriatr Psychiatr.* 2001;9:113–135.
118. Pohjasvaara T, Vataja R, Leppavuori A, Kaste M, Erkinjuntti T. Depression is an independent predictor of poor long-term functional outcome post-stroke. *Europ J Neurol.* 2001;8:315–319.
119. Sinclair P, Lyness J, King D, Cox C, Caine E. Depression and self-reported functional status in older primary care patients. *Am J Psychiatr.* 2001;158:416–419.
120. Hays J, Steffens D, Flint E, Bosworth H, George L. Does social support buffer functional decline in elderly patients with unipolar depression? *Am J Psychiatr.* 2001;158:1850–1855.
121. Li Y, Meyer J, Thornby J. Longitudinal follow-up of depressive symptoms among normal versus cognitively impaired elderly. *Intl J Geriatr Psychiatr.* 2001;16:718–727.
122. Lyketsos C, Baker L, Warren A, Steele C, Brandt J, Steinberg M. Major and minor depression in Alzheimer's disease: prevalence and impact. *J Neuropsychiatr Clin Neurosci.* 1997;9:556–561.
123. Lyketsos C, Steele C, Galik E, et al. Physical aggression in dementia patients and its relationship to depression. *Am J Psychiatr.* 1999;156: 66–71.
124. Gonzales-Salvador T, Aragano C, Lyketsos C, Barba A. The stress and psychological morbidity of the Alzheimer patient caregiver. *Intl J Geriatr Psychiatr.* 1999;14:701–710.
125. Geerlings S, Beekman A, Beeg D, Twisk J, van Tilburg W. Duration and severity of depression predict mortality in older adults in the community. *Psychol Med.* 2002;32:609–618.
126. Henderson A, Korten A, Jacomb P, et al. The course of depression in the elderly: a longitudinal community based study in Australia. *Psychol Med.* 1997;27:119–129.
127. Takeida K, Nishi M, Miyake H. Zung's depression scale as a predictor of death in elderly people: a cohort study in Hokkaido, Japan. *J Epidemiol.* 1999;9:240–244.
128. Penninx B, Geerlings S, Deeg D, van Eijk J, van Tilling W, Beekman A. Minor and major depression and the risk of death in older persons. *Arch Gen Psychiatr.* 2001;56:889–895.
129. Schulz R, Beach S, Ives D. Association between depression and mortality in older adults: The Cardiovascular Health Study. *Arch Intl Med.* 2000;160:1761–1768.
130. Fredman L, Schoenbach V, Kaplan B, Blazer D, James S. The association between depressive symptoms and mortality among older participants in the Epidemiologic Catchment Area-Piedmont Health Survey. *J Gerontol Soc Sci.* 1989;44:S149–S156.
131. Thomas C, Kelman H, Kennedy G. Depressive symptoms and mortality in elderly persons. *J Gerontol.* 1992;24:580–587.
132. Blazer D, Hybels C, Pieper C. The association of depression and mortality in elderly persons: a case for multiple independent pathways. *J Gerontol Med Sci.* 2001;56A:M505–M509.

133. Takeshita J, Masaki K, Ahmed I, et al. Are depressive symptoms a risk factor for mortality in elderly Japanese American men?: The Honolulu Asia Aging Study. *Am J Psychiatr.* 2002;159:1127–1132.
134. Whooley M, Browner W. Association between depressive symptoms and mortality in older women. Study of Osteoporotic Fractures Research Group. *Arch Intern Med.* 1999;158:2129–2135.
135. Saz P, Dewey M. Depression, depressive symptoms and mortality in persons aged 65 and over living in the community: a systematic review of the literature. *Intl J Geriatr Psychiatr.* 2001;16:622–630.
136. Hybels C, Pieper C, Blazer D. Gender differences in the relationship between subthreshold depression and mortality in a community sample of older adults. *Am J Geriatr Psychiatr.* 2002;10:283–291.
137. NCHS. *Death Rates for 72 Selected Causes by 5-year Age Groups, Race, and Sex: United States, 1979–1998.* Washington, DC: National Center for Health Statistics; 2001.
138. Conwell Y, Duberstein P, Caine E. Risk factors for suicide in later life. *Biol Psychiatr.* 2002;52:193–204.
139. Murphy GE, Wetzel RD. Suicide risk by birth cohort in the United States, 1949 to 1974. *Arch Gen Psychiatr.* 1980;37:519–523.
140. Blazer D, Bachar J, Manton K. Suicide in late life: review and commentary. *J Am Geriatr Soc.* 1986;34:519–526.
141. Raern M, Reneson B, Allebeck P, et al. Mental disorder in elderly suicides: a case-control study. *Am J Psychiatr.* 2002;159:450–455.
142. Conwell Y, Lyness J, Duberstein P, Cox C, Seidlitz L, DiGiorgio A. Completed suicide among older patients in primary care practices: a controlled study. *J Am Geriatr Soc.* 2000;48:23–29.
143. Turvey C, Conwell Y, Jones M, et al. Risk factors for late-life suicide: a prospective, community-based study. *Am J Geriatr Psychiatr.* 2002; 10:398–406.
144. De Leo D, Padoani W, Scocco P, et al. Attempted and completed suicide in older subjects: results from the WHO/EURO Multicentre study of suicidal behaviour. *Intl J Geriatr Psychiatr.* 2001;16:300–310.
145. Parkin D, Stengel E. Incidence of suicidal attempts in an urban community. *Br Med J.* 1965;2:133–138.
146. Huang B, Comoni-Huntley J, Hays J, Huntley R, Galanos A, Blazer D. Impact of depressive symptoms on hospitalization risk in community-dwelling older persons. *J Am Geriatr Soc.* 2000;48:1279–1284.
147. Unutzer J, Patrick D, Simon G, et al. Depressive symptoms and the cost of health services in HMO patients 65+ years and older. *JAMA.* 1997;277:1618–1623.
148. Luber M, Meyers B, Williams-Russo P, et al. Depression and service utilization in elderly primary care patients. *Am J Geriatr Psychiatr.* 2001;9:169–176.
149. Fischer L, Wei F, Rolnick S, et al. Geriatric depression, antidepressant treatment, and healthcare utilization in a health maintenance organization. *Am J Geriatr Soc.* 2002;50:307–312.
150. Starkstein S, Preziosi T, Bolduck P, Robinson R. Depression in Parkinson's disease. *J Nervous Mental Disord.* 1990;178:27–31.
151. Parmelee P, Katz I, Lawton M. The relation of pain to depression among institutionalized aged. *J Gerontol.* 1991;46:15–21.
152. Endberg S, Sereika S, Weber E, Engberg R, McDowell B, Reynolds C. Prevalence and recognition of depressive symptoms among homebound older adults with urinary incontinence. *J Geriatr Psychiatr Neurol.* 2001;14:130–139.
153. Gilman S, Abraham H. A longitudinal study of the order of onset of alcohol dependence and major depression. *Drug Alcohol Depend.* 2001;63:277–286.
154. Jorm A. Association of hypotension with positive and negative affect and depressive symptoms in the elderly. *Br J Psychiatr.* 2001;178:553–555.
155. Holsinger T, Steffens D, Phillips C, et al. Head injury in early adulthood and the lifetime risk of depression. *Arch Gen Psychiatr.* 2002; 59:17–22.
156. Barondes S. *Mood Genes: Hunting for Origins of Mania and Depression.* New York: WH Freeman; 1998.
157. Gatz M, Pedersen N, Plomin R, Nesselroade J, McCleam G. Importance of shared genes and shared environments for symptoms of depression in older adults. *J Abnorm Psychol.* 1992;101:701–708.
158. Hopkinson G. A genetic study of affective illness in patients over 50. *Br J Psychiatr.* 1964;110:244–252.
159. Blazer D, Burchette B, Fillenbaum G. APOE E4 and low cholesterol as risks for depression in a biracial elderly community sample. *Am J Geriatr Psychiatr.* 2002;10:515–520.
160. Nebes R, Vora I, Melzer C, et al. Relationship of deep white matter hyperintensities and apolipoprotein E genotype to depressive symptoms in older adults without clinical depression. *Am J Psychiatr.* 2001;158:878–884.
161. Desmond D, Moroney J, Lynch T, Chan S, Chin S, Mohr J. The natural history of CADASIL: a pooled analysis of previously published cases. *Stroke.* 1999;30:1230–1233.
162. Krishnan K. Biological risk factors in late life depression. *Biol Psychiatr.* 2002;52:185–192.
163. Krishnan K, Goli V, Ellinwood E, Blazer D, Nemeroff C. Leukoencephalopathy in patients diagnosed as major depressive. *Biol Psychiatr.* 1988;23:519–522.
164. Coffey C, Figiel G, Djang W. Subcortical hyperintensity on magnetic resonance imaging: a comparison of normal and depressed elderly subjects. *Am J Psychiatr.* 1990;147:187–189.
165. Kumar A, Mintz J, Bilker W, Gottlieb G. Autonomous neurobiological pathways to late-life depressive disorders: clinical and pathophysiological implications. *Neuropsychopharmacology.* 2002;26: 229–236.
166. Kumar A, Thomas A, Lavretsky H, et al. Frontal white matter biochemical abnormalities in late-life major depression detected with proton magnetic resonance spectroscopy. *Am J Psychiatr.* 2002;159: 630–636.
167. George M, Ketter T, Post R. Prefrontal cortex dysfunction in clinical depression. *Depression.* 1994;2:59–72.
168. Krishnan K, McDonald W, Doraiswamy P, et al. Neuroanatomical substrates of depression in the elderly. *Europ Arch Psychiatr Clin Neurosci.* 1993;243:41–46.
169. Krishnan K, McDonald W, Escalona P, et al. Magnetic imaging of the caudate nuclei in depression: preliminary observation. *Arch Gen Psychiatr.* 1992;49:553–557.
170. Husain M, McDonald W, Doraiswamy P, et al. A magnetic resonance imaging study of putamen nuclei in major depression. *Psychiatr Res.* 1991;40:95–99.
171. Lai T, Payne M, Byrum C, Steffens D, Krishnan K. Reduction of orbital fronal cortex volume in geriatric depression. *Biol Psychiatr.* 2000;48:971–975.
172. Steffens D, Payne M, Greenberg D, et al. Hippocampal volume and incident dementia in geriatric depression. *Am J Geriatr Psychiatr.* 2002; 10:62–71.
173. Nemeroff C, Knight D, Krishnan K, Slotkin T, Bissette G, Blazer D. Marked reduction in the number of platelet tritiated imipramine binding sites in geriatric depression. *Arch Gen Psychiatr.* 1988;45:919–923.
174. Tsukada H, Kakiuchi T, Nishiyama S, Ohba H, Harada N. Effects of aging on 5-HT(1A) receptors and their functional response to 5-HT(1A) agonist in the living brain: PET study with [carbonyl-(11)C]WAY-100635 in conscious monkeys. *Synapse.* 2001;42:242–251.
175. Davis K, David B, Mathe A, Mohs R, Rothpearl A. Age and the dexamethasone supression test in depression. *Am J Psychiatr.* 1984;141: 872–874.
176. Arborelius L, Owens M, Plotsky P, Nemeroff C. The role of corticotropin-releasing factor in depression and anxiety disorders. *J Endocrinol.* 1999;160:1–12.
177. Luisi S, Tonetti A, Bernardi F, et al. Effect of acute corticotropin releasing factor on pituitary-adrenocortical responsiveness in elderly women and men. *J Endocrinol Invest.* 1998;21:449–453.
178. Yaffe K, Ettinger B, Pressman A. Neuropsychiatric function and dehydroepiandrosterone sulfate in elderly women: a prospective study. *Biol Psychiatr.* 1998;43:694–700.
179. Seidman S, Araujo A, Roose S, et al. Low testosterone levels in elderly men with dysthymic disorder. *Am J Psychiatr.* 2002;159:456–459.
180. Seidman S, Spatz E, Rizzo C, Roose S. Testosterone replacement therapy for hypogonadal men with major depresive disorder: a randomized, placebo-controlled clinical trial. *J Clin Psychiatr.* 2001;62: 406–412.
181. Schwartz S, Feller A, Perlmuter L. Postprandial systolic blood pressure and subsyndromal depression. *Exp Aging Res.* 2001;27:309–318.
182. Sherwin B, Gelfand M. Sex steroids and affect in the surgical menopause: a double-blind, cross-over study. *Psychoneuroendocrinology.* 1985;10:325–335.
183. Seligman MEP. Learned helplessness. *Annu Rev Med.* 1972;23:407.
184. Seligman M, Maier S. Failure to escape traumatic shock. *J Exp Psychol.* 1967;74:1–15.

185. Kraaij V, de Wilde E. Negative life events and depressive symptoms in the elderly: a life span perspective. *Aging Mental Health*. 2001;5: 84–91.
186. Kraaij V, Arensman E, Spinhoven P. Negative life events and depression in elderly persons: a meta-analysis. *J Gerontol Psychol Soc Sci*. 2002;57B:P87–P94.
187. Brilman E, Ormel J. Life events, difficulties and onset of depressive episodes in later life. *Psychol Med*. 2001;31:859–869.
188. Cath S. Discussion notes. In: Berezin N, Cath S, eds. *Geriatric Psychiatry*. New York: International Universities Press; 1965.
189. Baltes P, Baltes M. *Successful Aging: Perspectives from the Behavioral Sciences*. Cambridge: Cambridge University Press; 1990.
190. Beck AT. *Depression*. New York: Harper & Row; 1967.
191. Devenand D, Kim M, Paykina N, Sackeim H. Adverse life events in elderly patients with major depression or dysthymia and in healthy-control subjects. *Am J Geriatr Psychiatr*. 2002;10:265–274.
192. Beck A. Cognitive model of depression. *J Cog Psychother*. 1987;1: 2–27.
193. Mazure C, Maciejewski P, Jacobs S, Bruce M. Stressful life events interacting with cognitive/personality styles to predict late-onset major depression. *Am J Geriatr Psychiatr*. 2002;10:297–304.
194. Chi I, Chou K. Social support and depression among elderly Chinese people in Hong Kong. *Intl J Aging Human Devel*. 2001;52:231–252.
195. George L, Blazer D, Hughes D, Fowler N. Social support and the outcome of major depression. *Br J Psychiatr*. 1989;154:478–485.
196. Livingston G, Manela M, Katona C. Depression and other psychiatric morbidity in carers of elderly people living at home. *Br Med J*. 1996; 312:153–156.
197. Clipp E, George L. Psychotropic drug use among caregivers of patients with dementia. *J Am Geriatr Soc*. 1990;38:227–235.
198. Beeson R, Horton-Deutsch S, Farran C, Neurndorfer M. Loneliness and depression in caregivers of persons with Alzheimer's disease or related disorders. *Issues Mental Health Nurs*. 2000;21:779–906.
199. Lewinsohn P, Rohde P, Seeley J, Fischer S. Age and depression: unique and shared effects. *Psychol Aging*. 1989;6:247–260.
200. Cumming E, Henry W. *Growing Old: The Process of Disengagement*. New York: Basic Books; 1961.
201. Fonda S, Wallace R, Herzog A. Changes in driving patterns and worsening depressive symptoms among older adults. *J Gerontol Psychol Soc Sci*. 2001;56B:S343–S351.
202. Braam A, van den Eeden P, Prince M, et al. Religion as a cross-cultural determinant of depression in elderly Europeans: results from the EURODEP collaboration. *Psychol Med*. 2001;31:803–814.
203. Koenig H, Cohen H, Blazer D, et al. Religious coping and depression in elderly hospitalized medically ill men. *Am J Psychiatr*. 1992;149: 1693–1700.
204. Koenig H, Cohen H, Blazer D, Kudler H, Krishnan K, Sibert T. Cognitive symptoms of depression and religious coping in elderly medical patients. *Psychosomatics*. 1995;36:369–375.
205. Koenig H, Meador K, Cohen H, Blazer D. Screening for depression in hospitalized elderly medical patients: taking a closer look. *J Am Geriatr Soc*. 1992;40:1013–1017.
206. Callahan C, Hendrie H, Nienaber N, Tierney W. Suicidal ideation among older primary care patients. *J Am Geriatr Soc*. 1996;44:1205–1209.
207. Callahan C, Nienaber N, Hendrie H, Tierney W. Depression of elderly outpatients: primary care physicians attitudes and practice patterns. *J Gen Intern Med*. 1992;7:26–31.
208. Callahan C, Hendrie H, Tierney W. The recognition and treatment of late-life depression: a view from primary care. *Intl J Psychiatr Med*. 1996;26:173–175.
209. Callahan C, Hendrie H, Dittus R, Brater D, Hui S, Tierney W. Improving treatment of late life depression in primary care: a randomized clinical trial. *J Am Geriatr Soc*. 1994;42:839–846.
210. Folstein M, Folstein S, McHugh P. Mini-Mental State: a practical method for grading the cognitive state of patients for the clinician. *J Psychiatr Res*. 1975;12:189–198.
211. Schoenfeld D, Malmrose L, Blazer D, Gold D, Seeman T. Self-rated health and mortality in the high-functioning elderly—a closer look at healthy individuals: MacArthur Field Study of Successful Aging. *J Gerontol Med Sci*. 1994;49A:M109–M115.
212. Branch L, Meyers A. Assessing physical function in the elderly. *Clin Geriatr Med*. 1987;3:29–51.

213. Fillenbaum G. *Multidimensional Functional Assessment of Older Adults: The Duke Older Americans Resources and Services Procedures*. Hillsdale, NJ: Erlbaum; 1988.
214. Blazer D. Social support and mortality in an elderly community population. *Am J Epidemiol*. 1982;115:684–694.
215. Forlenza O, Junior A, Hirala E, Ferreira R. Antidepressant efficacy of sertraline and imipramine for the treatment of major depression in elderly outpatients. *Sao Paolo Med J*. 2000;118:99–104.
216. Kyle C, Petersen H, Overo K. Comparison of the tolerability and efficacy of citalopram and amitriptyline in elderly depressed patients treated in general practice. *Depress Anxiety*. 1998;8:147–153.
217. Mulsant B, Pollock B, Nebes R, et al. A twelve-week, double-blind, randomized comparison of nortriptyline and paroxetine in older depressed inpatients and outpatients. *Am J Geriatr Psychiatr*. 2001; 9:406–414.
218. Salloway S, Boyle P, Correia S, et al. The relationship of MRI subcortical hyperintensities to treatment response in a trial of sertraline in geriatric depressed outpatients. *Am J Geriatr Psychiatr*. 2002;10: 107–111.
219. Taragano F, Allegri R, Vicario A, Bagnatti P, Lyketsos C. A double-blind, randomized clinical trial assessing the efficacy and safety of augmenting standard antidepressant therapy with nimodipine in the treatment of 'vascular depression.' *Intl J Geriatr Psychiatr*. 2001;16: 254–260.
220. Simpson S, Balwin R, Burns A, Jackson A. Regional cerebral volume measurements in late-life depression: relationship to clinical correlates, neuropschological impairment and response to treatment. *Intl J Geriatr Psychiatr*. 2001;16:469–476.
221. Reifler B, Teri L, Raskind M, Veith R, Barnes R. Double-blind trial of imipramine in Alzheimer's disease patients with and without depression. *Am J Psychiatr*. 1989;146:45–49.
222. Lyketsos C, Sheppard J, Steele C, et al. A randomized placebo-controlled, double-blind, clinical trial of sertraline in the treatment of depression complicating Alzheimer disease: initial results from the Depression in Alzheimer Disease Study (DIADS). *Am J Psychiatr*. 2000;157:1686–1689.
223. Nyth A, Gottfries C, Lyby K, et al. A controlled multicenter clinical study of citalopram and placebo in elderly depressed patients with and without concomitant dementia. *Acta Psychiatr Scand*. 1992;86: 138–145.
224. Ackerman D, Greenland S, Bystritsky A, Small G. Side effects and time course of response in a placebo-controlled trial of fluoxetine for the treatment of geriatric depression. *J Clin Psychopharmacol*. 2000; 20:658–665.
225. Williams J, Barrett J, Oxman T, et al. Treatment of dysthymia and minor depression in primary care: a randomized controlled trial in older adults. *JAMA*. 2000;284:1519–1526.
226. Oxman T, Sungupta A. Treatment of minor depression. *Am J Geriatr Psychiatr*. 2002;10:256–264.
227. Group HDTS. Effect of hypericum perforatum (St. John's wort) in major depressive disorder: a randomized controlled trial. *JAMA*. 2002; 287:1807–1814.
228. Feighner J, Cohn J. Double-blind comparative trials of fluoxetine and doxepin in geriatric patients with major depression. *J Clin Psychiatr*. 1985;46:20–25.
229. Cohn C, Shrivastava R, Mendels J. Double-blind multicenter comparison of sertraline and amitriptyline in elderly depressed patients. *J Clin Psychiatr*. 1990;51:28–33.
230. Katona C, Hunder B, Bray J. A double-blind comparison of paroxetine and imipramine in the treatment of depression with dementia. *Intl J Geriatr Psychiatr*. 1998;13:100–180.
231. Nyth A, Gottfried C, Lyby K. A controlled multicenter clinical study of citalopram and placebo in elderly depressed patients with and without concomitant dementia. *Acta Psychiatr Scand*. 1992;86:138–145.
232. Rahman M, Akhton M, Savia N, Kellet J, Ashford J. A double-blind, randomized comparison of fluvoxamine and dothiepin in the treatment of depression in the elderly. *Br J Clin Pract*. 1991;45:255–258.
233. Mahapatra S, Hackett D. A randomized, double-blind, paralled-group comparison of venlafaxine and dothiepin in geriatric patients with major depression. *Intl J Clin Pract*. 1997;51:209–213.
234. Hoyberg O, Maragakis B, Mullin J, et al. A double-blind multicentre comparison of mirtazapine and amitriptyline in elderly depressed patients. *Acta Psychiatr Scand*. 1996;93:184–190.

235. Schatzberg A, Kremer C, Rodrigues H, Murphy G. Double-blind, randomized comparison of mirtazapine and paroxetine in elderly depressed patients. *Am J Geriatr Psychiatr.* 2002;10:541–550.
236. Branconnier R, Cole J, Ghazviain S, Spera K, Oxenkrug O. Clinical pharmacology of buproprion and imipramine in elderly depressives. *J Clin Psychiatr.* 1983;44:130–133.
237. Weihs K, Settle E, Batey S, Houser T, Donahue R, Ascher J. Buproprion sustained release versus paroxetine for the treatment of depression in the elderly. *J Clin Psychiatr.* 2001;61:196–202.
238. Baldwin D, Hawley C, Mellors K, Group C-S. A randomized, double-blind controlled comparison of nefazodone and paroxetine in the treatment of depression: safety, tolerability and efficacy in continuation phase treatment. *J Psychopharmacol.* 2001;15:161–165.
239. Alexopoulos G, Katz I, Reynolds C, Carpenter D, Docherty J. The Expert Consensus Guideline Series: pharmacotherapy of depressive disorders in older patients. *Postgrad Med.* (special issue) 2001:1–86.
240. Schneider L, Small G, Clary C. Estrogen replacement therapy and antidepressant response to sertraline in older depressed women. *Am J Geriatr Psychiatr.* 2001;9:393–399.
241. Morales A, Nolan J, Nelson J, Yen S. Effects of replacement dose of dehydroepiandrosterone in men and women of advancing age. *J Clin Endocrinol Metab.* 1994;78:1360–1367.
242. Pollock B. Geriatric psychiatry: psychopharmacology: general principles. In: Sadock B, Sadock V, eds. *Kaplan & Sadock's Comprehensive Textbook of Psychiatry/VII.* Baltimore, MD: Williams and Wilkins; 2000:3086–3090.
243. Greenblatt D, van Moltke L, Harmatz J, Shader R. Drug interactions with newer antidepressants: role of human cytochromes P450. *J Clin Psychiatr.* 1998;59(suppl 15):19–27.
244. Kirby D, Harigan S, Ames D. Hyponatraemia in elderly psychiatric patients treated with selective serotonin reuptake inhibitors and venlafaxine: a retrospective controlled study in an inpatient unit. *Intl J Geriatr Psychiatr.* 2002;17:231–237.
245. Thapa P, Gideon P, Cost T, Milam A, Ray W. Antidepressants and the risk of falls among nursing home residents. *N Engl J Med.* 1998;339:918–920.
246. Gillman P. The serotonin syndrome and its treatment. *J Psychopharmacol.* 1999;13:100–109.
247. de Abajo F, Rodriguez L, Montero D. Association between selective serotonin reuptake inhibitors and upper gastrointestinal bleeding: population based case-control study. *Br Med J.* 1999;319:1106–1109.
248. Flint A, Rifat S. The treatment of psychotic depression in later life: a comparison of pharmacotherapy and ECT. *J Geriatr Psychiatr.* 1998;13:23–28.
249. Godber C, Rosenvinge H, Wilkinson D, Smithes J. Depression in old age: prognosis after ECT. *Intl J Geriatr Psychiatr.* 1987;2:19–24.
250. Benbow S. The use of electroconvulsive therapy in old-age psychiatry. *Intl J Geriatr Psychiatr.* 1987;2:25–30.
251. Fraser R, Glass I. Unilateral and bilateral ECT in elderly patients. *Acta Psychiatr Scand.* 1980;62:13–31.
252. Benbow S. The role of electroconvulsive therapy in the treatment of depressive illness in old age. *Br J Psychiatr.* 1989;155:147–152.
253. Cattan R, Barry P, Mead G, Reefe W, Gay A. Electroconvulsive therapy in octogenerians. *J Am Geriatr Soc.* 1990;38:753–758.
254. O'Conner M, Knapp R, Husain M, et al. The influence of age on the response of major depression to electroconvulsive therapy: a C.O.R.E. Report. *Am J Geriatr Psychiatr.* 2001;9:382–390.
255. McNamara B, Ray J, Arthurs O, Boniface S. Transcranial magnetic stimulation for depression and other psychiatric disorders. *Psychol Med.* 2001;31:1141–1146.
256. Dannon P, Dolberg O, Schreiber S, Grunhaus L. Three and six-month outcome following courses of either ECT or rTMS in a population of severely depressed individuals—preliminary report. *Biol Psychiatr.* 2002;51:687–690.
257. Moser D, Jorge R, Manes F, Paradiso S, Benjamin M, Robinson R. Improved exective functioning following repetitive transcranial magnetic stimulation. *Neurology.* 2002;58:1288–1290.
258. Camacho T, Roberts R, Lazarus N, Kaplan G, Cohen R. Physical activity and depression: evidence from the Alameda County Study. *Am J Epidemiol.* 1991;134:220–231.
259. Blumenthal J, Babyak M, Moore K, et al. Effects of exercise training on older patients with major depression. *Arch Intern Med.* 1999;159:2349–2356.

260. Singh N, Clements K, Kingh M. The efficacy of exercise as a long-term antidepressant in elderly subjects: a randomized controlled trial. *J Gerontol Med Sci.* 2001;56A:M497–M504.
261. Sumaya I, Rienzi B, Beegan J, Moss D. Bright light treatment decreases depression in institutionalized older adults: a placebo-controlled crossover study. *J Gerontol Med Sci.* 2001;56A:M356–M360.
262. Walker D, Clarke M. Cognitive behavioral psychotherapy: a comparison between younger and older adults in two inner city mental health teams. *Aging Mental Health* 2001;5:197–199.
263. Alvidrez J, Arean P. Physician willingness to refer older depressed patients for psychotherapy. *Intl J Psychiatr Med.* 2002;32:21–35.
264. Landreville P, Landry J, Baillargeon L, Guerette A, Matteau E. Older adults' acceptance of psychological and pharmacological treatments for depression. *J Gerontol Psychol Sci.* 2001;56B:P285–P291.
265. Thompson L, Gallagher D, Breckenridge J. Comparative effectiveness of psychotherapies for depressed elders. *J Consult Clin Psychol.* 1987;55:385–390.
266. Karel M, Hinrichsen G. Treatment of depression in late life: psychotherapeutic interventions. *Clin Psychol Rev.* 2000;20:707–729.
267. Lynch T, Aspnes A. Individual and group psychotherapy. In: Blazer D, Steffens D, Busse E, eds. *American Psychiatric Press Textbook of Geriatric Psychiatry.* Washington, DC: American Psychiatric Press. In Press.
268. Teasdale J, Moore R, Hayhurst H. Metacognitive awareness and prevention of relapse in depression: empirical evidence. *J Consult Clin Psychol.* 2002;70:275–287.
269. Thompson L, Coon D, Gallagher-Thompson D. Comparision of desipramine and cognitive/behavioral therapy in the treatment of elderly outpatients with mild-to-moderate depression. *Am J Geriatr Psychiatr.* 2001;9:225–240.
270. Frank E, Frank N, Cornes C. Interpersonal psychotherapy in the treatment of late life depression. In: Klerman G, Weissman M, eds. *New Applications of Interpersonal Psychotherapy.* Washington, DC: American Psychiatric Press; 1993.
271. Frank E, Spanier C. Interpersonal psychotherapy for depression: overview, clinical efficacy, and future directions. *Clin Psychol Sci Pract.* 1995;2:349–369.
272. Reynolds C, Frank E, Perel J, et al. Nortriptyline and interpersonal psychotherapy as maintenance therapies for recurrent major depression: a randomized controlled trial in patients older than 59 years. *JAMA.* 1999;281:39–45.
273. Reynolds C, Frank E, Dew M, et al. Treatment of 70(+)-year olds with recurrent major depression. Excellent short-term but brittle long-term response. *Am J Geriatr Psychiatr.* 1999;7:64–69.
274. Myers W. *Dynamic Therapy of the Older Patient.* New York: Aronson; 1984.
275. Gallagher D, Thompson L. Treatment of major depressive disorder in older outpatients with brief psychotherapies. *Psychother Theory Res Prac.* 1982;19:482–490.
276. Fry P. Structured and unstructured reminiscence training and depression among the elderly. *Clin Gerontol.* 1983;1:15–37.
277. Perrotta P, Meacham J. Can a reminiscing intervention alter depression: nature, prevalence, and relationship to treatment response. *Intl J Aging Hum Dev.* 1982;14:23–30.
278. Burns D. *Feeling Good.* New York: New American Library; 1980.
279. Scogin F, McElreath L. Efficacy of psychosocial treatments for geriatric depression: a quantitative review. *J Consult Clin Psychol.* 1994;57:69–73.
280. Scogin F, Hamblin D, Beutler L. Bibliotherapy for depressed older adults: a self-help alternative. *Gerontologist.* 1987;27:383–387.
281. Scogin F, Jamison C, Davis N. Two-year follow-up of bibliotherapy for depression in older adults. *J Consult Clin Psychol.* 1990;58:665–667.
282. Jamison C, Scogin F. The outcome of cognitive bibliotherapy with depressed adults. *J Consult Clin Psychol.* 1995;63:644–650.
283. Saiger G. Group psychotherapy with older adults. *Psychiatry.* 2001;64:132–145.
284. Rokke P, Tomhave J, Jocic Z. The role of client choice and target selection in self-management therapy for depression in older adults. *Psychol Aging.* 1999;14:155–169.
285. Jarvik L, Mintz J, Steuer J. Treating geriatric depression: a 26-week interim analysis. *J Am Geriatr Soc.* 1982;30:713–717.

286. Steuer J. Cognitive-behavioral and psychodynamic group psychotherapy in treatment of geriatric depression. *J Consult Clin Psychol.* 1984; 52:180–189.
287. Lynch T, Morse J, Mendelson T. Dialectical behavior therapy in depressed elderly. *Am J Geriatr Psychiatr.* In press.
288. Lenze E, Dew M, Mazumba S, et al. Combined pharmacological and psychotherapy as maintenance treatment for late-life depression: effects on social adjustment. *Am J Psychiatr.* 2002;159:466–468.
289. Mulsant B, Alexopoulos G, Reynolds CR, et al. Pharmacological treatment of depression in older primary care patients: the PROSPECT algorithm. *Intl J Geriatr Psychiatr.* 2001;16:585–592.
290. Szanto K, Mulsant B, Houck P, Miller M, Mazumdar S, Reynolds C. Treatment outcome in suicidal vs. non-suicidal elderly patients. *Am J Geriatr Psychiatr.* 2001;9:261–268.
291. Blazer D. Self-efficacy and depression in late life: a primary prevention proposal. *Aging Mental Health.* 2002;6:319–328.
292. Alexopoulos G. New concepts for prevention and treatment of late life depression. *Am J Psychiatr.* 2001;158:835–838.
293. Rybarczyk B, De Marco G, DeLa Cruz M, Lapidos S. Comparing mind-body wellness interventions for older adults with chronic illness: classroom versus home instruction. *Behav Med.* 1999;24: 181–190.
294. Reynolds III C, Charney D. Editorial: unmet needs in the diagnosis and treatment of mood disorders in late life. *Biol Psychiatr.* 2002; 52:146.
295. Putnam R. *Bowling Alone.* New York: Simon & Schuster; 2000.

Received September 27, 2002
Accepted October 4, 2002

[28]

Negative life events and depressive symptoms in the elderly: a life span perspective

V. KRAAIJ & E. J. DE WILDE

Leiden University, Leiden, the Netherlands

Abstract
This study suggests that negative life events may have long-term consequences for people's well-being. A community sample of 194 elderly people was interviewed by means of the Geriatric Depression Scale and the Negative Life Events Questionnaire. Depressed mood at old age was related to the reporting of negative socio-economic circumstances as well as emotional abuse and neglect during childhood, and to the reporting of negative socio-economic circumstances, sexual abuse, emotional abuse and neglect, relational stress and problem behaviour of significant others during (late) adulthood. Depression scores were especially high when subjects reported the experience of many events during adulthood and late adulthood. On top of this, the interaction effect between the number of negative life events experienced in childhood and adulthood indicated that there was a much stronger association between the number of negative life events experienced in adulthood and depressive symptoms in late life, for those who experienced more negative life events in childhood, than for those who did not. It is suggested that incorporating life histories into the diagnostic interview is advisable.

Introduction

Despite high prevalence rates, depression in the elderly is often not recognized or diagnosed properly and the elderly appear to be overlooked by psychiatry in this respect (Beekman et al., 1997a; Gurland & Cross, 1982; Koenig et al., 1995; Ruegg et al., 1988). In the general population, approximately 10–15% of the elderly suffer from depressive complaints warranting intervention (Beekman et al., 1997b; Cappeliez, 1988; Gurland & Cross, 1982; van Marwijk, 1995; O'Hara et al., 1985; Ruegg et al., 1988). When using the stricter diagnostic criteria of a depressive disorder (e.g. DSM criteria), studies show prevalence rates of 0.8–8% (Beekman et al., 1997b; Blazer et al., 1987; Cappeliez, 1988; Gurland & Cross, 1982; Livingston & Hinchliffe, 1993; van Marwijk, 1995; O'Hara et al., 1985; Ruegg et al., 1988). Certain specific groups show even higher prevalence rates: about 30–40% of elderly psychiatric inpatients have a major mood disorder (Ruegg et al., 1988).

A substantial amount of research has been carried out on risk factors of depression in the elderly. For instance, female gender (de Beer & de Lange, 1993; Green et al., 1992; Katona, 1993), low socio-economic status (de Beer & de Lange, 1993; Katona, 1993; O'Hara et al., 1985), living alone (Beekman et al., 1995; de Beer & de Lange, 1993; Katona, 1993; O'Hara et al., 1985; van Ojen, 1995), low levels of social support (de Beer & de Lange, 1993; Green et al., 1992; Katona, 1993), a history of depressive episodes (Beekman et al., 1995; de Beer & de Lange, 1993; van Ojen, 1995), illness and disabilities (Beekman et al., 1995; de Beer & de Lange, 1993; Katona, 1993; van Ojen, 1995) and cognitive impairments (Beekman et al., 1995; de Beer & de Lange, 1993; Katona, 1993; van Ojen, 1995) have all been found to be related to depression in late life. Negative life events have also been the focus of past research. Those studies show adverse life events, such as loss experiences, severe illness of self or others, relational stress and sudden unexpected events, to be related to depression in late life (for a review see Kraaij et al., 2001; Kurlowicz, 1993; Murrell et al., 1988; Orrell & Davies, 1994; Parkes, 1992). However, the studies that are available have mainly focused on the influence of *recent* negative life events. Events occurring earlier in life remain largely unstudied, with a few exceptions. Catastrophic events experienced in early childhood and extreme experiences during the Second World War have been found to be related to depression in late life (Beekman et al., 1995). Furthermore, negative socio-economic circumstances during childhood and adulthood, and severe illness of significant others and negative events with relationships in adulthood, appeared to be related to depressive symptoms in late life (Kraaij et al., 1997). It is remarkable that not more studies have focused on the influence of earlier experiences, since elderly people constitute the age group with the highest possible accumulation of negative life events. Moreover, in adult studies, events such as physical, sexual and emotional abuse or loss experiences are found to have a longlasting effect on emotional well-being (Beitchman et al., 1992; Bifulco et al., 1992; Brown & Harris, 1993; Lloyd, 1980).

The aims of the present study are threefold. The first aim is to get a clearer view of the prevalence of negative life events elderly people have experienced at different developmental periods in their lives. The second aim is to examine the relationship of the events in these developmental periods to depressive symptoms in late life. To study the accumulation of negative life events, the total number of specific events experienced throughout life and the total number of events experienced in different developmental periods, and their relationship to late life depression, will be examined. The final aim is to explore whether elderly people with higher depression scores have a lifetime career of experiencing negative life events. The reinforcing effect of experiencing events in different developmental periods will be studied.

Method

Sample and procedure

A group of people aged 65 and over was randomly selected from the community register of the city of Leiden in the Netherlands. The only criterion that was used to select the addresses was that the individuals had to be 65 years of age or older. The selected people were informed by letter and invited by telephone call to participate in the study. They were told that the study was about how elderly people feel and whether events from both childhood and later life are still important at old age. They were invited for a 2-hour interview. A total of 920 letters were sent. Four hundred and eighty-seven people chose not to participate (e.g. they said that they had received too many requests for participation in various studies or that they found research useless). Another 239 people could not be reached (e.g. the telephone number was incorrect or the telephone was disconnected) or could not participate due to practical reasons (e.g. the respondent was deaf, did not speak the Dutch language or appeared to be confused). A total of 194 elderly people were interviewed at their homes after providing informed consent. The response rate was therefore 28%. Because the total instrument was quite extensive and elderly people have less experience in filling out questionnaires, all information was gathered by means of an oral interview (including the self-report instruments). The mean age of the respondents was 76.5 years (standard deviation (SD) 7.25, range 65–94) and 52% were female. Forty-four per cent had a single household, 90% were living independently and 76% were religious. 'Good' or 'very good' health was reported by 59%.

Measures

Data were collected on demographic characteristics. Perceived general health was measured by a question from Statistics Netherlands (Centraal Bureau voorde Statistiek (CBS), 1990). Depressive symptoms were measured by the Geriatric Depression Scale (GDS) (Brink et al., 1982), consisting of 30 dichotomous questions. Scores range from 0 to 30, with a high score indicating more depressive symptoms. Since the GDS excludes items that are confounded with normal ageing and diseases associated with old age, but assesses primarily psychological components of depression, it is very suitable for assessing depression in the elderly. The GDS has a high reliability (Cronbach's alpha coefficient: 0.94), good validity and high levels of sensitivity and specificity (Kok, 1994; Olin et al., 1992; Yesavage et al., 1983).

Negative life events were measured by the Negative Life Events Questionnaire. This questionnaire is an adaptation of the Life Events Questionnaire, an instrument used in the World Health Organization multicentre study on parasuicide (Kerkhof et al., 1994). The adapted version is extended with negative life events specific to elderly people (e.g. dementia of a partner and wartime-related events) and by the inclusion of an additional developmental period (late adulthood). The Negative Life Events Questionnaire contains 107 items on negative life events concerning self or significant others (i.e. parents, siblings, partner, children and important people such as a close friend or a confidant). The questionnaire is a lifetime instrument as the occurrence of all events is being questioned for different developmental periods, i.e. childhood (0–15 years), adulthood (16–49 years), late adulthood (50 years to 1 year prior to the interview) and the year prior to the interview. Questions are formulated in a detailed way in order to minimize judgement and subjective estimates (e.g. with regard to physical abuse one of the questions is not 'Were you ever physical abused?' but instead 'Were you ever severely beaten, kicked or deliberately wounded by [one of] your parents?'). If the answer is positive, the following question concerns the period(s) in which this event occurred. The time periods, including the specified age ranges, were provided to the respondent on a card. The items were classified into the following 10 clusters: death of significant others (e.g. death of father, and death of child); severe illness of self (e.g. chronic or life-threatening illness of self, and self admitted to a psychiatric institution); severe illness of significant others (e.g. chronic or life-threatening illness of parent, and partner admitted to a psychiatric institution); negative socio-economic circumstances (e.g. financial problems of partner, and unwanted unemployment of self); sexual abuse (e.g. sexual contact with parent, and unwanted sexual intercourse with partner); physical abuse (e.g. severe beating by parent, and severe beating by partner); emotional abuse and neglect (e.g. neglect by parents, and humiliation or torment by partner); crime, disaster and war events (e.g. natural disaster, imprisonment during war, and experience of bombardments); relational stress (e.g. divorce from partner, and broken relationship with child); and problem behaviour of significant others (e.g. suicide attempt by parent, and addiction by partner).

Each cluster score reflected the number of events experienced within a life event cluster. All 10 life event cluster scores were obtained for the four different developmental periods separately and for the whole life span overall. In addition, the total number of events of all 10 clusters, experienced within each developmental period, was calculated (period score). From every cluster score and period score two scorings were obtained. First, a dichotomy score was created with the following two categories: no event reported (score: 0); and one or more events reported (score: 1). This score reflected the experience of some event within the cluster or period. Secondly, a score was obtained which reflected the number of events experienced within each cluster or period (quantity score). It was assumed that there was a positive, but not a linear, relationship between life events and depression: therefore optimal scaling was used on the number of life events reported on the categorical regression with optimal scaling (CATREG) (SPSS Inc., 1998). In CATREG, the original categories of the variables are replaced by category quantifications, resulting from the optimal transformation of the variable. If the variables are assumed to be 'numerical', then the CATREG solution is identical to that of linear regression analyses. However, if the variables are assumed to be nominal or ordinal, CATREG optimally transforms the variables; this implies that the explained variance is as large as possible. Depression was assumed to be numerical and cluster score and period score were assumed to be ordinal. For every cluster score and period score optimal scaling was performed. In the final solution quantification scores were all lower than 4.

Summarizing, four types of scores could be obtained: (1) a dichotomy cluster score, reflecting the experience of some event within the life event cluster; (2) a quantity cluster score, reflecting the quantity of events experienced within the life event cluster; (3) a dichotomy period score, reflecting the experience of some event within the developmental period; and (4) a quantity period score, reflecting the quantity of events experienced within the developmental period.

In the present study, both dichotomy scores and quantity scores were used to study the relationship with depressive symptoms. The first gives insight into the experience versus non-experience of negative life events; the latter gives insight into the quantity of negative life events experienced. Due to the infrequent occurrence of certain life events within certain developmental periods, dichotomy scores were used when studying the relationship between specific negative life events per developmental period and depressive symptoms. In all other cases the quantity scores were used.

Data analysis

Simple statistics were used to determine the frequencies of the different clusters of negative life events. The bivariate relationship between the various clusters of negative life events and depressive symptoms was examined using Pearson correlations. The multivariate relationship between the event clusters (quantity of events experienced throughout life) and depressive symptoms was examined using a hierarchical regression analysis. In order to control for given demographic variables that do not resemble life events, age and gender were entered in the first step, followed in the second step by the event clusters. The multivariate relationship between the quantity of events experienced in every developmental period and depressive symptoms was examined, again using a hierarchical regression analysis. In order to study the reinforcing effect of experiencing events in different developmental periods, first-order interactions of the quantity of events experienced in the four different developmental periods were also entered in this hierarchical regression analysis. In the first step gender and age were entered; in the second step the different period scores were entered; followed in the third step by the interaction terms.

Results

Prevalence of depressive symptoms and negative life events

A score of 11 or higher on the GDS is taken as an indication of depression. In the present sample the mean GDS score was 5.9 (SD 4.86) and 16% had a score of 11 or higher.

The percentage of respondents who experienced one event or more per cluster in the various developmental periods and the whole life span are presented in Table 1. Seventy-seven per cent of the respondents experienced at least one negative life event during childhood. During adulthood and late adulthood almost all respondents (respectively 99.5% and 100%) experienced some negative life event. In the year prior to the interview 60% experienced at least one negative event.

All elderly people had experienced the death of a significant other. Approximately one-quarter of the respondents reported the death of a significant other during childhood and in the year prior to the interview.

TABLE 1. Respondents who experienced one or more events per negative life event cluster

Event cluster	Childhood (0–15 years) %	(n)	Adulthood (16–49 years) %	(n)	Late adulthood (50 years to past year) %	(n)	Year prior to the interview (past year) %	(n)	Throughout life %	(n)
Death of significant others	24.9	(47)	86.7	(163)	96.8	(182)	23.0	(43)	100.0	(188)
Severe illness—self	11.2	(21)	27.3	(51)	29.9	(56)	18.7	(35)	50.3	(94)
Severe illness—others	23.4	(44)	55.9	(105)	70.7	(133)	28.7	(54)	85.1	(160)
Socio-economic circumstances	33.0	(62)	25.1	(47)	7.0	(13)	2.1	(4)	45.5	(85)
Sexual abuse	3.2	(6)	10.6	(20)	4.8	(9)	0.5	(1)	14.9	(28)
Physical abuse	5.3	(10)	3.2	(6)	0.5	(1)	1.1	(2)	6.9	(13)
Emotional abuse/neglect	22.3	(42)	27.7	(52)	13.3	(25)	6.4	(12)	38.3	(72)
Crime/disaster/war	29.9	(56)	86.1	(161)	14.4	(27)	0.5	(1)	95.7	(179)
Relational stress	19.7	(37)	48.4	(91)	55.9	(105)	20.2	(38)	75.0	(141)
Problem behaviour of significant others	6.3	(12)	13.8	(26)	18.1	(34)	5.3	(10)	26.6	(50)
Total	77.0	(144)	99.5	(187)	100.0	(188)	60.4	(113)	100.0	(188)

Approximately half of the respondents reported that they had had a severe illness, with the highest percentage during adulthood and late adulthood (respectively 27% and 30%). The majority of the respondents had experienced a severe illness of someone close, again with the highest percentage during adulthood and late adulthood (respectively 56% and 71%). Negative socio-economic circumstances were reported mainly during childhood (by one-third) and during adulthood (by one-quarter). In the later stages of life few financial problems were reported.

Several elderly people appeared to be victims of abuse. Fifteen per cent of the respondents reported that they had been sexually abused during their life. This most frequently occurred in adulthood (11%), followed by late adulthood (5%) and childhood (3%). One respondent reported that they had been sexually abused in the year prior to the interview. Seven per cent of the elderly reported that they had been victims of physical abuse. Physical abuse was mainly experienced during childhood and adulthood (respectively 5% and 3%). Emotional abuse and neglect were reported by over one-third of the respondents (38%). This form of abuse was experienced in all developmental periods.

Almost all respondents had experienced crime, disaster and war events. These were mainly experienced in childhood (30%) and adulthood (86%), represented by the periods of World Wars I and II. Over the life span relational stress was reported by three-quarters of the respondents; 20% experienced this during childhood and in the year prior to the interview and approximately half experienced this during adulthood and late adulthood. Finally, around one-quarter of the respondents reported that they had experienced problem behaviour of significant others, with the majority experiencing this during adulthood and late adulthood (respectively 14% and 18%).

Relationship between negative life events per developmental period and depressive symptoms in late life

The relationship between the negative life events and depressive symptoms is presented in Table 2. The

TABLE 2. Relationship between negative life events per developmental period (dichotomy score) and depressive symptoms in late life

Event cluster	Childhood (0–15 years)	Adulthood (16–49 years)	Late adulthood (50 years to past year)	Year prior to the interview (past year)
Death of significant others	0.124	0.044	—	-0.003
Severe illness—self	-0.024	0.085	0.076	0.174*
Severe illness—others	0.101	0.081	0.122	0.184*
Socio-economic circumstances	0.179*	0.180*	0.212**	—
Sexual abuse	—	0.234**	0.315***	—
Physical abuse	0.064	—	—	—
Emotional abuse/neglect	0.200**	0.263***	0.278***	0.238**
Crime/disaster/war	-0.089	0.098	-0.088	—
Relational stress	0.069	0.229**	0.199**	0.150*
Problem behaviour of significant others	0.079	0.256***	0.206**	0.119

Note. n=187–189; Pearson correlation, two-tailed; *p < 0.05; **p < 0.01; ***p < 0.001; —, dichotomy less than 5–95%, no correlation calculated.

dichotomy cluster scores were used. All significant Pearson correlations were positive, indicating that the experience of one negative life event or more was related to a higher depression score. Negative socio-economic circumstances and emotional abuse and neglect during childhood were significantly correlated with depressive symptoms. Negative socio-economic circumstances, sexual abuse, emotional abuse and neglect, relational stress and problem behaviour of significant others during adulthood and late adulthood correlated significantly with depressive symptoms. Severe illness of both self and others, emotional abuse and neglect and relational stress in the year prior to the interview were significantly correlated with depressive symptoms in late life.

Relationship between specific negative life events throughout life and depressive symptoms in late life

The relationship between the specific negative life events experienced throughout life and depressive symptoms is presented in Table 3. The quantity cluster scores were used. First, the bivariate relationship was analysed by Pearson correlations. Almost all event clusters correlated significantly with depressive symptoms. Only physical abuse and crime, disaster and war events were not related to depressive symptoms. Secondly, the multivariate relationship between the negative life event clusters and depressive symptoms was studied using hierarchical regression analysis. After controlling for age and gender the following event clusters were found to be significant: death of significant others; sexual abuse; and relational stress ($F=5.22$; degrees of freedom (df)=12, 174; $p<0.001$). The total amount of explained variance was 27%.

Relationship between total quantity of negative life events per developmental period and depressive symptoms in late life

The relationship between the total quantity of all negative life events experienced in the various developmental periods and depressive symptoms is presented in Table 4. The quantity period scores were used. First, the bivariate relationship was analysed by Pearson correlations. In all periods a significant correlation with depressive symptoms in late life was found. Secondly, the multivariate relationship between

TABLE 3. Relationship between specific negative life events throughout life (quantity score) and depressive symptoms in late life

Event cluster (throughout life)	Bivariate (r)[a]	Multivariate (beta)[b]
Death of significant others	0.237**	0.167*
Severe illness—self	0.143*	0.041
Severe illness—others	0.209**	0.101
Socio-economic circumstances	0.248**	0.091
Sexual abuse	0.343***	0.174*
Physical abuse	0.046	-0.117
Emotional abuse/neglect	0.307***	0.097
Crime/disaster/war	-0.073	-0.043
Relational stress	0.355***	0.216*
Problem behaviour of significant others	0.238**	0.026

[a]Pearson correlation, two-tailed.
[b]Hierarchical regression analysis (corrected for age and gender).
Note. $n=187-188$; *$p < 0.05$; **$p < 0.01$; ***$p < 0.001$.

TABLE 4. Relationship between total quantity of negative life events per developmental period (quantity score) and depressive symptoms in late life

Period	Bivariate (r)[a]	Multivariate (beta)[b]
Childhood (0–15)	0.155*	0.063
Adulthood (16–49)	0.402***	0.251**
Late adulthood (50 to past year)	0.413***	0.294***
Year prior to interview (past year)	0.303***	0.132
Interaction childhood–adulthood		0.156*
Interaction childhood–late adulthood		0.008
Interaction childhood–past year		-0.019
Interaction adulthood–late adulthood		0.038
Interaction adulthood–past year		0.034
Interaction late adulthood–past year		-0.149

[a]Pearson correlation, two-tailed.
[b]Hierarchical regression analysis (corrected for age and gender).
Note. $n=187-188$; *$p < 0.05$; **$p <0.01$; ***$p < 0.001$.

the quantity of events experienced in the different developmental periods and depressive symptoms was examined using hierarchical regression analysis. In order to study the reinforcing effect of experiencing events in various developmental periods, interaction terms of the quantity of events experienced in the different developmental periods were also entered in the regression analysis. After controlling for age and gender, the quantity of events experienced during the following periods were significant: adulthood; late adulthood; and the interaction of childhood and adulthood ($F=7.51$; df=12, 174; $p<0.001$). The total amount of explained variance was 34%. The interaction effect between the number of negative life events experienced in childhood and adulthood indicated that there was a much stronger association between the number of negative life events experienced in adulthood and depressive symptoms in late life, for those who experienced more negative life events in childhood, than for those who did not.

Finally, all negative life events experienced throughout life were summed. After optimal scaling this total life score was correlated with depressive symptoms. A significant positive correlation was found ($r=0.47$, $p<0.001$).

Discussion

The pressure on the health care system by the elderly will increase by cohort growth of this population and by better recognition of depression. It is important to identify risk factors for elderly depression in order to aid the prevention of depression in the elderly and to design effective intervention programmes.

The present study focused on negative life events in this respect. The relationship between the number of depressive symptoms and negative life events reported in a randomly selected community sample of 194 elderly people in the Netherlands was investigated. The results show that all elderly people in this sample reported at least one negative life event during their lives. Most predominantly, these events concerned death and severe illness of significant others, crime, disaster and war events, and relational stress. The finding that 60% had experienced at least one negative life event in the year prior to the interview is in line with previous research (Davies, 1996).

Death of significant others, sexual abuse and relational stress, occurring throughout life, were all significantly related to depression scores, after controlling for age and gender. When studied using bivariate statistics, almost all (lifetime) life events were significantly related to depressive symptoms. This is in line with previous studies (for a review, see Kraaij et al., 2001; Kurlowicz, 1993; Murrell et al., 1988; Orrell & Davies, 1994; Parkes, 1992). Physical abuse and crime, disaster and war events were the only events that were not related to depressive symptoms in late life. Since no studies could be located that focused on the relationship between physical abuse and depression in late life this finding needs further confirmation by future studies. In line with the present study, Bramsen (1995) found no relationship between war events and depressive symptoms in a Dutch community sample of elderly people. Beekman et al. (1995), however, reported that, in their Dutch community sample of elderly people, extreme experiences during World War II which had had a lasting effect (1-item question) were associated with both major and minor depression. Possibly only certain specific war events have a long-lasting effect on emotional well-being. Further research is needed to explore these issues.

Elderly people who reported more depressive symptoms also reported more negative life events during all developmental periods. Depression scores were especially high when subjects reported more events during adulthood and late adulthood. On top of this, the interaction effect between the number of negative life events experienced in childhood and adulthood indicated that there was a much stronger association between the number of negative life events experienced in adulthood and depressive symptoms in late life, for those who experienced more negative life events in childhood, than for those who did not. This is in line with findings from previous studies which have reported that exposure to certain traumatic events in childhood (such as physical violence or parental divorce) signals a greater risk of psychiatric problems from subsequent trauma in adulthood (Breslau et al., 1999; Landerman et al., 1991). Possibly people who experience childhood trauma are more sensitive to further trauma. The sum of all negative life events experienced throughout life had the strongest relationship to depressive symptoms in late life. This is in line with previous research (Kraaij et al., 2001).

Before discussing the implications of these results, some methodological considerations have to be taken into account. The first issue concerns the representativeness of the group that was studied. The response rate was moderately low (28%). This low rate may have been due to other research projects being conducted in the same period. Another reason could have been the 'fear-inducing' statement in the invitation letter, which stated that people who were in treatment for emotional problems should discuss participation with their treatment provider (this was in accordance with the rules of the Ethical Committee). Despite the low response rate, there is no indication that people who were depressed were less willing to participate: 16% of the present sample scored above the cut-off score for depression of the GDS, which is in accordance with rates identified in other studies reporting on clinically relevant levels of depressive symptoms as measured with various self-report instruments (Beekman et al., 1995, 1997b; Cappeliez, 1988; Gurland & Cross, 1982; Løpine & Bouchez, 1998; van Marwijk, 1995; O'Hara et al.,

1985; Ruegg et al., 1988). Furthermore, the sample had a gender distribution comparable to that of the Dutch elderly population, and the subjects had the same assessment of their general health as the Dutch elderly population (CBS, 1997).

The second issue is that of the validity of the retrospective recollections of life events by these elderly subjects. There is evidence to suggest that depressed persons, in order to account for their current emotional state, may report more negative life events than non-depressed persons (Brown, 1972; Teasdale, 1983). It has also been suggested that elderly people may not remember early experiences accurately. However, Brewin et al. (1993) concluded in their review that there is little reason to link psychiatric status with less reliable or less valid recall of early experiences, and that much of our autobiographical recollection of the past is reasonably free of error, provided that we stick to remembering the broad outline of events and not detailed information. The present study focused on the broad outline of events only, since no questions regarding the details of an event were included. Another issue of concern is that the memory for dates and for the temporal order of events may be subject to error. Therefore, the present study did not date events precisely, but used four time periods.

The third point of concern is that the study had a cross-sectional design and negative life events were measured retrospectively. Therefore, no conclusions can be drawn regarding the causal direction of the relationship between life events and depressive symptoms. An important question is whether stress causes depression or depression-prone persons incur more life stress. Depressed people may experience more negative events as part of the social environment they create (Ingram et al., 1998). In order to solve these cause-and-effect issues and to disentangle the complex interplay between past experiences and psychological functioning, longitudinal research is needed. In addition, the total context of a stressful event should be taken into account in order to judge the independence of the event.

The main implication of the findings is that one loses valuable information when research or diagnostics is limited to recent negative life events only. In this study, depressed mood in elderly people is related to the report of negative socio-economic circumstances and emotional abuse and neglect during childhood, and to the report of negative socio-economic circumstances, sexual abuse, emotional abuse and neglect, relational stress and problem behaviour of significant others during (late) adulthood. The data suggest that these events may have long-term consequences for people's well-being and that incorporating life histories into the diagnostic interview and learning strategies to deal with these events is advisable at any age. Also, the quantity of all negative events experienced over the life span had the strongest relationship with depressive symptoms. This supports the notion that accumulating stress coincides with increased depressed mood, and it seems relevant to assess the number of negative life events experienced.

It is suggested here that special attention could be given to the subject of abuse. One in seven respondents reported that they had been sexually abused during their life. The highest percentage was reported during adulthood, followed by late adulthood and childhood. Seven per cent of the elderly reported that they had been victims of physical abuse, which was mainly experienced during childhood and adulthood. Emotional abuse and neglect were experienced by more than one-third of the respondents, occurring in all developmental periods. These results imply that assessment of such events should be part of a standard procedure in the depressed elderly.

Of course, life events should not be considered the sole causes of depression. Psychological and neurobiological mechanisms play an important role in the aetiology of depression in the elderly. Depressive episodes earlier in life may predict the recurrence of depressive episodes later in life (Fombonne, 1995). However, the present study suggests that possible traumatic experiences cannot be disregarded in this process. Further research should involve larger samples and clinical subgroups to make more (sophisticated) analyses possible. Future research should also focus on properties of stressors, such as the controllability and the severity of the event. Finally, the buffering role of aspects such as coping and social support should also be studied.

Depressed elderly people appear to carry a burden that has accumulated during a lifelong history of deaths of loved ones, abuse and relational problems. From the results of the present study, it seems fair to suggest that this 'social poverty' is an important contributor to the process. Prevention should therefore focus on skills to promote new and healthy social relationships.

References

BEEKMAN, A. T. F., DEEG, D. J. H., TILBURG, T. VAN, SMIT, J. H., HOOIJER, C. & TILBURG, W. VAN (1995). Major and minor depression in later life: a study of prevalence and risk factors. *Journal of Affective Disorders*, 36, 65–75.

BEEKMAN, A. T. F., DEEG, D. J. H., BRAAM, A. W., SMIT, J. H. & TILBURG, W. VAN (1997a). Consequences of major and minor depression in later life: a study of disability, well-being and service utilization. *Psychological Medicine*, 27, 1397–1409.

BEEKMAN, A. T. F., DEEG, D. J. H., TILBURG, T. G. VAN, SCHOEVERS, R. A., SMIT, J. H., HOOIJER, C. & TILBURG, W. VAN (1997b). Depressie bij ouderen in de Nederlandse bevolking: een onderzoek naar de prevalentie en risicofactoren [Depression in the elderly in the Dutch community: a study of prevalence and risk factors]. *Tijdschrift voor Psychiatrie*, 39, 294–307.

BEER, M. DE & LANGE, J. DE (1993). *Depressie bij ouderen: een literatuuronderzoek ten behoeve van de preventiepraktijk* in de AGGZ [Depression in the elderly: a literature study on behalf of prevention practice in the AGGZ]. Utrecht: Nederlands centrum Geestelijke volksgezondheid.

BEITCHMAN, J. H., ZUCKER, K. J., HOOD, J. E., DACOSTA, G. A., AKMAN, D. & CASSAVIA, E. (1992). A review of the long-term effects of child sexual abuse. *Child Abuse & Neglect, 16*, 101–118.

BIFULCO, A., HARRIS, T. & BROWN, G. W. (1992). Mourning or early inadequate care? Reexamining the relationship of maternal loss in childhood with adult depression and anxiety. *Development and Psychopathology, 4*, 433–449.

BLAZER, D. G., HUGHES, D. C. & GEORGE, L. K. (1987). The epidemiology of depression in an elderly community population. *Gerontologist, 27*, 281–287.

BRAMSEN, I. (1995). *The long-term psychological adjustment of World War II survivors in the Netherlands.* Dissertation, Leiden University, Leiden, the Netherlands.

BRESLAU, N., CHILCOAT, H. D., KESSLER, R. C. & DAVIS, G. C. (1999). Previous exposure to trauma and PTSD effects of subsequent trauma: results from the Detroit area survey of trauma. *American Journal of Psychiatry, 156*, 902–907.

BREWIN, C. R., ANDREWS, B. & GOTLIB, I. H. (1993). Psychopathology and early experience: a reappraisal of retrospective reports. *Psychological Bulletin, 113*, 82–98.

BRINK, T. L., YESAVAGE, J. A., HEERSEMA, P. H., ADEY, M. & ROSE, T. L. (1982). Screening tests for geriatric depression. *Clinical Gerontologist, 1*, 37–43.

BROWN, G. W. (1972). Life-events and psychiatric illness: some thoughts on methodology and causality. *Journal of Psychosomatic Research, 16*, 311–320.

BROWN, G. W. & HARRIS, T. O. (1993). Aetiology of anxiety and depressive disorders in an inner-city population. 1. Early adversity. *Psychological Medicine, 23*, 143–154.

CAPPELIEZ, P. (1988). Some thoughts on the prevalence and etiology of depressive conditions in the elderly. Special issue: Francophone research in gerontology in Canada. *Canadian Journal on Aging, 7*, 431–440.

CBS (1990). *Statistisch jaarboek 1990 [Statistical yearbook 1990]*. The Hague: sdu-uitgeverij.

CBS (1997). *Vademecum gezondheidsstatistiek Nederland [Handbook health statistics the Netherlands]* [online]. Available: http://statline.cbs.nl.

DAVIES, A. D. M. (1996). Life events, health, adaptation and social support in the clinical psychology of late life. In R. T. WOODS (Ed.), *Handbook of the clinical psychology of ageing* (pp. 115–140). Chichester: John Wiley.

FOMBONNE, E. (1995). Depressive disorders: time trends and possible explanatory mechanisms. In M. RUTTER & D. J. SMITH (Eds.), *Psychosocial disorders in young people: time trends and their causes* (pp. 544–615). Chichester: John Wiley.

GREEN, B. H., COPELAND, J. R. M., DEWEY, M. E., SHARMA, V., SAUNDERS, P. A., DAVIDSON, I. A., SULLIVAN, C. & MCWILLIAM, C. (1992). Risk factors for depression in elderly people: a prospective study. *Acta Psychiatrica Scandinavica, 86*, 213–217.

GURLAND, B. J. & CROSS, P. S. (1982). Epidemiology of psychopathology in old age: some implications for clinical services. *Psychiatric Clinics of North America, 5*, 11–26.

INGRAM, R. E., MIRANDA, J. & SEGAL, Z. V. (1998). *Cognitive vulnerability to depression.* New York: Guilford Press.

KATONA, C. (1993). The aetiology of depression in old age. *International Review of Psychiatry, 5*, 407–416.

KERKHOF, A. J. F. M., SCHMIDTKE, A., BILLE-BRAHE, U., DE LEO, D. & LÖNNQVIST, J. (1994). *Attempted suicide in Europe. Findings from the WHO multicentre study on parasuicide by the WHO regional office for Europe.* Leiden: DSWO Press.

KOENIG, H. G., FORD, S. M. & SIBERT, T. E. (1995). Screening for depression in elderly patients. In B.J. VELLAS, J. L. ALBAREDE & P. J. GARRY (Eds), *Moods and cognitive disorders. Facts and Research in Gerontology*, Supplement (pp. 119–130). New York: Springer Publishing.

KOK, R. M. (1994). Zelfbeoordelingsschalen voor depressie bij ouderen [Self-report instruments for depression in the elderly]. *Tijdschrift voor Gerontologie en Geriatrie, 25*, 150–156.

KRAAIJ, V., KREMERS, I. & ARENSMAN, E. (1997). The relationship between stressful and traumatic life events and depression in the elderly. *Crisis, 18*, 86–88.

KRAAIJ, V., ARENSMAN, E. & SPINHOVEN, Ph. (2001). Negative life events and depression in the elderly: a meta-analysis. *Journal of Gerontology: Psychological Sciences*, in press.

KURLOWICZ, L. H. (1993). Social factors and depression in late life. *Archives of Psychiatric Nursing, 7*, 30–36.

LANDERMAN, R., GEORGE, L. K. & BLAZER, D. G. (1991). Adult vulnerability for psychiatric disorders: interactive effects of negative childhood experiences and recent stress. *Journal of Nervous and Mental Disease, 179*, 656–663.

L'PINE, J. P. & BOUCHEZ, S. (1998). Epidemiology of depression in the elderly. *International Clinical Psychopharmacology, 13*, S7–S12.

LIVINGSTON, G. & HINCHLIFFE, A. C. (1993). The epidemiology of psychiatric disorders in the elderly. *International Review of Psychiatry, 5*, 317–326.

LLOYD, C. (1980). Life events and depressive disorder reviewed: events as precipitating factors. *Archives of General Psychiatry, 37*, 541–548.

MARWIJK, H. W. J. VAN (1995). *Depression in the elderly as seen in general practice: prevalence, diagnosis, and course.* Dissertation, Leiden University, Leiden, the Netherlands.

MURRELL, S. A., NORRIS, F. H. & GROTE, C. (1988). Life events in older adults. In L. H. COHEN (Ed.), *Life events and psychological functioning: theoretical and methodological issues* (pp. 96–122). Newbury Park, CA: Sage.

O'HARA, M. W., KOHOUT, F. J. & WALLACE, R. B. (1985). Depression among the rural elderly: a study of prevalence and correlates. *Journal of Nervous and Mental Disease, 173*, 582–589.

OJEN, R. L. VAN (1995). *Origins of depression: a study in the elderly population.* Dissertation, Vrije Universiteit Amsterdam, Amsterdam, the Netherlands.

OLIN, J. T., SCHNEIDER, L. S., EATON, E. M., ZEMANSKY, M. F. & POLLOCK, V. E. (1992). The Geriatric Depression Scale and the Beck Depression Inventory as screening instruments in an older adult outpatient population. *Psychological Assessment, 4*, 190–192.

ORRELL, M. W. & DAVIES, A. D. M. (1994). Life events in the elderly. *International Review of Psychiatry, 6*, 59–71.

PARKES, C. M. (1992). Bereavement and mental health in the elderly. *Reviews in Clinical Gerontology, 2*, 45–51.

RUEGG, R. G., ZISOOK, S. & SWERDLOW, N. R. (1988). Depression in the aged: an overview. *Psychiatric Clinics of North America, 11*, 83–99.

SPSS INC. (1998). *SPSS categories 8.0.* Chicago, IL: SPSS Inc.

TEASDALE, J. D. (1983). Negative thinking in depression: cause, effect or reciprocal relationship? *Advances in Behavior Research and Therapy, 5*, 3–25.

YESAVAGE, J. A., BRINK, T. L., ROSE, T. L., LUM, O., HUANG, V., ADEY, M. & LEIRER, O. VON (1983). Development and validation of a geriatric depression screening scale: a preliminary report. *Journal of Psychiatric Research, 17*, 37–49.

[29]

COMPREHENSIVE CONCEPTUALIZATION OF COGNITIVE BEHAVIOUR THERAPY FOR LATE LIFE DEPRESSION

Ken Laidlaw

Royal Edinburgh Hospital, UK

Larry W. Thompson

Pacific Graduate School of Psychology, Palo Alto, USA

Dolores Gallagher-Thompson

Stanford University School of Medicine, USA

Abstract. Cognitive behaviour therapy (CBT) has proven efficacy as a treatment for depression in older people. An important debate amongst therapists working with older people is whether CBT needs to be adapted to ensure optimal treatment outcome and, if so, what adaptations are necessary. It is accepted that psychotherapy with older people can differ from psychotherapy with younger people in a number of important respects because of the higher likelihood of chronic conditions, changes in cognitive capacity, potential loss experiences and different cohort belief systems. As psychotherapists are often much less comfortable dealing with physical problems, they may become negatively biased in terms of outcome when patients present with co-morbid health issues. The impact of loss experiences in older people can also be overemphasized in their importance by inexperienced therapists and can result in lowered expectations for therapy outcome. Consequently, there is a need to develop a model that addresses age related issues within a coherent cognitive therapy framework suitable for older people. This paper describes a CBT model that is augmented with applied gerontological knowledge, taking account of cohort beliefs, intergenerational linkages, sociocultural context, health status/beliefs and role investments/transitions. Clinical examples are used throughout to illustrate clinical implications of the model.

Keywords: Cognitive behavioural therapy, gerontology, generativity, cohort, late life depression, longevity, successful ageing.

Reprint requests to Ken Laidlaw, Section of Clinical and Health Psychology, University of Edinburgh, Kennedy Tower, Royal Edinburgh Hospital, Morningside Park, Edinburgh EH10 5HF, UK. E-mail: klaidlaw@srv1.med.ed.ac.uk

Depression in later life

Treatment for depression in older people is commonly managed by GPs in Primary Care settings (Rothera, Jones, & Gordon, 2002) with infrequent referrals to secondary specialist services (Laidlaw, Davidson, & Arbuthnot, 1998; Collins, Katona, & Orrell, 1997; Orrell, Collins, Shergill, & Katona, 1995). Although GPs primarily use antidepressants to treat depression in older people, many prescribe sub-therapeutic dosages of antidepressants because of fears about side effects (Katona & Livingston, 2002; Isometsa, Seppala, Henriksson, Kekki, & Lonnqvist, 1998; Heeren, Derksen, Heycop, & Van Gent, 1997; Orrell et al., 1995). Additionally, amongst older people there is a low rate of compliance with antidepressant prescriptions because they may already be using a large number of medications for a range of conditions (Katona & Livingston, 2002; Unutzer, Katon, Sullivan, & Miranda, 1999). With many older people now expressing a preference for psychotherapy as a treatment for depression (Landreville, Landry, Baillargeon, Guerett, & Matteau, 2001), it is clear that psychotherapeutic alternatives constitute a welcome addition to the treatment of late life depression (Gerson, Belin, Kaufman, Mintz, & Jarvik, 1999).

Cognitive Behaviour Therapy (CBT) is a very relevant form of psychotherapy with older people (Morris & Morris, 1991) as it is an active, directive time-limited, structured problem-solving treatment approach whose primary aim is symptom reduction. The application of CBT with older people is comprehensively described in Laidlaw, Thompson, Dick-Siskin and Gallagher-Thompson (2003). Primarily, research into CBT for late life depression has largely focused on outcome, while generally ignoring the importance of process issues.

Why do we need a conceptualization of CBT specific to older adults?

Since CBT outcome research demonstrates that unmodified and non-adapted CBT is efficacious for older people (Laidlaw, 2003a, 2001; Gatz et al., 1998; Koder, Brodaty, & Anstey, 1996; Scogin & McElreath, 1994), one might enquire as to why a specific CBT conceptualization, that modifies and extends the bounds of therapeutic investigation, is really needed with older adults. There are, however, a number of reasons why a specific conceptualization framework is needed. For example, at the end of an empirical review of CBT efficacy with older people, Koder et al. (1996) conclude, "The debate is not whether CT is applicable to elderly depressed patients, but rather how to modify existing CT programmes so that they incorporate differences in thinking styles in elderly people and age-related psychological adjustment". Koder et al. (1996) also argue that Life Review and Reminiscence can be usefully incorporated into CBT treatment programmes. Likewise, earlier cognitive therapy researchers have also stated that cognitive therapy needed to be adapted for use with older people, suggesting that "abstract" elements of therapy such as cognitive restructuring may not be beneficial, or perhaps even possible with many older people (Church, 1983, 1986; Steuer & Hammen, 1983). This is potentially confusing for some therapists as it suggests that unless one substantially alters one's practice, standard CBT approaches are not applicable with older people.

Further, because of an overemphasis on negative changes in later life, such as loss, bereavement and physical illnesses, some therapists may be sceptical about applying "standard" CBT (Laidlaw, 2003a). Padesky (1998) suggests the ultimate effectiveness of CBT may be enhanced or undermined by a therapist's own set of beliefs. Certainly, changes in cognitive capacity, potential loss experiences and different cohort belief systems can leave some therapists feeling out of their depths, and at a loss as to how to apply psychological interventions in the face of "external" rather than internal difficulties.

Many experienced therapists working in the field consider standard CBT conceptualizations are inadequate as a description of the complexity of the age-specific issues facing their clients. The comprehensive conceptualization framework applied here with older people provides an answer to such criticisms and applies gerontological knowledge that is consistent with clinical emphasis important to any therapist working with their patient. Simply put, the more authentic and collaborative the understanding that develops between the patient and the therapist, the better the outcome is likely to be (Persons, 1989). Hence, the current paper seeks to find a way to incorporate age-related differences within standard CBT frameworks using a comprehensive conceptualization framework for older people. For CBT with older people, modifications rather than adaptations may be all that is required (Laidlaw et al., 2003). Modifications suggest that treatment outcome can be enhanced by consideration of certain client specific variables, whereas adaptations require that substantive changes are necessary to a treatment model in order for it to be effective with any specific client group (Laidlaw, 2001). In summary, there is a need to develop a conceptualization model for older people that addresses age related issues within a coherent cognitive therapy framework suitable for older people (Grant & Casey, 1995).

A comprehensive conceptualization of CBT for older people

A brief description of each element of the conceptualization framework of CBT for late life depression is illustrated in Figure 1. At the centre of this conceptualization framework is the standard CBT model for depression (Beck, Rush, Shaw, & Emery, 1979), reflecting the focus that is placed upon standard CBT techniques for treatment interventions. Each element of the conceptualization framework is discussed in greater detail below and clinical examples are used to illustrate key issues.

Cohort

Cohort beliefs are those beliefs held by groups of people born in similar years or similar time periods (Neugarten & Datan, 1973). Cohort beliefs are the shared beliefs and experiences (cultural and developmental) of age specific generations (Smyer & Qualls, 1999). It follows that certain cohort beliefs may impact on the process and outcome of psychotherapy. Knight (1996) emphasizes this when he states that working with older adults entails learning something of the folkways of people born many years before. People born at the beginning of the 20th century will have different cultural and socio-historical experiences to those born at the end of the 20th century and hence may develop different cohort beliefs. It is, however, more than just a "generation gap". Historical events can have had tremendous impact on developmental experiences, leading people to develop different expectancies and beliefs about life. Laidlaw et al. (2003) state "Understanding cohort experiences, and taking these into account when working psychotherapeutically with older people, is no more difficult and no less important than when working with cohorts such as ethnic minority groups." Cohort differences become apparent if one reflects on the experiences of someone growing up in the 1930s, where

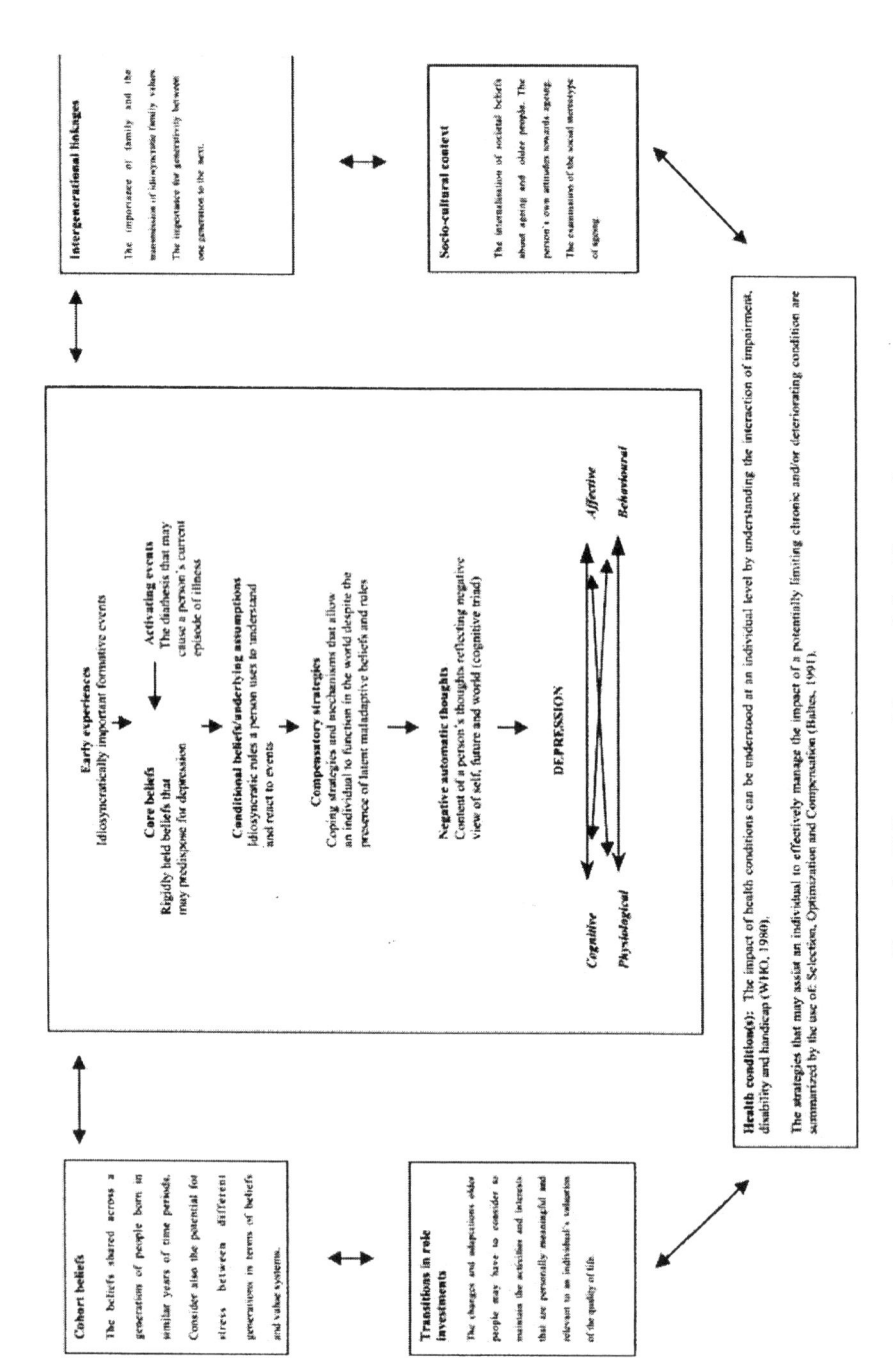

Figure 1. CBT conceptual framework for older people

great historical events like the Great Depression or World War II occurred and became shared socio-historical experiences. Cohort experiences produce potential for misunderstandings and miscommunication between generations. Cohort beliefs of older generations can also sometimes clash with the therapist's beliefs. For example, beliefs about lifestyle choices, and gender roles may differ markedly, making therapists feel uncomfortable.

Combining cohort beliefs with idiosyncratic core beliefs provides an age and generational context to therapy work. For instance, discussing how depression was understood within a specific age cohort and how this relates to personal beliefs about failure can provide a therapist with an opportunity to provide psychoeducation about depression. It may also help one to discover more about the individual's belief system and coping strategies. Lebowitz and Neiderehe (1992) state, "The stigma of mental illness is especially strong in the current cohort of elderly people, who tend to associate mental disorder with personal failure, spiritual deficiency, or some other stereotypic view." For instance, Mr Robson had been experiencing depression since he retired from a lifetime working with a local firm of builders. Mr Robson also experienced significant problems with agoraphobia and rarely left his house. Although Mr Robson was a keen gardener, he found it extremely difficult to be seen outside by people walking past his front garden. It appeared that Mr Robson had always strongly ascribed to the cohort belief that depression was a shameful mental illness. Thus he avoided people seeing him for fear that others were judging him as deficient and mentally abnormal. This cohort belief was extremely painful and he could not avoid experiencing deep feelings of shame and guilt. The impact of these emotions prevented him from managing his depressive symptoms, further confirming his belief that he was weak and a failure as a man. The therapist sought to normalize Mr Robson's fears by explaining that his generational cohort may have shared similar beliefs, but such perspectives would no longer be shared generally by society; especially, given changes in knowledge about mental illnesses. This intervention also introduced some flexibility into a belief system that was rigid and maladaptive. It is noteworthy that treating his avoidance as simple agoraphobia would have probably resulted in a misdirected effort on the part of the therapist.

Transitions in role investments

Active engagement in life is considered an important determinant of successful ageing (Rowe & Kahn, 1998) and often for an older adult this means maintaining close relationships with family and loved ones. For an older adult, remaining invested and involved in activities and interests that are personally meaningful, purposeful and relevant (Rowe & Kahn, 1998) is likely to improve quality of life and especially mental and emotional functioning (Laidlaw, 2003b; Vaillant, 2002). Role investment is therefore an important variable to evaluate in any conceptualization with older adults. Also, at this stage in one's life there may be transitions that an individual needs to navigate in order to successfully adapt to age related changes. Champion and Power (1995) state that vulnerability to depression is related to the extent to which an individual invests in certain highly valued roles and goals. Over investment, that is investment in certain roles and goals to the exclusion of all others, may constitute vulnerability for the development of depression. Champion and Power (1995) recognize a gender bias in the sorts of roles and goals that are invested in. Women are more likely to invest in interpersonal relationships and men are more likely to invest in areas of achievement-orientation, such as work. An important role transition for some, though not all older people, is signalled by occupational retirement. Generativity, the concern for and commitment to the wellbeing of one generation for another (Erikson, 1997), is considered an important element in the successful ageing of an individual (Vaillant, 2002). Mr Kirk was a successful expatriate engineer who prior to retirement was strongly invested in his work, like many men of his generation. His work provided an important method of self-definition, validation and indication of self-worth. An key role for Mr Kirk was a generative one; he liked to pass on knowledge and experience to his fellow workers (his company employed him to consult and teach younger engineers prior to his retirement) and to his adult children. On retiring from engineering, Mr Kirk returned "home" to Scotland. On his return, Mr Kirk quickly became depressed as a number of important roles had become lost to him. His adult children had remained abroad and he no longer felt needed. He applied to provide voluntary advice to a local engineering college but he was rejected because of his age. For Mr Kirk, CBT interventions focused upon reconstructing a new way of maintaining a sense of investment in activities of personal meaning. Hence, transitioning from one way of achieving meaning to an alternative way that was adaptive to the change in circumstances. Thus, an important element of therapy was finding ways in which he could continue to feel important and valuable to society. Mr Kirk invested his time in voluntary activities by joining the board of a local charity and importantly investing his time in education, enrolling in an Open University course. By investing in these activities, Mr Kirk gained a new sense of value that linked meaningful values from the past. He was able to maintain a sense of continued growth and potential, an aspect of life that is so important for successful ageing and longevity (Vaillant, 2002).

Intergenerational linkages

With the change in family and society demographics (increased longevity, smaller family sizes, increased rates of divorce and subsequent re-marriage) grand parents and great-grandparents perform an important role in our societies, providing strong intergenerational linkages across families (Bengtson & Boss, 2000; Bengtson 2001). Older generations tend to value continuity and transmission of values, whereas younger generations tend to value autonomy and independence (Bengtson et al., 2000). Intergenerational relationships can often create tensions, especially when older generations do not always either approve of, or understand, changes in family structures or marital relationships (Bengston et al., 2000).

For many older people, intergenerational linkages may be confusing and distressing as they clash with cherished cohort beliefs about the notions of family. Neugarten, Moore, & Lowe (1965) introduced the concept of the social clock in which people have certain socially influenced (and hence cohort) notions about the timetable for accomplishing life's tasks. For example, older generations may express disappointment or disapproval at their adult children if they have not settled down and started a family by their thirties. The increase in longevity may result in certain life stages being reached at different ages for different generation cohorts, resulting in misunderstandings and tensions across generations. Levine (1996) notes that older women may have different expectations about marital fulfilment and roles in society compared to younger women. Levine (1996) also notes that differences in expectations may become an important relationship issue to address in therapy.

Thompson (1996) notes that it is common for relationship strains between older adults and their adult-children to precipitate a depressive episode. Parents, regardless of the age of their children, often still retain a sense of responsibility for things that affect their children.

In depression, this sense of responsibility can become magnified. For example, Mr Ross felt a sense of having let his youngest son down when he learnt that his son had separated from his wife. He stated, "I've obviously not done the right things by him" and "If we had stayed, we might have been able to help . . . we might have prevented the divorce." Cognitive methods of thought challenging were the principal, and successful, method of dealing with this presentation. Eventually, Mr Ross was able to state, "I lived in the same district as my oldest son and that did not prevent him from divorcing." Mr. Ross was also able to see why his youngest son had originally hid his marital difficulties from him. He was able to accept eventually that this was not because his son didn't respect or need his father's advice, but probably because the son felt he had failed at his marriage. Mr Ross was also able to state that he understood that this was a common and understandable reaction on the part of anyone experiencing marital difficulties.

Socio-cultural context

The variable of interest here is primarily people's attitudes towards their own ageing. Often patients will explicitly state that "growing old is a terrible thing". Statements such as this may appear to be realistic appraisals of a difficult time of life, but in fact reveal the internalization of socio-cultural negative stereotypes about growing old. As Levy (2003) states "when individuals reach old age, the ageing stereotypes internalized in childhood, and then reinforced for decades, become self-stereotypes." Many older people have an implicit assumption (that can be challenged in therapy) that old age inevitably means loss and decrepitude. As one gets older, the growing sense of dread about what ageing will bring can often be accompanied by an increased vigilance for the first signs of the "the slippery slope". Thus many older people have a latent and potentially maladaptive vulnerability about ageing that has been reinforced and often endorsed by themselves and society for decades. Hence, older people may assume that if they are unhappy or depressed that this is a normal part of ageing. Unfortunately, beliefs such as these often prevent individuals from seeking treatment or at the very least making the most of treatment when it is offered (Unutzer et al., 1999). Therapists ought to explore the socio-cultural context of the patient when they are socializing the patient into therapy. Formulations of beliefs about ageing are very important if therapy is to proceed in a timely and efficacious fashion. The socio-cultural context also takes into account the values of the therapist. One must work to develop a realistic understanding of ways of working with older people. There are many erroneous "age related" negative cognitions that may sound "understandable" to younger therapists: such as, "Old age is a terrible time", "All my problems are to do with my age", "I'm too old to change my ways now". To avoid endorsing such concepts, it is important that therapists ask themselves a few key questions: "Would I accept this cognition as fact in a younger patient?" and "Would I accept the limitations this person places on his expected outcome in therapy in someone younger?"

Physical health

Increasing age brings with it an increased likelihood of developing chronic medical conditions. However, it does not follow that all older people have a chronic medical condition that has a limiting functional effect. In any formulation it is important to enquire about the presence and impact of medical conditions (Zeiss, Lewinsohn, Rohde, & Seeley, 1996). Equally, it is important to enquire about patients' understanding about diseases and to examine what they think will be the outcome of any chronic condition. In the cognitive model for late life depression, health status is formulated using the WHO (1980) classification of disease where physical ill-health is understood in terms of three components: impairment, disability and handicap. This is an extremely useful way for therapists to conceptualize illness. In this system, impairment refers to any loss/abnormality of body structure, appearance, organ or system. For example, in the case of someone having a stroke, the impairment would refer to the damage caused to neural tissue caused by the vascular event. Disability is the impact of the impairment on the individual's ability to carry out "normal" activities. So, following a stroke, the person may now find it difficult to dress himself without assistance. Handicap can be thought of as the social impact that the impairment or disease has on the individual. Consequences of handicap are reflected in the disadvantages an individual experiences in his interaction with, and adaptation to, the environment. Thus the person who experienced the stroke may find that other people now treat him differently, and he increasingly feels excluded from normal communications. The notion of handicap is useful for looking at the consequences of disease for an individual. Indeed, it highlights the loss of opportunity to participate in society that many older people will experience should they develop certain disease conditions. In this tripartite framework, it is apparent that the way a person copes with the disability and handicap components is under much more conscious control by the individual as compared to impairment component. The usefulness of this system to psychotherapists is that it allows one to consider the consequences of impairment or disease for an individual. While this system of classification has recently been superseded by a framework that more explicitly focuses on a more complex way of formulating health status (WHO, 2001), the simplicity of this model makes it useful.

A further helpful way of conceptualizing ill health is via Baltes' (1991) components of successful ageing. In this latter framework, individuals select a limited set of behaviours that they optimize to allow them to compensate for any limitations due to illness (SOC: selection, optimization and compensation). Use of these strategies can enable an older adult to accommodate to the changes associated with ageing and promote maximal independent functioning even in the presence of a chronic disabling condition. The model is exemplified by Baltes (1991), with reference to the concert pianist Arthur Rubinstein who continued to perform at an exceptional level late into life. When asked for the secrets of his success, Rubinstein mentioned three strategies. First, he reduced the scope of his repertoire (an example of selection), and secondly, Rubinstein, practised this repertoire more intensely than would have been the case when he was younger (an example of optimization). Finally, Rubinstein used "tricks" such as slowing down his speed of playing just immediately prior to playing the fast segments of his repertoire, thereby giving his audience the impression of faster play than was actually the case; an example of compensation for the effects of ageing on speed. Thus the psychological consequences of physical illnesses can be dealt with by first understanding the disability and handicap experience by the individual and then managing this by developing creative solutions using the SOC model (Baltes, 1991).

Concluding thoughts

Within this comprehensive conceptualization framework, a developmental approach is adopted across the entire lifespan of the individual. Later life is seen as another stage of life that shares similarities with all other stages of life. Transitions and challenges will have to be faced by the individual in order to maximize his emotional and physical independence. Adopting this perspective gives CBT therapists a rationale for treatment. The authors have found that mapping out the various domains has helped many therapists specializing in the field to conduct assessments, and consequently interventions, in a more focused manner. For example, the explication of the physical domain has provided therapists with a treatment rationale even where depression is considered to be a "biological" effect of illness, such as in stroke or heart disease. An important attribute of this conceptualization framework is that elements overlap and interact. Indeed, as outlined earlier, cohort beliefs may influence how an individual reacts to a change in health status ("I must not be a burden to my family"), and may determine some aspects of an individual's sociocultural beliefs ("Growing older is growing weaker").

The above conceptual model, although comprehensive, is clear and readily accounts for the complex nature of older people's experiences. This is thought to be an important feature as often CBT therapists unfamiliar to working with older people are vulnerable to feeling deskilled when working in the midst of such complexities. Such as, when working with a depressed older client, presenting with a range of physical illnesses, multiple loss experiences, and age related negative thoughts (such as "It is depressing to be old"). It is in the light of these challenges that cognitive therapists who work with older people need a specific age related conceptualization that integrates CBT interventions within a gerontological cognitive framework. The age stereotype of ageing equates this phase of life with decrepitude, and this needs to be addressed in order for a patient to challenge erroneous thinking that may prevent him from fully making changes in his life. Thus in applying CBT using this conceptualization, one challenges the age stereotype in a problem focused, specific and pragmatically oriented way, allowing older adults to get the maximal quality of life possible in their circumstances.

Acknowlegements

The authors wish to acknowledge the extremely helpful editorial suggestions made by Ian James on earlier drafts of the paper. We also wish to thank our anonymous reviewers.

References

BALTES, P. B. (1991). The many faces of human ageing: Toward a psychological culture of old age. *Psychological Medicine, 21*, 837–854.

BECK, A. T., RUSH, A. J., SHAW, B. F., & EMERY, G. (1979). *Cognitive therapy of depression*. New York: Guildford Press.

BENGSTON, V. L. (2001). Beyond the nuclear family: The increasing importance of multigenerational bonds. *Journal of Marriage and the Family, 63*, 1–16.

BENGTSON, V., BIBLARZ, T., CLARKE, E., GIARUSSO, R., ROBERTS, R., RICHLIN-KLONSKY, J., & SILVERSTEIN, M. (2000). Intergenerational relationships and aging: Families, cohorts, and social change. In J. M. Clair & R. Allman (Eds.), *The gerontological prism: Developing interdisciplinary bridges*. New York: Baywood Publishing Co.

BENGSTON, V. L., & BOSS, P. (2000). What living longer means to families. In National Council On Family Relations (Ed.), *Public policy through a family lens: Sustaining families in the 21st century*. Minnesota: NCFR.

CHAMPION, L. A., & POWER, M. J. (1995). Social and cognitive approaches to depression: Towards a new synthesis. *British Journal of Clinical Psychology, 34*, 485–503.

CHURCH, M. (1983). Psychological therapy with elderly people. *Bulletin of the British Psychological Society, 36,* 110–112.
CHURCH, M. (1986). Issues in psychological therapy with elderly people. In I. Hanley & M. Gilhooley (Eds.), *Psychological therapies for the elderly.* London: Croom Helm.
COLLINS, E., KATONA, C., & ORRELL, M. W. (1997). Management of depression in the elderly by general practitioners: Referral for psychological treatments. *British Journal of Clinical Psychology, 36,* 445–448.
ERIKSON, E. H. (1997). *The life cycle completed: Extended version with new chapters on the ninth stage of development by Joan M. Erikson.* New York: W. W. Norton.
GATZ, M., FISKE, A., FOX, L. S., KASKIE, B., KASL-GODLEY, J. E., MCCALLUM, T. J., & WETHERELL, J. L. (1998). Empirically validated psychological treatments for older adults. *Journal of Mental Health and Aging, 4,* 9–46.
GRANT, R. W., & CASEY, D. A. (1995). Adapting cognitive behavioral therapy for the frail elderly. *International Psychogeriatrics, 7,* 561–571.
GERSON, S., BELIN, T. R., KAUFMAN, M. S., MINTZ, J., & JARVIK, L. (1999). Pharmacological and psychological treatments for depressed older patients: A meta-analysis and overview of recent findings. *Harvard Review of Psychiatry, 7,* 1–28.
HEEREN, T. J., DERKSEN, B. F., HEYCOP, T. H., & VAN GENT, P. (1997). Treatment, outcome and predictors of response in elderly depressed in-patients. *British Journal of Psychiatry, 170,* 436–440.
ISOMETSA, E., SEPPALA, I., HENRIKSSON, M., KEKKI, P., & LONNQVIST, J. (1998). Inadequate dosaging in general practice of tricyclic vs other antidepressants for depression. *Acta Psychiatrica Scandinavia, 98,* 429–431.
KATONA, C., & LIVINGSTON, G. (2002). *Drug treatment in old age psychiatry.* London: Martin Dunitz.
KNIGHT, B. (1996). *Psychotherapy with older adults* (2nd ed.). London: Sage Publications.
KODER, D. A., BRODATY, H., & ANSTEY, K. J. (1996). Cognitive therapy for depression in the elderly. *International Journal of Geriatric Psychiatry, 11,* 97–107.
LAIDLAW, K. (2001). An empirical review of cognitive therapy for late life depression: Does research evidence suggest adaptations are necessary for cognitive therapy with older adults? *Clinical Psychology and Psychotherapy, 8,* 1–14.
LAIDLAW, K. (2003a). Depression in older people. In M. J. Power (Ed.), *Mood disorders: A handbook of science and practice.* Chichester: John Wiley & Sons.
LAIDLAW, K. (2003b). Impact of mental health and illness on successful ageing. In M. Kovacs (Ed.), *Late life depression and anxiety.* Budapest: Springer.
LAIDLAW, K., DAVIDSON, K. M., & ARBUTHNOT, C. (1998). GP referrals to clinical psychology and treatment for depression: A pilot study. *Newsletter of the Psychologist Special Interest Group in Elderly People (PSIGE), 67,* 6–8.
LAIDLAW, K., THOMPSON, L. W., DICK-SISKIN, L., & GALLAGHER-THOMPSON, D. (2003). *Cognitive behaviour therapy with older people.* Chichester: John Wiley & Sons.
LANDREVILLE, P., LANDRY, J., BAILLARGEON, L., GUERETTE, A., & MATTEAU, E. (2001). Older adults' acceptance of psychological and pharmacological treatments for depression. *Journal of Gerontology; Psychological Sciences, 50B,* P285–P291.
LEBOWITZ, B. D., & NIEDEREHE, G. (1992). Concepts and issues in mental health and aging. In J. E. Birren, R. B. Sloane & G. D. Cohen (Eds.), *Handbook of mental health and aging* (2nd ed.). San Diego: Academic Press.
LEVINE, L. (1996). "Things were different then": Countertransference issues for younger female therapists working with older female clients. *Social Work in Health Care, 22,* 73–88.
LEVY, B. R. (2003). Mind matters: Cognitive and physical effects of ageing self-stereotypes. *Journal of Gerontology: Psychological Sciences, 58B,* P203–P211.
MORRIS, R. G., & MORRIS, L. W. (1991). Cognitive and behavioural approaches with the depressed elderly. *International Journal of Geriatric Psychiatry, 6,* 407–413.

NEUGARTEN, B. L., & DATAN, N. (1973). Sociological perspectives on the life cycle. Reprinted in D. Neugarten (Ed.) (1996), *The meanings of age: Selected papers of Bernice Neugarten.* Chicago: University of Chicago Press.

NEUGARTEN, B. L., MOORE, J. W., & LOWE, J. C. (1965). Age norms, age constraints and adult socialization. Reprinted in D. Neugarten (Ed.) (1996), *The meanings of age: Selected papers of Bernice Neugarten.* Chicago: University of Chicago Press.

ORRELL, M., COLLINS, E., SHERGILL, S., & KATONA, C. (1995). Management of depression in the elderly by general practitioners: Use of antidepressants. *Family Practice, 12,* 5–11.

PADESKY, C. A. (1998). *Protocols and personalities: The therapist in cognitive therapy.* Paper presented at the European Association of Behavioural and Cognitive Therapies, Cork, Ireland.

PERSONS, J. B. (1989). *Cognitive therapy in practice: A case formulation approach.* New York: W. W. Norton.

ROTHERA, I., JONES, R., & GORDON, C. (2002). An examination of the attitudes and practice of general practitioners in the diagnosis and treatment of depression in older people. *International Journal of Geriatric Psychiatry, 17,* 354–358.

ROWE, J. W., & KAHN, R. L. (1998). *Successful aging.* New York: Pantheon Books.

SCOGIN, F., & MCELREATH, L. (1994). Efficacy of psychosocial treatments for geriatric depression: A quantitative review. *Journal of Consulting and Clinical Psychology, 62,* 69–74.

SMYER, M. A., & QUALLS, S. H. (1999). *Aging and mental health.* Oxford: Blackwell Publishers.

STEUER, J. L., & HAMMEN, C. L. (1983). Cognitive-behavioral group therapy for the depressed elderly: Issues and adaptations. *Cognitive Therapy and Research, 7,* 285–296.

THOMPSON, L. W. (1996). Cognitive-behavioral therapy and treatment for later life depression. *Journal of Clinical Psychiatry, 57* (Suppl 5), 29–37.

UNUTZER, J., KATON, W., SULLIVAN, M., & MIRANDA, J. (1999). Treating depressed older adults in primary care: Narrowing the gap between efficacy and effectiveness. *Milbank Quarterly, 77,* 225–256.

VAILLANT, G. E. (2002). *Aging well: Surprising guideposts to a happier life from the Landmark Harvard Study of Adult Development.* Boston: Little Brown & Co.

WHO (1980). *International classification of impairments, disabilities and handicaps: A manual of classification relating to the consequences of disease.* Geneva: World Health Organization.

WHO (2001). *International classification of functioning, disability and health.* Geneva: World Health Organization.

ZEISS, A. M., LEWINSOHN, P. M., ROHDE, P., & SEELEY, J. R. (1996). Relationship of physical disease and functional impairment to depression in older people. *Psychology and Aging, 11,* 572–581.

[30]

A Randomized, Controlled Trial of a Group Intervention To Reduce Fear of Falling and Associated Activity Restriction in Older Adults

Sharon Tennstedt,[1] Jonathan Howland,[2] Margie Lachman,[3]
Elizabeth Peterson,[4] Linda Kasten,[1] and Alan Jette[5]

[1]New England Research Institutes, Watertown, Massachusetts.
[2]Boston University School of Public Health.
[3]Brandeis University, Waltham, Massachusetts.
[4]University of Illinois at Chicago.
[5]Sargent College of Health and Rehabilitation Sciences, Boston University.

A randomized, single-blind controlled trial was conducted to test the efficacy of a community-based group intervention to reduce fear of falling and associated restrictions in activity levels among older adults. A sample of 434 persons age 60+ years, who reported fear of falling and associated activity restriction, was recruited from 40 senior housing sites in the Boston metropolitan area. Data were collected at baseline, and at 6-week, 6-month, and 12-month follow-ups. Compared with contact control subjects, intervention subjects reported increased levels of intended activity ($p < .05$) and greater mobility control ($p < .05$) immediately after the intervention. Effects at 12 months included improved social function ($p < .05$) and mobility range ($p < .05$). The intervention had immediate but modest beneficial effects that diminished over time in the setting with no booster intervention.

FEAR of falling is a serious consequence of falls that has not been addressed adequately in the medical literature. In addition to the physical consequences of falls (Baker, 1985; Kellogg International Work Group, 1987; Lamb, Miller, & Meradez, 1987; Tideiksaar, 1989), a number of investigators and clinicians have reported fear of falling following a fall (Murphy & Isaacs, 1982; Nevitt, Cummings, Kidd, & Black, 1989; Tinetti, Speechly, & Ginter, 1988). Results of several studies suggest that fear of falling is prevalent among community-dwelling older adults and may be independent of fall injuries (Maki, Holliday, & Topper, 1991). Investigations by Howland and colleagues (1993), Tinetti, deLeon, Doucette, and Baker (1994), and Arfken, Lash, Birge, and Miller (1994) indicate that from 30–50% of independently living elderly persons are afraid of falling. In the study by Howland and colleagues (1993), this fear ranked first when compared to the fear of being robbed in the street, forgetting an important appointment, losing a cherished item, or experiencing financial difficulties. The results of focus groups conducted to explore the etiology of fear of falling among elders suggested that many older adults do not discuss their fear of falling, or fall experiences, with support group members (family, friends, and health care providers) because they perceive the falls as sentinel events in precipitating nursing home admissions (Walker & Howland, 1992).

Restricted physical and social activity following a fall has been reported by several studies (Kellogg International Work Group, 1987; Nevitt, Cummings, & Hudes, 1991; Vellas, Cayla, Bocquet, de Pemille, & Albarede, 1987).

This restriction of activity might be due in part to fall-related injury. However, activity limitation due to fear of falling has also been noted as a consequence of falls, independent of injury, prior falls, age, gender, or health status (Howland et al., 1993; Kellogg International Work Group, 1987).

Fear of falling may itself become a risk factor for falls when this fear restricts activity to the point of causing deconditioning and associated muscle weakness (Hindmarsh & Estes, 1989). Indeed, Campbell, Borrie, and Spears (1989) have identified restricted activity as a risk factor for falls among older adults, and Maki and colleagues (1991) have shown an association between fear of falling and decreased postural performance, also a potential contributor to falls. In a cohort of community-dwelling elderly, Tinetti and colleagues (1994) found fear of falling marginally related to ADL–IADL functioning. However, falls-efficacy, or the degree of confidence in performing common daily activities without falling, was independently correlated with ADL–IADL functioning as well as higher order physical and social functioning. That is, persons who were afraid of falling or lacked confidence to perform activities without falling functioned at a lower level and were less active.

Thus, there is substantial evidence that fear of falling has a broad range of negative consequences for the physical, social, and mental health status of independently living older adults. Of the several fall prevention trials, including the FICSIT trials, previously reported in the literature (Alkalay, Alkalay, & Carmela, 1984; Buchner et al., 1993; Fiatarone et al., 1994; Hornbrook, Stevens, & Wingfield,

1993; Hornbrook et al., 1994; Lord, Ward, Williams, & Strudwick, 1995; Mulrow et al., 1994; Obonya, Drummond, & Isaacs, 1983; Province et al., 1995; Reinsch, MacRae, Lachenbruch, & Tobis, 1992; Tinetti et al., 1994; Wolf et al., 1988; Wolf-Klein et al., 1996; Wolfson et al., 1993), only four included fear of falling among the outcomes of interest (Hornbrook et al., 1994; Reinsch et al., 1992; Tinetti et al., 1994; Wolf-Klein et al., 1996). Results of these four trials have been mixed. A randomized trial of a multifactorial intervention to reduce the risk of falling among elders living in the community resulted in a significant decrease in both falls and fear of falling for treatment group subjects relative to controls (Tinetti et al., 1994). Another randomized trial of efficacy of Tai Chi exercise for falls reduction also found significant reductions in fear of falling for intervention subjects relative to controls (Wolf-Klein et al., 1996). In two other trials for fall-reduction interventions, however, one yielded no change in fear of falling among the treatment group (Reinsch et al., 1992), whereas the other showed an increase in fear of falling among intervention subjects (Hornbrook et al., 1994).

Given the prevalence and impact of fear of falling on older adults, intervention to reduce this fear is desirable. Programs that reduce the risk of falling may not always reduce fear of falling because this fear is, to some extent, independent of the risk of falling (Maki et al., 1991). Given that fear of falling can exist in the absence of a history or risk of falls, it is an important clinical problem for intervention. However, intervention for the fear of falling may be constrained because health care providers are not aware of the prevalence and intensity of this fear among their older patients and because older patients are reluctant to talk about falls and fear of falling with physicians and nurses (Vellas et al., 1987).

This article reports results of a randomized controlled trial of an intervention designed specifically to reduce the fear of falling among community-dwelling older persons who manifested this fear. The cognitive-behavioral intervention program was designed to reduce fear of falling by increasing self-efficacy and the sense of control over falling. This was accomplished by strategies for (a) restructuring misconceptions to promote a view of falls risk and fear of falls as controllable; (b) setting realistic goals for increasing activity; (c) changing the environment to reduce falls risk; and (d) promoting physical exercise to increase strength and balance. The primary aim of the intervention was to reduce fear of falling. The secondary aim was to increase physical, social, and functional activity. Three hypotheses were tested:

1. Fear of falling will decrease in intervention subjects as compared to control subjects.
2. Self-efficacy and a sense of control regarding risk of falling will increase in intervention subjects as compared to control subjects.
3. Physical and social activity will increase in intervention subjects as compared to control subjects.

Intervention effects at the 6-week (post-intervention), 6-month, and 12-month follow-ups are reported.

METHODS

Participants

Participants were recruited through public or publicly subsidized senior housing sites in the greater Boston area. This was done to facilitate participation by persons who, because of their fear of falling, might have restricted outside mobility. Eligibility criteria included: age ≥ 60 years; absence of any major physical or health condition that would preclude participation in the intervention; English-speaking; and self-reported restriction in activity due to fear of falling. This latter criterion was assessed by asking, "Are you worried or concerned that you might fall?" "As a result of this concern, have you stopped doing some of the things you used to do or like to do?" The word "fear" was not used in these questions based on pretrial focus group feedback that persons "worry" about falling but do not describe themselves as "afraid of falling." This was confirmed by early recruitment efforts and is consistent with Bandura's (1982) theory that self-reports of global states, such as fear, do not predict actual behavior.

The unit of randomization was the senior housing site. Forty sites were recruited for participation and pair-matched on the basis of number of units and percent minority residents, with one site in each pair randomly assigned to the intervention group and the other site to a placebo attention control group. Participants were recruited in-person through self-response to posted notices of the program and individual referrals by housing managers, social workers, and case managers for the state-funded home care program. Eligibility was determined and written informed consent obtained by the interventionist during home visits. The trial comprised 434 persons, with 216 assigned to the intervention group and 218 to the attention control group. The study was approved by the Institutional Review Boards at the New England Research Institutes and Boston University Medical Center.

The Intervention

The objective of the intervention (titled "A Matter of Balance") was to promote activity (functional, physical, social) by reducing fear of falling. The intervention was a structured group program consisting of eight 2-hour sessions scheduled twice a week for 4 weeks. To diversify group activities, several techniques were used: videotape, lecture, group discussion, mutual problem solving, role playing, exercise training, assertiveness training, home assignments, and behavioral contracting. The early sessions focused on changing attitudes and self-efficacy prior to attempting changes in actual behavior. This cognitive restructuring (Lachman, Weaver, Bandura, Elliott, & Lewkowicz, 1992; Rodin, 1983) approach involved instilling adaptive beliefs such as greater perceived control, greater confidence in one's abilities, and more realistic assessment of failures. This approach was used to educate participants about their self-conceptions regarding falls and risk of falling and to promote a realistic and adaptive view. The initial cognitive restructuring component of the intervention used a documentary-style video (produced specifically for the program) to present older adults expressing fears about falling in contrast to others expressing positive attitudes. Subsequent program content used varying activities to promote an adaptive conception of fear of falling with training exercises on how to shift from maladaptive (self-defeating) to adaptive (motivating) cognitions.

The cognitive restructuring approach to changing attitudes about activity restrictions related to fear of falling was reinforced by didactic material regarding incidence of falls and risks of falling, skill training in falls prevention, and what to do if one falls. The benefits of exercise to improve strength and balance in order to reduce falls risk as well as the physical and psychological costs of inactivity were emphasized. Strength training exercises (using wide elastic bands for resistance) were included in six of the eight sessions to instruct and encourage subjects to continue them independently. Approximately 30 minutes were devoted to these exercises in each of the six sessions. Assertiveness techniques were taught in the context of encouraging discussion with health care providers and family of concerns about falling and actual falls. Finally, in order to individualize the intervention, an additional approach was the use of behavioral contracts and goal-setting regarding desirable changes (e.g., correcting identified home hazards; engaging in physical exercise; resuming a formerly restricted activity).

The intervention was conducted at 20 sites between October 1994 and July 1996. Each intervention program was conducted by one of two trained facilitators. Average group membership was 10.8 participants.

The social contact control.—To test for the effect of social contact on the outcomes, a single 2-hour group session was provided for subjects in the control group. This session consisted of a didactic presentation regarding incidence and risk factors for falls, a video (produced by AARP) on home hazards that increase fall risk, and steps that can be taken to reduce risk. The approach included group discussion but did not address fear of falling or any restricted activity related to this fear. No training was provided in cognitive restructuring techniques, exercise, assertiveness, or behavioral self-management.

Twenty attention control groups were conducted, also between October 1994 and July 1996, with average group size of 10.9 participants. The social contact control programs were conducted by the same facilitators who conducted the intervention programs.

Measures

Outcomes variables.—There were two outcomes of interest: the proximate outcome of fear of falling and the distal outcome of physical, social, and functional activities. Three scales were used to measure the subject's fear or worry about falling. Because of the concern that subjects might not directly report their concerns about falling as fear, we used a modified version of the Falls Efficacy Scale developed by Tinetti, Richman, and Powell (1990) to measure fear of falling. This scale was based on Bandura's (1987) theory of self-efficacy, which has been shown empirically to predict behavior (Bandura, 1982; Mischel,

1968). This instrument assesses confidence in performing, without falling, each of 10 activities considered essential to independent living: cleaning house, getting dressed and undressed, preparing simple meals, taking a bath or shower, simple shopping, getting in or out of a chair, going up and down stairs, walking around the neighborhood, reaching into cabinets or closets, and hurrying to answer the phone. Two additional items were included—carrying bundles from the store and exercising. Using a revised scoring procedure (Tinetti et al., 1994), subjects rated their degree of confidence from 1 (not at all sure) to 4 (very sure). The confidence score is the average level of confidence they have across all activities, ranging from 1–4, a higher score indicating greater confidence. Cronbach alphas for this modified scale ranged from .90 to .93 across waves. Perceived control over falling was assessed by a four-item scale developed for this study, consisting of items revised from existing control inventories that have focused on other domains such as fear of memory loss (Lachman et al., 1992). Items focused on control over the environment and ability to do things to prevent falls and reduce fear of falling: "I can reduce my risk of falling"; "I can overcome my fear of falling"; "There are things I can do to keep myself from falling"; and "Falling is something I can control." Responses ranged from (1) strongly disagree to (4) strongly agree. Item scores were averaged to obtain a scale score, with higher scores indicating a greater sense of control. Cronbach alphas ranged from .70 to .76 across waves. A five-item scale to measure subjects' perceived ability to manage risk of falls or actual falls was also developed for the purposes of this study. On a 4-point scale with (1) being not at all sure to (4) very sure, subjects reported their perceived ability to: "find a way to get up if you fall"; "find ways to reduce falls"; "protect yourself if you fall"; "increase your physical strength"; and "get more steady on your feet." Cronbach alphas ranged from .76 to .84 across waves. The number of falls was collected at baseline and each follow-up with the question, "How many times have you fallen all the way down to the floor or ground, or fallen and hit an object like a chair or stair?" (Kellogg International Work Group, 1987; Nevitt et al., 1991). At baseline, the reporting period was the previous 3 months; at each follow-up, the reporting period was the time interval since the previous interview.

The distal behavioral outcome was measured with two scales, the abbreviated Sickness Impact Profile (SIP) (Bergner, Bobbit, Carter, & Gilson, 1981); and a seven-item scale measuring intended activity. The SIP indicates the changes in a person's behavior because of health problems. The abbreviated SIP consists of 68 items covering behaviors involved in carrying out one's life activities in six categories. Subjects respond affirmatively to those items that describe current dysfunction. Each of the items is assigned a utility weight based on estimates of the severity of each type of dysfunction. This allows for calculation of continuous scores expressed as a percent of the maximum dysfunctional score for each of six subscales and for an overall score. Two dimension scores for physical function (sum of 3 categories: somatic autonomy, mobility range, mobility control) and psychosocial function (sum of 3 categories: social behavior, emotional stability, and psychological autonomy and communication) were also calculated as per Bergner and colleagues (1981). The Intended Activity scale, developed for this study, asks subjects to rate how sure they are that they will perform various activities in the coming week. Rated from (1) not at all sure to (4) very sure, the activities included light and heavy housework, home repairs, lawn or yard care, walking outside the home, light sport, and strenuous sport or recreational activities. Higher scores indicate higher activity levels. Cronbach alphas ranged from .59 to .64 across waves.

Predisposing variables.—Those predisposing characteristics of subjects that might influence their likelihood of participation in the intervention or the outcomes include the following sociodemographic and health characteristics: age, gender, marital status, years of education, race, and recent history of falls. Recent falls history was assessed by asking, "(H)ow many times have you fallen all the way down to the floor or ground, or fallen and hit an object like a chair or stair, in the past 3 months?"

Process variables.—Attendance as well as reason for absence or dropout was recorded by the interventionists for each subject to document intervention dose. Interventionists also kept detailed logs of each session as well as a record of falls reported by the subjects during the intervention period. To assess adherence by the interventionists to the standardized intervention protocol, the investigators selected intervention sessions for observation. Finally, other community-level activities regarding falls prevention were monitored as they might contribute to observed change in the outcomes.

Data collection.—Data were gathered at baseline, 6 weeks (i.e., 1–2 weeks following the intervention), 6 months, and 12 months. Interviews were conducted by telephone using computer-assisted telephone interviewing (CATI) by interviewers blinded to the intervention status of the subjects.

Analysis

Sociodemographic, health, and fall-related variables at baseline were compared, using chi-square and t tests as appropriate, to detect significant differences between subjects in the intervention and control groups. In addition, because 37% of intervention subjects were considered not compliant with the intervention (attended ≤ 4 sessions), baseline measures of compliant intervention subjects were compared to those intervention subjects considered noncompliant for significant differences.

Analysis of variance was used to examine the effect of the intervention on change in fall-related and activity measures immediately post-intervention (6 weeks), 6 months, and 12 months after the baseline interview. A mixed model was used to account for the possible dependence of observations within each housing site, with the treatment (intervention or social contact control) modeled as a fixed effect and the site as a random effect within treatment. Time and Treatment × Time interactions were also included as fixed effects. The effect of the intervention was measured by the interaction of Treatment and Time. Baseline scores were included to control for initial differences between subjects. When a significant treatment effect was seen, linear contrasts were created to measure short-term change (baseline to 6 weeks) and long-term change (baseline to 6 months and baseline to 12 months). Following the principle of intention-to-treat, effects are reported for the entire sample. Results of the analysis of treatment effects comparing treatment subjects considered compliant with control subjects are reported as well. When demographic covariates (age, gender, education, race, marital status) were included in the models, the results were not changed. Therefore, results of these models are not reported.

Sample size and power.—Logistical considerations determined that each group had approximately 12 participants. Power calculations were based on this number in 20 intervention and 20 control sites. This provided 80% power at alpha = .05 to detect differences between the control and intervention groups' mean change scores of 7–8% for the attitude scales and differences of approximately 15% for the SIP and its subscales.

RESULTS

Sample Characteristics

The baseline characteristics of subjects enrolled in the trial are displayed in Table 1. There were no significant differences between subjects assigned to the intervention versus the control group. Consistent with characteristics of residents of senior housing, the participants were predominately female, not married, with a mean age of 78 years. Just over 9% were minorities, 3% lower than the 12% rate of minorities in the greater Boston area. On average, most had less than a high school education.

In terms of falls, the majority (75.1%) reported no falls in the previous 3 months; 9.4% reported two or more falls in the previous 3 months. Whereas rates of falling in most studies of community populations (e.g., Blake et al., 1988; Lord, Ward, Williams, & Anstey, 1994; Reinsch et al., 1992; Tinetti et al., 1994) are reported on an annualized basis, this rate is similar to a 3-month rate reported by Cummings, Nevitt, and Kidd (1988). On average, participants expressed being "slightly" to "somewhat afraid" that they might fall and hurt themselves. In contrast, however, they were more reserved in their reported confidence to perform common activities without falling. They reported similar levels of confidence in being able to manage an actual fall and in the control they had over reducing fall risk or their fear of falling.

In respect to activity and functional status, subjects on average expressed reservation (i.e., "a little sure") that they would perform a range of daily activities. Based on the total SIP score, these subjects were more functionally disabled than adult populations with a variety of clinical conditions (de Bruin, Diederiks, de Witte, Stevens, & Philipsen, 1994; Deyo & Centor, 1986; MacKenzie, Charlson, DiGioia, & Kelley, 1986) yet, as might be expected, less disabled than nursing home residents (Gerety et al., 1994).

Table 1. Baseline Sample Characteristics, n = 434

	Value	Range	Coding
Demographic			
Age: mean (± SD) years	77.8 (7.71)	60–100	years
Gender: female	389 (89.6%)		0 = female, 1 = male
Marital status: married	33 (7.6%)		0 = married, 1 = not married
Race: White	394 (90.8%)		0 = non-White, 1 = White
Education mean (± SD) years	10.7 (2.8)	0–18	years
Fall-related			
Falls efficacy scale	2.62 (0.74)	1–4	4 = greater confidence
Falls control	3.44 (0.93)	1–5	5 = higher perceived ability
Falls management	2.15 (0.72)	1–4	4 = higher ability to manage falls
No. of falls in past 3 months: 1	63 (15.5%)		number of falls
≥2	38 (9.4%)		
Function			
SIP total score	30.0 (16.5)	0–100	higher = more dysfunction
Physical subscale	29.2 (16.9)	0–100	higher = more dysfunction
Mobility range	47.0 (30.9)	0–100	higher = more dysfunction
Mobility control	53.4 (27.0)	0–100	higher = more dysfunction
Somatic autonomy	11.1 (13.3)	0–100	higher = more dysfunction
Psychosocial	31.4 (21.0)	0–100	higher = more dysfunction
Social behavior	50.8 (26.9)	0–100	higher = more dysfunction
Psychological autonomy	26.1 (27.6)	0–100	higher = more dysfunction
Emotional stability	19.4 (23.6)	0–100	higher = more dysfunction
Intended activity	1.78 (0.45)	1–4	4 = high

Focusing on the Social Behavior and Mobility Range scores of the SIP as indicators of activity level, subjects generally reported moderate levels of restricted activity. In contrast, the Somatic Autonomy score indicated that subjects reported minimal restriction with self-care activities, but the mean score for the Mobility Control subscale indicated a moderate level of mobility limitations such as walking inside and outside the house; duration of standing; and transfer or kneeling, stooping, or bending without support.

Compliance and Attrition

A measure of compliance with the intervention protocol was attendance at the group sessions. Based on the content of the program, attendance at 5 or more sessions was considered necessary for achieving a treatment effect. Of the 216 intervention subjects, 137 (63.4%) attended 5–8 sessions, 44 (20.4%) attended 1–4 sessions, and 35 (16.2%) subjects attended no sessions. Self-reported reasons for absence were typically illness or conflicting appointment or activity—usually health care-related. A comparison of subjects who attended fewer than 5 sessions with those who attended 5 or more sessions (see Table 2) revealed that subjects who attended fewer than than 5 sessions had a higher total SIP score as well as higher scores for the Physical subscale and Social Behavior score of the Psychosocial subscale indicating greater limitations in behavior. Consistent with this, a lower score on the Intended Activity scale also indicated lower activity level. That is, these subjects were generally less active than those who participated more fully in the intervention program. This greater restriction in activity, however, was not attributed to recent falls or a lower

Table 2. Comparison of Subjects Who Attended ≥ 5 Sessions With Subjects Who Attended < 5 Sessions

	≥ 5 Sessions (n = 137)	< 5 Sessions (n = 79)	p value
Gender: male	7.3%	15.2%	NS*
Age: years	77.8	77.2	NS
Any recent falls: yes	24.1%	35.4%	NS
Falls efficacy	2.70	2.52	NS
Intended activity	1.84	1.63	<.001
Sickness Impact Profile (SIP)			
Total score	28.1	33.6	<.05
Physical subscale score	26.8	33.0	<.01
Somatic autonomy	8.9	13.8	<.05
Mobility range	44.0	54.7	<.05
Mobility control	51.2	55.6	NS
Psychosocial subscale score	30.5	34.7	NS
Social behavior	49.5	57.6	<.05
Emotional stability	19.7	21.1	NS
Psychological autonomy and communication	24.6	28.0	NS

*NS = not significant.

falls efficacy, nor to gender or age, which did not differ by compliance status.

Of the 434 subjects enrolled in the trial, 388 (89.4%) completed the 6-week follow-up interview, 333 (76.7%) completed the 6-month follow-up, and 341 (78.6%) completed the 12-month follow-up. Forty-seven (10.8%) subjects died during the trial. Lack of follow-up for other reasons was similar in each group.

Effect of Intervention on Outcomes

The mean change scores in fall-related and activity outcome measures for the intervention and control subjects are displayed in Table 3. Looking first at the entire intervention group versus the social contact control group, subjects in the intervention group reported increased levels of intended activity and less health-related dysfunction with mobility control immediately after the intervention period. In addition, in contrast to control subjects, those in the intervention group had reductions in total dysfunction and general physical dysfunction that were of borderline significance. Data from the 12-month follow-up show intervention effects of improved mobility range, although of borderline significance. The unadjusted mean change scores for all of these SIP scores are small, however, and probably do not represent clinically meaningful change (MacKenzie et al., 1986).

The mean change scores for compliant intervention subjects compared to control subjects indicate more extensive effects of the intervention (also shown in Table 3). Some differences in change score that were insignificant for the full intervention sample are statistically significant for the sample of compliant intervention subjects. Those intervention subjects who attended 5 or more sessions of the program reported a significant increase in falls efficacy and perceived ability to manage falls immediately after the intervention. Increases in falls efficacy and ability to manage falls were significant at the 12-month contact as well. In addition, subjects who complied with the intervention had slight (not clinically important) reductions in physical and total dysfunction SIP scores and larger reductions in mobility range and social behavior dysfunction at the end of 12 months, whereas control subjects showed increased dysfunction in all of these areas. The 12-month change scores for mobility range and social behavior indicate change sufficient to represent clinically important improvement (MacKenzie et al., 1986).

These analyses were repeated with covariates including gender, age, education level, race, and marital status. Although certain covariates were significantly related to some of the scores, the treatment effects were the same as reported here.

Table 4 contains effect sizes for the significant mean change scores reported in Table 3. In general, the effect sizes are small (Cohen, 1988). The largest intervention effect was achieved for perceived ability to manage falls across all three follow-up periods.

Safety Monitoring

Because of concern that potentially increased activity levels among intervention subjects might result in increased incidence of falls, the number of falls reported by subjects in both the intervention and control groups was monitored. There was no statistically significant difference either in the number of subjects who reported a fall or in the mean number of falls reported by intervention subjects versus control subjects during the interval between baseline and 6-week follow-up (.25 vs .19) baseline and 6-month follow-up (.58 vs .52), or baseline and 12-month follow-up (1.03 vs 1.07). Subjects who reported multiple falls in the 3 months prior to baseline were more likely than subjects reporting no falls (64% vs 16%) to report multiple falls between baseline and 12-month follow-up ($p = .001$). However, there was no statistically significant difference in the number of falls reported by multiple fallers in the intervention group versus the control group.

DISCUSSION

In contrast to previous trials that attempted to reduce falls or the risk of falls, this intervention trial was directed

Table 3. Mean Change Scores: Comparing Intended and Compliant Intervention Subjects to the Attention Control Group

	6-Week Follow-up			6-Month Follow-up			12-Month Follow-up		
$N =$	Control 190	Intended 198	Compliant 131	Control 168	Intended 175	Compliant 120	Control 176	Intended 170	Compliant 118
Number of falls	-0.23	-0.21	-0.25	-0.14	0.01	-0.03	0.16	0.32	0.27
Falls efficacy	-0.04	0.12	0.15**	-0.07	-0.04	0.01	-0.12	-0.04	0.09**
Falls management	0.12	0.25	0.37***	0.09	0.16	0.28*	0.02	0.15	0.26**
Control fear of falling	0.11	0.26	0.38	-0.03	0.09	0.15	0.03	0.07	0.20
Intended activity	-0.02	0.09*	0.09+	-0.07	-0.01	0.00	-0.07	-0.04	-0.02
SIP: Total score	0.60	-2.52+	-2.63+	-0.24	1.59	1.20	2.92	1.50	-0.43*
SIP Physical score	0.32	-2.63+	-2.74+	-0.37	1.37	1.06	3.35	1.56	-0.21*
Somatic autonomy	-0.18	-1.23	-1.41	-0.40	1.41	0.31	3.01	2.26	1.15
Mobility control	1.78	-3.70*	-3.55*	-0.52	2.69	2.68	5.13	3.57	1.74
Mobility range	0.30	-4.82	-4.92	-0.16	-0.47	1.23	2.48	-2.18+	-5.48*
SIP Psychosocial score	0.76	-2.32	-2.44	-0.35	1.97	1.45	1.92	1.41	-0.82
Psychological autonomy and communication	-0.41	-1.87	-1.51	-0.93	3.99+	2.47	-0.01	2.09	0.67
Social behavior	1.83	-3.53	-3.57+	1.62	0.64	0.78	4.36	-0.55	-4.03*
Emotional stability	0.96	-1.75	-2.78	2.20	-0.01	0.44	2.38	1.42	-1.19

+$p < .075$; *$p < .05$; **$p < .01$; ***$p < .001$.

Table 4. Effect Sizes: Comparing Intended and Compliant Intervention Subjects to the Attention Control Group

	N =	6-Week Follow-up			6-Month Follow-up			12-Month Follow-up		
		Control 190	Intended 198	Compliant 131	Control 168	Intended 175	Compliant 120	Control 176	Intended 170	Compliant 118
Falls efficacy				0.20						0.12
Falls management				0.51			0.39			0.36
Intended activity			0.20							
SIP: Total score										0.03
SIP physical score										0.01
Mobility control			0.14	0.13						
Mobility range										0.18
SIP psychosocial score										
Social behavior										0.15

at reducing fear of falling and associated restrictions in physical and social activity. Using a cognitive-behavioral approach, the 8-session intervention showed an immediate effect on increasing the level of intended activities and mobility control. These effects decayed by the 6-month follow-up.

Consistent with the rules of clinical trials, intervention effects were analyzed in the entire sample. These analyses revealed modest, if not minimal, immediate effects and no maintenance of effects over time. However, because of the rate of noncompliance with the intervention and the fact that the noncompliant subjects were less active (both current and intended activities) than compliant subjects, we were interested in whether the results would differ when the analysis was restricted to compliant subjects. The results of that analysis show more extensive immediate intervention effects, particularly on falls efficacy and attitudes toward managing falls. Further, these effects were maintained at the 12-month follow-up. In addition, subjects who attended five or more sessions also reported improvements in mobility and social behavior. Therefore, although all subjects reported lower levels of intended activity at the 12-month follow-up, subjects attending the intervention program reported improved functioning. In comparison, the control subjects reported increased dysfunction at 12 months. These 12-month intervention effects are entirely consistent with the approach of cognitive restructuring (Lachman et al., 1992; Rodin, 1983) in trying to change attitudes and self-efficacy prior to attempting to change behaviors.

It is quite understandable that individuals who are more disabled and are not very active—in addition to being concerned about falling—would be less likely to participate fully in an intervention that is an activity in and of itself. However, these results suggest that extra effort directed toward encouraging and facilitating their participation in the intervention, as well as increased intervention focus on reasons for and consequences of restricted activity, might enhance the impact of the intervention for a vulnerable population. Anecdotal data from the interventionists also suggest that an in-home, individual, rather than group intervention might be necessary to reach the population with greater fear of falling and restricted activity, some of whom refused to leave their apartment at all.

The cognitive changes in attitudes and self-efficacy observed in the compliant intervention group are particularly noteworthy given the study population. The subjects in cognitive training trials (Lachman et al., 1992; Rodin, 1983) that have used a cognitive restructuring approach are generally of a higher educational level than the subjects in this trial. Likely associated with their lower educational level, these subjects were less introspective and less experienced with cognitively oriented exercises. The interventionists reported that the cognitive restructuring exercises were the most challenging components of the intervention, whereas the behavioral exercises and skill training components were the easiest to conduct. Yet the changes in the cognitive outcomes (i.e., falls efficacy, ability to manage falls) showed the greatest immediate and sustained effect of the intervention for persons attending five or more sessions.

The fact that decay of intervention effect in changes in attitude and self-efficacy was detected at 6 months argues for a booster session, possibly at 3 months after the intervention. At least one, perhaps two, sessions are indicated to reinforce the desired changes in attitude and self-efficacy regarding falls and fall management. Also focusing on the desired behavioral changes in the booster sessions might reduce decay of increased intended activity as well as have an earlier effect on social and physical functioning.

This intervention was not designed to decrease falls per se. However, by decreasing activity restriction, which is associated with physical deconditioning, the intervention might reduce risk of falls. There was no significant difference between intervention and control subjects in the number of falls for up to 12 months. This might be interpreted as the intervention having no effect on reduction in falls or falls risk. However, if indeed the intervention participants increased their activity levels, they might have increased their risk of falls as well. Therefore, the fact that their incidence of falls was not greater than that for control subjects suggests that perhaps there is some secondary impact of the intervention on reducing falls risk. This study relied on self-report to collect data on numbers of falls for intervals ranging from 6 weeks to 12 months, as compared to other studies that have used monthly calendars (Tinetti et al., 1994) or weekly return postcards (Cummings et al., 1988). Recognizing the limited accuracy of recall regarding falls, as reported by Cummings et al. (1988), the number of falls in this study might be underreported. However, there is no evidence to suggest differential reporting by intervention versus control subjects that might change the interpretation of results.

The absence of any meaningful change in targeted outcomes for control subjects provides further support of the efficacy of the intervention. However, the design limitation of the one-session attention control condition did not make it possible to control entirely for the effect of social contact on attitudinal and behavioral changes in the intervention group. It is possible that the supportive atmosphere and interaction of the group intervention contributed to the observed changes in fears about falling. Yet, because of the carefully constructed design of the content of the attention control session (i.e., nothing regarding fear of falling, restricted activity, or changing maladaptive attitudes), it is reasonable to conclude that the cognitive restructuring approach and skill training of the intervention made a substantial contribution to the observed effects.

In summary, the results of this study and others (Campbell et al., 1989; Howland et al., 1993; Maki et al., 1991; Reinsch et al., 1992; Tinetti et al., 1994) have established the importance of fear of falling as a targeted outcome for intervention. The results of this trial indicate that short-term changes can be achieved in maladaptive attitudes and beliefs about falling and in activity levels and functioning. The results indicate the need for a booster session a few months after the intervention to maintain the changes in attitude and self-efficacy and to foster quicker change in behavior and activity levels. Further, the fact that this intervention was conducted with a vulnerable population suggests that it could be conducted with similar effectiveness and efficacy with healthier, more functional—yet still afraid of falling—populations.

ACKNOWLEDGMENTS

This research was performed through the Boston University Roybal Center Consortium for Research in Applied Gerontology, funded by the National Institute on Aging (Grant No. AG11669).

The authors acknowledge the contributions of Dr. Mary Bandura to the design and content of the intervention.

Address correspondence to Dr. Sharon Tennstedt, Institute for Studies on Aging, New England Research Institutes, 9 Galen Street, Watertown, MA 02172. E-mail: sharont@neri.org

REFERENCES

Alkalay, L., Alkalay, J., & Carmela, S. (1984). Reducing falls among the elderly in a small community. *The Practitioner, 227,* 698.

Arfken, C. L., Lash, H. W., Birge, S. J., & Miller, J. P. (1994). The prevalence and correlates of fear of falling in elderly persons living in the community. *American Journal of Public Health, 84,* 565–570.

Baker, S. P. (1985). Fall injuries in the elderly. *Clinical Geriatric Medicine, 1,* 501–512.

Bandura, A. (1982). Self-efficacy mechanism in human agency. *American Psychologist, 37,* 122–147.

Bandura, A. (1987). Reflections on self-efficacy. In S. Rachman (Ed.), *Advances in behavior research and therapy* (pp. 237–269). Oxford, U.K.: Pergamon.

Bergner, M., Bobbit, R., Carter, W., & Gilson, B. S. (1981). The Sickness Impact Profile: Development and final revision of a health status measure. *Medical Care, 18,* 787–805.

Blake, A. J., Morgan, K., Bendall, M. J., Dallosso, H., Arie, T. H., Fentem, P. H., & Bassey, E. J. (1988). Falls by elderly people at home: Prevalence and associated factors. *Age and Ageing, 17,* 365–372.

Buchner, D. M., Cress, M. E., Wagner, E. H., de Lateur, B. J., Price, R., & Abrass, I. B. (1993). The Seattle FICSIT move it study: The effect of exercise on gait and balance in older adults. *Journal of the American Geriatrics Society, 41,* 489–497.

Campbell, A. J., Borrie, M. J., & Spears, G. F. (1989). Risk factors for falls in a community-based prospective study of people 70 years and older. *Journal of Gerontology: Medical Sciences, 44,* M112–M117.

Cohen, J. (1988). *Statistical power analysis for the behavioral sciences* (2d ed.). Hillsdale, NJ: Lawrence Erlbaum Associates.

Cummings, S., Nevitt, M., & Kidd, S. (1988). Forgetting falls: The limited accuracy of recall of falls in the elderly. *Journal of the American Geriatrics Society, 36,* 613–616.

de Bruin, A. F., Diederiks, J. P. M., de Witte, L. P., Stevens, F. C. J., & Philipsen, H. (1994). The development of a short generic version of the Sickness Impact Profile. *Journal of Clinical Epidemiology, 47,* 407–418.

Deyo, R. A., & Centor, R. M. (1986). Assessing the responsiveness of functional scales to clinical change: An analogy to diagnostic test performance. *Journal of Chronic Disease, 39,* 897–906.

Fiatarone, M. A., O'Neill, E. F., Ryan, N. D., Clements, K. M., Solares, G. R., Nelson, M. E., Roberts, S. B., Kehayias, J. J., Lipsitz, L. A., & Evans, W. J. (1994). Exercise training and nutritional supplementation for physical frailty in very elderly people. *New England Journal of Medicine, 330,* 1769–1775.

Gerety, M. B., Cornell, J. E., Mulrow, C. D., Tuley, M., Hazuda, H. P., Lichtenstein, M., Aguilar, C., Kadri, A. A., & Rosenberg, J. (1994). The Sickness Impact Profile for nursing homes. *Journal of Gerontology: Medical Sciences, 49,* M2–M8.

Hindmarsh, J. J., & Estes, E. H. Jr. (1989). Falls in older persons: Causes and interventions. *Archives of Internal Medicine, 149,* 2217–2222.

Hornbrook, M. C., Stevens, V. J., & Wingfield, D. J. (1993). Seniors' program for injury control and prevention. *Journal of the American Geriatrics Society, 41,* 309–314.

Hornbrook, M. C., Stevens, V. J., Wingfield, D. J., Hollis, J. F., Greenlick, M. R., & Ory, M. G. (1994). Preventing falls among community-dwelling older persons: Results from a randomized trial. *The Gerontologist, 34,* 16–23.

Howland, J., Peterson, E. W., Levin, W. C., Fried, L., Pordon, D., & Bak, S. (1993). Fear of falling among the community dwelling elderly. *Journal of Aging and Health, 5,* 229–243.

Kellogg International Work Group. (1987). The prevention of falls in later life. A report of the Kellogg International Work Group on the prevention of falls by the elderly. *Danish Medical Bulletin, 34* (Suppl 4), 1–24.

Lachman, M. E., Weaver, S. L., Bandura, M., Elliott, E., & Lewkowicz, C. (1992). Improving memory and control beliefs through cognitive restructuring and self-generated strategies. *Journal of Gerontology: Psychological Sciences, 47,* P293–P299.

Lamb, K., Miller, J., & Meradez, M. (1987). Falls in the elderly: Causes and prevention. *Orthopaedic Nursing, 6,* 45–49.

Lord, S. R., Ward, J. A., Williams, P., & Anstey, K. J. (1994). Physiological factors associated with falls in older community-dwelling women. *Journal of the American Geriatrics Society, 42,* 1110–1117.

Lord, S. R., Ward, J. A., Williams, P., & Strudwick, M. (1995). The effect of a 12 month exercise trial on balance, strength and falls in older women: A randomized controlled trial. *Journal of the American Geriatrics Society, 43,* 1198–1206.

MacKenzie, C. R., Charlson, M. E., DiGioia, D., & Kelley, K. (1986). Can the Sickness Impact Profile measure change? An example of scale assessment. *Journal of Chronic Disease, 39,* 429–438.

Maki, B. E., Holliday, P. J., & Topper, A. K. (1991). Fear of falling and postural performance in the elderly. *Journal of Gerontology: Medical Sciences, 46,* M123–M131.

Mischel, W. (1968). *Personality and assessment.* New York: Wiley.

Mulrow, C., Gerety, M. B., Kanten, D., Cornell, J. E., DeNino, L. A., Chiodo, L., Aguilar, C., O'Neil, M. B., Rosenberg, J., & Solis, R. M. (1994). A randomized trial of physical rehabilitation for very frail nursing home residents. *Journal of the American Medical Association, 271,* 519–524.

Murphy, J., & Isaacs, B. (1982). The post-fall syndrome: A study of 36 elderly patients. *Gerontology, 28,* 265–270.

Nevitt, M. C., Cummings, S. R., & Hudes, E. S. (1991). Risk factors for injurious falls: A prospective study. *Journal of Gerontology: Medical Sciences, 46,* M164–M170.

Nevitt, M. C., Cummings, S. R., Kidd, S., & Black, D. (1989). Risk factors for falls among elderly persons living in the community. *New England Journal of Medicine, 319,* 1701–1706.

Obonya, T., Drummond, M., & Isaacs, B. (1983). Domiciliary physiotherapy for older people who have fallen. *International Rehabilitative Medicine, 5,* 157–160.

Province, M., Hadley, E., Hornbrook, M., Lipsitz, L. A., Miller, J. P., Mulrow, C. D., Ory, M. G., Sattin, R. W., Tinetti, M. E., & Wolf, S. L. (1995). The effects of exercise on falls in elderly patients: A preplanned meta-analysis of the FICSIT trials. *Journal of the American Medical Association, 273,* 1341–1347.

Reinsch, S., MacRae, P., Lachenbruch, P. A., & Tobis, J. (1992). Attempts to prevent falls and injury: A prospective community study. *The Gerontologist, 32,* 450–456.

Rodin, J. (1983). Behavioral medicine: Beneficial effects of self control training in aging. *International Review of Applied Psychology, 32,* 153–181.

Tideiksaar, R. (1987). Fall prevention in the home. *Topics in Geriatric Rehabilitation, 3,* 57–64.

Tideiksaar, R. (1989). Geriatric falls: Assessing the cause, preventing recurrence. *Geriatrics, 44*(7), 57–61, 64.

Tinetti, M. E., Baker, D. I., McAvay, G., Claus, E., Garrett, P., Gottschalk, M., Koch, M., Tramork, K., & Horowitz, R. (1994). A multifactorial intervention to reduce the risk of falling among elderly people living in the community. *New England Journal of Medicine, 331,* 821–827.

Tinetti, M. E., deLeon, C. F. M., Doucette, J. T., & Baker, D. I. (1994). Fear of falling and fall-related efficacy in relationship to functioning among community-living elders. *Journal of Gerontology: Medical Sciences, 49,* M140–M147.

Tinetti, M. E., Richman, D., & Powell, L. (1990). Falls efficacy as a measure of fear of falling. *Journal of Gerontology: Psychological Sciences, 45,* P239–P243.

Tinetti, M. E., Speechley, M., & Ginter, S. F. (1988). Risk factors for falls among elderly persons living in the community. *New England Journal of Medicine, 319,* 1701–1707.

Vellas, B., Cayla, F., Bocquet, H., de Pemille, F., & Albarede, J. L. (1987). Prospective study of restriction of activity in old people after falls. *Age and Ageing, 16,* 189–193.

Walker, J. E., & Howland, J. (1992). Exploring dimensions of the fear of falling: Use of focus group interview. *Gerontology, 15,* 1–3.

Wolf, S. L., Barnhart, H. X., Kutner, N. G., McNeely, E., Coogler, C., & Xu, T. The Atlanta FICSIT Group. (1996). Reducing frailty and falls in older persons: An investigation of Tai Chi and computerized balance training. *Journal of the American Geriatrics Society, 44,* 489–497.

Wolf-Klein, G. P., Silverstone, F. A., Basavaraju, N., Foley, C. J., Pascaru, A., & Ma, P. H. (1988). Prevention of falls in the elderly population. *Archives of Physical Medicine and Rehabilitation, 69,* 689–691.

Wolfson, L. I., Whipple, R., Judge, J., Amerman, P., Derby, C., & King, M. (1993). Training balance and strength in the elderly to improve function. *Journal of the American Geriatrics Society, 41,* 341–343.

Received September 26, 1997
Accepted April 28, 1998

[31]

The Effects of Late-Life Spousal Bereavement Over a 30-Month Interval

Larry W. Thompson and Dolores Gallagher-Thompson
Older Adult and Family Research and Resource Center
Division of Gerontology, Stanford University School of Medicine
and Geriatric Research, Education and Clinical Center
Veterans Administration Medical Center
Palo Alto, California

Andrew Futterman
Holy Cross College

Michael J. Gilewski
Veterans Affairs Outpatient Clinic
Los Angeles

James Peterson
Andrus Gerontology Center
University of Southern California, Los Angeles

Self-report measures of grief, depression, and general psychopathology were studied in widows and widowers over a 2.5-year period following death of their partner. A comparison sample of men and women was also followed for the same period. Differences in severity of depression and psychopathology previously reported at 2 months postloss (Gallagher, Breckenridge, Thompson, & Peterson, 1983) diminished to nonsignificant levels at 12 and 30 months. However, significant differences between bereaved and comparison subjects on measures of grief were still apparent 30 months after spousal loss. A main effect of gender for depression and psychopathology (but not for grief) was found at 2 and 12 months: Women reported more distress than men regardless of bereavement status. Results indicate that the experience of grief persists for at least 30 months in both older men and women who have lost their spouse.

It is well documented that both younger and older bereaved individuals typically show many symptoms characteristic of depression (Breckenridge, Gallagher, Thompson, & Peterson, 1986; Gallagher, Breckenridge, Thompson, & Peterson, 1983; Lund, Caserta & Dimond, 1986; Murrell & Himmelfarb, 1989; Pearlin, 1982; Reich, Zautra & Guarnaccia, 1989; W. Stroebe, M. Stroebe, & Domittner, 1985; Zisook & Schuchter, 1986) and report more physical complaints than nonbereaved individuals (Maddison & Viola, 1968; Thompson, Breckenridge, Gallagher, & Peterson, 1984) in the months immediately following a loss. This negative impact of bereavement on mental and physical health has been called the *loss effect* (W. Stroebe & M. Stroebe, 1987). Although physical health changes have received considerable attention as a consequence of bereavement, we focus on measures of psychological distress in this article.

This research was supported in part by Grants MH37196 from the National Institute of Mental Health and AG01759 from the National Institute on Aging to Larry W. Thompson.
Parts of this article were presented in November 1988 at the annual scientific meeting of the Gerontological Society in San Francisco.
We thank Bernice Marcopulous for her thoughtful criticism of an earlier version of this article.
Correspondence concerning this article should be addressed to Larry W. Thompson, Older Adult and Family Research and Resource Center, Gerontology Research Program (182C/MP), Veterans Administration Medical Center, 3801 Miranda Avenue, Palo Alto, California 94304.

Gender may influence the response to loss and the magnitude of the loss effect, though the extent and nature of this influence is controversial. One set of studies suggests that women demonstrate more emotional distress than men in bereavement (e.g., Gallagher, Breckenridge, Thompson, Peterson, 1983). This finding is in keeping with more generally observed sex differences in depressive symptomatology (see Nolen-Hoeksema, 1987, for review). Another set of studies suggests that although widows may report more distress, it is the widowers who actually suffer more (M. Stroebe & W. Stroebe, 1983). Yet other studies point to broad similarities in the bereavement response of men and women (Lund et al., 1986; Van Zandt, Mou, & Abbott, 1989).

The duration of time following loss and the method of mental and physical health assessment are two additional important determinants of the degree of loss effect (W. Stroebe & M. Stroebe, 1987). Although the bereaved may report poorer physical health and more depressive symptomatology at two to four months following loss (Gallagher, Breckenridge, Thompson, et al., 1983; Parkes & Weiss, 1983; Thompson et al., 1984), by 2 years post-loss most studies suggest that bereaved and nonbereaved persons are comparable on indexes of depression (Lund, Caserta, & Dimond, 1989; W. Stroebe & M. Stroebe, 1987).

When asked about their adjustment to loss in more specific terms, however, as opposed to describing their general mood (e.g., on a depression inventory), studies present a different picture (see Wortman & Silver, 1989, for a review). Even 2 to 4 years after loss, bereaved individuals still frequently report difficulties adapting to the loss (Lund, Dimond, Caserta, Johnson, Poulton, & Connolly, 1985; Parkes & Weiss, 1983; Zisook & Schuchter, 1986). Such findings, coupled with reported differences between the symptomatology of grief and depression on depression scales (Breckenridge et al., 1986; Gallagher, Breckenridge, Thompson, Dessonville, & Amaral, 1982), point to the importance of assessing the bereavement response by using specific measures of grief and adaptation to loss in addition to general measures of psychological distress, especially later in bereavement. Few studies have reported on changes in both grief and other measures of distress.

Although several studies have evaluated bereavement effects longitudinally (Falleti, Gibbs, Clark, Pruchno, Caserta, & Berman, 1989; Heyman & Gianturco, 1973; Lund et al., 1986, 1989; Maddison & Viola, 1968; Parkes & Weiss, 1983; W. Stroebe et al., 1985; Van Zandt et al., 1989; Zisook & Schuchter, 1986), only a few studies have compared an older sample of widows and widowers with an appropriate comparison sample (e.g., Faletti et al., 1989; Lund et al., 1989; Van Zandt et al., 1989).

Our study reports the effects of spousal bereavement on psychological distress over a 2½ year period in a community sample of older men and women (over 55 years of age). In this study we used standardized measures of grief, depression, and psychopathology, permitting an examination of different dimensions of psychological distress. We used a comparison community sample of elderly men and women who were not currently undergoing spousal bereavement, but who had recently experienced death of a close friend or family member, thus permitting an evaluation of bereavement effects on psychological distress independent of normal aging effects.

Three hypotheses were proposed:

1. The first hypothesis predicted that elders who have suffered the loss of their spouse would report higher levels of distress at 2, 12, and 30 months than would elders who have not suffered a similar loss. More specifically, we hypothesized that measures of grief would show greater differences between bereaved individuals and controls than would measures of depression and general psychopathology. This is in keeping with findings reported previously (Gallagher, Breckenridge, Thompson, et al., 1983) and studies indicating long-term difficulties in resolving grief and issues of loss (Lund et al., 1985; Parkes & Weiss, 1983; Wortman & Silver, 1989; Zisook & Schuchter, 1986).

2. The second hypothesis predicted that the bereaved individuals and controls would demonstrate differential change in measures of psychological distress over time. It was anticipated that bereaved elders would report less distress at 12 and 30 months following loss than they had at 2 months. Similar measures among comparison controls, however, were not expected to change.

3. The third hypothesis predicted that women would report greater psychological distress than men at 2, 12, and 30 months, regardless of bereavement status. This is in keeping with previously reported findings of gender differences in mental health (Gallagher, Breckenridge, Thompson, et al., 1983). More generally, it is also in keeping with gender differences in depressive symptomatology reported by Nolen-Hoeksema (1987).

Method

Subjects

Two hundred and twelve bereaved elders (99 men and 113 women) and a comparison control sample of 162 elders (84 men and 78 women) participated in this study. Details of the sampling procedure and group demographics have been described in earlier studies (Gallagher, Breckenridge, Thompson, 1983; Thompson et al., 1984). Briefly, to obtain participants for the bereaved sample, death certificates at the Los Angeles County Health Department were searched periodically, and all spouses of persons over 55 who had died within the preceding 2 to 4 weeks were mailed a description of the project and a stamped postcard with which willingness to be interviewed could be indicated. Mailings were sent to 2,450 persons. Of the 735 who responded (30%), 212 met the age criteria and also resided within a reasonable distance from the research center to permit home interviews. Participants for the comparison sample were recruited from senior centers, residential facilities for elders, and the Emeriti Center mailing list of the University of Southern California. These were adults over age 55, who either were currently married or, if currently single, had not lost a spouse through death or divorce within the past 5 years. However, to be eligible for participation in the study, each control respondent had to have experienced the death of either another family member or a close friend within the past 5 years. Both bereaved and comparison samples can be characterized as Caucasian, well educated (80% had some high school), and of moderate socioeconomic status (most had income between $10,000 and $30,000). The age range of all subjects was 55–83 years. The two groups were roughly comparable in age: Means for bereaved and comparison samples were 68.20 years (SD = 7.84 years) and 70.11 years (SD = 7.65 years), respectively. Subjects in both groups had been married for many years: the mean number of years married for the bereaved group was 38.68 years (SD = 13.08), and the mean for the comparison sample (including those who were no longer married or were living alone) was 37.43 years (SD = 14.02).

Procedure

Structured interviews were conducted at three times following the loss of spouse, at approximately 2 months, 12 months, and 30 months. Interviews and measures were completed in the subjects' homes unless they requested to come to the research center. In the interviews the following were reviewed: demographic characteristics, religious beliefs and practices, coping strategies used in response to spousal loss, prior stressful life events, utilization of social supports, upheaval in routines of daily living, judgments of subjects' marital relationship, and self-ratings of psychological and physical health status. Comparable interviews were conducted at identical intervals with the comparison subjects. (Copies of all measures are available on request.)

Four self-report measures of psychological distress obtained at all times of measurement were considered in our analyses, as follows: (a) the Beck Depression Inventory (BDI; Beck, Ward, Mendelson, Mock, & Erbaugh, 1961); (b) the Global Severity Scale of mental health symptoms on the Brief Symptom Inventory (BSI; Derogatis, 1977; Derogatis & Spencer, 1982); (c) rating of current grief on the Texas Inventory of Grief–Revised (TIGCUR; Faschingbauer, 1981; Faschingbauer, Devaul, & Zisook, 1977); and (d) rating of past grief on the Texas Inventory of Grief—Revised (TIGPAST; Faschingbauer, 1981; Faschingbauer et al., 1977).

The BDI is a multiple-choice symptom scale developed to assess the severity of depression. Twenty-one items tap aspects of depressive features, such as sleep and appetite problems, sadness, guilt and self-reproach, suicidal ideation, and loss of interest in everyday activities. Reliability and concurrent validity (with psychiatric diagnoses) have been demonstrated in older adult samples (Gallagher, Breckenridge, Steinmetz, & Thompson, 1983; Gallagher, Nies, & Thompson, 1982).

The BSI is a 53-item version of the Hopkins Symptom Checklist (HSCL–90; Derogatis, 1977) developed by Derogatis and Spencer (1982). The BSI yields scores on nine dimensions of psychopathology (e.g., psychoticism, anxiety, phobic reaction). In our report, the Global Severity Index, an average of the nine scales, was used (BSISEV). Adequate psychometric properties of this instrument and index have been demonstrated in several populations and are reviewed in Derogatis and Spencer (1982). Norms for this measure with the elderly are reported in Hale, Cochran, and Hedgepeth (1984).

The TIG is a self-report measure of both past disruption due to loss and current feelings of grief. Ratings of agreement with descriptive statements (e.g., "I was unusually irritable after the person died," "I miss this person terribly") are made on Likert-type scales (1 = *entirely false*, 5 = *entirely true*). Eight items comprise the past disruption scale, (TIGPAST) with scores potentially ranging from 0 to 40; 13 items comprise the current grief scale (TIGCUR), with scores ranging on this scale from 0 to 65. Reliabilities from .70 to .90 have been reported for the two TIG subscales; these and other psychometric properties are reviewed in Faschingbauer (1981) and Faschingbauer et al. (1977). Bereaved subjects were instructed to fill out the form with their spouse in mind. Control subjects were asked to think of a recent death of a significant person in their life, identify that person by relationship (e.g., sister, brother, mother, father, in-law, close friend, etc.), indicate how many months ago the death occurred, and complete the measure with that death in mind. Higher scores on all measures are indicative of greater psychological distress.

Design

To test hypotheses relating to group and gender differences and to change across time in distress following the loss of spouse, a $2 \times 2 \times 3$ multivariate profile analysis of repeated measures (Morrison, 1976) was used. In this design, group (bereaved vs. controls) and gender (male vs. female) were the between-subjects, independent variables; the four indexes of psychological distress were within-subject, dependent variables measured at 2, 12, and 30 months. This design is doubly multivariate (Bock, 1975): First, there are multiple dependent variables that are analyzed through multivariate analysis of variance (MANOVA); second, each variable is measured more than once in a repeated-measures fashion. Taken together, each of these repeated-measures are treated as a multivariate profile and analyzed through a MANOVA. Analyses involved ordinary least squares estimation and associate listwise-deletion procedures (Wilkinson, 1989). In all analyses, multivariate tests were conducted first, by using the F approximation of the Wilks's lambda likelihood ratio (Rao, 1973). When multivariate tests were significant, univariate tests were then examined by using the Bonferroni procedure to maintain Type I error at nominal levels (Bray & Maxwell, 1985).

We completed two sets of analyses to test the hypotheses: The first compared the bereaved group and the *total* control group across the 30-month period, but included only the BDI and the BSISEV scores. These analyses permitted us to evaluate bereavement and gender effects and their interaction with time on measures of depression and general psychopathology.

The second set of analyses included the two grief measures as well, but a restricted sample of the controls was used in the comparison with the bereaved samples. This was done because legitimate concerns could be raised as to whether spousal loss is distinctly different from the grief experienced because of other losses, and therefore comparisons between the two might be inappropriate. This issue has received attention indirectly (e.g., Wortman & Silver, 1989), but there have been few empirical studies comparing the impact of spousal loss with the loss of other family members. Bass, Noelker, Townsend, and Deimling (1990) reported that conjugal compared with parental loss results in lower well-being and reported health changes along with increased difficulty in adjustment, but acknowledged some controversy in the literature even about this and suggested that "whether and how the relationship between survivors and deceased relatives may influence the bereavement experience" (1990, p. 33) should be a useful point of departure for subsequent studies.

For purposes of this article, we considered that grief in general can be viewed on a continuum, regardless of the source of loss. Note that the TIG was designed to measure the level of grief, irrespective of the nature of the relationship between the bereaved and the deceased. To our knowledge, prior research comparing intensity of grief following loss of spouse as opposed to other relatives has not been assessed by using a measure designed specifically to report levels of the grief experience. However, because there may be some concern on the part of the readers regarding this comparison, we decided to include only those control subjects who were reporting a loss that presumably would be most similar to the loss of a spouse. Therefore, in our sample we felt the comparison controls for the grief measures should be restricted to subjects who were reporting their level of grief for the loss of another immediate family member.

Results

Of the 374 subjects (212 bereaved, 162 controls) who began the study, 224 (60%; 123 bereaved, 101 controls) completed all of the self-report measures at all three times. This level of subject attrition is similar to that of other bereavement studies involving elders; for example, Lund et al. (1986) had a 34% attrition rate at the end of 2 years.

Table 1 shows the means and standard deviations of each distress measure at 2, 12, and 30 months for those subjects who remained in the study. Inspection of the means for the BDI indicates that all four groups were within normal ranges at each time of measurement, with the exception of the bereaved women at 2 months following the loss of the spouse. Bereaved women then had a mean BDI score of 10.65, which is in the mild depression range clinically (Gallagher, Breckenridge, Thompson, & Peterson, 1983). The BSISEV scores were very similar to means for normal community samples in this age range at all time points (Hale et al., 1984). The level of current grief (TIGCUR) reported by bereaved elders at 2 months ($M = 43.39$ for men and women combined) appeared to be somewhat higher than that reported for two younger adult samples (Faschingbauer, 1981). However, TIGCUR means at 12 and 30 months (Ms = 37.97 and 35.80, respectively, for men and women combined) were more similar to those reported by Faschingbauer (1981) for the time period covering the 1st year of bereavement ($M = 37.10$) and the period from 1 to 5 years following spousal loss ($M = 34.28$). Comparisons between the two samples also appeared to be similar on the measure reflecting the level of disruption at the time of the loss (TIGPAST). Unfortunately, more specific age and time comparisons could not be made with the data presented by Faschingbauer because finer-grained breakdowns of his data (by age and time since loss) were not available.

Table 1
Means and Standard Deviations for Self-Report Measures of Depression, General Psychopathology, and Grief Obtained From Elderly Widows, Widowers, and Control Subjects

	Bereaved				Controls			
	Men (n = 42)		Women (n = 81)		Men (n = 51)		Women (n = 50)	
Time point	M	SD	M	SD	M	SD	M	SD
2 months postloss								
BDI	7.66	6.26	10.65	8.23	4.34	4.21	7.78	6.76
BSISEV	.51	.51	.62	.54	.38	.44	.49	.42
TIGCUR	43.97	10.36	44.66	12.10	27.08	11.15	30.59	13.60
TIGPAST	18.57	6.73	19.73	6.89	11.49	5.57	13.71	8.89
12 months postloss								
BDI	6.50	9.43	8.10	7.18	5.65	5.41	6.56	6.41
BSISEV	.38	.33	.47	.40	.36	.35	.42	.42
TIGCUR	38.87	13.40	39.07	11.20	24.64	11.02	29.66	12.60
TIGPAST	18.85	12.02	19.33	6.59	11.40	5.30	14.02	6.85
30 months postloss								
BDI	5.28	5.28	7.22	6.31	6.24	6.88	6.62	5.83
BSISEV	.36	.45	.49	.52	.41	.46	.41	.42
TIGCUR	36.12	10.12	35.98	11.46	26.24	11.55	30.09	11.43
TIGPAST	17.64	7.36	17.67	7.37	12.00	5.02	13.14	7.47

Note. Grief measures are included here for the total control group, although analyses of grief measures reported in the text were completed by using the restricted comparison control group reported in Table 2. BDI = Beck Depression Inventory; BSISEV = global severity rating of the Brief Symptom Inventory; TIGCUR = rating of current grief on the Texas Inventory of Grief–Revised; TIGPAST = rating of grief at the time of the loss on the Texas Inventory of Grief–Revised.

Overall Severity of Distress Among Bereaved and Control Elders

Hypothesis 1 predicted that scores on measures of psychological distress would be greater in the bereaved compared with the control group. In particular, this hypothesis predicted that this effect would be more evident in measures of grief rather than measures of symptoms of depression or general psychopathology. To test this hypothesis, we considered results from both sets of analyses. In the first set of analyses the MANOVA completed on the entire sample, using only the BDI and BSISEV scores, yielded an overall main effect for group that was not significant, $F(2, 233) = 0.76$. The interaction of Group × Time for these two measures was highly significant, but this is reported later. In contrast, when the grief measures were included, while using the restricted comparison sample, the main effect of bereavement summed across all three measurement times was highly significant, $F(4, 116) = 19.95$, $p < .001$. A closer look at the univariate analyses indicated that this was due primarily to the measures of current grief, $F(1, 169) = 63.90$, $p < .001$, and past grief, $F(1, 169) = 38.17$, $p < .001$, rather than the measures of depression, $F(1, 169) = 1.48$, and general psychopathology, $F(1, 169) = 2.273$. Table 2 provides the means and standard deviations for the spousally bereaved and their control counterparts who reported grief due to the death of an immediate family member. As can be seen in both Tables 1 and 2, the TIGCUR and TIGPAST were higher for the spousally bereaved than for the two comparison groups throughout the 30-month period, whereas the BDI and the BSISEV measures were elevated for the bereaved group only during the early portion of the bereavement period. Thus, Hypothesis 1 is generally supported. However, Group × Time analyses revealed significant differences between groups on the depression and general psychopathology measures at specific time points, as well.

Differential Change in Psychological Distress of Bereaved and Control Elders

Hypothesis 2 predicted a decrease in psychological distress over a 30-month period among bereaved elders, whereas little change was expected among members of the comparison group. The test of this hypothesis was the Bereavement Status × Time of Measurement interaction effect in the MANOVA. Both sets of analyses yielded highly significant interactions, $F(4, 231) = 2.90$, $p < .05$, and $F(8, 162) = 4.64$, $p < .001$, for the first and second sets, respectively). In the first set a significant linear, $F(1, 234) = 5.641$, $p < .02$, and quadratic, $F(1, 234) = 4.671$, $p < .05$, trend was observed for the BDI, as well as significant quadratic trend for the BSISEV, $F(1, 234) = 4.891$, $p < .05$. Inspection of Table 1 indicates that the bereaved showed a greater decline in measures of psychological distress over the 2½ year period of the study than did the controls. In the second set of analyses, univariate tests of the linear and quadratic trends (i.e., orthogonal polynomials) demonstrated that the multivariate Group × Time effect was attributable primarily to a significant Group × Quadratic Trend in BDI, $F(1, 169) = 5.58$, $p < .02$, and a Group × Linear Trend in TIGCUR, $F(1, 169) = 25.39$, $p < .001$.

A comparison of adjacent times of measurement in the first set of analyses (i.e., 2 vs. 12 months, and 12 vs. 30 months)

Table 2
Measures of Depression, General Psychopathology, and Grief for Elderly Widows and Widowers Compared With Control Subjects Who Had Lost an Immediate Family Member

	Bereaved				Controls			
	Men ($n = 42$)		Women ($n = 81$)		Men ($n = 24$)		Women ($n = 26$)	
Time point	M	SD	M	SD	M	SD	M	SD
2 months postloss								
BDI	7.66	6.26	10.65	8.23	4.38	4.91	7.04	6.59
BSISEV	.51	.51	.62	.54	.27	.34	.40	.43
TIGCUR	43.97	10.36	44.66	12.10	25.00	10.25	28.11	12.70
TIGPAST	18.57	6.73	19.73	6.89	10.55	4.84	11.77	6.47
12 months postloss								
BDI	6.50	9.43	8.10	7.18	5.75	6.16	7.19	6.85
BSISEV	.38	.33	.47	.40	.35	.38	.36	.44
TIGCUR	38.87	13.40	39.07	11.20	24.29	10.17	26.88	11.10
TIGPAST	18.85	12.02	19.33	6.59	12.62	5.31	13.19	7.12
30 months postloss								
BDI	5.28	5.28	7.22	6.31	5.08	6.24	5.96	5.84
BSISEV	.36	.45	.49	.52	.33	.49	.40	.41
TIGCUR	36.12	10.12	35.98	11.46	24.25	9.02	29.19	10.87
TIGPAST	17.64	7.36	17.67	7.37	11.37	5.30	12.79	6.72

Note. BDI = Beck Depression Inventory; BSISEV = global severity rating of the Brief Symptom Inventory; TIGCUR = rating of current grief on the Texas Inventory of Grief–Revised; TIGPAST = rating of grief at the time of the loss of the Texas Inventory of Grief–Revised.

showed a group effect on change in the BDI from 2 to 12 months, $F(1, 234) = 7.78$, $p < .01$, but no effect thereafter from 12 to 30 months, $F(1, 234) = 1.20$. An inspection of Table 1 shows that the BDI scores for the bereaved subjects were higher initially but, as will be seen in subsequent analyses, by the end of 1 year there was no difference between bereaved and control subjects. A similar pattern was evident for the BSISEV. There was a significant decline from 2 to 12 months, $F(1, 234) = 4.44$, $p < .05$, but no effect from 12 to 30 months, $F(1, 234) = 0.10$. This picture was still apparent for the BDI and BSISEV in the reduced sample that included the two grief measures (Table 2).

Simple effects of time within each group further illustrates the nature of this interaction. For the bereaved group, there was a highly significant decline from 2 to 12 months on both the BDI, $F(1, 121) = 12.34$, $p < .005$, and the BSISEV, $F(1, 121) = 7.27$, $p < .01$, as expected, with no significant decline from 12 to 30 months on either measure, $F(1, 121) = 0.17$ and $F(1, 121) = 0.11$, for the BDI and the BSISEV, respectively. Control subjects, on the other hand, showed no significant changes on any of these comparisons. In contrast, the TIGCUR was highly significant for the period from 12 to 30 months, $F(1, 169) = 4.55$, $p < .05$, as well as from 2 to 12 months, $F(1, 169) = 7.50$, $p < .01$. As expected, the control subjects showed no change across time for TIGCUR. There was no significant change across time for TIGPAST for the control group. Turning now to a comparison of groups at each time of measurement, the effect of bereavement status on overall psychological distress was significant at all three times; at 2 months, $F(4, 166) = 25.18$, $p < .001$; at 12 months, $F(4, 166) = 13.39$, $p < .001$; and at 30 months, $F(4, 166) = 8.95$, $p < .001$. Once again, univariate tests highlighted a different pattern for the symptoms of depression and general psychopathology than for the measures of grief. Significant differences in grief between bereaved and control subjects were apparent throughout; at 2 months: TIGCUR, $F(1, 220) = 91.83$, $p < .001$; TIGPAST, $F(1, 220) = 46.97$, $p < .001$; at 12 months: TIGCUR, $F(1, 220) = 65.09$, $p < .001$; TIGPAST, $F(1, 220) = 36.87$, $p < .001$; and at 30 months: TIGCUR, $F(1, 220) = 32.52$, $p < .001$; TIGPAST, $F(1, 220) = 30.33$, $p < .001$. As Table 1 illustrates, the bereaved sample reported higher levels of both current and past grief than the controls at 2, 12, and 30 months following loss. It is noteworthy that although there was a steady decline in TIGCUR throughout the study, the spousally bereaved were still showing significantly higher current and past grief at 30 months than were their control counterparts who were grieving the death of a nonspouse family member.

The effect of bereavement on symptoms of depression and general psychopathology, on the other hand, was significant only at 2 months following loss: BDI, $F(1, 169) = 5.20$, $p < .05$; BSISEV, $F(1, 169) = 5.04$, $p < .05$. Bereaved subjects reported more severe depression and more severe psychopathology. At both 12 and 30 months following loss, the univariate values were nonsignificant: BDI, $F(1, 169) = 0.05$, at 12 months; BDI, $F(1, 169) = 0.89$, at 30 months; BSISEV, $F(1, 169) = 0.66$, at 12 months; and BSISEV, $F(1, 169) = 1.04$, at 30 months. This pattern was identical for the larger sample in which only the BDI and BSISEV scores were included for analyses.

Thus, Hypothesis 2 is supported. Bereaved subjects showed greater declines across time than did the controls for measures of current grief, depression, and general psychopathology, and the only change in the measure of past grief was a slight increase for the control group. By the end of 1 year, depression and psychopathology had decreased to a point near the control group levels and showed minimal declines thereafter. The level of current grief, on the other hand, continued to decrease significantly throughout the 30-month period but was still higher than the levels for the control group at the end of 2½ years. The measure of past grief was also higher for the bereaved than for the controls, at all times of measurement.

Gender Differences in Psychological Distress

In the first set of analyses, the MANOVA indicated that the overall main effect of gender was significant, $F(2, 233) = 3.67$, $p < .05$. Univariate analyses showed that both the BDI, $F(1, 234) = 7.32$, $p < .01$, and the BSISEV, $F(1, 234) = 4.15$, $p < .05$, were significantly higher in women than in men. Gender was also assessed at 2, 12, and 30 months separately in the MANOVA. Women reported greater depression at 2 months, $F(1, 234) = 9.95$, $p < .01$, and 12 months, $F(1, 234) = 7.84$, $p < .01$, but not at 30 months, $F(1, 234) = 0.85$. The BSISEV was higher for women at 2 months, $F(1, 234) = 9.07$, $p < .01$; but not at 12 months, $F(1, 234) = 2.45$; or 30 months, $F(1, 234) = 1.08$. The interaction between gender and bereavement status was not significant, $F(2, 233) = 0.66$.

In contrast, the second set of analyses, which included the grief measures, did not yield a significant overall main effect of gender, $F(4, 166) = 1.43$. In view of the gender effects seen earlier, and the fact that sex differences are frequently reported on depression measures, it seemed reasonable to evaluate the four measures separately for these two groups. As noted previously, univariate analysis showed a significant gender effect for the BDI, $F(1, 169) = 5.73$, $p < .02$, and the BSISEV, $F(1, 169) = 4.70$, $p < .05$, at 2 months, but this effect was not apparent for TIGCUR, $F(1, 169) = 0.33$, or TIGPAST $F(1, 169) = 2.56$. There was no evidence of a Gender × Time, Gender × Group, or third order interaction for any of the four measures. At 12 months the effect of gender on the BDI was still significant, $F(1, 169) = 5.16$, $p < .05$, but there was no difference for the BSISEV, $F(1, 169) = 0.83$, TIGCUR, $F(1, 169) = 0.07$, or TIGPAST, $F(1, 169) = 0.62$. As with the analyses at 2 months, none of the interactions were significant. By 30 months there was no gender effect on any of the measures.

Looking within the spousally bereaved group only, at 2 months the overall effect of gender in the MANOVA was significant, $F(4, 118) = 2.45$, $p < .05$. Once again, this was due to the difference for the BDI, $F(1, 121) = 4.63$, $p < .05$, and the BSISEV, $F(1, 121) = 4.84$, $p < .05$. There was no significant effect of gender for the TIGCUR, $F(1, 121) = 8.23$, and the TIGPAST, $F(1, 121) = 2.23$. At 12 months the MANOVA for gender was again significant, $F(4, 118) = 2.64$, $p < .05$. Univariate analyses showed a significant effect for the BDI, $F(1, 121) = 8.474$, $p < .005$, but not for the BSISEV, $F(1, 121) = 2.15$, the TIGCUR, $F(1, 121) = 0.06$, or the TIGPAST, $F(1, 121) = 0.18$. There was no significant gender effect at 30 months. The Gender × Bereavement Status interaction effect on psychological distress was nonsignificant at all three times of measurement: at 2 months, $F(4, 166) = 0.52$; at 12 months, $F(4, 166) = 0.44$; and at 30 months, $F(4, 166) = 1.08$.

Thus, in general these data suggest that women report more symptoms of depression and overall psychopathology than men, particularly in the 1st year of bereavement, but do not report more grief following loss. In fact, as Tables 1 and 2 show, the level of grief among widowers and widows at 2, 12, and 30 months was approximately equal.

Discussion

Results indicate that significant differences in psychological distress were found on several standardized measures at 2, 12, and 30 months following death of the spouse between bereaved and comparison subjects who also reported grief due to the loss of an immediate family member. Although severity of depression and psychopathology in older spousally bereaved men and women returned to the level of the comparison sample by 12 months, differences in the severity of self-reported current and past grief between these two groups remained for 30 months post-loss.

These findings highlight important differences between grief and depression over the bereavement course, especially as time goes on and 2 to 3 years have passed. These data are consistent with other reports pointing out that although depression or psychopathology may subside over the first 12 months, distress over issues relating to the loss itself is likely to persist for a number of years (Parkes & Weiss, 1983).

Women, regardless of bereavement status, reported more depression and symptoms of psychopathology than men, but gender differences were minimal in the expression of grief. A possible explanation for this might be that behavioral expressions of grief, such as weeping for the lost spouse, yearning for their presence, remembering the spouse fondly, and so on, are consistent with both male and female gender roles, but expressions of depression are not. This explanation finds support in two recent studies and in a recent review of the depression literature: Futterman, Gallagher, Thompson, Lovett, and Gilewski (1990) found that both widowers and widows similarly exaggerate the positive attributes of their lost spouse and marriage. Cornelius (1984), in a study of implicit rules or "scripts" that constrain emotional expression, found that men and women use similar scripts in determining the appropriateness and meaningfulness of weeping. Taken together, these findings suggest that both men and women express longing for their lost spouse in similar ways.

Nolen-Hoeksema (1987), on the other hand, presented a comprehensive review of the gender differences in depression literature and described a clear pattern of results: Women report more depressive symptoms than men. She provides a potential explanation for this consistent finding: Women ruminate over depressive thoughts and overreport depression, whereas men deny such thoughts and underreport depression. Different gender-related behavioral styles such as these are compatible with findings of gender differences in depression, regardless of bereavement status. Following loss or any other stressor, men and women will exhibit different tendencies to express depressive symptomatology.

Clinically, these results are instructive for a number of reasons. First, they emphasize the need for a broader-based assessment of the grieving person. In addition to the evaluation of more general mood and psychopathological symptomatology, this should include a more direct assessment of symptoms of grief and loss, reflecting the intensity of yearning for the person who died and how this might have an impact on various facets of current social adjustment.

Second, these findings may have implications for the development of models of normal grieving (c.f. Wortman & Silver, 1989, for a detailed evaluation of current theories of coping with loss). Thus, although a sizeable proportion of elderly persons undergoing bereavement can be expected to report minimal symptoms of general distress within the 1st year, it appears that adaptation to the loss of a spouse, if measured specifically in terms of grief resolution, may take much longer than 2 or 3 years, if it ever occurs. That is, contrary to theories suggesting stages of grief culminating in grief-resolution, it may be that thoroughly working through the pain relating to the loss of a spouse of 20 to 30 years is not something to be expected. As Wortman and Silver (1989) suggested, complete grief-resolution simply may not occur. On the contrary, perhaps, the normal grief response may involve living with grief long after the loss occurs and learning to mentally "compartmentalize" distress associated with the loss and recognize appropriate times to express it.

These results also have implications for the bereavement researcher. W. Stroebe and M. Stroebe (1987) suggested that when evaluating bereavement-specific aspects of loss (e.g., yearning for the deceased) it is not essential to have a comparison sample. When assessing bereavement response among elders, however, this suggestion may not be valid. More often than not, elders have had to deal with losses of significant others prior to the loss of their spouse (Heyman & Gianturco, 1973). It is not surprising, therefore, that the control subjects in our sample reported some grief on current and past grief inventories. Although their level of grief was not equal to that found in the spousally bereaved sample, it was not insignificant (either then or at 12 and 30 months), suggesting that other losses clearly have their own long-term impact.

There are several limitations to be noted regarding this study. The first concerns generalizability of findings because this sample consisted of a well-educated Caucasian group who volunteered to participate in longitudinal research. We do not know the extent to which their experience is similar to that of other social or ethnic groups, or to the less socially advantaged. Second, it would be desirable to have followed these subjects longer, to determine if subjective grief remains high for an even greater number of years and thus empirically test whether or not spousal grief ever really ends. Finally, careful longitudinal research is needed to investigate the long-term effects of other types of major losses, such as death of one's adult child, which may cause even more profound grief than loss of a spouse.

References

Bass, D. M., Noelker, L. S., Townsend, A. L., & Deimling, G. T. (1990). Losing an adult relative: Perceptual differences between spouses and adult children. *Omega, 21,* 21–40.

Beck, A. T., Ward, C. H., Mendelson, M., Mock, J. E., & Erbaugh, J. (1961). An inventory for measuring depression. *Archives of General Psychiatry, 4,* 561–571.

Bock, R. D. (1975). *Multivariate statistical methods in behavioral research.* New York: McGraw-Hill.

Bray, J. H., & Maxwell, S. E. (1985). *Multivariate analysis of variance.* Beverly Hills: Sage.

Breckenridge, J. N., Gallagher, D., Thompson, L. W., & Peterson, J. (1986). Characteristic depressive symptoms of bereaved elders. *Journal of Gerontology, 41,* 163–168.

Cornelius, R. (1984). A rule model of adult emotional expression. In C. Z. Malatesta & C. E. Izard (Eds.), *Emotion in adult development* (pp. 213–235). Beverly Hills: Sage.

Derogatis, L. (1977). *SCL-90: Administration, scoring, and procedures manual—1.* Baltimore: Johns Hopkins University School of Medicine.

Derogatis, L., & Spencer, P. (1982). *The Brief Symptom Inventory (BSI) administration, scoring and procedures manual.* Baltimore, MD: Johns Hopkins University School of Medicine.

Falleti, M. V., Gibbs, J. M., Clark, M. C., Pruchno, R. A., & Berman, E. C. (1989). Longitudinal course of bereavement in older adults. In D. A. Lund (Ed.), *Older bereaved spouses: Research with practical applications* (pp. 37–51). New York: Hemisphere.

Faschingbauer, T. R. (1981). *Texas Inventory of Grief–Revised manual.* Houston, TX: Honeycomb.

Faschingbauer, T. R., Devaul, R. D., & Zisook, S. (1977). Development of the Texas Inventory of Grief. *American Journal of Psychiatry, 134,* 696–698.

Futterman, A., Gallagher, D., Thompson, L. W., Lovett, S., & Gilewski, M. (1990). Retrospective assessment of marital adjustment and depression during the first two years of spousal bereavement. *Psychology and Aging, 5,* 277–283.

Gallagher, D., Breckenridge, J. N., Steinmetz, J., & Thompson, L. W. (1983). The Beck Depression Inventory and the Research Diagnostic Criteria. *Journal of Consulting and Clinical Psychology, 51,* 945–946.

Gallagher, D., Breckenridge, J. N., Thompson, L. W., Dessonville, C., & Amaral, P. (1982). Similarities and differences between normal grief and depression in older adults. *Essence, 5,* 127–140.

Gallagher, D., Breckenridge, J., Thompson, L. W., & Peterson, J. A. (1983). Effects of bereavement on indicators of mental health in elderly widows and widowers. *Journal of Gerontology, 38,* 565–571.

Gallagher, D., Nies, G., & Thompson, L. W. (1982). Reliability of the Beck Depression Inventory with older adults. *Journal of Consulting and Clinical Psychology, 50,* 152–153.

Hale, W. D., Cochran, C. D., & Hedgepeth, B. (1984). Norms for the elderly in the Brief Symptom Inventory. *Journal of Consulting and Clinical Psychology, 52,* 321–322.

Heyman, D. K., & Gianturco, D. T. (1973). Long-term adaptation by the elderly to bereavement. *Journal of Gerontology, 28,* 359–362.

Lund, D. A., Caserta, M. S., & Dimond, M. F. (1986). Gender differences through two years of bereavement among the elderly. *The Gerontologist, 26,* 314–320.

Lund, D. A., Caserta, M. S., & Dimond, M. F. (1989). Impact of spousal bereavement on subjective well-being of older adults. In D. A. Lund (Ed.), *Older bereaved spouses: Research with practical applications* (pp. 3–15). New York: Hemisphere.

Lund, D. A., Dimond, M. F., Caserta, M. S., Johnson, R. J., Poulton, J. L., & Connelly, J. R. (1985). Identifying elderly with coping difficulties after two years of bereavement. *Omega, 16,* 213–224.

Maddison, D. C., & Viola, A. (1968). The health of widows in the year following bereavement. *Journal of Psychosomatic Research, 12,* 297–306.

Morrison, D. F. (1976). *Multivariate methods in statistics.* New York: McGraw-Hill.

Murrell, S. A., & Himmelfarb, S. (1989). Effects of attachment bereavement and pre-event conditions on subsequent depressive symptoms in older adults. *Psychology and Aging, 4,* 166–172.

Nolen-Hoeksema, S. (1987). Sex differences in unipolar depression: Evidence and theory. *Psychological Bulletin, 101,* 259–282.

Parkes, C. M., & Weiss, R. S. (1983). *Recovery from bereavement.* New York: Basic Books.

Pearlin, L. (1982). Discontinuities in the study of aging. In T. K. Hareven & K. J. Adams (Eds), *Aging and life course transitions* (pp. 55–74). New York: Guilford Press.

Rao, C. R. (1973). *Linear statistical inference and its applications* (2nd ed.). New York: Wiley.

Reich, J. W., Zautra, A. J., & Guarnaccia, C.-A1 (1989). Effects of disability and bereavement on the mental health and recovery of older adults. *Psychology and Aging, 4,* 57–65.

Stroebe, M. S., & Stroebe, W. (1983). Who suffers more? Sex differences in health risks of the widowed. *Psychological Bulletin, 93,* 279–301.

Stroebe, M. S., & Stroebe, W. (1989). Who participates in bereavement research?: A review and empirical study. *Omega, 20,* 1–29.

Stroebe, W., & Stroebe, M. S. (1987). *Bereavement and health: The psychological and physical consequences of partner loss.* Cambridge, England: Cambridge University Press.

Stroebe, W., Stroebe, M. S., & Domittner, G. (1985). *The impact of recent bereavement on the mental and physical health of young widows and widowers.* Tübingen, Federal Republic of Germany: Psychological Institute, Tübingen University.

Thompson, L. W., Breckenridge, J. N., Gallagher, D., & Peterson, J. A. (1984). Effects of bereavement on self-perceptions of physical health in elderly widows and widowers. *Journal of Gerontology, 39,* 309–314.

Van Zandt, S., Mou, R., & Abbott, R. (1989). Mental and physical health of rural bereaved and nonbereaved elders: A longitudinal study. In D. A. Lund (Ed.), *Older bereaved spouses: Research with practical applications* (pp. 25–35). New York: Hemisphere.

Wilkinson, L. (1989). *Systat: Version 4.* Evanston, IL: Systat.

Wortman, C. B., & Silver, R. C. (1989). The myths of coping with loss. *Journal of Consulting and Clinical Psychology, 57,* 349–357.

Zisook, S., & Schuchter, S. R. (1986). The first four years of widowhood. *Psychiatric Annals, 15,* 288–294.

Received May 11, 1990
Revision received January 24, 1991
Accepted January 25, 1991 ∎

[32]

Explanation for low prevalence of PTSD among older Finnish war veterans: social solidarity and continued significance given to wartime sufferings

A. HAUTAMÄKI[1] & P. G. COLEMAN[2]

[1]*Swedish School of Social Science, University of Helsinki, Finland &* [2]*School of Medicine, University of Southampton, UK*

Abstract

A relatively low rate of Post-Traumatic Stress Disorder (PTSD) (<10%), has been reported among Finnish veterans of World War II. Possible explanations for this are explored by means of depth interviews with 30 veterans (mean age of 77 years), staying at a Disabled Veterans Hospital and at a Rehabilitation Centre, drawing on an Attachment Theory perspective. The Impact of Event Scale, the General Health Questionnaire, as well as health survey, medical problems, and war experience questions, were administered as part of the interview. A low rate of PTSD symptomatology was also reported in this sample alongside a relatively high level of subjective well-being. Without exception, they spoke freely about the war, often with emotion. Themes that received emphasis in their accounts included the Finnish fighting spirit and the strong reciprocal bonds of loyalty that were felt during the war. The war now featured prominently as part of their integrity as old men, representing a honourable task that they had been called on to fulfil. The significance they attributed to the war had not waned with time. Although this study of older war veterans, in common with other such studies, does not consider the less resilient who have not survived to old age, it does suggest that the strong community spirit built up in the war and continued in Finnish veterans' association after the war together with the continuing esteem of Finnish society, has contributed to the high levels of well-being expressed by the survivors.

Introduction

The 20th century has witnessed particularly horrific forms of warfare in various parts of the world, but also a recognition that traumatic experiences cause disorders of psychological functioning, and in most recent years a growing awareness of just how long-lasting the effects of so-called Post-Traumatic Stress Disorder (PTSD) can be. One of the best-selling books of 1999 in the UK was Pat Barker's 'Another World'; the main character of which is a 101-year-old veteran of World War I (WWI), increasingly tormented in his advanced old age by memories from that war. This reflects increasing evidence from clinical psychologists that PTSD, far from subsiding in late life, may re-emerge with greater force once the defences of a busy working life have been removed (Bender, 1997; Hunt, 1997; Coleman & Mills, 1997). Attention has also been given to the psychological effects on subsequent generations particularly with regard to the holocaust of European Jews (Hass, 1990; Bar-On, 1995).

At the same time longitudinal studies of adulthood and aging witness to variation in experience and consequences, this applies just as strongly to the effects of warfare. For some individuals there are gains as well as losses, and for some, the former predominate (Aldwin *et al.*, 1994). Social factors, including attitudes to the wars in question, also effect outcome. Thus, US veterans of World War II (WWII) fare much better in terms of mental health than veterans of the Korean War, which by comparison is a forgotten and unpopular war (Fontana & Rosenheck, 1994). This suggests that variation in experience of trauma is also likely to occur at the level of group, generation, society, or culture.

There have as yet, been few studies of the effects of trauma in different societies. Opportunities have been missed to carry out comparative studies on the consequences of WWI and WWII on mental health across Europe. Partly, this is itself attributable to the different attitudes to the war among the eventual victors, their defeated enemies, as well as in the occupied countries. For example, in Germany, studies on the effects of war trauma have concentrated on the victims of Nazi persecution, whereas the experiences of ordinary German soldiers and civilians have tended to be ignored (Kruse & Schmit, 1999). One can only speculate what the long-term consequence of this social neglect of memories may have been for the war generation and subsequent generations.

On the basis of studies with older British WWII

veterans, Hunt (1997) suggests that war experience is best resolved in the long-term, not by avoidance, but by its incorporation into a continuous narrative, which allows traumatic memories to be interpreted and controlled. An important part of this process is the giving of meaning and significance to the original events. For such stories to develop it is important that the meaning given stands the test of time. In this paper, we report on an exploratory study of a sample of Finnish war veterans, which forms part of a pilot study for cross-national research on the long-term effects of war memories and their transmission across northern Europe including Russia. In it, we seek to develop a methodology for the study of the long-term consequences of war experience, and to explore social and personal factors associated with the resolution of war trauma.

Finland is of particular interest in this regard because of the relatively low level of continuing PTSD related to WWII, which has been reported (Ponteva, 1998a). The warfare between Finland and Russia was among the earliest notable engagements of WWII. It aroused much public interest across Europe at the time, as well as subsequently, but before describing our study it is important to provide some historical background.

Finland and the Second World War

Finland was drawn into the Second World War after being attacked by the Soviet Union, which aimed to occupy the country. This attack started the so-called 'Winter War' (30th November 1939–13th March 1940). A strong will to defend their country sprang up among the Finns, spoken of then and now in terms of the 'Spirit of the Winter War' ('Talvisodan henki'). This phase of the war, in which the Soviet forces were repulsed, lasted for '105 days of honour' (Jarho, 1991). After an interval of over one year there followed the 'Continuation War' (25th June 1941–4th September 1944), also against the USSR, but which involved Finland in conflict with the allies of the USSR in association with Germany. After the negotiation of peace terms with the USSR, the 'Lapland War' (15th September 1944–27th April 1945), was fought to remove German forces from Northern Finland.

The immediate consequences of WWII for Finland were grave. A part of Eastern Finland, i.e. Eastern Karelia, was lost to the USSR, and high war reparations had to be paid as well. Nevertheless, the nation kept its independence. Finland was not occupied, and it was saved from massive aerial bombing (Jarho & Saari, 1991). Most of the losses were in combat at the front, involving men born between 1896–1926. The final account of numbers involved in the war is as follows: out of 700,000 men and women serving, 200,000 were wounded, injured or suffered chronic disease, and 86,000 perished. The figures show that almost half of those in the war were either injured or killed.

Thus, when compared with many other European countries, Finland experienced some definite advantages with regard to the psychosocial effects of WWII (Jarho, 1991). The number of prisoners of war (POWs), as well as the number of civilian victims, was rather low. The 'Spirit of the Winter War' survived relatively intact, creating solidarity among the Finns and uniting a young nation that had only recently engaged from bitter civil war following independence from Russia in 1917. The Finnish people in general, considered the wars inevitable and legitimate, and the war veterans were paid credit as honoured and honourable citizens.

However, the disabled victims had to be taken care of, in a societal and social situation in which, in terms of Jarho (1991), "there was lack of everything–except hard work." During the wars, the Finnish Red Cross accompanied by members of the women's voluntary defence services, played a central role in care and rehabilitation. The disabled war veterans themselves also began to take charge of their own affairs and founded 'The Disabled War Veterans Association' in 1940. The watchword of the organization echoed the code of comradeship from the front: "One does not abandon one's brother." The association took a leading role in building up and carrying out both medical care, and social and vocational rehabilitation of the disabled veterans (Jarho & Saari, 1991). This generous system of care continues, allowing three weeks of paid stay in a rehabilitation centre a year to veterans and their spouses.

As Jarho (1991) notes, post-war attitudes among Finnish people were very sympathetic to disabled veterans, encouraging them to take the decisive step back to civilian life. The spiritual and material support from the society at large, in combination with their own initiative and persistence, created a good system of after-care and rehabilitation: "As a result of social and vocational rehabilitation over 70% worked in their earlier or in a more demanding profession than before the wars. Only 10% remained unable to work. The disabled got married like other veterans (80%). Nearly all of them were members of their own association—99%—and it has always been non-political" (Jarho, 1991).

PTSD among Finnish war veterans

In Finland a rather low prevalence of PTSD (lower than 10%) among war veterans (POWs included), has been found (Ponteva, 1993; 1998b; Hautamäki, 1998). Disabled war veterans also seem to show the same pattern. The prevalence seems to be below 10%, even for prisoners of war (Ponteva 1998a; 1998b). The results clearly differ from the US National Vietnam Veterans Readjustment Study (Kulka et al., 1988), which show lifetime PTSD prevalence rates of 30%, with a current rate of 15%. They also differ from Hamilton and Canteen's (1987) US results, according to which 16% of a sample of naval veterans fulfilled PTSD-criteria, and Hunt's (1997) UK results, in which 19% scored above both the clinically derived PTSD cut-off point and the General Health Questionnaire (GHQ; 4/5).

How can this resilience of the old Finnish war veterans i.e. a subjectively experienced well-being in spite of a multiplicity of medical problems and physical restraints brought about by the aging process, be explained? Ponteva (1998a) concludes as follows: "Possible explanations are shortness of captivity, a fair stress-tolerance of Finnish people, the mainly physical nature of stress during the captivity and a rapid return to civil work after the war." However, a further reason for the low prevalence of PTSD might be the significance and the meaning given to the wars at the time, and subsequently. This study explores the attribution of meaning to war experience in a sample of elderly Finnish war veterans. In the absence of proper longitudinal studies of the effects of war experience, examination of retrospective accounts remains valuable evidence for theory development.

Methods

The participants

The sample (N=30) was drawn on the basis of voluntary participation from residents of Kauniala Hospital for Disabled Veterans (N=10), and from visitors to Siuntio Rehabilitation Centre (N=20), both situated in Southern Finland. Kauniala Hospital of Disabled Veterans is the only private veterans' hospital in Finland, owned by 'The Association of War-Disabled Brothers'. The mean age of the sample was 77 years, with a range from 71 to 94 years.

Of the 30 participants, 33% currently lived in an institution. The majority, 57%, had completed only primary education, 16% secondary education, and 27% university education. The scarcity of vocational education is related to the rapid return of most of the men to civil work after the wars, leaving no time for further education. There were no ex-POWs among the sample, which accords with the low overall incidence of captivity during the wars.

In addition to sampling biases based on voluntary participation, the importance of selective survival as a potential bias has to be acknowledged. Those with higher levels of biological, psychological and socio-economic functioning, have a greater probability to survive (Staudinger & Fleeson, 1996). However, without access to longitudinal or cohort-comparative data, it is not possible to speculate further.

Procedure

All participants were interviewed by two female interviewers, (a qualified psychologist and social worker), during their stay at Siuntio Centre and Kauniala Hospital. Some assistance was required by most of the participants because of physical incapacities, mental frailty, or general poor health. The interview format allowed for exploration of the subjective meanings and interpretations given to the questionnaire items by the respondents. Those participating were generally eager to cooperate and willing to share their wartime experiences. They often stated that it was their continued intention 'to let younger generations know'.

Four English questionnaires, translated into Finnish, were administered as part of the interview.

(1) The Impact of Event Scale (Horowitz et al., 1979) assesses the impact of the traumatic event in terms of psychological and psychosomatic symptoms. It yields three essential elements of PTSD: intrusion, avoidance, and numbing of feelings.

(2) The MOS SF–36 Health Survey Scale (UK version) was administered as an assessment of health and well-being perceived from the patient's point of view (Jenkinson et al., 1993). It includes measures of physical functioning, role limitations due to emotional problems, role limitations due to physical problems, social functioning, mental health, bodily pain, vitality, and general health perception.

(3) The General Health Questionnaire (GHQ–28; Goldberg, 1978) was included as an additional assessment of mental health. The GHS is commonly used in research to assess the influence of external events that might be expected to increase stress (e.g. natural disasters, persistent daily hassles).

(4) A Medical Problems Questionnaire comprising 18 items developed for use in a British longitudinal study of aging and which has been used in further community studies (Jerram & Coleman, 1999), was also administered.

The interview began with detailed questions on military career and war experience, adapted from Hunt's (1997) UK study. But throughout these questions and also at other times in the interview schedule, participants were encouraged to elaborate on the war events and experiences they recounted and the meaning they held for them, then and now. The interviewers supported the feelings expressed and encouraged further elucidation where appropriate. Permission was obtained for these interviews to be recorded and transcribed.

Analysis of transcripts

In order to assess resolution of the traumas and losses experienced during the war, discourse markers from the Adult Attachment Interview (AAI) were applied to the transcripts (Main & Goldwyn, in press; Crittenden, 1999). Crittenden (1997a) looks upon attachment patterns as strategies for organizing information processing and behaviour in response to danger or threat. These strategies can be evaluated in terms of their likely success in coping with danger and providing safety (Crittenden, 1997a; 1997b; 1997c). In this study, the interview transcripts were examined for signs of the strategies used to cope with the affective arousal related to the trauma/loss. Was the respondent still preoccupied by it, was he trying to dismiss it, or had he processed the trauma/loss to an adaptive resolution? A judgement was also made about the extent to which the trauma/loss was adequately contained or not (Crittenden, 1999). As Crittenden (1997a) succinctly proposes, the experience of PTSD is associated with alternating failing strategies e.g. avoidance alternating with intense re-experiencing, but neither strategy capable of warding off the seemingly overwhelming danger.

Discourse markers were analyzed in the transcripts only in context of trauma and/or loss, and in relation to the question of the degree of containment. Criteria for the use of a dismissive style in seeking to contain the effects of trauma and/or loss included:

- Omitting emotionally arousing episodes or images.
- Distancing the self and feelings by moving levels of description to semantic generalizations.
- Omitting negative affects and switching into false positive affects whenever distress emerged (Crittenden, 1999).

Examples of discourse markers of a preoccupied way of handling trauma were:

- Involving the interviewer strongly in taking sides in the interview situation.
- Recalling intense, affectively arousing episodes e.g. in the form of long run-on sentences, and in such a preoccupied way that the boundaries of time and place between the past reality and the present interview situation were lost.
- Never arriving at semantic conclusions concerning the episodes recounted (Crittenden, 1999).

A trauma/loss that is contained and processed to adaptive resolution is indicated by discourse markers, which express the capacity to remember and actually feel the affectively arousing episodes, as well as to arrive at adequate semantic conclusions. A veteran may endow the past traumatic experiences with meaning by providing a semantic generalization that applies in the present. This may be different from the meaning it had at the time of the war.

Results

Traumatic war memories and mental health in the sample

As in previous Finnish studies, the prevalence of traumatic memories was limited to a relatively small number of participants (Ponteva, 1993; Achte et al., 1995). On the Impact of Event Scale, only eight of the sample of 30 reported scores above 15 and only two (6.7%) scored above the PTSD cut-off point of 30. Similarly, only three (10%) scored above the GHQ cut-off point of four for mental disturbance, which approximates to the 8-12% rates for this age group reported by Goldberg (1978). Moreover, these were different people to those indicating PTSD symptoms. The values of the MOS SF-36 Health Survey Scales (apart from physical functioning which was low in this disabled sample) were high, exceeding those cited in UK population surveys (Garratt et al., 1993). An exploratory factor analysis of the questionnaire data collected in this study indicated three distinct factors: a physical functioning factor, a general mental health factor, evident from the SF-36 (lack of emotional role limitations and vitality) and some GHQ items, and a PTSD factor including GHQ items on severe depression, anxiety and insomnia.

The PTSD-values were not associated with age. Educational level, however, was related, so that those with only primary education had significantly higher PTSD scores than those with university education ($p < 0.01$). In accordance with Hunt's (1997) results, avoidance and intrusion were the essential constituents of the PTSD values. Two avoidance items {13 & 9}: 'I tried not to think about the war', 'I tried not to talk about the war', and one intrusion item {10}, 'Pictures about the war popped into my mind', comprised the most economic model (tested by regression analysis) to explain the PTSD scores. In some individual cases, one could discern traces of the original intense emotional arousal. One disabled war veteran, severely wounded on several occasions, described an easily activated hyper-alertness (PTSD score of 26), as follows:

- One had always a kind of feeling... of being constantly on the alert... was afraid that there's going to be a mobilization... or a confrontation. This feeling got in your blood for good...

This respondent also referred to continuing disturbing dreams about the war:

- Well, sometimes I do have a dream about the war. It was only a week ago when I saw a dream that went something like this: I was fighting in Kriev in a trench... then suddenly I had a confrontation with two Russians... the other one, who was on the left hand side from me, tried to hide himself... When I retreated, they both followed me... And I shot them with sustained fire—like this—waving my arms from one side to the other... and the guy dropped dead right there. Then somebody grabbed me by the arm—still in my dream—and that's when I woke up... screaming... yeah.
- And if I don't sleep, I'm kind of drowsing, and I see... all sorts of... funny situations. Occasionally I dream of real tough confrontations and... some other time I'm amid our own boys somewhere out there, planning raids and how it's going to be.

Van der Kolk and Fisler (1995) describe PTSD as a "combination of learned conditioning, problems with modulation of arousal, and shattered meaning propositions". Problems with modulation of arousal are related to the regulation of affects, and shattered meaning propositions are connected to the semantic transformation of cognitive information (Crittenden, 1997c). The statements of this disabled war veteran particularly express problems with modulation of arousal. More generally, the statements expressed some difficulties in adapting to the presence of safety, even if it is more than 50 years since the daily presence of a deadly threat.

In general, these Finnish war veterans were both capable and willing to share even the hardest experiences e.g. the death of a good comrade or being themselves severely wounded. They did it in a way indicating a rather completed working-through, expressing ego-filtered sorrow related to the atrocities of the war, such as trembling voices and tears, and even crying when remembering the death of a good friend. Neither numbing nor any significant avoidance of the recall of traumatic episodes or feelings triggered by them could be discerned in the narratives told by them, or in the ways they told their story. Criteria indicating avoidance from the Adult Attachment Interview were not evident in this sample when they spoke about war experiences. These might have included a tendency to swiftly change topics, failing to recall topics, staying on the level of idealized semantic generalizations or switching into false bright affect by strained humour and jokes, whenever distress emerged (Main & Goldwyn, in press; Crittenden, 1999). On the contrary, they appeared to find relief in talking about and sharing their wartime experiences.

Neither did they indicate problems with guilt often found to be associated with combat-related PTSD (Kubany, 1994), nor personalized hate in regard to the Russians. The logic for killing that they expressed emphasized the necessities of survival, of 'either us or them, me or him'. When asked about the stress of killing, one severely wounded, disabled war veteran (PTSD score of 26) answered as follows:

- No, it was not at all stressful. I only felt that now he is out of my way. Since it was an enemy which we considered very dangerous... I sort of felt glad, when I saw an enemy falling down or wounded, because he would not be on my way any more.

The same attitude applied also to the unintentional killing of woman soldiers used by the Soviet army. As another badly wounded disabled war veteran, (65% invalidity after the war, 85% now, but with a PTSD score of only 1), elaborated on the surprise discovery of women's bodies among the dead enemy soldiers:

- Well, listen, it was the same situation, they were there our enemies, that's it.
- Q: Does it mean that their sex did not matter?
- No, it didn't matter, not in the least. Of course, if I really re-consider it thoroughly, so maybe the only thing that occurred to me was why do the Russians use these young and beautiful women?

This particular respondent, however, then hesitated somewhat in his conclusion, remembering, on the basis of a scar on one women's stomach which indicated a caesarean section, that the soldiers could have been mothers:

- At least the one I just told about... probably she had been a mother. In fact, all of these three could have been mothers, they were of that age, over twenty, but definitely less than thirty years of age.

The interviewer had the distinct impression that an internal conflict between two value systems, that of instrumental, rational and efficient warfare and that which Ruddick (1990) termed 'the politics of peace', resting on maternal thinking, was emerging in the mind of the respondent.

The interview situation offered opportunities to discern motives lying behind avoidance of the issue of war e.g. not wishing to be bored by the old stories as compared with panicking in response to affect-triggering stimuli. As stated before, avoidance and distancing were not observed in this sample. However, most veterans reported the difficult years immediately after the war, which were characterized by PTSD symptomatology that was later relieved. A former leading officer and engineer and business executive, now a senior swimmer champion, who was not wounded (PTSD score of 0), described the process as follows:

- I can say that surely the war left some kind of mark on me, because more than ten years after the war, if I had drank more than moderately... or let's say a lot of alcoholic beverages... those war memories popped into my mind... they just returned. I found myself always in Hatjalahti, fighting against the Russians. Or so my wife told me.
- Q: Does it mean that the war operations came back into your mind?
- Yes, some twelve years after the war, I guess. Since then they didn't come back.

This front veteran also describes his current feelings to the wars in the following way:

- Nowadays when I watch war films, I watch them as an 'outsider'. I do like to watch them, but I feel 'cool', in fact without any feelings. I don't dream any more of these things. It's the past, and those times are gone forever.

The significance given to the war

It is crucial for both individual and group resilience, how the individuals and the group can make sense of a crisis situation and endow it with meaning (Antonovsky & Sourani, 1988). We therefore paid particular attention to the collective significance and the accompanying individual meaning given to the war, and how these attitudes may have protected against subjective distress. Finnish literature on the war suggested that strong collective meanings had developed.

However, these should not be over-idealized. The fighting spirit expressed by our sample seemed to be more a kind of grumbling, everyday persistence, and tenacity ('guts' or 'stamina', 'sisu' in Finnish), drawn on in order to safeguard the autonomy of the young nation. As one disabled veteran, who had received three severe wounds during the Continuation War (PTSD score of 26) put it:

- For our independence... yes. And the fact that I said before that I don't accept that any foreign state—not Sweden, not Russia—should rule us, but we decide on our own affairs. It is not widely known, but the Finnish nation is so different compared with other nations... I kept thinking in the way that we have, to maintain our independence and manage ourselves and the affairs of our own country. If it's not possible, then we're going to fight for these values. That's how I felt about the war.

The interviews also expressed a strong code of reciprocal bonds of loyalty and solidarity between the Finnish soldiers 'you never leave or abandon your pal, nor reject his bids for help (and, reciprocally he will help you)' (Lindgren, 1998). As exemplified by one story told by one disabled veteran, who was also severely wounded on three occasions (PTSD score of 26):

- The commander of our battalion, Major Kunnas said to me that he'll go himself to check up on the nearby hill that the boys won't advance too far. I said to him: 'Sir, better not to go yourself there...when the enemy sees that a high-ranking officer moves about there, they'll try to shoot you down!' But the Major didn't listen to me. He did not get far when he was hit in the chest by the enemy's bullet. Wounded he collapsed under a pine and I said to the guys: 'I'm going to get the captain out from there!' The boys said 'damn it, you won't!' I insisted. 'For sure, I'm going!', and I grabbed a small sled and took a machine gun with me. At Christmas time that year '39, there was a lot of snow, and I advanced by crawling in a snowy track. When I was near to the captain... there was this small 'Vickers', its caterpillar tread had been shot broken... from there I saw a guy coming out... with the intention of stabbing the major with his bayonet. I straightened myself up on the sled in a way that I could aim my gun at him, and then I shot him right there—that...boy. I managed to lift Major Kunnas up on that sled... and simultaneously a hell of a concentrated grenade fire fell on both sides of the path, but not a single one hit our track. Major Kunnas bled really badly, but I could not staunch it out there... didn't have any bandage, or anything like that. There was blood all over me, when I came back, and the boys said: 'You're wounded!'. 'Check Major Kunnas first!' I replied. He was still breathing...but in his chest...there was a big hole. And suddenly he just died there... collapsed in that sled.

Other respondents also mentioned admired and well-known Finnish military leaders, who set a good, even reckless heroic example. A former leading officer (engineer and business executive, now a senior swimmer champion, not wounded, PTSD = 0) gave an example of the emerging 'team spirit' uniting, what he called, 'the discordant Finnish people' as follows:

- Certain team spirit develops easily in a group of young men. It can be described by the worn-out phrase: 'We don't leave a friend behind!'. However discordant the Finnish people are, it was interesting to see that disagreements in the front were extremely rare. Before we came into contact with the enemy, we had to build, you could say, a kind of a half-done dugout. In my team, there was a communist, who had been sentenced for murder, but he was a skilful building worker. Now when you start to build a shelter, it is evident that a building worker's professional skills are for good use. The man in question was freed from prison and sent to the front. I ordered him to be the foreman for the building team. I was criticized a bit for this order; how on earth a murderer could be a foreman? I said: 'He's the best builder of all of us! He really knows how to build!'. As far as I can recall this was the only critique on me. The shelter that we built could have resisted any kind of fire. From the nearby primary school, we brought all available mattresses, and then we built a roof with wooden legs on our shelter. As for the murderer, he was cooperative and good, when he saw that he was trusted. Maybe he was a quick-tempered man and done what he had done, but he defended his native country well.

The greatest sorrow in the interviews was expressed when the respondents remembered the death of a comrade. The following excerpt is from the interview of a former leading officer (engineer and business executive, now a senior swimmer champion, not wounded, PTSD = 0). He described himself as a rational, rather cool, and detached person, as a person in complete control of himself. Nevertheless, when asked how much stress it caused him to have a friend killed in action, he indicated a different picture:

- It was shocking. When the enemy tanks attacked our front line, I was lucky to be in Vyborg. Unfortunately, my platoon had to bear the attack of tanks. I had lent my own rifle to one soldier called Blom. When I returned from Vyborg he had been killed in action... I was told that his last words were: 'I wonder if Susi is angry, because the strap of his rifle is now snapped in two?' These were his last... he was worried that because I had lent my own rifle... that... one would be, that is...

(The interview was interrupted by a long silence, during which the respondent had tears in eyes and the voice wavered, and he gradually collected himself).

Resilience and integrity in old age

In spite of many medical problems and physical restraints, these Finnish war veterans were characterized by a remarkably high psychological well-being. Age did not correlate significantly with any of the indicators of health and well-being. Adaptive resources of the aging self were well in evidence (Brandstädter et al., 1993). Many had adopted instrumental activities for example, within war veteran associations, which were relevant for maintaining self-esteem and identity. They also seemed to have succeeded in adjusting their personal goals and essential frames of self-evaluation to changes in resources and functional capacities e.g. creating new niches within the veteran associations of the institutional settings. Additionally, they usually limited their social comparison to their own age group and, even only to other disabled war veterans of the hospital.

In Erikson's terms (Erikson, 1963; 1982) 'ego integrity' in late life is the result of successfully exploring and resolving earlier and current identity issues, this time at a more complex level of integration than in adolescence, as the aging person faces up to the challenge of finite reality. These war veterans had gone to war as young as seventeen years of age, before even having had the time to achieve an identity (Marcia, 1964). The wars then are likely to have been crucial for many in forming their identity. Certainly, the war experience, and the losses associated with it, seemed to be well integrated in their life narratives.

In answer to questions such as 'In what way did the war influence your life?' and 'Do you think your life would have been different if the war had not occurred?', the veterans realistically admitted the losses associated with the war. The losses were, in general, defined as first, the loss of one's youth and a shortened educational career, and second, all those unattainable things that the individual would have liked to be or to have in his life. However, most veterans, even the disabled ones, did not harbour a grudge. They seemed to have been capable of integrating the losses and gains of the war in relation to their aging process, into a coherent life narrative, which provided their lives with meaning. Most of them indicated that the suffering of wartime was necessary and deeply meaningful. This was expressed in sometimes striking ways. A former lawyer, not wounded in the war, and with a PTSD score of 6, had difficulties to endow the question 'What aspects of the war did you find most interesting?' with significance and retorted (with tears in his eyes and voice wavering):

- As I am a peaceful man, I did not find it interesting. You just had to be there. It was the task of our generation—to save Finland as an independent nation. And now our children and grandchildren have a good country to live in.

Most Finnish war veterans seemed to accept—the disabled veterans very stoically—the necessities that had been governing their lives across their life-course. A severely wounded war veteran (65% invalidity after the war, 85% now, and with a PTSD score of 1) answered the question 'If you could live your life anew, would there be things you would do in a different way?' as follows:

- No. This is life. This is my life. With me, it's like that. OK! I would like to reply that this has been my destiny and my way. You can't restore that, it is so that the Lord determines the length and the quality of your days.

He had tripped on a landmine in the 'Continuation War', and lost one eye, arm and leg, yet still had a respected leadership position in the War Veteran Association of the Hospital of the Disabled War Veterans. He told the interviewer about the recurrent dreams he had during the years after the war:

- I was always running around with two healthy feet, even if I did not have any!

He was married and when asked, if he had any children, he proudly stated:

- I have no children. I have three sons!

A very vigorous and vital 94-year-old war veteran (military rank of captain, wounded in the head, 45% invalidity), who was proud to call himself a professional soldier, had been awarded with several medals of honour for his bravery, with a PTSD score of 2, summed up his life as follows:

- I was so well prepared for the war that it has been my vocation... and I did my job so well that nobody has ever said to me 'You failed!' and I was always in front, always in the front line!

He had a similarly positive view of his present life at the veterans' hospital:

- They really take such good care of me... Yeah, here I am such a good pal with everyone. Everybody is saying 'Hey, Peter! Hallo, Peter! Do you feel fine and how are you? All the doctors sit here from time to time... I'm treated so well here... surely the others are treated well, too? But I feel so good here! The head nurse called me up recently and asked me 'Have you got your uniform and your badges of honour here?' I said 'As this wardrobe is so small I have not brought them here.' She responded 'It's not! You must have your uniform and your badges of honour on you!'... and that she will check personally that they will be brought here.

Looking retrospectively at his life, he summed it up:

- I cannot say anything else, but, I have had such a good life! I've been involved in so many things, that only very few have had the possibility for. For in my life—from the beginning of this century, when I was born—and which I now have lived through as a whole... so many things have happened here in Finland!

Discussion

The Finnish war veterans interviewed in this study were characterized by both a low prevalence of PTSD and a remarkably high subjective well-being in spite of many medical problems and physical restraints. The low prevalence of PTSD is in accordance with previous research findings in Finland (Ponteva, 1993; Ponteva, 1998a; 1998b), and was supported by further interview material collected. The war veterans expressed ego-filtered sorrow that seemed to result from some genuine working-through—having assimilated war experiences into their life narratives. There was little use of the coping strategy of avoidance in their retrospective accounts, and therefore no evidence relevant to Hunt's hypothesis, derived from his study of British English war veterans (Hunt, 1997), that avoidance breaks down with advancing age.

The high level of general well-being is reflected in other age-related developmental characteristics. For example, if wisdom is defined in terms of the Stoic philosopher Epictetus, as the appreciation of necessities and the willingness to accommodate one's life to the necessities perceived, the respondents in this study gave ample examples of wisdom—for a nuanced analysis of wisdom as one predictor of life satisfaction in old age, see Ardelt (1997).

The sample interviewed in this study was small and it is likely that those veterans who participated were more eager to share their wartime experiences, and less likely to find it too anxiety provoking. However, the educational level of the sample, which can also serve as an indicator of socio-economic functioning, is similar to that for the age cohort of Finnish men. This, and the fact that the figures for PTSD are comparable to larger and more representative Finnish surveys, suggests that we are justified in examining the qualitative data in our sample for possible explanation of the general findings on low PTSD levels among Finnish war veterans.

In the first place, these veterans have been capable of endowing the sufferings caused by the war with lasting meaning. This process does not, however, occur in a social vacuum, but in the matrices of social relations. Meaning plays a key role in linking cultural symbolic structures and systems to individual development (Heymans, 1994). In this study, meaning has been looked upon in terms of cultural symbolic systems (how the wars in their aftermath have been evaluated in Finland), and as a part of the lifespan development of the individual war veterans, as they have been trying to create a sense of integrity in understanding their life and themselves in the face of death. It is important to stress that the strong meaning of WWII has not waned for these men, in the way it has, for example, for many British veterans for whom the changes in British society has led them to question the sacrifices they made (Coleman & McCulloch, 1990).

Furthermore, most Finnish war veterans seem to have experienced the wars as a deeply collective endeavour, defined strongly as a joint responsibility (Saari, 1997). The community spirit was fostered by a patriotism based on the definition of the war as the ultimate survival fight of a small nation, on and for, one's own territory. In Lindgren's (1998) survey of the motives influencing combat behaviour, consequences of eventual occupation ranked first, followed by responsibility towards companion in arms and love of the fatherland.

The collective nature of the war and the resulting feeling of community spirit appear to have provided socially supportive networks—a kind of secure base in terms of Bowlby's attachment theory (Bowlby, 1969, 1982; Ainsworth et al., 1978)—which helped the soldiers to endure and cope with the stresses of warfare. After the war, the Finnish veteran associations have constituted a tightly knit social network, in which the veterans have been able to share their experiences, talk and write about those experiences that radically changed and moulded their youth, and, for the disabled war veterans, the rest of their life. They have been able, if only gradually, to assimilate the war experience and the losses associated with it in their life narratives.

The aging self is characterized by accommodative processes, whereby personal goals and frames of self-evaluation are gradually adjusted to changes in action resources and functional capacities (Brandtstädter et al., 1993, 323). The reference points and groups chosen for self-evaluative comparisons concerning physical and psychological functioning, varied among the respondents. The residents of Kauniala Hospital (i.e. the disabled veterans), seemed to compare themselves first and foremost with other disabled war veterans, while the out-patients of the Siuntio Rehabilitation Centre compared themselves with (elderly) people in general. When interviewed about their health, some participants even asked, 'it depends— compared to whom?' This may partly explain why the assessment made by the war veterans about subjective well-being did not have much to do with their actual physical performance. It also helps to explain the resilience paradox, also found in this study, the discrepancy between an increasing number of losses and physical constraints on the one hand, and maintenance of adaptive functioning of the self and subjective well-being on the other (Baltes & Baltes, 1990; Brandtstädter et al., 1993).

What might the implications of these findings on Finnish war veterans be for the management of war-related PTSD? As psychotherapists, including both Erikson and Frankl have observed, suffering can be born provided it can be made meaningful. The initial process of finding meaning, as well as its sustenance, over long periods depends on social support. Finland seems to be a good example of a society that has preserved its original perception of its WWII wars against the Soviet Union virtually intact. It has also provided the organizations and facilities, which demonstrate in practical terms Finland's continuing positive evaluation of its war veterans. Within them, the veterans have been able to share and discuss their experiences. Programmes for prevention and treatment of late-life PTSD clearly require active collaboration with veterans' organizations.

Greater problems are likely to occur in societies where support from such organizations has become weaker with time. Changes and/or threats to meaning also need to be taken into account and worked through at an individual level. Even well established societal meanings can be undermined by later generations. Of course, there is justice in letting other voices be heard, and psychological benefit as well. For example, some of the myths created around Britain's heroic resistance against Nazi Germany have made it very difficult for individuals, whose experiences do not match, to tell their own stories of the war. Meaning making must also be tempered by a respect for truth (Coleman, 1999).

Interestingly, the Finnish male ideal is characterized more by an avoidant attachment style— one should have 'sisu' (stamina) and never complain (Hautamäki, 2000). Yet in this sample, more than 50 years after the wars, war matters were openly discussed and accompanied by ego-filtered expressions of feeling. This suggests that there has been a thorough processing of the traumatic material, and that a reserved orientation to more strong emotional states together with a gradual working through in supportive relationships may in the long-run be a successful combination.

It is important to bear in mind that the voice of those perhaps less resilient Finns has not been heard in this research. As part of this study three Finnish female war veterans, voluntary civilians working as helping and service personnel in the women's voluntary defence services at the front, were interviewed. After the war, they, as most women at that time, had married war veterans. Two of these women spoke about very difficult marriages with husbands apparently traumatized by the war in ways not understood thoroughly by psychiatric practitioners at that time. During the years after the war, their husbands had been attempting unsuccessfully, to soothe themselves with the help of drugs and alcohol, enacting and acting out in their family life their internal nameless terrors, thereby creating some of the unfortunate family hells of the '50s and '60s in Finland.

It is crucial for both individual and group resilience, how the individuals and the group as a whole can make sense of a crisis situation, and endow it with collective and personalized meaning. The war veterans experienced the war for Finland as meaningful thus, legitimating the deep sufferings and heavy personal losses. This has also been the historical verdict passed by the Finnish people. One of the most well-known Finnish novelists, Väinö Linna, finishes his novel, 'The Unknown Soldier'—bought and read more in Finland than any other single book except the Bible and the ABC—by capturing this blessing in one dense description of the retreating, rugged and dead tired Finnish soldiers. The war was lost, but the independence of Finland as a nation was saved (Linna, 1954, 1996):

"Later the autumn sun warmed the ground and the men sleeping on it. Lingonberry plants glistened in the sunlight, and slowly the rumble of cart wheels faded into the all-embracing silence of the pine forest. The weary men slept and a benevolent sky looked down on them. It was by no means angry with them. It may even have felt a kind of sympathy for them. They were good men."

Acknowledgements

We should like to acknowledge financial assistance received from the Swedish School of Social Sciences, University of Helsinki, in carrying out this study, and the support of its research director, Tom Sandlund.

References

ACHTE, K., JARHO, L. & PONTEVA, M. (1995). Muistio: Maamme 2. maailmansodan veteraanien pitkäaikaiset traumaperäiset stressihäiriöt (TPSH). TPSH:n-esiintyminen veteraaneilla, sen sisältö sekä tutkimus—ja korvausperusteet. Asiantuntijalausunto Sotainvalidien Veljesliiton hallitukselle.

AINSWORTH, M. D. S., BLEHAR, M., WATERS, E. & WALL, S. (1978). *Patterns of attachment: a psychological study of the strange situation*. Hillsdale, NJ: Erlbaum Assoc.

ALDWIN, C. M., LEVENSON, M. R. & SPIRO III, A. (1994). Vulnerability and resilience to combat exposure: can stress have lifelong effects? *Psychology and Aging*, 9, 34–44.

ANTONOVSKY, A. & SOURANI, T. (1988). Family sense of coherence and family adaptation. *Journal of Marriage and the Family*, 50, 79–92.

ARDELT, M. (1997). Wisdom and life satisfaction in old age. *Journal of Gerontology*, 52B, 15–27.

BALTES, P. B. & BALTES, M. M. (1990). Psychological perspectives on successful aging: The model of selective optimization with compensation. In P. B. BALTES & M. M. BALTES (Eds.). *Successful aging: perspectives from the behavioral sciences* (pp. 1–34). New York: Cambridge University Press.

BAR-ON, D. (1995). *Fear and hope. Three generations of the Holocaust*. Cambridge MA: Harvard University Press.

BENDER, M. P. (1997). Bitter harvest: the implications of continuing war-related stress on reminiscence theory and practice. *Aging and Society*, 17, 337–348.

BOWLBY, J. (1969/1982). *Attachment and loss. Vol. 1: Attachment.* New York: Basic Books.

BRÄNDTSTÄDTER, J., WENTURA, D. & GREVE, W. (1993). Adaptive resources of the aging self: outlines of an emergent perspective. *International Journal of Behavioral Development*, 16, 323–349.

COLEMAN, P. G. (1999). Creating a life story: the task of reconciliation. *The Gerontologist*, 39, 133–139.

COLEMAN, P. G. & MCCULLOCH, A. W. (1990) Societal change, values and social support: exploratory studies into adjustment in late life. *Journal of Aging Studies*, 4, 321–332.

COLEMAN, P. G. & MILLS, M. A. (1997). Listening to the story. Life review and the painful past in day and residential care settings. In: L. HUNT, M. MARSHALL, & C. ROWLINGS, C. (Eds.). *Past trauma in late life: European perspectives on therapeutic work with older people* (pp. 171–183). London: Jessica Kingsley.

CRITTENDEN, P. M. (1997a). Truth, error, omission, distortion, and deception: the application of attachment theory to the assessment and treatment of psychological disorder. In S. M. C. DOLLINGER, & L. F. DILALLA (Eds.). *Assessment and intervention across the lifespan* (pp. 35–76). Hillsdale, NJ: Erlbaum.

CRITTENDEN, P. M. (1997b). Patterns of attachment and sexuality: risk of dysfunction versus opportunity for creative integration. (47–93). In L. ATKINSON, & K. J. ZUCKERMAN (Eds.). *Attachment and psychopathology*. New York: Guilford Press.

CRITTENDEN, P. M. (1997c). Toward an integrative theory of trauma: a dynamic-maturational approach. In D. CICCHETTI, & S. TOTH (Eds.). *The Rochester symposium on developmental psychopathology. Vol. 10. Risk, trauma, and mental processes,* (pp. 34–84). Rochester: University of Rochester.

CRITTENDEN, P. M. (1999). Adult Attachment Interview. Manual. Unpublished manuscript.

ERIKSON, E. H. (1963). *Childhood and society*. New York: Norton.

ERIKSON, E. H. (1982). *The life cycle completed. A review.* New York: Norton.

FONTANA, A. & ROSENHECK, R. (1994). Traumatic war stressors and psychiatric symptoms among World War II, Korean and Vietnam War veterans. *Psychology and Aging, 9,* 27–33.

GARRATT, A. M., RUTA, D. A., ABDALLA, M. I., BUCKINGHAM, J. K., RUSSELL, I. T. (1993). The SF 36 health survey questionnaire: an outcome measure suitable for routine use within the NHS? *British Medical Journal, 306,* 1440–1444.

GOLDBERG, D. (1978). *Manual of the General Health Questionnaire*. NFER-Nelson.

HAMILTON, J. D. & CANTEEN, W. (1987). Post-traumatic stress disorder in World War II naval veterans. *Hospital and Community Psychiatry, 38,* 197–199.

HASS, A. (1990) *In the shadow of the Holocaust. The second generation.* Cornell: Cornell University Press.

HAUTAMÄKI, A. (1998). International workshop on long-term effects of war memories. *SSKH informerar (Newsletter of the Swedish School of Social Science, University of Helsinki),* May 1998, 28–34.

HAUTAMÄKI, A. (2000). The ecology of transmission of attachment and mentalising across three consecutive generations in Finland: mechanisms of continuity and discontinuity in normative and non-normative samples. Unpublished research plan.

HEYMANS, P. G. (1994). Developmental tasks in an young adult woman: Emotions, life-events and changes. University of Utrecht. Unpublished manuscript.

HOROWITZ, M. J., WILNER, N. & ALWAREZ, W. (1979). Impact of Event Scale: a measure of subjective distress. *Psychosomatic Medicine, 41,* 207–218.

HUNT, N. (1997). Trauma of war. Long-term psychological effects of war in World War Two veterans. *The Psychologist, 10,* 357–360.

JARHO, L. (1991). *Psychosocial aspects of war disabilities.* Paper presented at the 20th General Assembly of the World Veterans Federation, Special session: Psychosocial effects of war and the maintenance of peace, October 20–24, 1991, Helsinki, Finland.

JARHO, L. & SAARI, J. (1991). 50 years of medical care for disabled war veterans in Finland—still more than 20 years of work ahead. *WISMIC Newsletter, 3, (2),* 14–15.

JENKINSON, C., COULTER, A. & WRIGHT, L. (1993). Short form 36 (SF 36) questionnaire: Normative data for adults of working age. *British Medical Journal, 306,* 1437–1440.

JERRAM, K. L. & COLEMAN, P. G. (1999) The big five personality traits and reporting of health problems and health behaviour in old age. *British Journal of Health Psychology, 4,* 181–192.

KRUSE, A. & SCHMIT, E. (1999) *Coping styles in holocaust survivors.* Paper given at the European Congress of Gerontology, July 1999, Berlin.

KUBANY, E. S. (1994) A cognitive model of guilt typology in combat-related PTSD. *Journal of Trauma and Stress, 7,* 3–19.

KULKA, R. A., SCHLENGER, W. E., FAIRBANK, J. A., HOUGH, R. L., JORDAN, B. K. et al. (1988). *Contractual Report of Findings from the National Vietnam Veterans Readjustment Study.* Research Triangle Park, NC: Research Triangle Institute.

LINDGREN, G. (1998). Ihmisten johtaminen sodassa. Kyselytutkimus viime sotien veteraanien kokemuksista. Suomen Reserviupseeriliitto.

LINNA, V. (1954/1996). *The unknown soldier.* Porvoo: WSOY.

MAIN, M. & GOLDWYN, R. (in press) Adult attachment classification systems. In: M. MAIN (Ed .). *A typology of human attachment organization: Assessed in discourse, drawing and interviews.* Cambridge: Cambridge University Press.

MARCIA, J. E. (1964). *Determination and construct validity of ego identity status.* The Ohio State University, Clinical Psychology Doctoral dissertation. University Microfilms, Inc. Ann Arbor, Michigan.

PONTEVA, M. (1993). Sodan aiheuttamat psyykkiset vammat. Suomen Lääkärilehti 6/1993.

PONTEVA, M. (1998a). *The long-term consequences of war captivity—The Finnish experiences.* Abstract of a paper presented at the WVF's First International Conference on the Psycho-Social Consequences of War, 1998.

PONTEVA, M. (1998b). *Private communication.* Swedish School of Social Science, University of Helsinki, Spring, 1998.

RUDDICK, S. (1990). *Maternal thinking: towards a politics of peace.* London: The Women's Press.

SAARI, S. (1997). *Private communication,* University of Helsinki, Autumn 1997.

STAUDINGER, U. M. & FLEESON, W. (1996). Self and personality in old and very old age: A sample case of resilience? *Development and Psychopathology, 8,* 867–885.

VAN DER KOLK, B. A. & FISLER, R. (1995). Dissociation and the fragmentary nature of traumatic memories: Overview and exploratory study. *Journal of Traumatic Stress, 8,* 505–525.

[33]

A preliminary investigation of self-reported personality disorders in late life: prevalence, predictors of depressive severity, and clinical correlates

J. Q. MORSE[1] & T. R. LYNCH[2]

[1]*Department of Psychiatry, Western Psychiatric Institute and Clinic &* [2]*Department of Psychology, Duke University and Department of Psychiatry, Duke University Medical Center, North Carolina, USA*

Abstract
Previous research suggests that personality disorders, particularly in clusters A and C, persist into late life, are particularly prevalent in late-life depressed samples, and negatively impact treatment of late-life depression. The present study examined the self-reported personality disorder traits of a sample of 65 depressed elders using the Wisconsin Personality Disorder Inventory IV (WISPI IV). As expected, clusters A and C were most prevalent and the presence of a personality disorder predicted the maintenance or re-emergence of depressive symptoms, as did hopelessness and ambivalence regarding emotional expression. No specific personality disorder traits were associated with clinical features of late-life depression (age of onset, number of previous episodes) while some personality disorder traits were associated with psychological correlates of depression (hopelessness, ambivalence regarding emotional expression, thought suppression). A theoretical explanation for the cluster prevalence based on self-verification is discussed along with a profile of elderly patients who may have poor depression treatment course if they exhibit personality disorder traits, particularly interpersonal rigidity or avoidance, chronic hopelessness, and emotional inhibition.

Introduction

Despite earlier misconceptions that all personality disorders might 'burn out' in late life, an initial meta-analysis (Abrams & Horowitz, 1996) of 11 studies indicated an overall prevalence rate of 10%. In these studies, the most commonly diagnosed personality disorders were obsessive-compulsive, dependent and 'not otherwise specified'. With the addition of five studies, a revised meta-analysis suggested an overall prevalence rate for late-life personality disorders of 20% (Abrams & Horowitz, 1999). Across the included studies, the most frequently diagnosed disorders were paranoid, self-defeating, and schizoid. Other studies not included in the meta-analysis or published after it was completed support the initial conclusion that cluster C personality disorders are most commonly diagnosed in late life (Kenan et al., 2000; Kunik et al., 1994; Vine & Steingart, 1994) as well as the previous finding of relatively high rates of personality disorder 'not otherwise specified' compared with other individual personality disorder diagnoses (Kenan et al., 2000; Kunik et al., 1994). Therefore, reasonable conclusions from the meta-analyses and other studies are that the overall prevalence rate is between 10 and 20%, that the highest prevalence may be in clusters A and/or C, and that personality dysfunction in older adults may underestimated by focusing on those who meet full criteria for any one disorder.

Further complicating estimates of prevalence of personality disorders in late life is the high co-morbidity between depressive disorders and personality disorders in elderly samples (Abrams, 1996; Kunik et al., 1994; Thompson, Gallagher & Czirr, 1988). Elderly with a diagnosis of major depression have more personality disorders than 'normal' elderly, especially in cluster C (Abrams, Alexopoulos & Young, 1987; Agbayewa, 1996; Devanand et al., 1994). Estimates of personality disorder co-morbidity in late-life depression range from 24% (Kunik et al., 1994) to 61% (Molinari & Marmion, 1995). Some studies reported on remitted or recovered depressed patients, which may account for some of the variability in prevalence estimates. Additional research on personality disorders in late life has suggested that early-onset late-life depression is associated with greater personality psychopathology than late-onset late-life depression (Abrams et al., 1994; Camus et al., 1997).

In adult samples, patients with comorbid personality disorder diagnoses respond less favorably than non-personality disordered patients to a variety of empirically supported treatments for depression, including antidepressant medications, interpersonal psychotherapy, placebo, and combined medication plus therapy (Duggan, Lee & Murray, 1990; Hardy et al., 1995; Ilardi, Craighead & Evans, 1997; Pilkonis & Frank, 1988; Shea et al., 1990; Thase, 1996). Though there are fewer studies, there is preliminary evidence of similar patterns for late-life depression patients also diagnosed with personality disorders. Personality psychopathology has generally been associated with poorer response to treatment (Fiorot, Boswell & Murray, 1990; Thompson et al., 1988; but not Kunik et al., 1993) and 'chronicity'—meaning relapse or staying continuously ill (Stek et al., 2002; Vine & Steingart, 1994). Comorbid personality disorder has been inconsistent in predicting simple relapse, predicting significantly in one study (Brodaty et al., 1993) but not in another (Molinari & Marmion, 1995). In addition, personality disorders in the elderly are associated with impaired functioning after affective symptoms improve (Abrams et al., 1998), impaired social support (Vine & Steingart, 1994), and decreased quality of life, suicide, and disability (Lyness et al., 1993).

Overall, personality disorders are clearly relevant in late life, are likely to be particularly prevalent in depressed geriatric patient samples and are likely to negatively impact the treatment of depression in these samples. The present study used a self-report measure of personality disorder characteristics, the Wisconsin Personality Disorder Inventory IV (WISPI; Klein, 1996), to characterize personality disorder features in an elderly sample. While the WISPI has been well validated in adult samples (Klein et al., 1993; Barber & Morse, 1994), its internal consistency in and norms for outpatient elderly samples have not yet been established. The present study provides preliminary psychometric information about the WISPI in elderly samples and attempts to predict maintenance or re-emergence of depressive symptoms from the presence or absence of personality disorder. The relations between personality disorder characteristics and features of late-life depression (age of onset and number of episodes) and psychological correlates of depression (suicidal ideation, hopelessness, thought suppression, and ambivalence regarding emotional expression) are examined in an exploratory analysis.

Based on the previous research findings, we expected the highest frequency of high WISPI personality disorder z-scores to be in clusters C and A, particularly obsessive-compulsive, dependent, paranoid, and schizoid personality disorders, and to generate the highest frequency of personality disorder cases in these clusters. Secondly, we hypothesized that the presence of a personality disorder would predict experiencing significant depressive symptoms.

Methods

Participants

Participants were recruited from the NIMH Clinical Research Center (CRC) naturalistic study of late-life depression. For initial inclusion in the CRC study subjects met criteria for major depressive episode (unipolar) using the Duke Depression Evaluation Schedule for the Elderly (George et al., 1989) and had a Mini-Mental Status Exam (MMSE; Folstein, Folstein & McHugh, 1975) score of 25 or greater. For the current study, participants with recent MMSE scores below 25, a diagnosis of Alzheimer's disease, or receiving current ECT were excluded. Sixty-five elderly depressed patients participated in the current study. The average age was 70.3 ($\pm$ 6.3) with 14.1 ($\pm$ 2.9) years of education. Most participants were married (52.3%, $n=34$), Caucasian (89.2%, $n=58$) and female (69.2%, $n=45$). The modal household income was more than $50,000; the median household income was between $30,001 and $40,000.

Procedure

Surveys with business reply envelopes were mailed to participants in the CRC for the study of Depression in Late Life at Duke University Medical Center in two waves. Participants were paid $10 for completing the first set of questionnaires, which included the Affect Intensity Measure (Larsen, 1984), the Adult Suicide Ideation Questionnaire (Reynolds, 1991), the White Bear Suppression Inventory (Wegner & Zanakos, 1994), the Beck Hopelessness Scale (Beck et al., 1974) and the Ambivalence regarding Emotional Expression Questionnaire (King & Emmons, 1990). They received the second set of questionnaires, including the Wisconsin Personality Disorders Inventory IV (Klein, 1996), approximately two weeks later. They were paid $15 for completing the second set of questionnaires. Participants received one or two reminder phone calls if they had not returned the questionnaire packets. The return rate for the first packet was 52% and 71% for the second. Though not high, this return rate is reasonable for mail surveys. There were no differences in demographics or questionnaire measures between those who completed only the first questionnaire packet and those who completed both questionnaire packets.

As participants in the present study were enrolled in an ongoing treatment study of late-life depression where they received antidepressant therapy, their self-report data was linked with their depression symptom scores on the Montgomery Asberg Depression Rating Scale (MADRS; Montgomery & Asberg, 1979) from each psychiatrist appointment. It should be noted that the design of the present study was essentially cross-sectional rather than intentionally prospective, meaning that patients in the larger longitudinal study participated in the present study at various time points during their treatment for depression. Most often, patients completed the WISPI a month before their next psychiatrist appointment (length of time between completing WISPI and next psychiatrist appointment: mode = 30 days, range 18–244 days [almost eight months], median 67 days [just over two months]). Available follow-up data ranged from no more appointments (next appointment after completing the WISPI was last recorded appointment for the patient) to 2.8 years of appointments (mode 2.4 years, median 2.1 years). Patient MADRS scores after participating in the present study were examined to see if the presence or absence of personality disorder predicted the re-emergence of or maintenance of depressive symptoms. The larger study in which patients were treated is a longitudinal treatment study with physician-choice of antidepressant not a clinical trial comparing medications or treatments and does not include either placebos or operationalized definitions of treatment phases. In this sense, the present study examines the impact of personality disorder on more naturalistic treatment of late-life depression at various points in this chronic illness.

Measures

Affect Intensity Measure (AIM; Larsen, 1984) This 40-item self-report scale measures the characteristic intensity with which the respondent experiences his or her emotions and is considered a measure of temperament. Items focus on intensity instead of frequency of emotional experiences and items are rated on a six-point Likert scale ranging from 'never' (1) to always (6). Good test-retest reliabilities have been reported for one, two, and three-month intervals (Larsen, 1984). In the current sample, the internal consistency was $\alpha = 0.88$.

Adult Suicide Ideation Questionnaire (ASIQ; Reynolds; 1991) This 25-item self-report measure asks the respondents to rate the frequency of certain thoughts about suicide (e.g., 'I thought it would be better if I were not alive'). Items are rated on a seven-point Likert scale ranging from 'I never had this thought' (0) to 'almost every day' (6). The ASIQ has been used with age-mixed adult samples, including college students, and has reported high internal consistency and test-retest reliability. Further, the ASIQ significantly correlates with other measures of depression, hopelessness, and self-esteem. In the current sample, the internal consistency was $\alpha = 0.96$.

White Bear Suppression Inventory (WBSI; Wegner & Zanakos, 1994) This 15-item self-report scale measures the tendency of the respondent to engage in thought suppression. Items are rated on a five-point Likert scale from strongly disagree (1) to strongly agree (5). The WBSI correlates significantly with self-report measures of obsessive thinking, depression and anxiety in student samples and exhibits good test-retest reliability and internal consistency in the same samples (Wegner & Zanakos, 1994). In the current sample, the internal consistency was $\alpha = 0.93$.

Beck Hopelessness Scale (BHS; Beck et al., 1974) The BHS is a commonly used measure of hopelessness, particularly in the context of depression. It contains 20 true/false items, some of which are reverse coded. It has good internal consistency in hospitalized patients with a recent suicide attempt and also correlates strongly with clinical ratings of hopelessness in patient samples (Beck *et al.*, 1974). In the current sample, the internal consistency was α (KR20) = 0.90.

Ambivalence Regarding Emotional Expression Questionnaire (AEQ; King & Emmons, 1990) This 28-item self-report measure was generated from personal strivings related to emotions with items specifically worded to capture ambivalence regarding expressing emotions. Items are rated on a five-point Likert scale from never (1) to very often (5). No items are reverse coded, but the AEQ shows significant negative correlations with social desirability in a student sample (King & Emmons, 1990). Both internal consistency and test-retest reliability were adequate in a student sample (King & Emmons, 1990). In the current sample, the internal consistency was $\alpha = 0.94$

Montgomery Asberg Depression Rating Scale (MADRS; Montgomery & Asberg, 1979) This 10-item clinician rating scale assesses depressive symptoms and is designed to be sensitive to change and to response to treatment (Montgomery & Asberg, 1979). Items are rated on a scale from zero (no symptom) to six (severe symptom) where the rater decides whether the rating lies on the defined scale steps (0, 2, 4, 6) or between them (1, 3, 5). It has good internal consistency (Maier & Phillipp, 1985) and good inter-rater reliability (Montgomery & Asberg, 1979). Participants were categorized as experiencing low initial depressive severity if their MADRS score at the first appointment following WISPI completion was ≤ 10; as experiencing a re-emergence of depressive symptoms if baseline MADRS was ≤ 10

TABLE 1. Definitions and distribution of cases experiencing maintenance or re-emergence of significant depressive symptoms

	Any follow-up MADRS ≥ 15		
Initial MADRS ≤ 10	No	Yes	Totals
No	Continuously well $n = 27$	Depressive symptom re-emergence $n = 12$	$n = 39$
Yes	Depression improved $n = 10$	Maintenance of depressive symptoms $n = 14$	$n = 24$
Total	$n = 37$	$n = 26$	$n = 63*$

*Two patients had no follow-up appointments in the larger study (the last appointment was immediately before completing the WISPI)

and any follow-up MADRS score was ≥ 15; and as maintaining depressive severity if their MADRS at baseline and follow-up was ≥ 15 (see Table 1).

Wisconsin Personality Disorders Inventory IV (Klein, 1996) This is a 214 item self-report measure of personality disorder characteristics and behaviors with 2–3 items for each DSM criterion. Two hundred and four of the items reflect DSM IV personality disorder criteria and the criteria for passive-aggressive personality disorder from DSM-III-R. An additional 10 items make up the Marlowe Crowne Scale for social desirability. Items were worded to reflect the personality disorder criteria from the perspective of interpersonal theory (Structural Analysis of Social Behavior; Benjamin, 1974) and distinguish the personality disorders with overlapping criteria. Items are rated on a 10-point scale from 'never or not at all true of you' (1) to 'always or extremely true of you' (10). Good internal consistency and test-retest reliability has been reported in student and clinical samples (Klein et al., 1993; Barber & Morse, 1994). Z-scores can be calculated from norms provided for both normal and outpatient samples (Klein et al., 1993). In the current sample, the internal consistency for the individual WISPI scales ranged from $\alpha = 0.64$ (antisocial personality disorder) to $\alpha = 0.91$ (dependent personality disorder). Though participants completed the WISPI on pencil-and-paper questionnaires, the data was entered into text files that could be scored by the WISPI program. The scoring program provides the mean and standard deviation for each WISPI scale, z-scores for the personality disorder scales, personality disorder diagnoses met based on one or two items per criteria, and percent of necessary and exclusionary criteria met for each personality disorder according to Benjamin's (1993) interpersonal theory of personality disorders. Klein and colleagues (1993) suggest that cases be identified in a two step process: first examining the person's ipsatized scores to highlight specific scales to be considered as marked peaks within the profile and then using a cutoff of + 1.96 on the z-scores relative to the non-clinical norms to identify cases. For the present study, a personality disorder diagnosis was considered present if the patient endorsed the required number of DSM criteria and if the resulting z-score compared with non-clinical norms was greater than 1.90. Assignment to a cluster was based on the pattern of z-scores compared with non-clinical norms; cases with single elevations (no other z-score greater than 1.5) or elevations within the same cluster were assigned to that cluster. Where there were significant elevations in two clusters, both cluster assignments were made. In addition, a personality disorder severity rating was made on Tryer & Johnson's (1996) scale, which ranges from zero, meaning no personality disorder, to three, indicating diffuse personality disorder. Personality disorder severity (Tryer & Johnson, 1996) scores were assigned by examining z-scores based on the non-clinical sample (Klein et al., 1993) and whether the patient endorsed enough items to meet DSM criteria for that same personality disorder. Patients with z-scores ≥ 1.90 and meeting DSM criteria for disorders in more than one cluster received a three (diffuse personality disorder). Patients with a single z-score ≥ 1.90, no other z-score ≥ 1.5 in a different cluster, and who met DSM criteria received a two (simple personality disorder). Patients who had a z-score ≥ 1.90 but who did not meet DSM criteria or patients who had a z-score ≥ 1.5 but < 1.90 and met DSM criteria received a one (personality difficulty/sub-threshold personality disorder). All remaining patients received a zero (no personality disorder). A cutoff of 1.90 instead of 1.96 was used to capture two cases meeting DSM criteria and having z-scores between 1.90 and 1.96.

Results

Descriptive statistics as well as internal consistency scores for the WISPI scales are presented in Table 2. Though the internal consistency scores in the present elderly sample are lower than those reported by Klein et al. (1993) they are generally adequate. Mean personality disorder scores in order from highest to lowest: obsessive-compulsive, schizoid, paranoid, avoidant, histrionic, narcissistic, dependent, passive-aggressive, borderline, schizotypal, antisocial, mostly supporting the hypothesis that personality disorders in clusters A and C would have the highest scores. Only dependent personality disorder traits were

TABLE 2. Mean, standard deviation and internal consistency scores for WISPI personality disorder scales in the present sample and compared with Klein et al. (1993) outpatient norms

	n	Present sample					Klein norms	
		Mean	SD	Min	Max	α	Mean	SD
Paranoid	65	2.70	1.50	1.00	7.40	0.89	−0.54	1.01
Schizoid	65	3.01	1.39	1.00	6.47	0.82	−0.16	1.10
Schizotypal	65	1.64	0.80	1.00	4.05	0.83	−0.70	0.65
Histrionic	65	2.63	0.98	1.07	4.83	0.77	−0.37	0.82
Narcissistic	65	2.14	0.99	1.00	4.58	0.85	−0.81	0.77
Antisocial	65	1.19	0.29	1.00	2.00	0.64	−0.81	0.32
Borderline	65	1.94	0.88	1.00	5.35	0.76	−1.02	0.59
Avoidant	65	2.68	1.49	1.00	6.13	0.91	−0.96	0.73
Dependent	65	2.14	1.30	1.00	6.94	0.92	−0.99	0.81
Obsessive-compulsive	64	3.19	1.31	1.05	6.26	0.84	−0.48	0.92
Passive-aggressive	65	2.04	0.93	1.00	5.11	0.83	−0.78	0.78
Marlowe Crowne Social Desirability	65	7.53	1.06	5.00	10.00	0.51	–	–

expected to receive relatively higher scores but did not do so.

Compared to Klein and colleagues' (1993) patient sample, the present elderly sample endorses lower levels of personality disorder psychopathology as shown by the negative mean z-scores for each scale presented in Table 2. In terms of personality disorder severity, 70.8% ($n = 46$) patients were not diagnosed with a personality disorder, 6.2% ($n = 4$) with personality difficulty or sub-threshold personality disorder, 15.4% ($n = 10$) with simple personality disorder, and 7.7% ($n = 5$) with diffuse personality disorder. Of those with personality disorders (personality disorder severity ≥ 2), 16.9% ($n = 11$) were classified in Cluster A, 1.5% ($n = 1$) in Cluster B, and 10.8% ($n = 7$) in Cluster C. The five cases with diffuse personality disorders included four assigned to both clusters A and C and one assigned to both clusters B and C. This distribution of personality disorder cases confirms the hypothesis that clusters A and C would be the most frequently represented clusters. Overall, 76.9% ($n = 50$) of the sample did not receive a personality disorder diagnosis while the remaining 23.1% ($n = 15$) did.

Logistic regressions were examined in an attempt to predict experiencing significant depressive symptoms from the presence or absence of a personality disorder. Whether or not the person experienced significant depressive symptoms (MADRS ≥ 15) during the remainder of the larger treatment study was the dependent variable, representing maintenance or re-emergence of marked depressive symptoms. Whether or not the person was experiencing minimal depressive symptoms (MADRS ≤ 10) at the first appointment after WISPI completion was entered first and presence of personality disorder second. Initial depressive symptoms predicted later depressive symptoms ($b = 1.15$, Wald $\chi^2(1) = 4.51$, $p < 0.05$; OR = 3.15). While personality disorder severity did not predict later symptoms after controlling for initial symptoms ($b = 0.37$, Wald $\chi^2(1) = 1.84$, $p > 0.10$), presence of personality disorder diagnosis did ($b = 1.37$, Wald $\chi^2(1) = 4.21$, $p < 0.05$; OR = 3.95). Confirming expectations, patients with a personality disorder were almost four times more likely to experience maintenance or re-emergence of significant depressive symptoms than those without personality disorders. Clinical features of depression and late-life depression variables were entered into similar regressions. Only hopelessness and ambivalence regarding emotional expression predicted experiencing later depressive symptoms (hopelessness: $b = 0.13$, Wald $\chi^2(1) = 4.24$, $p < 0.05$; OR = 1.14; ambivalence: $b = 0.60$, Wald $\chi^2(1) = 4.26$, $p < 0.05$; OR = 1.81). When entered together simultaneously, all three effects became trends (hopelessness: $b = 0.09$, Wald $\chi^2(1) = 1.91$, $p > 0.10$; OR = 1.10; ambivalence: $b = 0.43$, Wald $\chi^2(1) = 1.98$, $p > 0.10$; OR = 1.54; personality disorder: $b = 1.12$, Wald $\chi^2(1) = 2.53$, $p > 0.10$; OR = 3.06), suggesting that all may be relevant for predicting re-emergence or maintenance of depressive symptoms, but that none have significant unique predictive power when controlling for the others. Examining the odds ratios suggests that despite the absence of unique prediction of maintenance or re-emergence of depressive symptoms, presence of personality disorder may confer greater risk than hopelessness or ambivalence regarding emotional expression.

Exploratory correlations between personality disorder scales and clinical features and psychological correlates of depression are presented in Table 3. Age of onset and number of previous depressive episodes were not significantly related with any personality disorder scales or with personality disorder severity. With a Bonferroni correction for the number of correlations computed, only borderline and avoidant personality disorder traits were significantly associated with hopelessness and no personality disorder traits were significantly associated with suicidal ideation or intense negative emotions. Ambivalence regarding emotional expression was significantly related to paranoid, narcissistic and obsessive-compulsive personality disorder traits while thought suppression was significantly associated

TABLE 3. Correlations between WISPI scores and other measures

	WBSI	AIM	Ambiv	Hopelessness	SI	Onset Age	# Episodes	MADRS	PD Severity
PAR	**0.45******	0.17	**0.42******	0.31*	0.42***	−0.13	−0.03	0.11	**0.59******
SCZ	0.39***	0.07	0.37**	0.33**	0.34**	−0.27*	0.08	0.19	**0.56******
SZT	0.35**	0.28*	0.32**	0.17	0.09	−0.12	0.03	−0.03	**0.62******
HIS	0.27*	0.32**	0.28*	0.04	0.09	−0.21	0.13	−0.04	0.31*
NAR	**0.46******	0.22	**0.43******	0.31**	0.32*	−0.17	0.08	0.01	**0.52******
ANT	0.20	0.05	0.15	0.12	0.08	−0.10	0.06	0.03	0.25*
BOR	**0.45******	0.29*	**0.39******	**0.48******	0.34**	−0.29*	0.31*	0.16	**0.42***
AVO	**0.46******	0.09	0.38**	**0.49******	0.35**	−0.28*	0.09	0.13	**0.59******
DEP	0.23	0.15	0.20	0.31*	0.19	−0.02	0.02	0.15	**0.62******
OBS	**0.49******	0.21	**0.43******	0.38**	0.22	−0.29*	0.05	0.20	**0.54******
PAS	0.37**	0.09	0.31*	0.30*	0.14	−0.09	−0.07	0.09	**0.57******
MCSD	−0.26*	−0.11	−0.25*	−0.31*	−0.41***	0.21	−0.04	−0.28*	−0.07
PD severity	0.19	0.09	0.24	0.22	0.14	−0.21	−0.20	0.04	–

*$p \leq 0.05$. **$p \leq 0.01$. ***$p \leq 0.001$. ****$p \leq 0.0001$. Correlations in bold are significant with Bonferroni correction ($p \leq 0.0004$)

with paranoid, borderline, narcissistic, avoidant, and obsessive-compulsive personality disorder traits. Interestingly, none of the personality disorder scales were significantly related to depression scores at the next psychiatrist appointment. This may be partially due to the fact that patients completed the WISPI when it was mailed to them and came to an appointment one month later, on average. However, none of the personality disorder scales or any other measures were associated with the length of time between the date the patient completed the self-report measures and the date of his or her next psychiatrist appointment.

Discussion

The frequency of self-reported clinically meaningful personality dysfunction reported in this study of depressed elderly subjects is similar to that found in prior meta-analyses (Abrams & Horowitz, 1996; 1999). As hypothesized, the highest personality disorder scores found in this elderly sample were within Clusters A and C. In addition, patients diagnosed with a personality disorder were almost four times more likely to experience maintenance or re-emergence of depressive symptoms than those without personality disorder diagnoses. Interestingly, more long-standing demographic or trait-like variables, such as early onset, chronic depression, or affect intensity, were not correlated with the presence of any particular personality disorder or personality disorder severity.

A theoretical explanation for cluster prevalence

The DSM-IV states that 'some types of personality disorders (notably, antisocial and borderline personality disorders) tend to become less evident or to remit with age, whereas this appears to be less true for some other types (e.g., obsessive-compulsive)' (p.632; American Psychiatric Association, 1994).

Findings from our study support these clinical observations, yet explanations of these apparent age-related changes have remained essentially atheoretical. It could be that environmental feedback or reinforcement shapes the expression of personality pathology (see Lynch & Aspnes, 2001).

Experimental evidence from both clinical and non-clinical samples with students and adults suggests that individuals favor information that confirms their self-view over other reinforcers, particularly if that self-view is extreme, and that individuals become anxious or withdraw when they cannot dismiss disconfirming feedback (Giesler, Josephs & Swann, 1996; Pelham & Swann, 1994; Ritts & Stein, 1995; Swann, 1997; Swann, de la Ronde & Hixon, 1994). Unfortunately, development and emotional growth involves learning from failure and contradiction; ignoring disconfirming social feedback may exacerbate personality psychopathology. That is, an environmental feedback hypothesis suggests that while a person controls mental and social interactions to avoid aversive feedback, avoidance may reinforce pathology. For example, by repeatedly staying away from interpersonal situations a patient with avoidant personality disorder never learns that she can cope in social situations and a patient with paranoid personality disorder never learns that others are not exploiting or deceiving him. By avoiding social interaction as much as possible a patient with schizoid personality disorder removes the opportunity for social reinforcement of any kind and consequently becomes even more detached. While not always avoiding social interactions, a patient with obsessive-compulsive personality disorder is likely to favor occupational feedback that supports rigid and detail-oriented behavior and may not discover that being flexible can have beneficial consequences. We consider it probable that decades of reinforcement without disconfirming feedback function to maintain and exaggerate personality pathology.

In contrast, cluster B disorders are thought to decline with age. Older adults may have less energy for the impulsive or reckless behavior characterized by cluster B disorders (Abrams et al., 2001) or those who exhibit reckless or violent behavior may die earlier (Fishbain, 1991). Alternatively, disconfirming environmental feedback may punish or extinguish maladaptive behaviors. For example, self-injury (a symptom of borderline personality disorder) is not only difficult to hide but may also elicit negative social feedback, which may slowly shape these behaviors out of a person's repertoire.

Personality disorder and depressive symptom maintenance or re-emergence

There is growing empirical evidence that personality disorders are associated with poorer treatment response, including antidepressant medications and psychotherapy. In findings similar to the present study, Thompson, Gallagher and Czirr (1988) reported that the likelihood of treatment failure was approximately four times greater for older adult depressed patients diagnosed with personality disorders (37%) compared to those without (9.5%). Despite controlling for initial depressive severity, our findings provide additional evidence for these observations, suggesting that older depressed patients with a comorbid personality disorder are generally less responsive to treatment. In the current sample, only hopelessness, ambivalence regarding emotional expression, and the presence or absence of a personality disorder diagnosis predicted the maintenance or re-emergence of depressive symptoms. Hopelessness has been liked to depression theoretically (Abramson, Metalsky & Alloy, 1989) and empirically both cross-sectionally (Beck et al., 1988; Trenteseau et al., 1989) and longitudinally (Alford et al., 1995; McCranie & Riley, 1992) and to poor treatment outcome (Whisman et al., 1995). Similarly, personality disorders are frequently comorbidly diagnosed with depression (Agbayewa, 1996; Devanand et al., 1994; Shea et al., 1990) and personality disorder diagnosis can predict depressive relapse (Brodaty et al., 1993; Hardy et al., 1995; Ilardi et al., 1997). However, the finding that ambivalence regarding emotional expression may predict poor treatment response in the form of maintenance or re-emergence of depressive symptoms is new. It may be that hopelessness and personality disorder status are interrelated. One study found that among psychiatric inpatients, patients with the most hopeless cognitive styles were those with personality disorders, severe depression, and aversive and controlling family histories (Rose et al., 1994). In the current sample, hopelessness correlated with borderline and avoidant personality disorder traits, which may suggest poor interpersonal skills that make it difficult to ask for or take advantage of social supports or treatment. On the other hand, ambivalence regarding emotional expression correlated with paranoid, narcissistic and obsessive-compulsive personality disorder traits, which may suggest a rigidity that predicts later difficulty. Treatments such as dialectical behavior therapy that specifically target personality pathology (e.g., non-compliance, ineffective interpersonal skills, rigid coping) may prove more useful in treating depressed elders exhibiting personality disorder traits, chronic hopelessness, or ambivalence regarding emotional expression.

Psychological variables and personality pathology

To our knowledge, this is the first study to examine the relations between ambivalence regarding emotional expression and thought suppression and personality disorder pathology in older adults. Both ambivalence regarding emotional expression (i.e., the desire to express and suppress emotions simultaneously) and the tendency to suppress unwanted emotional thoughts were associated with paranoid, narcissistic, and obsessive-compulsive personality disorder traits and thought suppression was also related to borderline and avoidant traits. In non-clinical samples older adults have been shown to experience fewer negative emotions and to have more functional and adaptive control over their emotions than their younger counterparts (Gross et al., 1997). However, in a late-life clinical sample, higher levels of thought suppression were associated with higher depressive symptoms following treatment (Rosenthal et al., 2003). Results from the present study support the notion that thought and emotion inhibition may be an ineffective emotion regulation style that is related to personality pathology and poor treatment response.

Limitations

Several factors limit the generalizability of the results of the present study and suggest directions for future research. Much of the study was cross-sectional in nature, limiting causal conclusions. Future research on the impact of personality disorders on treatment for late-life depression would benefit from a prospective design that assesses personality disorder traits both at baseline and at first remission. In addition, measures were primarily self-reported and depressive measures used in longitudinal analyses did not include structured diagnostic interviews. The absence of structured interviews and the use of a self-reported measure of personality disorder traits (WISPI), particularly in a sample where the psychometric properties of the WISPI are unknown, is problematic. However, we have not used the WISPI to arrive at specific personality disorder diagnoses but rather the less specific presence or absence of personality disorder in general. This more conservative use of the WISPI seems reasonable and should certainly be confirmed with future research which employs diagnostic interviews and which investigates the concurrent validity of the WISPI in older adults. These limitations notwithstanding, this study is the first we know to utilize the WISPI to characterize personality disorder characteristics of a geriatric depressed sample. Despite the self-report nature of the WISPI, it generated clinically meaningful groups based on the presence or absence of significant personality disorder traits, which significantly predicted poor treatment course.

In conclusion, results from this preliminary study support previous observations that Cluster A and C disorders are more likely to occur in older adults and that the presence of personality disorder pathology would negatively impact recovery from depression among older adults. Though it would be ideal to assess personality disorders with a complete diagnostic interview, the negative impact of the presence of a personality disorder may be evidenced in self-report measures. These preliminary results further suggest a clinical profile for depressed older patients who exhibit personality disorder pathology and may be at risk for poor treatment outcome that includes hopelessness, concern or difficulty expressing emotion, and interpersonal avoidance or rigidity. These clinical indicators may be helpful for treatment providers in identifying older patients who are at greatest risk for maintenance of or re-emergence of depressive symptoms during the course of treatment.

Acknowledgements

This research was supported by the Duke Mental Health Clinical Research Center, which was performed pursuant to NIMH grant P50 MH60451 and RO1 MH54846 and manuscript preparation was supported by grant NIMH K23 MH01614 to Thomas R. Lynch. Manuscript preparation by Dr. Morse was supported by a postdoctoral training fellowship from NIMH grant T32 MH 18269, Clinical Research Training for Psychologists (PI: Paul A. Pilkonis, PhD). We would like to thank Paul Pilkonis for his helpful comments on earlier drafts of this manuscript and Mai El-Khoury and David Rak for their invaluable help in data collection.

References

ABRAMS, R.C. & HOROWITZ, S.V. (1996). Personality disorders after age 50: a meta-analysis. *Journal of Personality Disorders, 10*, 271–281.

ABRAMS, R.C. & HOROWITZ, S.V. (1999). Personality disorders after age 50: a meta-analytic review of the literature. In: E. ROSOWSKY, R.A. ZWEIG & R.C. ABRAMS (Eds.), *Personality disorders in older adults: emerging issues in diagnosis and treatment* (pp. 55–68). LEA Series in Personality and Clinical Psychology. Mahwah, NJ: Erlbaum.

ABRAMS, R.C. (1996). Personality disorders in the elderly. *International Journal of Geriatric Psychiatry, 11*, 759–763.

ABRAMS, R.C., ALEXOPOULOS, G.S. & YOUNG, R.C. (1987). Geriatric depression and DSM-III-R personality disorder criteria. *Journal of the American Geriatrics Society, 35*, 383–386.

ABRAMS, R.C., ALEXOPOULOS, G.S., SPIELMAN, L.A., KLAUSNER, E. & KAKUMA, T. (2001). Personality disorder symptoms predict global functioning and quality of life in elderly depressed patients. *American Journal of Geriatric Psychiatry, 9*, 67–71.

ABRAMS, R.C., ROSENDAHL, E., CARD, C. & ALEXOPOULOS, G.S. (1994). Personality disorder correlates of late and early onset depression. *Journal of the American Geriatrics Society, 42*, 727–731.

ABRAMS, R.C., SPIELMAN, L.A., ALEXOPOULOS, G.S. & KLAUSNER, E. (1998). Personality disorder symptoms and functioning in elderly depressed patients. *American Journal of Geriatric Psychiatry, 6*, 24–30.

ABRAMSON, L.Y., METALSKY, G.I. & ALLOY, L.B. (1989). Hopeless depression: a theory-based subtype of depression. *Psychological Review, 96*, 358–372.

AGBAYEWA, M.O. (1996). Occurrence and effects of personality disorders in depression: are they the same in the old and young? *Canadian Journal of Psychiatry, 41*, 223–226.

ALFORD, B.R., LESTER, J.M., RATEL, R.J., BUCHANAN, J.P. & GIUNTA, L.C. (1995). Hopelessness predicts future depressive symptoms: a prospective analysis of cognitive vulnerability and cognitive content specificity. *Journal of Clinical Psychology, 51*, 331–339.

AMERICAN PSYCHIATRIC ASSOCIATION. (1994). *Diagnostic and statistical manual of mental disorders*, (fourth edition). Washington, DC: American Psychiatric Association.

BARBER, J.P. & MORSE, J.Q. (1994). Validation of the Wisconsin Personality Disorders Inventory with the SCID-II and PDE. *Journal of Personality Disorders, 8*, 307–319.

BECK, A.T., WEISSMAN, A., LESTER, D. & TREXLER, L. (1974). The measurement of pessimism: The Hopelessness Scale. *Journal of Consulting and Clinical Psychology, 42*, 861–864.

BECK, A.T., RISKIND, J.H., BROWN, G. & STEER, R.A. (1988). Levels of hopelessness in DSM-III disorders: a partial test of content specificity in depression. *Cognitive Therapy and Research, 12*, 459–469.

BENJAMIN, L.S. (1974). Structural analysis of social behavior. *Psychological Review, 81*, 392–425.

BENJAMIN, L.S. (1993). *An interpersonal approach to the DSM personality disorders*. New York: Guilford Press.

BRODATY, H., HARRIS, L., PETERS, K., WILHELM, K., HICKIE, I., BOYCE, P. et al. (1993). Prognosis of depression in the elderly: a comparison with younger patients. *British Journal of Psychiatry, 163*, 589–596.

CAMUS, V., DE MENDONCA LIMA, C.A., GAILLARD, M., SIMEONE, I. & WERTHEIMER, J. (1997). Are personality disorders more frequent in early onset geriatric depression? *Journal of Affective Disorders, 46*, 297–302.

DEVANAND, D.P., NOBLER, M.S., SINGER, T., KIERSKY, J.E., TURRET, N., ROSE, S.P. et al. (1994). Is dysthymia a different disorder in the elderly? *American Journal of Psychiatry, 151*, 1592–1599.

DUGGAN, C.F., LEE, A.S. & MURRAY, R.M. (1990). Does personality predict long-term outcome in depression? *British Journal of Psychiatry, 157*, 19–24.

FIOROT, M., BOSWELL, P. & MURRAY, E.J. (1990). Personality and response to psychotherapy in depressed elderly women. *Behavior, Health, and Aging*, 1, 51–63.

FISHBAIN D.A. (1991). Personality disorder diagnoses in old age. *Journal of Clinical Psychiatry*, 52, 477–478.

FOLSTEIN, M.F., FOLSTEIN, S.E. & McHUGH, P.R. (1975). Mini-Mental State: a practical method for grading the cognitive state of patients for the clinician. *Journal of Psychiatric Research*, 12, 189–198.

GEORGE, L.K., BLAZER, D.G., HUGHES, D.C. & FOWLER, N. (1989). Social support and the outcome of major depression. *British Journal of Psychiatry*, 154, 478–485.

GIESLER R.B., JOSEPHS R.A. & SWANN W.B. JR. (1996). Self-verification in clinical depression: the desire for negative evaluation. *Journal of Abnormal Psychology*, 105, 358–368.

GROSS J.J., CARSTENSEN L.L., PASUPATHI M., HSU, A.Y.C., TSAI, J. & SKORPEN, C.G. (1997). Emotion and aging: experience, expression, and control. *Psychology and Aging*, 12, 590–599.

HARDY, G.E., BARKHAM, M., SHAPIRO, D.A., STILES, W.B., REES, A. & REYNOLDS, S. (1995). Impact of cluster C personality disorders on outcomes of contrasting brief psychotherapies for depression. *Journal of Consulting and Clinical Psychology*, 63, 997–1004.

ILARDI, S.S., CRAIGHEAD, W.E. & EVANS, D.D. (1997). Modeling relapse in unipolar depression: the effects of dysfunctional cognitions and personality disorders. *Journal of Consulting and Clinical Psychology*, 65, 381–391.

KENAN, M.M., KENDJELIC, E.M., MOLINARI, V.A., WILLIAMS, W., NORRIS, M. & KUNIK, M.E. (2000). Age-related differences in the frequency of personality disorders among inpatient veterans. *International Journal of Geriatric Psychiatry*, 15, 831–837.

KING, L.A. & EMMONS, R.A. (1990). Conflict over emotional expression: psychological and physical correlates. *Journal of Personality and Social Psychology*, 66, 998–1006.

KLEIN, M.H. (1996). *The Wisconsin Personality Disorders Inventory IV*.

KLEIN, M.H., BENJAMIN, L.S., ROSENFELD, R., TREECE, C., HUSTED, J. & GREIST, J.H. (1993). The Wisconsin Personality Disorders Inventory: development, reliability, and validity. *Journal of Personality Disorders*, 7, 285–303.

KUNIK, M.E., MULSANT, B.H., RIFAI, A.H., SWEET, R.A., PASTERNAK, R., ROSEN, J. et al. (1993). Personality disorders in elderly inpatients with major depression. *American Journal of Geriatric Psychiatry*, 1, 38–45.

KUNIK, M.E., MULSANT, B.H., RIFAI, A.H., SWEET, R.A., PASTERNAK, R. & ZUBENKO, G.S. (1994). Diagnostic rate of comorbid personality disorder in elderly psychiatric inpatients. *American Journal of Psychiatry*, 151, 603–605.

LARSEN, R.J. (1984). Theory and measurement of affect intensity as an individual difference characteristic. *Dissertation Abstracts International*, 85, 2297B. (University Microfilms No. 84-22112).

LYNCH, T.R. & ASPNES, A. (2001). Personality disorders in older adults: diagnostic and theoretical issues. *Clinical Geriatrics*, 9, 64–70.

LYNESS, J.M., CAINE, E.D., CONWELL, Y., KING, D.A. & COX, C. (1993). Depressive symptoms, medical illness, and functional status in depressed psychiatric inpatients. *American Journal of Psychiatry*, 150, 910–915.

MAIER, W. & PHILLIPP, M. (1988). Comparative analysis of observer depression scales. *Acta Psychiatrica Scandinavica*, 72, 239–254.

McCRANIE, E.W. & RILEY, W.T. (1992). Hopelessness and persistence of depression in an inpatient sample. *Cognitive Therapy and Research*, 16, 699–708.

MOLINARI, V. & MARMION, J. (1995). Relationship between affective disorders and axis II diagnoses in geropsychiatric patients. *Journal of Geriatric Psychiatry and Neurology*, 8, 61–64.

MONTGOMERY, S.A. & ASBERG, M. (1979). A new depression scale designed to be sensitive to change. *British Journal of Psychiatry*, 134, 382–389.

PELHAM B.W. & SWANN W.B. JR. (1994) The juncture of intrapersonal and interpersonal knowledge: self-certainty and interpersonal congruence. *Personality and Social Psychology Bulletin*, 20, 349–357.

PILKONIS, P.A. & FRANK, E. (1988). Personality pathology in recurrent depression: nature, prevalence and relationship to treatment response. *American Journal of Psychiatry*, 145, 435–441.

REYNOLDS, W.M. (1991). Psychometric characteristics of the Adult Suicidal Ideation Questionnaire in college students. *Journal of Personality Assessment*, 56, 289–307.

RITTS V. & STEIN J.R. (1995). Verification and commitment in marital relationships: an exploration of self-verification theory in community college students. *Psychological Reports*, 76, 383–386.

ROSE, D.T., ABRAMSON, L.Y., HODULIK, C.J., HALBERSTADT, L. & LEFF, G. (1994). Heterogeneity of cognitive style among depressed inpatients. *Journal of Abnormal Psychology*, 103, 419–429.

ROSENTHAL, M.Z., CHEAVENS, J.S., COMPTON, J.S., THORP, S.R. & LYNCH, T.R. (2004). Thought suppression and treatment outcome in late-life depression. *Aging & Mental Health*, in press.

SHEA, M.T., PILKONIS, P.A., BECKMAN, E., COLLINS, J.F., ELKIN, I., SOTSKY, S.M. et al. (1990). Personality disorders and treatment outcome in the NIMH Treatment of Depression Collaborative Research Program. *American Journal of Psychiatry*, 147, 711–718.

STEK, M.L., VAN EXEL, E., VAN TILBURG, W., WESTENDORP, R.G.J. & BEEKMAN, A.T.F. (2002). The prognosis of depression in old age: outcome six to eight years after clinical treatment. *Aging and Mental Health*, 6, 282–285.

SWANN, W.B. JR. (1997). The trouble with change: self-verification and allegiance to the self. *Psychological Science*, 8, 177–180.

SWANN, W.B. JR., DE LA RONDE C. & HIXON J.G. (1994). Authenticity and positivity strivings in marriage and courtship. *Journal of Personality & Social Psychology*, 66, 857–869.

THASE, M.E. (1996). The role of axis II comorbidity in the management of patients with treatment-resistant depression. *The Psychiatric Clinics of North America*, 19, 287–309.

THOMPSON, L.W., GALLAGHER, D. & CZIRR, R. (1988). Personality disorder and outcome in the treatment of late life depression. *Journal of Geriatric Psychiatry*, 21, 133–153.

TRENTESEAU, J.A., HYER, L., VERENES, D. & WARSAW, J. (1989). Hopelessness among later-life patients. *Journal of Applied Gerontology*, 8, 355–364.

TYRER, P. & JOHNSON, T. (1996). Establishing the severity of personality disorder. *American Journal of Psychiatry*, 153, 1593–1597.

VINE, R.G. & STEINGART, A.B. (1994). Personality disorder in the elderly depressed. *Canadian Journal of Psychiatry*, 39, 392–398.

WEGNER, D.M. & ZANAKOS, S. (1994). Chronic thought suppression. *Journal of Personality*, 62, 615–640.

WHISMAN, M.A., MILLER, I.W., NORMAN, W.H. & KEITNER, G.I. (1995). Hopeless depression in depressed inpatients: symptomology, patient characteristics, and outcome. *Cognitive Therapy & Research*, 19, 377–389.

Name Index

Abbott, R. 363
Abeles, R.P. 67
Abraham, I.L. 208
Abrams, R.C. 302, 381–2, 386–7
Abramson, L.Y. 128, 251, 387
Abson, V. 13
Achte, K. 374
Adamowicz, J. 189
Agbayewa, M.O. 381, 387
Ainsworth, M.D.S. 378
Akerberg, H. 87
Akiyama, H. 119
Aksari, P. 42
Albarede, J.L. 353
Albert, M.L. 232
Albert, M.S. 42
Albert, S.M. 57, 302
Albrecht, R. 123
Aldwin, C.M. 371
Alessi, C.A. 212, 217
Alex, L. 85–93
Alexander, G.E. 40, 57
Alexopoulos, G.S. 198, 302, 323, 381
Alexopoulos, P. 189
Alford, B.R. 387
Alfred, D. 208
Alkalay, J. 353
Alkalay, L. 353
Allen, C. 187, 237, 242
Alloy, L.B. 128, 387
Altman, D.G. 199
Amaral, P. 364
Ambrose, Anne F. 143–51
Anderson, S. 187
Andres, D. 4
Andres, R. 57
Aneshensel, C. 264
Anson, O. 90
Anstey, K.J. 32, 342, 356
Antonovsky, A. 86–7, 90, 375
Antonovsky, H. 86
Antonucci, T.C. 68, 119
Arbuckle, T.Y. 4

Arbuthnot, C. 342
Ardelt, M. 378
Arenberg, D. 11
Arfken, C.L. 353
Argyle, N. 254
Arkin, S.M. 185–6
Armor, D.J. 97
Aroian, K.J. 89
Aronstein, Z. 211, 216
Asberg, M. 383
Ashley, J. 209
Aspnes, A. 386
Åström, S. 301, 242
Aveni, A. 115
Azariah, R. 90

Bach-Peterson, Julie 260, 269–75
Bäckman, L. 22, 185
Baer, J.S. 95
Bahro, M. 252
Baillargeon, L. 342
Baillon, S. 237, 242
Baines, S. 200
Baker, D.I. 95, 353
Baker, S.P. 353
Ballard, C. 187
Baltes, Margret M. 32, 63–81, 85, 91, 125–6, 127, 378
Baltes, Paul B. 12, 25–33, 49–81, 85–6, 118, 123, 127, 360
Bandura, A. 116, 124, 354–55
Bandura, M. 372
Banerji, N. 11
Banham, K.M. 128
Bank, L. 11
Barber, J.P. 382, 384
Barer, B.M. 96
Barker, Pat 371
Barnes, R.F. 253–4
Bar-On, D. 371
Barrett, T.J. 12
Barron, C.R. 86
Barthel, D.W. 87

Barton, E.M. 58
Bass, D.M. 165, 365
Basso, M.R. 36
Bauer, T. 86
Beard, C.M. 41
Beck, A.T. 86, 343–4, 382–3, 387
Beck, C. 237, 242
Becker, J.T. 39
Beckett, L.A. 95
Beekman, A.T.F. 317, 333, 338
Beer, M. de 333
Beiser, M. 52, 66
Beitchman, J.H. 334
Belin, T.R. 342
Bell, B. 11
Benbow, S.M. 188
Bender, M.P. 185, 187–8, 371
Bengtson, V.L. 52–4, 346
Benjamin, L.C. 242
Benjamin, L.S. 384
Benjamin, S. 248
Benson, D.F. 232
Bent, L. 12
Bent, N. 11–13
Bentler, P.M. 26
Berg, A. 189, 242
Berg, S. 11, 22
Berger, A.K. 140
Bergman, L.R. 32
Bergmann, K. 247–8, 269
Bergner, M. 355–6
Berkman, Lisa F. 42, 95–101, 253, 317
Berkowitz, B. 22
Berlin, I. 51
Berman, E.C. 364
Bickel, H. 57
Bifulco, A. 334
Birchmore, T. 210
Bird, M. 186, 189, 210
Birge, S.J. 353
Birnie, J. 187
Birren, J.E. 11, 52, 115
Bjoervell, H. 87
Black, B.S. 302
Black, D. 353
Black, F.W. 186
Blake, A.J. 356
Blanchard-Fields, F. 121, 127
Blazer, Dan G. 95, 104, 315–31, 333
Bledin, K. 188

Bleeker, J.K. 95
Blenkner, M. 269
Bloom, J.R. 95
Blum, K. 22
Blumenkrantz, J. 4
Blumenthal, J.A. 158–9
Bobbit, R. 355
Bock, R.D. 365
Bocquet, H. 353
Boehm, S. 210
Bonaiuto, S. 22, 41
Bond, J. 189
Bonneh, D.Y. 90
Borawski-Clark, E. 95
Borchelt, M. 26
Boring, E.G. 25
Bornstein, R. 57, 36
Borrie, M.J. 353
Boss, P. 346
Boswell, P. 382
Bosworth, H.B. 11, 22
Botwinick, J. 22
Bouchez, S. 338
Bould, S. 85
Bourgeois, M.S. 185
Boustani, Malaz 299–313
Bovbjerg, V.E. 95
Bowlby, J. 251, 378
Bowling, A. 201
Boyd, S.L. 194
Bradburn, N.M. 248
Bradway, K. 4, 8
Braehler, E. 90
Bramsen, I. 338
Brandstädter, J. 56, 67, 125, 377–8
Bray, J.H. 365
Breckenridge, J.N. 363–5
Bredin, Kathleen 163–81
Brennan, F.P. 279
Breslau, N. 338
Breuil, V. 198, 286–7
Brewin, C.R. 251, 339
Brim, O.G. Jr. 49–50, 68, 57–8
Brink, T.L. 334
Britton, Peter G. 247–56, 190
Brod, M. 302, 310
Brodaty, Henry 277–84, 342, 382, 387
Brodman, E. 13
Brody, E.M. 257, 261, 252
Brody, I.M. 250

Brook, P. 197
Brooker, D. 209, 302
Bross, L.S. 86
Brotons, M. 208
Brown, A.L. 64
Brown, D.C. 210
Brown, G.W. 251, 334, 339
Brown, J. 128
Bruce, Martha L. 95–101
Bruin, A.F. de 356
Brun, A. 40
Bryant, L.L. 86
Buchner, D.M. 353
Buckland, S. 252
Buettner, L. 212
Bulka, D. 121
Burgener, S.C. 237
Burgess, P.W. 21
Burgio, L.D. 209, 310
Burkhardt, M.A. 91
Burnight, K.P. 11–12
Burns, A. 188
Buschke, Herman 143–51
Buschmann, M.T. 208
Bush, H.A. 91
Bushke, M. 12
Busse, E.W. 57
Butler, R.N. 11
Butler, S.M. 42
Butt, D.S. 52, 66
Butterworth, Margaret 197–203

Cacioppo, J.T. 96
Cafferata, G.L. 258
Caine, E.D. 165
Callahan, C.M. 41
Callahan, L.F. 86
Camberg, L. 209
Camp, C. 127, 185–6
Campbell, A.J. 353, 360
Campbell, D.T. 221, 293
Camus, V. 382
Canteen, W. 372
Cantor, M.H. 250
Cantor, N. 117
Cappeliez, P. 333, 338
Carmel, S. 90
Carmela, S. 353
Carroll, J.B. 6, 25
Carstensen, Laura L. 85, 91, 115–31

Carter, W. 355
Casarett, D. 310
Casby, J.A. 208
Caserta, M.S. 253, 363–4
Casey, D.A. 343
Cattell, R.B. 63
Cayla, F. 353
Centor, R.M. 356
Chafetz, P.K. 210
Chaikelson, J. 4
Challis, D. 253
Chamberlain, K. 90
Champion, L.A. 345
Chandler, M.J. 59
Chang, B.L. 165, 282
Change, C.H. 302
Chappell, N.L. 237, 241–2
Charles, Susan T. 85, 115–31
Charlson, M.E. 356
Charness, N. 59
Charpentier, P.A. 96–7
Chatel, D. 128
Chenoweth, L. 208
Cheston, R. 185, 187–8
Chetwynd, A. 22
Chin-A-Loy, S.S. 90
Chipuer, H. 33
Chiverton, P. 165
Chown, S. 11
Christopher, K.A. 89–90
Chrosniak, L. 127
Chu, P. 165, 282
Church, M. 342
Churchill, M. 209
Cicero, L.A. 116
Cicero, M.T. 50–51, 55, 75
Clague, S. 210
Clare, L. 185–6, 201
Clark, C. 310
Clark, E. 253
Clark, J.W. 11
Clark, M.C. 364
Clark, M.E. 208
Clarke, M. 85
Cleary, T.A. 212
Clement, F.J. 11
Clements, Karen M. 153–60
Clipp, E. 115
Cobb, J.L. 41–2
Cochran, C.D. 365

Cohen, C.I. 188
Cohen, D. 252
Cohen, J. 358
Cohen, R.D. 95
Cohen, S. 85
Cohen-Mansfield, Jiska 205–25, 302
Coleman, P.G. 371–80
Collins, A.H. 274
Collins, E. 342
Colsher, P.L. 11
Connolly, J.R. 364
Cook, M.J. 85, 90
Cook, T.D. 221
Cooley, C.N. 257
Coon, David W. 285–7
Cooper, B. 57
Coper, H. 55, 60, 62
Coppel, D.B. 248, 251–2
Corballis, M.C. 115
Cornelius, R. 368
Cornelius, S.W. 33, 63
Cornoni-Huntley, J. 96
Corso, J.F. 32
Costa, P.T. 11, 57
Cotrell, V. 183, 187
Court, J.H. 6
Courtice, K. 247
Covi, L. 97
Coward, D.D. 86–7, 90–91
Craighead, W.E. 382
Craik, F.I.M. 25, 60, 62
Crapo, L.M. 57
Crawford, J.R. 3–9
Crimmins, E.M. 95
Crittenden, P.M. 373–5
Cronbach, J.L. 302, 356
Cross, P.S. 333, 338
Cross, S. 118, 126
Crumbaugh, J.C. 87
Cumming, E. 123, 128
Cummings, J.L. 232
Cummings, S.R. 353, 356, 359–60
Cunningham, W. 115
Cutrona, C.E. 251
Czirr, R. 381, 387

D'Amico, D. 86
D'Andrade, R.G. 116
Damon, A. 11
Dancy, B.L. 91

Dannefer, D. 57
Darby, S.J. 210
Darwin, Charles 53
Datan, N. 343
Davidson, K.M. 342
Davies, A.D.M. 333, 338
Davies, B. 253
Davies, Steve 197–203
Davis, R. 252
Dean, A. 264
Dean, J. 121
Deary, Ian J. 3–9
Deci, E.L. 116
Deickmann, L. 238
Deimling, G.T. 247, 249–50, 252–3, 365
Del Ser, T. 42
Dening, T.R. 85, 90
Denney, A. 208
Denney, N.W. 58
Derby, Carol A. 143–51
Derksen, B.F. 342
Derogatis, L.R. 97, 264, 364–5
Dessonville, C. 364
Detterman, D.K. 25
Deutsch, G. 39
Devanand, D.P. 381, 387
Devaul, R.D. 364
Dewilde, E.J. 333–40
Deyo, R.A. 356
Diamond, M.C. 43, 173
Dick-Siskin, L. 342
Diederiks, J.P.M. 356
Dietch, J.T. 186
Diggle, Peter 11–23
DiGioia, D. 356
Dimond, M.F. 363–4
Dingley, C.E. 91
Dintzer, L. 251
Dirken, J.M. 11
Dittmann-Kohli, F. 61, 69
Dixon, R.A. 11, 25, 59, 65–6, 69, 118
Dobbs, Debra 299–313
Domittner, G. 363
Donaldson, C. 188, 237
Donlan, C. 12–13
Doucette, J.T. 353
Douvan, E. 66
Douzjian, M. 243
Doyle, C. 210
Drew, N. 242

Dröes, R.M. 165
Drummond, M. 280, 354
Duggan, C.F. 382
Dunn, L.A. 242
Dyer, J.G. 86

Eagles, J.M. 248, 254
Eaton, W. 317
Eckert, J. Kevin 299–313
Edelman, P. 302
Edwards, D.R. 126
Edwards, H. 87, 90
Eggers, R. 21
Eichorn, D.H. 4
Eisdorfer, C. 252
Ekman, I. 90
Ekman, P. 121
Elder, G. 115
Ellermann, C.R. 87
Elliott, E. 354
Eloniema-Sulkava, U. 165, 282
Emery, G. 343
Emmons, R.A. 382–3
Endicott, J. 248
Englund, E. 40
Ensel, W. 264
Epictetus 378
Epstein, S. 54
Erbaugh, J. 364
Erdman, A.J. Jr. 13
Erikson, E.H. 54, 346, 377–8
Erikson, J.M. 54
Eriksson, K.A. 61
Erlen, J.A. 90
Estes, E.H. Jr. 353
Evans, D.A. 11, 22, 41, 43
Evans, D.D. 382
Everitt, D.E. 237
Everson, S.A. 90
Ewart, C. 153, 155

Fabrigoule, C. 43
Fagerberg, B. 90
Fairburn, C.G. 188
Fairchild, J.K. 310
Fairclough, D.L. 86
Falleti, M.V. 364
Farmer, M.E. 42
Faschingbauer, T.R. 364–5
Fatheringham, J. 247

Featherman, D.L. 50, 57, 59, 64, 69, 74
Feil, N. 187
Feldman, P.H. 310
Felton, B.J. 66
Femia, E.E. 85
Ferguson, S.A. 127
Fernsler, J.I. 90
Ferrario, J. 211
Fiatarone Singh, Maria A. 153–60, 353
Field, D. 119, 124
Filipp, S.H. 40, 66
Finch, C.E. 57
Fingerman, K. 118
Fiorot, M. 382
Firth-Cozens, J. 238
Fishbain, D.A. 387
Fisher, S.E. 310
Fiske, D.W. 293
Fisler, R. 357
Fitting, M. 248–82, 253
Fleeson, W. 89, 91, 373
Folsom, James C. 197, 193–5
Folstein, M.F. 87, 185, 197–8, 261, 302, 382
Folstein, S.E. 87, 261, 302, 382
Fombonne, E. 339
Fontana, A. 371
Forner, A. 11–12
Fossler, R.J. 86
Foster, N.L. 40
Fozard, J.L. 25, 32
Francis, N. 14
Frank, E. 382
Frankl, V.E. 86–7, 378
Fratiglioni, Laura 41–2, 135–41
Fredrickson, B.L. 119–20, 124, 126
Freedman, J.L. 126
Freedman, M. 232
Freire, Paulo 164
Freud, A. 116
Freud, Sigmund 128
Freund, A. 125
Friedland, R. 43
Friel-McGowin, D.F. 252
Fries, B.E. 302
Fries, J.F. 56–7, 74
Friesen, W.V. 121
Fritz, C. 209
Fruge, E. 253
Fulton, B.R. 302
Fung, H. 116, 119, 124–6

Furby, L. 302
Futterman, Andrew 363–70

Gallagher, D. 363–5, 368, 381, 387
Gallagher-Thompson, Delores 187, 347–51, 363–70
Galper, Y. 22
Gardiner, E. 188, 237–44
Garratt, A.M. 374
Garrison, J. 274
Gatz, M. 117, 342
Geerlings, M.I. 41–2
Geigy, J.R. 27
Geiselmann, B. 91
Gendron, C. 165, 282
Gent, P. van 342
George, L.K. 104, 248–9, 261, 382
Gerdner, L.A. 208, 218
Gerety, M.B. 356
Gerson, S. 342
Gianturco, D.T. 364, 369
Gibbons, L.E. 302, 310
Gibbs, J.M. 364
Gibson, L.M. 90
Giesler, R.B. 386
Gilden, D. 86
Gilewski, Michael J. 11, 363–70
Gilhooly, M.L.M. 247–50, 252–4
Gilleard, C.J. 169, 197–8, 238, 247–53, 253
Gilliard, J. 185
Gilloran, A. 189
Gilmore, G.C. 212, 217
Gilson, B.S. 354
Ginter, S.F. 353
Glatt, S.L. 41
Glosser, G. 253
Goddaer, J. 208
Gold, D. 4
Goldberg, D.P. 238, 248, 373–4
Goldstein, H. 239
Goldwyn, R. 375
Gollwitzer, P.M. 126
Gonzalez, A. 115
Gonzalez-Salvador, T. 307, 310
Gordon, C. 52, 342
Gottlieb, B.H. 277
Gottman, John M. 121–2
Gould, E. 43
Grad de Alarcon, J. 247, 269–70
Grady, C.L. 38–9

Graff, J. 122
Grafstrom, M. 242
Granick, S. 25, 33
Grant, R.W. 343
Grasby, P.M. 38
Graves, A.B. 37, 42
Green, Alisa 277–84
Green, B.H. 333
Green, R. 22
Greenberg, J. 128
Greene, J.G. 247, 249, 251, 254
Greenhouse, S.W. 11
Greenough, W.T. 64
Greenwald, A.G. 54
Gresham, M. 165, 282
Greve, W. 125
Gribbin, K. 11
Groene, R.W. 211
Groom, F. 238
Gross, J. 116, 119, 121, 128, 387
Guarnaccia, C. 363
Guerett, A. 342
Guess, H.A. 302
Gunzelmann, T. 90
Gur, R.C. 33, 37
Gur, R.E. 33
Gurland, B.J. 41–2, 90, 333, 338
Gustafson, Y. 85–93
Guthke, J. 57
Gutmann, D. 59–60
Gwilliam, C. 185
Gwyther, L.P. 248–50, 261

Haddad, P.M. 188
Hagberg, B. 86
Haitsma, K. van 302
Hakim-Larson, J. 121
Hale, W.D. 365
Haley, William E. 285–7
Hall, Charles B. 143–51
Hall, L. 209
Hallberg, I.R. 189, 266
Hamilton, J.D. 372
Hammen, C.L. 251, 342
Hanley, I.G. 185, 211
Hansson, U.W. 189
Hardin, J.M. 310
Hardy, G.E. 238, 382, 387
Hare, J. 209
Harris, L. 66

Harris, T.O. 334
Hartmaier, S.L. 302
Hashtroudi, S. 127
Hass, A. 371
Hastings, T.J. 115
Haugh, H. 21
Hauser, P.M. 22
Hausman, C. 187
Hautamäki, A. 372–80
Havighurst, R.J. 51, 57, 123
Heagerty, P. 302
Heard, K. 210
Hebert, R. 279, 282
Heck, E. 300
Heckhausen, J. 65–6, 118, 125
Hedgepeth, B. 365
Heeren, T.J. 342
Heidrich, S.M. 86
Heil, F.E. 56
Heim, A.W. 13–14
Heiman, R. 126
Helfrich, H. 127
Helmchen, H. 25, 123
Henriksson, M. 342
Henrion, R. 87
Henry, J.P. 57, 59–60
Henry, W.E. 123, 128
Herbster, A.N. 39
Heron, A. 11
Herrnstein, R.J. 25
Hertzog, C. 11, 27, 28, 33
Hess, T.M. 127
Hewett, L.J. 186
Heycop, T.H. 342
Heyman, D.K. 364, 369
Heymans, P.G. 378
Higgins, E.T. 116–17
Hilgard, E.R. 25
Hill, L.R. 41
Hill, R.D. 185
Himmelfarb, S. 363
Hinchliffe, A.C. 213, 279, 282, 333
Hindmarsh, J.J. 353
Hinton, L. 212
Hirdman, Y. 91
Hiris, J. 95
Hirschfield, M.J. 249, 251
Hixon, J.G. 386
Hofer, S.M. 25, 27, 30, 32
Holden, U.P. 186, 198, 200

Holland, Fiona 11–23
Holliday, P.J. 353
Holliday, S.G. 59
Holm, A. 213
Holm, M.B. 208
Holmberg, S.K. 212, 216
Holtkamp, C.C. 209
Hömberg, V. 25
Honzik, M.P. 4
Hope, R.A. 188
Hope, T. 188, 243
Horn, J.L. 21, 25, 27, 30, 32, 63
Hornbrook, M.C. 353–4
Horowitz, A. 249–51
Horowitz, M.J. 373
Horowitz, S.V. 381, 386
House, J.S. 96, 100, 264
Howe, A. 274
Howland, Jonathan 353–61
Hoyer, W.J. 59
Hudes, E.S. 353
Hudis, I.E. 274
Hughes, C.P. 198
Hultsch, D.F. 11, 32, 43
Humphreys, L.G. 4
Hunt, E. 60
Hunt, J.V. 4
Hunt, N. 371–4, 378
Husband, H.J. 185
Hussian, R.A. 210–11

Ilardi, S.S. 382, 387
Ingram, R.E. 339
Isaacowitz, Derek M. 85, 115–31
Isaacs, B. 248–50, 254, 353–4
Isometsa, E. 342

Jackson, G.A. 241
Jackson, J.S. 58, 119
Jackson, S.E. 238
Jacobs, B. 57
Jacobs, J.W. 270–72
Jacoby, R. 248
Jagger, C. 85
Jahnke, H.C. 127
James, W. 116
Jänicke, B. 55
Jarho, L. 372
Jarvik, L.F. 11, 22, 342
Jay, G. 33

Jenkins, H. 237, 242
Jenkinson, C. 372
Jensen, A.R. 3
Jerram, K.L. 373
Jerusalem, M. 67
Jette, Alan 353–61
Johansson, B. 11, 22, 85
Johnson, B.D. 212
Johnson, C.L. 247
Johnson, J.R. 242
Johnson, M. 127
Johnson, M.M.S. 242
Johnson, R.J. 364
Johnson, S.A 115
Johnson, T. 384
Jones, I.G. 247
Jones, J.M. 115, 127
Jones, R. 342
Jones, S. 186
Jonsen, E. 85–93
Josephs, R.A. 386
Josephsson, S. 186
Jung, C. 128

Kagan, J. 49
Kahan, J. 253 279, 282
Kahana, E. 22, 259
Kahn, R.L. 52–3, 55, 57, 68, 86, 119, 247, 264, 269–72, 345
Kahneman, D. 127
Kane, R.L. 310–11
Kangas, J. 4, 8
Kanmark, T. 95
Kaplan, G.A. 95
Kareholt, I. 95
Karlawish, J.H.T. 310
Karlsson, J. 88
Karp, Anita 135–141
Kasl, S.V. 96–7
Kasper, J.D. 302
Kasten, Linda 353–61
Katon, W. 342
Katona, C. 286–7, 333, 342
Katz, Mindy J. 143–151
Katz, S. 261
Katzman, R. 33–34, 42–3, 144
Kaufman, M.S. 342
Kausler, D.H. 20
Kay, D.W.K. 269
Keady, J. 184

Kekki, P. 342
Kelley, K. 356
Kemperman, G. 57
Kenan, M.M. 381
Kennedy, G. 184
Kerkhof, A.J.F.M. 334
Kessler, R.C. 96
Kidd, S. 353, 356
Kiecolt-Glaser, J.K. 96
Kilstoff, K. 208
Kim, E.J. 208
Kindermann, T. 60, 58
King, L.A. 382–3
Kinney, C.K. 91
Kinsella, G. 186
Kitagawa, E.M. 22
Kitayama, S. 126
Kittner, S.J. 42
Kitwood, Tom 163–81, 183–4, 188–8, 243
Kivnick, H. 54
Klaas, D. 90
Klapper, J. 302
Klauer, T. 54, 66
Kleban, M.H. 25, 121
Klein, M.H. 382, 384–5
Kleinman, L. 302
Kleven, M. 4
Kliegl, R. 26, 33, 58–62, 68, 57
Klocinski, J. 310
Kluckhorn, F. 127
Knight, B. 343
Knop, J. 12
Koch, G.G. 302
Koder, D.A. 342
Koenig, H.G. 317, 333
Kohler, P.O. 299
Kok, R.M. 334
Kolk, B.A. van der 375
Kondo, K. 57
Korczyn, A.D. 22, 41
Koschera, Annette 277–84
Koss, E. 212, 217
Kozma, A. 60
Kraaij, V. 333–40
Kraepelin, Emil 164
Krampe, R.T. 33
Krampen, G. 56
Krantz, D. 228
Krause, N. 95
Kruse, A. 371

Kruyssen, D.C. 95
Kubany, E.S. 375
Kucera, H. 14
Kuehl, K.P. 85
Kuhn, D. 302
Kulka, R.A. 66, 372
Kulys, R. 251
Kunik, M.E. 381–2
Kunzmann, U. 85, 91
Kurlowicz, L.H. 333, 338
Kuslansky, Gail 143–51
Kuypers, J.A. 53

Labouvie-Vief, G.V. 11–12, 49, 52, 58–9, 65, 121, 127
Lachenbruch, P.A. 354
Lachman, J.L. 12
Lachman, M.E. 66, 353–61
Lachman, R. 12
LaCroix, A.Z. 95
Laidlaw, Ken 341–51
Lam, D.H. 185
Lamb, K. 353
Lamers, L.M. 95
Landerman, R. 104, 338
Landreville, P. 342
Landry, J. 342
Lang, F.R. 85, 90, 118–19, 123–5
Lange, B. 67
Lange, J. de 333
Langer, Ellen J. 51–2, 293–8
Langius, A. 87, 90
Lansen, P. 11
Larsen, R.J. 382–3
Larson, E. 186
Lash, H.W. 353
Lauver, D. 90
Lawton, M.P. 68, 121, 257, 261, 264, 302
Lebowitz, B.D. 345
Lee, A.S. 382
Lee, D.J. 123
Leenders, I.M. 95
Lefcourt, H. 293
Lehr, U. 52, 57, 68
Lemke, J.H. 300
Lemke, S. 239
Lemmon, Helen 3–9
Leon, C.F.M. de 353
Lerner, R.M. 49, 56

Letenneur, l. 41
Levenson, A. 90
Levenson, Robert W. 121–2
Levin, E. 252–4
Levine, L. 346
Levine, R. 115
Levy, B.R. 347
Lewin, L.M. 210
Lewinsohn, P.M. 252, 347
Lewkowicz, C. 354
Liang, K.Y. 12, 302
Lichtenstein, E. 95
Lichtenstein, P. 8
Lieberman, M.A. 22, 128
Liebman, Joshua L. 115, 128
Lin, N. 264
Lind, M.G. 90
Lindenberger, Ulman 12, 25–33, 58, 61, 127
Lindgren, G. 376, 378
Linna, Väinö 379
Lintern, T. 301
Lipman, R.S. 97, 264
Lippi, A. 22
Lipton, Richard B. 143–51
Little, T.D. 85
Livingston, G. 286–7, 333, 342
Lloyd, C. 334
LoGiuodice, D. 279, 282
Logsdon, Rebecca G. 302, 310, 198
Longino, C.F. Jr. 85
Lonnqvist, J. 342
Løpine, J.P. 338
Lord, S.R. 32, 354, 356
Lovell, B.B. 212
Lovett, S. 368
Loving, G.L. 85
Lowe, C. 21
Lowe, J.C. 346
Lowenthal, M.F. 269–71
Lucas, M.J. 262
Lund, D.A. 363–5
Lundberg, O. 95
Lundervold, D. 210
Lundman, B. 85–93
Lusty, K. 185
Lutz, A. 124
Lyketsos, C.G. 307, 212
Lynch, T.R. 381–9
Lyness, J.M. 382

Lyons, D. 241

McArdle, J.J. 27
McAvay, Gail 95–101
McCallion, P. 211, 280
McCrae, R.R. 11
McCranie, E.W. 387
McCulloch, A.W. 378
McCurry, Susan M. 280, 282, 302, 310
MacDonald, A.J.D. 247
McDonald-Miszczak, L. 11
Mace, N.L. 247, 251, 262
McElreath, L. 342
MacFarland, R.A. 25, 33
MacFarlane, J. 123
McGrath, J.E. 126
McGuinness, T.M. 86
Machin, E. 247, 249, 251
McHugh, P.R. 87, 185, 264, 302, 382
McInnes, Lynn 11–23
MacKenzie, C.R. 356, 358
McKitrick, L.A. 186
McLearn, G.E. 8
MacLullich, A.M.J. 8
McMinn, B.G. 212
McNiel, K. 153, 158
MacPherson, R. 237, 242
MacRae, P. 354
Maddison, D.C. 363–4
Maddox, G.L. 56–7
Magai, C. 188
Magnusson, D. 32
Maguire, C.P. 185
Maholick, L.T. 87
Mahoney, R.I. 87
Maier, W. 383
Main, M. 375
Maki, B.E. 353–4, 360
Malmberg, B. 85
Mandl, H. 64
Manly, J.J. 57
Maoz, B. 90
Marcia, J.E. 377
Markides, K.S. 123
Markus, H. 54, 66, 118, 126
Marmion, J. 381–2
Marriot, A. 279, 282
Marshack, A. 115
Marsiske, M. 86
Marwijk, H.W.J. van 333, 338

Maslach, C. 238
Maslow, A.H. 116
Maslow, K. 300
Mason, K. 12
Mason, W. 12
Matteau, E. 342
Matteson, M.A. 211, 216
Matthews, E.A. 213
Mattis, S. 230, 232–3
Maxwell, S.E. 365
Mayer, K.U. 25, 123
Mayer, R. 210
Mayer, U. 26, 33, 122
Mayo, R. de 251
Meacham, J.A. 59
Medelson, M. 364
Medina, John 115
Mednick, S.A. 12
Meier, A. 87, 90
Mellors, M.P. 90
Mendes de Lyon, C.F. 95
Mentes, J.C. 211
Meradez, M. 353
Meredith, L.S. 103–14
Mermelstein, R. 95
Mesulam, M.M. 230
Metalsky, G.I. 128, 387
Metzner, H. 96
Meyer, D.L. 212
Meyerowitz, B. 117
Middleton, J. 217
Middleton, M. 213
Miesen, B.M.L. 187
Miller, E. 186
Miller, J. 353
Miller, N.E. 270
Mills, M.A. 187, 189, 371
Mingrone, M. 126
Minkler, M. 119, 124
Mintz, J. 342
Miranda, J. 342
Mischel, W. 355
Mishara, B.L. 210
Mishima, M. 212
Mitchell, R.G. 185
Mitchell, Robert A. 194
Mittelman, Mary S. 280, 282, 285–7
Moch, S.D. 91
Mock, J. 364
Mohide, E.A. 280, 282

Molenberghs, S. 19
Molinari, V. 381–2
Mollica, R. 310
Monahan, D.J. 237
Moniz-Cook, E. 188, 280, 282, 237–44
Montgomery, S.A. 383
Moore, B. 22
Moore, J.W. 346
Moos, R.H. 300–301, 239
Mor, V. 95
Mori, E. 42
Morris, J.N. 302
Morris, Lorna W. 242, 247–56, 342
Morris, Robin G. 186, 189, 242, 247–56, 280, 282, 342
Morris, S.A. 302
Morrison, D.F. 365
Morrison, J.H. 40
Morse, C.K. 11
Morse, J.Q. 381–9
Mortel, K.F. 41, 57
Mortensen, E.L. 4
Mortimer, J.A. 36, 42
Mosher-Ashley, P.M. 57
Mou, S. 363
Mozley, C.G. 189
Mullan, Joseph T. 257–68
Mullen, B. 67
Mullen, R. 185
Mulrow, C. 354
Munbodh, R. 247
Murphy, J. 353
Murray, E.J. 382
Murray, R.M. 382
Murrell, A.J. 126
Murrell, S.A. 333, 338, 363
Myer, G. 22

Nabholz, S. 90
Nagi, S.Z. 97
Namazi, K.H. 212
Neisser, U. 66
Nesbitt, B.J. 86
Nesselroade, J.R. 12, 27, 32–3,
Nettelbeck, T. 25
Neugarten, B.L. 57, 343, 346
Nevitt, M.C. 353, 355–6
Newbigging, K. 249
Niederehe, G. 253, 345
Nies, G. 365

Nilsson, M. 301
Nisbet, J.D. 4
Noelker, L.S. 365
Nolan, M. 252
Nolen-Hoeksema, S. 363–4, 368
Norberg, A. 85–93, 301, 242
Norem, J. 117
Norris, A.E. 89
Novak, M. 237, 241–2
Nurius, P. 66, 126
Nygren, B. 85–93

O'Hara, M.W. 333, 338
O'Hara, R. 57
Obonya, T. 354
Oden, M.H. 11
Ojen, R.L. van 333
Okawa, M. 212
Olin, J.T. 334
Olson, J. 209
Orbist, W.D. 21
Orrell, Martin 197–203, 333, 338, 342
Osman, P. 22
Ostwald, S.K. 280, 282
Ott, A. 41
Ott, B.R. 299, 302
Owens, W.A. 4, 11

Padesky, C.A. 342
Pagel, M.D. 248–9, 251
Palmer, C.V. 213
Palmore, E. 12, 51, 53, 123
Pancoast, D.L. 274
Park, D. 127
Parker, M.G. 95
Parkes, C.M. 251, 333, 338, 363–4, 368
Parmelee, P.A. 68
Pasamanick, B. 273
Pascucci, M.A. 85
Pasquier, Florence 227–36
Pasupathi, M. 122
Patel, V. 243
Patrick, D.L. 302
Patterson, S.L. 274
Pattie, A.H. 197–8
Pavalko, E.K. 103
Payton, A. 11
Pearlin, Leonard I. 257–68, 363
Pearson, R.C.A. 40
Pedersen, N.L. 8

Pelham, B.W. 386
Pemille, F. de 353
Pendleton, N. 11
Pereda, M. 36
Perkins, R.E. 281
Perlmutter, M. 59, 118
Persons, J.B. 343
Peterson, Elizabeth 353–61
Peterson, James 50, 363
Petrie, K. 90
Petrie, T. 252
Pfeiffer, E. 97, 248
Phair, L. 301
Phibbs, E. 188
Philipsen, H. 356
Phillipp, M. 383
Phillips, C.D. 310
Piaget, Jean 216
Pickett-Cooper, P.K. 208
Pietrukowicz, M.E. 242
Pilkonis, P.A. 382
Pincus, T. 86
Plassman, B.L. 4–5
Plomin, R. 8, 56
Plutzky, M. 269
Polich, M. 97
Ponteva, M. 372–4, 378
Post-White, J. 90
Poulshock, S.W. 247, 249–52, 253–4
Poulton, J.L. 364
Powell, D.H. 11
Powell, L.S. 247, 355
Power, M.J. 345
Praag, H. van 57
Preisser, John S. 299–313
Prencipe, M. 41
Proctor, R. 241
Prohovnik, I. 40
Province, M. 354
Pruchno, R.A. 261, 364
Pugliesi, K.L. 262
Pyszczynski, T. 128

Qualls, S.H. 343
Quayhagen, M. 264
Quayhagen, M.P. 280, 282, 264

Rabbitt, Patrick M. 11–23, 25
Rabins, P.V. 247, 251, 262, 302
Ragneskog, H. 208

Rajagopal, D. 121
Rakowski, W. 95
Rao, C.R. 365
Rappaport, H. 86
Raven, J. 6, 8
Raven, J.C. 6, 8, 13–14
Ready, R.E. 299, 307
Reed, P.G. 86–7, 90–91
Reed, Peter S. 299–313
Reedy, M. 54
Reever, Karen E. 269–75
Reeves, K.E. 260
Reich, J.W. 363
Reifler, B.V. 186
Reiger, D.A. 128
Reimanis, G. 22
Reinert, G. 30, 33
Reinsch, S. 354, 356, 360
Reisenzein, R. 72
Reivitch, M. 21
Rennemark, M. 86
Resch, N.L. 261
Reynolds, W.M. 382–3
Rice, K. 185
Richardson, E.D. 95
Richardson, G.E. 96
Richman, D. 355
Rickels, K. 97
Rieckmann, N. 85
Riegel, K.F. 22
Riegel, R.M. 22
Riley, M.W. 38, 57
Riley, T.A. 90
Riley, W.T. 387
Riordan, J. 280, 282, 185
Ripich, D.N. 280, 282
Ritts, V. 386
Robbins, C. 96
Robert, S. 96
Roberts, J. 280, 282
Robins, J.M. 12
Robinson, K.M. 280
Rocca, W.A. 22, 57
Rodin, Judith 293–8, 354, 359
Roether, D. 57–9
Rogers, J. 40
Rogers, J.C. 210
Rogers, W. 103–14
Rohde, P. 347
Romeis, J.C. 258

Ronde, C. de la 386
Roodin, P.A. 59
Rose, C.L. 11
Rose, D.T. 387
Rose, J.F. 91
Rosen, W.G. 198
Rosenberg, M. 263
Rosenheck, R. 371
Rosenthal, M.Z. 387
Roth, David L. 285–7
Rothbart, M.K. 116
Rothera, I. 342
Rotnitzky, A. 12
Roux, G. 91
Rovner, B.W. 213–14
Rowe, J.W. 52–3, 55, 57, 95, 96, 345
Rowe, M. 208
Royan, Lindsay 197–203
Rubin, D.B. 12
Rubinstein, Arthur 74, 348
Ruch, F.L. 293
Ruddick, S. 357
Rudinger, G. 32
Ruegg, R.G. 333, 339
Runci, S. 209, 215
Rush, A.J. 343
Ryan, R.M. 116, 124
Rybash, J.M. 59
Ryff, C.D. 52–3, 55, 60, 126
Rypma, B. 38

Saari, J. 372
Saari, S. 378
Sagy, S. 86, 90
Sainsbury, P. 247, 269–70
Saito, Y. 95
Salmon, D.P. 232
Salthouse, T.A. 25–6, 28, 33, 60, 62, 64
Sanden Eriksson, B. 90
Sandman, P.O. 301
Sands, L. 302
Sanford, J.R.A. 249, 270
Sangl, J. 258
Sarvimäki, A. 85–6, 89–90
Satlin, A. 212
Satz, P. 36
Schaefer, J.A. 301
Schaie, K.W. 11–12, 25, 27, 32–3, 49, 56–8
Schaller, J.R. 186
Schapiro, M.B. 40

Scharfstein, D.O. 12
Scharlach, A.E. 262
Scheibel, A.B. 21
Scheibel, M.E. 21
Scherder, E. 208
Scherr, P.A. 95
Schlesselman, J.J. 12
Schmid, U. 72
Schmidt, L.R. 57
Schmit, E. 371
Schoeberlein, S. 121
Schofield, P.W. 37, 42
Scholey, K. 187
Schooler, C. 263–4
Schuchter, S.R. 363–4
Schulsinger, F. 12
Schulz, R. 300, 297, 251, 187
Schulze, G. 55
Schumacher, J. 90
Schwartz, A.N. 54
Schwartzman, A.E. 4–5
Schwarzer, R. 67
Scilley, K. 310
Scogin, F. 342
Scott, K. 90
Sears, D. 115
Seckl, J.R. 8
Seeley, J.R. 347
Seeman, Teresa 95–101
Seligman, M.E.P. 293
Semple, Shirley J. 257–68
Seppala, I. 342
Settersten, R.A. Jr. 91
Shallice, T. 21
Shamoian, C.A. 302
Shanas, E. 257
Shankar, K. 199
Shaw, B.F. 343
Shaw, T.G. 21
Shea, M.T. 382, 387
Shema, S.J. 95
Sherbourne, C.Donald 87, 103–14
Shergill, S. 342
Sherman, S. 297
Shindelman, L.W. 251
Shmotkin, D. 118
Shock, N.W. 55, 57
Shweder, R.A. 116
Silber, E. 252
Silver, M. 238, 242

Silver, R.C. 363–5, 369
Simon, L. 128
Simonsick, E.M. 95
Sinason, V. 187
Singer, T. 12
Singer, W. 65
Singh, Nalin A. 153–60
Sival, R.C. 211
Skaff, Marilyn M. 257–68
Skeldon, R. 125
Skolnik, B.E. 21
Sliwinski, Martin 12, 143–51
Sloane, Philip D. 307, 299–313
Small, B.J. 11, 22
Smircina, M.T. 57
Smith, A.D. 120, 127
Smith, Brewster 67
Smith, J. 50, 58–9, 59–60, 71, 85, 91
Smith, M.H. 85
Smyer, M.A. 343
Snowden, J. 241
Snowdon, D.A. 4–5, 22, 40, 42–3
Snyder, M. 208–9, 220
Sokoloff, L. 11
Solomon, K. 188
Solomon, S. 128
Someren, E. van 217
Sonn, U. 87
Sourani, T. 375
Sowarka, D. 58–9, 85
Spada, H. 50
Spears, G.F. 353
Specht, V.C. 237
Spector, Aimee 186, 197–203
Spector, J. 242
Speechly, M. 353
Spencer, P. 364–5
Spiers, N.A. 85
Spiro, A. 33
Stambul, H.B. 97
Starace, F. 36
Starr, John M. 3–9
Staudinger, U.M. 59, 63, 71, 86, 89, 124, 373
Steele, H. 188
Steffens, D. 317
Stein, J.R. 386
Steingart, A.B. 381–2
Steinhagen-Thiessen, E. 25–6, 123
Steinmetz, J. 365
Stek, M.L. 382

Stelmach, G.E. 25
Stenbock-Hult, B. 85–6, 89–90
Stern, R. 36, 39
Stern, Yaakov 35–47
Sternberg, R.J. 25, 59
Steuer, J. 253, 342
Stevens, F.C.J. 356
Stevens, V.J. 353
Stewart, A.L. 302
Stewart, K.W. 11
Stewart, S.T. 12
Stokes, G. 188
Stoller, E.P. 262
Stollery, B. 22
Stone, R. 258
Stones, M.J. 60
Stoppe, G. 42
Storandt, M. 22
Stouffer Calderon, K. 85
Strawbridge, W.J. 95
Strodtbeck, F. 127
Stroebe, M. 363, 369
Stroebe, W. 363–4, 369
Strother, C.R. 25
Strudwick, M. 354
Styron, William 315
Suddendorf, T. 115
Suhr, J. 187
Sulkava, R. 41
Sullivan, M. 88, 116, 342
Suls, J.N. 53
Sunderland, T. 252
Swaab, D.F. 57
Swann, W.B. Jr. 386
Swanson, E.A. 208
Syme, S.L. 86
Szemanski, A. 11
Szwarbo, P. 188

Tabloski, P.A. 208
Tak, Y. 90
Tarnopolsky, A. 248
Tarrier, N. 188
Taulbee, Lucille R. 197, 193–5
Taylor, D.W. 12
Taylor, S. 128
Teasdale, J.D. 339
Tennstedt, Sharon 353–61
Teresi, J.A. 43
Teri, Linda 41, 167–8, 187, 189, 212, 302

Terman, L.M. 11
Thase, M.E. 382
Thoits, P.A. 95
Thomae, H. 56–7, 68
Thomas, D.W. 208
Thompson, Larry W. 56, 71, 187, 341–51, 363–70, 381–2, 387
Thorgrimsen, Lene 197–203
Thorpe, L. 212
Thorslund, M. 95
Tideiksaar, R. 353
Timbury, G.C. 247, 254
Tinetti, M.E. 95, 353–6, 359–60
Tobin, S.S. 247, 251
Tobis, J. 354
Todd, P. 259
Tokar, A.V. 11
Tomkins, S.S. 116
Topper, A.K. 353
Törestad, B. 32
Tornstam, L. 86, 91
Toseland, R.W. 187
Tower, R.B. 86
Townsend, A.L. 365
Tranel, D. 187
Trenteseau, J.A. 387
Truax, P. 189
Tryer, P. 384
Tuddenham, R.D. 4
Turk-Charles, S. 117, 120–21
Turner, H.A. 262, 264
Tversky, A. 127
Twibell, R.S. 209

Uchino, B.N. 96
Uhlenhuth, E.H. 97
Umberson, D. 96
Unger, Jennifer B. 95–101
Unutzer, J. 342, 347
Uomoto, Jay M. 187
Upchurch, S. 86, 90

Vaillant, G.E. 345–6
Vellas, B. 353–4
Verbeck, G. 19
Verghese, Joe 143–51
Verhey, F.R.J. 185
Vernon, P.A. 25
Veroff, J. 66
Vickers, A.J. 199

Vine, R.G. 381–2
Viola, A. 363–4
Vnek, N. 127
Voe, M. de 121
Voitenko, V.P. 11
Vygotsky, L. 57

Wagnild, G.M. 86–7, 89–91
Wahl, H.W. 57, 69, 72–3
Walker, J.E. 353
Wallace, R.B. 11, 95
Walsh, D.A. 33
Walton, P. 302
Wang, Hui-Xin 135–41
Ward, C. 364
Ward, J.A. 356
Ward, S.R. 354
Ware, C.J.G. 188
Ware, J.E. Jr. 87–8, 103–14
Waring, E.M. 251
Warner, N. 185
Watson, P. 12
Watson, T.S. 210
Weaver, S.L. 354
Wechsler, D. 145–6, 228–30, 233
Wegner, D.M. 382–3
Weinert, F.E. 64
Weintraub, S. 230
Weiss, A.D. 25
Weiss, R.S. 363–4, 368
Weissman, M. 317
Welden, S. 187
Welford, A.T. 32
Wells, D.L. 211
Werner, P. 208–9, 211–13
West, R.L. 22
Wexler, D. 253
Whall, A. 212
Whalley, Lawrence J. 3–9, 57
Wheaton, B. 263
Whisman, M.A. 387
Whitbourne, S.K. 55, 60
White, L. 41
White, R.W. 116
Wicklund, R.A. 126
Wilber, K.H. 237
Wilcock, G.K. 201
Wilcox, V.L. 95, 97
Wilkin, W.R. 4
Wilkinson, L. 365

Williams, Christianna S. 299–313
Williams, D.P. 310
Williams, P. 32, 354, 356
Williams, R.H. 51
Williams, S.J. 86
Willis, S.L. 33, 58
Wills, T.A. 67
Wilson, B.A. 185
Wilson, K.B. 311
Wimo, A. 213
Winblad, Bengt 135–41, 301
Wingfield, D.J. 353
Winzelberg, G.S. 310
Wirths, C.G. 51
Wisocki, P. 58
Witte, L.P. de 356
Witucki, J.M. 209
Wolf, S.L. 354
Wolff, H.G. 13
Wolf-Klein, G.P. 354
Wolfson, L.I. 354
Wood, J.V. 67
Woodruff, R.S. 302
Woods, B. 301
Woods, P. 209
Woods, R.T. 183–92, 197–203, 237–44
Wortman, C.B. 96, 251, 363–7, 369
Wunderlich, G.S. 299
Wurf, E. 54, 114

Yale, R. 187
Yalom, I. 128
Yarrow, M.R. 11
Yates, K. 280
Yesavage, J.A. 187, 334
Yoshitake, T. 139
Young, H.M. 86–7, 89–91
Young, R.C. 302, 381
Young, R.F. 259
Young, S.H. 209

Zajonc, R. 117
Zanakos, S. 382–3
Zandt, S. van 363–4
Zanetti, O. 167–8, 185–6, 200
Zarit, J.M. 250, 253, 258, 259
Zarit, Steven H. 11, 85, 167–8, 247, 249–50, 259–60, 269–75
Zautra, A.J. 363
Zeger, S.L. 12, 302
Zeiss, A.M. 347
Zelinski, E.M. 11–12
Zgola, J.M. 301
Zhang, M. 41
Zimbardo, P.G. 115, 293
Zimmerman, Sheryl 299–313
Zisook, S. 363–4
Zisselman, M.H. 209, 212
Zung, W.W.K. 145–7